MAZDA MX-5 MIATA
1990-09 REPAIR MANUAL

~~Deleted~~

P9-CLC-014

Covers U.S. and Canadian models of Mazda MX-5 Miata
1990 through 2009

Does not include information specific to turbocharged models

by Alan Ahlstrand

CHILTON *Automotive Books*

PUBLISHED BY **HAYNES NORTH AMERICA, Inc.**

Manufactured in USA
©2010 Haynes North America, Inc.
ISBN-13: 978-1-56392-886-4
ISBN-10: 1-56392-886-8
Library of Congress Control Number 2010935070

Haynes Publishing Group
Sparkford Nr Yeovil
Somerset BA22 7JJ England

Haynes North America, Inc
861 Lawrence Drive
Newbury Park
California 91320 USA

ABCDE
FGHIJ
KLMNO
PQRST

Chilton is a registered trademark of W.G. Nichols, Inc., and has been licensed to Haynes North America, Inc.

Contents

Mechanic, author and photographer with a 1996 Mazda Miata

ACKNOWLEDGEMENTS

Wiring diagrams provided by Valley Forge Technical Communications.

All rights reserved. No part of this book may be reproduced or transmitted in any form or by any means, electronic or mechanical, including photocopying, recording or by any information storage or retrieval system, without permission in writing from the copyright holder.

While every attempt is made to ensure that the information in this manual is correct, no liability can be accepted by the authors or publishers for loss, damage or injury caused by any errors in, or omissions from, the information given.

About this manual

ITS PURPOSE

The purpose of this manual is to help you get the best value from your vehicle. It can do so in several ways. It can help you decide what work must be done, even if you choose to have it done by a dealer service department or a repair shop; it provides information and procedures for routine maintenance and servicing; and it offers diagnostic and repair procedures to follow when trouble occurs.

We hope you use the manual to tackle the work yourself. For many simpler jobs, doing it yourself may be quicker than arranging an appointment to get the vehicle into a shop and making the trips to leave it and pick it up. More importantly, a lot of money can be saved by avoiding the expense the shop must pass on to you to cover its labor and overhead costs. An added benefit is the sense of satisfaction and accomplishment that you feel after doing the job yourself.

USING THE MANUAL

The manual is divided into Chapters. Each Chapter is divided into numbered Sections. Each Section consists of consecutively numbered paragraphs.

At the beginning of each numbered Section you will be referred to any illustrations which apply to the procedures in that Section. The reference numbers used in illustration captions pinpoint the pertinent Section and the Step within that Section. That is, illustration 3.2 means the illustration refers to Section 3 and Step (or paragraph) 2 within that Section.

Procedures, once described in the text, are not normally repeated. When it's necessary to refer to another Chapter, the reference will be given as Chapter and Section number. Cross references given without use of the word "Chapter" apply to Sections and/or paragraphs in the same Chapter. For example, "see Section 8" means in the same Chapter.

References to the left or right side of the vehicle assume you are sitting in the driver's seat, facing forward.

Even though we have prepared this manual with extreme care, neither the publisher nor the author can accept responsibility for any errors in, or omissions from, the information given.

→**NOTE**

A *Note* provides information necessary to properly complete a procedure or information which will make the procedure easier to understand.

CAUTION

A *Caution* provides a special procedure or special steps which must be taken while completing the procedure where the Caution is found. Not heeding a Caution can result in damage to the assembly being worked on.

WARNING

A *Warning* provides a special procedure or special steps which must be taken while completing the procedure where the Warning is found. Not heeding a Warning can result in personal injury.

Introduction to the Mazda Miata

These models are available in a two-door convertible body styles only. A removable hardtop is optional.

Engines used in these vehicles include a 1.6 liter, a 1.8 liter and a 2.0 liter inline four. Multi-port fuel injection (MPFI) is used on all models. Later models are equipped with the On Board Diagnostic Second Generation (OBD-II) computerized engine management system that controls virtually every aspect of engine operation. OBD-II monitors emissions system components for signs of degradation and engine operation for any malfunction that could affect emissions, turning on the Service Engine Soon light if any faults are detected.

The engine drives the rear wheels through either a five-speed or six-speed manual or four-speed or six-speed automatic transmission via a driveshaft, differential and driveaxles.

The rack-and-pinion steering is mounted in front of the engine. Power assisted steering is optional.

The front suspension is composed of upper and lower control arms, coil spring/shock absorber assemblies and a stabilizer bar. The rear suspension is independent, with upper and lower control arms, coil springs, shock absorber units and a stabilizer bar.

The brakes are four wheel disc, with an Anti-lock Brake System (ABS) optional.

Vehicle identification numbers

Modifications are a continuing and unpublicized part of vehicle manufacturing. Since spare parts manuals and lists are compiled on a numerical basis, the individual vehicle numbers are essential to correctly identify the component required.

VEHICLE IDENTIFICATION NUMBER (VIN)

On 1997 and earlier and 2002 and later models, this very important identification number is stamped on a plate attached to the left side of the dashboard and is visible through the driver's side of the windshield (see illustration). On 1999 through 2001 models, the VIN is stamped on a plate located in the center of the firewall. The VIN also appears on the Vehicle Certificate of Title and Registration. It contains valuable information such as where and when the vehicle was manufactured, the model year and the body style.

ENGINE IDENTIFICATION NUMBER

The engine identification number can be found stamped on a pad at the right rear or left rear of the cylinder block (see illustration).

AUTOMATIC TRANSMISSION NUMBER

The ID number is stamped into the casting next to the neutral safety switch (see illustration).

MANUAL TRANSMISSION NUMBER

The vehicle ID number can be found on the case (see illustration).

VEHICLE EMISSIONS CONTROL INFORMATION (VECI) LABEL

This label is found in the engine compartment. See Chapter 6 for more information on this label.

The Vehicle Identification Number (VIN) is visible through the driver's side of the windshield (1997 and earlier and 2002 and later models)

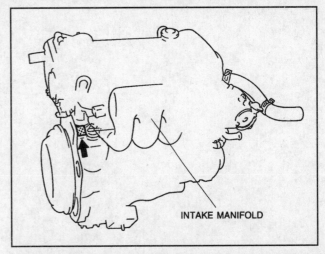

Engine identification number location (1997 and earlier/2006 and later models shown, 1999 through 2005 models on opposite side)

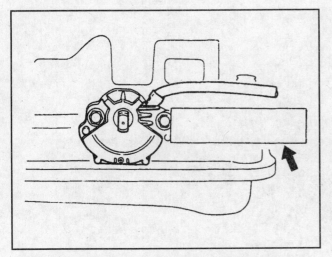

Automatic transmission identification number location

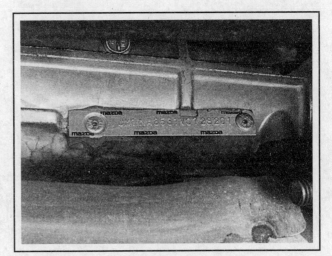

The VIN is also on a plate attached to the manual transmission

Buying parts

Replacement parts are available from many sources, which generally fall into one of two categories - authorized dealer parts departments and independent retail auto parts stores. Our advice concerning these parts is as follows:

Retail auto parts stores: Good auto parts stores will stock frequently needed components which wear out relatively fast, such as clutch components, exhaust systems, brake parts, tune-up parts, etc. These stores often supply new or reconditioned parts on an exchange basis, which can save a considerable amount of money. Discount auto parts stores are often very good places to buy materials and parts needed for general vehicle maintenance such as oil, grease, filters, spark plugs, belts, touch-up paint, bulbs, etc. They also usually sell

tools and general accessories, have convenient hours, charge lower prices and can often be found not far from home.

Authorized dealer parts department: This is the best source for parts which are unique to the vehicle and not generally available elsewhere (such as major engine parts, transmission parts, trim pieces, etc.).

Warranty information: If the vehicle is still covered under warranty, be sure that any replacement parts purchased - regardless of the source - do not invalidate the warranty!

To be sure of obtaining the correct parts, have engine and chassis numbers available and, if possible, take the old parts along for positive identification.

MAINTENANCE TECHNIQUES

There are a number of techniques involved in maintenance and repair that will be referred to throughout this manual. Application of these techniques will enable the home mechanic to be more efficient, better organized and capable of performing the various tasks properly, which will ensure that the repair job is thorough and complete.

Fasteners

Fasteners are nuts, bolts, studs and screws used to hold two or more parts together. There are a few things to keep in mind when working with fasteners. Almost all of them use a locking device of some type, either a lockwasher, locknut, locking tab or thread adhesive. All threaded fasteners should be clean and straight, with undamaged threads and undamaged corners on the hex head where the wrench fits. Develop the habit of replacing all damaged nuts and bolts with new ones. Special locknuts with nylon or fiber inserts can only be used once. If they are removed, they lose their locking ability and must be replaced with new ones.

Rusted nuts and bolts should be treated with a penetrating fluid to ease removal and prevent breakage. Some mechanics use turpentine in a spout-type oil can, which works quite well. After applying the rust penetrant, let it work for a few minutes before trying to loosen the nut or bolt. Badly rusted fasteners may have to be chiseled or sawed off or removed with a special nut breaker, available at tool stores.

If a bolt or stud breaks off in an assembly, it can be drilled and removed with a special tool commonly available for this purpose. Most automotive machine shops can perform this task, as well as other repair procedures, such as the repair of threaded holes that have been stripped out.

Flat washers and lockwashers, when removed from an assembly, should always be replaced exactly as removed. Replace any damaged washers with new ones. Never use a lockwasher on any soft metal surface (such as aluminum), thin sheet metal or plastic.

Fastener sizes

For a number of reasons, automobile manufacturers are making wider and wider use of metric fasteners. Therefore, it is important to be able to tell the difference between standard (sometimes called U.S. or SAE) and metric hardware, since they cannot be interchanged.

All bolts, whether standard or metric, are sized according to diameter, thread pitch and length. For example, a standard 1/2 - 13 x 1 bolt is 1/2 inch in diameter, has 13 threads per inch and is 1 inch long. An M12 - 1.75 x 25 metric bolt is 12 mm in diameter, has a thread pitch of 1.75 mm (the distance between threads) and is 25 mm long. The two bolts are nearly identical, and easily confused, but they are not interchangeable.

In addition to the differences in diameter, thread pitch and length, metric and standard bolts can also be distinguished by examining the bolt heads. To begin with, the distance across the flats on a standard bolt head is measured in inches, while the same dimension on a metric bolt is sized in millimeters (the same is true for nuts). As a result, a standard wrench should not be used on a metric bolt and a metric wrench should not be used on a standard bolt. Also, most standard bolts have slashes

radiating out from the center of the head to denote the grade or strength of the bolt, which is an indication of the amount of torque that can be applied to it. The greater the number of slashes, the greater the strength of the bolt. Grades 0 through 5 are commonly used on automobiles. Metric bolts have a property class (grade) number, rather than a slash, molded into their heads to indicate bolt strength. In this case, the higher the number, the stronger the bolt. Property class numbers 8.8, 9.8 and 10.9 are commonly used on automobiles.

Strength markings can also be used to distinguish standard hex nuts from metric hex nuts. Many standard nuts have dots stamped into one side, while metric nuts are marked with a number. The greater the number of dots, or the higher the number, the greater the strength of the nut.

Metric studs are also marked on their ends according to property class (grade). Larger studs are numbered (the same as metric bolts), while smaller studs carry a geometric code to denote grade.

It should be noted that many fasteners, especially Grades 0 through 2, have no distinguishing marks on them. When such is the case, the only way to determine whether it is standard or metric is to measure the thread pitch or compare it to a known fastener of the same size.

Standard fasteners are often referred to as SAE, as opposed to metric. However, it should be noted that SAE technically refers to a non-metric fine thread fastener only. Coarse thread non-metric fasteners are referred to as USS sizes.

Since fasteners of the same size (both standard and metric) may have different strength ratings, be sure to reinstall any bolts, studs or nuts removed from your vehicle in their original locations. Also, when replacing a fastener with a new one, make sure that the new one has a strength rating equal to or greater than the original.

Tightening sequences and procedures

Most threaded fasteners should be tightened to a specific torque value (torque is the twisting force applied to a threaded component such as a nut or bolt). Overtightening the fastener can weaken it and cause it to break, while undertightening can cause it to eventually come loose. Bolts, screws and studs, depending on the material they are made of and their thread diameters, have specific torque values, many of which are noted in the Specifications at the end of each Chapter. Be sure to follow the torque recommendations closely. For fasteners not assigned a specific torque, a general torque value chart is presented here as a guide. These torque values are for dry (unlubricated) fasteners threaded into steel or cast iron (not aluminum). As was previously mentioned, the size and grade of a fastener determine the amount of torque that can safely be applied to it. The figures listed here are approximate for Grade 2 and Grade 3 fasteners. Higher grades can tolerate higher torque values.

Fasteners laid out in a pattern, such as cylinder head bolts, oil pan bolts, differential cover bolts, etc., must be loosened or tightened in sequence to avoid warping the component. This sequence will normally be shown in the appropriate Chapter. If a specific pattern is not given, the following procedures can be used to prevent warping.

Initially, the bolts or nuts should be assembled finger-tight only. Next, they should be tightened one full turn each, in a criss-cross or diagonal pattern. After each one has been tightened one full turn, return to the first one and tighten them all one-half turn, following the same

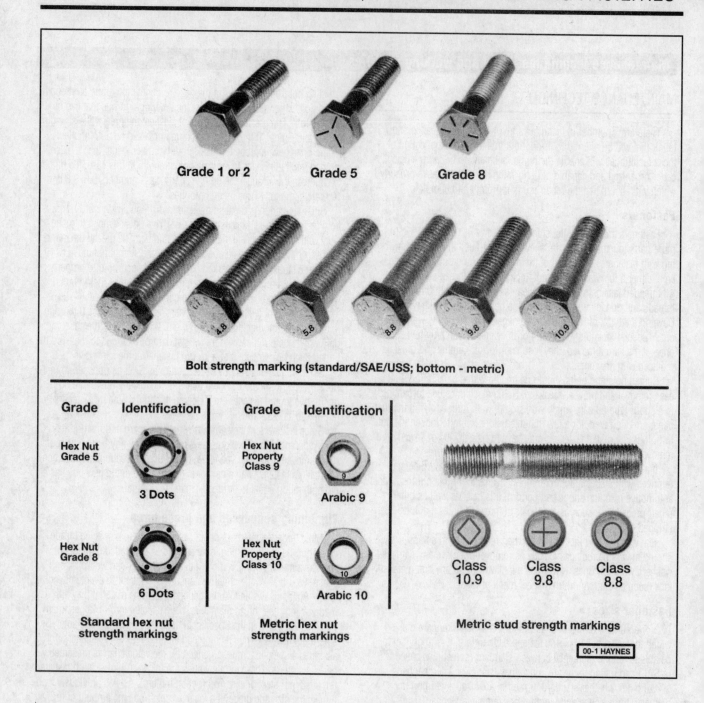

Grade 1 or 2   Grade 5   Grade 8

Bolt strength marking (standard/SAE/USS; bottom - metric)

Grade	Identification	Grade	Identification
Hex Nut Grade 5	3 Dots	Hex Nut Property Class 9	Arabic 9
Hex Nut Grade 8	6 Dots	Hex Nut Property Class 10	Arabic 10

Standard hex nut strength markings

Metric hex nut strength markings

Class 10.9   Class 9.8   Class 8.8

Metric stud strength markings

00-1 HAYNES

pattern. Finally, tighten each of them one-quarter turn at a time until each fastener has been tightened to the proper torque. To loosen and remove the fasteners, the procedure would be reversed.

Component disassembly

Component disassembly should be done with care and purpose to help ensure that the parts go back together properly. Always keep track of the sequence in which parts are removed. Make note of special characteristics or marks on parts that can be installed more than one way, such as a grooved thrust washer on a shaft. It is a good idea to lay the disassembled parts out on a clean surface in the order that they were removed. It may also be helpful to make sketches or take instant photos of components before removal.

When removing fasteners from a component, keep track of their locations. Sometimes threading a bolt back in a part, or putting the washers and nut back on a stud, can prevent mix-ups later. If nuts and bolts cannot be returned to their original locations, they should be kept in a compartmented box or a series of small boxes. A cupcake or muffin tin is ideal for this purpose, since each cavity can hold the bolts and nuts from a particular area (i.e. oil pan bolts, valve cover bolts, engine

Metric thread sizes	Ft-lbs	Nm
M-6	6 to 9	9 to 12
M-8	14 to 21	19 to 28
M-10	28 to 40	38 to 54
M-12	50 to 71	68 to 96
M-14	80 to 140	109 to 154

Pipe thread sizes		
1/8	5 to 8	7 to 10
1/4	12 to 18	17 to 24
3/8	22 to 33	30 to 44
1/2	25 to 35	34 to 47

U.S. thread sizes		
1/4 - 20	6 to 9	9 to 12
5/16 - 18	12 to 18	17 to 24
5/16 - 24	14 to 20	19 to 27
3/8 - 16	22 to 32	30 to 43
3/8 - 24	27 to 38	37 to 51
7/16 - 14	40 to 55	55 to 74
7/16 - 20	40 to 60	55 to 81
1/2 - 13	55 to 80	75 to 108

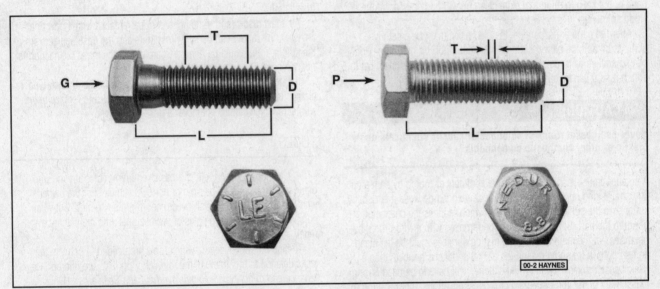

00-2 HAYNES

Standard (SAE and USS) bolt dimensions/grade marks

G   Grade marks (bolt strength)
L   Length (in inches)
T   Thread pitch (number of threads per inch)
D   Nominal diameter (in inches)

Metric bolt dimensions/grade marks

P   Property class (bolt strength)
L   Length (in millimeters)
T   Thread pitch (distance between threads in millimeters)
D   Diameter

mount bolts, etc.). A pan of this type is especially helpful when working on assemblies with very small parts, such as the carburetor, alternator, valve train or interior dash and trim pieces. The cavities can be marked with paint or tape to identify the contents.

Whenever wiring looms, harnesses or connectors are separated, it is a good idea to identify the two halves with numbered pieces of masking tape so they can be easily reconnected.

Gasket sealing surfaces

Throughout any vehicle, gaskets are used to seal the mating surfaces between two parts and keep lubricants, fluids, vacuum or pressure contained in an assembly.

Many times these gaskets are coated with a liquid or paste-type gasket sealing compound before assembly. Age, heat and pressure can sometimes cause the two parts to stick together so tightly that they are very difficult to separate. Often, the assembly can be loosened by striking it with a soft-face hammer near the mating surfaces. A regular hammer can be used if a block of wood is placed between the hammer and the part. Do not hammer on cast parts or parts that could be easily damaged. With any particularly stubborn part, always recheck to make sure that every fastener has been removed.

Avoid using a screwdriver or bar to pry apart an assembly, as they

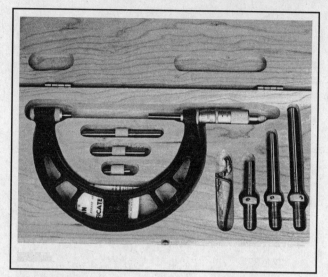

Micrometer set

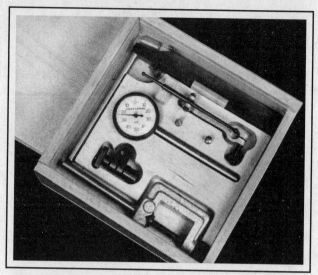

Dial indicator set

can easily mar the gasket sealing surfaces of the parts, which must remain smooth. If prying is absolutely necessary, use an old broom handle, but keep in mind that extra clean up will be necessary if the wood splinters.

After the parts are separated, the old gasket must be carefully scraped off and the gasket surfaces cleaned. Stubborn gasket material can be soaked with rust penetrant or treated with a special chemical to soften it so it can be easily scraped off.

✳ CAUTION:

Never use gasket removal solutions or caustic chemicals on plastic or other composite components.

A scraper can be fashioned from a piece of copper tubing by flattening and sharpening one end. Copper is recommended because it is usually softer than the surfaces to be scraped, which reduces the chance of gouging the part. Some gaskets can be removed with a wire brush, but regardless of the method used, the mating surfaces must be left clean and smooth. If for some reason the gasket surface is gouged, then a gasket sealer thick enough to fill scratches will have to be used during reassembly of the components. For most applications, a non-drying (or semi-drying) gasket sealer should be used.

Hose removal tips

✳ WARNING:

If the vehicle is equipped with air conditioning, do not disconnect any of the A/C hoses without first having the system depressurized by a dealer service department or a service station.

Hose removal precautions closely parallel gasket removal precautions. Avoid scratching or gouging the surface that the hose mates against or the connection may leak. This is especially true for radiator hoses. Because of various chemical reactions, the rubber in hoses can bond itself to the metal spigot that the hose fits over. To remove a hose, first loosen the hose clamps that secure it to the spigot. Then, with slip-joint pliers, grab the hose at the clamp and rotate it around the spigot. Work it back and forth until it is completely free, then pull it off. Silicone or other lubricants will ease removal if they can be applied

between the hose and the outside of the spigot. Apply the same lubricant to the inside of the hose and the outside of the spigot to simplify installation.

As a last resort (and if the hose is to be replaced with a new one anyway), the rubber can be slit with a knife and the hose peeled from the spigot. If this must be done, be careful that the metal connection is not damaged.

If a hose clamp is broken or damaged, do not reuse it. Wire-type clamps usually weaken with age, so it is a good idea to replace them with screw-type clamps whenever a hose is removed.

TOOLS

A selection of good tools is a basic requirement for anyone who plans to maintain and repair his or her own vehicle. For the owner who has few tools, the initial investment might seem high, but when compared to the spiraling costs of professional auto maintenance and repair, it is a wise one.

To help the owner decide which tools are needed to perform the tasks detailed in this manual, the following tool lists are offered: *Maintenance and minor repair, Repair/overhaul* and *Special.*

The newcomer to practical mechanics should start off with the *maintenance and minor repair* tool kit, which is adequate for the simpler jobs performed on a vehicle. Then, as confidence and experience grow, the owner can tackle more difficult tasks, buying additional tools as they are needed. Eventually the basic kit will be expanded into the *repair and overhaul* tool set. Over a period of time, the experienced do-it-yourselfer will assemble a tool set complete enough for most repair and overhaul procedures and will add tools from the special category when it is felt that the expense is justified by the frequency of use.

Maintenance and minor repair tool kit

The tools in this list should be considered the minimum required for performance of routine maintenance, servicing and minor repair work. We recommend the purchase of combination wrenches (box-end and open-end combined in one wrench). While more expensive than open end wrenches, they offer the advantages of both types of wrench.

Combination wrench set (1/4-inch to 1 inch or 6 mm to 19 mm)
Adjustable wrench, 8 inch
Spark plug wrench with rubber insert

Spark plug gap adjusting tool
Feeler gauge set
Brake bleeder wrench
Standard screwdriver (5/16-inch x 6 inch)
Phillips screwdriver (No. 2 x 6 inch)
Combination pliers - 6 inch
Hacksaw and assortment of blades
Tire pressure gauge
Grease gun

Oil can
Fine emery cloth
Wire brush
Battery post and cable cleaning tool
Oil filter wrench
Funnel (medium size)
Safety goggles
Jackstands (2)
Drain pan

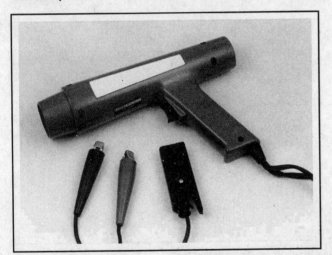

Dial caliper

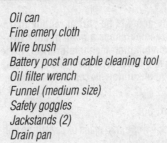

Hand-operated vacuum pump

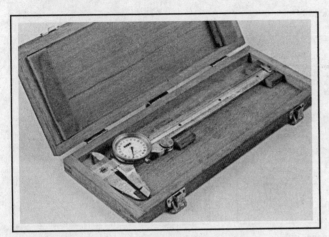

Timing light

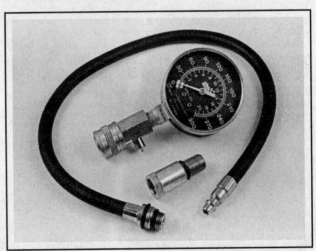

Compression gauge with spark plug hole adapter

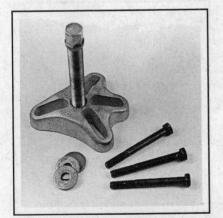

Damper/steering wheel puller

General purpose puller

Hydraulic lifter removal tool

➡Note: If basic tune-ups are going to be part of routine maintenance, it will be necessary to purchase a good quality stroboscopic timing light and combination tachometer/dwell meter. Although they are included in the list of special tools, it is mentioned here because they are absolutely necessary for tuning most vehicles properly.

Repair and overhaul tool set

These tools are essential for anyone who plans to perform major repairs and are in addition to those in the maintenance and minor repair tool kit. Included is a comprehensive set of sockets which, though expensive, are invaluable because of their versatility, especially when various extensions and drives are available. We recommend the 1/2-inch drive over the 3/8-inch drive. Although the larger drive is bulky and more expensive, it has the capacity of accepting a very wide range of large sockets. Ideally, however, the mechanic should have a 3/8-inch drive set and a 1/2-inch drive set.

Valve spring compressor

Valve spring compressor

Ridge reamer

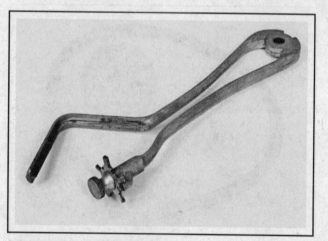

Piston ring groove cleaning tool

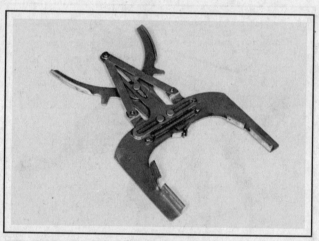

Ring removal/installation tool

Ring compressor

Cylinder hone

Brake hold-down spring tool

Torque angle gauge

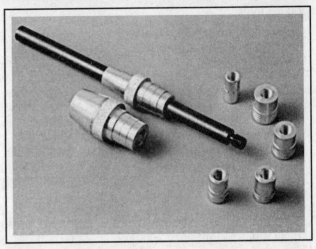

Clutch plate alignment tool

Socket set(s)
Reversible ratchet
Extension - 10 inch
Universal joint
Torque wrench (same size drive as sockets)
Ball peen hammer - 8 ounce
Soft-face hammer (plastic/rubber)
Standard screwdriver (1/4-inch x 6 inch)
Standard screwdriver (stubby - 5/16-inch)
Phillips screwdriver (No. 3 x 8 inch)
Phillips screwdriver (stubby - No. 2)
Pliers - vise grip
Pliers - lineman's
Pliers - needle nose
Pliers - snap-ring (internal and external)
Cold chisel - 1/2-inch
Scribe
Scraper (made from flattened copper tubing)
Centerpunch
Pin punches (1/16, 1/8, 3/16-inch)
Steel rule/straightedge - 12 inch
Allen wrench set (1/8 to 3/8-inch or 4 mm to 10 mm)
A selection of files
Wire brush (large)
Jackstands (second set)
Jack (scissor or hydraulic type)

➡Note: Another tool which is often useful is an electric drill with a chuck capacity of 3/8-inch and a set of good quality drill bits.

Special tools

The tools in this list include those which are not used regularly, are expensive to buy, or which need to be used in accordance with their manufacturer's instructions. Unless these tools will be used frequently, it is not very economical to purchase many of them. A consideration would be to split the cost and use between yourself and a friend or friends. In addition, most of these tools can be obtained from a tool rental shop on a temporary basis.

This list primarily contains only those tools and instruments widely available to the public, and not those special tools produced by the vehicle manufacturer for distribution to dealer service departments. Occasionally, references to the manufacturer's special tools are included in the text of this manual. Generally, an alternative method of doing the job without the special tool is offered. However, sometimes there is no alternative to their use. Where this is the case, and the tool cannot be purchased or borrowed, the work should be turned over to the dealer service department or an automotive repair shop.

Valve spring compressor
Piston ring groove cleaning tool
Piston ring compressor
Piston ring installation tool
Cylinder compression gauge
Cylinder ridge reamer
Cylinder surfacing hone
Cylinder bore gauge
Micrometers and/or dial calipers
Hydraulic lifter removal tool
Balljoint separator
Universal-type puller
Impact screwdriver
Dial indicator set
Stroboscopic timing light (inductive pick-up)
Hand operated vacuum/pressure pump
Tachometer/dwell meter
Universal electrical multimeter
Cable hoist
Brake spring removal and installation tools
Floor jack

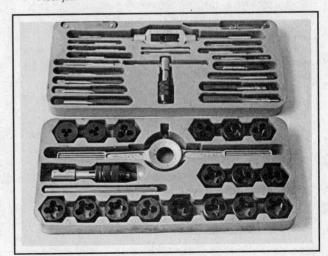

Tap and die set

Buying tools

For the do-it-yourselfer who is just starting to get involved in vehicle maintenance and repair, there are a number of options available when purchasing tools. If maintenance and minor repair is the extent of the work to be done, the purchase of individual tools is satisfactory. If, on the other hand, extensive work is planned, it would be a good idea to purchase a modest tool set from one of the large retail chain stores. A set can usually be bought at a substantial savings over the individual tool prices, and they often come with a tool box. As additional tools are needed, add-on sets, individual tools and a larger tool box can be purchased to expand the tool selection. Building a tool set gradually allows the cost of the tools to be spread over a longer period of time and gives the mechanic the freedom to choose only those tools that will actually be used.

Tool stores will often be the only source of some of the special tools that are needed, but regardless of where tools are bought, try to avoid cheap ones, especially when buying screwdrivers and sockets, because they won't last very long. The expense involved in replacing cheap tools will eventually be greater than the initial cost of quality tools.

Care and maintenance of tools

Good tools are expensive, so it makes sense to treat them with respect. Keep them clean and in usable condition and store them properly when not in use. Always wipe off any dirt, grease or metal chips before putting them away. Never leave tools lying around in the work area. Upon completion of a job, always check closely under the hood for tools that may have been left there so they won't get lost during a test drive.

Some tools, such as screwdrivers, pliers, wrenches and sockets, can be hung on a panel mounted on the garage or workshop wall, while others should be kept in a tool box or tray. Measuring instruments, gauges, meters, etc. must be carefully stored where they cannot be damaged by weather or impact from other tools.

When tools are used with care and stored properly, they will last a very long time. Even with the best of care, though, tools will wear out if used frequently. When a tool is damaged or worn out, replace it. Subsequent jobs will be safer and more enjoyable if you do.

HOW TO REPAIR DAMAGED THREADS

Sometimes, the internal threads of a nut or bolt hole can become stripped, usually from overtightening. Stripping threads is an all-too-common occurrence, especially when working with aluminum parts, because aluminum is so soft that it easily strips out.

Usually, external or internal threads are only partially stripped. After they've been cleaned up with a tap or die, they'll still work. Sometimes, however, threads are badly damaged. When this happens, you've got three choices:

1) Drill and tap the hole to the next suitable oversize and install a larger diameter bolt, screw or stud.

2) Drill and tap the hole to accept a threaded plug, then drill and tap the plug to the original screw size. You can also buy a plug already threaded to the original size. Then you simply drill a hole to the specified size, then run the threaded plug into the hole with a bolt and jam nut. Once the plug is fully seated, remove the jam nut and bolt.

3) The third method uses a patented thread repair kit like Heli-Coil or Slimsert. These easy-to-use kits are designed to repair damaged threads in straight-through holes and blind holes. Both are available as kits which can handle a variety of sizes and thread patterns. Drill the hole, then tap it with the special included tap. Install the Heli-Coil and the hole is back to its original diameter and thread pitch.

Regardless of which method you use, be sure to proceed calmly and carefully. A little impatience or carelessness during one of these relatively simple procedures can ruin your whole day's work and cost you a bundle if you wreck an expensive part.

WORKING FACILITIES

Not to be overlooked when discussing tools is the workshop. If anything more than routine maintenance is to be carried out, some sort of suitable work area is essential.

It is understood, and appreciated, that many home mechanics do not have a good workshop or garage available, and end up removing an engine or doing major repairs outside. It is recommended, however, that the overhaul or repair be completed under the cover of a roof.

A clean, flat workbench or table of comfortable working height is an absolute necessity. The workbench should be equipped with a vise that has a jaw opening of at least four inches.

As mentioned previously, some clean, dry storage space is also required for tools, as well as the lubricants, fluids, cleaning solvents, etc. which soon become necessary.

Sometimes waste oil and fluids, drained from the engine or cooling system during normal maintenance or repairs, present a disposal problem. To avoid pouring them on the ground or into a sewage system, pour the used fluids into large containers, seal them with caps and take them to an authorized disposal site or recycling center. Plastic jugs, such as old antifreeze containers, are ideal for this purpose.

Always keep a supply of old newspapers and clean rags available. Old towels are excellent for mopping up spills. Many mechanics use rolls of paper towels for most work because they are readily available and disposable. To help keep the area under the vehicle clean, a large cardboard box can be cut open and flattened to protect the garage or shop floor.

Whenever working over a painted surface, such as when leaning over a fender to service something under the hood, always cover it with an old blanket or bedspread to protect the finish. Vinyl covered pads, made especially for this purpose, are available at auto parts stores.

Jacking and towing

JACKING

✳✳ WARNING:

The jack supplied with the vehicle should only be used for raising the vehicle when changing a tire or placing jackstands under the frame. Never work under the vehicle or start the engine while the jack is being used as the only means of support.

The vehicle must be on a level surface with the wheels blocked and the transmission in Park. Apply the parking brake if the front of the vehicle must be raised. Make sure no one is in the vehicle as it's being raised with the jack.

Remove the jack and lug nut wrench and spare tire from the trunk.

To replace the tire, loosen the lug nuts one-half turn, but leave them in place until the tire is raised off the ground.

Position the jack under the side of the vehicle at the indicated jacking points. There's a front and rear jacking point on each side of the vehicle (see illustration).

Turn the jack handle clockwise until the tire clears the ground. Remove the lug nuts and pull the tire off. Clean the mating surfaces of the hub and wheel, then install the spare. Clean the lug nut threads,

The head of the jack should engage the notch in the rocker panel flange - there's one at the front and one at the rear on each side of the vehicle

then replace the lug nuts with the beveled edges facing in and tighten them snugly. Don't attempt to tighten them completely until the vehicle is lowered or it could slip off the jack.

✳✳ CAUTION:

Don't use oil on the lug nut threads. It may cause the lug nuts to loosen or seize.

Turn the jack handle counterclockwise to lower the vehicle. Remove the jack and tighten the lug nuts in a criss-cross pattern. If possible, tighten the nuts with a torque wrench (see Chapter 1 for the torque figures). If you don't have access to a torque wrench, have the nuts checked by a service station or repair shop as soon as possible.

✳✳ CAUTION:

The compact spare included with these vehicles is intended for temporary use only. Have the tire repaired and reinstall it on the vehicle at the earliest opportunity and don't exceed 50 mph with the spare tire on the car.

Stow the tire, jack and wrench and unblock the wheels.

TOWING

We recommend these vehicles be towed from the rear, with the rear wheels off the ground. If it's absolutely necessary, these vehicles can be towed from the front with the front wheels off the ground, provided that speeds don't exceed 35 mph and the distance is less than 35 miles; the transmission can be damaged if these mileage/speed limitations are exceeded.

Equipment specifically designed for towing should be used. It must be attached to the main structural members of the vehicle, not the bumpers or brackets.

Safety is a major consideration when towing and all applicable state and local laws must be obeyed. A safety chain must be used at all times.

The parking brake must be released and the transmission must be in Neutral. The steering must be unlocked (ignition switch in the Acc position). Remember that power steering and power brakes won't work with the engine off.

Anti-theft audio system

Some of these models are equipped with an anti-theft feature that will render the stereo inoperative if stolen. If the power source to the stereo is cut off, the stereo will be inoperative. Even if the power source is immediately reconnected, the stereo will not function.

If your vehicle is equipped with this anti-theft system, do not disconnect the battery, remove the stereo or remove related components unless you have the individual activation code number for the stereo.

Booster battery (jump) starting

➡**Note: The battery is located in the luggage compartment on 2005 and earlier models. On 2006 and later models it's located in the engine compartment.**

Observe these precautions when using a booster battery to start a vehicle:

a) *Before connecting the booster battery, make sure the ignition switch is in the Off position.*
b) *Turn off the lights, heater and other electrical loads.*
c) *Your eyes should be shielded. Safety goggles are a good idea.*
d) *Make sure the booster battery is the same voltage as the dead one in the vehicle.*
e) *The two vehicles MUST NOT TOUCH each other!*
f) *Make sure the transaxle is in Neutral (manual) or Park (automatic).*
g) *If the booster battery is not a maintenance-free type, remove the vent caps and lay a cloth over the vent holes.*

Connect the red jumper cable to the positive (+) terminals of each battery (see illustration).

Connect one end of the black jumper cable to the negative (-) terminal of the booster battery. The other end of this cable should be connected to a good ground on the vehicle to be started, such as a bolt or bracket on the body.

Start the engine using the booster battery, then, with the engine running at idle speed, disconnect the jumper cables in the reverse order of connection.

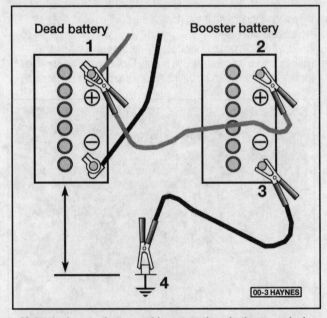

Make the booster battery cable connections in the numerical order shown (note that the negative cable of the booster battery is NOT attached to the negative terminal of the dead battery)

Automotive chemicals and lubricants

A number of automotive chemicals and lubricants are available for use during vehicle maintenance and repair. They include a wide variety of products ranging from cleaning solvents and degreasers to lubricants and protective sprays for rubber, plastic and vinyl.

CLEANERS

Carburetor cleaner and choke cleaner is a strong solvent for gum, varnish and carbon. Most carburetor cleaners leave a dry-type lubricant film which will not harden or gum up. Because of this film it is not recommended for use on electrical components.

Brake system cleaner is used to remove brake dust, grease and brake fluid from the brake system, where clean surfaces are absolutely necessary. It leaves no residue and often eliminates brake squeal caused by contaminants.

Electrical cleaner removes oxidation, corrosion and carbon deposits from electrical contacts, restoring full current flow. It can also be used to clean spark plugs, carburetor jets, voltage regulators and other parts where an oil-free surface is desired.

Demoisturants remove water and moisture from electrical components such as alternators, voltage regulators, electrical connectors and fuse blocks. They are non-conductive and non-corrosive.

Degreasers are heavy-duty solvents used to remove grease from the outside of the engine and from chassis components. They can be sprayed or brushed on and, depending on the type, are rinsed off either with water or solvent.

LUBRICANTS

Motor oil is the lubricant formulated for use in engines. It normally contains a wide variety of additives to prevent corrosion and reduce foaming and wear. Motor oil comes in various weights (viscosity ratings) from 0 to 50. The recommended weight of the oil depends on the season, temperature and the demands on the engine. Light oil is used in cold climates and under light load conditions. Heavy oil is used in hot climates and where high loads are encountered. Multi-viscosity oils are designed to have characteristics of both light and heavy oils and are available in a number of weights from 0W-20 to 20W-50.

Gear oil is designed to be used in differentials, manual transmissions and other areas where high-temperature lubrication is required.

Chassis and wheel bearing grease is a heavy grease used where increased loads and friction are encountered, such as for wheel bearings, ball-joints, tie-rod ends and universal joints.

High-temperature wheel bearing grease is designed to withstand the extreme temperatures encountered by wheel bearings in disc brake equipped vehicles. It usually contains molybdenum disulfide (moly), which is a dry-type lubricant.

White grease is a heavy grease for metal-to-metal applications where water is a problem. White grease stays soft under both low and high temperatures (usually from -100 to +190-degrees F), and will not wash off or dilute in the presence of water.

Assembly lube is a special extreme pressure lubricant, usually containing moly, used to lubricate high-load parts (such as main and rod bearings and cam lobes) for initial start-up of a new engine. The assembly lube lubricates the parts without being squeezed out or washed away until the engine oiling system begins to function.

Silicone lubricants are used to protect rubber, plastic, vinyl and nylon parts.

Graphite lubricants are used where oils cannot be used due to contamination problems, such as in locks. The dry graphite will lubricate metal parts while remaining uncontaminated by dirt, water, oil or acids. It is electrically conductive and will not foul electrical contacts in locks such as the ignition switch.

Moly penetrants loosen and lubricate frozen, rusted and corroded fasteners and prevent future rusting or freezing.

Heat-sink grease is a special electrically non-conductive grease that is used for mounting electronic ignition modules where it is essential that heat is transferred away from the module.

SEALANTS

RTV sealant is one of the most widely used gasket compounds. Made from silicone, RTV is air curing, it seals, bonds, waterproofs, fills surface irregularities, remains flexible, doesn't shrink, is relatively easy to remove, and is used as a supplementary sealer with almost all low and medium temperature gaskets.

Anaerobic sealant is much like RTV in that it can be used either to seal gaskets or to form gaskets by itself. It remains flexible, is solvent resistant and fills surface imperfections. The difference between an anaerobic sealant and an RTV-type sealant is in the curing. RTV cures when exposed to air, while an anaerobic sealant cures only in the absence of air. This means that an anaerobic sealant cures only after the assembly of parts, sealing them together.

Thread and pipe sealant is used for sealing hydraulic and pneumatic fittings and vacuum lines. It is usually made from a Teflon compound, and comes in a spray, a paint-on liquid and as a wrap-around tape.

CHEMICALS

Anti-seize compound prevents seizing, galling, cold welding, rust and corrosion in fasteners. High-temperature anti-seize, usually made with copper and graphite lubricants, is used for exhaust system and exhaust manifold bolts.

Anaerobic locking compounds are used to keep fasteners from vibrating or working loose and cure only after installation, in the absence of air. Medium strength locking compound is used for small nuts, bolts and screws that may be removed later. High-strength locking compound is for large nuts, bolts and studs which aren't removed on a regular basis.

Oil additives range from viscosity index improvers to chemical treatments that claim to reduce internal engine friction. It should be noted that most oil manufacturers caution against using additives with their oils.

Gas additives perform several functions, depending on their chemical makeup. They usually contain solvents that help dissolve gum and varnish that build up on carburetor, fuel injection and intake parts. They also serve to break down carbon deposits that form on the inside surfaces of the combustion chambers. Some additives contain upper cylinder lubricants for valves and piston rings, and others contain chemicals to remove condensation from the gas tank.

MISCELLANEOUS

Brake fluid is specially formulated hydraulic fluid that can withstand the heat and pressure encountered in brake systems. Care must be taken so this fluid does not come in contact with painted surfaces or plastics. An opened container should always be resealed to prevent contamination by water or dirt.

Weatherstrip adhesive is used to bond weatherstripping around doors, windows and trunk lids. It is sometimes used to attach trim pieces.

Undercoating is a petroleum-based, tar-like substance that is designed to protect metal surfaces on the underside of the vehicle from corrosion. It also acts as a sound-deadening agent by insulating the bottom of the vehicle.

Waxes and polishes are used to help protect painted and plated surfaces from the weather. Different types of paint may require the use of different types of wax and polish. Some polishes utilize a chemical or abrasive cleaner to help remove the top layer of oxidized (dull) paint on older vehicles. In recent years many non-wax polishes that contain a wide variety of chemicals such as polymers and silicones have been introduced. These non-wax polishes are usually easier to apply and last longer than conventional waxes and polishes.

CONVERSION FACTORS

LENGTH (distance)

Inches (in)	X 25.4	= Millimeters (mm)	X 0.0394	= Inches (in)
Feet (ft)	X 0.305	= Meters (m)	X 3.281	= Feet (ft)
Miles	X 1.609	= Kilometers (km)	X 0.621	= Miles

VOLUME (capacity)

Cubic inches (cu in; in³)	X 16.387	= Cubic centimeters (cc; cm³)	X 0.061	= Cubic inches (cu in; in³)
Imperial pints (Imp pt)	X 0.568	= Liters (l)	X 1.76	= Imperial pints (Imp pt)
Imperial quarts (Imp qt)	X 1.137	= Liters (l)	X 0.88	= Imperial quarts (Imp qt)
Imperial quarts (Imp qt)	X 1.201	= US quarts (US qt)	X 0.833	= Imperial quarts (Imp qt)
US quarts (US qt)	X 0.946	= Liters (l)	X 1.057	= US quarts (US qt)
Imperial gallons (Imp gal)	X 4.546	= Liters (l)	X 0.22	= Imperial gallons (Imp gal)
Imperial gallons (Imp gal)	X 1.201	= US gallons (US gal)	X 0.833	= Imperial gallons (Imp gal)
US gallons (US gal)	X 3.785	= Liters (l)	X 0.264	= US gallons (US gal)

MASS (weight)

Ounces (oz)	X 28.35	= Grams (g)	X 0.035	= Ounces (oz)
Pounds (lb)	X 0.454	= Kilograms (kg)	X 2.205	= Pounds (lb)

FORCE

Ounces-force (ozf; oz)	X 0.278	= Newtons (N)	X 3.6	= Ounces-force (ozf; oz)
Pounds-force (lbf; lb)	X 4.448	= Newtons (N)	X 0.225	= Pounds-force (lbf; lb)
Newtons (N)	X 0.1	= Kilograms-force (kgf; kg)	X 9.81	= Newtons (N)

PRESSURE

Pounds-force per square inch (psi; lbf/in²; lb/in²)	X 0.070	= Kilograms-force per square centimeter (kgf/cm²; kg/cm²)	X 14.223	= Pounds-force per square inch (psi; lbf/in²; lb/in²)
Pounds-force per square inch (psi; lbf/in²; lb/in²)	X 0.068	= Atmospheres (atm)	X 14.696	= Pounds-force per square inch (psi; lbf/in²; lb/in²)
Pounds-force per square inch (psi; lbf/in²; lb/in²)	X 0.069	= Bars	X 14.5	= Pounds-force per square inch (psi; lbf/in²; lb/in²)
Pounds-force per square inch (psi; lbf/in²; lb/in²)	X 6.895	= Kilopascals (kPa)	X 0.145	= Pounds-force per square inch (psi; lbf/in²; lb/in²)
Kilopascals (kPa)	X 0.01	= Kilograms-force per square centimeter (kgf/cm²; kg/cm²)	X 98.1	= Kilopascals (kPa)

TORQUE (moment of force)

Pounds-force inches (lbf in; lb in)	X 1.152	= Kilograms-force centimeter (kgf cm; kg cm)	X 0.868	= Pounds-force inches (lbf in; lb in)
Pounds-force inches (lbf in; lb in)	X 0.113	= Newton meters (Nm)	X 8.85	= Pounds-force inches (lbf in; lb in)
Pounds-force inches (lbf in; lb in)	X 0.083	= Pounds-force feet (lbf ft; lb ft)	X 12	= Pounds-force inches (lbf in; lb in)
Pounds-force feet (lbf ft; lb ft)	X 0.138	= Kilograms-force meters (kgf m; kg m)	X 7.233	= Pounds-force feet (lbf ft; lb ft)
Pounds-force feet (lbf ft; lb ft)	X 1.356	= Newton meters (Nm)	X 0.738	= Pounds-force feet (lbf ft; lb ft)
Newton meters (Nm)	X 0.102	= Kilograms-force meters (kgf m; kg m)	X 9.804	= Newton meters (Nm)

VACUUM

Inches mercury (in. Hg)	X 3.377	= Kilopascals (kPa)	X 0.2961	= Inches mercury
Inches mercury (in. Hg)	X 25.4	= Millimeters mercury (mm Hg)	X 0.0394	= Inches mercury

POWER

Horsepower (hp)	X 745.7	= Watts (W)	X 0.0013	= Horsepower (hp)

VELOCITY (speed)

Miles per hour (miles/hr; mph)	X 1.609	= Kilometers per hour (km/hr; kph)	X 0.621	= Miles per hour (miles/hr; mph)

FUEL CONSUMPTION *

Miles per gallon, Imperial (mpg)	X 0.354	= Kilometers per liter (km/l)	X 2.825	= Miles per gallon, Imperial (mpg)
Miles per gallon, US (mpg)	X 0.425	= Kilometers per liter (km/l)	X 2.352	= Miles per gallon, US (mpg)

TEMPERATURE

Degrees Fahrenheit = (°C x 1.8) + 32   Degrees Celsius (Degrees Centigrade; °C) = (°F - 32) x 0.56

*It is common practice to convert from miles per gallon (mpg) to liters/100 kilometers (l/100km), where mpg (Imperial) x l/100 km = 282 and mpg (US) x l/100 km = 235

FRACTION/DECIMAL/MILLIMETER EQUIVALENTS

DECIMALS TO MILLIMETERS

Decimal	mm	Decimal	mm
0.001	0.0254	0.500	12.7000
0.002	0.0508	0.510	12.9540
0.003	0.0762	0.520	13.2080
0.004	0.1016	0.530	13.4620
0.005	0.1270	0.540	13.7160
0.006	0.1524	0.550	13.9700
0.007	0.1778	0.560	14.2240
0.008	0.2032	0.570	14.4780
0.009	0.2286	0.580	14.7320
		0.590	14.9860
0.010	0.2540		
0.020	0.5080		
0.030	0.7620		
0.040	1.0160	0.600	15.2400
0.050	1.2700	0.610	15.4940
0.060	1.5240	0.620	15.7480
0.070	1.7780	0.630	16.0020
0.080	2.0320	0.640	16.2560
0.090	2.2860	0.650	16.5100
		0.660	16.7640
0.100	2.5400	0.670	17.0180
0.110	2.7940	0.680	17.2720
0.120	3.0480	0.690	17.5260
0.130	3.3020		
0.140	3.5560		
0.150	3.8100	0.700	17.7800
0.160	4.0640	0.710	18.0340
0.170	4.3180	0.720	18.2880
0.180	4.5720	0.730	18.5420
0.190	4.8260	0.740	18.7960
		0.750	19.0500
0.200	5.0800	0.760	19.3040
0.210	5.3340	0.770	19.5580
0.220	5.5880	0.780	19.8120
0.230	5.8420	0.790	20.0660
0.240	6.0960		
0.250	6.3500		
0.260	6.6040	0.800	20.3200
0.270	6.8580	0.810	20.5740
0.280	7.1120	0.820	21.8280
0.290	7.3660	0.830	21.0820
		0.840	21.3360
0.300	7.6200	0.850	21.5900
0.310	7.8740	0.860	21.8440
0.320	8.1280	0.870	22.0980
0.330	8.3820	0.880	22.3520
0.340	8.6360	0.890	22.6060
0.350	8.8900		
0.360	9.1440		
0.370	9.3980		
0.380	9.6520		
0.390	9.9060		
		0.900	22.8600
0.400	10.1600	0.910	23.1140
0.410	10.4140	0.920	23.3680
0.420	10.6680	0.930	23.6220
0.430	10.9220	0.940	23.8760
0.440	11.1760	0.950	24.1300
0.450	11.4300	0.960	24.3840
0.460	11.6840	0.970	24.6380
0.470	11.9380	0.980	24.8920
0.480	12.1920	0.990	25.1460
0.490	12.4460	1.000	25.4000

FRACTIONS TO DECIMALS TO MILLIMETERS

Fraction	Decimal	mm	Fraction	Decimal	mm
1/64	0.0156	0.3969	33/64	0.5156	13.0969
1/32	0.0312	0.7938	17/32	0.5312	13.4938
3/64	0.0469	1.1906	35/64	0.5469	13.8906
1/16	0.0625	1.5875	9/16	0.5625	14.2875
5/64	0.0781	1.9844	37/64	0.5781	14.6844
3/32	0.0938	2.3812	19/32	0.5938	15.0812
7/64	0.1094	2.7781	39/64	0.6094	15.4781
1/8	0.1250	3.1750	5/8	0.6250	15.8750
9/64	0.1406	3.5719	41/64	0.6406	16.2719
5/32	0.1562	3.9688	21/32	0.6562	16.6688
11/64	0.1719	4.3656	43/64	0.6719	17.0656
3/16	0.1875	4.7625	11/16	0.6875	17.4625
13/64	0.2031	5.1594	45/64	0.7031	17.8594
7/32	0.2188	5.5562	23/32	0.7188	18.2562
15/64	0.2344	5.9531	47/64	0.7344	18.6531
1/4	0.2500	6.3500	3/4	0.7500	19.0500
17/64	0.2656	6.7469	49/64	0.7656	19.4469
9/32	0.2812	7.1438	25/32	0.7812	19.8438
19/64	0.2969	7.5406	51/64	0.7969	20.2406
5/16	0.3125	7.9375	13/16	0.8125	20.6375
21/64	0.3281	8.3344	53/64	0.8281	21.0344
11/32	0.3438	8.7312	27/32	0.8438	21.4312
23/64	0.3594	9.1281	55/64	0.8594	21.8281
3/8	0.3750	9.5250	7/8	0.8750	22.2250
25/64	0.3906	9.9219	57/64	0.8906	22.6219
13/32	0.4062	10.3188	29/32	0.9062	23.0188
27/64	0.4219	10.7156	59/64	0.9219	23.4156
7/16	0.4375	11.1125	15/16	0.9375	23.8125
29/64	0.4531	11.5094	61/64	0.9531	24.2094
15/32	0.4688	11.9062	31/32	0.9688	24.6062
31/64	0.4844	12.3031	63/64	0.9844	25.0031
1/2	0.5000	12.7000	1	1.0000	25.4000

Safety first!

Regardless of how enthusiastic you may be about getting on with the job at hand, take the time to ensure that your safety is not jeopardized. A moment's lack of attention can result in an accident, as can failure to observe certain simple safety precautions. The possibility of an accident will always exist, and the following points should not be considered a comprehensive list of all dangers. Rather, they are intended to make you aware of the risks and to encourage a safety conscious approach to all work you carry out on your vehicle.

ESSENTIAL DOS AND DON'TS

DON'T rely on a jack when working under the vehicle. Always use approved jackstands to support the weight of the vehicle and place them under the recommended lift or support points.

DON'T attempt to loosen extremely tight fasteners (i.e. wheel lug nuts) while the vehicle is on a jack - it may fall.

DON'T start the engine without first making sure that the transmission is in Neutral (or Park where applicable) and the parking brake is set.

DON'T remove the radiator cap from a hot cooling system - let it cool or cover it with a cloth and release the pressure gradually.

DON'T attempt to drain the engine oil until you are sure it has cooled to the point that it will not burn you.

DON'T touch any part of the engine or exhaust system until it has cooled sufficiently to avoid burns.

DON'T siphon toxic liquids such as gasoline, antifreeze and brake fluid by mouth, or allow them to remain on your skin.

DON'T inhale brake lining dust - it is potentially hazardous (see Asbestos below).

DON'T allow spilled oil or grease to remain on the floor - wipe it up before someone slips on it.

DON'T use loose fitting wrenches or other tools which may slip and cause injury.

DON'T push on wrenches when loosening or tightening nuts or bolts. Always try to pull the wrench toward you. If the situation calls for pushing the wrench away, push with an open hand to avoid scraped knuckles if the wrench should slip.

DON'T attempt to lift a heavy component alone - get someone to help you.

DON'T rush or take unsafe shortcuts to finish a job.

DON'T allow children or animals in or around the vehicle while you are working on it.

DO wear eye protection when using power tools such as a drill, sander, bench grinder, etc. and when working under a vehicle.

DO keep loose clothing and long hair well out of the way of moving parts.

DO make sure that any hoist used has a safe working load rating adequate for the job.

DO get someone to check on you periodically when working alone on a vehicle.

DO carry out work in a logical sequence and make sure that everything is correctly assembled and tightened.

DO keep chemicals and fluids tightly capped and out of the reach of children and pets.

DO remember that your vehicle's safety affects that of yourself and others. If in doubt on any point, get professional advice.

STEERING, SUSPENSION AND BRAKES

These systems are essential to driving safety, so make sure you have a qualified shop or individual check your work. Also, compressed suspension springs can cause injury if released suddenly - be sure to use a spring compressor.

AIRBAGS

Airbags are explosive devices that can CAUSE injury if they deploy while you're working on the vehicle. Follow the manufacturer's instructions to disable the airbag whenever you're working in the vicinity of airbag components.

ASBESTOS

Certain friction, insulating, sealing, and other products - such as brake linings, brake bands, clutch linings, torque converters, gaskets, etc. - may contain asbestos or other hazardous friction material. Extreme care must be taken to avoid inhalation of dust from such products, since it is hazardous to health. If in doubt, assume that they do contain asbestos.

FIRE

Remember at all times that gasoline is highly flammable. Never smoke or have any kind of open flame around when working on a vehicle. But the risk does not end there. A spark caused by an electrical short circuit, by two metal surfaces contacting each other, or even by static electricity built up in your body under certain conditions, can ignite gasoline vapors, which in a confined space are highly explosive. Do not, under any circumstances, use gasoline for cleaning parts. Use an approved safety solvent.

Always disconnect the battery ground (-) cable at the battery before working on any part of the fuel system or electrical system. Never risk spilling fuel on a hot engine or exhaust component. It is strongly recommended that a fire extinguisher suitable for use on fuel and electrical fires be kept handy in the garage or workshop at all times. Never try to extinguish a fuel or electrical fire with water.

FUMES

Certain fumes are highly toxic and can quickly cause unconsciousness and even death if inhaled to any extent. Gasoline vapor falls into this category, as do the vapors from some cleaning solvents. Any draining or pouring of such volatile fluids should be done in a well ventilated area.

When using cleaning fluids and solvents, read the instructions on the container carefully. Never use materials from unmarked containers.

Never run the engine in an enclosed space, such as a garage. Exhaust fumes contain carbon monoxide, which is extremely poisonous. If you need to run the engine, always do so in the open air, or at least have the rear of the vehicle outside the work area.

THE BATTERY

Never create a spark or allow a bare light bulb near a battery. They normally give off a certain amount of hydrogen gas, which is highly explosive.

Always disconnect the battery ground (-) cable at the battery before working on the fuel or electrical systems.

If possible, loosen the filler caps or cover when charging the battery from an external source (this does not apply to sealed or maintenance-free batteries). Do not charge at an excessive rate or the battery may burst.

Take care when adding water to a non maintenance-free battery and when carrying a battery. The electrolyte, even when diluted, is very corrosive and should not be allowed to contact clothing or skin.

Always wear eye protection when cleaning the battery to prevent the caustic deposits from entering your eyes.

HOUSEHOLD CURRENT

When using an electric power tool, inspection light, etc., which operates on household current, always make sure that the tool is correctly connected to its plug and that, where necessary, it is properly grounded. Do not use such items in damp conditions and, again, do not create a spark or apply excessive heat in the vicinity of fuel or fuel vapor.

SECONDARY IGNITION SYSTEM VOLTAGE

A severe electric shock can result from touching certain parts of the ignition system (such as the spark plug wires) when the engine is running or being cranked, particularly if components are damp or the insulation is defective. In the case of an electronic ignition system, the secondary system voltage is much higher and could prove fatal.

HYDROFLUORIC ACID

This extremely corrosive acid is formed when certain types of synthetic rubber, found in some O-rings, oil seals, fuel hoses, etc. are exposed to temperatures above 750-degrees F (400-degrees C). The rubber changes into a charred or sticky substance containing the acid. *Once formed, the acid remains dangerous for years. If it gets onto the skin, it may be necessary to amputate the limb concerned.*

When dealing with a vehicle which has suffered a fire, or with components salvaged from such a vehicle, wear protective gloves and discard them after use.

Troubleshooting

CONTENTS

Section   Symptom

Engine and performance

1 Engine will not rotate when attempting to start
2 Engine rotates but will not start
3 Starter motor operates without turning engine
4 Engine hard to start when cold
5 Engine hard to start when hot
6 Starter motor noisy or engages roughly
7 Engine starts but stops immediately
8 Engine 'lopes' while idling or idles erratically
9 Engine misses at idle speed
10 Excessively high idle speed
11 Battery will not hold a charge
12 Alternator light stays on
13 Alternator light fails to come on when key is turned on
14 Engine misses throughout driving speed range
15 Hesitation or stumble during acceleration
16 Engine stalls
17 Engine lacks power
18 Engine backfires
19 Engine surges while holding accelerator steady
20 Pinging or knocking engine sounds when engine is under load
21 Engine diesels (continues to run) after being turned off
22 Low oil pressure
23 Excessive oil consumption
24 Excessive fuel consumption
25 Fuel odor
26 Miscellaneous engine noises

Cooling system

27 Overheating
28 Overcooling
29 External coolant leakage
30 Internal coolant leakage
31 Abnormal coolant loss
32 Poor coolant circulation
33 Corrosion

Clutch

34 Fails to release (pedal pressed to the floor - shift lever does not move freely in and out of Reverse)
35 Clutch slips (engine speed increases with no increase in vehicle speed)
36 Grabbing (chattering) as clutch is engaged
37 Squeal or rumble with clutch engaged (pedal released)
38 Squeal or rumble with clutch disengaged (pedal depressed)
39 Clutch pedal stays on floor when disengaged

Manual transmission

40 Noisy in Neutral with engine running
41 Noisy in all gears
42 Noisy in one particular gear
43 Slips out of gear
44 Oil leaks
45 Difficulty engaging gears
46 Noise occurs while shifting gears

Section   Symptom

Automatic transmission

47 Fluid leakage
48 General shift mechanism problems
49 Transmission will not downshift with the accelerator pedal pressed to the floor
50 Engine will start in gears other than Park or Neutral
51 Transmission slips, shifts rough, is noisy or has no drive in forward or Reverse gears

Driveshaft

53 Knock or clunk when transmission is under initial load (just after transmission is put into gear)
52 Leaks at front of driveshaft
54 Metallic grating sound consistent with vehicle speed
55 Vibration
56 Scraping noise

Rear axle and differential

57 Noise - same when in drive as when vehicle is coasting
58 Knocking sound when starting or shifting gears
59 Noise when turning
60 Vibration
61 Oil leaks

Brakes

62 Vehicle pulls to one side during braking
63 Noise (high-pitched squeal)
64 Excessive brake pedal travel
65 Brake pedal feels spongy when depressed
66 Excessive effort required to stop vehicle
67 Pedal travels to the floor with little resistance
68 Brake pedal pulsates during brake application
69 Brakes drag (indicated by sluggish engine performance or wheels being very hot after driving)
70 Rear brakes lock up under light brake application
71 Rear brakes lock up under heavy brake application

Suspension and steering

72 Vehicle pulls to one side
73 Shimmy, shake or vibration
74 Excessive pitching and/or rolling around corners or during braking
75 Wandering or general instability
76 Excessively stiff steering
77 Excessive play in steering
78 Lack of power assistance
79 Steering wheel fails to return to straight-ahead position
80 Steering effort not the same in both directions (power system)
81 Noisy power steering pump
82 Miscellaneous noises
83 Excessive tire wear (not specific to one area)
84 Excessive tire wear on outside edge
85 Excessive tire wear on inside edge
86 Tire tread worn in one place

This Section provides an easy reference guide to the more common problems that may occur during the operation of your vehicle. Various symptoms and their probable causes are grouped under headings denoting components or systems, such as Engine, Cooling system, etc. They also refer to the Chapter and/or Section that deals with the problem.

Remember that successful troubleshooting isn't a mysterious 'black art' practiced only by professional mechanics, it's simply the result of knowledge combined with an intelligent, systematic approach to a problem. Always use a process of elimination starting with the simplest solution and working through to the most complex - and never overlook the obvious. Anyone can run the gas tank dry or leave the lights on overnight, so don't assume that you're exempt from such oversights.

Finally, always establish a clear idea why a problem has occurred and take steps to ensure that it doesn't happen again. If the electrical system fails because of a poor connection, check all other connections in the system to make sure they don't fail as well. If a particular fuse continues to blow, find out why - don't just go on replacing fuses. Remember, failure of a small component can often be indicative of potential failure or incorrect functioning of a more important component or system.

ENGINE AND PERFORMANCE

1 Engine will not rotate when attempting to start

1 Battery terminal connections loose or corroded. Check the cable terminals at the battery; tighten cable clamp and/or clean off corrosion as necessary (see Chapter 1).
2 Battery discharged or faulty. If the cable ends are clean and tight on the battery posts, turn the key to the On position and switch on the headlights or windshield wipers. If they won't run, the battery is discharged.
3 Automatic transmission not engaged in park (P) or Neutral (N).
4 Broken, loose or disconnected wires in the starting circuit. Inspect all wires and connectors at the battery, starter solenoid and ignition switch (on steering column).
5 Starter motor pinion jammed in flywheel ring gear. If manual transmission, place transmission in gear and rock the vehicle to manually turn the engine. Remove starter (Chapter 5) and inspect pinion and flywheel (Chapter 2).
6 Starter solenoid faulty (Chapter 5).
7 Starter motor faulty (Chapter 5).
8 Ignition switch faulty (Chapter 12).
9 Engine seized. Try to turn the crankshaft with a large socket and breaker bar on the pulley bolt.

2 Engine rotates but will not start

1 Fuel tank empty.
2 Battery discharged (engine rotates slowly). Check the operation of electrical components as described in previous Section.
3 Battery terminal connections loose or corroded. See previous Section.
4 Fuel not reaching fuel injectors. Check for clogged fuel filter or lines and defective fuel pump. Also make sure the tank vent lines aren't clogged (Chapter 4).
5 Faulty camshaft position sensor (Chapter 5).
6 Low cylinder compression. Check as described in Chapter 2.
7 Water in fuel. Drain tank and fill with new fuel.
8 Dirty or clogged fuel injectors.
9 Wet or damaged ignition components (Chapters 1 and 5).
10 Worn, faulty or incorrectly gapped spark plugs (Chapter 1).
11 Broken, loose or disconnected wires in the ignition circuit.
12 Broken, loose or disconnected wires at the ignition coil(s) or faulty coil(s) (Chapter 5).
13 Timing belt or chain failure or wear affecting valve timing (Chapter 2).

3 Starter motor operates without turning engine

1 Starter pinion sticking. Remove the starter (Chapter 5) and inspect.
2 Starter pinion or flywheel/driveplate teeth worn or broken. Remove the inspection cover on the left side of the engine and inspect.

4 Engine hard to start when cold

1 Battery discharged or low. Check as described in Chapter 1.
2 Fuel not reaching the fuel injectors. Check the fuel filter and lines (Chapters 1 and 4).
3 Defective spark plugs (Chapter 1).
4 Intake manifold vacuum leaks. Make sure all mounting bolts/nuts are tight and all vacuum hoses connected to the manifold are attached properly and in good condition.

5 Engine hard to start when hot

1 Air filter dirty (Chapter 1).
2 Bad engine ground connection.
3 Fuel not reaching the injectors (Chapter 4).
4 Loose connection in the ignition system (Chapter 5).

6 Starter motor noisy or engages roughly

1 Pinion or flywheel/driveplate teeth worn or broken. Remove the inspection cover and inspect.
2 Starter motor mounting bolts loose or missing.

7 Engine starts but stops immediately

1 Loose or damaged wiring in the ignition system.
2 Intake manifold vacuum leaks. Make sure all mounting bolts/nuts are tight and all vacuum hoses connected to the manifold are attached properly and in good condition.

8 Engine "lopes" while idling or idles erratically

1 Vacuum leaks. Check mounting bolts at the intake manifold or plenum for tightness. Make sure that all vacuum hoses are connected and in good condition. Use a stethoscope or a length of fuel hose held against your ear to listen for vacuum leaks while the engine is running. A hissing sound will be heard. A soapy water solution will also detect leaks. Check the intake manifold or plenum gasket surfaces.
2 Leaking EGR valve or plugged PCV valve (Chapter 6).

3   Air filter clogged (Chapter 1).
4   Leaking head gasket. Perform a cylinder compression check (Chapter 2).
5   Timing belt or chain worn (Chapter 2).
6   Camshaft lobes worn (Chapter 2).
7   Valves burned or otherwise leaking (Chapter 2).
8   Ignition system not operating properly (Chapters 1 and 5).
9   Dirty or clogged injectors (Chapter 4).
10 Throttle position sensor out of adjustment (Chapter 4).

9   Engine misses at idle speed

1   Spark plugs faulty or not gapped properly (Chapter 1).
2   Faulty spark plug wires (Chapter 1).
3   Wet or damaged camshaft position sensor components (Chapter 1).
4   Short circuits in ignition, coil(s) or spark plug wires.
5   Sticking or faulty emissions systems (Chapter 6).
6   Clogged fuel filter and/or foreign matter in fuel. Replace the fuel filter (Chapter 1).
7   Vacuum leaks at intake manifold or hose connections. Check as described in Section 8.
8   Incorrect idle speed or idle mixture.
9   Low or uneven cylinder compression. Check as described in Chapter 2.
10 Clogged or dirty fuel injectors (Chapter 4).
11 Leaky EGR valve (Chapter 6).

10   Excessively high idle speed

1   Sticking throttle linkage (Chapter 4).
2   Idle speed incorrect.

11   Battery will not hold a charge

1   Drivebelt defective or not adjusted properly (Chapter 1).
2   Battery cables loose or corroded (Chapter 1).
3   Alternator not charging properly (Chapter 5).
4   Loose, broken or faulty wires in the charging circuit (Chapter 5).
5   Short circuit causing a continuous drain on the battery (Chapter 12).
6   Battery defective internally.
7   Faulty regulator (Chapter 5).

12   Alternator light stays on

1   Fault in alternator or charging circuit (Chapter 5).
2   Drivebelt defective or not properly adjusted (Chapter 1).

13   Alternator light fails to come on when key is turned on

1   Faulty bulb (Chapter 12).
2   Defective alternator (Chapter 5).
3   Fault in the printed circuit, dash wiring or bulb holder (Chapter 12).

14   Engine misses throughout driving speed range

1   Fuel filter clogged and/or impurities in the fuel system. Check fuel filter (Chapter 1) or clean system (Chapter 4).
2   Faulty or incorrectly gapped spark plugs (Chapter 1).
3   Incorrect ignition timing (Chapter 5).

4   Disconnected ignition system wires or damaged ignition system components (Chapter 5).
5   Defective spark plug wires (Chapter 1).
6   Emissions system components faulty (Chapter 6).
7   Low or uneven cylinder compression pressures. Check as described in Chapter 2.
8   Weak or faulty ignition coil(s) (Chapter 5).
9   Weak or faulty ignition system (Chapter 5).
10 Vacuum leaks at intake manifold or vacuum hoses (see Section 8).
11 Dirty or clogged fuel injector (Chapter 4).

15   Hesitation or stumble during acceleration

1   Ignition timing incorrect (Chapter 5).
2   Ignition system not operating properly (Chapter 5).
3   Dirty or clogged fuel injectors (Chapter 4).
4   Low fuel pressure. Check for proper operation of the fuel pump and for restrictions in the fuel filter and lines (Chapter 4).

16   Engine stalls

1   Idle speed incorrect (Chapter 4).
2   Fuel filter clogged and/or water and impurities in the fuel system (Chapter 1).
3   Damaged or wet ignition system wires or components.
4   Emissions system components faulty (Chapter 6).
5   Faulty or incorrectly gapped spark plugs (Chapter 1). Also check the spark plug wires (Chapter 1).
6   Vacuum leak at the intake manifold or plenum or vacuum hoses. Check as described in Section 8.

17   Engine lacks power

1   Incorrect ignition timing (Chapter 5).
2   Check for faulty spark plug wires (Chapter 1).
3   Faulty or incorrectly gapped spark plugs (Chapter 1).
4   Air filter dirty (Chapter 1).
5   Spark timing control system not operating properly.
6   Faulty ignition coil(s) (Chapter 5).
7   Brakes binding (Chapters 1 and 9).
8   Automatic transmission fluid level incorrect, causing slippage (Chapter 1).
9   Clutch slipping (Chapter 8).
10 Fuel filter clogged and/or impurities in the fuel system (Chapters 1 and 4).
11 EGR system not functioning properly (Chapter 6).
12 Use of sub-standard fuel. Fill tank with proper octane fuel.
13 Low or uneven cylinder compression pressures. Check as described in Chapter 2.
14 Air (vacuum) leak at intake manifold or plenum (check as described in Section 8).

18   Engine backfires

1   EGR system not functioning properly (Chapter 6).
2   Ignition timing incorrect (Chapter 5).
3   Vacuum leak (refer to Section 8).
4   Damaged valve springs or sticking valves (Chapter 2).
5   Intake air (vacuum) leak (see Section 8).

19 Engine surges while holding accelerator steady

1 Intake air (vacuum) leak (see Section 8).
2 Fuel pump not working properly.

20 Pinging or knocking engine sounds when engine is under load

1 Incorrect grade of fuel. Fill tank with fuel of the proper octane rating.
2 Ignition timing incorrect (Chapter 5) or problem in the ignition system (Chapter 5).
3 Carbon build-up in combustion chambers. Remove cylinder head and clean combustion chambers (Chapter 2).
4 Incorrect spark plugs (Chapter 1).
5 Electronic Spark Control (ESC) system not functioning properly (Chapter 6).

21 Engine diesels (continues to run) after being turned off

1 Idle speed too high (Chapter 4).
2 Ignition timing incorrect (Chapter 5).
3 Incorrect spark plug heat range (Chapter 1).
4 Intake air (vacuum) leak (see Section 8).
5 Carbon build-up in combustion chambers. Remove the cylinder head and clean the combustion chambers (Chapter 2).
6 Valves sticking (Chapter 2).
7 Valve clearance incorrect (Chapter 1).
8 EGR system not operating properly (Chapter 6).
9 Leaking fuel injector(s) (Chapter 4).
10 Check for causes of overheating (Section 27).

22 Low oil pressure

1 Improper grade of oil.
2 Oil pump regulator valve not operating properly (Chapter 2).
3 Oil pump worn or damaged (Chapter 2).
4 Engine overheating (refer to Section 27).
5 Clogged oil filter (Chapter 1).
6 Clogged oil strainer (Chapter 2).
7 Oil pressure gauge not working properly (Chapter 2).

23 Excessive oil consumption

1 Loose oil drain plug.
2 Loose bolts or damaged oil pan gasket (Chapter 2).
3 Loose bolts or damaged oil pump body gasket (Chapter 2).
4 Front or rear crankshaft oil seal leaking (Chapter 2).
5 Loose bolts or damaged valve cover gasket (Chapter 2).
6 Loose oil filter (Chapter 1).
7 Loose or damaged oil pressure switch (Chapter 2).
8 Pistons and cylinders excessively worn (Chapter 2).
9 Piston rings not installed correctly on pistons (Chapter 2).
10 Worn or damaged piston rings (Chapter 2).
11 Intake and/or exhaust valve oil seals worn or damaged (Chapter 2).
12 Worn valve stems.
13 Worn or damaged valves/guides (Chapter 2).

24 Excessive fuel consumption

1 Dirty or clogged air filter element (Chapter 1).
2 Incorrect ignition timing (Chapter 5).
3 Incorrect idle speed (Chapter 4).
4 Low tire pressure or incorrect tire size (Chapter 10).
5 Fuel leakage. Check all connections, lines and components in the fuel system (Chapter 4).
6 Dirty or clogged fuel injectors (Chapter 4).
7 Problem in the fuel injection system (Chapter 4).

25 Fuel odor

1 Fuel leakage. Check all connections, lines and components in the fuel system (Chapter 4).
2 Fuel tank overfilled. Fill only to automatic shut-off.
3 Charcoal canister filter in Evaporative Emissions Control system clogged (Chapter 6).
4 Vapor leaks from Evaporative Emissions Control system lines (Chapter 6).

26 Miscellaneous engine noises

1 A strong dull noise that becomes more rapid as the engine accelerates indicates worn or damaged crankshaft bearings or an unevenly worn crankshaft. To pinpoint the trouble spot, remove the spark plug wire from one plug at a time and crank the engine over. If the noise stops, the cylinder with the removed plug wire indicates the problem area. Replace the bearing and/or service or replace the crankshaft (Chapter 2).
2 A similar (yet slightly higher pitched) noise to the crankshaft knocking described in the previous paragraph, that becomes more rapid as the engine accelerates, indicates worn or damaged connecting rod bearings (Chapter 2). The procedure for locating the problem cylinder is the same as described in Paragraph 1.
3 An overlapping metallic noise that increases in intensity as the engine speed increases, yet diminishes as the engine warms up indicates abnormal piston and cylinder wear (Chapter 2). To locate the problem cylinder, use the procedure described in Paragraph 1.
4 A rapid clicking noise that becomes faster as the engine accelerates indicates a worn piston pin or piston pin hole. This sound will happen each time the piston hits the highest and lowest points in the stroke (Chapter 2). The procedure for locating the problem piston is described in Paragraph 1.
5 A metallic clicking noise coming from the water pump indicates worn or damaged water pump bearings or pump. Replace the water pump with a new one (Chapter 3).
6 A rapid tapping sound or clicking sound that becomes faster as the engine speed increases indicates valve tapping or stuck valve lifters. This can be identified by holding one end of a section of hose to your ear and placing the other end at different spots along the rocker arm cover. The point where the sound is loudest indicates the problem valve. Inspect the lifters (Chapter 2).
7 A steady metallic rattling or rapping sound coming from the area of the timing belt or chain cover indicates a worn, damaged or out-of-adjustment timing belt or chain. Replace the belt or chain and related components (Chapter 2).

COOLING SYSTEM

27   Overheating

1   Insufficient coolant in system (Chapter 1).
2   Drivebelt defective or not adjusted properly (Chapter 1).
3   Radiator core blocked or radiator grille dirty and restricted (Chapter 3).
4   Thermostat faulty (Chapter 3).
5   Fan not functioning properly (Chapter 3).
6   Radiator cap not maintaining proper pressure. Have cap pressure tested by gas station or repair shop.
7   Ignition timing incorrect (Chapter 5).
8   Defective water pump (Chapter 3).
9   Improper grade of engine oil.
10 Inaccurate temperature gauge (Chapter 3).

28   Overcooling

1   Thermostat faulty (Chapter 3).
2   Inaccurate temperature gauge (Chapter 3).

29   External coolant leakage

1   Deteriorated or damaged hoses. Loose clamps at hose connections (Chapter 1).
2   Water pump seals defective. If this is the case, water will drip from the weep hole in the water pump body (Chapter 3).
3   Leakage from radiator core or header tank. This will require the radiator to be professionally repaired (see Chapter 3 for removal procedures).
4   Engine drain plugs or water jacket freeze plugs leaking (see Chapters 1 and 2).
5   Leak from coolant temperature switch (Chapter 3).
6   Leak from damaged gaskets or small cracks (Chapter 2).
7   Damaged head gasket. This can be verified by checking the condition of the engine oil as noted in Section 30.

30   Internal coolant leakage

➡Note: Internal coolant leaks can usually be detected by examining the oil. Check the dipstick and inside the valve cover for water deposits and an oil consistency like that of a milkshake.

1   Leaking cylinder head gasket. Have the system pressure tested or remove the cylinder head (Chapter 2) and inspect.
2   Cracked cylinder bore or cylinder head. Dismantle engine and inspect (Chapter 2).
3   Loose cylinder head bolts (tighten as described in Chapter 2).

31   Abnormal coolant loss

1   Overfilling system (Chapter 1).
2   Coolant boiling away due to overheating (see causes in Section 27).
3   Internal or external leakage (see Sections 29 and 30).
4   Faulty radiator cap. Have the cap pressure tested.
5   Cooling system being pressurized by engine compression. This could be due to a cracked head or block or leaking head gasket(s).

32   Poor coolant circulation

1   Inoperative water pump. A quick test is to pinch the top radiator hose closed with your hand while the engine is idling, then release it. You should feel a surge of coolant if the pump is working properly (Chapter 3).
2   Restriction in cooling system. Drain, flush and refill the system (Chapter 1). If necessary, remove the radiator (Chapter 3) and have it reverse flushed or professionally cleaned.
3   Thermostat sticking (Chapter 3).
4   Insufficient coolant (Chapter 1).

33   Corrosion

1   Excessive impurities in the water. Soft, clean water is recommended. Distilled or rainwater is satisfactory.
2   Insufficient antifreeze solution (refer to Chapter 1 for the proper type and ratio of water to antifreeze).
3   Infrequent flushing and draining of system. Regular flushing of the cooling system should be carried out at the specified intervals as described in Chapter 1.

CLUTCH

34   Fails to release (pedal pressed to the floor - shift lever does not move freely in and out of Reverse)

1   Clutch contaminated with oil. Remove clutch plate and inspect.
2   Clutch plate warped, distorted or otherwise damaged.
3   Diaphragm spring fatigued. Remove clutch cover/pressure plate assembly and inspect.
4   Leakage of fluid from clutch hydraulic system. Inspect master cylinder, operating (release) cylinder and connecting lines.
5   Air in clutch hydraulic system. Bleed the system.
6   Insufficient pedal stroke. Check and adjust as necessary.
7   Piston seal in operating (release) cylinder deformed or damaged.
8   Lack of grease on pilot bushing.
9   Damaged transmission input shaft splines.

35   Clutch slips (engine speed increases with no increase in vehicle speed)

1   Worn or oil soaked clutch plate.
2   Clutch plate not broken in. It may take 30 or 40 normal starts for a new clutch to seat.
3   Diaphragm spring weak or damaged. Remove clutch cover/pressure plate assembly and inspect.
4   Flywheel warped or scored (Chapter 2).
5   Debris in master cylinder preventing the piston from returning to its normal position.

36   Grabbing (chattering) as clutch is engaged

1   Oil on clutch plate. Remove and inspect. Repair any leaks.
2   Worn or loose engine or transmission mounts. They may move slightly when clutch is released. Inspect mounts and bolts.
3   Worn splines on transmission input shaft. Remove clutch components and inspect.

4   Warped pressure plate or flywheel. Remove clutch components and inspect.

5   Diaphragm spring fatigued. Remove clutch cover/pressure plate assembly and inspect.

6   Clutch linings hardened or warped.

7   Clutch lining rivets loose.

8   Engine and transmission not in alignment. Check for foreign object between bellhousing and engine block. Check for loose bellhousing bolts.

37   Squeal or rumble with clutch engaged (pedal released)

1   Release bearing binding on transmission shaft. Remove clutch components and check bearing. Remove any burrs or nicks, clean and lubricate before reinstallation.

2   Clutch rivets loose.

3   Clutch plate cracked.

4   Fatigued clutch plate torsion springs. Replace clutch plate.

38   Squeal or rumble with clutch disengaged (pedal depressed)

1   Worn or damaged release bearing.

2   Worn or broken pressure plate diaphragm fingers.

3   Worn or damaged pilot bearing.

39   Clutch pedal stays on floor when disengaged

1   Binding release fork or release bearing. Inspect release fork or remove clutch components as necessary.

2   Faulty clutch master cylinder or release cylinder.

MANUAL TRANSMISSION

➡Note: All manual transmission service information is located in Chapter 7, unless otherwise noted.

40   Noisy in Neutral with engine running

1   Input shaft bearing worn.

2   Damaged main drive gear bearing.

3   Insufficient transmission oil (Chapter 1).

4   Transmission lubricant in poor condition. Drain and fill with proper grade oil. Check old lubricant for water and debris (Chapter 1).

5   Noise can be caused by variations in engine torque.

41   Noisy in all gears

1   Any of the above causes, and/or:

2   Worn or damaged output gear bearings or shaft.

42   Noisy in one particular gear

1   Worn, damaged or chipped gear teeth.

2   Worn or damaged synchronizer.

43   Slips out of gear

1   Transmission loose on engine.

2   Stiff shift lever seal.

3   Shift linkage binding.

4   Broken or loose input gear bearing retainer.

5   Dirt between clutch lever and engine housing.

6   Worn linkage.

7   Damaged or worn check balls, fork rod ball grooves or check springs.

8   Worn mainshaft or countershaft bearings.

9   Loose engine mounts (Chapter 2).

10 Excessive gear end play.

11 Worn synchronizers.

44   Oil leaks

1   Excessive amount of lubricant in transmission (see Chapter 1 for correct checking procedures). Drain lubricant as required.

2   Case retaining bolts loose or gaskets damaged.

3   Rear oil seal or speedometer oil seal damaged.

4   To pinpoint a leak, first remove all built-up dirt and grime from the transmission. Degreasing agents and/or steam cleaning will achieve this. With the underside clean, drive the vehicle at low speeds so the air flow will not blow the leak far from its source. Raise the vehicle and determine where the leak is located.

45   Difficulty engaging gears

1   Clutch not releasing completely.

2   Loose or damaged shift linkage. Make a thorough inspection, replacing parts as necessary.

3   Insufficient transmission oil (Chapter 1).

4   Transmission oil in poor condition. Drain and fill with proper grade oil. Check oil for water and debris (Chapter 1).

5   Worn or damaged shift forks.

6   Sticking or jamming gears.

46   Noise occurs while shifting gears

1   Check for proper operation of the clutch (Chapter 8).

2   Faulty synchronizer assemblies. Measure baulk ring-to-gear clearance. Also, check for wear or damage to baulk rings or any parts of the synchromesh assemblies.

AUTOMATIC TRANSMISSION

➡Note: Due to the complexity of the automatic transmission, it's difficult for the home mechanic to properly diagnose and service. For problems other than the following, the vehicle should be taken to a reputable mechanic.

47   Fluid leakage

1   Automatic transmission fluid is a deep red color, and fluid leaks should not be confused with engine oil which can easily be blown by air flow to the transmission.

2   To pinpoint a leak, first remove all built-up dirt and grime from the transmission. Degreasing agents and/or steam cleaning will achieve this. With the underside clean, drive the vehicle at low speeds so the air flow will not blow the leak far from its source. Raise the vehicle and determine where the leak is located. Common areas of leakage are:

   a) *Fluid pan: tighten mounting bolts and/or replace pan gasket as necessary (Chapter 1).*
   b) *Rear extension: tighten bolts and/or replace oil seal as necessary.*
   c) *Filler pipe: replace the rubber oil seal where pipe enters transmission case.*
   d) *Transmission oil lines: tighten fittings where lines enter transmission case and/or replace lines.*
   e) *Vent pipe: transmission overfilled and/or water in fluid (see checking procedures, Chapter 1).*
   f) *Speedometer connector: replace the O-ring where speedometer sensor enters transmission case.*

48   General shift mechanism problems

Chapter 7 deals with checking and adjusting the shift linkage on automatic transmissions. Common problems which may be caused by out of adjustment linkage are:

   a) *Engine starting in gears other than P (Park) or N (Neutral).*
   b) *Indicator pointing to a gear other than the one actually engaged.*
   c) *Vehicle moves with transmission in P (Park) position.*

49   Transmission will not downshift with the accelerator pedal pressed to the floor

Chapter 7, Part B deals with adjusting the throttle valve cable installed on automatic transmissions.

50   Engine will start in gears other than Park or Neutral

Chapter 7, Part B deals with adjusting the Park/Neutral start switch installed on automatic transmissions.

51   Transmission slips, shifts rough, is noisy or has no drive in forward or Reverse gears

1   There are many probable causes for the above problems, but the home mechanic should concern himself only with one possibility; fluid level.

2   Before taking the vehicle to a shop, check the fluid level and condition as described in Chapter 1. Add fluid, if necessary, or change the fluid and filter if needed. If problems persist, have a professional diagnose the transmission.

DRIVESHAFT

52   Leaks at front of driveshaft

Defective transmission rear seal. See Chapter 7 for replacement procedure. As this is done, check the splined yoke for burrs or roughness that could damage the new seal. Remove burrs with a fine file or whetstone.

53   Knock or clunk when transmission is under initial load (just after transmission is put into gear)

1   Loose or disconnected rear suspension components. Check all mounting bolts and bushings (Chapters 1 and 11).

2   Loose driveshaft bolts. Inspect all bolts and nuts and tighten them securely.

3   Worn or damaged universal joint bearings. Replace driveshaft (Chapter 8).

4   Worn sleeve yoke and mainshaft spline.

54   Metallic grating sound consistent with vehicle speed

Pronounced wear in the universal joint bearings. Replace U-joints or driveshaft, as necessary.

55   Vibration

1   Install a tachometer inside the vehicle to monitor engine speed as the vehicle is driven. Drive the vehicle and note the engine speed at which the vibration (roughness) is most pronounced. Now shift the transmission to a different gear and bring the engine speed to the same point.

2   If the vibration occurs at the same engine speed (rpm) regardless of which gear the transmission is in, the driveshaft is NOT at fault since the driveshaft speed varies.

3   If the vibration decreases or is eliminated when the transmission is in a different gear at the same engine speed, refer to the following probable causes.

4   Bent or dented driveshaft. Inspect and replace as necessary.

5   Undercoating or built-up dirt, etc. on the driveshaft. Clean the shaft thoroughly.

6   Worn universal joint bearings. Replace the U-joints or driveshaft as necessary.

7   Driveshaft and/or companion flange out of balance. Check for missing weights on the shaft. Remove driveshaft and reinstall 180-degrees from original position, then recheck. Have the driveshaft balanced if problem persists.

8   Loose driveshaft mounting bolts/nuts.

9   Worn transmission rear bushing.

56   Scraping noise

Make sure the dust cover on the sleeve yoke isn't rubbing on the transmission extension housing.

REAR AXLE AND DIFFERENTIAL

➡ **Note: For differential servicing information, refer to Chapter 8, unless otherwise specified.**

57   Noise - same when in drive as when vehicle is coasting

1   Road noise. No corrective action available.

2   Tire noise. Inspect tires and check tire pressures (Chapter 1).

3   Front wheel bearings worn or damaged (Chapter 10).

4   Insufficient differential oil (Chapter 1).

5   Defective differential.

58 Knocking sound when starting or shifting gears

Defective or incorrectly adjusted differential.

59 Noise when turning

Defective differential.

60 Vibration

See probable causes under Driveshaft. Proceed under the guidelines listed for the driveshaft. If the problem persists, check the rear wheel bearings by raising the rear of the vehicle and spinning the wheels by hand. Listen for evidence of rough (noisy) bearings. Remove and inspect (Chapter 8).

61 Oil leaks

1 Pinion oil seal damaged (Chapter 8).
2 Driveaxle oil seals damaged (Chapter 8).
3 Loose cover bolts or filler plug on differential (Chapter 1).
4 Clogged or damaged breather on differential.

BRAKES

→Note: Before assuming a brake problem exists, make sure the tires are in good condition and inflated properly, the front end alignment is correct and the vehicle is not loaded with weight in an unequal manner. All service procedures for the brakes are included in Chapter 9, unless otherwise noted.

62 Vehicle pulls to one side during braking

1 Defective, damaged or oil contaminated brake pad on one side. Inspect as described in Chapter 1. Refer to Chapter 9 if replacement is required.
2 Excessive wear of brake pad material or disc on one side. Inspect and repair as necessary.
3 Loose or disconnected front suspension components. Inspect and tighten all bolts securely (Chapters 1 and 10).
4 Defective caliper assembly. Remove caliper and inspect for stuck piston or damage.
5 Brake pad-to-disc adjustment needed. Inspect automatic adjusting mechanism for proper operation.
6 Scored or out of round disc.
7 Loose caliper mounting bolts.

63 Noise (high-pitched squeal)

1 Brake pads worn out. This noise comes from the wear sensor rubbing against the disc. Replace pads with new ones immediately!
2 Glazed or contaminated pads.
3 Dirty or scored disc.
4 Bent support plate.

64 Excessive brake pedal travel

1 Partial brake system failure. Inspect entire system and correct as required.

2 Insufficient fluid in master cylinder. Check (Chapter 1) and add fluid - bleed system if necessary.
3 Air in system. Bleed system.
4 Excessive lateral disc play.
5 Defective check valve. Replace valve and bleed system.

65 · Brake pedal feels spongy when depressed

1 Air in brake lines. Bleed the brake system.
2 Deteriorated rubber brake hoses. Inspect all system hoses and lines. Replace parts as necessary.
3 Master cylinder mounting nuts loose. Inspect master cylinder bolts (nuts) and tighten them securely.
4 Master cylinder faulty.
5 Incorrect pad clearance.
6 Defective check valve. Replace valve and bleed system.
7 Clogged reservoir cap vent hole.
8 Deformed rubber brake lines.
9 Soft or swollen caliper seals.
10 Poor quality brake fluid. Bleed entire system and fill with new approved fluid.

66 Excessive effort required to stop vehicle

1 Power brake booster not operating properly.
2 Excessively worn pads. Check and replace if necessary.
3 One or more caliper pistons seized or sticking. Inspect and rebuild as required.
4 Brake pads contaminated with oil or grease. Inspect and replace as required.
5 New pads installed and not yet seated. It'll take a while for the new material to seat against the disc.
6 Worn or damaged master cylinder or caliper assemblies. Check particularly for frozen pistons.
7 Also see causes listed under Section 65.

67 Pedal travels to the floor with little resistance

Little or no fluid in the master cylinder reservoir caused by leaking caliper piston(s) or loose, damaged or disconnected brake lines. Inspect entire system and repair as necessary.

68 Brake pedal pulsates during brake application

→Note: Brake pedal pulsation during operation of the Anti-Lock Brake System (ABS) is normal.

1 Disc not within specifications. Check for excessive lateral runout and parallelism. Have the discs resurfaced or replace them with new ones. Also make sure that all discs are the same thickness.
2 Wheel bearings damaged or worn (Chapter 10).

69 Brakes drag (indicated by sluggish engine performance or wheels being very hot after driving)

1 Output rod adjustment incorrect at the brake pedal.
2 Obstructed master cylinder compensator. Disassemble master cylinder and clean.
3 Master cylinder piston seized in bore. Overhaul master cylinder.
4 Caliper assembly in need of overhaul.

5 Brake pads or shoes worn out.
6 Piston cups in master cylinder or caliper assembly deformed. Overhaul master cylinder.
7 Parking brake assembly will not release.
8 Clogged brake lines.
9 Brake pedal height improperly adjusted.

70 Rear brakes lock up under light brake application

1 Tire pressures too high.
2 Tires excessively worn (Chapter 1).

71 Rear brakes lock up under heavy brake application

1 Tire pressures too high.
2 Tires excessively worn (Chapter 1).
3 Front brake pads contaminated with oil, mud or water. Clean or replace the pads.
4 Front brake pads excessively worn.
5 Defective master cylinder or caliper assembly.

SUSPENSION AND STEERING

→Note: All service procedures for the suspension and steering systems are included in Chapter 10, unless otherwise noted.

72 Vehicle pulls to one side

1 Tire pressures uneven (Chapter 1).
2 Defective tire (Chapter 1).
3 Excessive wear in suspension or steering components (Chapter 10).
4 Front end alignment incorrect.
5 Front brakes dragging. Inspect as described in Section 69.
6 Wheel lug nuts loose.
7 Worn upper or lower control arm bushings.

73 Shimmy, shake or vibration

1 Tire or wheel out of balance or out of round. Have them balanced on the vehicle.
2 Worn or damaged wheel bearings (Chapter 10).
3 Shock absorbers and/or suspension components worn or damaged. Check for worn bushings in the upper and lower links.
4 Wheel lug nuts loose.
5 Incorrect tire pressures.
6 Excessively worn or damaged tire.
7 Loosely mounted steering gear housing.
8 Steering gear improperly adjusted.
9 Loose, worn or damaged steering components.
10 Worn balljoint.

74 Excessive pitching and/or rolling around corners or during braking

1 Defective shock absorbers. Replace as a set.
2 Broken or weak springs and/or suspension components.
3 Worn or damaged stabilizer bar or bushings.
4 Worn or damaged upper or lower links or bushings.

75 Wandering or general instability

1 Improper tire pressures.
2 Worn or damaged bushings.
3 Incorrect front end alignment.
4 Worn or damaged steering linkage.
5 Improperly adjusted steering gear.
6 Out of balance wheels.
7 Loose wheel lug nuts.
8 Worn rear shock absorbers.
9 Fatigued or damaged rear springs.

76 Excessively stiff steering

1 Lack of lubricant in power steering fluid reservoir, where appropriate (Chapter 1).
2 Incorrect tire pressures (Chapter 1).
3 Front end out of alignment.
4 Steering gear out of adjustment or lacking lubrication.
5 Worn or damaged wheel bearings.
6 Worn or damaged steering gear.
7 Interference of steering column with turn signal switch.
8 Low tire pressures.
9 Worn or damaged balljoints.
10 Worn or damaged steering linkage.

77 Excessive play in steering

1 Worn wheel bearings (Chapter 10).
2 Steering gear improperly adjusted.
3 Incorrect front end alignment.
4 Steering gear mounting bolts loose.
5 Worn steering linkage.

78 Lack of power assistance

1 Drivebelt faulty or not adjusted properly (Chapter 1).
2 Fluid level low (Chapter 1).
3 Hoses or pipes restricting the flow. Inspect and replace parts as necessary.
4 Air in power steering system. Bleed system.
5 Defective power steering pump.

79 Steering wheel fails to return to straight-ahead position

1 Incorrect front end alignment.
2 Tire pressures low.
3 Steering gears improperly engaged.
4 Steering column out of alignment.
5 Worn or damaged balljoint.
6 Worn or damaged steering linkage.
7 Insufficient oil in steering gear.
8 Lack of fluid in power steering pump.

80 Steering effort not the same in both directions (power system)

1 Leaks in steering gear.
2 Clogged fluid passage in steering gear.

81 Noisy power steering pump

1 Insufficient oil in pump.
2 Clogged hoses or oil filter in pump.
3 Loose pulley.
4 Worn or improperly adjusted drivebelt (Chapter 1).
5 Defective pump.

82 Miscellaneous noises

1 Improper tire pressures.
2 Insufficiently lubricated balljoint or steering linkage.
3 Loose or worn steering gear, steering linkage or suspension components.
4 Defective shock absorber.
5 Defective wheel bearing.
6 Damaged spring.
7 Loose wheel lug nuts.
8 Worn or damaged rear driveaxle CV joint.
9 Worn or damaged rear shock absorber mounting bushing.
10 Worn rear hub bearing.
11 See also causes of noises at the rear axle and driveshaft.

83 Excessive tire wear (not specific to one area)

1 Incorrect tire pressures.
2 Tires out of balance. Have them balanced on the vehicle.
3 Wheels damaged. Inspect and replace as necessary.
4 Suspension or steering components worn (Chapter 1).

84 Excessive tire wear on outside edge

1 Incorrect tire pressure
2 Excessive speed in turns.
3 Wheel alignment incorrect.

85 Excessive tire wear on inside edge

1 Incorrect tire pressure.
2 Wheel alignment incorrect.
3 Loose or damaged steering components (Chapter 1).

86 Tire tread worn in one place

1 Tires out of balance. Have them balanced on the vehicle.
2 Damaged or buckled wheel. Inspect and replace if necessary.
3 Defective tire.

1
TUNE-UP AND ROUTINE MAINTENANCE

Reference to other Chapters
CHECK ENGINE light - See Chapter 6

Typical engine compartment components (1996 model shown)

1	Main fuse/relay box	6	Clutch fluid reservoir	11	Radiator cap
2	Windshield washer fluid reservoir	7	Air cleaner assembly	12	Upper radiator hose
3	PCV valve	8	Power steering fluid dipstick	13	Coolant reservoir
4	Engine oil dipstick	9	Engine oil filler cap	14	Evaporative emissions canister
5	Brake fluid reservoir	10	Spark plug		

Typical engine compartment components (2006 model shown)

1	Brake fluid reservoir	5	Drivebelt	9	Windshield washer fluid reservoir
2	Underhood fuse/relay box	6	Power steering fluid reservoir	10	Oil filler cap
3	Air filter housing	7	Expansion tank cap	11	Engine oil dipstick
4	Upper radiator hose	8	Battery (under cover)		

Typical front underside components

1	Radiator drain plug	4	Steering gear boot	7	Engine oil drain plug
2	Drivebelts	5	Front disc brake caliper	8	Shock absorber
3	Lower radiator hose	6	Manual transmission check/fill plug		

Typical rear underside components

1	Exhaust system hanger	4	Rear differential check/fill plug	7	Rear differential drain plug
2	Muffler	5	Fuel filter (under cover)	8	Shock absorber
3	Driveaxle boot	6	Catalytic converter		

1 Mazda Miata Maintenance schedule

The maintenance intervals in this manual are provided with the assumption that you, not the dealer, will be doing the work. These are the minimum maintenance intervals recommended by the factory for vehicles that are driven daily. If you wish to keep your vehicle in peak condition at all times, you may wish to perform some of these procedures even more often. Because frequent maintenance enhances the efficiency, performance and resale value of your car, we encourage you to do so. If you drive in dusty areas, tow a trailer, idle or drive at low speeds for extended periods or drive for short distances (less than four miles) in below freezing temperatures, shorter intervals are also recommended.

When your vehicle is new, it should be serviced by a factory authorized dealer service department to protect the factory warranty. In many cases, the initial maintenance check is done at no cost to the owner.

EVERY 250 MILES OR WEEKLY, WHICHEVER COMES FIRST

Check the engine oil level (Section 4)
Check the engine coolant level (Section 4)
Check the windshield washer fluid level (Section 4)
Check the brake/clutch fluid level (Section 4)
Check the tires and tire pressures (Section 5)

EVERY 3000 MILES OR 3 MONTHS, WHICHEVER COMES FIRST

All items listed above plus:
Change the engine oil and oil filter (Section 6)
Rotate the tires (Section 7)

EVERY 7500 MILES OR 6 MONTHS, WHICHEVER COMES FIRST

Check the power steering fluid level (Section 8)
Check the automatic transmission fluid level (Section 9)
Inspect and replace if necessary the windshield wiper blades (Section 10)
Check the clutch pedal for proper height and freeplay (Section 11)
Check and service the battery (Section 12)
Check and adjust if necessary the engine drivebelts (Section 13)
Inspect and replace if necessary all underhood hoses (Section 14)
Check the cooling system (Section 15)

EVERY 15,000 MILES OR 12 MONTHS, WHICHEVER COMES FIRST

All items listed above plus:
Inspect the brake system (Section 16)*
Replace the air filter (Section 17)

Check the manual transmission lubricant level (Section 18)
Inspect the steering and suspension components (Section 19)*
Check the driveaxle boots (Section 20)

EVERY 30,000 MILES OR 24 MONTHS, WHICHEVER COMES FIRST

All items listed above plus:
Inspect the fuel system (Section 21)
Replace the spark plugs (Section 22)
Inspect and replace if necessary the spark plug wires (Section 23)
Service the cooling system (drain, flush and refill)* (Section 24)
Inspect the fuel evaporative emissions control system (Section 25)
Inspect the exhaust system (Section 26)
Change the automatic transmission fluid (Section 27)**
Change the manual transmission lubricant (Section 28)**
Check and replace if necessary the PCV valve (Section 29)
* Except 2006 and later models with "F22" marked on the cooling system pressure cap

EVERY 60,000 MILES OR 48 MONTHS, WHICHEVER COMES FIRST

Service the cooling system (drain, flush and refill) (2006 and later models with "F22" marked on the cooling system pressure cap)
Replace the fuel filter (2005 and earlier models only) (Section 30)
Replace the timing belt (Chapter 2A)
*This item is affected by "severe" operating conditions as described below. If your vehicle is operated under "severe" conditions, perform all maintenance indicated with an asterisk (*) at 3000 mile/3 month intervals. Severe conditions are indicated if you mainly operate your vehicle under one or more of the following conditions:

Operating in dusty areas
Towing a trailer
Idling for extended periods and/or low speed operation
Operating when outside temperatures remain below freezing and when most trips are less than four miles

**If operated under one or more of the following conditions, change the manual or automatic transmission fluid and differential lubricant every 15,000 miles:

In heavy city traffic where the outside temperature regularly reaches 90-degrees F (32-degrees C) or higher
In hilly or mountainous terrain
Frequent trailer pulling

EVERY 75,000 MILES

Check and, if necessary, adjust the valves (2006 and later models) (Section 31)

2 Introduction

This Chapter is designed to help the home mechanic maintain the Mazda Miata for peak performance, economy, safety and long life.

Included is a master maintenance schedule, followed by sections dealing specifically with each item on the schedule. Visual checks, adjustments, component replacement and other helpful items are included. Refer to the accompanying illustrations of the engine compartment and the underside of the vehicle for the location of various components.

Servicing your Miata in accordance with the mileage/time maintenance schedule and the following Sections will provide it with a planned maintenance program that should result in a long and reliable service life. This is a comprehensive plan, so maintaining some items but not others at the specified service intervals will not produce the same results.

As you service your Miata, you will discover that many of the procedures can - and should - be grouped together because of the nature of the particular procedure you're performing or because of the close proximity of two otherwise unrelated components to one another.

For example, if the vehicle is raised for any reason, you should inspect the exhaust, suspension, steering and fuel systems while you're under the vehicle. When you're rotating the tires, it makes good sense to check the brakes and wheel bearings since the wheels are already removed.

Finally, let's suppose you have to borrow or rent a torque wrench. Even if you only need to tighten the spark plugs, you might as well check the torque of as many critical fasteners as time allows.

The first step of this maintenance program is to prepare yourself before the actual work begins. Read through all Sections pertinent to the procedures you're planning to do, then make a list of and gather together all the parts and tools you will need to do the job. If it looks as if you might run into problems during a particular segment of some procedure, seek advice from your local parts store or dealer service department.

3 Tune-up general information

The term tune-up is used in this manual to represent a combination of individual operations rather than one specific procedure.

If, from the time the vehicle is new, the routine maintenance schedule is followed closely and frequent checks are made of fluid levels and high wear items, as suggested throughout this manual, the engine will be kept in relatively good running condition and the need for additional work will be minimized.

More likely than not, however, there will be times when the engine is running poorly due to lack of regular maintenance. This is even more likely if a used vehicle, which has not received regular and frequent maintenance checks, is purchased. In such cases, an engine tune-up will be needed outside of the regular routine maintenance intervals.

The first step in any tune-up or engine diagnosis to help correct a poor running engine would be a cylinder compression check. A check of the engine compression (Chapter 2, Part B) will give valuable information regarding the overall performance of many internal components and should be used as a basis for tune-up and repair procedures. If, for instance, a compression check indicates serious internal engine wear, a conventional tune-up will not help the running condition of the engine and would be a waste of time and money.

The following series of operations are those most often needed to bring a generally poor running engine back into a proper state of tune.

MINOR TUNE-UP

Clean, inspect and test the battery (Section 12)
Check all engine related fluids (Section 4)
Check and adjust the drivebelts (Section 13)
Replace the spark plugs (Section 22)
Inspect the spark plug and coil wires (Section 23)
Check all underhood hoses (Section 14)
Check the cooling system (Section 15)
Check the air filter (Section 17)

MAJOR TUNE-UP

All items listed under Minor tune-up, plus . . .
Check the ignition system (Section 23)
Check the charging system (Chapter 5)
Check the fuel system (Section 21)
Replace the air filter (Section 17)
Replace the spark plug wires (Section 23)

4 Fluid level checks (every 250 miles or weekly)

1 Fluids are an essential part of the lubrication, cooling, brake, clutch and other systems. Because these fluids gradually become depleted and/or contaminated during normal operation of the vehicle, they must be periodically replenished. See *Recommended lubricants and fluids* and *Capacities* in this Chapter's Specifications before adding fluid to any of the following components.

➡**Note: The vehicle must be on level ground before fluid levels can be checked.**

4.2a Engine oil dipstick location (2005 and earlier models)

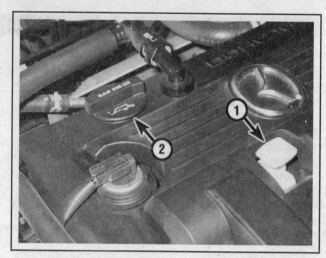

4.2b Dipstick (1) and oil filler cap (2) (2006 and later models)

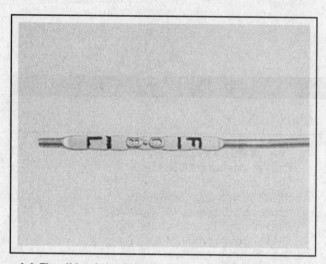

4.4 The oil level should be at or near the F mark - if it isn't, add enough oil to bring the level to near the F mark (typical)

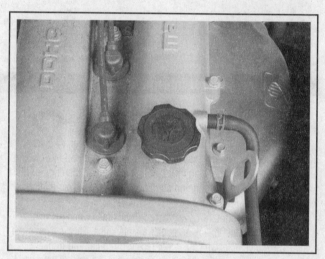

4.6 Location of the threaded oil filler cap (2005 and earlier models)

ENGINE OIL

▶ **Refer to illustrations 4.2a, 4.2b, 4.4 and 4.6**

2   Locate the dipstick (see illustrations).

3   The oil level should be checked before the vehicle has been driven, or about 5 minutes after the engine has been shut off. If the oil is checked immediately after driving the vehicle, some of the oil will remain in the upper engine components, producing an inaccurate reading on the dipstick.

4   Pull the dipstick from the tube and wipe all the oil from the end with a clean rag or paper towel. Insert the clean dipstick all the way back into its metal tube and pull it out again. Observe the oil at the end of the dipstick. At its highest point, the level should be between the L (Low) and F (Full) marks (see illustration).

5   It takes slightly less than 14 ounces of oil to raise the level from the L mark to the F mark on the dipstick. Do not allow the level to drop below the L mark or oil starvation may cause engine damage. Con-

versely, overfilling the engine (adding oil above the F mark) may cause oil fouled spark plugs, oil leaks or oil seal failures.

6   Remove the threaded cap from the valve cover to add oil (2005 and earlier models, see illustration; 2006 and later models, see illustration 4.2b). Use a funnel to prevent spills. After adding the oil, install the filler cap hand tight. Start the engine and look carefully for any small leaks around the oil filter or drain plug. Stop the engine and check the oil level again after it has had sufficient time to drain from the upper block and cylinder head galleys.

7   Checking the oil level is an important preventive maintenance step. A continually dropping oil level indicates oil leakage through damaged seals, from loose connections, or past worn rings or valve guides. If the oil looks milky in color or has water droplets in it, a cylinder head gasket may be blown. The engine should be checked immediately. The condition of the oil should also be checked. Each time you check the oil level, slide your thumb and index finger up the dipstick before wiping off the oil. If you see small dirt or metal particles clinging to the dipstick, the oil should be changed (Section 6).

4.9a On 2005 and earlier models, the coolant reservoir is located in the left front corner of the engine compartment

4.9b On 2006 and later models, the coolant expansion tank is located at the front of the engine compartment

4.14a On 2005 and earlier models, the windshield washer fluid reservoir tank is located in the right rear corner of the engine compartment

ENGINE COOLANT

▶ Refer to illustrations 4.9a and 4.9b

❊❊ WARNING:

Do not allow antifreeze to come in contact with your skin or painted surfaces of the vehicle. Flush contaminated areas immediately with plenty of water. Don't store new coolant or leave old coolant lying around where it's accessible to children or pets - they're attracted by its sweet smell and may drink it. Ingestion of even a small amount of coolant can be fatal! Wipe up garage floor and drip pan spills immediately. Keep antifreeze containers covered and repair cooling system leaks as soon as they're noticed.

8 All vehicles covered by this manual are equipped with a pressurized coolant recovery system. On 2006 and later models, the expansion tank is under the same pressure as the rest of the cooling system.

9 The coolant level should be checked before the vehicle has been driven when the engine is cool. It must be between the F (Full) and L (Low) marks on the reservoir (see illustrations). Use only ethylene-glycol type coolant and soft (demineralized) water in the mixture ratio recommended by your owner's manual. Do not use supplemental inhibitor additives. If only a small amount of coolant is required to bring the system up to the proper level, water can be used. However, repeated additions of water will dilute the recommended antifreeze and water solution. In order to maintain the proper ratio of antifreeze and water, it is advisable to top up the coolant level with the correct mixture. Refer to this Chapter's Specifications for the recommended ratio.

10 If the coolant level drops within a short time after replenishment, there may be a leak in the system. Inspect the radiator, hoses, engine coolant filler cap, drain plugs, air bleeder plugs and water pump. If no leak is evident, have the radiator cap pressure tested by your dealer.

❊❊ WARNING:

Never remove the radiator cap or the coolant recovery reservoir cap when the engine is running or has just been shut down, because the cooling system is hot. Escaping steam and scalding liquid could cause serious injury.

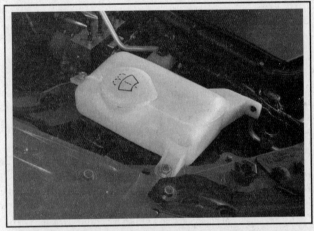

4.14b On 2006 and later models, the windshield washer fluid reservoir is located at the right front corner of the engine compartment

11 If it is necessary to open the radiator cap, wait until the system has cooled completely, then wrap a thick cloth around the cap and turn it to the first stop. If any steam escapes, wait until the system has cooled further, then remove the cap.

12 When checking the coolant level, always note its condition. It should be relatively clear. If it is brown or rust colored, the system should be drained, flushed and refilled. Even if the coolant appears to be normal, the corrosion inhibitors wear out with use, so it must be replaced at the specified intervals.

13 Do not allow antifreeze to come in contact with your skin or painted surfaces of the vehicle. Flush contacted areas immediately with plenty of water.

WINDSHIELD/WINDOW WASHER FLUID

▶ Refer to illustrations 4.14a and 4.14b

14 Fluid for the windshield washer system is stored in a plastic reservoir which is located either in the right front or right rear corner of the engine compartment (see illustrations). In milder climates, plain water can be used to top up the reservoir, but the reservoir should be kept no more than two-thirds full to allow for expansion should the water freeze.

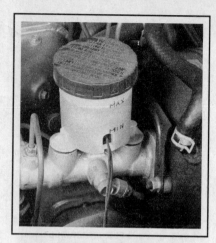

4.17a The brake fluid level should be kept between the MIN and MAX marks on the translucent plastic reservoir - remove the cap to add fluid

4.17b The clutch fluid reservoir is located next to the brake reservoir - the same type of fluid is used in the clutch and brake systems

4.17c On 2006 and later models, the clutch master cylinder uses fluid from the brake fluid reservoir

In colder climates, the use of a specially designed windshield washer fluid, available at your dealer and any auto parts store, will help lower the freezing point of the fluid. Mix the solution with water in accordance with the manufacturer's directions on the container. Do not use regular antifreeze. It will damage the vehicle's paint.

BATTERY ELECTROLYTE

→Note: The battery is located in the luggage compartment on 2005 and earlier models. On 2006 and later models, it's located in the engine compartment.

15 On models not equipped with a sealed battery, unscrew the filler/vent cap and check the electrolyte level. It must be between the upper and lower levels. If the level is low, add distilled water. Install and securely retighten the cap.

✳✳ **CAUTION:**

Overfilling the cells may cause electrolyte to spill over during periods of heavy charging, causing corrosion or damage.

BRAKE/CLUTCH FLUID

◆ **Refer to illustrations 4.17a, 4.17b and 4.17c**

16 On 2005 and earlier models, separate reservoirs are used for the brake and clutch hydraulic systems. The brake reservoir is mounted in front of the brake power booster unit in the engine compartment and the clutch reservoir is mounted to its left. On 2006 and later models, the clutch master cylinder gets its fluid supply from the brake fluid reservoir.

17 To check the fluid level of either reservoir, simply look at the MAX and MIN marks on the reservoir (see illustrations). The level should be

at or near the MAX fill line on the reservoir.

18 If the level is low, wipe the top of the reservoir cap with a clean rag to prevent contamination of the brake and clutch systems before lifting the cap.

19 Add only the specified brake fluid to the reservoir (refer to *Recommended lubricants and fluids* in this Chapter's Specifications or to your owner's manual). Mixing different types of brake fluid can damage the system. Fill the master cylinder reservoir only to the MAX level.

✳✳ **WARNING:**

Use caution when filling the reservoir - brake fluid can harm your eyes and damage painted surfaces. Do not use brake fluid that has been opened for more than one year (even if the cap has been on) or has been left open. Brake fluid absorbs moisture from the air. Excess moisture can cause a dangerous loss of braking.

20 While the reservoir cap is removed, inspect the fluid for contamination. If deposits, dirt particles or water droplets are present, the system should be bled until it is purged of all old fluid (see Chapter 8 for clutch system bleeding and Chapter 9 for brake system bleeding).

21 After filling the reservoir to the proper level, make sure the cap is properly seated to prevent fluid leakage and/or system pressure loss.

22 The fluid in the brake master cylinder will drop slightly as the brake pads at each wheel wear down during normal operation. If the fluid requires repeated replenishing to keep it at the proper level, this is an indication of leakage in the brake or clutch hydraulic systems, which should be corrected immediately. Check all brake lines and connections, along with the wheel cylinders and booster (see Section 16). Check all clutch fluid lines and connections, along with the clutch master cylinder (see Chapter 8).

23 If, upon checking the master cylinder fluid level, you discover the reservoir empty or nearly empty, the brake and clutch system must be diagnosed immediately (see Chapters 8 and 9).

5   Tire and tire pressure checks (every 250 miles or weekly)

▶ **Refer to illustrations 5.2, 5.3, 5.4a, 5.4b and 5.8**

1   Periodic inspection of the tires may spare you from the inconvenience of being stranded with a flat tire. It can also provide you with vital information regarding possible problems in the steering and suspension systems before major damage occurs.

2   Normal tread wear can be monitored with a simple, inexpensive device known as a tread depth indicator (see illustration). When the tread depth reaches the specified minimum, replace the tire(s).

3   Note any abnormal tread wear (see illustration). Tread pattern irregularities such as cupping, flat spots and more wear on one side than the other are indications of front end alignment and/or balance problems. If any of these conditions are noted, take the vehicle to a tire shop or service station to correct the problem.

4   Look closely for cuts, punctures and embedded nails or tacks. Sometimes a tire will hold its air pressure for a short time or leak down very slowly even after a nail has embedded itself into the tread. If a slow

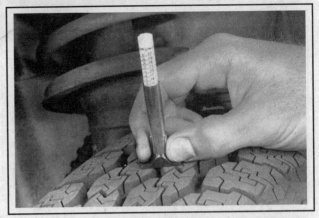

5.2 A tire tread depth indicator should be used to monitor tire wear - they are available at auto parts stores and service stations and cost very little

UNDERINFLATION

CUPPING

OVERINFLATION

INCORRECT TOE-IN OR EXTREME CAMBER

Cupping may be caused by:
- **Underinflation and/or mechanical irregularities such as out-of-balance condition of wheel and/or tire, and bent or damaged wheel.**
- **Loose or worn steering tie-rod or steering idler arm.**
- **Loose, damaged or worn front suspension parts.**

FEATHERING DUE TO MISALIGNMENT

5.3 This chart will help you determine the condition of your tires, the probable cause(s) of abnormal wear and the corrective action necessary

5.4a If a tire loses air on a steady basis, check the valve core first to make sure it's snug (special inexpensive wrenches are commonly available at auto parts stores)

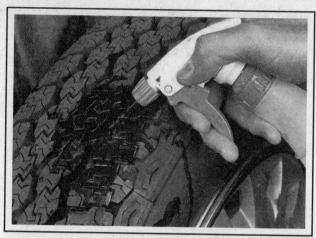

5.4b If the valve core is tight, raise the corner of the vehicle with the low tire and spray a soapy water solution onto the tread as the tire is turned slowly - slow leaks will cause small bubbles to appear

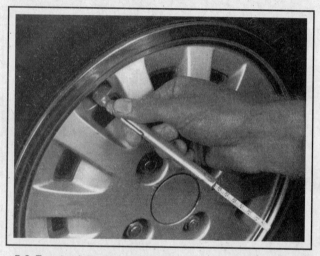

5.8 To extend the life of your tires, check the air pressure at least once a week with an accurate gauge (don't forget the spare!)

leak persists, check the valve stem core to make sure it is tight (see illustration). Examine the tread for an object that may have embedded itself into the tire or for a plug that may have begun to leak (radial tire punctures are repaired with a plug that is installed in a puncture). If a puncture is suspected, it can be easily verified by spraying a solution of soapy water onto the puncture area (see illustration). The soapy solution will bubble if there is a leak. Unless the puncture is inordinately large, a tire shop or gas station can usually repair the punctured tire.

5   Carefully inspect the inner sidewall of each tire for evidence of brake fluid leakage. If you see any, inspect the brakes immediately.

6   Correct tire air pressure adds miles to the lifespan of the tires, improves mileage and enhances overall ride quality. Tire pressure cannot be accurately estimated by looking at a tire, particularly if it is a radial. A tire pressure gauge is therefore essential. Keep an accurate gauge in the glovebox. The pressure gauges fitted to the nozzles of air hoses at gas stations are often inaccurate.

7   Always check tire pressure when the tires are cold. "Cold," in this case, means the vehicle has not been driven over a mile in the three hours preceding a tire pressure check. A pressure rise of four to eight pounds is not uncommon once the tires are warm.

8   Unscrew the valve cap protruding from the wheel or hubcap and push the gauge firmly onto the valve (see illustration). Note the reading on the gauge and compare this figure to the recommended tire pressure shown on the tire placard on the driver's door frame. Be sure to reinstall the valve cap to keep dirt and moisture out of the valve stem mechanism. Check all four tires and, if necessary, add enough air to bring them up to the recommended pressure levels.

9   Don't forget to keep the spare tire inflated to the specified pressure (consult your owner's manual). Note that the air pressure specified for the compact spare is significantly higher than the pressure of the regular tires.

6   Engine oil and oil filter change (every 3000 miles or 3 months)

▶ Refer to illustrations 6.2, 6.6, 6.7, 6.12a, 6.12b and 6.14

1   Frequent oil changes are the best preventive maintenance the home mechanic can give the engine, because aging oil becomes diluted and contaminated, which leads to premature engine wear.

2   Make sure that you have all the necessary tools before you begin this procedure (see illustration). You should also have plenty of rags or newspapers handy for mopping up any spills.

3   Access to the underside of the vehicle is greatly improved if the vehicle can be lifted on a hoist, driven onto ramps or supported by jackstands.

✳✳ WARNING:

Do not work under a vehicle which is supported only by a bumper, hydraulic or scissors-type jack.

4   If this is your first oil change, get under the vehicle and familiarize yourself with the location of the oil drain plug. The engine and exhaust components will be warm during the actual work, so try to anticipate any potential problems before the engine and accessories are hot.

5   Park the vehicle on a level spot. Start the engine and allow it to reach its normal operating temperature (the needle on the temperature gauge should be at least above the bottom mark). Warm oil and sludge will flow out more easily. Turn off the engine when it's warmed up. Remove the filler cap in the valve cover.

6   Raise the vehicle and support it on jackstands, then remove the engine under-cover (see illustration).

✳✳ WARNING:

To avoid personal injury, never get beneath the vehicle when it is supported by only by a jack. The jack provided with your vehicle is designed solely for raising the vehicle to remove and replace the wheels. Always use jackstands to support the vehicle when it becomes necessary to place your body underneath the vehicle.

7   Being careful not to touch the hot exhaust components, place the drain pan under the drain plug in the bottom of the pan and remove the plug (see illustration). You may want to wear gloves while unscrewing the plug the final few turns if the engine is really hot.

8   Allow the old oil to drain into the pan. It may be necessary to move the pan farther under the engine as the oil flow slows to a trickle. Inspect the old oil for the presence of metal shavings and chips.

9   After all the oil has drained, wipe off the drain plug with a clean rag. Even minute metal particles clinging to the plug would immediately contaminate the new oil.

10 Clean the area around the drain plug opening, reinstall the plug and tighten it to the torque listed in this Chapter's Specifications.

11 Move the drain pan into position under the oil filter.

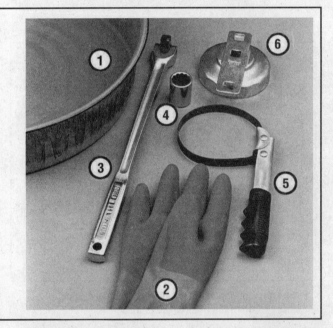

6.2   These tools are required when changing the engine oil and filter

1   **Drain pan** - It should be fairly shallow in depth, but wide in order to prevent spills

2   **Rubber gloves** - When removing the drain plug and filter, it is inevitable that you will get oil on your hands (the gloves will prevent burns)

3   **Breaker bar** - Sometimes the oil drain plug is pretty tight and a long breaker bar is needed to loosen it

4   **Socket** - To be used with the breaker bar or a ratchet (must be the correct size to fit the drain plug)

5   **Filter wrench** - This is a metal band-type wrench, which requires clearance around the filter to be effective

6   **Filter wrench** - This type fits on the bottom of the filter and can be turned with a ratchet or beaker bar (different size wrenches are available for different types of filters)

6.6   Typical engine under-cover bolt locations (2006 and later models)

6.7   Use a proper size box-end wrench or socket to remove the oil drain plug and avoid rounding it off

6.12a On 2005 and earlier models, the oil filter is located on the right side of the engine block

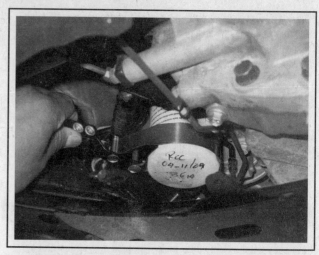

6.12b On 2006 and later models, the oil filter is located on the left side of the engine block

6.14 Lubricate the oil filter gasket with clean engine oil before installing the filter on the engine

12 Loosen the oil filter (see illustrations) by turning it counterclockwise with a filter wrench. Any standard filter wrench should work. Once the filter is loose, use your hands to unscrew it from the block. Just as the filter is detached from the block, immediately tilt the open end up to prevent the oil inside the filter from spilling out.

✳✳ WARNING:

The engine exhaust components may still be hot, so be careful.

13 With a clean rag, wipe off the mounting surface on the block. If a residue of old oil is allowed to remain, it will smoke when the block is

heated up. It will also prevent the new filter from seating properly. Also make sure that the none of the old gasket remains stuck to the mounting surface. It can be removed with a scraper if necessary.

14 Compare the old filter with the new one to make sure they are the same type. Smear some engine oil on the rubber gasket of the new filter and screw it into place (see illustration). Because overtightening the filter will damage the gasket, do not use a filter wrench to tighten the filter. Tighten it by hand until the gasket contacts the seating surface. Then seat the filter by giving it an additional 3/4-turn.

15 Remove all tools, rags, etc. from under the vehicle, being careful not to spill the oil in the drain pan, then lower the vehicle.

16 Add new oil to the engine through the oil filler cap in the valve cover. Use a spout or funnel to prevent oil from spilling onto the top of the engine. Pour three quarts of fresh oil (four quarts in the 1.8L or 2.0L engine) into the engine. Wait a few minutes to allow the oil to drain into the pan, then check the level on the oil dipstick (see Section 4 if necessary). If the oil level is at or near the F mark, install the filler cap hand tight, start the engine and allow the new oil to circulate.

17 Allow the engine to run for about a minute. While the engine is running, look under the vehicle and check for leaks at the oil pan drain plug and around the oil filter. If either is leaking, stop the engine and tighten the plug or filter slightly.

18 Wait a few minutes to allow the oil to trickle down into the pan, then recheck the level on the dipstick and, if necessary, add enough oil to bring the level to the F mark.

19 During the first few trips after an oil change, make it a point to check frequently for leaks and proper oil level.

20 The old oil drained from the engine cannot be reused in its present state and should be discarded. Check with your local refuse disposal company, disposal facility or environmental agency to see if they will accept the oil for recycling. Don't pour used oil into drains or onto the ground. After the oil has cooled, it can be drained into a suitable container (capped plastic jugs, topped bottles, milk cartons, etc.) for transport to one of these disposal sites.

7   Tire rotation (every 3000 miles or 3 months)

▶ **Refer to illustration 7.2**

1   The tires should be rotated at the specified intervals and whenever uneven wear is noticed. Since the vehicle will be raised and the tires removed anyway, check the brakes (see Section 16) at this time.

2   Radial tires must be rotated in a specific pattern (see illustration).

3   Refer to the information in *Jacking and towing* at the front of this manual for the proper procedures to follow when raising the vehicle and changing a tire. If the brakes are to be checked, do not apply the parking brake as stated. Make sure the tires are blocked to prevent the vehicle from rolling.

4   Preferably, the entire vehicle should be raised at the same time. This can be done on a hoist or by jacking up each corner and then lowering the vehicle onto jackstands placed under the frame rails. Always use four jackstands and make sure the vehicle is firmly supported.

5   After rotation, check and adjust the tire pressures as necessary and be sure to check the lug nut tightness.

6   For further information on the wheels and tires, refer to Chapter 10.

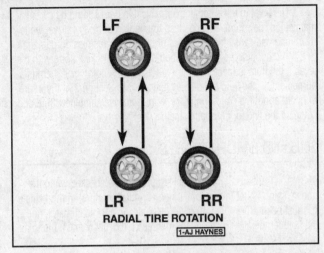

7.2 The recommended tire rotation pattern for these vehicles

8   Power steering fluid level check (every 7500 miles or 6 months)

▶ **Refer to illustrations 8.2a, 8.2b and 8.4**

1   Unlike manual steering, the power steering system relies on fluid which may, over a period of time, require replenishing.

2   Locate the power steering fluid reservoir (see illustrations).

3   For the check, the front wheels should be pointed straight ahead and the engine should be off.

4   To check the fluid level on 2005 and earlier models, remove the dipstick from the reservoir, wipe it off, then reinsert it and remove it, noting the fluid level (see illustration). It should be between the L and H

mark; if it isn't, add the recommended fluid, but don't overfill the reservoir.

5   The fluid level on 2006 and later models is checked by looking at the translucent reservoir; the fluid level should be between the MIN and MAX marks.

6   If additional fluid is required, pour the specified type into the reservoir, using a funnel to prevent spills. Be careful not to overfill the reservoir.

7   If the reservoir requires frequent fluid additions, all power steering hoses, hose connections, the power steering pump and the steering gear should be carefully checked for leaks.

8.2a On 2005 and earlier models, the power steering fluid reservoir is located in the left front of the engine compartment

8.2b On 2006 and later models, the power steering fluid reservoir is located at the front of the engine, between the air filter housing and the battery

8.4 On 2005 and earlier models, the power steering fluid level should be between the L and H marks on the dipstick

9   Automatic transmission fluid level check (every 7500 miles or 6 months)

1   The level of the automatic transmission fluid should be carefully maintained. Low fluid level can lead to slipping or loss of drive, while overfilling can cause foaming, loss of fluid and transmission damage.

2   The condition of the fluid should also be checked along with the level. If the fluid is black or a dark reddish brown color, or if it emits a burned smell, the fluid should be changed (see Section 27). If you are in doubt about the condition of the fluid, purchase some new fluid and compare the two for color and smell.

2005 AND EARLIER MODELS

3   The transmission fluid level should only be checked when the transmission is hot (at its normal operating temperature). If the vehicle has just been driven over 10 miles (15 miles in a frigid climate), and the fluid temperature is about 150-degrees F (65-degrees C), the transmission is hot.

✸✸ CAUTION:

If the vehicle has just been driven for a long time at high speed or in city traffic in hot weather, or if it has been pulling a trailer, an accurate fluid level reading cannot be obtained. Allow the fluid to cool down for about 30 minutes.

4   If the vehicle has not just been driven, park the vehicle on level ground, set the parking brake and start the engine. While the engine is idling, depress the brake pedal and move the selector lever through all the gear ranges, beginning and ending in Park.

5   With the engine still idling, remove the dipstick from its tube near the right rear corner of the engine. Check the level of the fluid on the dipstick and note its condition.

6   Wipe the fluid from the dipstick with a clean rag and reinsert it back into the filler tube until the cap seats.

7   Pull the dipstick out again and note the fluid level. If the level is below the lower notch, add the specified automatic transmission fluid through the dipstick tube with a funnel.

8   Add just enough of the recommended fluid to fill the transmission to the proper level. It takes about one pint to raise the level from the low notch to the full notch on the dipstick when the fluid is hot, so add the fluid a little at a time and keep checking the level until it is correct.

2006 AND LATER MODELS

▸ **Refer to illustration 9.10**

➟**Note: It is important that the vehicle be raised at both ends so that it is level.**

➟**Note: The transmission fluid temperature must be below 140-degrees F when beginning this procedure.**

9   With the vehicle raised and safely supported, place a drain pan under the transmission.

10 Start the engine and let it run at idle speed for about one minute, then turn it off. Remove the overflow plug from the overflow tube at the bottom left side of the transmission fluid pan. Some fluid will probably drain out initially (the fluid that collected in the overflow tube); don't consider this fluid part of the checking procedure. After this fluid has spilled out, if transmission fluid continues to drip from the overflow

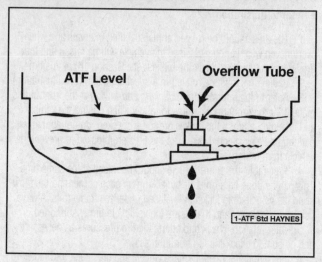

9.10 When the automatic transmission fluid level is correct, fluid will steadily drip from the overflow tube in the transmission fluid pan (2006 and later models)

tube (see illustration), proceed to Step 13.

11 If fluid does not continue to drip out, remove the fill plug from the left side of the transmission case, near the bellhousing. Add the recommended type of automatic transmission fluid through the fill hole until fluid just starts to drip from the overflow tube.

➟**Note: A suction gun or fluid pump will be required to add the fluid.**

12 Install the fill plug, using a new sealing ring, and tighten it to the torque listed in this Chapter's Specifications.

➟**Note: Be sure to install the sealing washer so its flat side seats against the case.**

13 Start the engine, then depress the brake pedal and move the shift lever through all of the gear ranges two times, then return the shift lever to Park.

➟**Note: Pause for two seconds in each range.**

14 Allow the engine to run until the transmission fluid temperature is between 122 and 140-degrees F. This can be verified by using a scan tool plugged into the diagnostic connector (see Chapter 6), or by using the following procedure:

a) Locate the Transmission Control Module (TCM); it's under the left end of the instrument panel, attached to a bracket near the steering column. In the wiring harness to the TCM is a two-terminal check connector; using a jumper wire, bridge the two terminals of the connector.

b) Depress the brake pedal and shift from Neutral to Drive four times, pausing 1.5 seconds in each position, ending up back in Neutral. The AT warning light on the instrument panel should illuminate for two seconds, then one of three things will happen, indicating the fluid temperature range:

1) If the AT warning light goes out, the fluid temperature is below 122-degrees F.

2) If the light remains on, the fluid temperature is between 122 and 140-degrees F.

3) If the light blinks on and off (1 second intervals), the fluid temperature is above 140-degrees F.

15 Check to see if fluid is dripping from the overflow tube. If it is, the fluid level is correct. Turn the engine off and reinstall the overflow plug, tightening it to the torque listed in this Chapter's Specifications.

➥Note: Be sure to install the sealing washer so its flat side seats against the pan.

16 If fluid is not dripping from the overflow tube, turn off the engine and repeat Steps 11 through 15.

17 If the transmission fluid temperature was checked by bridging the terminals of the TCM check connector, don't forget to remove the jumper wire.

10 Windshield wiper blade inspection and replacement (every 7500 miles or 6 months)

▶ Refer to illustrations 10.5, 10.6 and 10.7

1   The windshield wiper and blade assembly should be inspected periodically for damage, loose components and cracked or worn blade elements.

2   Road film can build up on the wiper blades and affect their efficiency, so they should be washed regularly with a mild detergent solution.

3   The action of the wiping mechanism can loosen bolts, nuts and fasteners, so they should be checked and tightened, as necessary, at the same time the wiper blades are checked.

4   If the wiper blade elements are cracked, worn or warped, or no longer clean adequately, they should be replaced with new ones.

5   Remove the wiper blade assembly from the arm by pushing on the release lever, then sliding the assembly down and out of the hook in the end of the arm (see illustration).

6   Detach the blade insert element and pull it out of the right end of the wiper frame (see illustration).

7   Insert the new element end with the small protrusions into the right side of the wiper frame (see illustration). Slide the element fully into place, then seat the protrusions in the end of the frames to secure it.

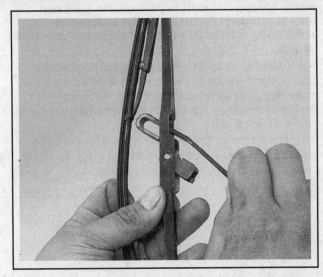

10.5 Push on the release lever and slide the wiper assembly down out of the hook in the end of the wiper arm

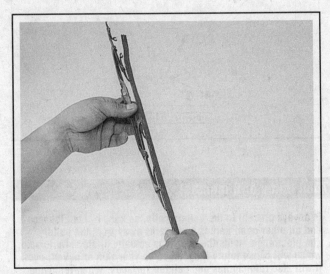

10.6 After detaching the end of the element, slide it out of the end of the frame

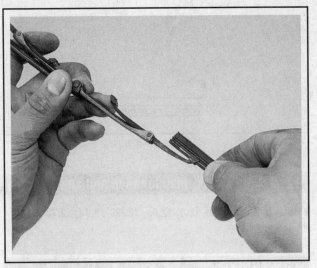

10.7 Insert the end of the element with the protrusions in first

11 Clutch pedal height and freeplay - check and adjustment (every 7500 miles or 6 months)

2005 AND EARLIER MODELS

▶ **Refer to illustration 11.1**

1   To check the clutch pedal height, measure the horizontal distance from the center of the clutch pedal surface to the carpet or pad on the firewall (see illustration). The height should be within the limits listed in this Chapter's Specifications. If it isn't, it must be adjusted.

2   To adjust the clutch pedal height, disconnect the clutch switch electrical connector.

3   Loosen the switch locknut (see illustration 11.1).

4   Turn the clutch switch until the pedal height is correct.

5   Tighten the locknut and recheck the pedal height to verify it is correct.

➡**Note: Whenever the pedal height is adjusted it will most likely be necessary to adjust the freeplay because increasing or decreasing pedal height will cause a similar change in pedal freeplay.**

6   Check the clutch pedal freeplay by lightly pushing the clutch pedal down and, with a small steel ruler, measure the distance that it moves freely before the clutch resistance is felt (see illustration 11.1). The freeplay should be within the limits listed in this Chapter's Specifications. If it isn't, it must be adjusted.

7   To adjust the clutch pedal freeplay, loosen the locknut on the pedal end of the clutch pushrod (see illustration 11.1).

8   Turn the pushrod until pedal freeplay is correct.

9   Tighten the locknut and recheck the pedal freeplay to verify it is correct.

10 Complete this procedure by checking the disengagement height (from the upper surface of the pedal to the floor carpet). The disengagement height should be equal to or more than the minimum listed in this Chapter's Specifications.

2006 AND LATER MODELS

▶ **Refer to illustration 11.11**

11 To check the clutch pedal stroke, measure the distance that the pedal travels from its normal position to its fully depressed position (see illustration). Measure the distance from the lower edge of the pedal and compare your measurement to the pedal stroke listed in this Chapter's Specifications. If the pedal stroke is incorrect, loosen the adjuster bolt locknut at the top of the pedal and adjust the stroke by turning the adjuster bolt. When the stroke is correct, tighten the locknut.

12 To check the clutch pedal freeplay, push on the pedal with your hand until you feel resistance. The distance that the pedal travels from its normal position to the point at which you feel resistance is its freeplay. Measure this freeplay and compare it to the pedal freeplay listed in this Chapter's Specifications. If the freeplay is incorrect, loosen the pushrod locknut (see illustration 11.11) and adjust the freeplay by turning the adjuster rod. When the freeplay is correct, tighten the locknut.

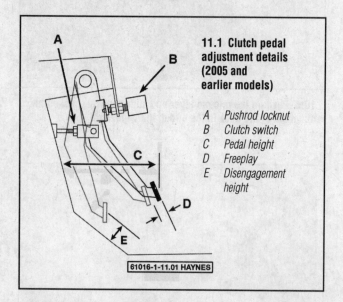

11.1 Clutch pedal adjustment details (2005 and earlier models)

A   Pushrod locknut
B   Clutch switch
C   Pedal height
D   Freeplay
E   Disengagement height

61016-1-11.01 HAYNES

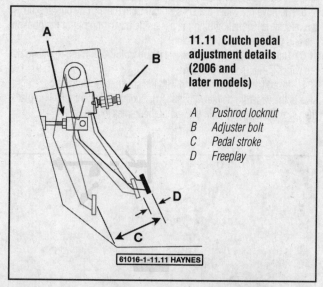

11.11 Clutch pedal adjustment details (2006 and later models)

A   Pushrod locknut
B   Adjuster bolt
C   Pedal stroke
D   Freeplay

61016-1-11.11 HAYNES

12 Battery check, maintenance and charging (every 7500 miles or 6 months)

▶ **Refer to illustrations 12.1, 12.6a, 12.6b, 12.7a, 12.7b and 12.8**

✳✳ **WARNING:**

Certain precautions must be followed when checking and servicing the battery. Hydrogen gas, which is highly flammable, is always present in the battery cells, so keep lighted tobacco and all other open flames and sparks away from the battery. The electrolyte inside the battery is actually dilute sulfuric acid, which will cause injury if splashed on your skin or in your eyes. It will also ruin clothes and painted surfaces. When removing the battery cables, always detach the negative cable first and hook it up last!

12.1 Tools and materials required for battery maintenance

1 *Face shield/safety goggles* - *When removing corrosion with a brush, the acidic particles can easily fly up into your eyes*
2 *Baking soda* - *A solution of baking soda and water can be used to neutralize corrosion*
3 *Petroleum jelly* - *A layer of this on the battery posts will help prevent corrosion*
4 *Battery post/cable cleaner* - *This wire brush cleaning tool will remove all traces of corrosion from the battery posts and cable clamps*
5 *Treated felt washers* - *Placing one of these on each post, directly under the cable clamps, will help prevent corrosion*
6 *Puller* - *Sometimes the cable clamps are very difficult to pull off the posts, even after the nut/bolt has been completely loosened. This tool pulls the clamp straight up and off the post without damage*
7 *Battery post/cable cleaner* - *Here is another cleaning tool which is a slightly different version of number 4 above, but it does the same thing*
8 *Rubber gloves* - *Another safety item to consider when servicing the battery; remember that's acid inside the battery*

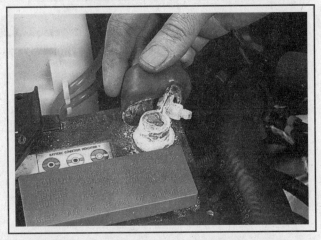

12.6a Battery terminal corrosion usually appears as light, fluffy powder

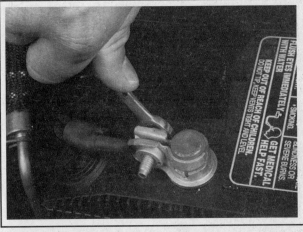

12.6b Removing a cable from the battery post with a wrench - sometimes a pair of special battery pliers are required for this procedure if corrosion has caused deterioration of the nut hex (always remove the ground (-) cable first and hook it up last!)

➡Note: The battery is located in the luggage compartment on 2005 and earlier models. On 2006 and later models, it's located in the engine compartment.

1   A routine preventive maintenance program for the battery in your vehicle is the only way to ensure quick and reliable starts. But before performing any battery maintenance, make sure that you have the proper equipment necessary to work safely around the battery (see illustration).

2   There are also several precautions that should be taken whenever battery maintenance is performed. Before servicing the battery, always turn the engine and all accessories off and disconnect the cable from the negative terminal of the battery.

3   The battery produces hydrogen gas, which is both flammable and explosive. Never create a spark, smoke or light a match around the battery. Always charge the battery in a ventilated area.

4   Electrolyte contains poisonous and corrosive sulfuric acid. Do not allow it to get in your eyes, on your skin on your clothes. Never ingest it. Wear protective safety glasses when working near the battery. Keep children away from the battery.

5   Note the external condition of the battery. If the positive terminal and cable clamp on your vehicle's battery is equipped with a rubber protector, make sure that it's not torn or damaged. It should completely cover the terminal. Look for any corroded or loose connections, cracks in the case or cover or loose hold-down clamps. Also check the entire length of each cable for cracks and frayed conductors.

6   If corrosion, which looks like white, fluffy deposits (see illustration) is evident, particularly around the terminals, the battery should be removed for cleaning. Loosen the cable clamp bolts with a wrench, being careful to remove the ground cable first, and slide them off the terminals (see illustration). Then disconnect the hold-down clamp bolt and nut, remove the clamp and lift the battery from the engine compartment.

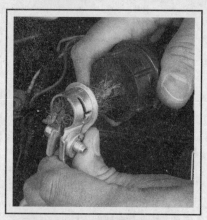

12.7a When cleaning the cable clamps, all corrosion must be removed (the inside of the clamp is tapered to match the taper on the post, so don't remove too much material)

12.7b Regardless of the type of tool used to clean the battery posts, a clean, shiny surface should be the result

12.8 Make sure the battery clamp nut and bolt are tight

7   Clean the cable clamps thoroughly with a battery brush or a terminal cleaner and a solution of warm water and baking soda (see illustration). Wash the terminals and the top of the battery case with the same solution but make sure that the solution doesn't get into the battery. When cleaning the cables, terminals and battery top, wear safety goggles and rubber gloves to prevent any solution from coming in contact with your eyes or hands. Wear old clothes too - even diluted, sulfuric acid splashed onto clothes will burn holes in them. If the terminals have been extensively corroded, clean them up with a terminal cleaner (see illustration). Thoroughly wash all cleaned areas with plain water.

8   Make sure that the battery tray is in good condition and the hold-down nut and bolt are tight (see illustration). If the battery is removed from the tray, make sure no parts remain in the bottom of the tray when the battery is reinstalled. When reinstalling the hold-down clamp bolt or nut, do not overtighten it.

9   Information on removing and installing the battery can be found in Chapter 5. Information on jump starting can be found at the front of this manual.

CLEANING

10   Corrosion on the hold-down components, battery case and surrounding areas can be removed with a solution of water and baking soda. Thoroughly rinse all cleaned areas with plain water.

11   Any metal parts of the vehicle damaged by corrosion should be covered with a zinc-based primer, then painted.

CHARGING

✳✳ WARNING:

When batteries are being charged, hydrogen gas, which is very explosive and flammable, is produced. Do not smoke or allow open flames near a charging or a recently charged battery. Wear eye protection when near the battery during charging. Also, make sure the charger is unplugged before connecting or disconnecting the battery from the charger.

12   Slow-rate charging is the best way to restore a battery that's discharged to the point where it will not start the engine. It's also a good way to maintain the battery charge in a vehicle that's only driven a few miles between starts. Maintaining the battery charge is particularly important in the winter when the battery must work harder to start the engine and electrical accessories that drain the battery are in greater use.

13   It's best to use a one or two-amp battery charger (sometimes called a "trickle" charger). They are the safest and put the least strain on the battery. They are also the least expensive. For a faster charge, you can use a higher amperage charger, but don't use one rated more than 1/10th the amp/hour rating of the battery. Rapid boost charges that claim to restore the power of the battery in one to two hours are hardest on the battery and can damage batteries not in good condition. This type of charging should only be used in emergency situations.

14   The average time necessary to charge a battery should be listed in the instructions that come with the charger. As a general rule, a trickle charger will charge a battery in 12 to 16 hours.

13   Drivebelt check, adjustment and replacement (every 7500 miles or 6 months)

▶ **Refer to illustrations 13.1, 13.3 and 13.4**

1   The drivebelts are located at the front of the engine (see illustration).

2   Because of their composition and the high stresses to which they are subjected, drivebelts stretch and deteriorate as they get older. They must therefore be periodically inspected.

2005 AND EARLIER MODELS

Check

3   With the engine off, open the hood and locate the drivebelts. With a flashlight visually check the belts. Look for cracking, fraying, separa-

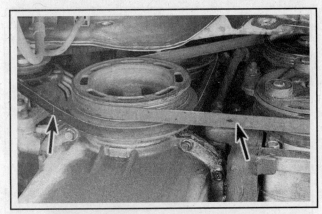

13.1 Drivebelts stretch and deteriorate as they age and must be carefully inspected (typical 2005 and earlier model shown)

tion, tears and glazing, which gives the belt a shiny appearance (see illustration). Both sides of the belt should be inspected, which means you will have to twist the belt to check the underside. Use your fingers to feel the belt where you can't see it. If any of the above conditions are evident, replace the belt (go to Step 8).

4   To check the tension of each belt in accordance with factory specifications, apply moderate pressure (22 pounds) midway between the specified pulleys. Measure the deflection (see illustration) and compare your measurement to the specified drivebelt deflection for either a used or new belt.

➡Note: A "used" belt is defined as any belt which has been operated more than five minutes on the engine; a "new" belt is one that has been used for less than five minutes.

Adjustment

▶ Refer to illustrations 13.5 and 13.6

5   If the alternator/water pump belt must be adjusted, loosen the alternator mounting bolts located above and under the alternator. Tighten the adjusting bolt to push the alternator away from the engine and tighten the belt (see illustration). Tighten the mounting bolts. Measure the belt deflection in accordance with the above method. Repeat this step until the drivebelt is properly adjusted.

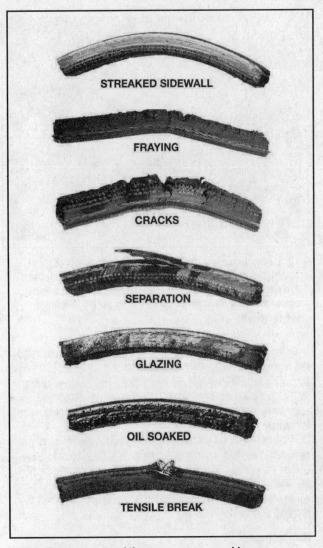

13.3 Here are some of the more common problems associated with drivebelts (check belts very carefully to prevent an untimely breakdown)

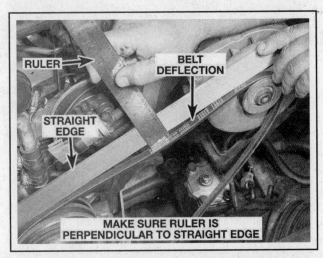

13.4 Measuring drivebelt deflection with a straightedge and ruler

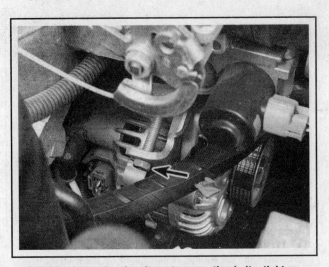

13.5 After loosening the alternator mounting bolts, tighten the adjusting bolt to tension the drivebelt

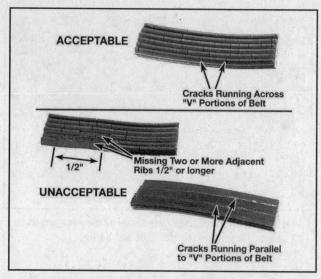

13.6 After loosening the bolt (A) and two locknuts (B) that secure the pump, turn the adjusting bolt (C) to tension the drivebelt (vehicles with air conditioning that do not have power steering have an adjustable idler pulley to tension the drivebelt)

13.13 Small cracks in the underside of a V-ribbed belt are acceptable - lengthwise cracks, or missing pieces that cause the belt to make noise, are cause for replacement

6   Adjust the power steering pump belt by loosening the bolt and two locknuts that secure the pump to the engine. Adjust the belt tension by turning the adjusting bolt (see illustration). Tighten the adjusting locknut and the pump bolt and nut. Measure the belt deflection in accordance with the above method. Repeat this step until the drivebelt is properly adjusted.

7   Vehicles that do not have power steering but are equipped with air conditioning have an idler pulley installed above the compressor. Loosen the idler pulley locknut and turn the adjusting bolt to tension the drivebelt. Tighten the locknut. Measure the belt deflection in accordance with the above method. Repeat this step until the drivebelt is properly adjusted.

Replacement

8   To replace a belt, follow the above procedures to loosen the drivebelt enough to slip the belt off the crankshaft pulley and remove it. If you are replacing the alternator/water pump belt, you will have to remove the power steering and/or air conditioning belt first because of

the way they are arranged on the crankshaft pulley. Because of this and because belts tend to wear out more or less together, it is a good idea to replace both belts at the same time. Mark each belt and its appropriate pulley groove so the replacement belts can be installed in their proper positions.

9   Take the old belts to the parts store in order to make a direct comparison for length, width and design.

10   After replacing the drivebelt, make sure that it fits properly. When installing a multi-ribbed belt, make sure that it is centered - it must not overlap either edge of the pulley.

11   Adjust the drivebelt(s) in accordance with the procedure outlined above.

2006 AND LATER MODELS

Check

♦ **Refer to illustrations 13.13 and 13.14**

12   With the engine stopped, inspect the full length of the drivebelt for cracks and separation of the belt plies. It will be necessary to turn the engine (using a wrench or socket and bar on the crankshaft pulley bolt) in order to move the belt from the pulleys so that the belt can be inspected thoroughly. Twist the belt between the pulleys so that both sides can be viewed. Also check for fraying and glazing, which gives the belt a shiny appearance. Check the pulleys for nicks, cracks, distortion and corrosion.

13   Note that it is not unusual for a ribbed belt to exhibit small cracks in the edges of the belt ribs, and unless these are extensive or very deep, belt replacement is not essential (see illustration).

14   It's not necessary to adjust the serpentine drivebelt because the automatic tensioner maintains the correct tension. However, you can determine whether the belt should be replaced by checking the orientation of the indicator mark on the tensioner in relation to the stationary index mark on the tensioner mounting bracket (see illustration). As long as the arrow on the tensioner is pointing at the stationary index mark, the belt is okay. But if the arrow is pointing at the upper end of the stationary mark, or has already moved above it, replace the belt.

13.14 Note the relationship of the small arrow on the tensioner and the stationary index mark on the tensioner bracket. If the arrow is pointing at the upper end of the mark, or is already beyond the mark, replace the belt

Replacement

Drivebelt

▶ **Refer to illustration 13.17**

15 Remove the battery and the battery tray (see Chapter 5).

16 Remove the air filter housing (see Chapter 4).

17 Note the routing of the drivebelt. Make a sketch to ensure that you install the new belt exactly the same way as the old belt. Rotate the tensioner clockwise (see illustration) and remove the drivebelt.

18 Rotate the tensioner clockwise and, using your sketch of the correct routing for the belt, install the new drivebelt. After you release the tensioner, verify that the belt is correctly tensioned (see illustration 13.14).

19 Install the battery tray and battery (see Chapter 5).

Automatic tensioner

20 Remove the drivebelt (see Steps 15 through 17).

21 Rotate the tensioner pulley by hand in its operational direction (clockwise) and verify that it rotates smoothly. If it doesn't, replace it.

22 Remove the tensioner assembly mounting bolts (see illustration 13.15) and remove the tensioner assembly.

23 Installation is the reverse of removal. Be sure to tighten the tensioner assembly mounting bolts securely.

13.17 To remove or install a new serpentine drivebelt, rotate the tensioner clockwise and remove the drivebelt from the pulleys. To replace the tensioner, remove the drivebelt, then remove the two tensioner mounting bolts

14 Underhood hose check and replacement (every 7500 miles or 6 months)

✳ CAUTION:

Replacement of air conditioning hoses must be left to a dealer service department or air conditioning shop that has the equipment to depressurize the system safely. Never remove air conditioning components or hoses until the system has been depressurized.

GENERAL

1 High temperatures in the engine compartment can cause the deterioration of the rubber and plastic hoses used for engine, accessory and emission systems operation. Periodic inspection should be made for cracks, loose clamps, material hardening and leaks.

2 Information specific to the cooling system hoses can be found in Section 15.

3 Some, but not all, hoses are secured to the fittings with clamps. Where clamps are used, check to be sure they haven't lost their tension, allowing the hose to leak. If clamps aren't used, make sure the hose has not expanded and/or hardened where it slips over the fitting, allowing it to leak.

VACUUM HOSES

4 It's quite common for vacuum hoses, especially those in the emissions system, to be color coded or identified by colored stripes molded into them. Various systems require hoses with different wall thickness, collapse resistance and temperature resistance. When replacing hoses, be sure the new ones are made of the same material.

5 Often the only effective way to check a hose is to remove it completely from the vehicle. If more than one hose is removed, be sure to label the hoses and fittings to ensure correct installation.

6 When checking vacuum hoses, be sure to include any plastic T-fittings in the check. Inspect the fittings for cracks and the hose where it fits over the fitting for distortion, which could cause leakage.

7 A small piece of vacuum hose (1/4-inch inside diameter) can be used as a stethoscope to detect vacuum leaks. Hold one end of the hose to your ear and probe around vacuum hoses and fittings, listening for the hissing sound characteristic of a vacuum leak.

✳ WARNING:

When probing with the vacuum hose stethoscope, be very careful not to come into contact with moving engine components such as the drivebelts, cooling fan, etc.

FUEL HOSE

✳✳ WARNING:

Gasoline is extremely flammable, so take extra precautions when you work on any part of the fuel system. Don't smoke or allow open flames or bare light bulbs near the work area, and don't work in a garage where a gas-type appliance (such as a water heater or clothes dryer) is present. Since gasoline is carcinogenic, wear fuel-resistant gloves when there's a possibility of being exposed to fuel, and, if you spill any fuel on your skin, rinse it off immediately with soap and water. Mop up any spills immediately and do not store fuel-soaked rags where they could ignite. When you perform any kind of work on the fuel system, wear safety glasses and have a Class B type fire extinguisher on hand. The fuel system is under constant pressure, so, before any lines are disconnected, the fuel system pressure must be relieved (see Chapter 4).

8 Check all rubber fuel lines for deterioration and chafing. Check especially for cracks in areas where the hose bends and just before fittings, such as where a hose attaches to the fuel filter.

9 High quality fuel line, specifically designed for fuel injection systems, must be used for fuel line replacement.

✳✳ WARNING:

Never use anything other than the proper fuel line for fuel line replacement.

10 Spring-type clamps are commonly used on fuel lines. These clamps often lose their tension over a period of time, and can be sprung during removal. Replace all spring-type clamps with screw clamps whenever a hose is replaced.

METAL LINES

11 Sections of metal line are often used for fuel line between the fuel pump and fuel injection unit. Check carefully to be sure the line has not been bent or crimped and that cracks have not started in the line.

12 If a section of metal fuel line must be replaced, only seamless steel tubing should be used, since copper and aluminum tubing don't have the strength necessary to withstand normal engine vibration.

13 Check the metal brake lines where they enter the master cylinder and brake proportioning unit (if used) for cracks in the lines or loose fittings. Any sign of brake fluid leakage calls for an immediate thorough inspection of the brake system.

15 Cooling system check (every 7500 miles or 6 months)

▸ **Refer to illustration 15.4**

1 Many major engine failures can be attributed to a faulty cooling system. If the vehicle is equipped with an automatic transmission, the cooling system also cools the transmission fluid and thus plays an important role in prolonging transmission life.

2 The cooling system should be checked with the engine cold. Do this before the vehicle is driven for the day or after the engine has been shut off for at least three hours.

3 Remove the radiator cap by turning it to the left until it reaches a stop. If you hear a hissing sound (indicating there is still pressure in the system), wait until it stops. Now press down on the cap with the palm of your hand and continue turning to the left until the cap can be

removed. Thoroughly clean the cap, inside and out, with clean water. Also clean the filler neck on the radiator. All traces of corrosion should be removed. The coolant inside the radiator should be relatively transparent. If it's rust colored, the system should be drained and refilled (see Section 24). If the coolant level isn't up to the top, add additional antifreeze/coolant mixture (see Section 4).

4 Carefully check the large upper and lower radiator hoses along with the smaller diameter heater hoses which run from the engine to the firewall. Inspect each hose along its entire length, replacing any hose which is cracked, swollen or shows signs of deterioration. Cracks may become more apparent if the hose is squeezed (see illustration). Regardless of condition, it's a good idea to replace hoses with new ones every two years.

Check for a chafed area that could fail prematurely.

Check for a soft area indicating the hose has deteriorated inside.

Overtightening the clamp on a hardened hose will damage the hose and cause a leak.

Check each hose for swelling and oil-soaked ends. Cracks and breaks can be located by squeezing the hose.

15.4 Hoses, like drivebelts, have a habit of failing at the worst possible time - to prevent the inconvenience of a blown radiator or heater hose, inspect them carefully as shown here

5   Make sure that all hose connections are tight. A leak in the cooling system will usually show up as white or rust colored deposits on the areas adjoining the leak. If wire-type clamps are used at the ends of the hoses, it may be a good idea to replace them with more secure screw-type clamps.

6   Use compressed air or a soft brush to remove bugs, leaves, etc.

from the front of the radiator or air conditioning condenser. Be careful not to damage the delicate cooling fins or cut yourself on them.

7   Every other inspection, or at the first indication of cooling system problems, have the cap and system pressure tested. If you don't have a pressure tester, most gas stations and repair shops will do this for a minimal charge.

16 Brake check (every 15,000 miles or 12 months)

♦ Refer to illustration 16.6

✳✳ WARNING:

The dust created by the brake system is harmful to your health. Never blow it out with compressed air and don't inhale any of it. An approved filtering mask should be worn when working on the brakes. Do not, under any circumstances, use petroleum-based solvents to clean brake parts. Use brake system cleaner only!

➡**Note: For detailed photographs of the brake system, refer to Chapter 9.**

1   In addition to the specified intervals, the brakes should be inspected every time the wheels are removed or whenever a defect is suspected. Any of the following symptoms could indicate a potential brake system defect: The vehicle pulls to one side when the brake pedal is depressed; the brakes make squealing or dragging noises when applied; brake travel is excessive; the pedal pulsates; brake fluid leaks, usually onto the inside of the tire or wheel.

2   The disc brake pads have built-in wear indicators which should make a high-pitched squealing or scraping noise when they are worn to the replacement point. When you hear this noise, replace the pads immediately or expensive damage to the discs can result.

3   Loosen the wheel lug nuts.

4   Raise the vehicle and place it securely on jackstands.

5   Remove the wheels (see *Jacking and towing* at the front of this book, or your owner's manual, if necessary).

6   There are two pads - an outer and an inner - in each caliper. The pads are visible by looking at the top of the caliper (see illustration).

7   Check the pad thickness by measuring the pad lining. If the lining material is less than the thickness listed in this Chapter's Specifications, replace the pads.

➡**Note: Keep in mind that the lining material is riveted or bonded to a metal backing plate and the metal portion is not included in this measurement.**

8   If it is difficult to determine the exact thickness of the remaining pad material by the above method, or if you are at all concerned about the condition of the pads, remove the caliper(s), then remove the pads from the calipers for further inspection (see Chapter 9).

9   Once the pads are removed from the calipers, clean them with brake cleaner and re-measure them with a small steel pocket ruler or a vernier caliper.

10   Measure the disc thickness with a micrometer to make sure that

16.6 Look through the opening in the caliper to determine the thickness of remaining pad material for both inner and outer pads

it still has service life remaining. If any disc is thinner than the specified minimum thickness, replace it (see Chapter 9). Even if the disc has service life remaining, check its condition. Look for scoring, gouging and burned spots. If these conditions exist, remove the disc and have it resurfaced (see Chapter 9).

11   Before installing the wheels, check all brake lines and hoses for damage, wear, deformation, cracks, corrosion, leakage, bends and twists, particularly in the vicinity of the rubber hoses at the calipers. Check the clamps for tightness and the connections for leakage. Make sure that all hoses and lines are clear of sharp edges, moving parts and the exhaust system. If any of the above conditions are noted, repair, reroute or replace the lines and/or fittings as necessary (see Chapter 9).

12   Install the wheels and lug nuts.

13   Remove the jackstands and lower the vehicle.

14   Tighten the wheel lug nuts to the torque listed in this Chapter's Specifications.

BRAKE BOOSTER CHECK

15   Sit in the driver's seat and perform the following sequence of tests.

16   With the engine stopped, depress the brake pedal several times - the travel distance should not change.

17 With the brake fully depressed, start the engine - the pedal should move down a little when the engine starts.

18 Depress the brake, stop the engine and hold the pedal in for about 30 seconds - the pedal should neither sink nor rise.

19 Restart the engine, run it for about a minute and turn it off. Then firmly depress the brake several times - the pedal travel should decrease with each application.

20 If your brakes do not operate as described above when the preceding tests are performed, the brake booster is either in need of repair or has failed. Refer to Chapter 9 for the removal procedure.

PARKING BRAKE

21 Slowly pull up on the parking brake and count the number of clicks you hear until the handle is up as far as it will go. The adjustment is correct if you hear the specified number of clicks. If you hear more or fewer clicks, it's time to adjust the parking brake (refer to Chapter 9).

22 An alternative method of checking the parking brake is to park the vehicle on a steep hill with the parking brake set and the transmission in Neutral. If the parking brake cannot prevent the vehicle from rolling, it is in need of adjustment (see Chapter 9).

17 Air filter replacement (every 15,000 miles or 12 months)

▶ Refer to illustrations 17.2a, 17.2b, 17.2c and 17.2d

1 The air filter is located inside a housing on the left front corner of the engine compartment.

2 To remove the air filter, remove the bolts or clips attaching the air filter cover to the box, then lift the cover up and remove the air filter element (see illustrations).

3 Inspect the outer surface of the filter element. If it is dirty, replace it. If it is only moderately dusty, it can be reused by blowing it clean from the back to the front surface with compressed air. Because it is a pleated paper type filter, it cannot be washed or oiled. If it cannot be cleaned satisfactorily with compressed air, discard and replace it. While the cover is off, be careful not to drop anything down into the housing.

※※ CAUTION:

Never drive the vehicle with the air filter removed. Excessive engine wear could result and backfiring could even cause a fire under the hood.

17.2a Remove the cover bolts (2005 and earlier model shown)

4 Wipe out the inside of the housing with a damp cloth.

5 Place the new filter into the housing, making sure it seats properly.

6 Installation of the cover is the reverse of removal.

17.2b Remove the cover and lift the element out (2005 and earlier model shown)

17.2c On 2006 and later models, release the filter housing clips . . .

17.2d . . . separate the housing halves and replace the filter element

18 Manual transmission and differential lubricant level check (every 15,000 miles or 12 months)

▶ **Refer to illustrations 18.1a, 18.1b and 18.1c**

1 Remove the oil level check/fill plug (see illustrations).
2 Insert a finger into the hole and feel the oil level. It should be up to the bottom of the hole. If the oil level is low, add oil until it is at the proper level.

❋❋ **WARNING:**

Do not overfill.

3 Install the oil level check/fill plug. Tighten the plug to the torque listed in this Chapter's Specifications.
4 Drive the vehicle a short distance, then check carefully for leaks.

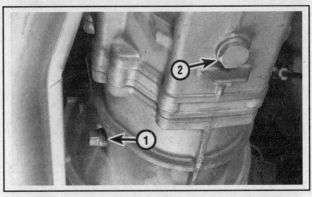

18.1a Manual transmission oil check/fill plug (1) and drain plug (2) (2005 and earlier models)

18.1b Manual transmission oil check/fill plug (1) and drain plug (2) (2006 and later models)

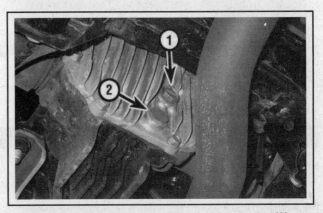

18.1c Differential oil check/fill plug (1) and drain plug (2) (2006 and later models)

19 Steering and suspension check (every 15,000 miles or 12 months)

➡ **Note: For detailed illustrations of the steering and suspension components, refer to Chapter 10.**

WITH THE WHEELS ON THE GROUND

1 With the vehicle stopped and the front wheels pointed straight ahead, rock the steering wheel gently back and forth. If freeplay is excessive, a front wheel bearing, main shaft yoke, intermediate shaft yoke, lower arm balljoint or steering system joint is worn or the steering gear is out of adjustment or broken. Refer to Chapter 10 for the appropriate repair procedure.
2 Other symptoms, such as excessive vehicle body movement over rough roads, swaying (leaning) around corners and binding as the steering wheel is turned, may indicate faulty steering and/or suspension components.
3 Check the shock absorbers by pushing down and releasing the vehicle several times at each corner. If the vehicle does not come back to a level position within one or two bounces, the shocks/struts are worn and must be replaced. When bouncing the vehicle up and down, listen for squeaks and noises from the suspension components. Additional information on suspension components can be found in Chapter 10.

UNDER THE VEHICLE

▶ **Refer to illustrations 19.7 and 19.8**

4 Raise the vehicle with a floor jack and support it securely on jackstands. See *Jacking and towing* at the front of this manual for the proper jacking points.
5 Check the tires for irregular wear patterns and proper inflation. See Section 5 in this Chapter for information regarding tire wear and Chapter 10 for the wheel bearing replacement procedures.
6 Inspect the universal joint between the steering shaft and the steering gear housing. Check the steering gear housing for grease leakage or oozing. Make sure that the dust seals and boots are not damaged and that the boot clamps are not loose. Check the steering linkage for looseness or damage. Check the tie-rod ends for excessive play. Look for loose bolts, broken or disconnected parts and deteriorated rubber bushings on all suspension and steering components. While an assistant turns the steering wheel from side to side, check the steering components for free movement, chafing and binding. If the steering components do not seem to be reacting with the movement of the steering wheel, try to determine where the slack is located.

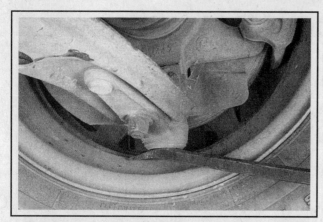

19.7 Move the lower arm up and down with a prybar to make sure there is no play in the balljoint (if there is, replace it)

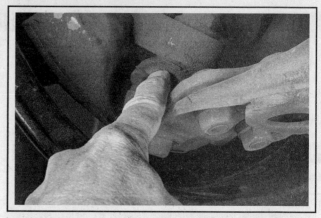

19.8 Push on the balljoint boot to check for damage

7   Check the balljoints for wear by placing a 7-inch thick wooden block under each tire. Lower the jack until there is about half a load on the coil spring. Make sure that the front wheels are in a straight forward position and block the wheel with chocks. Move each lower arm up and down with a pry bar (see illustration) to ensure that its balljoint has no play. If any balljoint does have play, replace it. See Chapter 10 for the front balljoint replacement procedure.

8   Inspect the balljoint boots for damage and leaking grease (see illustration). Replace the balljoints with new ones if they are damaged (see Chapter 10).

20 Driveaxle boot check (every 15,000 miles or 12 months)

▶ Refer to illustration 20.2

1   The rear driveaxle boots are very important because they prevent dirt, water and foreign material from entering and damaging the constant velocity (CV) joints. Oil and grease can cause the boot material to deteriorate prematurely, so it's a good idea to wash the boots with soap and water.

2   Inspect the boots for tears and cracks as well as loose clamps (see illustration). If there is any evidence of cracks or leaking lubricant, they must be replaced as described in Chapter 8.

20.2 Flex the driveaxle boots by hand to check for cracks and/or leaking grease

21 Fuel system check (every 30,000 miles or 24 months)

▶ Refer to illustrations 21.2 and 21.5

❊❊ WARNING:

Certain precautions should be observed when inspecting or servicing the fuel system components. Work in a well ventilated area and do not allow open flames (cigarettes, appliance pilot lights, etc.) near the work area. Mop up spills immediately and do not store fuel soaked rags where they could ignite. It is a good idea to keep a dry chemical (Class B) fire extinguisher near the work area any time the fuel system is being serviced.

1   If you smell gasoline while driving or after the vehicle has been sitting in the sun, inspect the fuel system immediately.

2   Remove the gas filler cap and inspect if for damage and corrosion. The gasket should have an unbroken sealing imprint. If the gasket is damaged or corroded, remove it and install a new one (see illustration).

3   Inspect the fuel feed and return lines for cracks. Make sure that the threaded flare-nut type connectors which secure the metal fuel lines to the fuel injection system are tight.

4   Since some components of the fuel system - the fuel tank and

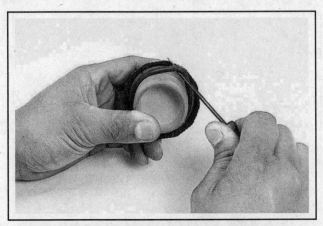

21.2 Use a small screwdriver to carefully pry out the old gasket - take care not to damage the cap

21.5 Inspect the filler/tank connecting hose for cracks and make sure the clamps are tight

part of the fuel feed and return lines, for example - are underneath the vehicle, they can be inspected more easily with the vehicle raised on a hoist. If that's not possible, raise the vehicle and support it securely on jackstands.

5   With the vehicle raised and safely supported, inspect the gas tank and filler neck for punctures, cracks and other damage. The hose connecting the filler neck to the tank is particularly critical. Sometimes this hose will leak because of loose clamps or deteriorated rubber (see illustration). These are problems a home mechanic can usually rectify.

❊❊ WARNING:

Do not, under any circumstances, try to repair a fuel tank (except rubber components). A welding torch or any open flame can easily cause fuel vapors inside the tank to explode.

6   Carefully check all rubber hoses and metal lines leading away from the fuel tank. Check for loose connections, deteriorated hoses, crimped lines and other damage. Carefully inspect the lines from the tank to the fuel injection system. Repair or replace damaged sections as necessary (see Chapter 4).

22 Spark plug check and replacement (every 30,000 miles or 24 months)

CHECK

♦ **Refer to illustrations 22.1, 22.4a and 22.4b**

1   Spark plug replacement requires a spark plug socket which fits onto a ratchet wrench. This socket is lined with a rubber grommet to protect the porcelain insulator of the spark plug and to hold the plug while you insert it into the spark plug hole. You will also need a wire-type feeler gauge to check and adjust the spark plug gap and a torque wrench to tighten the new plugs to the specified torque (see illustration).

2   If you are replacing the plugs, purchase the new plugs, adjust them to the proper gap and then replace each plug one at a time.

➡ **Note: When buying new spark plugs, it's essential that you obtain the correct plugs for your specific vehicle. This information can be found in the Specifications Section in this Chapter's Specifications, on the Vehicle Emissions Control Information (VECI) label located on the underside of the hood or in the owner's manual. If these sources specify different plugs, purchase the spark plug type specified on the VECI label because that information is provided specifically for your engine.**

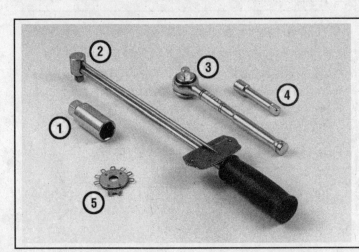

22.1 Tools required for changing spark plugs

1   **Spark plug socket** - *This will have special padding inside to protect the spark plug porcelain insulator*
2   **Torque wrench** - *Although not mandatory, use of this tool is the best way to ensure that the plugs are tightened properly*
3   **Ratchet** - *Standard hand tool to fit the plug socket*
4   **Extension** - *Depending on model and accessories, you may need special extensions and universal joints to reach one or more of the plugs*
5   **Spark plug gap gauge** - *This gauge for checking the gap comes in a variety of styles. Make sure the gap for your engine is included*

22.4a Spark plug manufacturers recommend using a wire-type gauge when checking the gap - if the wire does not slide between the electrodes with a slight drag, adjustment is required

22.4b To change the gap, bend the side electrode only, as indicated by the arrows, and be very careful not to crack or chip the porcelain insulator surrounding the center electrode

22.6 When removing the spark plug wires, pull only on the boot and use a twisting/pulling motion

22.8 Use a spark plug socket with a long extension to unscrew the spark plug

3   Inspect each of the new plugs for defects. If there are any signs of cracks in the porcelain insulator of a plug, don't use it.

4   Check the electrode gaps of the new plugs. Check the gap by inserting the wire gauge of the proper thickness between the electrodes at the tip of the plug (see illustration). The gap between the electrodes should be identical to that listed in this Chapter's Specifications or on the VECI label. If the gap is incorrect, use the notched adjuster on the feeler gauge body to bend the curved side electrode slightly (see illustration).

5   If the side electrode is not exactly over the center electrode, use the notched adjuster to align them.

❋❋ CAUTION:

If the gap of a new plug must be adjusted, bend only the base of the ground electrode - do not touch the tip.

➡Note: It is not recommended to adjust the gap on platinum or iridium spark plugs. If the gap exceeds the value listed in this Chapter's Specifications, replace the spark plug.

REPLACEMENT

2000 and earlier models

◗ Refer to illustrations 22.6, 22.8, 22.9, 22.10a and 22.10b

6   To prevent the possibility of mixing up spark plug wires, work on one spark plug at a time. Remove the wire and boot from one spark plug. Grasp the boot - not the cable - as shown, give it a half twisting motion and pull straight up (see illustration).

7   If compressed air is available, blow any dirt or foreign material away from the spark plug area before proceeding.

8   Remove the spark plug (see illustration).

9   Whether you are replacing the plugs at this time or intend to reuse the old plugs, compare each old spark plug with the chart shown (see illustration) to determine the overall running condition of the engine.

A normally worn spark plug should have light tan or gray deposits on the firing tip.

A carbon fouled plug, identified by soft, sooty, black deposits, may indicate an improperly tuned vehicle. Check the air cleaner, ignition components and engine control system.

An oil fouled spark plug indicates an engine with worn piston rings and/or bad valve seals allowing excessive oil to enter the chamber.

This spark plug has been left in the engine too long, as evidenced by the extreme gap- Plugs with such an extreme gap can cause misfiring and stumbling accompanied by a noticeable lack of power.

A physically damaged spark plug may be evidence of severe detonation in that cylinder. Watch that cylinder carefully between services, as a continued detonation will not only damage the plug, but could also damage the engine.

A bridged or almost bridged spark plug, identified by a build-up between the electrodes caused by excessive carbon or oil build-up on the plug.

22.9 Inspect the spark plug to determine engine running conditions

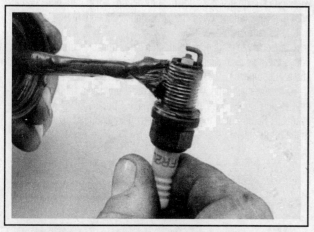
22.10a Apply a thin coat of anti-seize compound to the spark plug threads

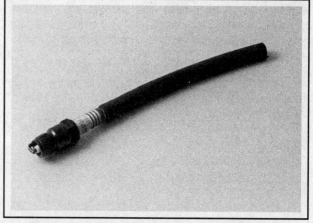
22.10b A length of snug-fitting rubber hose will save time and prevent damaged threads when installing the spark plugs

10 Prior to installation, it's a good idea to coat the spark plug threads with anti-seize compound (see illustration). Also, it's often difficult to insert spark plugs into their holes without cross-threading them. To avoid this possibility, fit a short piece of snug-fitting rubber hose over the end of the spark plug (see illustration). The flexible hose acts as a universal joint to help align the plug with the plug hole. Should the plug begin to cross-thread, the hose will slip on the spark plug, preventing thread damage. Tighten the plug to the torque listed in this Chapter's Specifications.

11 Attach the plug wire to the new spark plug, again using a twisting motion on the boot until it is firmly seated on the end of the spark plug.

12 Follow the above procedure for the remaining spark plugs, replacing them one at a time to prevent mixing up the spark plug wires.

2001 through 2005 models

13 Remove the two ignition coils (see Chapter 5).

14 Spark plug replacement is identical to the procedure for earlier models, except that there are only two spark plug wires; the two coils are installed directly on top of the other two plugs.

15 Install the two ignition coils (see Chapter 5).

2006 and later models

16 Remove the four ignition coils (see Chapter 5).

17 Spark plug replacement is identical to the procedure for earlier models, except that there are no spark plug wires; each coil is installed directly on top of each plug.

18 Install the four ignition coils (see Chapter 5).

23 Spark plug wire check and replacement (every 30,000 miles or 24 months)

▸ Refer to illustration 23.8

➡Note: This Section applies to 2000 and earlier models, which use four replaceable spark plug wires. Some of it also applies to 2001 through 2005 models, which use two coil-over-plug type ignition coils, each of which uses a short spark plug wire to connect it to one other plug. However, these plug wires are not separately serviceable; each of them is an integral part of the coil, so if the wire is damaged, you must replace the coil itself. This procedure does not apply to 2006 and later models; they use four coil-over-plug units with no spark plug wires.

1   The spark plug wires should be checked whenever new spark plugs are installed.

2   Begin this procedure by making a visual check of the spark plug wires while the engine is running. In a darkened garage (make sure there is ventilation) start the engine and observe each plug wire. Be careful not to come into contact with any moving engine parts. If there is a break in the wire, you will see arcing or a small spark at the damaged area. If arcing is noticed, make a note to obtain new wires, then allow the engine to cool and check the ignition coil unit.

3   The spark plug wires should be inspected one at a time to prevent mixing up the order, which is essential for proper engine operation. Each original plug wire should be numbered to help identify its location. If the number is illegible, a piece of tape can be marked with the correct number and wrapped around the plug wire.

4   Disconnect the plug wire from the spark plug. A removal tool can be used for this purpose or you can grasp the rubber boot, twist the boot half a turn and pull the boot free. Do not pull on the wire itself.

5   Check inside the boot for corrosion, which will look like a white crusty powder.

6   Push the wire and boot back onto the end of the spark plug. It should fit tightly onto the end of the plug. If it doesn't, remove the wire and use pliers to carefully crimp the metal connector inside the wire boot until the fit is snug.

7   Using a clean rag, wipe the entire length of the wire to remove

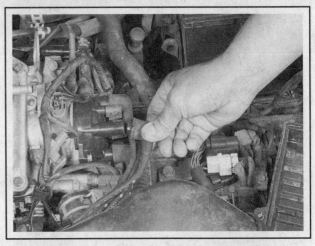

23.8 Pull only on the boot when removing ignition wires from the coils

built-up dirt and grease. Once the wire is clean, check for burns, cracks and other damage. Do not bend the wire sharply, because the conductor might break.

8   Disconnect the wire from the ignition coil unit. Disconnect the wires one at a time so they don't get mixed up. Again, pull only on the boot (see illustration). Check for corrosion and a tight fit. Replace the wire in its correct coil.

9   Inspect the remaining spark plug wires, making sure that each one is securely fastened at its ignition coil and spark plug when the check is complete.

10 If new spark plug wires are required, purchase a set for your specific engine model. Pre-cut wire sets with the boots already installed are available. Remove and replace the wires one at a time to avoid mix-ups in the firing order.

24 Cooling system servicing (draining, flushing and refilling) (see Maintenance Schedule for service interval)

❋❋ WARNING:

Do not allow engine coolant (antifreeze) to come in contact with your skin or painted surfaces of the vehicle. Rinse off spills immediately with plenty of water. Antifreeze is highly toxic if ingested. Never leave antifreeze laying around in an open container or in puddles on the floor; children and pets are attracted by it's sweet smell and may drink it. Check with local authorities about disposing of used antifreeze. Many communities have collection centers which will see that antifreeze is disposed of safely.

1   Periodically, the cooling system should be drained, flushed and

refilled to replenish the antifreeze mixture and prevent formation of rust and corrosion, which can impair the performance of the cooling system and cause engine damage. When the cooling system is serviced, all hoses and the radiator cap should be checked and replaced if necessary.

DRAINING

▸ Refer to illustrations 24.4 and 24.5

2   Apply the parking brake and block the wheels. If the vehicle has just been driven, wait several hours to allow the engine to cool down

24.4 On most models you will have to remove a cover for access to the radiator drain fitting located at the bottom of the radiator - before opening the valve, push a short section of 3/8-inch ID hose onto the plastic fitting to prevent the coolant from splashing (2005 and earlier model shown)

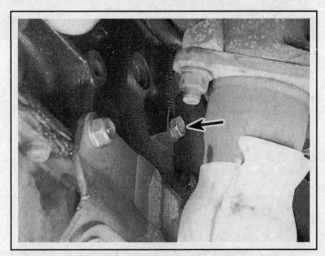

24.5 After draining the radiator, be sure to fully drain the cooling system by removing the block drain plug (arrow) located on the side of the engine block (2005 and earlier model shown)

before beginning this procedure.

3   Once the engine is completely cool, remove the cooling system pressure cap.

4   Move a large container under the radiator drain to catch the coolant. Attach a 3/8-inch inner diameter hose to the drain fitting to direct the coolant into the container (some models are already equipped with a hose), then open the drain fitting (see illustration).

5   On 2005 and earlier models, after the coolant stops flowing out of the radiator, move the container under the engine block drain plug (see illustration). Loosen the plug and allow the coolant in the block to drain.

➡**Note: There is no engine block drain plug on 2006 and later models.**

6   While the coolant is draining, check the condition of the radiator hoses, heater hoses and clamps (refer to Section 14 if necessary).

7   Replace any damaged clamps or hoses (see Chapter 3).

FLUSHING

8   Once the system is completely drained, flush the radiator with fresh water from a garden hose until water runs clear at the drain. The flushing action of the water will remove sediments from the radiator but will not remove rust and scale from the engine and cooling tube surfaces.

9   These deposits can be removed by the chemical action of a cleaner. Follow the procedure outlined in the manufacturer's instructions. If the radiator is severely corroded, damaged or leaking, it should be removed (see Chapter 3) and taken to a radiator repair shop.

10 On 2005 and earlier models, remove the overflow hose from the coolant recovery reservoir. Drain the reservoir and flush it with clean water, then reconnect the hose.

REFILLING

11 Close and tighten the radiator drain. Install and tighten the block drain plug.

12 Place the heater temperature control in the maximum heat position.

13 On 2005 and earlier models, fill the radiator with the proper type of coolant until it's full. Also fill the coolant reservoir up to the LOW or MIN mark. On 2006 and later models, fill the cooling system until the coolant level in the expansion tank is up to the F mark.

14 Install the pressure cap, then start the engine and allow it to idle until it reaches normal operating temperature.

✴✴ CAUTION:

If the temperature gauge indicates an overheating condition, stop the engine and allow it to cool completely, then recheck the coolant level.

15 Once the engine has warmed up, increase the engine speed to 2500 rpm and hold it there for five minutes, then increase the engine speed to 3000 rpm for five seconds and allow it to return to idle.

16 Repeat Step 15 four times, then stop the engine and allow it to cool completely.

17 Recheck the coolant level, adding as necessary. If additional coolant is required, repeat Steps 14 through 16.

25 Evaporative emissions control system check (every 30,000 miles or 24 months)

♦ **Refer to illustrations 25.2a and 25.2b**

1   The function of the evaporative emissions control system is to draw fuel vapors from the gas tank and fuel system, store them in a charcoal canister and then burn them during normal engine operation.

2   The most common symptom of a fault in the evaporative emissions system is a strong fuel odor in the engine compartment. If a fuel odor is detected, inspect the charcoal canister, which is located at the right front corner of the engine compartment on 1997 and earlier mod- els (see illustration), and under the vehicle, near the fuel tank on 1999 and later models (see illustration).

➡ **Note: On 1999 through 2005 models, the earlier style EVAP canister shown in illustration 25.2a is used in addition to the newer style under-vehicle canister, but it's referred to as the "catch tank."**

3   The evaporative emissions control system is explained in more detail in Chapter 6.

25.2a Typical early style EVAP canister (1997 and earlier models)/catch tank (1999 through 2005 models), which is located in the right front corner of the engine compartment

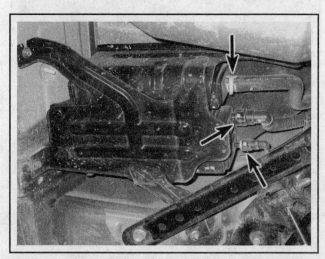

25.2b Typical later style under-vehicle EVAP canister (1999 and later models), which is located near the fuel tank (exact location varies with model year)

26 Exhaust system check (every 30,000 miles or 24 months)

1   With the engine cold (at least three hours after the vehicle has been driven), check the complete exhaust system from its starting point at the engine to the end of the tailpipe. This should be done on a hoist where unrestricted access is available.

2   Check the pipes and connections for evidence of leaks, severe corrosion or damage. Make sure that all brackets and hangers are in good condition and tight.

3   At the same time, inspect the underside of the body for holes, cor- rosion, open seams, etc. which may allow exhaust gases to enter the pas- senger compartment. Seal all body openings with silicone or body putty.

4   Rattles and other noises can often be traced to the exhaust sys- tem, especially the mounts and hangers. Try to move the pipes, muffler and catalytic converter. If the components can come in contact with the body or suspension parts, secure the exhaust system with new mounts.

5   Check the running condition of the engine by inspecting inside the end of the tailpipe. The exhaust deposits here are an indication of engine state-of-tune. If the pipe is black and sooty or coated with white deposits, the engine is in need of a tune-up, including a thorough fuel system inspection.

27 Automatic transmission fluid and filter change (every 30,000 miles or 24 months)

♦ **Refer to illustration 27.8**

1   At the specified intervals, the automatic transmission fluid should be drained and replaced.

2   Before beginning work, purchase the specified transmission fluid (see *Recommended fluids and lubricants* in this Chapter's Specifica- tions).

3   Other tools necessary for this job include jackstands to support the vehicle in a raised position, wrenches, drain pan capable of holding at least eight quarts, newspapers and clean rags.

4   The fluid should be drained immediately after the vehicle has been driven. Hot fluid is more effective than cold fluid at removing built up sediment.

✳✳ **WARNING:**

Fluid temperature can exceed 350-degrees F in a hot transmis- sion. Wear protective gloves.

5   After the vehicle has been driven to warm up the fluid, raise it and support it securely on jackstands.

➡**Note: On 2006 and later models, it is important that the vehicle be raised at both ends so that it is level for the fluid level checking procedure.**

6   Position a drain pan under the transmission pan.

1997 AND EARLIER MODELS

7   Remove the rear and side fluid pan bolts. Loosen the front pan bolts about four turns, then pry the pan loose and allow the fluid to drain. Remove the front pan bolts and carefully lower the pan and drain out the remaining fluid.

8   Clean the fluid pan and the gasket mating surface of the transmission. Reinstall the pan using a new gasket. Tighten the bolts a little at a time, in a criss-cross pattern, to the torque listed in this Chapter's Specifications.

➡**Note: The manufacturer recommends using new bolts.**

9   Lower the vehicle. Using a funnel, add new fluid through the dipstick tube (see this Chapter's Specifications for the recommended type and amount). It's best to add fluid a little at a time, continually checking the level on the dipstick (see Section 9). It's important to not overfill the transmission.

10 Start the engine and shift the selector lever through all positions, ending in Park. Be sure the parking brake is applied.

11 With the engine idling, check the fluid level. Add fluid as necessary to bring the level between the notches on the dipstick.

1999 AND LATER MODELS

12 Remove the drain plug and allow the fluid to drain. On 2006 and later models, also remove the overflow plug from the left side of the pan.

13 Once the fluid has stopped draining, reinstall the drain plug, using a new sealing washer.

➡**Note: Be sure to install the sealing washer so its flat side seats against the pan. Tighten the plug to the torque listed in this Chapter's Specifications.**

1999 through 2005 models

14 Lower the vehicle. Using a funnel, add new fluid through the dipstick tube (see this Chapter's Specifications for the recommended type

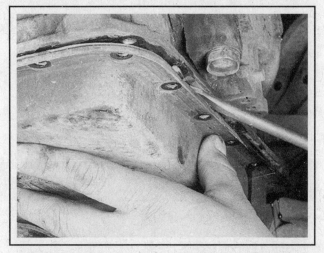

27.8 On 1997 and earlier models, pry the pan free and let it hang down so the transmission can drain (1999 and later models have a drain plug)

and amount). It's best to add fluid a little at a time, continually checking the level on the dipstick (see Section 9). It's important to not overfill the transmission.

15 Start the engine and shift the selector lever through all positions, ending in Park. Be sure the parking brake is applied.

16 With the engine idling, check the fluid level. Add fluid as necessary to bring the level between the notches on the dipstick.

2006 and later models

17 Remove the fill plug from the left side of the transmission case, near the bellhousing. Add the recommended type of automatic transmission fluid through the fill hole until fluid just starts to drip from the overflow tube.

➡**Note: A suction gun or fluid pump will be required to add the fluid.**

18 Install the fill plug, using a new sealing ring, and tighten it to the torque listed in this Chapter's Specifications.

➡**Note: Be sure to install the sealing washer so its flat side seats against the case.**

19 Adjust the fluid level as described in Section 9, beginning with Step 13.

<hr>

28 Manual transmission lubricant change (every 30,000 miles or 24 months)

1   At the specified intervals, the manual transmission lubricant should be drained and replaced.

2   Before beginning work, purchase the specified lubricant (see *Recommended fluids and lubricants* in this Chapter's Specifications) and a new drain plug washer/seal.

3   Other tools necessary for this job include jackstands to support the vehicle in a raised position, wrenches, drain pan capable of holding at least four quarts, newspapers and clean rags.

4   The oil should be drained immediately after the vehicle has been driven. Hot oil is more effective than cold oil at removing built up sediment.

✳ **WARNING:**

Oil temperature can exceed 350-degrees F in a hot transmission. Wear protective gloves.

5   After the vehicle has been driven to warm up the oil, raise the vehicle and support it securely on jackstands. Make sure it is safely supported and as level as possible.

6   Move the necessary equipment under the vehicle, being careful not to touch any of the hot exhaust components.

7   Place the drain pan under the transmission drain plug. Remove the check/fill plug, then loosen the drain plug (2005 and earlier models, see illustration 18.1a; 2006 and later models, see illustration 18.1b).

8   Carefully unscrew the drain plug and washer with your fingers. Be careful not to burn yourself on the oil.

9   Allow the oil to drain completely. Clean the drain plug then reinstall it with a new washer. Tighten the drain plug to the torque listed in this Chapter's Specifications.

10 With the engine off, add new oil to the transmission through the check/fill plug hole (see *Recommended fluids and lubricants* in this Chapter's Specifications for oil type and transmission capacity). A hand pump or suction gun will be required to do this. Add oil until it is level with the bottom of the hole.

12 Install the check/fill plug and tighten it to the torque listed in this Chapter's Specifications.

29 Positive Crankcase Ventilation (PCV) valve and hose check and replacement (every 30,000 miles or 24 months)

▶ Refer to illustrations 29.2 and 29.4

➡Note: While this procedure applies to all models, it is extremely difficult to access the PCV valve on 2006 and later models because it is located on the left side of the engine block, underneath the intake manifold. You must remove the intake manifold (see Chapter 2A) to remove, check or replace the PCV valve on these models.

1   The PCV valve and hose is located in the valve cover.

2   Pull the PCV valve from the cover (see illustration).

3   With the engine idling at normal operating temperature, place your finger over the end of the valve. If there's no vacuum at the valve, check for a plugged hose or valve. Replace any plugged or deteriorated hoses.

4   Turn off the engine. Remove the PCV valve from the hose. Blow low-pressure air through the valve from the valve cover (cylinder head) end. If air will not pass through the valve in this direction, replace it with a new one (see illustration).

5   When purchasing a replacement PCV valve, make sure it's for your particular vehicle and engine size. Compare the old valve with the new one to make sure they're the same.

29.2 Grasp the hose securely and pull the PCV valve out of the cover (2005 and earlier model shown)

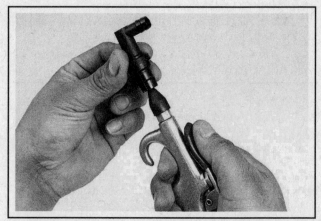

29.4 To check the PVC valve, blow low-pressure air through the cylinder head side of the valve - air should pass through easily - then blow through the intake manifold side of the valve and verify that air passes through with difficulty

30 Fuel filter replacement (every 60,000 miles or 48 months)

▶ Refer to illustrations 30.3, 30.4 and 30.5

❋❋ **WARNING:**

Gasoline is extremely flammable, so take extra precautions when you work on any part of the fuel system. Don't smoke or allow open flames or bare light bulbs near the work area, and don't work in a garage where a gas-type appliance (such as a water heater or a clothes dryer) is present. Since gasoline is carcinogenic, wear fuel-resistant gloves when there's a possibility of being exposed to fuel, and, if you spill any fuel on your skin, rinse it off immediately with soap and water. Mop up any spills immediately and do not store fuel-soaked rags where they could ignite. The fuel system is under constant pressure, so, if any fuel lines are to be disconnected, the fuel pressure in the system must be relieved first. When you perform any kind of work on the fuel system, wear safety glasses and have a Class B type fire extinguisher on hand.

❋❋ **WARNING:**

Pressure in the fuel lines is very high even when the engine is off. Relieve fuel system pressure as described in Chapter 4 before disconnecting the lines to remove the filter.

30.3 Remove this cover for access to the fuel filter

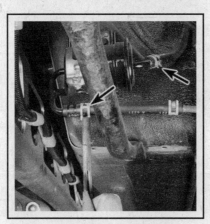

30.4 After relieving fuel pressure, squeeze the clamps and disconnect the hoses (arrows)

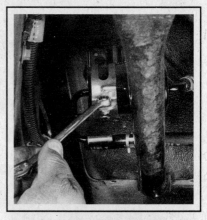

30.5 Loosen the clamp bolt and remove the filter from the bracket

❄❄ **CAUTION:**

If the radio in your vehicle is equipped with an anti-theft system, make sure you have the correct activation code before disconnecting the battery.

➡ Note: This procedure applies only to 2005 and earlier models. On 2006 and later models, the fuel filter is an integral component of the fuel pump/fuel level sending unit, and cannot be serviced separately.

1   Relieve the fuel system pressure (see Chapter 4), then disconnect the negative battery cable.

2   The fuel filter is mounted behind the fuel tank at the right rear of the vehicle.

3   Remove the fuel filter cover (see illustration).

4   Disconnect the fuel hoses from the fuel filter (see illustration).

5   Loosen the clamp bolt and remove the old filter from the bracket (see illustration).

6   Note that the inlet and outlet pipes are clearly labeled on their respective ends. Make sure the new filter is installed so that it's facing the proper direction as noted above.

7   Installation is the reverse of the removal procedure. Be sure to push the fuel lines all the way onto the fittings.

31 Valve clearance - check and adjustment (every 75,000 miles)

➡ Note: This procedure applies only to 1999 and later models.

CHECK

▶ **Refer to illustrations 31.3a and 31.3b**

1   Remove the valve cover (see Chapter 2A).

2   Set the engine to TDC on the compression stroke for cylinder No 1.

❄❄ **CAUTION:**

Turn the engine only in the normal direction of rotation - clockwise - from the front of the vehicle.

3   Using feeler gauges, measure the clearances of the indicated valves (see illustration) between the base of the cam lobe and the lifter (see illustration). Record all four clearances. The desired clearances are given in this Chapter's Specifications. Note that the clearances for intake and exhaust valves are different.

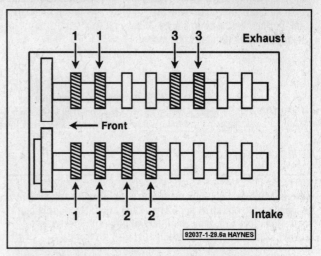

31.3a When the No. 1 piston is at TDC on the compression stroke, the valve clearance for the No. 1 and No. 3 cylinder exhaust valves and the No. 1 and No. 2 intake valves can be measured

31.3b Measure the clearance between the base of the camshaft lobe and the bucket using feeler gauges (2.0L engine only)

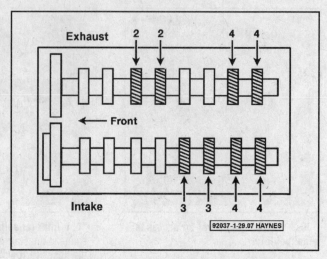

31.4 When the No. 4 piston is at TDC on the compression stroke, the valve clearance for the No. 2 and No. 4 exhaust valves and the No. 3 and No. 4 intake valves can be measured

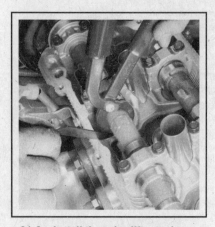

31.6a Install the valve lifter tool as shown and squeeze the handles together to depress the valve lifter, then hold the lifter down with the smaller tool so the shim can be removed (1999 through 2005 models)

31.6b Keep pressure on the lifter with the smaller tool and remove the shim with a small screwdriver (1999 through 2005 models) . . .

31.6c . . . a pair of tweezers or a magnet (as shown here) (1999 through 2005 models)

4 Turn the crankshaft clockwise 360-degrees to bring cylinder number 4 to TDC on the compression stroke, then measure the clearances for the indicated valves (see illustration).

ADJUSTMENT

➡**Note: 1999 through 2005 models use replaceable adjustment shims that ride on top of the lifters. 2006 and later models don't have shims; instead, they use lifters of different thickness to provide proper valve clearance.**

1999 through 2005 models

▶ **Refer to illustrations 31.6a, 31.6b, 31.6c and 31.7**

5 If any of the valve clearances were out of specification, turn the

crankshaft pulley until the camshaft lobe above the first valve which you intend to adjust is pointing upward, away from the shim.

6 Position the notch in the valve lifter toward the center of the engine, then depress the valve lifter with the special valve lifter tools (see illustration). Place the special valve lifter tool in position as shown, with the longer jaw of the tool gripping the lower edge of the cast lifter boss and the upper, shorter jaw gripping the upper edge of the lifter itself. Depress the valve lifter by squeezing the handles of the valve lifter tool together, then hold the lifter down with the smaller tool and remove the larger one. Remove the adjusting shim with a small screwdriver or a pair of tweezers (see illustrations). Note that the wire hook on the end of some valve lifter tool handles can be used to clamp both handles together to keep the lifter depressed while the shim is removed.

7 Measure the thickness of the shim with a micrometer (see illustration).

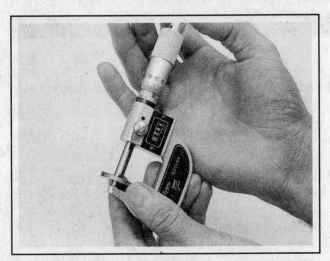

31.7 Measure the shim thickness with a micrometer (1999 through 2005 models)

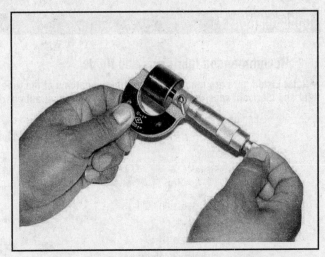

31.13 Measure the thickness of each lifter head with a micrometer (2006 and later models)

8   To calculate the correct thickness of a replacement shim that will place the valve clearance within the specified value, use the following formula:

$N = T + (A - V)$

T = thickness of the old shim
A = valve clearance measured
N = thickness of the new shim
V = desired valve clearance

9   Select a shim with a thickness as close as possible to the valve clearance calculated.

10   Place the special valve lifter tool in position as shown in illustration 31.6a, with the longer jaw of the tool gripping the lower edge of the cast lifter boss and the upper, shorter jaw gripping the upper edge of the lifter itself. Press down the valve lifter by squeezing the handles of the valve lifter tool together and install the new adjusting shim (note that the wire hook on the end of one valve lifter tool handle can be used to clamp the handles together to keep the lifter depressed while the shim is inserted). Release the tool and measure the clearance with a feeler gauge to make sure that your calculations are correct.

11   Repeat this procedure until all the valves which are out of clearance have been corrected.

2006 and later models

▶ **Refer to illustration 31.13**

12   If adjustment is required, the lifter(s) must be changed by remov-ing the camshaft(s) over the affected valve(s) (see Chapter 2A).

13   If the valve clearance was too small, a lifter with a thinner head must be installed. If the clearance was too large, a lifter with a thicker head must be installed. The lifters might have a number indicating their thickness on the inside, but if not, a micrometer will be needed to establish lifter thickness (see illustration).

14   To calculate the correct thickness of a replacement shim that will place the valve clearance within the specified value, use the following formula:

$N = T + (A - V)$

T = thickness of the old lifter
A = valve clearance measured
N = thickness of the new lifter
V = desired valve clearance

15   With the correct thickness lifters installed in the cylinder head, reinstall the camshafts (see Chapter 2A).

16   Check that the valve clearances are now correct, as described in Steps 2 through 4. If any clearances are still not within specification, carry out the adjustment procedure again.

17   It will be helpful for future adjustment if a record is kept of the thickness of lifter installed at each position. The lifters required can be purchased in advance once the clearances and the existing thicknesses are known.

Specifications

Recommended lubricants and fluids

→Note: Listed here are manufacturer recommendations at the time this manual was written. Manufacturers occasionally upgrade their fluid and lubricant specifications, so check with your local auto parts store for current recommendations.

Engine oil	
Type	API grade "certified for gasoline engines"
Viscosity	See accompanying chart
Engine coolant	50/50 mixture of ethylene glycol based antifreeze and water*
Fuel	Unleaded gasoline, 87 octane or higher
Automatic transmission fluid	
2005 and earlier	DEXRON III or M-III automatic transmission fluid
2006 and later	Mazda Genuine JWS 3309 automatic transmission fluid
Manual transmission lubricant	
5-speed	API GL-4 or GL-5, SAE 75W-90 gear oil
6-speed	API GL-4, SAE 75W-90 gear oil
Brake/clutch fluid	DOT 3 brake fluid
Power steering fluid	
1997 and earlier	DEXRON II automatic transmission fluid
1999 and later	M-III or DEXRON II automatic transmission fluid

2006 and later models: If the cooling system pressure cap is labeled "F22," the system is filled with pre-mixed long life coolant. It is compatible with other types of coolant, but it is recommended that only F22 coolant be used. It should never be diluted with water.

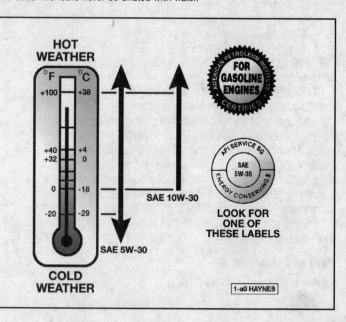

ENGINE OIL VISCOSITY CHART

For best fuel economy and cold starting, select the lowest SAE viscosity grade for the expected temperature range

Capacities*

Engine oil (including filter)	
1.6L engine	3.6 quarts
1.8L engine	4.0 quarts
2.0L engine	
2006 through 2008	
With automatic or 5-speed manual transmission	4.7 quarts
With six-speed manual transmission	4.8 quarts
2009	
Without oil cooler	4.7 quarts
With oil cooler	4.8 quarts

Capacities* (continued)

Engine coolant	6.3 quarts
Transmission lubricant	
Manual	2.1 quarts
Automatic (oil pan)	
1997 and earlier	4.2 quarts
1999 through 2005	7.1 quarts
2006 and later	7.8 quarts

All capacities approximate. Add as necessary to bring up to appropriate level.

Ignition system

Spark plug type	
1997 and earlier	NGK BKR5E11, BKR6E11 or equivalents
1999 through 2005	NGK BKR5E or BKR6E; Denso K16PR or K20PR; Champion RC10YC4 or RC8YC4
2006 and later	L3G2 18 110 or L3Y1 18 110
Spark plug gap	
2005 and earlier	0.040 to 0.043 inch
2006 and 2007	0.050 to 0.053 inch
2008 and later	0.050 to 0.057 inch
Spark plug wire resistance	400 ohms per inch
Engine firing order	1-3-4-2

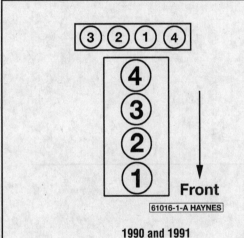

1990 and 1991

1992 and later

Cylinder and coil terminal locations

Accessory drivebelt deflection

1997 and earlier	
Used belt	
Alternator and water pump (crankshaft-to-alternator pulley)	
1993 and earlier	0.35 to 0.39 inch
1994 through 1997	0.24 to 0.29 inch
Power steering pump	0.36 to 0.39 inch
Power steering pump and air conditioning compressor (crankshaft-to-power steering pump pulleys)	0.36 to 0.39 inch
Air conditioning compressor	0.36 to 0.39 inch

Accessory drivebelt deflection (continued)

1997 and earlier (continued)
    New belt
        Alternator and water pump (crankshaft-to-alternator pulley)

1993 and earlier	0.32 to 0.35 inch
1994 through 1997	0.22 to 0.27 inch
Power steering pump	0.32 to 0.35 inch

        Power steering pump and air conditioning compressor
            (crankshaft-to-power steering

pump pulleys)	0.32 to 0.35 inch
Air conditioning compressor	0.32 to 0.35 inch

1999 through 2005
    Used belt

Alternator	0.24 to 0.29 inch

        Power steering pump and/or air

conditioning compressor	0.36 to 0.39 inch

    New belt

Alternator	0.22 to 0.27 inch

        Power steering pump and/or air conditioning compressor

1999 and 2000	0.32 to 0.35 inch
2001 through 2005	0.28 to 0.31 inch

Clutch pedal

2005 and earlier

Height (including carpet)	6.89 to 7.28 inches
Freeplay	0.02 to 0.12 inch
Disengagement height (minimum - including carpet)	2.68 inches

2006 and later

Stroke	5.12 inches
Freeplay	0.20 to 0.59 inch
Disengagement stroke	3.15 to 4.33 inches

Brakes

Disc brake pad lining thickness (minimum)	3/32-inch

Parking brake adjustment

1993 and earlier	5 to 7 clicks
1994 through 1997	7 to 9 clicks
1999 through 2005	5 to 7 clicks
2006 and later	1 to 3 clicks

Valve clearances

1997 and earlier models	Not adjustable

1999 through 2005 models

Intake	0.008 to 0.009 inch
Exhaust	0.012 to 0.013 inch

2006 and later models

Intake	0.0087 to 0.0110 inch
Exhaust	0.0106 to 0.0129 inch

Torque specifications	Ft-lbs (unless otherwise indicated)

➡**Note: One foot-pound (ft-lb) of torque is equivalent to 12 inch-pounds (in-lbs) of torque. Torque values below approximately 15 foot-pounds are expressed in inch-pounds, because most foot-pound torque wrenches are not accurate at these smaller values.**

Engine oil drain plug	23 to 30
Spark plugs	
1993 and earlier	132 to 204 in-lbs
1994 through 2005	132 to 192 in-lbs
2006 and later	96 to 120 in-lbs
Automatic transmission	
1997 and earlier	
Oil pan bolts	52 to 69 in-lbs
Oil strainer/filter	
1993 and earlier	
Bolts	27 to 34 in-lbs
Nuts	44 to 60 in-lbs
1994 through 1997	58 to 69 in-lbs
1999 through 2005	
Oil pan drain plug	14 to 16
2006 and later	
Oil pan drain plug and overflow plug	13 to 16
Filler plug	20 to 30
Manual transmission	
Check/fill plug	19 to 28
Drain plug	29 to 43
Wheel lug nuts	66 to 86

Notes

2A
ENGINE

Section

Reference to other Chapters

1 General information

This Part of Chapter 2 is devoted to in-vehicle repair procedures for all engines. Information concerning engine removal and installation and engine overhaul can be found in Part B of this Chapter.

The following repair procedures are based on the assumption that the engine is installed in the vehicle. If the engine has been removed from the vehicle and mounted on a stand, many of the Steps outlined in this Part of Chapter 2 will not apply.

2 Repair operations possible with the engine in the vehicle

Many major repair operations can be accomplished without removing the engine from the vehicle.

Clean the engine compartment and the exterior of the engine with some type of degreaser before any work is done. It will make the job easier and help keep dirt out of the internal areas of the engine.

Depending on the components involved, it may be helpful to remove the hood to improve access to the engine as repairs are performed (refer to Chapter 11 if necessary). Cover the fenders to prevent damage to the paint. Special pads are available, but a substitute such as a thick bedspread or blanket will also work.

If vacuum, exhaust, oil or coolant leaks develop, indicating a need for gasket or seal replacement, the repairs can generally be made with the engine in the vehicle. The intake and exhaust manifold gaskets, oil pan gasket, crankshaft oil seals and cylinder head gasket are all accessible with the engine in place.

Exterior engine components, such as the intake and exhaust manifolds, the oil pan, the oil pump, the water pump, the starter motor, the alternator, and the fuel system components can be removed for repair with the engine in place.

Since the cylinder head can be removed without pulling the engine, camshaft and valve component servicing can also be accomplished with the engine in the vehicle. Replacement of the timing belt and sprockets is also possible with the engine in the vehicle.

In extreme cases caused by a lack of necessary equipment, repair or replacement of piston rings, pistons, connecting rods and rod bearings is possible with the engine in the vehicle. However, this practice is not recommended because of the engine cleaning and other preparation work, such as driveshaft, steering, stabilizer bar, and engine mount members that may require partial disassembly or removal for access to the engine.

3 Top Dead Center (TDC) - locating

→**Note: The TDC marks align when no. 1 cylinder is at TDC on its exhaust stroke, as well as when it's on the compression stroke. Piston position must be determined by feeling for compression at the number one spark plug hole, then aligning the ignition timing marks as described in Step 8.**

1 Top Dead Center (TDC) is the highest point in the cylinder that each piston reaches traveling up-and-down as the crankshaft turns. Each piston reaches TDC on the compression stroke and again on the exhaust stroke, but TDC generally refers to piston position on the compression stroke.

2 Positioning the piston(s) at TDC is an essential part of many procedures such as camshaft and timing belt/sprocket removal.

3 Before beginning this procedure, be sure to place the transmission in Neutral and apply the parking brake or block the rear wheels. Also, disable the ignition system by detaching the primary (low voltage) wires from the coil (see Chapter 5). Remove the spark plugs (see Chapter 1).

2005 AND EARLIER MODELS

▶ **Refer to illustration 3.6**

4 In order to bring any piston to TDC, the crankshaft must be turned using one of the methods outlined below. When looking at the front of the engine, normal crankshaft rotation is clockwise.

a) *The preferred method is to turn the crankshaft with a socket and ratchet attached to the bolt threaded into the front of the crankshaft.*

b) *A remote starter switch, which may save some time, can also be used. Follow the instructions included with the switch. Once the piston is close to TDC, use a socket and ratchet as described in the previous paragraph.*

c) *If an assistant is available to turn the ignition switch to the Start position in short bursts, you can get the piston close to TDC without a remote starter switch. Make sure your assistant is out of the vehicle, away from the ignition switch, then use a socket and ratchet as described in Paragraph a) to complete the procedure.*

5 Install a compression gauge in the no. 1 spark plug hole (closest to the front of the vehicle). As the no. 1 piston rises to the top of its compression stroke, compression pressure will be indicated on the gauge.

6 Turn the crankshaft (see Step 4) until the notch in the crankshaft sprocket is aligned with the T on the timing plate (located at the front of the engine) (see illustration).

7 If compression pressure was not indicated on the gauge as the marks were aligning, the number one piston is at TDC on the exhaust stroke.

8 To get the piston to TDC on the compression stroke, turn the

crankshaft one complete turn (360-degrees) clockwise. The ignition timing marks should now be aligned, indicating that the number one piston is at TDC on the compression stroke.

9   After the number one piston has been positioned at TDC on the compression stroke, TDC for any of the remaining pistons can be located by turning the crankshaft and following the firing order.

2006 AND LATER MODELS

▶ **Refer to illustrations 3.13, 3.14 and 3.16**

➡**Note: You will need two Mazda Special Service Tools for this procedure: the camshaft holding tool (SST #303-465/49 UN30 3465) and the timing pin (SST #303-507).**

10   Disconnect the battery negative cable (see Chapter 5).
11   Remove the valve cover (see Section 4).
12   Using a wrench or socket on the crankshaft pulley bolt, rotate the crankshaft clockwise until the intake valves for no. 1 cylinder have opened and just closed again.
13   A TDC timing hole is located near the lower right front corner of the engine block to provide a means of accurately positioning the no. 1 cylinder at TDC. When you locate this hole, remove the timing pin plug (see illustration).
14   Screw in the timing pin (see illustration). You can purchase this tool from a Mazda dealer or a suitable equivalent tool from an aftermarket tool supplier.

✳✳ CAUTION:

We don't recommend trying to fabricate a timing pin with a bolt because, while you would be able to determine the correct bolt diameter and thread pitch, it is impossible to determine the length of the bolt. These pins come in several lengths, depending on the engine family. There is no way to determine the correct pin length without comparing it to a factory or aftermarket tool designed to be used with this engine. Using a bolt of the wrong length could damage the engine.

15   Turn the engine forwards slowly until the crankshaft comes into contact with the timing pin - in this position, the engine is set to TDC on no. 1 cylinder.
16   The camshafts each have a machined slot at the transmission end

3.6 To bring the number one piston to TDC, align the timing notch on the edge of the crankshaft pulley with the T-degree mark

of the engine; both slots will be completely horizontal, and at the same height as the cylinder head machined surface, when the engine is at TDC on no. 1 cylinder. Use the Mazda special service tool to check this position, and to positively locate the camshafts in position. Instead of purchasing the factory tool, you can fabricate your own tool (see illustration) from a strip of metal 5 mm thick (while the strip's thickness is critical, its length and width are not, but should be approximately 180 to 230 mm long by 20 to 30 mm wide).

✳✳ CAUTION:

Never use the camshaft alignment tool as a means to stop the engine from rotating - engine damage can result.

17   Before rotating the crankshaft again, make sure that the tools are removed. When the procedure you are doing is completed, do not forget to install the blanking plug.
18   Once no. 1 cylinder has been positioned at TDC on the compression stroke, TDC for any of the other cylinders can then be located by rotating the crankshaft clockwise 180-degrees at a time and following the firing order (see this Chapter's Specifications).

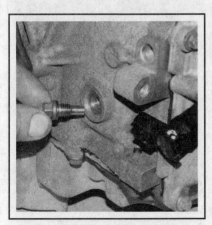

3.13 Remove the timing hole plug . . .

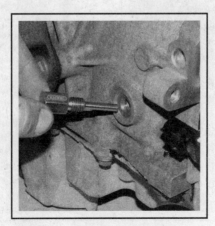

3.14 . . . and insert the timing peg tool

3.16 Slide the special tool or a suitable metal bar into the slots in the ends of the camshafts

4 Valve cover - removal and installation

2005 AND EARLIER MODELS

Removal

1 Disconnect the negative cable from the battery (see Chapter 5).

2 Detach the Positive Crankcase Ventilation (PCV) valve and breather hoses from the valve cover.

3 Label the spark plug wires, then remove them from the spark plugs.

4 Remove the bolts attaching the valve cover to the cylinder head in the reverse order of the tightening sequence (see illustration 4.11).

5 Disconnect any tubing or other connected components and move them out of the way, and remove the valve cover. If the cover sticks, knock it loose with a rubber mallet or a hammer and a block of wood. Do not pry between the sealing surfaces.

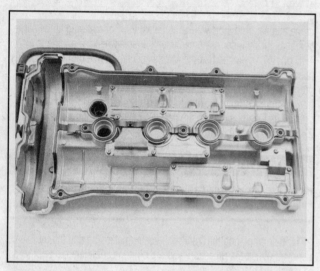

4.7 Press the valve cover gasket into the groove by hand

Installation

♦ **Refer to illustrations 4.7, 4.9 and 4.11**

6 The mating surfaces of the housing or cylinder head and cover must be clean when the cover is installed. Carefully use a gasket scraper to remove all traces of sealant and old gasket material - be careful to not gouge the gasket surfaces when cleaning. Then clean the mating surfaces with a rag soaked with lacquer thinner or acetone. If there is residue or oil on the mating surfaces when the cover is installed, oil leaks may develop.

7 If a new valve cover gasket is being installed, apply silicone sealant in the groove of the valve cover and press the new gasket into the groove (see illustration).

8 If the valve cover gasket is being reused, remove the gasket, make sure the groove is clean and the gasket is clean. Apply RTV sealant in the groove of the valve cover, and reinstall the gasket.

9 Apply a light coating of RTV sealant to the areas shown (see illustration).

10 Position the valve cover in place and insert the bolts by hand, starting the threads several turns before using a wrench.

11 Following the recommended sequence (see illustration), tighten the bolts in two or three steps to the torque listed in this Chapter's Specifications.

12 Reinstallation of the remaining parts is the reverse of removal.

13 Run the engine and check for oil leaks.

2006 AND LATER MODELS

Removal

♦ **Refer to illustrations 4.19a, 4.19b, 4.23a and 4.23b**

14 Disconnect the cable from the negative battery terminal (see Chapter 5).

15 Remove the engine cover.

16 Disconnect the PCV hose from the valve cover (see Chapter 6).

4.9 Apply RTV sealant to the corners where the cam bearing caps and crank angle sensor cap meet the cylinder head

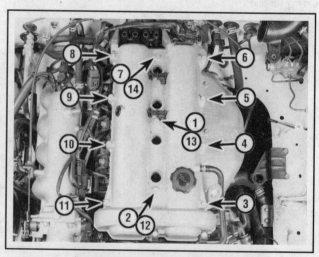

4.11 Valve cover bolt TIGHTENING sequence

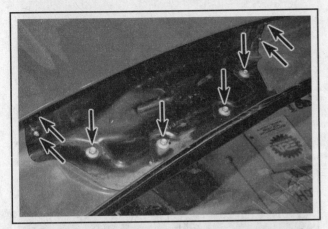

4.19a To detach the strut reinforcement plate from the cowl area, remove these four bolts; the four bolts on the ends are accessed from the firewall side

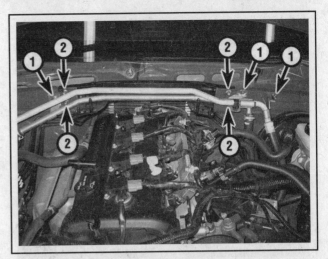

4.19b To detach the strut reinforcement plate from the firewall, remove the bolts (1) that secure the cooler and heater pipe brackets and pull the pipes forward slightly, then remove the four bolts (2) from the firewall

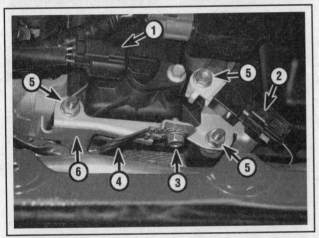

4.23a Details of the small mounting bracket at the rear part of the valve cover

1	*Camshaft Position (CMP)*	*4*	*Ground wires*
	sensor electrical connector	*5*	*Mounting bracket fastener*
2	*Electrical connector*	*6*	*Mounting bracket*
3	*Ground bolt*		

17 Remove the strut bar (see Chapter 10).

18 Remove the windshield wiper motor and linkage assembly (see Chapter 12).

19 Remove the strut bar reinforcement plate (see illustrations).

20 Disconnect the electrical connector from the Oil Control Valve (OCV) (see Chapter 6).

21 Remove all four ignition coils from the valve cover (see Chapter 5).

22 Disconnect the electrical connector from the Camshaft Position (CMP) sensor (see Chapter 6).

23 Remove the valve cover bolts (see illustrations) and remove the valve cover.

Installation

♦ **Refer to illustrations 4.24a, 4.24b, 4.24c and 4.25**

24 Remove and inspect the valve cover gaskets (see illustrations). You don't have to replace these gaskets unless they're already leaking or

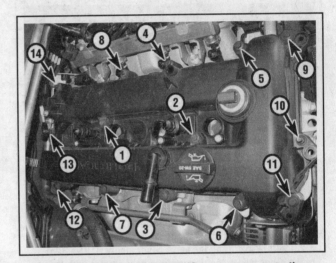

4.23b Valve cover bolt TIGHTENING sequence; remove the bolts in the reverse order of the tightening sequence

4.24a The valve cover on 2006 and later models uses several gaskets, including the main gasket . . .

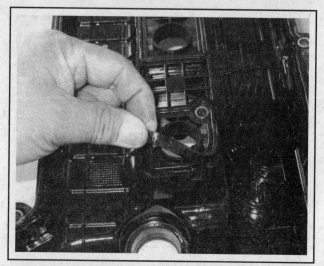

4.24b . . . the spark plug hole gaskets . . .

4.24c . . . and the gasket for the Oil Control Valve (OCV)

4.25 Before installing the valve cover, apply RTV sealant to the areas where the timing chain cover mates with the cylinder head

they're damaged. But, it's always a good practice to replace all the valve cover gaskets on a high-mileage engine.

25 Before installing the valve cover, be sure to apply silicone sealant to the indicated surfaces (see illustration).

26 Install the valve cover, then tighten the valve cover bolts in the indicated tightening sequence (see illustration 4.23b) to the torque listed in this Chapter's Specifications.

27 Installation is otherwise the reverse of removal.

5 Intake manifold - removal and installation

WARNING:

The engine must be completely cool before beginning this procedure.

1 Relieve the fuel system pressure (see Chapter 4), then disconnect the cable from the negative terminal of the battery (see Chapter 5).

2 Drain the cooling system (see Chapter 1).

3 Remove the air intake duct assembly (see Chapter 4).

2005 AND EARLIER MODELS

Removal

▶ Refer to illustrations 5.7 and 5.8

4 Disconnect the accelerator cable and remove the throttle body from the intake assembly (see Chapter 4).

5 Label and detach all wire harness, control cables and hoses connected to the intake manifold.

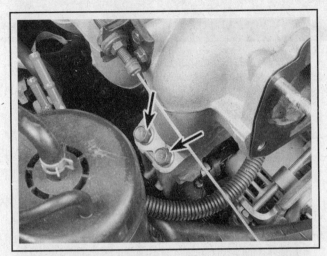

5.7 Unbolt the intake manifold support bracket at the top and at the bottom

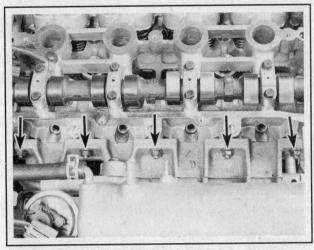

5.8 Remove the intake manifold mounting nuts (upper nuts shown; lower nuts hidden)

6   Remove the fuel rail, injectors and injector wiring harness (see Chapter 4).

7   Under the intake manifold, remove the intake manifold bracket (see illustration).

8   Remove the intake manifold mounting bolts/nuts, while supporting the intake manifold from above the engine (see illustration).

9   Remove the intake manifold.

Installation

10 Carefully use a gasket scraper to remove all traces of old gasket material and any sealant from the manifold and cylinder head, then clean the mating surfaces with gasket cleaner or solvent - be careful to not gouge the gasket surfaces when cleaning. If the gasket was leaking, have the manifold checked for warpage at an automotive machine shop and resurfaced if necessary.

11 Install a new gasket, then position the manifold on the head and install the nuts/bolts.

12 Tighten the nuts/bolts in three or four equal steps to the torque listed in this Chapter's Specifications. Work from the center out towards the ends, while alternating upper to lower bolts/nuts to avoid warping the manifold.

13 Reinstall the remaining parts in the reverse order of removal.

14 Before starting the engine, check the throttle linkage for smooth operation.

15 Refill the coolant system (see Chapter 1), reconnect the battery, start the engine and check for leaks.

16 Road test the vehicle and check for proper operation of all accessories, including the cruise control system (if equipped).

2006 AND LATER MODELS

➡Note: The plenum/intake runner assembly has a lot of components, hoses and wiring attached or connected to it. Clearly label things as you disconnect and/or remove them to avoid confusion when installing the plenum/intake runner.

17 Remove the engine cover.

18 Remove the left part of the strut bar (see Chapter 10).

19 Detach the cooler and heater pipes from the firewall (see illustration 4.19b). Slide back the heater hose clamp, disconnect the heater hose from the heater pipe and set the hose and pipe aside.

20 Remove the throttle body (see Chapter 4).

21 Disconnect the electrical connectors from the ignition coils (see Chapter 5), the fuel injectors (see Chapter 4) and any other sensors with electrical wiring that share the main engine harness, then set the harness aside.

22 Disconnect the fuel supply line quick-connect fitting from the fuel rail (see Chapter 4).

23 Disconnect all hoses connected to the intake manifold.

24 Remove the fuel rail and injectors (see Chapter 4).

25 Raise the front of the vehicle and place it securely on jackstands. Remove the engine compartment under-cover.

26 Disconnect the electrical connector from the EGR valve and disconnect the connectors from all other electrical components attached to the underside of the plenum/intake runner assembly. Detach all electrical harnesses from the plenum/intake runner and set them aside.

27 Disconnect all coolant and heater hoses connected to the EGR valve, the thermostat and the underside of the plenum/intake runner and set them aside.

28 Disconnect the electrical connectors from the air conditioning compressor (see Chapter 3) and from the knock sensor.

29 Remove the upper and lower plenum/intake runner fasteners. Remove the plenum/intake runner and the plenum gasket.

30 Remove the intake manifold, then remove the intake manifold gasket.

31 If you're replacing the plenum/intake runner, remove all components from the old plenum and install them on the new one.

32 Installation is the reverse of removal. Be sure to use a new gasket and tighten all fasteners to the torque listed in this Chapter's Specifications.

33 Refill the coolant system (see Chapter 1), reconnect the battery, start the engine and check for leaks.

6 Exhaust manifold - removal and installation

※※ WARNING:

The engine must be completely cool before beginning this procedure.

REMOVAL

2005 and earlier models

▶ Refer to illustrations 6.3 and 6.7

1 Disconnect the negative cable from the battery (see Chapter 5).

2 Unplug the oxygen sensor electrical connector from the exhaust manifold. If you are installing a new manifold, remove the sensor (see Chapter 6).

3 Remove the heat shield bolts and remove the heat shield from the manifold (see illustration).

4 Apply penetrating oil to the exhaust manifold mounting bolts/nuts and to the exhaust pipe nuts.

5 Raise the vehicle and support it securely on jackstands (see Chapter 1).

6 Disconnect the exhaust pipe from the exhaust manifold. Lower the vehicle.

7 Remove the manifold bolts/nuts and detach the manifold from the cylinder head (see illustration).

➡Note: If any bolts/nuts are difficult to remove, reapply penetrating oil to the bolts/nuts and let them soak for at least 15 minutes. If any bolts or studs break during removal, you may be able to use vise-grip pliers after the manifold is removed to unscrew the broken bolt/stud. If unable to remove the broken bolt/stud, see your automotive parts store for stud removal tools. Replace any damaged parts with factory parts, or parts specifically designed for exhaust system application.

2006 and later models

8 Remove the battery and battery tray (see Chapter 5).

9 Remove the drivebelt (see Chapter 1).

10 Raise the vehicle and place it securely on jackstands. Remove the engine compartment under-cover.

11 Remove the right side of the strut bar (see Chapter 10).

12 Remove the alternator (see Chapter 5).

13 Remove the upper heat shield bolts, then remove the upper shield. Remove the lower heat shield bolts and remove the lower heat shield from the exhaust manifold.

14 Disconnect the electrical connectors from the upstream and downstream oxygen sensors (see Chapter 6).

15 Move the coolant line and heater hose aside.

16 Disconnect the crankcase ventilation hose from the cylinder head and move it aside.

17 Remove the nuts from the exhaust manifold flange and pull off the exhaust pipe.

18 Remove the exhaust manifold fasteners and remove the exhaust manifold from the cylinder head.

19 Replace the exhaust manifold gasket and the sealing ring that fits inside the exhaust pipe flange. You might have to free the sealing ring from the flange with a small screwdriver; make sure that you don't damage the exhaust pipe flange.

INSTALLATION

20 Use a scraper to remove all traces of old gasket material and carbon deposits from the manifold and cylinder head mating surfaces. If the gasket was leaking, have the manifold checked for warpage at an automotive machine shop and resurfaced if necessary.

※※ CAUTION:

When scraping, be very careful not to gouge or scratch the delicate aluminum cylinder head manifold mounting surface.

21 Position a new exhaust manifold gasket over the studs on the cylinder head.

22 Install the manifold and thread the mounting bolts/nuts into place.

23 Working from the center out, tighten the bolts/nuts to the torque listed in this Chapter's Specifications in several equal steps.

24 Reinstall the remaining parts in the reverse order of removal. If reinstalling the oxygen sensor, use a special anti-seize thread lubricant available at your automotive parts store.

25 Run the engine and check for exhaust leaks.

6.3 Remove the exhaust manifold heat shield

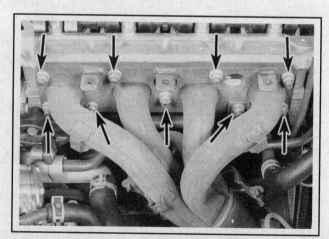

6.7 Remove the exhaust manifold nuts

7 Timing belt and sprockets - removal, inspection and installation

➡ Note: This procedure applies to 2005 and earlier models only.

REMOVAL

▶ **Refer to illustrations 7.10, 7.11, 7.12a, 7.12b, 7.12c, 7.15, 7.16a, 7.16b, 7.19a and 7.19b**

❋❋ CAUTION:

The timing system is complex. Severe engine damage will occur if you make any mistakes. Do not attempt this procedure unless you are highly experienced with this type of repair. If you are at all unsure of your abilities, consult an expert. Double-check all your work and be sure everything is correct before you attempt to start the engine.

1 Disconnect the negative cable from the battery (see Chapter 5).
2 Drain the cooling system (see Chapter 1).
3 Remove the engine under cover shield.
4 Remove the air intake duct.
5 Disconnect the upper radiator hose and the small coolant hoses from the thermostat housing (see Chapter 3).
6 Remove the power steering and/or air conditioning drivebelt (see Chapter 1).
7 Remove the alternator drivebelt (see Chapter 1).
8 Remove the ignition coil assembly and spark plug wires.
9 Remove the spark plugs from all cylinders.
10 Remove the water pump pulley (see illustration).
11 Remove the four crankshaft pulley plate bolts and remove the crankshaft pulley (see illustration).
12 Remove the valve cover (see Section 4). Remove the timing belt upper cover, middle cover, and lower cover (see illustrations).
13 Using a socket and breaker bar on the crankshaft sprocket bolt, rotate the crankshaft to align the crankshaft and camshaft sprocket timing marks (see illustrations 7.29a and 7.29b).
14 Remove the crankshaft sprocket center bolt and the crankshaft pulley hub.

➡ Note: To prevent the crankshaft from turning, fabricate a holding tool that will bolt to the crankshaft pulley hub.

15 If reusing the timing belt, paint match marks on the pulley and belt and an arrow indicating direction of travel on the belt (see illustration).

7.10 Remove the bolts and take off the water pump pulley

7.11 Remove the four bolts from the crankshaft pulley plate and remove the pulley

7.12a Remove the upper timing belt cover . . .

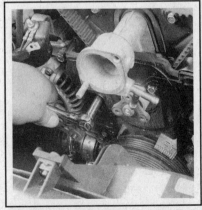
7.12b . . . the center timing belt cover . . .

7.12c . . . and the lower timing belt cover

7.15 Paint a directional arrow on the timing belt if you're going to reuse it

16 Loosen the timing belt tensioner (see illustrations). Cover the tensioner with a rag to protect it while prying the tensioner outward with a prybar. Temporarily tighten the tensioner with the spring fully extended.

17 Remove the timing belt.

18 If necessary, remove the crankshaft sprocket using two prybars or screwdrivers placed behind the sprocket to apply even pressure on the sprocket to slide it off the crankshaft.

19 If necessary, remove the camshaft sprocket bolts and remove the sprockets from the camshafts. Prevent the camshaft from turning by placing a wrench on the hex surface on the shaft (see illustrations).

INSPECTION

▸ Refer to illustration 7.22

❋❋ CAUTION:

Do not bend, twist or turn the timing belt inside out. Do not allow it to come in contact with oil, coolant or fuel. Do not use

timing belt tension to keep the camshaft or crankshaft from turning when installing the sprocket bolts. Do not turn the crankshaft or camshaft more than a few degrees (necessary for tooth alignment) while the timing belt is removed.

20 Check the tensioner and idler pulley bearings for smooth operation and excessive play. Inspect the tensioner spring for damage. Replace the components, if necessary.

21 If the timing belt was broken during engine operation, the belt may have been fouled by debris or may have been damaged by a defective component in the area of the timing belt; check for belt material in the teeth of the sprockets. Any defective parts or debris in the sprockets must be cleaned out of all the sprockets before installing the new belt or the belt will not mesh properly when installed.

22 If the belt teeth are cracked or pulled off (see illustration), the crank angle sensor, water pump, oil pump or camshaft(s) may have seized.

23 If there is noticeable wear or cracks in the belt, check to see if there are nicks or burrs on the sprockets.

24 If there is wear or damage on only one side of the belt, check the belt guide and the alignment of all sprockets. Also check the oil seals at

7.16a To release the tension on the timing belt, loosen the timing belt tensioner pulley bolt . . .

7.16b . . . pry the pulley away from the belt with a padded bar and retighten the bolt

7.19a To remove the camshaft sprocket, hold the camshaft with a wrench on the hex while loosening the sprocket bolt . . .

7.19b . . . then pull the sprocket off the end of the camshaft

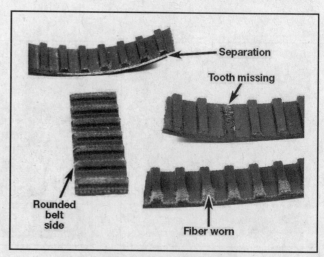

7.22 Inspect the timing belt for these conditions

the front of the engine and replace them if they are leaking.

25 Replace the timing belt with a new one if obvious wear or damage is noted or if it is the least bit questionable. Correct any problems which contributed to belt failure prior to belt installation.

➡Note: We recommend replacing the belt whenever it is removed, since belt failure can lead to expensive engine damage.

INSTALLATION

▶ Refer to illustrations 7.29a, 7.29b, 7.32 and 7.36

✳ CAUTION:

Before starting the engine, carefully rotate the crankshaft by hand through at least two full revolutions (use a socket and breaker bar on the crankshaft pulley center bolt). If you feel any resistance, STOP! There is something wrong - most likely, valves are contacting the pistons. You must find the problem before proceeding. Check your work and see if any updated repair information is available.

26 Remove all dirt and oil from the timing belt area at the front of the engine.

27 If they were removed, install the tensioner and idler pulley. The tensioner pulley should be pulled back against spring tension with the spring fully extended and the tensioner bolt temporarily tightened.

28 If they were removed, install the camshaft and crankshaft sprockets. Make sure the crankshaft sprocket Woodruff key is installed with the tapered side toward the oil pump body. Tighten the camshaft sprocket bolts to the torque listed in this Chapter's Specifications, referring to Step 19.

29 Align the camshaft sprocket and crankshaft sprocket timing marks (see illustrations). The notch on the rear flange of the crankshaft sprocket is aligned with the mark on the oil pump body. The "I" and "E" marks on the camshaft sprockets are aligned with the "E" and "I" marks on the rear timing belt cover and the second set of "E" and "I" marks are at approximately 12 o'clock.

➡Note: If necessary, rotate the crankshaft and camshaft sprockets slightly to achieve proper alignment.

30 Slip the timing belt over the crankshaft sprocket and camshaft sprockets, and position the belt so it's tight on the side opposite the tensioner pulley and between the camshaft sprockets. If the original belt is being reinstalled, align the marks made during removal with the marks on the sprockets, and be sure to install the timing belt so that it will rotate in the same direction as removed (the direction of rotation was marked during removal).

31 Install the crankshaft pulley hub and crankshaft sprocket bolt.

32 Rotate the crankshaft 1-5/6 turns clockwise and align the crankshaft sprocket timing mark (notch) with the tension set mark on the oil pump body (see illustration).

✳ CAUTION:

If you feel resistance while rotating the engine by hand, do not continue. The valves may be contacting the pistons due to incorrect valve timing. Recheck the camshaft and crankshaft sprockets to be sure they are correctly aligned with their marks.

7.29a Align the notch on the rear flange of the crankshaft sprocket with the pointer on the oil pump body (arrow)

7.29b Align the intake camshaft E mark with the E pointer on the rear timing belt cover (arrows), the I mark will be at approximately 12 o'clock; align the exhaust camshaft I mark with the I pointer on the rear timing belt cover (arrows), the E mark will be at approximately 12 o'clock

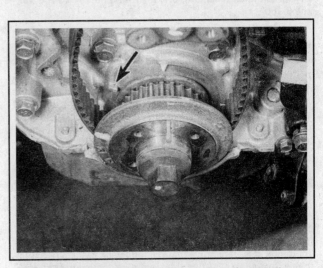

7.32 Rotate the crankshaft 1-5/6 turns clockwise and align the crankshaft sprocket timing mark with the tension set mark (arrow)

7.36 Check the timing belt deflection at a point midway between the camshaft sprockets

33 Loosen the tensioner pulley bolt and allow the tensioner spring to apply tension to the timing belt.

➡ Note: The tensioner pulley spring applies the proper tension to the belt.

34 Tighten the tensioner pulley bolt to the torque listed in this Chap-ter's Specifications.

35 Turn the crankshaft 2-1/6 turns clockwise and verify that the crankshaft sprocket timing mark and the camshaft sprocket timing marks are correctly aligned (see illustrations 7.29a and 7.29b). If the timing marks do not align, remove the timing belt and repeat the instal-lation procedure.

36 Check the timing belt tension by applying moderate force by hand (about 20 pounds force) midway between the camshaft sprockets and measure the belt deflection (see illustration). Belt deflection should be 3/8 inch to 7/16 inch.

37 If belt deflection is not correct, repeat the installation procedure. If the proper tension is still not obtained, replace the tensioner spring with a new spring and reset belt tension as described above.

38 Tighten the crankshaft sprocket bolt to the torque listed in this Chapter's Specifications, referring to Step 14.

39 Reinstall the remaining parts in the reverse order of removal. Run the engine and check for proper operation.

✳✳ CAUTION:

DO NOT start the engine until you are absolutely certain that the timing belt is installed correctly. Serious and costly engine dam-age could occur if the belt is improperly installed.

8   Timing chain and sprockets - removal, inspection and installation

➡ Note: This procedure applies to 2006 and later models only.

REMOVAL

◆ Refer to illustrations 8.6, 8.7, 8.11, 8.12, 8.13, 8.14, 8.16a and 8.16b

✳✳ CAUTION:

The timing system is complex. Severe engine damage will occur if you make any mistakes. Do not attempt this procedure unless you are highly experienced with this type of repair. If you are at all unsure of your abilities, consult an expert. Double-check all your work and be sure everything is correct before you attempt to start the engine.

✳✳ CAUTION:

The crankshaft pulley will have to be removed in order to remove the timing chain cover. Once the crankshaft pulley bolt is loosened, the crankshaft timing chain sprocket will be loosened as well. At this point, the engine is no longer timed. Therefore, it is imperative that you follow the procedure outlined in this Section EXACTLY in order to protect the engine and to re-time it correctly. Failure to do so could cause severe engine damage.

➡ Note: The crankshaft pulley bolt is very tight. Mazda uses several special tools to hold the crankshaft pulley (holding tool, SST #205-126; bolts, SST #205-072-02/49 UN20 507202) while loosening the pulley bolt. You might be able to obtain similar tools in the aftermarket, but make sure that they are suitable equivalents; trying to remove the crank pulley bolt without the right tools could damage the engine.

1 Warm up the engine, then drain the engine oil (see Chapter 1).
2 Remove the battery and the battery tray (see Chapter 5).
3 Remove the air filter housing (see Chapter 4).
4 Remove the valve cover (see Section 4).
5 While the drivebelt is still installed, loosen the water pump pulley bolts and the idler pulley bolt. Remove the drivebelt and the drivebelt tensioner (see Chapter 1).
6 Remove the water pump pulley (see Chapter 3) and the drivebelt idler pulley (see illustration).
7 Remove the larger front engine under-cover (see illustration).
8 Disconnect the Crankshaft Position (CKP) sensor electrical con-nector, unclip the wiring harness and move it away from the timing chain cover. Remove the (CKP) sensor (see Chapter 6).

✳✳ CAUTION:

Be sure to follow the procedure for removing the CKP sensor outlined in Chapter 6. Failure to do so could adversely affect ignition timing, fuel injection and other engine control systems.

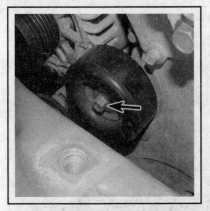

8.6 To remove the drivebelt idler pulley from the timing chain cover, remove this bolt

8.7 Front engine under cover bolts

8.11 Use a factory tool or a suitable aftermarket tool (shown) to hold the crankshaft pulley while loosening (and tightening) the crank pulley bolt

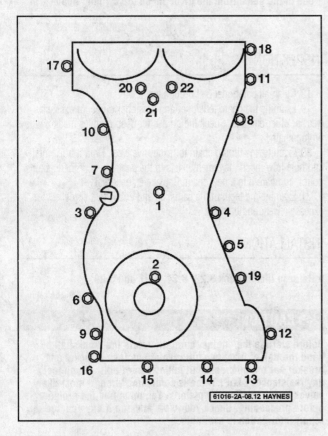

8.12 Timing chain cover bolt tightening sequence

8.13 Use a large wrench on the hexagonal portion of the camshaft to hold the cam in place while loosening (or tightening) the sprocket bolt

➡Note: The purpose of the timing pin is to stop the crankshaft at TDC, NOT to lock down the crank while you loosen the crank pulley bolt. You must immobilize the crank pulley while loosening the pulley bolt. Using the pin as a crank holding tool will only damage the pin.

❊❊ **CAUTION:**

In order to keep the crankshaft in the correct position, do NOT remove the timing pin until after the crankshaft pulley has been reinstalled later in this procedure. Do NOT try to rotate the crankshaft for any reason while the timing pin is installed. Doing so could damage the engine.

9   Remove the cylinder block lower blind plug on the right side of the engine and screw the special timing pin into the hole (see Section 3).

10 Facing the front of the engine, turn the crankshaft clockwise until the crank stops (a crank balance weight contacts the timing pin). The No. 1 cylinder is now in the TDC position.

11 The crankshaft pulley must be immobilized while loosening the crank pulley bolt. Install the special holding tool on the crankshaft pulley to hold it (see illustration), then loosen and remove the crankshaft pulley bolt. Remove the crank pulley holding tool and remove the pulley.

12 Remove the timing chain cover bolts (see illustration) and remove the timing chain cover.

13 If you need to remove the camshaft sprockets, loosen the sprocket bolts now, before you loosen anything else. Using a wrench on the hexagonal portion of the camshaft, hold the cam in place while loosening the camshaft sprocket bolt (see illustration).

❊❊ **CAUTION:**

Allowing a camshaft to rotate during this Step could damage the valves.

8.14 Timing chain tensioner details:

1   *Insert a drill bit into this hole to lock the ratchet mechanism into place*
2   *Tensioner mounting bolts*

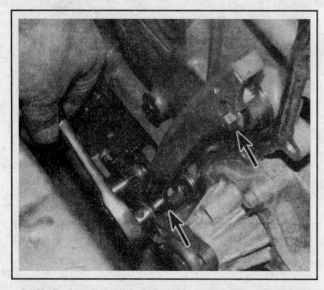

8.16b To detach the left chain guide, remove these two bolts

14 Carefully compress the timing chain tensioner and place a pin (a drill bit or paper clip will work) into the hole to hold it in the compressed position (see illustration).

☀☀ CAUTION:

Compress only the round plunger on the tensioner and not the ratchet mechanism (the ratchet is next to the plunger and has square sides).

15 Remove the two tensioner mounting bolts and remove the tensioner.
16 Remove the right and left timing chain guides (see illustrations), then remove the timing chain.
17 If you loosened the camshaft sprocket bolts, remove the camshaft sprockets now.

8.16a To remove the right chain guide, disengage the upper end of the guide from the pivot pin on the cylinder head

INSPECTION

18 Clean all components thoroughly and wipe dry.
19 Examine the chain tensioner and tensioner guide for excessive wear or other damage. Check the guides for deep grooves made by the timing chain.
20 Examine the timing chain for excessive wear. Hold it horizontally and note how much movement exists in the chain links. If there is any doubt, compare it to a new chain. Replace as necessary.
21 Examine the teeth of the camshaft and crankshaft sprockets for excessive wear and damage.

INSTALLATION

▶ **Refer to illustrations 8.22, 8.24, 8.27 and 8.29**

☀☀ CAUTION:

Before starting the engine, carefully rotate the crankshaft by hand through at least two full revolutions (use a socket and breaker bar on the crankshaft pulley center bolt). If you feel any resistance, STOP! There is something wrong - most likely, valves are contacting the pistons. You must find the problem before proceeding. Check your work and see if any updated repair information is available.

22 Before installing the timing chain tensioner, the piston must be compressed and locked until installation. If the ratchet needs to be reset, perform the following:
   a) *Remove the tensioner and place it lightly in a vise using the plunger and tensioner housing.*
   b) *Place a pick-type tool or small screwdriver in the hole (see illustration) closest to the ratchet to disengage the pawl from the ratchet mechanism.*
   c) *While holding the tool in place, push the ratchet back into the tensioner, then install a pin into the other hole to keep the plunger and ratchet compressed.*
   d) *Remove the tensioner from the vise.*

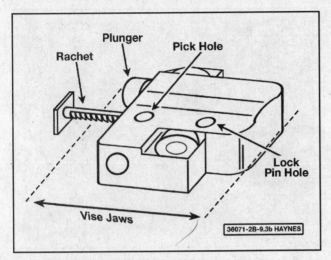

8.22 Timing chain tensioner details

23 Install the timing chain tensioner and tighten the tensioner mounting bolts securely. Do NOT remove the pin from the tensioner at this time; the plunger and ratchet must remain depressed until the timing chain is installed.

24 Install the left chain guide and the right chain guide (see illustration). Tighten the left chain guide bolts securely and make sure that the right chain guide is fully seated on its pivot pin.

25 Install the camshaft sprockets and timing chain as follows:

 a) *If you removed either camshaft sprocket, install it now and hand tighten the sprocket bolt. If you didn't remove either camshaft sprocket, loosen - but don't remove - the cam sprocket bolts.*

 b) *Thread the timing chain over the Variable Valve Timing (VVT) actuator/intake camshaft sprocket, then route the chain down the friction surface of the left chain guide, around the crankshaft sprocket, then up the friction surface of the right chain guide.*

 c) *Remove the bolt from the exhaust camshaft sprocket, pull the sprocket off the exhaust cam, thread the timing chain onto the sprocket, install the sprocket on the exhaust cam and install the sprocket bolt.*

 d) *Using a wrench on the hexagonal portion on each camshaft, hold the cam in place while tightening the camshaft sprocket bolts to the torque listed in this Chapter's Specifications (see illustration 8.13).*

✳✳ CAUTION:

Allowing a camshaft to rotate during this Step could damage the valves. Do not use the camshaft alignment tool or camshaft to hold the camshafts while tightening the camshaft sprocket bolts. Doing so could damage the alignment tool or camshaft and cause engine damage.

 e) *After you have installed the camshaft sprocket bolts, install the camshaft alignment tool again to hold the cams in position.*

26 Remove the pin to release the tensioner. Make sure that the tensioner plunger releases and pushes against the right chain guide (see illustration 8.14).

27 Install the timing chain cover as follows:

 a) *Clean the mating surfaces of all material.*

➡Note: Be careful not to gouge or use any abrasives on the mating surfaces.

8.24 Chain guide details:

| 1 | *Right chain guide pivot pin* | 2 | *Left chain guide mounting bolts* |

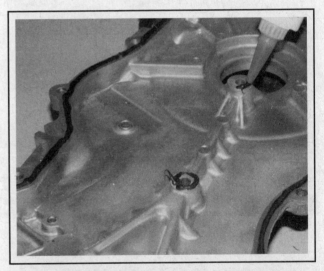

8.27 Apply a bead of RTV sealant to the mating surface of each of the mounting bolt bosses in the middle of the timing chain cover and to the mating surface around the edge of the cover

 b) *Install a new front crankshaft seal in the timing cover. Lay the timing chain cover flat on a clean work surface, align the new seal with the hole, then use a seal driver and carefully tap the new seal into position.*

 c) *Apply a bead of RTV sealant to the mating surfaces of the bolt hole bosses located in the middle of the timing chain cover and to the mating surface running around the edge of the cover (see illustration).*

 d) *Install the engine cover within 10 minutes of applying the sealant.*

 e) *Using the indicated tightening sequence (see illustration 8.12), gradually and evenly tighten the timing cover bolts to the torque listed in this Chapter's Specifications.*

28 Lightly coat the crankshaft front seal with clean engine oil, then install the crankshaft pulley. Install a new crankshaft pulley bolt and hand tighten it.

29 Install and align the crankshaft pulley as follows:

a) *Position the crank pulley so the hole in the pulley is aligned with the threaded hole in the timing chain cover. When the hole in the crank pulley is aligned with the hole in the timing cover, install a crankshaft pulley alignment bolt (M6 x 18 mm) through the pulley and into the timing chain cover (see illustration).*

※ **CAUTION:**

Failure to perform this step will result in a misaligned crank pulley, which will cause engine damage.

b) *Install the crankshaft pulley holding tool (see illustration 8.11) and tighten the crankshaft pulley bolt to the torque listed in this Chapter's Specifications.*

c) *With the crankshaft pulley alignment bolt installed, install the camshaft alignment tool and verify that the camshafts are still correctly aligned. If the tool cannot be installed into the slots in the back ends of the camshafts, the engine timing is incorrect.*

d) *The engine is correctly timed when the camshaft alignment tool, the timing pin and the crankshaft pulley alignment bolt tool are all simultaneously in their installed positions.*

30 When the engine is correctly timed, remove the crankshaft pulley holding tool and the threaded crankshaft alignment bolt from the pulley and front engine cover, remove the timing pin from the cylinder block, then remove the camshaft alignment tool.

31 Rotate the engine in a clockwise directions two complete revolu-

8.29 To properly align the crankshaft pulley, insert an M6 bolt through this timing alignment hole in the crankshaft pulley (the hole should be at 6 o'clock) and screw the bolt into the timing chain cover

tions by turning the crankshaft pulley bolt with a wrench or large socket.

32 Insert the cam alignment tool, the timing pin and the crank pulley alignment bolt one last time to verify that timing is absolutely correct.

33 With the engine at TDC on the compression stroke for cylinder no. 1, install the CKP sensor (see Chapter 6).

34 The remainder of installation is the reverse of removal.

9   Camshafts, oil seals and valve lifters - removal, inspection and installation

REMOVAL

▶ **Refer to illustrations 9.3, 9.5, 9.7a, 9.7b, 9.7c, 9.10a and 9.10b**

1   Disconnect the cable from the negative battery terminal (see Chapter 5).

2   Remove the valve cover (see Section 4).

3   1997 and earlier models only: Turn the engine over with a socket and breaker bar on the crankshaft pulley center bolt to position the base of each camshaft lobe against the hydraulic lifters. Measure the clearance between the cam lobe base and lifter with a feeler gauge (see illustration). If it's more than the limit listed in this Chapter's Specifications, the lifter needs to be replaced. Write down the locations of any lifters that need cleaning or replacement, then continue measuring until all lifters have been checked.

4   Remove the timing belt/chain cover(s) and the timing belt/chain (see Section 7 or 8).

5   Measure the thrust clearance (endplay) of the camshaft(s) with a dial indicator (see illustration). If the clearance is greater than the value listed in this Chapter's Specifications, replace the camshaft, cylinder head or both, whichever is worn.

6   2005 and earlier models only: Remove the rear timing belt cover (see illustration 9.37).

7   Remove the camshaft sprockets (see Section 7 or 8). Loosen the camshaft bearing cap bolts gradually, in five or six steps, in the sequence shown (see illustrations). Remove the camshaft bearing caps, marking or packaging to record their locations for correct reinstallation later. To further ensure correct reinstallation later, take note of the factory camshaft cap stamped numbers and direction arrows (see illustration).

8   2005 and earlier models only: Make note how far into the bearing cap the old oil seal is located and use this as a guide for installation depth later.

9   Mark the camshafts to ensure proper reinstallation later. Remove the camshafts. On 2005 and earlier models, remove the oil seals from the camshafts.

10   Using a magnet, lift out each valve lifter and set them in numbered boxes, plastic bags or other containers so they can be reinstalled in the same position during reassembly (see illustrations). 1997 and earlier models: If you're planning to store the lifters for some time, keep them upside down in a container of engine oil, but be sure to keep them in their original order.

※ **CAUTION:**

Do not scratch the lifters when removing them.

9.3 Measure the lifter-to-cam lobe clearance with a feeler gauge

9.5 Pry the camshaft back-and-forth to check the endplay (thrust clearance)

9.7a Loosen the camshaft bearing cap bolts, in several steps, in the sequence shown (2005 and earlier models)

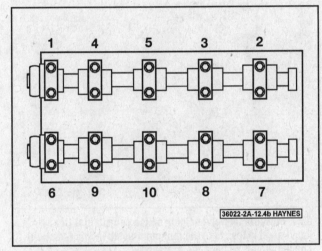

9.7b Loosen the camshaft bearing cap bolts, in several steps, in the sequence shown (2006 and later models)

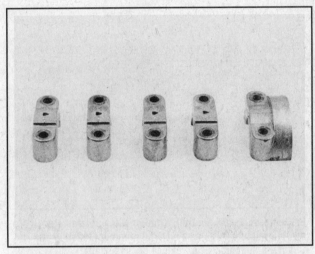

9.7c All cam bearing caps are marked I for intake or E for exhaust; the front cam bearing caps can be identified by their shapes; the others are numbered from front to rear of the engine and have arrowhead marks that point to the front

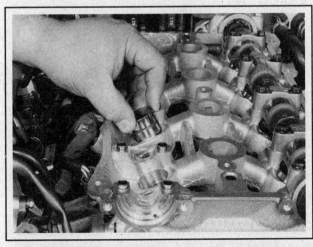

9.10a Pull the lifters out of their bores, using a magnet if necessary

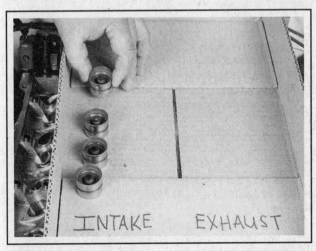

9.10b Mark a cardboard box or use a similar method to store the lifters and bearing caps so they can be reinstalled in their original locations

9.12a Lay a strip of Plastigage on each camshaft journal

9.12b Compare the width of the crushed Plastigage to the scale on the envelope to determine the oil clearance

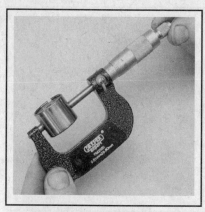

9.14 Measure the outside diameter of each lifter at several points

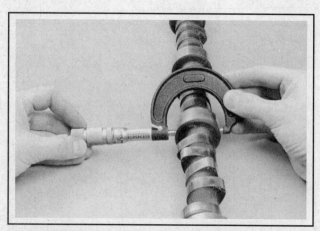

9.16 Measure each journal diameter with a micrometer (if any journal measures less than the minimum listed in this Chapter's Specifications, replace the camshaft)

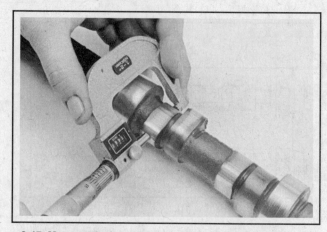

9.17 Measure the lobe heights on the camshaft(s) (if any lobe height is less than the minimum listed in this Chapter's Specifications, replace the camshaft)

INSPECTION

▶ Refer to illustrations 9.12a, 9.12b, 9.14, 9.16 and 9.17

11 Examine all parts, looking for signs of pitting, scoring or scuffing.
12 Check the oil clearance for each camshaft journal as follows:

a) *Clean the bearing caps and the camshaft journals with cleaning solvent and dry thoroughly.*

b) *Carefully lay the camshafts in place in the head. Do not install the lifters and do not use any lubrication.*

c) *Lay a strip of Plastigage on each journal (see illustration).*

d) *Install the camshaft bearing caps in the proper locations as removed with the arrows pointing as removed.*

e) *Tighten the bolts IN SEQUENCE (see illustration 9.27) to the torque listed in this Chapter's Specifications in two or three steps.*

➡**Note: Do not turn the camshaft while the Plastigage is in place.**

f) *Remove the camshaft bearing cap bolts IN THE OPPOSITE OF THE TIGHTENING SEQUENCE (see illustration 9.7a) and detach the caps.*

g) *Compare the width of the crushed Plastigage (at its widest point) to the scale on the Plastigage envelope (see illustration).*

h) *If the clearance is greater than specified, replace the camshaft and/or cylinder head.*

i) *Scrape off the Plastigage with your fingernail or the edge of a credit card - do not scratch or nick the journals or bearing caps.*

13 Inspect each lifter for scuffing and scoring marks. On 1997 and earlier models, press the lifter plunger in by hand, checking for movement. If the lifter plunger moves, replace the lifter.

14 Measure the outside diameter of each lifter (see illustration) and measure the lifter bore diameter. Compare your measurements with the values listed in this Chapter's Specifications. Replace any lifter that is worn excessively. Thoroughly clean each lifter by soaking it in solvent.

15 Visually examine the camshaft lobes and bearing journals for scoring marks, pitting, galling and evidence of overheating (blue, discolored areas). Look for flaking away of the hardened surface of each lobe.

16 Using a micrometer, measure the diameter of each camshaft journal (see illustration). If the diameter of any one journal is less than specified, replace the camshaft.

17 Using a micrometer, measure the height of each lobe (see illustration). If the height for any one lobe is less than the specified minimum, replace the camshaft.

18 Replace any parts that are worn beyond specifications.

9.26 Apply sealant between the seal housing portion of each front bearing cap and the cylinder head (arrows); don't get any sealant between the cam bearing portion of the bearing caps and the cylinder head

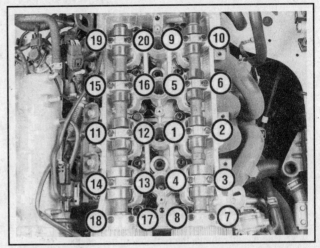

9.27a Camshaft bearing cap tightening sequence (2005 and earlier models)

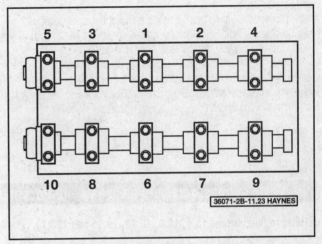

9.27b Camshaft bearing cap tightening sequence (2006 and later models)

VVT actuator (2006 and later models)

→Note: For more information about the VVT system, refer to Chapter 6.

19 Mark the orientation of the VVT actuator to the camshaft to ensure that the VVT actuator is installed in exactly the same relation to the cam.

20 Secure the camshaft in a bench vise. Use plastic jaw liners to protect the camshaft from damage.

21 Remove the VVT actuator bolt, remove the VVT actuator and remove the actuator washer. Discard the washer.

22 Using a new washer, install the VVT actuator. Be sure to align the marks that you made prior to disassembly.

23 Tighten the actuator bolt to the torque listed in this Chapter's Specifications.

INSTALLATION

♦ Refer to illustrations 9.26 and 9.27

24 Apply engine assembly lubricant or clean engine oil to the lifters and install them in the lifter bores, in their original locations. Check that the lifters travel smoothly in their bores.

25 Apply camshaft assembly lubricant or clean engine oil to the camshaft lobes and bearing journals. Install the camshafts. Make sure the exhaust camshaft is reinstalled on the exhaust manifold side of the engine, and the intake camshaft is reinstalled on the intake manifold side of the engine.

26 2005 and earlier models: Apply RTV sealant to the portions of the bearing cap surfaces that surround the camshaft seals (see illustration). Don't put any sealant on the portion of the cap that surrounds the camshaft journal.

27 Install the camshaft bearing caps in the proper order as marked when removed, in the stamped numerical order with the arrows pointing as removed. Then tighten the cap bolts in two or three steps IN SEQUENCE (see illustration) to the torque listed in this Chapter's Specifications.

28 2005 and earlier models: Apply clean engine oil to the lips of the new camshaft oil seals and install the oil seals (see Step 39).

29 Install the camshaft sprockets on their correct camshafts (see Section 7 or 8).

30 Install the timing belt (see Section 7) or timing chain (see Section 8)

31 1997 and earlier models: Before reinstalling the camshaft position sensor, install a new O-ring. Apply grease to the O-ring and apply grease or engine assembly lubricant to the sensor drive lugs. Refer to Chapter 5 and install the sensor.

32 Reinstall the remaining parts in the reverse order of removal.

33 Run the engine and the timing (see Chapter 5). Check the engine for proper operation and coolant leaks.

CAMSHAFT OIL SEALS (2005 AND EARLIER MODELS) - REPLACEMENT

♦ Refer to illustrations 9.37 and 9.38

34 Disconnect the cable from the negative battery terminal (see Chapter 5).

35 Block the rear wheels and set the parking brake.

9.37 Unbolt and remove the rear timing belt cover

9.38 Carefully pry the camshaft seal out of the bore - DO NOT nick or scratch the camshaft or seal bore

36 Position cylinder number one to TDC on the compression stroke (see Section 3).

37 Remove the timing belt, camshaft sprocket bolts and sprockets (see Section 7). Remove the rear timing belt cover (see illustration).

38 Carefully pry the camshaft seal out of the bore using a thin screwdriver or pointed tool (see illustration). Or drill a small hole in the seal midway between the camshaft and cylinder head; thread a small screw into the camshaft oil seal one or two threads and use the screw to pull the seal from the bore.

✳✳ **CAUTION:**

DO NOT nick or scratch the camshaft or seal bore.

39 Apply some clean engine oil to the lip of the new camshaft oil seal. Push the seal in slightly by hand.

40 Using a seal driver and hammer, lightly tap the seal in, flush to the edge of the camshaft cap or to the depth of the original seal.

41 Reinstall the remaining parts in the reverse order of removal.

42 Run the engine and check for proper operation.

10 Valve springs, retainers and seals - replacement

▶ Refer to illustrations 10.4, 10.9, 10.10, 10.15 and 10.17

➥**Note: Broken valve springs and defective valve stem seals can be replaced without removing the cylinder head. Several special tools and a compressed air source are normally required to perform this operation, so read through this Section carefully and rent or buy the tools before beginning the job. If compressed air isn't available, a length of nylon rope can be used to keep the valves from falling into the cylinder during this procedure.**

1 Refer to Section 9 and remove the camshafts. Remove the valve lifters from the defective valves. Keep the lifters in order so they may be reinstalled in their original location.

2 Remove the spark plug from the cylinder which has the defective component. If all of the valve stem seals are being replaced, all of the spark plugs should be removed.

3 Turn the crankshaft until the piston in the affected cylinder is at Top Dead Center (TDC) on the compression stroke (refer to Section 3 for instructions). If you are replacing all of the valve stem seals, begin with cylinder number one and work on the valves for one cylinder at a time. Move from cylinder-to-cylinder following the firing order sequence (see this Chapter's Specifications).

4 Thread an adapter into the spark plug hole (see illustration) and connect an air hose from a compressed air source. Most auto parts stores can supply the air hose adapter.

➥**Note: Many cylinder compression gauges utilize a screw-in fitting that may work with your air hose quick-disconnect fitting.**

5 Apply compressed air to the cylinder.

✳✳ **WARNING:**

The piston may be forced down by compressed air, causing the crankshaft to turn suddenly. If the wrench used when positioning the number one piston at TDC is still attached to the bolt in the crankshaft pulley end, damage or injury could occur if the crankshaft moves.

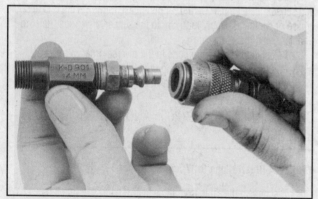

10.4 Thread an air hose adapter into the spark plug hole - adapters are commonly available from auto parts stores

10.9 Use a valve spring compressor to compress the springs, then remove the keepers from the valve stem with a magnet or small needle-nose pliers - a special adapter (not shown) is necessary to compress the spring

10.10 Remove the valve guide oil seal with an oil seal removal tool or a pair of pliers

10.15 Gently tap the seal into place with a hammer and a seal installer or deep socket

6   The valves should now be held in place by the air pressure.

7   If you do not have access to compressed air, an alternative method can be used. Position the piston at a point approximately 45-degrees before TDC on the compression stroke, then feed a long piece of nylon rope through the spark plug hole until it fills the combustion chamber. Be sure to leave the end of the rope hanging out of the engine so it can be removed easily.

8   Use a socket and breaker bar on the crankshaft pulley enter bolt to rotate the crankshaft in the normal direction of rotation (clockwise, when viewed from the front) until slight resistance is felt.

9   Stuff clean shop rags into any cylinder head holes above and below the valves to prevent parts and tools from falling into the engine, then use a valve spring compressor to compress the spring. Remove the keepers with small needle-nose pliers or a magnet (see illustration).

➡Note: A special valve spring compressor capable of compressing the valve springs with the head in place will be needed. Because the valves are recessed into the cylinder head, a special adapter is also necessary.

10   Remove the spring retainer and valve spring (mark the top end of the valve spring for later reinstallation). Measure the depth to the upper side of the valve stem oil seal, then remove the oil seal (see illustration).

➡Note: If using air pressure to hold the valve(s) fails to hold the valve in the closed position during this operation, the valve face and/or seat is probably damaged. If so, the cylinder head will have to be removed. The alternate procedure for holding the valves described above may be used, or the cylinder head will require removal for additional repair operations.

11   Wrap a rubber band or tape around the top of the valve stem so the valve won't fall into the combustion chamber, then release the air pressure.

➡Note: If a rope was used instead of air pressure, turn the crankshaft slightly in the direction opposite normal rotation.

12   Inspect the valve spring for cracks or damage. Inspect the valve stem for damaged or rough face or an unevenly worn stem tip. Rotate the valve in its guide and check the end of the valve stem for eccentric movement, which would indicate that the valve is bent.

13   Move the valve up-and-down in the guide and make sure there is no binding. If the valve stem binds, either the valve is bent or the guide is damaged.

10.17 Apply a small dab of grease to each keeper as shown here before installation - it'll hold them in place on the valve stem as the spring is released

14   Reapply air pressure to the cylinder to retain the valve in the closed position, then remove the tape or rubber band from the valve stem. If a nylon rope was used instead of air pressure, rotate the crankshaft in the normal direction of rotation until slight resistance is felt.

15   Lubricate the valve stem with engine oil or engine assembly lubricant and install a new oil seal using an oil seal installer tool or deep socket (see illustration), measuring the installed depth as necessary. Install the oil seal to the depth measured before seal removal (see Step 10).

16   Install the spring in position over the valve. Replace any springs not meeting the inspection above. Be sure the spring is installed as marked during removal (top of the spring is up) and also note that the end of the spring with a closer pitch is toward the cylinder head.

17   Install the valve spring retainer. Compress the valve spring and carefully position the keepers in the groove. Apply a small dab of grease to the inside of each keeper to hold it in place if necessary (see illustration).

18   Remove the pressure from the spring tool and make sure the keepers are seated.

19   Disconnect the compressed air hose and remove the adapter from the spark plug hole. If a nylon rope was used in place of air pressure, pull it out of the cylinder.

20   Refer to Section 9 and install the camshafts.

21   Install the rest of the parts in the reverse order of the removal procedure.

22   Start and run the engine, then check for oil leaks and unusual sounds coming from the valve cover area.

11 Cylinder head - removal and installation

❊❊ WARNING:

The engine must be completely cool before beginning this procedure.

REMOVAL

1 Disconnect the negative cable from the battery (see Chapter 5).
2 Drain the engine coolant (see Chapter 1).
3 Drain the engine oil and remove the oil filter (see Chapter 1).
4 Remove the air intake duct assembly.
5 Remove the spark plugs.
6 Remove the throttle valve cable (if so eqipped) and accelerator cable.
7 Remove the power brake booster vacuum hose, fuel hose, radiator hoses, the purge control vacuum hose (from intake manifold to firewall area), cruise control vacuum hose (as applicable), and the heater hoses. Mark the hoses for later reinstallation.
8 Remove all electrical connectors/wiring harness connections to the cylinder head. Mark the connectors for later reinstallation.
9 Remove water bypass tubing bolts/nuts (where applicable, the bypass tubing is mounted on engine head).
10 Remove the water pump pulley and drive belt.
11 Remove the fuel rail and injectors (see Chapter 4).
12 Remove the intake manifold (see Section 5).
13 Remove the exhaust manifold (see Section 6).
14 Remove the valve cover (see Section 4).
15 Remove the timing belt (see Section 7) or chain (see Section 8).
16 Remove the power steering pump and alternator drivebelt(s) (see Chapter 1).
17 Remove the alternator and alternator brackets (see Chapter 5).
18 Remove any sensors attached to the cylinder head (see Chapter 6).
19 Unbolt the power steering pump, as applicable, and lay it to the side without disconnecting the hoses (see Chapter 10).
20 Label and detach any remaining components that would interfere with cylinder head removal.
21 Using a breaker bar and the appropriate hex-bit driver or socket, loosen the cylinder head bolts in 1/4-turn increments, loosening in the reverse of the tightening sequence (see illustration 11.33) until they can be removed by hand.
22 Lift the cylinder head off the engine block. If it is stuck, very carefully pry up at the transmission end, away from the head gasket surface.
23 Remove all external components from the head to allow for thorough cleaning and inspection.

INSTALLATION

◆ **Refer to illustrations 11.27, 11.32 and 11.33**

❊❊ CAUTION:

On 2006 and later models, replace the cylinder head bolts with new ones.

24 The mating surfaces of the cylinder head and block must be perfectly clean when the head is installed.
25 Use a gasket scraper to remove all traces of carbon and old gasket material, then clean the mating surfaces with lacquer thinner or acetone. If any oil residue is on the mating surfaces when the head is installed, the gasket may not seal correctly and leaks could develop. When working on the block, stuff the cylinders with clean shop rags to prevent the entry of debris. Use a vacuum cleaner to remove material that falls into the cylinders.

❊❊ CAUTION:

Be careful not to gouge the soft aluminum of the cylinder head.

26 Check the block and head mating surfaces for nicks, deep scratches and other damage. If damage is slight, it can be removed with a file; if it's excessive, machining may be the only alternative.
27 On 2005 and earlier models, use a thread die of the correct thread size to chase (clean up) the head bolt threads (see illustration).
➡Note: **Cleaning up the threads using a thread die should not cut any metal from the threads. If you observe any metal cuttings while chasing the threads, stop and replace the bolt with a new bolt from an automotive parts store or dealer. Make sure the replacement bolt is an OEM (Original Equipment Manufacture) replacement cylinder head bolt specifically designed for this engine, and is the correct length and thread type. Discard the defective bolt.**

Use a tap of the correct thread size to chase the threads in the head bolt holes, then clean the holes with compressed air - make sure that no residue such as dirt, corrosion, and sealant remains in the holes and the threads are not damaged as this will affect torque readings, which affects the quality of the head installation job.

❊❊ WARNING:

Wear eye protection when using compressed air!

28 Install the components that were removed from the head.
29 Position the new gasket over the dowel pins in the block.
30 Carefully set the head on the block without disturbing the gasket.
31 Before installing the head bolts, apply a small amount of clean engine oil to the threads.
32 Install the bolts and tighten them finger tight (see illustration).
33 Tighten the bolts following the recommended sequence in several steps to the torque listed in this Chapter's Specifications (see illustration).
34 The remaining installation steps are the reverse of removal.
35 Refill the cooling system, install a new oil filter and add oil to the engine (see Chapter 1).
36 Run the engine and check for leaks. Set the ignition timing (see Chapter 5) and road test the vehicle.
37 Frequently recheck coolant level for the first few hundred miles to be sure that no leakage exists.

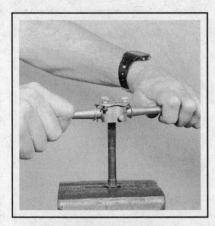
11.27 A die should be used to remove sealant and corrosion from the head bolt threads prior to installation

11.32 You'll need a torque angle gauge to tighten the cylinder head bolts on 2006 and later models

11.33 Cylinder head bolt TIGHTENING sequence

12 Oil pan - removal and installation

➡Note: Because of the lack of clearance between the oil pan and crossmember, oil pan removal is a very difficult procedure requiring the crossmember to be disconnected from the body and lowered. Read through the entire procedure and acquire the necessary tools and equipment before beginning.

2005 AND EARLIER MODELS

Removal

1 Disconnect the negative battery cable (see Chapter 5).
2 Drain the engine oil (see Chapter 1).
3 Remove the under cover from under the front of the vehicle.
4 Disconnect the steering column from the steering gear (see Chapter 10).

✳✳ WARNING:

On models equipped airbags, make sure the steering wheel is not rotated while the steering shaft is disconnected from the steering gear or damage to the airbag clock spring could occur resulting in airbag system failure and personal injury. To prevent the steering wheel from turning, place the ignition switch in the lock position and remove the key or wrap the seat belt around the steering wheel and buckle the belt into place.

5 Remove the dipstick and dipstick tube.
6 Support the engine from above with an engine support fixture. Remove the engine mounting nuts and raise the engine slightly (see Section 17).
7 Raise the vehicle and support it securely. Support the front crossmember with a heavy-duty jack, such as a transmission jack. Remove the crossmember nuts/bolts, then lower the crossmember until there's about four inches clearance between the steering gear and crossmember.

✳✳ CAUTION:

Don't strain any hoses (brakes, power steering or air conditioning) while lowering the crossmember.

8 Remove the oil pan-to-transmission and oil pan-to-engine bolts.
9 Remove the oil pan. If the oil pan is stuck, pry it loose very carefully by inserting a screwdriver or putty knife at the engine block ears.

✳✳ CAUTION:

Do not insert the screwdriver or prying tool between the oil baffle and the engine block. Be very careful not to scratch, bend, or otherwise damage the mating surfaces of the oil pan, baffle, and block or oil leaks could develop.

➡Note: Oil pan bolts may be of varying sizes. Mark, tag, or store each oil pan bolt/nut with the location removed from the oil pan for correct reinstallation later.

10 Unbolt the oil strainer from the oil pump.
11 Remove the baffle, prying as necessary against the main bearing journal or at the corners of the baffle.

Installation

◆ Refer to illustrations 12.15 and 12.17

12 Use a scraper to remove all traces of old gasket material and sealant from the block, baffle, oil pan and strainer. Clean the mating surfaces with gasket cleaner or equivalent solvent, available at automotive parts stores.

✳✳ CAUTION:

Be very careful not to scratch, bend, or otherwise damage the mating surfaces of the pan and block or oil leaks could develop.

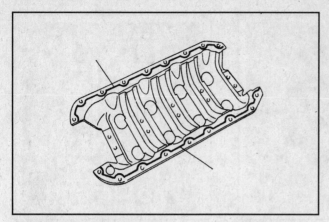

12.15 Apply a bead of sealant to the oil pan baffle flange to the inside of the bolt holes

13 Make sure the threaded bolt holes in the block are clean. Visually check the condition of the oil strainer.

14 Check the oil pan flange for cracks or distortion, particularly at the bolting flange.

15 Apply a continuous bead of silicone sealant to the bolting flange (lip) of the baffle inside the bolt holes (see illustration). Install the baffle.

➡**Note: Install the component within 5 minutes after applying the sealant.**

16 Install the oil strainer with a new gasket and tighten the bolts to the torque listed in this Chapter's Specification.

17 Apply RTV sealant to the new gaskets for the oil pump body and rear cover. Install the new gaskets on the oil pump body and rear cover on the engine block, inserting the projections on the gaskets into the notches (see illustration).

18 Apply a continuous bead of RTV sealant around the perimeter of the oil pan flange and inside the bolt holes.

➡**Note: Install the component within 5 minutes after applying the sealant.**

19 Carefully position the oil pan on the engine block and install the bolts/nuts. Working from the center out, tighten the oil pan-to-engine block bolts to the torque listed in this Chapter's Specifications in three or four steps. Tighten the oil pan-to-transmission bolts to the torque listed in Chapter 7 Specifications.

20 Let the RTV sealant set up approximately 12 hours before adding oil to the engine.

21 The remainder of installation is the reverse of removal. Be sure to add oil and install a new oil filter.

22 After sufficient time for the RTV sealant to set up, run the engine and check for oil leaks.

2006 AND LATER MODELS

Removal

♦ **Refer to illustration 12.35**

23 Remove the engine cover.
24 Drain the engine oil (see Chapter 1).
25 Remove the battery and the battery tray (see Chapter 5).
26 Remove the air filter housing (see Chapter 4).
27 Remove the drivebelt (see Chapter 1).
28 Remove the strut bar (see Chapter 10) and the strut bar reinforce-

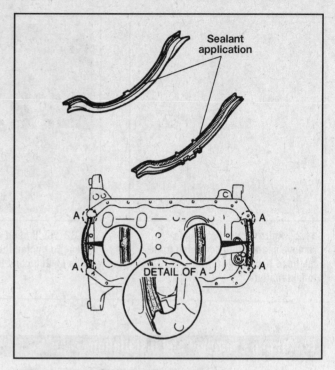

12.17 Oil pan end seal installation details

ment plate (see illustration 4.19a).

29 Disconnect and detach the clips for all wiring harnesses between the engine compartment and the engine, including the ignition coil and fuel injector harnesses. The engine will need to be lifted slightly, so make sure that no harnesses that might break remain connected.

30 Detach the power steering pump mounting bracket and set the bracket and pump aside. Don't disconnect the power steering hoses.

31 Loosen the front wheel lug nuts. Raise the vehicle and place it securely on jackstands. Remove the front wheels.

32 Remove the oil filter (see Chapter 1).

33 Remove the Crankshaft Position (CKP) sensor (see Chapter 6).

34 Remove the timing chain cover (see Section 8).

35 Remove the transverse member (see illustration).

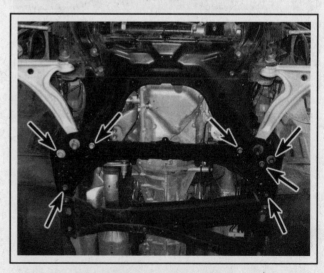

12.35 Transverse member mounting bolts

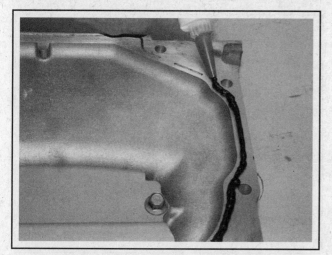

12.40 **Apply a bead of RTV sealant to the mating surface of the oil pan**

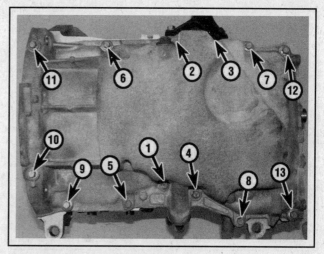

12.42 **Oil pan bolt tightening sequence**

36 Hook up an engine hoist to the engine lifting brackets.

37 Remove the engine mounting bracket nuts, then lift up the engine about an inch.

38 Gradually and evenly loosen and remove the oil pan bolts in the reverse order of the tightening sequence (see illustration 12.42), then remove the oil pan. You might need to use a rubber mallet to loosen the pan, which will stick to the block because of old sealant. Use a scraper to break the sealant around the oil pan, but make sure you don't damage the mating surfaces of the oil pan and cylinder block.

Installation

▶ **Refer to illustrations 12.40 and 12.42**

39 Before installation, thoroughly clean and degrease the mating surfaces of the block and the oil pan, then use a clean rag to wipe out the pan. If you're reusing the old oil pan bolts, make sure that you remove all of the old sealant from the bolts as well.

✳✳ CAUTION:

Failure to remove all old sealant from the oil pan bolts will affect the accuracy of the bolt tightening torque and could damage the block when the bolts are torqued.

40 Apply a 3.0 mm bead of RTV sealant to the oil pan flange so that the bead is around the inside edge of the bolt holes (see illustration).

➡**Note: The oil pan must be installed within four minutes of applying the sealant.**

41 Lift the oil pan into place and install (but do not tighten) all of the oil pan bolts.

42 Gradually and evenly tighten the oil pan bolts in the indicated sequence to the torque listed in this Chapter's Specifications (see illustration).

43 Installation is otherwise the reverse of removal. When installing the CKP sensor, make sure that you follow the procedure outlined in Chapter 6.

44 Let the RTV sealant set up approximately 12 hours before adding oil to the engine.

45 Install a new oil filter, lower the vehicle and refill the engine with oil (see Chapter 1).

46 Start the engine, allow it to warm up to its normal temperature, then check for signs of oil leaks.

13 Oil pump - removal, inspection and installation

➡**Note: If you are replacing the front oil seal only and not removing, inspecting, repairing or replacing the oil pump, the front oil seal can be replaced without oil pump removal as described in Section 14.**

2005 AND EARLIER MODELS

Removal

▶ **Refer to illustration 13.6**

1 Disconnect the negative battery cable (see Chapter 5).

2 Remove the under cover splash shield.

3 Remove the alternator (see Chapter 5). Remove the air conditioning compressor (without disconnecting the hoses) and secure it aside (see Chapter 3).

4 Remove the crankshaft pulley, water pump pulley, timing belt covers, timing belt, and crankshaft pulley hub (see Section 7). Remove the crankshaft sprocket using two prybars or screwdrivers placed behind the sprocket to apply even pressure on the sprocket to slide it off the crankshaft.

5 Remove the oil pan (see Section 12). Remove the oil pump strainer.

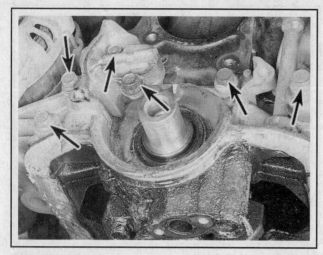

13.6 Remove the bolts (arrows) and separate the oil pump assembly from the engine block

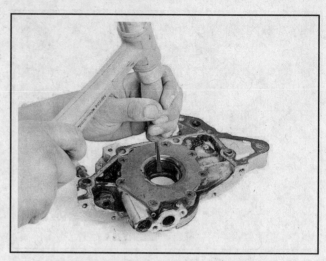

13.7 Remove the front oil seal using a screwdriver or punch - wrap the tool tip with tape to protect the oil pump bore

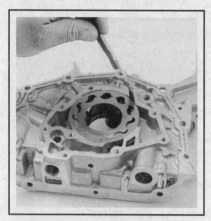

13.10a Measure the clearance between the oil pump driven rotor and the pump housing . . .

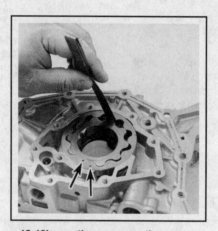

13.10b . . . then measure the clearance between the drive and driven rotor tips . . .

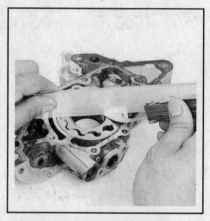

13.10c . . . using a straightedge, measure the endplay between the rotors and the pump housing

6   Remove the oil pump bolts/nuts from the engine block and separate the oil pump from the engine block (see illustration). You may have to pry carefully between the front main bearing cap and the pump housing with a screwdriver.

Inspection

◊ Refer to illustrations 13.7, 13.10a, 13.10b and 13.10c

7   Place the oil pump on a workbench. Note how far the oil seal is seated in the bore. Using a seal removal tool or a screwdriver taped or wrapped with a rag to protect the pump bore, remove the oil seal from the housing (see illustration).

✳✳ CAUTION:

Do not scratch the housing bore.

8   Remove the screws retaining the oil pump cover to the housing and remove the cover. Inspect the oil pump cover for distortion or damage.

9   Remove the oil pressure relief valve. Note or mark the direction of the components as installed, then remove the oil pump inner and outer rotors from the housing. Thoroughly clean all of the components in clean solvent.

10 Reinstall the oil pump inner and outer rotors into the oil pump housing (see illustrations) and measure the clearance of:

a) *The driven rotor-to-pump housing.*
b) *The drive rotor-to-driven rotor tips.*
c) *The rotor set-to-oil pump housing endplay.*

Compare your measurements to the clearance listed in this Chapter's Specifications.

11 Check the length of the oil pressure relief spring when removed from the oil pump. Compare the length measured with the free length listed in this Chapter's Specifications. Replace the spring if necessary.

12 Be sure the surfaces of the pump housing are clean and dry before reassembly.

13 Lightly coat the outer edge of a new oil seal with engine assembly lubricant or clean engine oil. Using a socket with an outside diameter slightly smaller than the outside diameter of the seal, carefully drive the new seal into place with a hammer. Make sure it's installed squarely

13.26 Remove the two bolts that secure the oil pump pickup tube

13.27 Remove the chain guide mounting bolts, the chain guide and the tensioner

13.28 Use a two-pin spanner to hold the oil pump sprocket, then remove the sprocket bolt

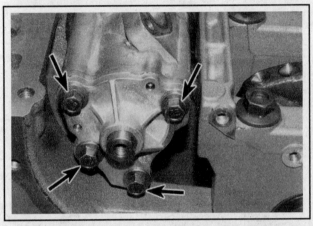

13.30 To remove the oil pump assembly, remove these four bolts

and driven in to the same depth as the original. If a socket is not available, a short section of large diameter pipe will also work. Apply engine assembly lubricant to the seal lip surface that contacts the crankshaft.

14 Lubricate the oil pressure relief valve piston with clean engine oil and reinstall the valve components into the pump case. Tighten the plug to the torque listed in this Chapter's Specifications.

15 Lubricate the rotor set with clean engine oil. Reinstall the rotors.

16 Pack the pump cavities with petroleum jelly (this will prime the pump and ensure good suction when the engine is started).

17 Install the cover, apply thread locking compound to the screw threads and tighten the screws securely.

18 Inspect the screen at the end of the oil pick-up tube for any debris that might plug it. Either clean the tube and screen completely or replace it with a new one at this time.

Installation

19 Use a scraper to remove all traces of gasket and sealant from the cover and engine block, then clean the mating surfaces with lacquer thinner or acetone.

20 Install new gasket with a thin coat of silicone sealant on the oil pump gasket surface. Reinstall the oil pump to the engine block.

➠**Note: Be sure the sealant doesn't plug or cover any oil passages.**

21 Install the bolts and tighten them to the torque listed in this

Chapter's Specifications.

22 Using a razor knife, trim the oil pump gasket flush with the oil pan sealing surface.

23 The remainder of installation is the reverse of the removal procedure.

2006 AND LATER MODELS

Removal

▶ **Refer to illustrations 13.26, 13.27, 13.28 and 13.30**

24 Remove the timing chain cover and timing chain (see Section 8).

25 Remove the oil pan (see Section 12).

26 Undo the two bolts securing the oil pump pick-up pipe to the pump (see illustration). Discard the O-ring/gasket.

27 Undo the two retaining bolts and remove the oil pump chain guide, then undo the retaining bolt and remove the oil pump chain tensioner (see illustration).

28 Hold the oil pump drive sprocket to prevent it from turning and slacken the sprocket retaining bolt (see illustration).

29 Undo the bolt and remove the oil pump sprocket complete with the oil pump drive chain.

30 Unbolt the pump from the cylinder block/crankcase (see illustration). Withdraw and discard the gasket.

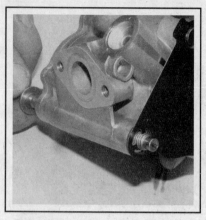

13.34 Use one of the oil pump mounting bolts to hold the new pump gasket in place

13.35 Install a new O-ring in the oil pump pick-up tube mounting flange

13.36 When installing the oil pump sprocket, align the flats on the oil pump sprocket with the flats on the oil pump driveshaft

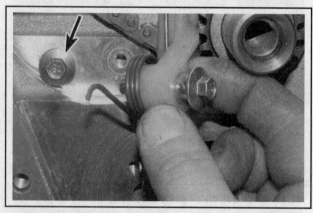

13.37 When installing the spring on the pump drive chain tensioner, make sure that the tensioner is hooked behind the bolt

Inspection

31 The pump is not rebuildable, so it should not be disassembled for inspection. If the pump is not functioning correctly, replace it.

Installation

▶ Refer to illustrations 13.34, 13.35, 13.36 and 13.37

32 Thoroughly clean and degrease all components, particularly the mating surfaces of the pump, the oil pan, and the cylinder block/crankcase. When using a scraper and solvent to remove all traces of old gasket/sealant from the mating surfaces, be careful to ensure that you do not scratch or damage the material of either component - any solvents used must be suitable for this application.

33 The oil pump must be primed on installation, by pouring clean engine oil into it, and rotating its inner rotor a few turns.

34 Fit the new gasket in place on the oil pump using one of the retaining bolts to locate it. Replace the pump to the cylinder block/crankcase and insert the retaining bolts, tightening them to the specified torque wrench setting (see illustration).

35 Fit the new O-ring/gasket in place and replace the pump pick-up pipe to the pump, tightening its retaining bolts securely (see illustration).

36 Install the oil pump drive chain complete with oil pump sprocket (see illustration) and tighten the retaining bolt to the specified torque setting. Hold the oil pump drive sprocket (using the same method as removal) to prevent it from turning when tightening the sprocket retaining bolt.

37 Install the oil pump chain tensioner to the cylinder block, making sure the spring is located correctly (see illustration). Tighten the retaining bolt securely.

38 Install the oil pump chain guide to the cylinder block and tighten the two retaining bolts securely.

39 Install the timing chain and timing chain cover (see Section 8).

40 Install the oil pan as described in Section 12.

14 Crankshaft front oil seal - replacement

2005 AND EARLIER MODELS

▶ Refer to illustrations 14.7 and 14.9

1 Disconnect the negative battery cable (see Chapter 5).
2 Remove the under cover splash shield.
3 Securely support the front of the vehicle on jackstands, and remove the front passenger side tire for access to the front cover.

4 Remove the crankshaft pulley, timing belt covers, timing belt, and crankshaft pulley hub (see Section 7).
5 Remove the crankshaft sprocket using two prybars or screwdrivers placed behind the gear to apply even pressure on the gear to slide it off the crankshaft.
6 Cut completely around the front oil seal lip with a razor knife, be careful not to damage the crankshaft sealing surface.
7 Note how far the seal is seated in the bore and the direction

14.7 Before removal of the old oil seal, note how far the seal is seated in the bore and the direction the oil seal lip faces. Remove the front oil seal with a screwdriver taped or wrapped with a rag to protect the crankshaft surface and engine block

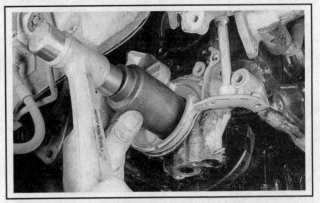

14.9 With the oil seal lips facing the correct direction as when removed, press the oil seal partially into place by hand. Using a seal driver or a large socket to fit the seal, tap the seal into the bore until it is flush with the face of the oil pump body, as noted before removal

the oil seal lip faces (the oil seal should be flush with the face of the oil pump body). Remove the front oil seal with a screwdriver taped or wrapped with a rag to protect the crankshaft surface and engine block (see illustration).

8   Clean the bore in the engine block and clean the crankshaft surface. Coat the outside of the new front oil seal with engine oil. Apply engine assembly lubricant or clean engine oil to the seal lip.

9   Press the oil seal in slightly by hand, with the oil seal lip facing the same direction as removed. Using a seal driver or a socket with an outside diameter slightly smaller than the outside diameter of the front oil seal, carefully tap the new seal into place with a hammer (see illustration) until the oil seal is flush with the face of the oil pump body. Make sure the oil seal is installed squarely.

10   Reinstall the crankshaft sprocket and timing belt (see Section 7).

11 The remainder of the installation is the reverse of the removal procedure.

12 Run the engine and check for oil leaks at the front oil seal.

2006 AND LATER MODELS

13 Remove the timing chain cover (see Section 8).

14 With the timing chain cover lying flat on a clean work bench, carefully pry out the seal with a seal removal tool or with a small screwdriver. Be careful not to gouge or scratch the aluminum timing cover.

15 Make sure that the seal bore is clean, then use a seal driver or a socket with the same outside diameter as the seal's outside diameter and carefully drive the seal into the bore (see illustration 14.9).

16 Install the timing chain cover.

---

15 Flywheel/driveplate - removal and installation

REMOVAL

▶ **Refer to illustration 15.3**

1   Raise the vehicle and support it securely on jackstands, then refer to Chapter 7 and remove the transmission.

2   If you're working on a model with a manual transmission, remove the clutch cover and clutch disc (see Chapter 8). Now is a good time to check/replace the clutch components and pilot bearing.

3   Use a center-punch or paint to make alignment marks on the flywheel/driveplate and engine rear plate to ensure correct reinstallation alignment later (see illustration).

4   Remove the bolts that secure the flywheel/driveplate to the crankshaft (see illustration 15.3). If the crankshaft turns, wedge a screwdriver in the ring gear teeth to jam the flywheel.

➡**Note:** Don't turn the crankshaft with the flywheel/driveplate removed, or you'll lose the alignment of flywheel to crankshaft. If you must turn the crankshaft (or if you're going to remove it), punch alignment marks on the flywheel and the rear end of the crankshaft near one of the bolt holes after removing the flywheel. This will allow the flywheel/driveplate to be realigned with the crankshaft.

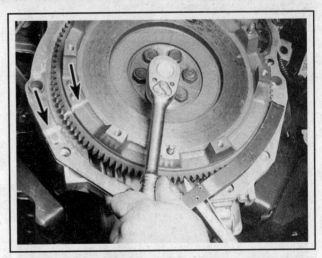

15.3 Marking the flywheel/driveplate and the rear plate (arrows) will preserve the alignment of flywheel and crankshaft as long as the crankshaft isn't turned; if you're going to turn the crankshaft, mark the flywheel and crankshaft near one of the bolt holes

5   Remove the flywheel/driveplate from the crankshaft. On the automatic transmission models, also remove the driveplate backing plate and adapter, taking note which sides of the driveplate the adapter plates are mounted on for correct reinstallation later. Since the flywheel is fairly heavy, be sure to support it while removing the last bolt.

6   Clean the flywheel to remove grease and oil. Inspect the surface for cracks, rivet grooves, burned areas and score marks. Light scoring can be removed with emery cloth. Check for cracked and broken ring gear teeth. Lay the flywheel on a flat surface and use a straightedge to check for warpage. If necessary, take the flywheel to an automotive machine shop to have it resurfaced.

7   Clean and inspect the mating surfaces of the flywheel/driveplate and the crankshaft. If the crankshaft rear seal is leaking, replace it before reinstalling the flywheel/driveplate (see Section 16).

INSTALLATION

8   Remove any thread sealant from the crankshaft flywheel bolt

holes and bolts.

> ❋❋ **CAUTION:**

If all the thread sealant cannot be removed from a bolt, replace that bolt. Do not apply new sealant when installing a new bolt.

9   For manual transmission models, position the flywheel at the crankshaft. For automatic transmission models, position the adapter, driveplate, and backing plate at the crankshaft. Be sure to align the marks made during removal. Before installing the bolts, apply thread sealant to the threads of any reused bolts, but not to new bolts.

10 Wedge a screwdriver in the ring gear teeth to keep the flywheel/driveplate from turning as you tighten the bolts to the torque listed in this Chapter's Specifications. Follow a criss-cross pattern and work up to the final torque in three or four steps.

11 The remainder of installation is the reverse of the removal procedure.

16 Rear main oil seal - replacement

2005 AND EARLIER MODELS

▶ **Refer to illustrations 16.4 and 16.5**

1   The transmission must be removed from the vehicle for this procedure (see Chapter 7).

2   Remove the flywheel/driveplate (see Section 15).

3   Cut completely around the rear main oil seal lip with a razor knife, be careful not to damage the crankshaft sealing surface.

4   Pry out the old seal with a screwdriver taped or wrapped in a rag, or use a seal removal tool to pry the seal out (see illustration).

5   Apply engine oil to the crankshaft seal journal and to the lip of the new seal. Carefully push the new seal part way into place by hand. Carefully tap into place using a flat punch, large socket, or a suitable short pipe or tubing of the correct diameter until the oil seal is flush with the edge of the rear cover (see illustration).

6   Reinstall the flywheel/driveplate (see Section 15).

7   The remaining steps are the reverse of removal.

2006 AND LATER MODELS

▶ **Refer to illustration 16.18**

8   Remove the transmission (see Chapter 7).

9   Remove the flywheel (see Section 15).

10 Remove the rear main seal housing bolts and remove the housing.

11 Wipe off the seal housing, lay it flat on a clean work bench surface and carefully pry out the old seal.

12 Using a small clean block of wood, carefully tap the new seal into the housing.

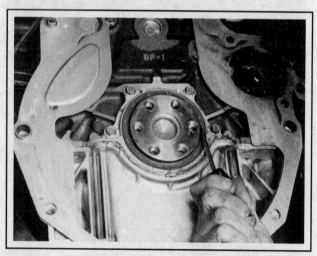

16.4 **The quick way to replace the rear main oil seal is to simply pry the old one out . . .**

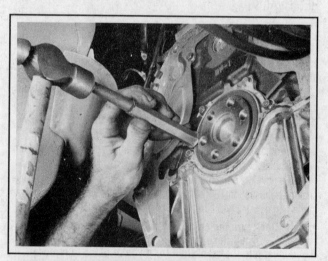

16.5 **. . . then lubricate the crankshaft journal and the lip of the new seal with engine oil and tap the new seal into place - the seal lip is stiff and can be easily damaged during installation if you're not careful**

13 Clean the mating surface for the seal housing on the cylinder block and the crankshaft. Carefully remove and polish any burrs or raised edges on the crankshaft that may have caused the seal to fail.

14 Lightly coat the inside lip of the new seal with clean engine oil. Then use a thin (but durable) two-inch wide plastic strip (or a two-liter plastic beverage bottle cut to size) around the inside circumference of the seal to act as a liner for installation.

15 With the plastic seal liner in place, carefully push the new rear seal and housing into position by sliding it onto the contact surface of the crankshaft.

16 Install the rear main seal housing bolts and finger tighten them while holding the housing in place.

17 Carefully remove the plastic liner or bottle so that the new seal contacts the crankshaft mating surface correctly.

18 Gradually and evenly tighten the rear main seal housing bolts in the indicated sequence (see illustration) to the torque listed in this Chapter's Specifications.

19 Installation is otherwise the reverse of removal.

20 Start the engine and check for signs of oil leakage.

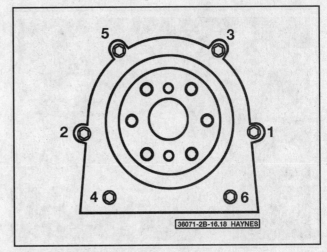

16.18 Tighten the rear main seal housing bolts in the indicated sequence

17 Engine mounts - check and replacement

1 Engine mounts seldom require attention, but broken or deteriorated mounts should be replaced immediately or the added strain placed on the driveline components may cause damage or wear.

❋❋ WARNING:

Do not remove any engine mounts or components of engine mounts if the engine is not properly supported as described. DO NOT place any part of your body directly under the engine when performing engine mount work and when the engine is supported only by a jack!

CHECK

◆ Refer to illustration 17.5

2 During the check, the engine must be raised slightly to remove the weight from the mounts.

3 Raise the vehicle and support it securely on jackstands, then position a jack with a block of wood under the engine oil pan or use an engine support fixture from above. Carefully raise the engine just enough to take the weight off the mounts.

❋❋ WARNING:

DO NOT place any part of your body under the engine when it's supported only by a jack! Support the engine just enough to take the weight off the engine mounts but without lifting the weight of the car from the jackstands.

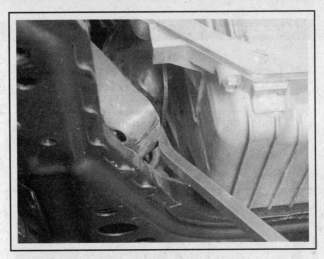

17.5 Pry between the inner and outer parts of the engine mount to check for movement

4 Check the mounts to see if the rubber is cracked, hardened or separated from the metal portion. Occasionally, the rubber will split down the center.

5 Check for relative movement between the mounts and the engine or frame, using a large screwdriver or prybar to attempt to move the mounts (see illustration). If movement is noted, lower the engine and tighten the mount fasteners.

6 Rubber preservative liquid, available from any automotive parts store, should be applied to the engine mounts (and other chassis rubber components) to help protect from deterioration.

17.8a The engine mount on each side is secured to the frame by a nut

17.8b The inner section of the mount is bolted to the engine block

REPLACEMENT

▶ **Refer to illustrations 17.8a and 17.8b**

7 Disconnect the negative battery cable from the battery, then raise the vehicle and support it securely on jackstands (if not already done). Support the engine as described in Step 3.

8 Replace the engine mounts as follows:

   a) *Remove the engine mount stud nuts to detach from the rubber mount from the mount bracket (see illustration).*
   b) *Unbolt the engine mounts from the engine block (see illustration).*
   c) *Reinstall the engine mounts by reversing the removal steps.*
   d) *Tighten all bolts/nuts securely.*

Specifications

General

Firing order	1-3-4-2

Timing belt (2005 and earlier models*)

Timing belt deflection	0.35 to 0.45 inches
* 2006 and later models have a timing chain	

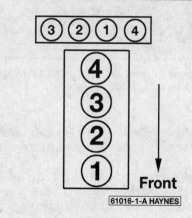

1990 and 1991

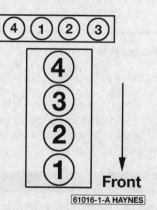

1992 and later

Cylinder and coil terminal location

Camshaft and lifters

Lobe height
    1993 and earlier   1.6019 inches minimum
    1994 through 1997
        Intake   1.7281 inches minimum
        Exhaust   1.7480 inches minimum
    1999 through 2005
        Intake   1.736 inches minimum
        Exhaust   1.760 inches minimum
    2006 and later
        With variable valve timing
            Intake   1.666 inches minimum
            Exhaust   1.616 inches minimum
        Without variable valve timing
            Intake   1.653 inches minimum
            Exhaust   1.612 inches minimum
Journal diameter
    1997 and earlier   1.0213 inches minimum
    1999 through 2005   1.0201 inches minimum
    2006 and later   0.982 inch minimum
Out-of-round limit   0.0012 inch maximum
Journal oil clearance
    2005 and earlier   0.0060 inch maximum
    2006 and later   0.0035 inch maximum
Endplay
    2005 and earlier   0.0080 inch maximum
    2006 and later   0.0098 inch maximum
Lifters
    Lifter diameter
        2005 and earlier   1.1795 to 1.1801 inches
        2006 and later   1.2193 to 1.2196 inches
    Lifter-to-bore clearance
        2005 and earlier   0.0071 inch maximum
        2006 and later   0.006 inch maximum
    Lifter-to-cam lobe clearance
        1997 and earlier   0.0059 inch maximum
        1999 and later   See Chapter 1 for valve clearance adjustment

Oil pump

2005 and earlier
    Driven rotor-to-housing clearance   0.087 inch maximum
    Drive rotor-to-driven rotor clearance   0.0079 inch maximum
    Rotor set-to-housing clearance (endplay)   0.0055 inch maximum
    Oil pump relief valve spring free length
        1992 and earlier   1.791 inches minimum
        1993 through 1997   1.809 inches minimum
        1999 through 2005   N/A
2006 and later   N/A (pump is not rebuildable)

➡Note: One foot-pound (ft-lb) of torque is equivalent to 12 inch-pounds (in-lbs) of torque. Torque values below approximately 15 foot-pounds are expressed in inch-pounds, because most foot-pound torque wrenches are not accurate at these smaller values.

2005 and earlier

Timing belt tensioner bolt	27 to 38
Timing belt idler pulley bolt	27 to 38
Timing belt cover bolts	69 to 95 in-lbs
Valve cover bolts	43 to 78 in-lbs
Camshaft bearing cap bolts	100 to 125 in-lbs
Camshaft seal plate bolts	69 to 95 in-lbs
Camshaft sprocket bolts	37 to 44
Crankshaft pulley bolts	109 to 151 in-lbs
Crankshaft sprocket bolt	
1990	80 to 87
1991 through 2005	116 to 122
Cylinder head bolts	56 to 60
End plate bolts	70 to 95 in-lbs
Exhaust manifold bolts/nuts	29 to 33
Exhaust manifold heat shield bolts/nuts	70 to 95 in-lbs
Exhaust pipe bracket bolts	47 to 66
Flywheel/driveplate bolts	71 to 75
Intake manifold bolts	14 to 18
Intake manifold bracket bolts	28 to 38
Oil pan-to-engine block bolts	70 to 95 in-lbs
Oil pump bolts	14 to 19
Oil pump strainer	70 to 95 in-lbs
Water pump pulley	70 to 95 in-lbs

2006 and later

Camshaft bearing cap bolts	
Step 1	44 to 80 in-lbs
Step 2	120 to 156 in-lbs
Crankshaft pulley/timing chain sprocket bolt	
Step 1	71 to 77
Step 2	Tighten an additional 87 to 93 degrees
Cylinder head bolts	
Step 1	44 in-lbs
Step 2	120 to 156 in-!bs
Step 3	33 to 34
Step 4	Tighten an additional 90 degrees (1/4-turn)
Step 5	Tighten an additional 90 degrees (1/4-turn)
Drivebelt idler pulley bolt	131 to 195 in-lbs
Exhaust manifold nuts	32 to 47
Intake manifold assembly	
Plenum/intake runner bolts	144 to 168 in-lbs
Intake manifold bolts	12 to 18
Oil cooler and oil filter adapter assembly	
Oil cooler bolt	25 to 29
Oil filter adapter bolts	15 to 22

➡Note: One foot-pound (ft-lb) of torque is equivalent to 12 inch-pounds (in-lbs) of torque. Torque values below approximately 15 foot-pounds are expressed in inch-pounds, because most foot-pound torque wrenches are not accurate at these smaller values.

2006 and later (continued)

Oil pan bolts	
Oil pan-to-engine bolts	13 to 17
Oil pan-to-transmission bolts	28 to 38
Oil pump chain tensioner bolts	71 to 102 in-lbs
Oil pump chain guide bolts	71 to 102 in-lbs
Oil pump sprocket bolt	15 to 22
Timing chain cover bolts	
18 shorter bolts	71 to 102 in-lbs
Four longer bolts	30 to 41 in-lbs
Timing chain guide bolts	71 to 102 in-lbs
Valve cover bolts	71 to 93 in-lbs
Variable valve timing actuator bolt	51 to 55
Water pump pulley bolts	15 to 19

Notes

Section

Reference to other Chapters

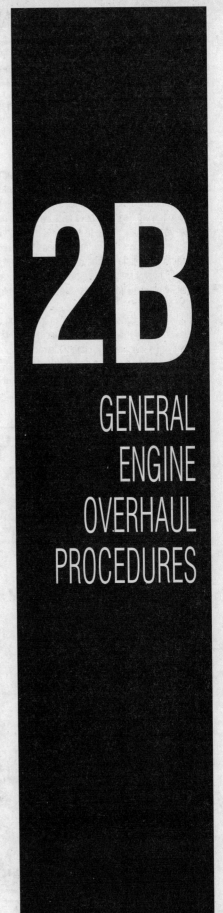

2B

GENERAL ENGINE OVERHAUL PROCEDURES

1 General information - engine overhaul

▶ **Refer to illustrations 1.1, 1.2, 1.3, 1.4, 1.5 and 1.6**

Included in this portion of Chapter 2 are general information and diagnostic testing procedures for determining the overall mechanical condition of your engine.

The information ranges from advice concerning preparation for an overhaul and the purchase of replacement parts and/or components to detailed, step-by-step procedures covering removal and installation.

The following Sections have been written to help you determine whether your engine needs to be overhauled and how to remove and install it once you've determined it needs to be rebuilt. For information concerning in-vehicle engine repair, see Chapter 2A.

It's not always easy to determine when, or if, an engine should be completely overhauled, because a number of factors must be considered.

High mileage is not necessarily an indication that an overhaul is needed, while low mileage doesn't preclude the need for an overhaul. Frequency of servicing is probably the most important consideration. An engine that's had regular and frequent oil and filter changes, as well as other required maintenance, will most likely give many thousands of miles of reliable service. Conversely, a neglected engine may require an overhaul very early in its service life.

Excessive oil consumption is an indication that piston rings, valve seals and/or valve guides are in need of attention. Make sure that oil leaks aren't responsible before deciding that the rings and/or guides are bad. Perform a cylinder compression check to determine the extent of the work required (see Section 3). Also check the vacuum readings under various conditions (see Section 4).

Check the oil pressure with a gauge installed in place of the oil pressure sending unit and compare it to this Chapter's Specifications (see Section 2). If it's extremely low, the bearings and/or oil pump are probably worn out.

Loss of power, rough running, knocking or metallic engine noises, excessive valve train noise and high fuel consumption rates may also point to the need for an overhaul, especially if they're all present at the same time. If a complete tune-up doesn't remedy the situation, major mechanical work is the only solution.

An engine overhaul involves restoring the internal parts to the specifications of a new engine. During an overhaul, the piston rings are replaced and the cylinder walls are reconditioned (rebored and/or honed) (see illustrations 1.1 and 1.2). If a rebore is done by an automotive machine shop, new oversize pistons will also be installed. The main

1.1 An engine block being bored - an engine rebuilder will use special machinery to recondition the cylinder bores

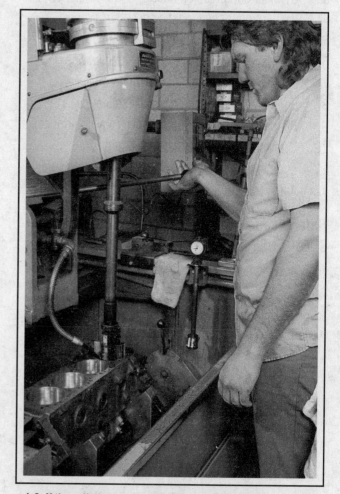

1.2 If the cylinders are bored, the machine shop will normally hone the engine on a machine like this

1.3 A crankshaft having a main bearing journal ground

1.4 A machinist checks for a bent connecting rod, using specialized equipment

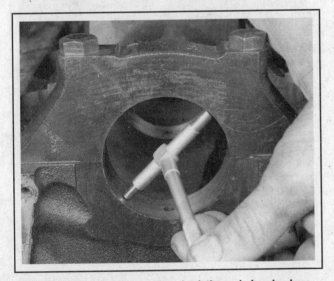

1.5 A bore gauge being used to check the main bearing bore

1.6 Uneven piston wear like this indicates a bent connecting rod

bearings and connecting rod bearings are generally replaced with new ones and, if necessary, the crankshaft may be reground to restore the journals (see illustration 1.3). Generally, the valves are serviced as well, since they're usually in less-than-perfect condition at this point. While the engine is being overhauled, other components, such as the starter and alternator, can be rebuilt as well. The end result should be a like-new engine that will give many trouble-free miles.

➡Note: Critical cooling system components such as the hoses, drivebelts, thermostat and water pump should be replaced with new parts when an engine is overhauled. The radiator should be checked carefully to ensure that it isn't clogged or leaking (see Chapter 3). If you purchase a rebuilt engine or short block, some rebuilders will not warranty their engines unless the radiator has been professionally flushed. Also, we don't recommend overhauling the oil pump - always install a new one when an engine is rebuilt.

Overhauling the internal components on today's engines is a difficult and time-consuming task that requires a significant amount of specialty tools and is best left to a professional engine rebuilder (see illustrations 1.4, 1.5 and 1.6). A competent engine rebuilder will handle the inspection of your old parts and offer advice concerning the reconditioning or replacement of the original engine. Never purchase parts or have machine work done on other components until the block has been thoroughly inspected by a professional machine shop. As a general rule, time is the primary cost of an overhaul, especially since the vehicle may be tied up for a minimum of two weeks or more. Be aware that some engine builders only have the capability to rebuild the engine you bring them while other rebuilders have a large inventory of rebuilt exchange engines in stock. Also be aware that many machine shops could take as much as two weeks time to completely rebuild your engine depending on shop workload. Sometimes it makes more sense to simply exchange your engine for another engine that's already rebuilt to save time.

2 Oil pressure check

▶ **Refer to illustrations 2.2a and 2.2b**

1   Low engine oil pressure can be a sign of an engine in need of rebuilding. A "low oil pressure" indicator (often called an "idiot light") is not a test of the oiling system. Such indicators only come on when the oil pressure is dangerously low. Even a factory oil pressure gauge in the instrument panel is only a relative indication, although much better for driver information than a warning light. A better test is with a mechanical (not electrical) oil pressure gauge.

2   Locate the oil pressure sending unit on the engine block:

a) On 1.6L and 1.8L engines, the oil pressure sending unit is located on the right side of the engine block, between the oil filter and the starter motor (see illustration).

b) On 2.0L engines, the oil pressure sending unit is located on the left side of the engine block, to the rear of the oil filter (see illustration).

3   Unscrew and remove the oil pressure sending unit and screw in the hose for your oil pressure gauge. If necessary, install an adapter fitting. Use Teflon tape or thread sealant on the threads of the adapter and/or the fitting on the end of your gauge's hose.

4   Connect a tachometer to the engine, according to the tachometer manufacturer's instructions.

5   Check the oil pressure with the engine running (normal operating temperature) at the specified engine speed, and compare it to this Chapter's Specifications. If it's extremely low, the bearings and/or oil pump are probably worn out.

2.2a On 1.6L and 1.8L engines, the oil pressure sending unit is located on the right side of the engine block, between the oil filter and the starter motor

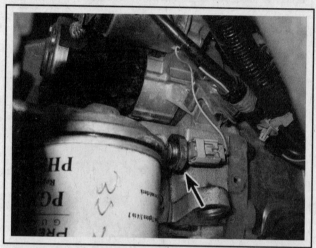

2.2b On 2.0L engines, the oil pressure sending unit is located on the left side of the engine block, to the rear of the oil filter

3 Cylinder compression check

▶ **Refer to illustration 3.6**

1   A compression check will tell you what mechanical condition the upper end of your engine (pistons, rings, valves, head gaskets) is in. Specifically, it can tell you if the compression is down due to leakage caused by worn piston rings, defective valves and seats or a blown head gasket.

➡**Note: The engine must be at normal operating temperature and the battery must be fully charged for this check.**

2   Disable the ignition system by unplugging the primary electrical connector from the electrical connector(s) from the ignition coil(s) (see Chapter 5). Also, disable the fuel system as described in Chapter 4, Section 2.

3   Clean the area around the spark plugs before you remove them (compressed air should be used, if available). The idea is to prevent dirt from getting into the cylinders as the compression check is being done.

4   Remove all of the spark plugs from the engine (see Chapter 1).

5   Block the throttle wide open.

6   Install a compression gauge in the spark plug hole (see illustration).

7   Crank the engine over at least seven compression strokes and watch the gauge. The compression should build up quickly in a healthy engine. Low compression on the first stroke, followed by gradually increasing pressure on successive strokes, indicates worn piston rings. A low compression reading on the first stroke, which doesn't build up during successive strokes, indicates leaking valves or a blown head gasket (a cracked head could also be the cause). Deposits on the undersides of the valve heads can also cause low compression. Record the highest gauge reading obtained.

8   Repeat the procedure for the remaining cylinders and compare the results to this Chapter's Specifications.

9   If the compression is lower than specified on any cylinder, add some engine oil (about three squirts from a plunger-type oil can) to that cylinder, through the spark plug hole, and repeat the test.

10 If the compression increases after the oil is added, the piston rings are definitely worn. If the compression doesn't increase significantly, the leakage is occurring at the valves or head gasket. Leakage past the valves may be caused by burned valve seats and/or faces or warped, cracked or bent valves.

11 If two adjacent cylinders have equally low compression, there's a strong possibility that the head gasket between them is blown. The appearance of coolant in the combustion chambers or the crankcase would verify this condition.

12 If one cylinder is slightly lower than the others, and the engine has a slightly rough idle, a worn lobe on the camshaft could be the cause.

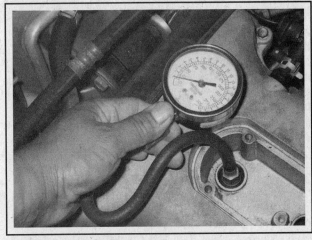

3.6 Use a compression gauge with a threaded fitting for the spark plug hole, not the type that requires hand pressure to maintain the seal

13 If the compression is unusually high, the combustion chambers are probably coated with carbon deposits. If that's the case, the cylinder head(s) should be removed and decarbonized.

14 If compression is way down or varies greatly between cylinders, it would be a good idea to have a leak-down test performed by an automotive repair shop. This test will pinpoint exactly where the leakage is occurring and how severe it is.

4   Vacuum gauge diagnostic checks

◆ **Refer to illustrations 4.4 and 4.6**

1   A vacuum gauge provides inexpensive but valuable information about what is going on in the engine. You can check for worn rings or cylinder walls, leaking head or intake manifold gaskets, restricted exhaust, stuck or burned valves, weak valve springs, improper ignition or valve timing and ignition problems.

2   Unfortunately, vacuum gauge readings are easy to misinterpret, so they should be used in conjunction with other tests to confirm the diagnosis.

3   Both the absolute readings and the rate of needle movement are important for accurate interpretation. Most gauges measure vacuum in inches of mercury (in-Hg). The following references to vacuum assume the diagnosis is being performed at sea level. As elevation increases (or atmospheric pressure decreases), the reading will decrease. For every 1,000 foot increase in elevation above approximately 2,000 feet, the gauge readings will decrease about one inch of mercury.

4   Connect the vacuum gauge directly to the intake manifold vacuum, not to ported (throttle body) vacuum (see illustration). Be sure no hoses are left disconnected during the test or false readings will result.

5   Before you begin the test, allow the engine to warm up completely. Block the wheels and set the parking brake. With the transaxle in Park, start the engine and allow it to run at normal idle speed.

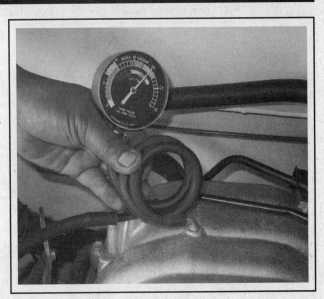

4.4 A simple vacuum gauge can be handy in diagnosing engine condition and performance

❊❊ WARNING:

Keep your hands and the vacuum gauge clear of the fans.

6   Read the vacuum gauge; an average, healthy engine should normally produce about 17 to 22 in-Hg with a fairly steady needle (see illustration). Refer to the following vacuum gauge readings and what they indicate about the engine's condition:

7   A low steady reading usually indicates a leaking gasket between the intake manifold and cylinder head(s) or throttle body, a leaky vacuum hose, late ignition timing or incorrect camshaft timing. Check ignition timing with a timing light and eliminate all other possible causes, utilizing the tests provided in this Chapter before you remove the timing chain cover to check the timing marks.

8   If the reading is three to eight inches below normal and it fluctuates at that low reading, suspect an intake manifold gasket leak at an intake port or a faulty fuel injector.

9   If the needle has regular drops of about two-to-four inches at a steady rate, the valves are probably leaking. Perform a compression check or leak-down test to confirm this.

10 An irregular drop or down-flick of the needle can be caused by a sticking valve or an ignition misfire. Perform a compression check or leak-down test and read the spark plugs.

11 A rapid vibration of about four in-Hg vibration at idle combined with exhaust smoke indicates worn valve guides. Perform a leak-down test to confirm this. If the rapid vibration occurs with an increase in engine speed, check for a leaking intake manifold gasket or head gasket, weak valve springs, burned valves or ignition misfire.

12 A slight fluctuation, say one inch up and down, may mean ignition problems. Check all the usual tune-up items and, if necessary, run the engine on an ignition analyzer.

13 If there is a large fluctuation, perform a compression or leak-down test to look for a weak or dead cylinder or a blown head gasket.

14 If the needle moves slowly through a wide range, check for a clogged PCV system, incorrect idle fuel mixture, throttle body or intake manifold gasket leaks.

15 Check for a slow return after revving the engine by quickly snapping the throttle open until the engine reaches about 2,500 rpm and let it shut. Normally the reading should drop to near zero, rise above normal idle reading (about 5 in-Hg over) and return to the previous idle reading. If the vacuum returns slowly and doesn't peak when the throttle is snapped shut, the rings may be worn. If there is a long delay, look for a restricted exhaust system (often the muffler or catalytic converter). An easy way to check this is to temporarily disconnect the exhaust ahead of the suspected part and redo the test.

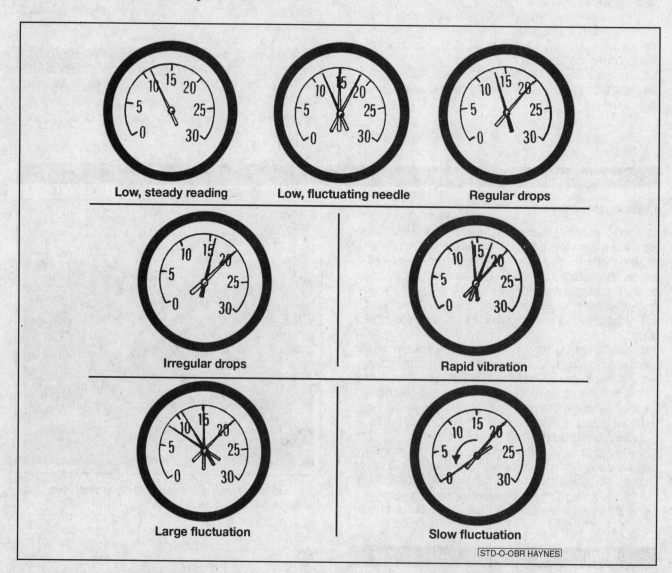

Low, steady reading   Low, fluctuating needle   Regular drops

Irregular drops   Rapid vibration

Large fluctuation   Slow fluctuation

STD-O-OBR HAYNES

4.6 Typical vacuum gauge readings

5   Engine rebuilding alternatives

The do-it-yourselfer is faced with a number of options when purchasing a rebuilt engine. The major considerations are cost, warranty, parts availability and the time required for the rebuilder to complete the project. The decision to replace the engine block, piston/connecting rod assemblies and crankshaft depends on the final inspection results of your engine. Only then can you make a cost effective decision whether to have your engine overhauled or simply purchase an exchange engine for your vehicle.

Some of the rebuilding alternatives include:

Individual parts - If the inspection procedures reveal that the engine block and most engine components are in reusable condition, purchasing individual parts and having a rebuilder rebuild your engine may be the most economical alternative. The block, crankshaft and piston/connecting rod assemblies should all be inspected carefully by a machine shop first.

Short block - A short block consists of an engine block with a crankshaft and piston/connecting rod assemblies already installed. All new bearings are incorporated and all clearances will be correct. The existing camshafts, valve train components, cylinder head and external parts can be bolted to the short block with little or no machine shop work necessary.

Long block - A long block consists of a short block plus an oil pump, oil pan, cylinder head, valve cover, camshaft and valve train components, timing sprockets and belt and timing cover. All components are installed with new bearings, seals and gaskets incorporated throughout. The installation of manifolds and external parts is all that's necessary.

Low mileage used engines - Some companies now offer low mileage used engines which is a very cost effective way to get your vehicle up and running again. These engines often come from vehicles which have been in totaled in accidents or come from other countries which have a higher vehicle turn over rate. A low mileage used engine also usually has a similar warranty like the newly remanufactured engines.

Give careful thought to which alternative is best for you and discuss the situation with local automotive machine shops, auto parts dealers and experienced rebuilders before ordering or purchasing replacement parts.

6   Engine removal - methods and precautions

▶ **Refer to illustrations 6.1, 6.2, 6.3 and 6.4**

✳✳ WARNING:

On 2006 and later models, the engine is removed from the bottom of the engine compartment, along with the transmission and crossmember, by raising the vehicle sufficiently to slide the assembly out; this procedure requires the use of a vehicle hoist. Only begin this procedure if all of the necessary equipment is at hand. With only a floor jack and jackstands, the vehicle can't safely be raised high enough for the engine/transmission/crossmember to slide out from underneath.

If you've decided that an engine must be removed for overhaul or major repair work, several preliminary steps should be taken. Read all removal and installation procedures carefully prior to committing to this job.

Locating a suitable place to work is extremely important. Adequate work space, along with storage space for the vehicle, will be needed. If a shop or garage isn't available, at the very least a flat, level, clean work surface made of concrete or asphalt is required.

Cleaning the engine compartment and engine before beginning the removal procedure will help keep tools clean and organized (see illustrations 6.1 and 6.2).

An engine hoist will also be necessary. Make sure the hoist is rated

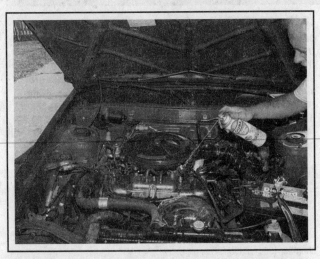

6.1 After tightly wrapping water-vulnerable components, use a spray cleaner on everything, with particular concentration on the greasiest areas, usually around the valve cover and lower edges of the block. If one section dries out, apply more cleaner

6.2 Depending on how dirty the engine is, let the cleaner soak in according to the directions and hose off the grime and cleaner. Get the rinse water down into every area you can get at; then dry important components with a hair dryer or paper towels

in excess of the combined weight of the engine and transaxle. Safety is of primary importance, considering the potential hazards involved in removing the engine from the vehicle.

If you're a novice at engine removal, get at least one helper. One person cannot easily do all the things you need to do to remove a big heavy engine and transaxle assembly from the engine compartment. Also helpful is to seek advice and assistance from someone who's experienced in engine removal.

Plan the operation ahead of time. Arrange for or obtain all of the tools and equipment you'll need prior to beginning the job (see illustrations 6.3 and 6.4). Some of the equipment necessary to perform engine removal and installation safely and with relative ease are (in addition to a vehicle hoist) a heavy duty floor jack (preferably fitted with a transaxle jack head adapter), complete sets of wrenches and sockets as described in the front of this manual, wooden blocks, plenty of rags and cleaning solvent for mopping up spilled oil, coolant and gasoline.

Plan for the vehicle to be out of use for quite a while. A machine shop can do the work that is beyond the scope of the home mechanic. Machine shops often have a busy schedule, so before removing the engine, consult the shop for an estimate of how long it will take to rebuild or repair the components that may need work.

6.3 Get an engine stand sturdy enough to firmly support the engine while you're working on it. Stay away from three-wheeled models; they have a tendency to tip over more easily, so get a four-wheeled unit.

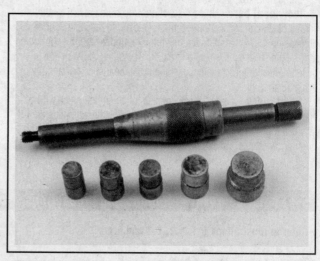

6.4 A clutch alignment tool is necessary if you plan to install a rebuilt engine mated to a manual transaxle

7 Engine - removal and installation

✳✳ WARNING:

These models are equipped with airbags. The airbag is armed and can deploy (inflate) anytime the battery is connected. To prevent accidental deployment (and possible injury), turn the ignition key to LOCK and disconnect the negative battery cable whenever working near airbag components. After the battery is disconnected, wait at least two minutes before beginning work (the system has a back-up capacitor that must fully discharge). See Chapter 12 for more information.

2005 AND EARLIER MODELS

♦ Refer to illustrations 7.21 and 7.22

✳✳ WARNING:

The engine must be completely cool before beginning this procedure.

➡Note: Read through the entire Section before beginning this procedure. The factory recommends removing the engine and transmission from the top as a unit, then separating the engine from the transmission on the shop floor; however, our experience was that the engine can be removed separately. To provide enough clearance at the front of the engine for separate removal, engine-mounted accessories, as well as the radiator, must be removed. Since the engine will have to be tilted up at the front during removal, an engine tilter device on the hoist will be helpful.

Removal

1 Relieve the fuel system pressure (see Chapter 4).
2 Disconnect the negative cable from the battery (see Chapter 5).
3 Place protective covers on the fenders and cowl.
4 Remove the air cleaner housing assembly and the resonance chamber (see Chapter 4).
5 Disconnect the accelerator cable (see Chapter 4).
6 Disconnect the cruise control cable, if equipped, from the throttle body.
7 Remove the drivebelts (see Chapter 1).

8   On power steering-equipped vehicles, unbolt the power steering pump. If clearance allows, tie the pump aside without disconnecting the hoses. If necessary, remove the pump (see Chapter 10).

9   Remove the alternator (see Chapter 5), water pump pulley (see Chapter 3) and crankshaft pulley (see Chapter 2A).

10 Remove the hood.

11 Raise the vehicle and support it securely on jackstands.

12 Remove the engine undercover to provide access to the bottom of the engine, then, on automatic transmission models, remove the driveplate-to-torque converter bolts (see Chapter 7B).

13 Remove the starter motor (see Chapter 5).

14 On air-conditioned models, unbolt the compressor and set it aside. Do not disconnect the refrigerant hoses.

➡Note: Wire the compressor out of the way with a coat hanger; don't let the compressor hang on the hoses.

15 Disconnect the exhaust pipe from the exhaust manifold.

16 Drain the cooling system and engine oil (see Chapter 1).

17 Lower the vehicle.

18 Disconnect the heater hoses.

19 Remove the cooling fan(s), the radiator hoses and the radiator (see Chapter 3).

20 Detach the fuel feed and return lines from the fuel rail. Plug or cap all open fittings.

21 Clearly label, then disconnect all vacuum lines, coolant and emissions hoses, wiring harness connectors, ground straps and fuel lines. Masking tape and/or a touch up paint applicator work well for marking items (see illustration). Take instant photos or sketch the locations of components and brackets.

22 Attach a lifting chain or sling to the engine. Position a hoist and connect the sling to it. Take up the slack until there is slight tension on the hoist (see illustration).

23 Recheck to be sure nothing except the mounts are still connecting the engine to the vehicle or to the transmission. Disconnect and label anything still remaining.

24 Support the front of the transmission with a floor jack. Place a block of wood on the jack head to prevent damage to the transmission. Remove the transmission-to-engine bolts, then disconnect the engine mounts (see Chapter 2A).

❋❋ WARNING:

Do not place any part of your body under the engine/transmission when it's supported only by a hoist or other lifting device.

➡Note: Some transmission-to-engine bolts are very hard to remove from the top or bottom. It will probably be necessary to use flexible sockets and a long extension on a ratchet.

25 Lift the engine up slightly, then move it forward to separate it from the transmission. If it does not move forward easily, check to be sure all transmission-to-engine bolts are removed. It may help to pry the engine loose from the transmission with a prybar. Also, it will be necessary to tilt the engine up at the front to provide enough clearance. When the engine is separated from the transmission, lift the engine straight up, out of the vehicle.

26 Move the engine away from the vehicle and carefully lower the hoist until the engine can be set on the floor; or remove the flywheel/driveplate and mount the engine on an engine stand.

➡Note: On automatic transmission-equipped models, mark the front and rear spacer plates and keep them with the driveplate.

Installation

27 Check the engine/transmission mounts. If they're worn or damaged, replace them.

28 On manual transmission models, inspect the clutch components (see Chapter 8). On automatic transmission models, inspect the converter seal and bushing.

29 On automatic transmission models, apply a film of grease to the nose of the converter. Make sure the converter is completely seated on the transmission input shaft and the front pump splines. To be sure of this, check the converter-to-bellhousing clearance as described in Chapter 7B, Section 5.

30 Attach the hoist to the engine and carefully lower the engine assembly into the engine compartment.

31 Carefully guide the engine into place against the transmission, then align the engine mounts with the mount brackets.

❋❋ CAUTION:

On manual transmission models, it will be necessary to guide the transmission input shaft into the clutch, which requires precise angling and alignment. Re-positioning the transmission with the jack may help. Do not use the bolts to force the engine and transmission into alignment. It may crack or damage major components.

32 Install the engine-to-transmission bolts and tighten them to the torque listed in the Chapter 7 Specifications.

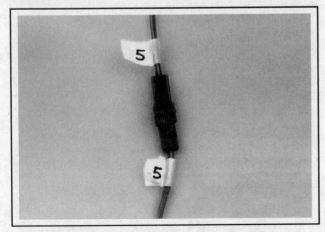

7.21 Label both ends of each wire and hose before disconnecting it

7.22 Attach the hoist chain to the engine lifting brackets

33 Install the mount bolts and tighten them securely.

34 Reinstall the remaining components and fasteners in the reverse order of removal.

35 Add coolant, oil, power steering and transmission fluids as needed (see Chapter 1).

36 Run the engine and check for proper operation and leaks. Shut off the engine and recheck the fluid levels.

2006 AND LATER MODELS

❋❋ WARNING:

The engine must be completely cool before beginning this procedure.

➡Note: Engine removal on these models is a difficult job, especially for the do-it-yourself mechanic working at home. Because of the vehicle's design, the manufacturer states that the engine/transmission and subframe have to be removed as a unit from the bottom of the vehicle, not the top. With a floor jack and jackstands, the vehicle can't be raised high enough and supported safely enough for the engine/transmission/subframe assembly to slide out from underneath. The manufacturer recommends that removal of the engine/transmission/subframe assembly only be performed on a frame-contact type vehicle hoist. The procedure is complicated and is not recommended for the home mechanic.

➡Note: Read through the entire Section before beginning this procedure. The engine and transmission are removed as a unit from below and then separated outside the vehicle.

➡Note: Keep in mind that during this procedure you'll have to adjust the height of the vehicle to perform certain operations.

➡Note: Removal and installation of the engine on these models is from the bottom of the vehicle, along with the transmission and the subframe.

Removal

37 Park the vehicle on a frame-contact type vehicle hoist, then engage the arms of the hoist with the jacking points of the vehicle. Raise the hoist arms until they contact the vehicle, but not so much that the wheels come off the ground.

38 Place protective covers on the fenders and cowl. Relieve the fuel system pressure (see Chapter 4).

39 Remove the battery, battery tray and duct (see Chapter 5).

40 Loosen the front wheel lug nuts, then raise the vehicle and remove the front wheels.

41 Remove the under-vehicle splash shields and inner fender liners.

42 Drain the cooling system, engine oil and transmission lubricant (see Chapter 1).

43 Remove the air filter housing (see Chapter 4).

44 Remove the throttle body (see Chapter 4).

45 Remove the PCM (see Chapter 6), the cooling duct and the air filter housing insulator.

46 Remove the radiator and coolant reservoir (see Chapter 3).

47 Remove the drivebelt (see Chapter 1).

48 Remove the alternator duct.

49 Disconnect the vacuum hose to the power brake booster.

50 Disconnect the hoses from the power steering pump and drain the fluid into a container.

51 Disconnect the fuel line from the fuel rail (see Chapter 4).

52 Disconnect the heater hoses from the heater core tubes at the firewall (see Chapter 3).

53 Remove the air conditioning compressor and support it out of the way with a length of rope from above.

❋❋ WARNING:

Do not disconnect the refrigerant lines.

54 Mark and disconnect any remaining wires or hoses between the engine and the chassis.

55 Remove the shift knob and center console.

56 If you're working on a model with an automatic transmission, disconnect the shift linkage from the manual lever on the transaxle. Also, remove the torque converter cover, mark the relationship of the torque converter and the driveplate, then remove the driveplate-to-torque converter fasteners.

57 If you're working on a model with a manual transmission, remove the clutch release cylinder and support it out of the way. Don't disconnect the hydraulic hose.

❋❋ CAUTION:

Do not depress the clutch pedal with the release cylinder removed.

58 Disconnect any hoses or wires between the engine/transmission and chassis from underneath the vehicle.

59 Remove the brake calipers and hang them from above with rope or wire. Don't disconnect the hoses and don't let the calipers hang by the hoses.

60 Remove the tunnel member (the cross-brace under the driveshaft).

61 Remove the exhaust pipe (see Chapter 4).

62 On models with a manual transmission, remove the cross-brace under the transmission.

63 Disconnect the steering intermediate shaft from the steering gear (see Chapter 10).

64 Remove the driveshaft (see Chapter 8).

65 Raise the vehicle on the hoist, then move a large, sturdy workbench under the vehicle. Slowly and carefully lower the vehicle onto jackstands or blocks placed on the workbench, which must contact the rear of the transmission and the subframe.

66 Remove the power plant frame (see Chapter 7A).

67 With the transmission and engine/subframe supported by the jackstands, remove the subframe-to-chassis bolts. Make sure nothing is still connected between the engine/transmission/subframe and the chassis, then slowly raise the vehicle on the hoist until it clears the engine/transmission assembly.

68 The transmission and engine can now be separated. An engine hoist can then be attached to the engine for transferring to an engine stand.

Installation

▶ **Refer to illustration 7.69**

69 Installation is the reverse of removal, noting the following points:

a) *Check the engine and transmission mounts. If they're worn, replace them.*

b) On manual transmission models, inspect the clutch components (see Chapter 8). On automatic transmission models, inspect the converter seal and bushing.

c) On automatic transmission models, apply a film of grease to the nose of the converter. Make sure the converter is completely seated on the transmission input shaft and the front pump splines. To be sure of this, check the converter-to-bellhousing clearance as described in Chapter 7B, Section 5.

d) When positioning the subframe beneath the vehicle, make a plumb bob from a piece of string and a nut. Hold the string at each subframe bolt hole on the body and verify that its corresponding subframe bolt hole is directly below it (see illustration). This will eliminate trying to adjust the subframe as the vehicle is lowered over it.

e) Tighten the subframe mounting bolts to the torque listed in this Chapter's Specifications. Tighten all other fasteners to the torque values specified in the chapters that deal with those components.

f) Refill the cooling system with the proper mixture of coolant. Refill the engine with the recommended oil, the transmission with the recommended lubricant and the power steering system with the recommended fluid (see Chapter 1).

g) Have the wheel alignment checked and, if necessary, adjusted.

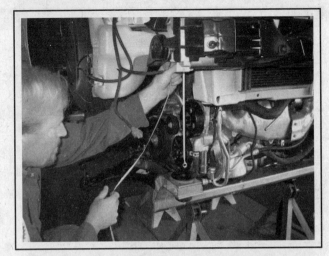

7.69 Use a plumb-bob to get the engine/transmission/subframe lined-up with the bolt holes in the body (typical)

8 Engine overhaul - disassembly sequence

1   It's much easier to remove the external components if the engine is mounted on a portable engine stand. A stand can often be rented quite cheaply from an equipment rental yard. Before the engine is mounted on a stand, the flywheel/driveplate should be removed from the engine.

2   If a stand isn't available, it's possible to remove the external engine components with it blocked up on the floor. Be extra careful not to tip or drop the engine when working without a stand.

3   If you're going to obtain a rebuilt engine, all external components must come off first, to be transferred to the replacement engine. These components include:

Clutch and flywheel (models with manual transaxle)
Driveplate (models with automatic transaxle)
Ignition system components
Emissions-related components
Engine mounts and mount brackets
Flywheel plate (spacer plate between flywheel/driveplate and engine block)
Intake/exhaust manifolds
Fuel injection components
Oil filter
Ignition coils and spark plugs
Thermostat and housing assembly
Water pump

➡ Note: When removing the external components from the engine, pay close attention to details that may be helpful or important during installation. Note the installed position of gaskets, seals, spacers, pins, brackets, washers, bolts and other small items.

4   If you're going to obtain a short block (assembled engine block, crankshaft, pistons and connecting rods), then remove the timing chain or belt, cylinder head(s), oil pan, oil pump pick-up tube, oil pump and water pump from your engine so that you can turn in your old short block to the rebuilder as a core. See Engine rebuilding alternatives for additional information regarding the different possibilities to be considered.

9 Pistons and connecting rods - removal and installation

REMOVAL

▶ **Refer to illustrations 9.1, 9.3 and 9.4**

➡**Note: Prior to removing the piston/connecting rod assemblies, remove the cylinder head and oil pan (see Chapter 2A).**

1   Use your fingernail to feel if a ridge has formed at the upper limit of ring travel (about 1/4-inch down from the top of each cylinder). If carbon deposits or cylinder wear have produced ridges, they must be completely removed with a special tool (see illustration). Follow the manufacturer's instructions provided with the tool. Failure to remove the ridges before attempting to remove the piston/connecting rod assemblies may result in piston breakage.

2   After the cylinder ridges have been removed, turn the engine so the crankshaft is facing up.

3   Before the connecting rods are removed, check the connecting rod endplay with feeler gauges. Slide them between the first connecting rod and the crankshaft throw until the play is removed (see illustration). Repeat this procedure for each connecting rod. The endplay is equal to the thickness of the feeler gauge(s). Check with an automotive machine shop for the endplay service limit (a typical endplay limit should measure between 0.005 to 0.015 inch [0.127 to 0.381 mm]). If the play exceeds the service limit, new connecting rods will be required. If new rods (or a new crankshaft) are installed, the endplay may fall under the minimum allowable. If it does, the rods will have to be machined to restore it. If necessary, consult an automotive machine shop for advice.

4   Check the connecting rods and caps for identification marks. If they aren't plainly marked, use paint or marker to clearly identify each rod and cap (1, 2, 3, etc., depending on the cylinder they're associated with) (see illustration).

5   Remove the connecting rod cap fasteners from the number one connecting rod.

6   Remove the number one connecting rod cap and bearing insert. Don't drop the bearing insert out of the cap.

7   Remove the bearing insert and push the connecting rod/piston assembly out through the top of the engine. Use a wooden dowel to push on the connecting rod. If resistance is felt, double-check to make sure that all of the ridge was removed from the cylinder.

8   Repeat the procedure for the remaining cylinders.

9   After removal, reassemble the connecting rod caps and bearing inserts in their respective connecting rods and install the cap fasteners finger tight. Leaving the old bearing inserts in place until reassembly will help prevent the connecting rod bearing surfaces from being accidentally nicked or gouged.

10 The pistons and connecting rods are now ready for inspection and overhaul at an automotive machine shop.

PISTON RING INSTALLATION

▶ **Refer to illustrations 9.13, 9.14, 9.15, 9.19a, 9.19b and 9.22**

11 Before installing the new piston rings, the ring end gaps must be checked. It's assumed that the piston ring side clearance has been checked and verified correct.

12 Lay out the piston/connecting rod assemblies and the new ring sets so the ring sets will be matched with the same piston and cylinder during the end gap measurement and engine assembly.

13 Insert the top (number one) ring into the first cylinder and square it up with the cylinder walls by pushing it in with the top of the piston (see illustration). The ring should be near the bottom of the cylinder, at the lower limit of ring travel.

14 To measure the end gap, slip feeler gauges between the ends of the ring until a gauge equal to the gap width is found (see illustration). The feeler gauge should slide between the ring ends with a slight amount of drag. A typical ring gap should fall between 0.010 and 0.020 inch (0.25 to 0.50 mm) for compression rings and up to 0.030 inch (0.76 mm) for the oil ring steel rails. If the gap is larger or smaller than specified, double-check to make sure you have the correct rings before proceeding.

9.1 Before you try to remove the pistons, use a ridge reamer to remove the raised material (ridge) from the top of the cylinders

9.3 Checking the connecting rod endplay (side clearance)

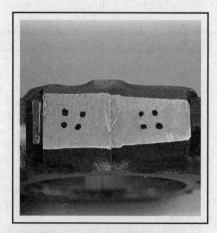

9.4 If the connecting rods and caps are not marked, mark the caps to the rods by cylinder number (for example, this would be the No. 4 connecting rod)

15 If the gap is too small, it must be enlarged or the ring ends may come in contact with each other during engine operation, which can cause serious damage to the engine. If necessary, increase the end gaps by filing the ring ends very carefully with a fine file. Mount the file in a vise equipped with soft jaws, slip the ring over the file with the ends contacting the file face and slowly move the ring to remove material from the ends. When performing this operation, file only by pushing the ring from the outside end of the file towards the vise (see illustration).

16 Excess end gap isn't critical unless it's greater than 0.040 inch (1.01 mm). Again, double-check to make sure you have the correct ring type.

17 Repeat the procedure for each ring that will be installed in the first cylinder and for each ring in the remaining cylinders. Remember to keep rings, pistons and cylinders matched up.

18 Once the ring end gaps have been checked/corrected, the rings can be installed on the pistons.

19 The oil control ring (lowest one on the piston) is usually installed first. It's composed of three separate components. Slip the spacer/ expander into the groove (see illustration). If an anti-rotation tang is used, make sure it's inserted into the drilled hole in the ring groove. Next, install the upper side rail in the same manner (see illustration). Don't use a piston ring installation tool on the oil ring side rails, as they may be damaged. Instead, place one end of the side rail into the groove between the spacer/expander and the ring land, hold it firmly in place and slide a finger around the piston while pushing the rail into the groove. Finally, install the lower side rail.

20 After the three oil ring components have been installed, check to make sure that both the upper and lower side rails can be rotated smoothly inside the ring grooves.

21 The number two (middle) ring is installed next. It's usually stamped with a mark which must face up, toward the top of the piston. Do not mix up the top and middle rings, as they have different cross-sections.

➡ **Note: Always follow the instructions printed on the ring package or box - different manufacturers may require different approaches.**

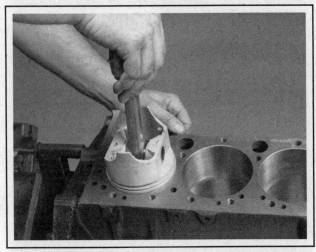

9.13 Install the piston ring into the cylinder then push it down into position using a piston so the ring will be square in the cylinder

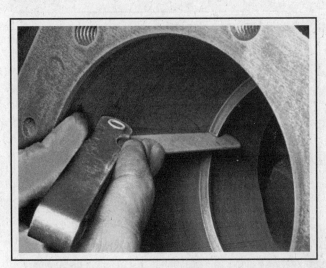

9.14 With the ring square in the cylinder, measure the ring end gap with a feeler gauge

9.15 If the ring end gap is too small, clamp a file in a vise as shown and file the piston ring ends - be sure to remove all raised material

9.19a Installing the spacer/expander in the oil ring groove

9.19b DO NOT use a piston ring installation tool when installing the oil control side rails

22 Use a piston ring installation tool and make sure the identification mark is facing the top of the piston, then slip the ring into the middle groove on the piston (see illustration). Don't expand the ring any more than necessary to slide it over the piston.

23 Install the number one (top) ring in the same manner. Make sure the mark is facing up. Be careful not to confuse the number one and number two rings.

24 Repeat the procedure for the remaining pistons and rings.

INSTALLATION

25 Before installing the piston/connecting rod assemblies, the cylinder walls must be perfectly clean, the top edge of each cylinder bore must be chamfered, and the crankshaft must be in place.

26 Remove the cap from the end of the number one connecting rod (refer to the marks made during removal). Remove the original bearing inserts and wipe the bearing surfaces of the connecting rod and cap with a clean, lint-free cloth. They must be kept spotlessly clean.

9.22 Use a piston ring installation tool to install the number 2 and the number 1 (top) rings - be sure the directional mark on the piston ring(s) is facing toward the top of the piston

Connecting rod bearing oil clearance check
▶ **Refer to illustrations 9.30, 9.35, 9.37 and 9.41**

27 Clean the back side of the new upper bearing insert, then lay it in place in the connecting rod.

28 Make sure the tab on the bearing fits into the recess in the rod. Don't hammer the bearing insert into place and be very careful not to nick or gouge the bearing face. Don't lubricate the bearing at this time.

29 Clean the back side of the other bearing insert and install it in the rod cap. Again, make sure the tab on the bearing fits into the recess in the cap, and don't apply any lubricant. It's critically important that the mating surfaces of the bearing and connecting rod are perfectly clean and oil free when they're assembled.

30 Position the piston ring gaps at the specified intervals around the piston as shown (see illustration).

31 Lubricate the piston and rings with clean engine oil and attach a piston ring compressor to the piston. Leave the skirt protruding about 1/4-inch to guide the piston into the cylinder. The rings must be compressed until they're flush with the piston.

32 Rotate the crankshaft until the number one connecting rod journal is at BDC (bottom dead center) and apply a liberal coat of engine oil to the cylinder walls.

33 With the arrow on top of the piston facing the front of the engine, gently insert the piston/connecting rod assembly into the number one cylinder bore and rest the bottom edge of the ring compressor on the engine block. Install the pistons with the cavity mark(s) or arrow facing toward the timing belt end of the engine.

34 Tap the top edge of the ring compressor to make sure it's contacting the block around its entire circumference.

35 Gently tap on the top of the piston with the end of a wooden or plastic hammer handle (see illustration) while guiding the end of the connecting rod into place on the crankshaft journal (a pair of wooden dowels would be helpful for this). The piston rings may try to pop out of the ring compressor just before entering the cylinder bore, so keep some downward pressure on the ring compressor. Work slowly, and if any resistance is felt as the piston enters the cylinder, stop immediately. Find out what's hanging up and fix it before proceeding. Do not, for any reason, force the piston into the cylinder - you might break a ring and/or the piston.

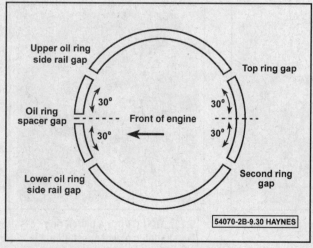

9.30 Position the piston ring end gaps as shown

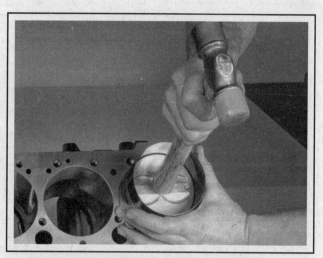

9.35 Use a plastic or wooden hammer handle to push the piston into the cylinder

36 Once the piston/connecting rod assembly is installed, the connecting rod bearing oil clearance must be checked before the rod cap is permanently installed.

37 Cut a piece of the appropriate size Plastigage slightly shorter than the width of the connecting rod bearing and lay it in place on the number one connecting rod journal, parallel with the journal axis (see illustration).

38 Clean the connecting rod cap bearing face and install the rod cap. Make sure the mating mark on the cap is on the same side as the mark on the connecting rod (see illustration 9.4).

39 Install the rod cap fasteners, and tighten them to the torque listed in this Chapter's Specifications.

➡**Note: Use a thin-wall socket to avoid erroneous torque readings that can result if the socket is wedged between the rod cap and the bolt or nut. If the socket tends to wedge itself between the fastener and the cap, lift up on it slightly until it no longer contacts the cap. DO NOT rotate the crankshaft at any time during this operation.**

40 Remove the fasteners and detach the rod cap, being very careful not to disturb the Plastigage.

41 Compare the width of the crushed Plastigage to the scale printed on the Plastigage envelope to obtain the oil clearance (see illustration). The connecting rod oil clearance is usually about 0.001 to 0.002 inch (0.025 to 0.05 mm). Consult an automotive machine shop for the clearance specified for the rod bearings on your engine.

42 If the clearance is not as specified, the bearing inserts may be the wrong size (which means different ones will be required). Before deciding that different inserts are needed, make sure that no dirt or oil was between the bearing inserts and the connecting rod or cap when the clearance was measured. Also, recheck the journal diameter. If the Plastigage was wider at one end than the other, the journal may be tapered. If the clearance still exceeds the limit specified, the bearing will have to be replaced with an undersize bearing.

✳✳ CAUTION:

When installing a new crankshaft always use a standard size bearing.

Final installation

43 Carefully scrape all traces of the Plastigage material off the rod journal and/or bearing face. Be very careful not to scratch the bearing - use your fingernail or the edge of a plastic card.

44 Make sure the bearing faces are perfectly clean, then apply a uniform layer of clean moly-base grease or engine assembly lube to both of them. You'll have to push the piston into the cylinder to expose the face of the bearing insert in the connecting rod.

45 Slide the connecting rod back into place on the journal, install the rod cap, install the fasteners and tighten them to the torque listed in this Chapter's Specifications.

46 Repeat the entire procedure for the remaining pistons/connecting rods.

47 The important points to remember are:

a) *Keep the back sides of the bearing inserts and the insides of the connecting rods and caps perfectly clean when assembling them.*
b) *Make sure you have the correct piston/rod assembly for each cylinder.*
c) *The arrow or mark on the piston must face the front of the engine.*
d) *Lubricate the cylinder walls liberally with clean oil.*
e) *Lubricate the bearing faces when installing the rod caps after the oil clearance has been checked.*

48 After all the piston/connecting rod assemblies have been correctly installed, rotate the crankshaft a number of times by hand to check for any obvious binding.

49 As a final step, check the connecting rod endplay, as described in Step 3. If it was correct before disassembly and the original crankshaft and rods were reinstalled, it should still be correct. If new rods or a new crankshaft were installed, the endplay may be inadequate. If so, the rods will have to be removed and taken to an automotive machine shop for resizing.

9.37 Place Plastigage on each connecting rod bearing journal parallel to the crankshaft centerline

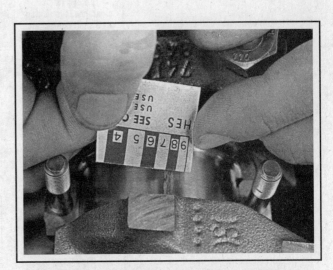

9.41 Use the scale on the Plastigage package to determine the bearing oil clearance - be sure to measure the widest part of the Plastigage and use the correct scale; it comes with both standard and metric scales

ENGINE BEARING ANALYSIS

Debris

Babbitt bearing embedded with debris from machinings

Microscopic detail of debris

Microscopic detail of gouges

Overplated copper alloy bearing gouged by cast iron debris

Aluminum bearing embedded with glass beads

Microscopic detail of glass beads

Damaged lining caused by dirt left on the bearing back

Misassembly

Excessive oil clearance is indicated by a short contact arc

Result of a lower half assembled as an upper - blocking the oil flow

Polished and oil-stained backs are a result of a poor fit in the housing bore

Result of a wrong, reversed, or shifted cap

Overloading

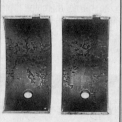

Damage from excessive idling which resulted in an oil film unable to support the load imposed

Damaged upper connecting rod bearings caused by engine lugging; the lower main bearings (not shown) were similarly affected

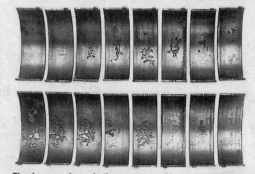

The damage shown in these upper and lower connecting rod bearings was caused by engine operation at a higher-than-rated speed under load

Misalignment

A warped crankshaft caused this pattern of severe wear in the center, diminishing toward the ends

A poorly finished crankshaft caused the equally spaced scoring shown

A bent connecting rod led to the damage in the "V" pattern

A tapered housing bore caused the damage along one edge of this pair

Lubrication

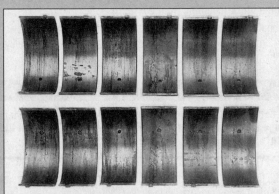

Result of dry start: The bearings on the left, farthest from the oil pump, show more damage

Result of a low oil supply or oil starvation

Severe wear as a result of inadequate oil clearance

Corrosion

Microscopic detail of corrosion

Corrosion is an acid attack on the bearing lining generally caused by inadequate maintenance, extremely hot or cold operation, or inferior oils or fuels

Microscopic detail of cavitation

Example of cavitation - a surface erosion caused by pressure changes in the oil film

Damage from excessive thrust or insufficient axial clearance

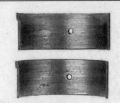

Bearing affected by oil dilution caused by excessive blow-by or a rich mixture

© 1986 Federal-Mogul Corporation
Copy and photographs courtesy of Federal Mogul Corporation

10 Crankshaft - removal and installation

REMOVAL

♦ Refer to illustrations 10.1 and 10.3

➡**Note: The crankshaft can be removed only after the engine has been removed from the vehicle. It's assumed that the flywheel or driveplate, crankshaft pulley, timing belt or timing chain, oil pan, oil pump body, oil filter and piston/connecting rod assemblies have already been removed. The rear main oil seal retainer must be unbolted and separated from the block before proceeding with crankshaft removal.**

1   Before the crankshaft is removed, measure the endplay. Mount a dial indicator with the indicator in line with the crankshaft and touching the end of the crankshaft as shown (see illustration).

2   Pry the crankshaft all the way to the rear and zero the dial indicator. Next, pry the crankshaft to the front as far as possible and check the reading on the dial indicator. The distance traveled is the endplay. A typical crankshaft endplay will fall between 0.003 to 0.010 inch (0.076 to 0.254 mm). If it is greater than that, check the crankshaft thrust surfaces for wear after it's removed. If no wear is evident, new main bearings should correct the endplay.

3   If a dial indicator isn't available, feeler gauges can be used. Gently pry the crankshaft all the way to the front of the engine. Slip feeler gauges between the crankshaft and the front face of the thrust bearing or washer to determine the clearance (see illustration).

4   Loosen the main bearing cap bolts 1/4-turn at a time each, until they can be removed by hand. Follow the reverse of the tightening sequence (see illustration 10.19a or 10.19b).

5   Remove the main bearing caps (or cap assembly) from the engine block.

6   Carefully lift the crankshaft out of the engine. It may be a good idea to have an assistant available, since the crankshaft is quite heavy and awkward to handle.

INSTALLATION

7   Crankshaft installation is the first step in engine reassembly. It's assumed at this point that the engine block and crankshaft have been cleaned, inspected and repaired or reconditioned.

8   Position the engine block with the bottom facing up.

9   Remove the original bearing inserts from the main bearing caps.

10 If they're still in place, remove the original bearing inserts from the block. Wipe the bearing surfaces of the block and main bearing caps with a clean, lint-free cloth. They must be kept spotlessly clean. This is critical for determining the correct bearing oil clearance.

Main bearing oil clearance check

♦ Refer to illustrations 10.17, 10.19a, 10.19b and 10.21

11 Without mixing them up, clean the back sides of the new upper main bearing inserts (with grooves and oil holes) and lay one in each main bearing saddle in the engine block. Each upper bearing (engine block) has an oil groove and oil hole in it.

✳✳ CAUTION:

The oil holes in the block must line up with the oil holes in the engine block inserts.

The thrust washers must be installed in the correct location.

➡**Note: The thrust washers are located on the 4th journal in the engine block (counting from the front).**

Clean the back sides of the lower main bearing inserts and lay them in the corresponding location in the main bearing caps. Make sure the tab on the bearing insert fits into the recess in the block.

✳✳ CAUTION:

Do not hammer the bearing insert into place and don't nick or gouge the bearing faces. DO NOT apply any lubrication at this time.

12 Clean the faces of the bearing inserts in the block and the crankshaft main bearing journals with a clean, lint-free cloth.

13 Check or clean the oil holes in the crankshaft, as any dirt here can go only one way - straight through the new bearings.

14 Once you're certain the crankshaft is clean, carefully lay it in position in the cylinder block.

10.1 Checking crankshaft endplay with a dial indicator

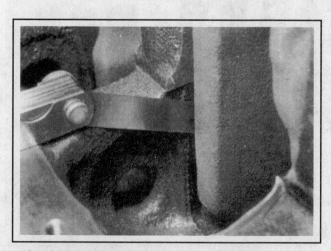

10.3 Checking the crankshaft endplay with feeler gauges at the thrust bearing journal

15 Before the crankshaft can be permanently installed, the main bearing oil clearance must be checked.

16 Cut several strips of the appropriate size of Plastigage. They must be slightly shorter than the width of the main bearing journal.

17 Place one piece on each crankshaft main bearing journal, parallel with the journal axis as shown (see illustration).

18 Clean the faces of the bearing inserts in the engine block and main bearing caps. Hold the bearing inserts in place and install the main bearing caps onto the crankshaft and cylinder block. DO NOT disturb the Plastigage.

19 Apply clean engine oil to all bolt threads prior to installation, then install all bolts finger-tight. Tighten the main bearing cap bolts in the sequence shown (see illustrations) progressing in steps, to the torque listed in this Chapter's Specifications. DO NOT rotate the crankshaft at any time during this operation.

20 Remove the bolts in the reverse order of the tightening sequence and carefully lift the main bearing bridge straight up and off the block. Do not disturb the Plastigage or rotate the crankshaft.

21 Compare the width of the crushed Plastigage on each journal to the scale printed on the Plastigage envelope to determine the main bearing oil clearance (see illustration). Check with an automotive machine shop for the oil clearance for your engine.

22 If the clearance is not as specified, the bearing inserts may be the wrong size (which means different ones will be required). Before deciding if different inserts are needed, make sure that no dirt or oil was between the bearing inserts and the caps or block when the clearance was measured. If the Plastigage was wider at one end than the other, the crankshaft journal may be tapered. If the clearance still exceeds the limit specified, the bearing insert(s) will have to be replaced with an undersize bearing insert(s).

✱✱ CAUTION:

When installing a new crankshaft always install a standard bearing insert set.

10.17 Place the Plastigage onto the crankshaft bearing journal as shown

10.19a Main bearing cap bolt tightening sequence - 1.6L and 1.8L engines

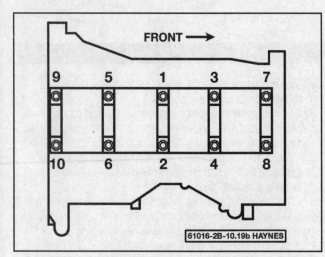

10.19b Main bearing cap assembly bolt tightening sequence - 2.0L engine

10.21 Use the scale on the Plastigage package to determine the bearing oil clearance - be sure to measure the widest part of the Plastigage and use the correct scale; it comes with both standard and metric scales

23 Carefully scrape all traces of the Plastigage material off the main bearing journals and/or the bearing insert faces. Be sure to remove all residue from the oil holes. Use your fingernail or the edge of a plastic card - don't nick or scratch the bearing faces.

Final installation

24 Carefully lift the crankshaft out of the cylinder block.

25 Clean the bearing insert faces in the cylinder block, then apply a thin, uniform layer of moly-base grease or engine assembly lube to each of the bearing surfaces. Be sure to coat the thrust faces as well as the journal face of the thrust bearing.

26 Make sure the crankshaft journals are clean, then lay the crankshaft back in place in the cylinder block.

27 Clean the bearing insert faces and apply the same lubricant to them. Clean the engine block and the mating surface of the bearing caps thoroughly. The surfaces must be free of oil residue.

28 Prior to installation, apply clean engine oil to all bolt threads, wiping off any excess, then install all bolts finger-tight.

29 Tighten the bolts to the torque listed in this Chapter's Specifications following the correct torque sequence (see illustration 10.19a or 10.19b).

30 Recheck the crankshaft endplay with a feeler gauge or a dial indicator. The endplay should be correct if the crankshaft thrust faces aren't worn or damaged and if new bearings have been installed.

31 Rotate the crankshaft a number of times by hand to check for any obvious binding. It should rotate with a running torque of 50 in-lbs or less. If the running torque is too high, correct the problem at this time.

32 Install the new rear main oil seal (see Chapter 2A).

11 Engine overhaul - reassembly sequence

1   Before beginning engine reassembly, make sure you have all the necessary new parts, gaskets and seals as well as the following items on hand:

Common hand tools
A 1/2-inch drive torque wrench
New engine oil
Gasket sealant
Thread locking compound

2   If you obtained a short block it will be necessary to install the cylinder head, the oil pump and pick-up tube, the oil pan, the water pump, the timing belt and timing cover, and the valve cover (see Chapter 2A). In order to save time and avoid problems, the external components must be installed in the following general order:

Thermostat and housing cover
Water pump
Intake and exhaust manifolds
Fuel injection components
Emission control components
Spark plug wires and spark plugs
Ignition distributor or coils
Oil filter
Engine mounts and mount brackets
Clutch and flywheel (manual transaxle)
Driveplate (automatic transaxle)

12 Initial start-up and break-in after overhaul

❋❋ WARNING:

Have a fire extinguisher handy when starting the engine for the first time.

1   Once the engine has been installed in the vehicle, double-check the engine oil and coolant levels.

2   With the spark plugs out of the engine and the ignition system and fuel pump disabled (see Chapter 4, Section 2), crank the engine until oil pressure registers on the gauge or the light goes out.

3   Install the spark plugs, hook up the plug wires and restore the ignition system and fuel pump functions.

4   Start the engine. It may take a few moments for the fuel system to build up pressure, but the engine should start without a great deal of effort.

5   After the engine starts, it should be allowed to warm up to normal operating temperature. While the engine is warming up, make a thorough check for fuel, oil and coolant leaks.

6   Shut the engine off and recheck the engine oil and coolant levels.

7   Drive the vehicle to an area with minimum traffic, accelerate from 30 to 50 mph, then allow the vehicle to slow to 30 mph with the throttle closed. Repeat the procedure 10 or 12 times. This will load the piston rings and cause them to seat properly against the cylinder walls. Check again for oil and coolant leaks.

8   Drive the vehicle gently for the first 500 miles (no sustained high speeds) and keep a constant check on the oil level. It is not unusual for an engine to use oil during the break-in period.

9   At approximately 500 to 600 miles, change the oil and filter.

10 For the next few hundred miles, drive the vehicle normally. Do not pamper it or abuse it.

11 After 2,000 miles, change the oil and filter again and consider the engine broken in.

GLOSSARY

B

Backlash - The amount of play between two parts. Usually refers to how much one gear can be moved back and forth without moving the gear with which it's meshed.

Bearing Caps - The caps held in place by nuts or bolts which, in turn, hold the bearing surface. This space is for lubricating oil to enter.

Bearing clearance - The amount of space left between shaft and bearing surface. This space is for lubricating oil to enter.

Bearing crush - The additional height which is purposely manufactured into each bearing half to ensure complete contact of the bearing back with the housing bore when the engine is assembled.

Bearing knock - The noise created by movement of a part in a loose or worn bearing.

Blueprinting - Dismantling an engine and reassembling it to EXACT specifications.

Bore - An engine cylinder, or any cylindrical hole; also used to describe the process of enlarging or accurately refinishing a hole with a cutting tool, as to bore an engine cylinder. The bore size is the diameter of the hole.

Boring - Renewing the cylinders by cutting them out to a specified size. A boring bar is used to make the cut.

Bottom end - A term which refers collectively to the engine block, crankshaft, main bearings and the big ends of the connecting rods.

Break-in - The period of operation between installation of new or rebuilt parts and time in which parts are worn to the correct fit. Driving at reduced and varying speed for a specified mileage to permit parts to wear to the correct fit.

Bushing - A one-piece sleeve placed in a bore to serve as a bearing surface for shaft, piston pin, etc. Usually replaceable.

C

Camshaft - The shaft in the engine, on which a series of lobes are located for operating the valve mechanisms. The camshaft is driven by gears or sprockets and a timing chain. Usually referred to simply as the cam.

Carbon - Hard, or soft, black deposits found in combustion chamber, on plugs, under rings, on and under valve heads.

Cast iron - An alloy of iron and more than two percent carbon, used for engine blocks and heads because it's relatively inexpensive and easy to mold into complex shapes.

Chamfer - To bevel across (or a bevel on) the sharp edge of an object.

Chase - To repair damaged threads with a tap or die.

Combustion chamber - The space between the piston and the cylinder head, with the piston at top dead center, in which air-fuel mixture is burned.

Compression ratio - The relationship between cylinder volume (clearance volume) when the piston is at top dead center and cylinder volume when the piston is at bottom dead center.

Connecting rod - The rod that connects the crank on the crankshaft with the piston. Sometimes called a con rod.

Connecting rod cap - The part of the connecting rod assembly that attaches the rod to the crankpin.

Core plug - Soft metal plug used to plug the casting holes for the coolant passages in the block.

Crankcase - The lower part of the engine in which the crankshaft rotates; includes the lower section of the cylinder block and the oil pan.

Crank kit - A reground or reconditioned crankshaft and new main and connecting rod bearings.

Crankpin - The part of a crankshaft to which a connecting rod is attached.

Crankshaft - The main rotating member, or shaft, running the length of the crankcase, with offset throws to which the connecting rods are attached; changes the reciprocating motion of the pistons into rotating motion.

Cylinder sleeve - A replaceable sleeve, or liner, pressed into the cylinder block to form the cylinder bore.

D

Deburring - Removing the burrs (rough edges or areas) from a bearing.

Deglazer - A tool, rotated by an electric motor, used to remove glaze from cylinder walls so a new set of rings will seat.

E

Endplay - The amount of lengthwise movement between two parts. As applied to a crankshaft, the distance that the crankshaft can move forward and back in the cylinder block.

F

Face - A machinist's term that refers to removing metal from the end of a shaft or the face of a larger part, such as a flywheel.

Fatigue - A breakdown of material through a large number of loading and unloading cycles. The first signs are cracks followed shortly by breaks.

Feeler gauge - A thin strip of hardened steel, ground to an exact thickness, used to check clearances between parts.

Free height - The unloaded length or height of a spring.

Freeplay - The looseness in a linkage, or an assembly of parts, between the initial application of force and actual movement. Usually perceived as slop or slight delay.

Freeze plug - See Core plug.

G

Gallery - A large passage in the block that forms a reservoir for engine oil pressure.

Glaze - The very smooth, glassy finish that develops on cylinder walls while an engine is in service.

H

Heli-Coil - A rethreading device used when threads are worn or damaged. The device is installed in a retapped hole to reduce the thread size to the original size.

I

Installed height - The spring's measured length or height, as installed on the cylinder head. Installed height is measured from the spring seat to the underside of the spring retainer.

J

Journal - The surface of a rotating shaft which turns in a bearing.

K

Keeper - The split lock that holds the valve spring retainer in position on the valve stem.

Key - A small piece of metal inserted into matching grooves machined into two parts fitted together - such as a gear pressed onto a shaft - which prevents slippage between the two parts.

Knock - The heavy metallic engine sound, produced in the combustion chamber as a result of abnormal combustion - usually detonation. Knock is usually caused by a loose or worn bearing. Also referred to as detonation, pinging and spark knock. Connecting rod or main bearing knocks are created by too much oil clearance or insufficient lubrication.

L

Lands - The portions of metal between the piston ring grooves.

Lapping the valves - Grinding a valve face and its seat together with lapping compound.

Lash - The amount of free motion in a gear train, between gears, or in a mechanical assembly, that occurs before movement can begin. Usually refers to the lash in a valve train.

Lifter - The part that rides against the cam to transfer motion to the rest of the valve train.

M

Machining - The process of using a machine to remove metal from a metal part.

Main bearings - The plain, or babbitt, bearings that support the crankshaft.

Main bearing caps - The cast iron caps, bolted to the bottom of the block, that support the main bearings.

O

O.D. - Outside diameter.

Oil gallery - A pipe or drilled passageway in the engine used to carry engine oil from one area to another.

Oil ring - The lower ring, or rings, of a piston; designed to prevent excessive amounts of oil from working up the cylinder walls and into the combustion chamber. Also called an oil-control ring.

Oil seal - A seal which keeps oil from leaking out of a compartment. Usually refers to a dynamic seal around a rotating shaft or other moving part.

O-ring - A type of sealing ring made of a special rubberlike material; in use, the O-ring is compressed into a groove to provide the sealing action.

Overhaul - To completely disassemble a unit, clean and inspect all parts, reassemble it with the original or new parts and make all adjustments necessary for proper operation.

P

Pilot bearing - A small bearing installed in the center of the flywheel (or the rear end of the crankshaft) to support the front end of the input shaft of the transmission.

Pip mark - A little dot or indentation which indicates the top side of a compression ring.

Piston - The cylindrical part, attached to the connecting rod, that moves up and down in the cylinder as the crankshaft rotates. When the fuel charge is fired, the piston transfers the force of the explosion to the connecting rod, then to the crankshaft.

Piston pin (or wrist pin) - The cylindrical and usually hollow steel pin that passes through the piston. The piston pin fastens the piston to the upper end of the connecting rod.

Piston ring - The split ring fitted to the groove in a piston. The ring contacts the sides of the ring groove and also rubs against the cylinder wall, thus sealing space between piston and wall. There are two types of rings: Compression rings seal the compression pressure in the combustion chamber; oil rings scrape excessive oil off the cylinder wall.

Piston ring groove - The slots or grooves cut in piston heads to hold piston rings in position.

Piston skirt - The portion of the piston below the rings and the piston pin hole.

Plastigage - A thin strip of plastic thread, available in different sizes, used for measuring clearances. For example, a strip of plastigage is laid across a bearing journal and mashed as parts are assembled. Then parts are disassembled and the width of the strip is measured to determine clearance between journal and bearing. Commonly used to measure crankshaft main-bearing and connecting rod bearing clearances.

Press-fit - A tight fit between two parts that requires pressure to force the parts together. Also referred to as drive, or force, fit.

Prussian blue - A blue pigment; in solution, useful in determining the area of contact between two surfaces. Prussian blue is commonly used to determine the width and location of the contact area between the valve face and the valve seat.

R

Race (bearing) - The inner or outer ring that provides a contact surface for balls or rollers in bearing.

Ream - To size, enlarge or smooth a hole by using a round cutting tool with fluted edges.

Ring job - The process of reconditioning the cylinders and installing new rings.

Runout - Wobble. The amount a shaft rotates out-of-true.

S

Saddle - The upper main bearing seat.

Scored - Scratched or grooved, as a cylinder wall may be scored by abrasive particles moved up and down by the piston rings.

Scuffing - A type of wear in which there's a transfer of material between parts moving against each other; shows up as pits or grooves in the mating surfaces.

Seat - The surface upon which another part rests or seats. For example, the valve seat is the matched surface upon which the valve face rests. Also used to refer to wearing into a good fit; for example, piston rings seat after a few miles of driving. .

Short block - An engine block complete with crankshaft and piston and, usually, camshaft assemblies.

Static balance - The balance of an object while it's stationary.

Step - The wear on the lower portion of a ring land caused by excessive side and back-clearance. The height of the step indicates the ring's extra side clearance and the length of the step projecting from the back wall of the groove represents the ring's back clearance.

Stroke - The distance the piston moves when traveling from top dead center to bottom dead center, or from bottom dead center to top dead center.

Stud - A metal rod with threads on both ends.

T

Tang - A lip on the end of a plain bearing used to align the bearing during assembly.

Tap - To cut threads in a hole. Also refers to the fluted tool used to cut threads.

Taper - A gradual reduction in the width of a shaft or hole; in an engine cylinder, taper usually takes the form of uneven wear, more pronounced at the top than at the bottom.

Throws - The offset portions of the crankshaft to which the connecting rods are affixed.

Thrust bearing - The main bearing that has thrust faces to prevent excessive endplay, or forward and backward movement of the crankshaft.

Thrust washer - A bronze or hardened steel washer placed between two moving parts. The washer prevents longitudinal movement and provides a bearing surface for thrust surfaces of parts.

Tolerance - The amount of variation permitted from an exact size of measurement. Actual amount from smallest acceptable dimension to largest acceptable dimension.

U

Umbrella - An oil deflector placed near the valve tip to throw oil from the valve stem area.

Undercut - A machined groove below the normal surface.

Undersize bearings - Smaller diameter bearings used with re-ground crankshaft journals.

V

Valve grinding - Refacing a valve in a valve-refacing machine.

Valve train - The valve-operating mechanism of an engine; includes all components from the camshaft to the valve.

Vibration damper - A cylindrical weight attached to the front of the crankshaft to minimize torsional vibration (the twist-untwist actions of the crankshaft caused by the cylinder firing impulses). Also called a harmonic balancer.

W

Water jacket - The spaces around the cylinders, between the inner and outer shells of the cylinder block or head, through which coolant circulates.

Web - A supporting structure across a cavity.

Woodruff key - A key with a radiused backside (viewed from the side).

Specifications

General

Displacement
1.6L	97 cubic inches
1.8L	112 cubic inches
2.0L	122 cubic inches

Cylinder compression pressure @ 300 rpm

1.6L
Standard	192 psi
Minimum	135 psi

1.8L
Standard	182 psi
Minimum	128 psi

2.0L
Standard	249 psi
Minimum	174 psi

Maximum variation between cylinders	28 psi

Oil pressure (warm)

1.6L and 1.8L
1000 rpm	29 to 42 psi
3000 rpm	43 to 56 psi
2.0L (at 3000 rpm)	49 to 85 psi

Torque specifications*   Ft-lbs (unless otherwise indicated)

➡**Note: One foot-pound (ft-lb) of torque is equivalent to 12 inch-pounds (in-lbs) of torque. Torque values below approximately 15 ft-lbs are expressed in inch-pounds, since most foot-pound torque wrenches are not accurate at these smaller values.**

Main bearing cap bolts

1.6L and 1.8L	40 to 43

2.0L

110 mm bolt stem length
Step 1	33 to 34
Step 2	Tighten an additional 175 to 185-degrees

104 mm bolt stem length
Step 1	27 to 61 inch-lbs
Step 2	17 to 19
Step 3	28 to 31
Step 4	Loosen all bolts completely
Step 5	27 to 61 inch-lbs
Step 6	159 to 194 inch-lbs
Step 7	Tighten an additional 87.5 to 92.5-degrees

Connecting rod cap nuts/bolts
1.6L	37 to 40
1.8L	35 to 36

2.0L
Step 1	20 to 23
Step 2	Tighten an additional 80 to 100-degrees
Oil jets	105 to 156 in-lbs
Subframe bolts (2006 and later models)	94 to 115

Refer to Part A for additional torque specifications.

Notes

Section

Reference to other Chapters

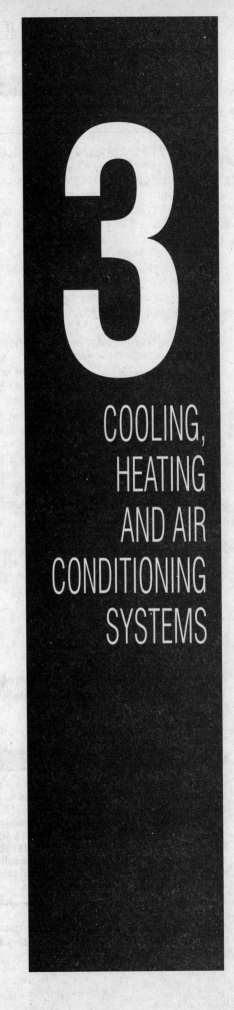

3

COOLING, HEATING AND AIR CONDITIONING SYSTEMS

1 General information

ENGINE COOLING SYSTEM

All vehicles covered by this manual employ a pressurized engine cooling system with thermostatically-controlled coolant circulation. An impeller type water pump mounted on the front of the block pumps coolant through the engine. The coolant flows around each cylinder and toward the rear of the engine. Cast-in coolant passages direct coolant around the intake and exhaust ports, near the spark plug areas and in proximity to the exhaust valve guides.

A wax-pellet type thermostat is located in the thermostat housing at the front of the engine. During warm up, the closed thermostat prevents coolant from circulating through the radiator. When the engine reaches normal operating temperature, the thermostat opens and allows hot coolant to travel through the radiator, where it is cooled before returning to the engine.

The cooling system is sealed by a pressure-type radiator cap. This raises the boiling point of the coolant, and the higher boiling point of the coolant increases the cooling efficiency of the radiator. If the system pressure exceeds the cap pressure-relief value, the excess pressure in the system forces the spring-loaded valve inside the cap off its seat and allows the coolant to escape through the overflow tube into a coolant reservoir. When the system cools, the excess coolant is automatically drawn from the reservoir back into the radiator.

The coolant reservoir does double duty as both the point at which fresh coolant is added to the cooling system to maintain the proper fluid level and as a holding tank for overheated coolant.

This type of cooling system is known as a closed design because coolant that escapes past the pressure cap is saved and reused.

HEATING SYSTEM

The heating system consists of a blower fan and heater core located within the heater box under the right end of the dashboard, the inlet and outlet hoses connecting the heater core to the engine cooling system and the heater/air conditioning control head on the dashboard. Hot engine coolant is circulated through the heater core. When the heater mode is activated, a flap door opens to expose the heater box to the passenger compartment. A fan switch on the control head activates the blower motor, which forces air through the core, heating the air.

AIR CONDITIONING SYSTEM

The air conditioning system consists of a condenser mounted in front of the radiator, an evaporator mounted adjacent to the heater core, a compressor mounted on the engine, a filter-drier which contains a high pressure relief valve and the plumbing connecting all of the above.

A blower fan forces the warmer air of the passenger compartment through the evaporator core (similar to a radiator in reverse), transferring the heat from the air to the refrigerant. The liquid refrigerant boils off into low pressure vapor, taking the heat with it when it leaves the evaporator. The compressor keeps refrigerant circulating through the system, pumping the warmed coolant through the condenser where it is cooled and then circulated back to the evaporator.

2 Antifreeze - general information

♦ Refer to illustration 2.4

❋❋ WARNING:

Do not allow antifreeze to come in contact with your skin or painted surfaces of the vehicle. Rinse off spills immediately with plenty of water. Antifreeze is highly toxic if ingested. Never leave antifreeze lying around in an open container or in puddles on the floor; children and pets are attracted by it's sweet smell and may drink it. Check with local authorities about disposing of used antifreeze. Many communities have collection centers which will see that antifreeze is disposed of safely. Never dump used antifreeze on the ground or into drains.

➡**Note: Non-toxic antifreeze is now manufactured and available at local auto parts stores, but even these types should be disposed of properly.**

➡**Note: If the cooling system pressure cap is labeled "F22," the system is filled with pre-mixed long life coolant. It is compatible with other types of coolant, but it is recommended that only F22 coolant be used. It should never be diluted with water.**

1 The cooling system should be filled with a water/ethylene-glycol based antifreeze solution, which will prevent freezing down to at least -20 degrees F, or lower if local climate requires it. It also provides protection against corrosion and increases the coolant boiling point.

2 The cooling system should be drained, flushed and refilled at the intervals listed in the Chapter 1 Maintenance schedule. The use of anti-freeze solutions for periods of longer than two years is likely to cause damage and encourage the formation of rust and scale in the system. If your tap water is hard (contains a lot of dissolved minerals), use distilled water with the antifreeze.

3 Before adding antifreeze to the system, check all hose connections, because antifreeze tends to search out and leak through very minute openings. Engines do not normally consume coolant. Therefore, if the level goes down, find the cause and correct it.

4   The exact mixture of antifreeze-to-water you should use depends on the relative weather conditions. The mixture should contain at least 50 percent antifreeze, but should never contain more than 70 percent antifreeze. Consult the mixture ratio chart on the antifreeze container before adding coolant. Hydrometers are available at most auto parts stores to test the ratio of antifreeze to water (see illustration) or antifreeze test strips are available instead of the hydrometer gauge. Use antifreeze which meets the vehicle manufacturer's specifications.

2.4 An inexpensive hydrometer can be used to test the condition of your coolant - also available are antifreeze test strips

3   Thermostat - check and replacement

✳✳ WARNING:

Do not attempt to remove the cooling system pressure cap, coolant or thermostat until the engine has cooled completely.

CHECK

1   Before assuming the thermostat is responsible for a cooling system problem, check the coolant level (see Chapter 1), drivebelt tension (see Chapter 1) and temperature gauge (or light) operation.

2   If the engine takes a long time to warm up (as indicated by the temperature gauge or heater operation), the thermostat is probably stuck open. Replace the thermostat with a new one.

3   If the engine runs hot, use your hand to check the temperature of the upper radiator hose. If the hose is not hot, but the engine is, the thermostat is probably stuck in the closed position, preventing the coolant inside the engine from traveling through the radiator. Replace the thermostat.

✳✳ CAUTION:

Do not drive the vehicle without a thermostat. The computer may stay in open loop and emissions and fuel economy will suffer.

4   If the hose is hot, it means that the coolant is flowing and the thermostat is open. Consult the *Troubleshooting* Section at the front of this manual for further diagnosis.

REPLACEMENT

5   Disconnect the negative cable from the battery (see Chapter 5).
6   Drain the coolant from the radiator (see Chapter 1).

2005 and earlier models

▶ Refer to illustrations 3.8 and 3.10

7   If you're working on a 1993 or earlier model, disconnect the thermoswitch electrical connector from the thermostat cover located at the front of the cylinder head.

8   Loosen the radiator hose clamp (do this with pliers on original-equipment spring-type clamps) and remove the radiator hose from the thermostat cover (see illustration).

➡Note: The radiator hose can be left attached to the thermostat cover, unless the thermostat cover itself is to be replaced.

9   Detach the thermostat cover from the engine. Be prepared for some coolant to spill as the gasket seal is broken.

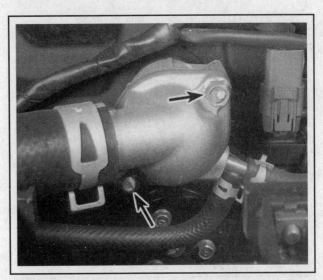

3.8 Remove the mounting bolts (arrows) and lift off the thermostat housing

3.10 The thermostat is installed with the spring end into the housing; note the position of the sub-valve (arrow)

10 Remove the thermostat, noting the direction in which it was installed in the block (see illustration).

11 Remove the gasket and thoroughly clean the sealing surfaces.

12 Install the thermostat with the spring end down (1993 and earlier) or toward the engine (1994 through 2005).

13 Fit a new gasket, aligning the gasket with the bolt holes in the block.

   a) *On 1993 and earlier models, install the gasket with the printed side facing down (toward the thermostat).*

   b) *On 1994 through 2005 models, install the gasket with the tab facing the thermostat cover.*

14 Installation is the reverse of removal. Tighten the thermostat cover fasteners to the torque listed in this Chapter's Specifications.

15 Refill the cooling system (see Chapter 1), run the engine and check for leaks and proper operation.

2006 and later models

16 Remove the throttle body (see Chapter 4).

17 Disconnect the bypass (upper) and radiator (lower) hoses from the thermostat cover.

18 Remove the thermostat housing cover bolts and remove the thermostat housing cover.

19 Remove and discard the thermostat housing cover gasket.

20 Installation is the reverse of removal. Be sure to use a new gasket and tighten the thermostat housing cover bolts to the torque listed in this Chapter's Specifications.

21 Refill the cooling system (see Chapter 1), run the engine and check for leaks and proper operation.

4 Engine cooling fan - replacement

✳✳ WARNING:

To avoid possible injury, keep clear of the fan blades, as they may start turning at any time!

2005 AND EARLIER MODELS

▶ **Refer to illustrations 4.2, 4.4, 4.5 and 4.6**

1 Disconnect the negative battery cable (see Chapter 5).

2 Remove the air intake duct (see illustration).

3 Disconnect the wiring connector at the fan motor.

4 Unbolt the left (radiator) fan shroud and lift the fan assembly from the engine compartment, then unbolt and remove the right (condenser) fan assembly (see illustration 4.2 and the accompanying illustration).

5 While holding the fan blades, remove the fan retaining nut (see illustration). Remove the fan from the fan motor.

6 Remove the fan motor from the fan shroud (see illustration).

7 Installation is the reverse of removal. When installing the fan shroud and the air intake duct, tighten the mounting bolts securely.

4.2 Remove the air intake duct (upper arrow) and the fan upper mounting bolts (lower arrows)

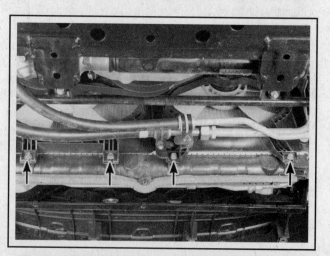

4.4 Remove the lower mounting bolts and lift out the fans

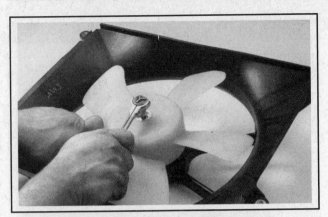

4.5 Hold the cooling fan blades and remove the fan retaining nut

4.6 Unclip the wiring harness and remove the screws retaining the motor to the shroud

2006 AND LATER MODELS

▶ Refer to illustration 4.11, 4.14 and 4.16

8 Disconnect the cable from the negative battery terminal (see Chapter 5).

9 Raise the vehicle and place it securely on jackstands. Remove the engine compartment under-cover.

10 Drain the engine coolant (see Chapter 1).

11 Remove the battery and the battery tray (see Chapter 5), then remove the battery cooling duct (see illustration).

12 Remove the air filter housing (see Chapter 4).

13 Remove the Powertrain Control Module (PCM).

14 Remove the Powertrain Control Module (PCM) cooling duct (see illustration).

15 Remove the coolant reservoir (see Section 5).

16 Disconnect the electrical connector from the fan motor (see illustration).

17 On vehicles with an automatic transmission, detach the ATF cooler hose.

18 Remove the cooling fan shroud and fan motor as a single assembly.

19 To remove the fan motor and/or fan from the cooling fan assembly, refer to Steps 5 and 6.

20 Installation is the reverse of removal.

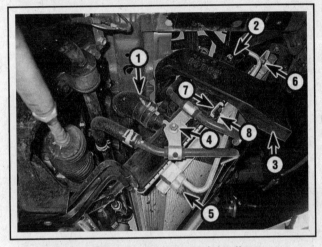

4.11 Radiator and condenser (right side) details:

1 Lower radiator hose
2 Battery cooling duct mounting screw
3 Battery cooling duct
4 Power steering cooler line bracket bolt
5 Refrigerant line flange bolt
6 Condenser mounting bolt
7 Condenser mounting clip
8 Condenser mounting clip bracket

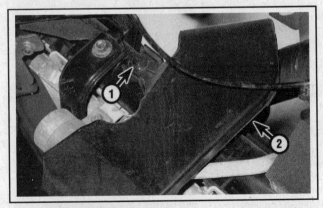

4.14 Radiator (left side) details:

1 PCM cooling duct mounting screw
2 PCM cooling duct

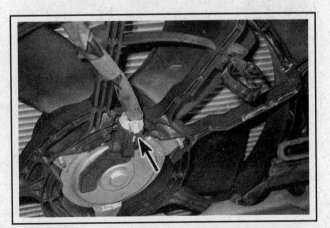

4.16 Fan motor electrical connector (2006 model shown, other models similar)

5 Radiator and coolant reservoir - removal and installation

✳✳ WARNING:

Do not start this procedure until the engine is completely cool.

COOLANT RESERVOIR

▸ **Refer to illustrations 5.1a and 5.1b**

1 If you're working on a 2006 or later model, drain the cooling system (see Chapter 1). Disconnect the coolant hoses from the coolant reservoir (see illustrations). Undo the mounting bolts and lift the reservoir out. Dump the coolant into a container and check the reservoir for cracks.

RADIATOR

2005 and earlier models

▸ **Refer to illustrations 5.5, 5.7a and 5.7b**

2 Disconnect the negative battery cable (see Chapter 5).
3 Drain the engine coolant into a container (see Chapter 1).
4 Remove the cooling fans (see Section 4).
5 Disconnect the reservoir hose from the filler neck, loosen the radiator hose clamps and remove the upper radiator hose (see illustration). Loosen the hose clamps and remove the lower radiator hose.
6 If equipped with an automatic transmission, disconnect the oil cooler hose from the radiator. Place a drip pan to catch the transmission fluid and cap the fittings.
7 Remove the radiator mounting bolts. On 1997 and earlier models, there are two bolts, one at each upper corner of the radiator. On some earlier models, there are also mounting pins at the lower left and right edges of the radiator (see illustrations). The radiators on 1999 through 2005 models are secured by two mounting brackets, one near each upper corner, which are secured to the radiator by nuts. To remove the radiator, lift it out from above. Watch out for dripping fluid and sharp fins.

5.1a Remove the reservoir mounting bolts (2005 and earlier models shown)

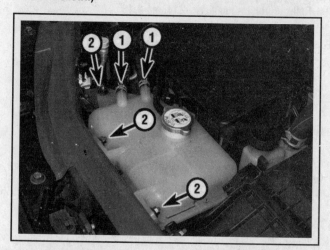

5.1b Coolant reservoir details (2006 and later models):

1 Coolant hoses (disconnect the third hose, which is underneath, after lifting up the reservoir)
2 Coolant reservoir mounting nuts

5.5 Disconnect the reservoir hose from the filler neck and the upper hose from the fitting

5.7a Remove the upper mounting bolt on each side (1990 through 1997 model shown; 1999 through 2005 models use a pair of small mounting brackets, one at each upper corner) . . .

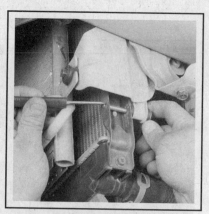

5.7b . . . then pry off the clip and pull out the mounting pin on each side to free the radiator (some earlier models)

2006 and later models

▸ **Refer to illustration 5.20**

8 Disconnect the cable from the negative battery terminal (see Chapter 5).

9 Raise the vehicle and place it securely on jackstands. Remove the engine compartment under-cover.

10 Drain the engine coolant (see Chapter 1).

11 Remove the battery and the battery tray (see Chapter 5), then remove the battery cooling duct (see illustration 4.11).

12 Remove the air filter housing (see Chapter 4).

13 Remove the Powertrain Control Module (PCM) (see Chapter 6).

14 Remove the Powertrain Control Module (PCM) cooling duct (see illustration 4.14).

15 Remove the coolant reservoir (see illustration 5.1b).

16 On vehicles with an automatic transmission, detach the ATF cooler hose.

17 Disconnect the electrical connector from the cooling fan motor (see illustration 4.16).

18 Loosen the hose clamps and disconnect the upper and lower radiator hoses from the radiator.

19 Remove the power steering cooler line and the air conditioning condenser (see Section 17). Do not disconnect the hoses from either the power steering coolant pipe or the condenser.

20 Remove the upper and lower radiator insulator mounting brackets (see illustration).

21 Remove the radiator and cooling fan shroud from below as a single assembly.

22 Detach the cooling fan shroud and cooling fan motor from the radiator.

All models

23 With the radiator removed, it can be inspected for leaks, damage and internal blockage. If in need of repairs, have a professional radiator shop or dealer service department perform the work as special techniques are required.

24 Bugs and dirt can be cleaned from the radiator with compressed air and a soft brush. Don't bend the cooling fins as this is done.

❋❋ WARNING:

Wear eye protection when using compressed air.

5.20 Radiator removal details (2006 and later models):

1   *Power steering cooler line (see Section 17 for details)*
2   *Condenser (see Section 17 for details)*
3   *Upper radiator insulator mounting bracket fasteners*
4   *Upper radiator insulator brackets (rubber insulators not visible in this photo)*
5   *Lower radiator insulator mounting bracket fasteners*
6   *Lower radiator insulator mounting brackets*
7   *Lower radiator insulators*

25 Installation is the reverse of the removal procedure. Be sure the bottom of the radiator is located properly. When installing the radiator fan shroud and the air intake duct, tighten the mounting bolts securely.

26 Fill the cooling system with the proper mixture of antifreeze and water (see Chapter 1).

27 Start the engine and check for leaks. Allow the engine to reach normal operating temperature, indicated by both radiator hoses becoming hot. Recheck the coolant level and add more if required.

28 On automatic transmission equipped models, check and add automatic transmission fluid as needed.

6   Water pump - check

1   A failure in the water pump can cause serious engine damage due to overheating. If the pump is defective, it should be replaced with a new or rebuilt unit

2   If you're working on a 2005 or earlier model, remove the timing belt cover(s) (see Chapter 2A).

3   Water pumps are equipped with weep or vent holes. If a failure occurs in the pump seal, coolant will leak from the hole. In most cases you'll need a flashlight to find the hole on the water pump from underneath to check for leaks. Any water coming from this hole is vented to the outside of the timing belt cover on the back side of the engine in order to not damage the timing belt.

4   Check the water pump shaft bearing for wear by grasping the pump hub and gently rocking the hub and shaft from side to side. If any looseness is apparent, excessive water pump shaft/bearing wear is possible.

5   If the water pump shaft bearings fail there may be a howling sound at the drivebelt end of the engine while it's running. Don't mistake drivebelt slippage, which causes a squealing sound, for water pump bearing failure. If a squealing sound is heard, check belt condition and belt tension.

7 Water pump - removal and installation

✳✳ WARNING:

Wait until the engine is completely cool before beginning this procedure. Do not allow antifreeze to come in contact with your skin or painted surfaces of the vehicle. Rinse off spills immediately with plenty of water. Antifreeze is highly toxic if ingested. Never leave antifreeze lying around in an open container or in puddles on the floor; children and pets are attracted by it's sweet smell and may drink it. Check with local authorities about disposing of used antifreeze. Many communities have collection centers which will see that antifreeze is disposed of safely.

2005 AND EARLIER MODELS

Removal

▶ **Refer to illustration 7.6**

1   Disconnect the negative battery cable from the battery (see Chapter 5).

2   Drain the cooling system (see Chapter 1). If the coolant is relatively new or in good condition, save it and reuse it.

3   Remove the water pump drivebelt, pulley, timing belt cover(s) and timing belt (see Chapter 2A).

4   Remove the water inlet pipe and gasket from the water pump.

5   Remove the water bypass pipe and O-ring, located on the water inlet pipe.

6   Remove the water pump mounting bolts (see illustration) and detach the water pump from the engine. If the water pump is stuck, gently tap it with a soft-faced hammer to break the seal.

Installation

7   Clean the bolt threads and the threaded holes in the engine to remove corrosion and sealant.

8   Remove all traces of old gasket material from the sealing surfaces.

9   Compare the new water pump to the old one to make sure they are identical.

10 Apply a thin film of silicone sealant to the new gasket and install it on the water pump.

11 Carefully mate the water pump to the engine.

12 Install the water pump mounting bolts. Tighten them to the torque listed in this Chapter's Specifications. Don't over-tighten them or the pump may be damaged.

13 Reinstall all parts removed for access to the water pump.

14 Refill the cooling system (see Chapter 1) and check the timing belt tension (see Chapter 2A). Run the engine and check for leaks.

2006 AND LATER MODELS

▶ **Refer to illustration 7.17**

15 Disconnect the cable from the negative battery terminal (see Chapter 5). Remove the battery and the battery tray (see Chapter 5).

16 Remove the air filter housing (see Chapter 4).

17 Loosen the water pump pulley bolts (see illustration).

18 Remove the drivebelt (see Chapter 1).

19 Remove the water pump pulley bolts and remove the pulley.

20 Remove the water pump bolts and remove the water pump.

21 Remove and discard the old water pump O-ring type gasket.

22 Clean off the mating surfaces of the water pump and the engine.

23 Using a new gasket, install the water pump and tighten the bolts to the torque listed in this Chapter's Specifications. Install the pulley, tightening the bolts as securely as possible at this time.

24 Install the drivebelt, then tighten the water pump pulley bolts to the torque listed in this Chapter's Specifications.

25 The remainder of installation is the reverse of removal.

26 Refill the cooling system (see Chapter 1).

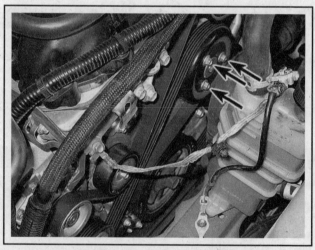

7.6 After removing the front covers and timing belt, remove the water pump mounting bolts and remove the water pump

7.17 Before removing the drivebelt, loosen the water pump pulley bolts

8 Coolant temperature gauge sending unit - check and replacement

✳✳ WARNING:

Do not start this procedure until the engine is completely cool.

1997 AND EARLIER MODELS

Check

▸ **Refer to illustration 8.3**

1 If the coolant temperature gauge is inoperative, check the fuses first (see Chapter 12).

2 If the temperature gauge indicates excessive temperature after running awhile, see the Troubleshooting Section in the front of the manual.

3 If the temperature gauge indicates HOT as soon as the engine is started cold, disconnect the electrical connector at the coolant gauge sending unit, located at rear of the engine (see illustration). If the gauge reading drops, replace the sending unit. If the reading remains high, the wire to the gauge may be shorted to ground or the gauge is faulty.

4 If the coolant temperature gauge fails to show any indication after the engine has been warmed up, (approximately 10 minutes) and the fuses are good, shut off the engine. Disconnect the electrical connector at the sending unit and, using a jumper wire, connect the wire to a clean ground on the engine. Briefly turn on the ignition without starting the engine. If the gauge now indicates HOT, replace the sending unit.

5 Additionally, the sending unit may be checked for resistance using an ohmmeter; with the engine coolant hot, resistance should be 190 to 260 ohms.

6 If the gauge fails to respond, the circuit may be open or the temperature gauge may be faulty.

Replacement

7 Drain the coolant (see Chapter 1).

8 Disconnect the wiring connector from the sending unit.

9 Using a deep socket or a wrench, remove the sending unit.

10 Install the new sending unit, and tighten it securely. Do not use thread sealer as it may electrically insulate the sending unit. Connect the electrical connector.

11 Refill the cooling system and check for coolant leakage and proper gauge operation.

1999 AND LATER MODELS

12 On these models, there is no coolant temperature gauge sending unit. This function is handled by the Engine Coolant Temperature (ECT) sensor, an information sensor for the Powertrain Control Module (PCM) (see Chapter 6).

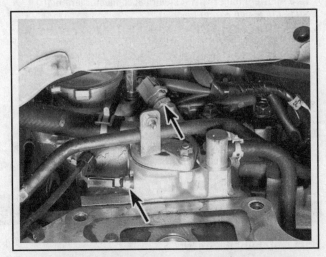

8.3 On 1997 and earlier models, the temperature gauge sending unit (left arrow) and the PCM temperature sensor (right arrow) are mounted on the rear of the engine (transmission removed for clarity)

9 Radiator cooling fan thermoswitch (1993 and earlier models) - replacement

1 Drain the cooling system (see Chapter 1).

2 To replace the main radiator cooling fan thermoswitch, disconnect the electrical connector and unscrew the switch from the thermostat housing.

3 Install the new switch with a new O-ring and tighten it securely. Connect the electrical connector.

4 Refill the cooling system.

10 Blower motor resistor - check and replacement

CHECK

▸ **Refer to illustrations 10.5 and 10.6**

➥**Note: This Section does not apply to 2006 and later models, on which the blower motor is electronically controlled. On all earlier models, the blower motor resistor is located on the blower motor housing.**

1 Make sure that the ignition key is turned to OFF.

2 Remove the trim panel below the glove box (see Chapter 11).

3 Disconnect the electrical connector from the blower motor resistor.

4 Refer to the accompanying connector terminal guide and check the continuity of the resistor side of the connector as follows:

5 On 1996 and earlier models, there should be continuity between

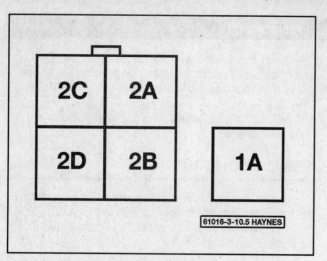

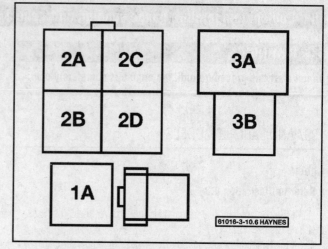

10.5 Blower motor resistor electrical connector terminal guide (1996 and earlier models)

10.6 Blower motor resistor electrical connector terminal guide (1997 through 2005 models)

terminals 1A and 2A, 1A and 2B, 1A and 2C, and 1A and 2D, respectively (see illustration).

6   On 1997 through 2005 models, there should be continuity between terminals 1A and 3A and between terminals 3B and 2B, but there should not be continuity between terminals 2B and 2A, 2A and 2C, and 2C and 2D (see illustration).

7   If the indicated continuity is not as specified, replace the resistor.

REPLACEMENT

8   Remove the old resistor from the blower motor housing. Install a new resistor and reconnect the electrical connector.

9   Start the engine, turn on the blower motor and verify that it works properly at all speeds.

10   Install the lower trim panel below the glove box (see Chapter 11).

11 Blower motor and housing - removal and installation

2005 AND EARLIER MODELS

Blower motor

▸ **Refer to illustrations 11.2, 11.3 and 11.5**

1   Remove the trim panel underneath the glove box (see Chapter 11).

2   Disconnect the electrical connector from the blower motor (see illustration).

3   Remove the three screws retaining the blower motor to the housing (see illustration).

4   Withdraw the blower motor straight down and out of the housing.

5   To remove the blower fan, remove the clip from the shaft and withdraw the fan from the motor (see illustration).

6   Installation is the reverse of removal.

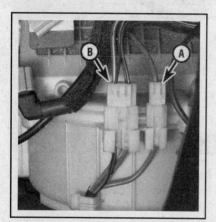

11.2 Unplug the power terminal connector (A) and the resistor terminal connector (B), then slip them out of the mounting bracket

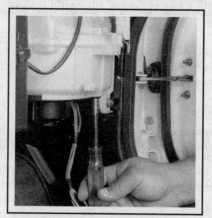

11.3 Remove the three screws and lower the blower motor from the housing

11.5 Remove the clip in the center of the fan to separate the fan from the motor

Blower housing

▶ **Refer to illustrations 11.9a and 11.9b**

7   Remove the glove box (see Chapter 11).
8   Disconnect the heater blower electrical connectors.
9   Unclip the seal at the left end of the blower unit (see illustration). Remove the upper bolt and two lower nuts and take the unit out (see illustration).
10 Installation is the reverse of removal.

2006 AND LATER MODELS

▶ **Refer to illustration 11.12**

11 Remove the trim panel below the glove box (see Chapter 11).
12 Disconnect the electrical connector from the blower motor (see illustration).
13 Remove the blower motor assembly mounting screws and remove the blower motor assembly.
14 Installation is the reverse of removal.

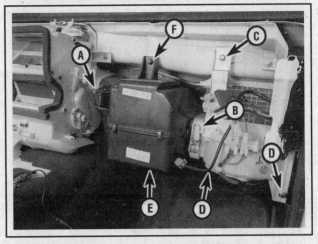

11.9a Blower and cooling unit mounting details

A   Cooling unit-to-heater unit seal plate
B   Cooling unit-to-blower housing seal plate
C   Blower housing upper mounting bolt
D   Blower housing lower mounting nuts (left nut hidden)
E   Cooling unit lower mounting nuts (hidden)
F   Cooling unit upper mounting bolt

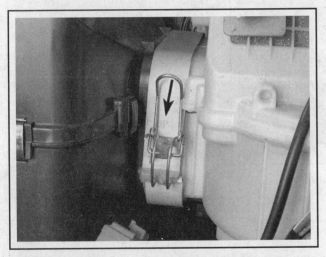

11.9b Each seal plate has an UP mark (arrow); this is the blower housing-to-cooling unit seal plate

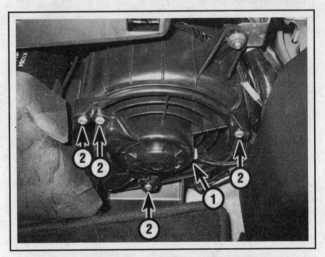

11.12 Blower motor details (2006 and later models):

1   Electrical connector
2   Blower motor mounting screws

12 Heater core - replacement

✳✳ WARNING:

All models are equipped with airbags. The airbag is armed and can deploy (inflate) anytime the battery is connected. To prevent accidental deployment (and possible injury), turn the ignition key to LOCK and disconnect the negative battery cable whenever working near airbag components. After the battery is disconnected, wait at least two minutes before beginning work (the system has a back-up capacitor that must fully discharge). For more information see Chapter 12.

✳✳ WARNING:

The air conditioning system is under high pressure. Do not loosen any hose fittings or remove any components until the system has been discharged. Air conditioning refrigerant should be properly discharged into an EPA-approved recovery/recycling unit by a dealer service department or an automotive air conditioning repair facility. Always wear eye protection when disconnecting air conditioning system fittings.

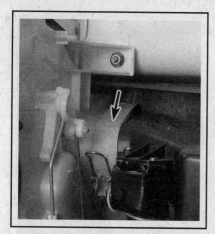

12.5 Location of the cooling unit-to-heater unit seal plate

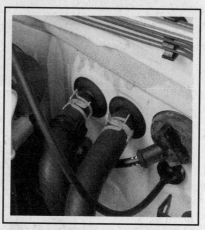

12.6 Disconnect the heater hoses from the heater unit in the engine compartment - these spring-clip type hose clamps can be removed with pliers

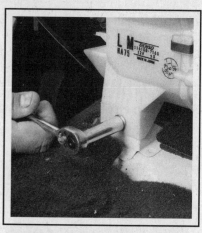

12.7a Remove the heater unit lower mounting nuts . . .

12.7b . . . and the upper mounting nuts

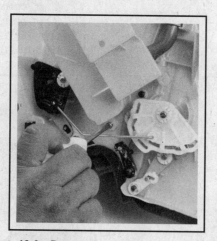

12.9a Remove the cover's lower screw . . .

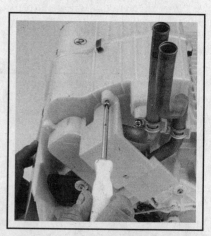

12.9b . . . and the upper screw and cover

2005 AND EARLIER MODELS

▶ **Refer to illustrations 12.5, 12.6, 12.7a, 12.7b and 12.9a through 12.9e**

1   Have the air conditioning system discharged and recovered by a qualified repair facility.

2   Disconnect the cable from the negative battery terminal (see Chapter 5).

3   Drain the engine coolant (see Chapter 1).

4   Remove the center console and the instrument panel (see Chapter 11)..

5   Unlatch the seal plate latch on the right side of the heater unit (see illustration 11.9a and the accompanying illustration).

6   Disconnect the heater hoses from the heater core by undoing the hose connections at the firewall (see illustration). Keep plenty of towels or rags on the carpeting to catch any coolant that may drip.

7   Remove the three nuts from the studs retaining the heater unit to the firewall (see illustrations).

8   Remove the heater unit from the firewall. The seal plate will come out with the heater unit as an assembly.

9   Remove the heater core from the heater unit (see illustrations).

10   Reassembly is the reverse of removal. When installing the heater hoses on the heater core, make sure the hose clamps are securely positioned. Refill the cooling system (see Chapter 1), then have the air conditioning system evacuated and recharged at the shop that discharged it.

2006 AND LATER MODELS

▶ **Refer to illustration 12.14**

11   Have the air conditioning system refrigerant discharged and recovered by a qualified repair facility.

12   Disconnect the cable from the negative battery terminal (see Chapter 5).

13   Drain the engine coolant (see Chapter 1).

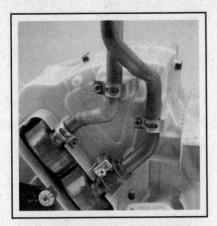

12.9c Remove these screws and the core tube clamps . . .

12.9d . . . and withdraw the core from the housing

12.9e Make sure the foam sealing material is in good condition

14 Remove the flange bolt that secures the air conditioning lines to the evaporator at the right part of the firewall (see illustration), then disconnect the lines. Remove and discard the old O-rings. Plug the open pipes immediately to prevent moisture and contaminants from entering the evaporator.

15 Loosen the hose clamps and disconnect the two heater hoses from the heater core pipes, next to the air conditioning lines on the firewall. Plug the open pipes immediately to prevent contaminants from entering the heater core.

16 Remove the instrument panel (see Chapter 11).

17 Remove the fasteners that secure the air distribution unit (the left housing) and the air conditioning unit (the right housing) to the firewall.

18 Remove the two nuts that secure the air distribution unit to the air conditioning unit and separate the two units.

19 The heater core is located in the air conditioning unit. Set the air distribution unit aside and disassemble the air conditioning unit as follows.

20 Remove the fasteners that secure the upper part of the housing to the lower part of the housing and remove the upper part.

21 Remove the heater core from the lower part of the housing.

22 Installation is the reverse of removal.

23 Refill the cooling system (see Chapter 1), then have the air conditioning system evacuated and recharged at the shop that discharged it.

12.14 Air conditioning high-pressure (1) and low-pressure (2) lines and heater hoses (3)

13 Heater and air conditioning control assembly - removal, installation and adjustment

❄❄ **WARNING:**

All models are equipped with airbags. The airbag is armed and can deploy (inflate) anytime the battery is connected. To prevent accidental deployment (and possible injury), turn the ignition key to LOCK and disconnect the negative battery cable whenever working near airbag components. After the battery is disconnected, wait at least two minutes before beginning work (the system has a back-up capacitor that must fully discharge). For more information see Chapter 12.

2005 AND EARLIER MODELS

Removal and installation

▶ Refer to illustrations 13.4a, 13.4b, 13.5, 13.6a and 13.6b

1 Disconnect the negative battery cable (see Chapter 5).
2 Remove the console (see Chapter 11).
3 Remove the center heater and radio control panel (see Chapter 11).

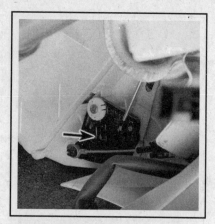

13.4a Airflow mode lever and wire - the set hole (arrow) is used for adjustment (2005 and earlier models shown)

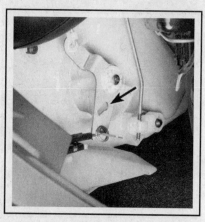

13.4b Air mix lever and wire - the set hole is used for adjustment (1997 and earlier models shown)

13.5 Free the air intake wire from the clip and detach it from the blower unit (1997 and earlier models shown)

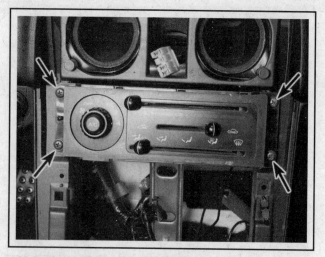

13.6a On 1997 and earlier models, remove the control unit mounting screws and pull it out partway . . .

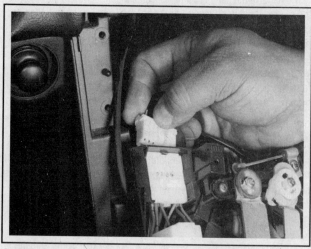

13.6b . . . then unplug the electrical connector and remove it the rest of the way

4   Disconnect the air mix wire and airflow mode wire from the heater unit behind the heater control (see illustrations).

5   Disconnect the air intake wire from the blower unit (see illustration).

6   On 1997 and earlier models, remove the heater control assembly screws (see illustration). Pull the assembly out of the dash and unplug its electrical connector (see illustration). On 1999 through 2005 models, the heater control assembly is not secured by mounting screws; it's secured by a pair of spring-type clips, one on each side. Using a small, tape-wrapped screwdriver, carefully pry off the small trim pieces that cover the gaps between the control assembly and the center trim panel. Insert a pair of special removal tools (Mazda SST #49 UN01 050, or a suitable aftermarket equivalent) into the gaps in accordance with the tool manufacturer's instructions, then pull the special removal tools out and to the rear simultaneously to slide out the control assembly.

7   Installation is the reverse of the removal procedure. When installation of the heater/air conditioning control assembly is complete, connect and adjust the heater control wires as follows.

Adjustment

8   To connect and adjust the air intake wire, set the REC-FRESH lever to the Fresh position, connect the air intake wire to the air intake link, set the REC-FRESH door to FRESH position and place a 0.20-inch diameter pin in the set hole. Clamp the wire in place and remove the pin. Check that the lever moves its full stroke.

9   To connect and adjust the air mix wire, set the temperature lever to the MAX HOT position, connect the air mix wire to the MIX door, set the door to the MAX HOT position and place a 0.20-inch diameter pin in the set hole (see illustration 13.4b). Clamp the wire in place and remove the pin. Check that the lever moves its full stroke.

10 To connect and adjust the airflow mode wire, set the MODE lever to the VENT position, connect the airflow mode wire to the MODE door, set the door to the VENT position and place a 0.20-inch diameter pin in the set hole (see illustration 13.4a). Clamp the wire in place and remove the pin. Check that the lever moves its full stroke.

2006 AND LATER MODELS

▶ **Refer to illustration 13.13**

11 Disconnect the cable from the negative battery terminal (see Chapter 5).

12 Remove the lower panel, the knee bolster, the sidewall trim pieces from both sides and the center panel unit (see Chapter 11).

13 Remove the heater and air conditioning control assembly from the center panel unit (see illustration).

14 Installation is the reverse of removal.

13.13 Heater and air conditioning control assembly mounting screws

14 Air conditioning and heating system - check and maintenance

☀ WARNING:

The air conditioning system is under high pressure. Do not loosen any hose fittings or remove any components until the system has been discharged. Air conditioning refrigerant should be properly discharged into an EPA-approved recovery/recycling unit by a dealer service department or an automotive air conditioning repair facility. Always wear eye protection when disconnecting air conditioning system fittings.

AIR CONDITIONING SYSTEM

▶ **Refer to illustration 14.1**

1 The following maintenance checks should be performed on a regular basis to ensure that the air conditioning system continues to operate at peak efficiency:

a) *Inspect the condition of the compressor drivebelt. If it is worn or deteriorated, replace it (see Chapter 1).*

b) *Check the drivebelt tension and, if necessary, adjust it (see Chapter 1).*

c) *Inspect the system hoses. Look for cracks, bubbles, hardening and deterioration. Inspect the hoses and all fittings for oil bubbles or seepage. If there is any evidence of wear, damage or leakage, replace the hose(s).*

d) *Inspect the condenser fins for leaves, bugs and any other foreign material that may have embedded itself in the fins. Use a fin comb or compressed air to remove debris from the condenser (see illustration).*

e) *Make sure the system has the correct refrigerant charge.*

2 It's a good idea to operate the system for about ten minutes at least once a month. This is particularly important during the winter months because long term non-use can cause hardening, and subsequent failure, of the seals.

3 Leaks in the air conditioning system are best spotted when the system is brought up to operating temperature and pressure, by running the engine with the air conditioning ON for five minutes. Shut the engine off and inspect the air conditioning hoses and connections. Traces of oil usually indicate refrigerant leaks.

4 Because of the complexity of the air conditioning system and the special equipment required to effectively work on it, accurate troubleshooting of the system should be left to a professional technician.

5 If the air conditioning system doesn't operate at all, check the fuse panel and the air conditioning relay, located in the fuse/relay box in the engine compartment.

6 The most common cause of poor cooling is simply a low system refrigerant charge. If a noticeable drop in cool air output occurs, the following quick check will help you determine if the refrigerant level is low.

14.1 The fins of the condenser can be cleaned with a fin comb - use the side of the tool with the correct fins-per-inch spacing for your core

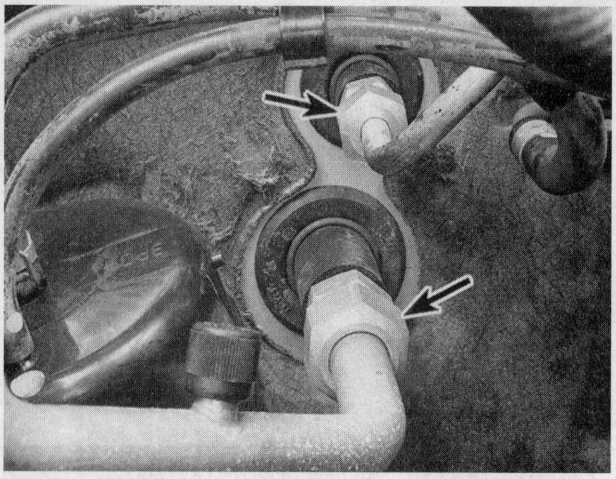

14.9 With the system operating, the evaporator outlet line (large tubing) should feel slightly cooler than the inlet line (small tubing)

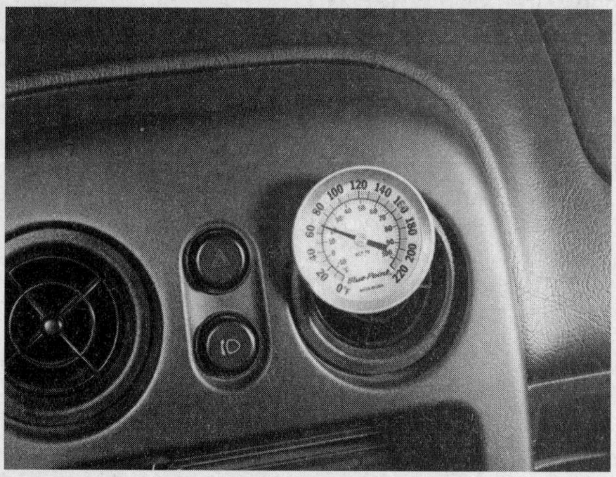

14.10 Check the temperature of the output air in the center register with a thermometer - it should be 35 to 40 degrees below the surrounding air temperature

Checking the refrigerant charge

Refer to illustrations 14.9, 14.10 and 14.11

7 Warm the engine up to normal operating temperature.

8 With the engine at fast idle, place the air conditioning temperature selector at the coldest setting and put the blower at the highest setting. Open the doors (to make sure the air conditioning system doesn't cycle off as soon as it cools the passenger compartment).

9 With the compressor engaged, the clutch will make an audible click and the center of the clutch will rotate. After the system reaches operating temperature, feel the two pipes connected to the evaporator at the firewall (see illustration).

10 The pipe leading from the condenser outlet to the evaporator (small tubing) should be cold, and the evaporator outlet line (the larger tubing that leads back to the compressor) should be slightly colder (3 to 10 degrees F). If the evaporator outlet is considerably warmer than the inlet, the system needs a charge. Insert a thermometer in the center air distribution duct while operating the air conditioning system (see illustration) - the temperature of the output air should be 35 to 40 degrees F below the ambient air temperature (down to approximately 40 degrees F). If the ambient (outside) air temperature is very high, say 110 degrees F, the duct air temperature may be as high as 60 degrees F, but generally the air conditioning is 35 to 40 degrees F cooler than the surrounding air. If the air isn't as cold as it used to be, the system probably needs a charge. Further inspection or testing of the system is beyond the scope of the home mechanic and should be left to a professional.

11 Inspect the sight glass (if equipped). If the refrigerant looks foamy when running, it's low (see illustration). When surrounding temperatures are very hot, bubbles may show in the sight glass even with the proper amount of refrigerant. With the proper amount of refrigerant, when the air conditioning is turned off, the sight glass should show refrigerant that foams, then clears.

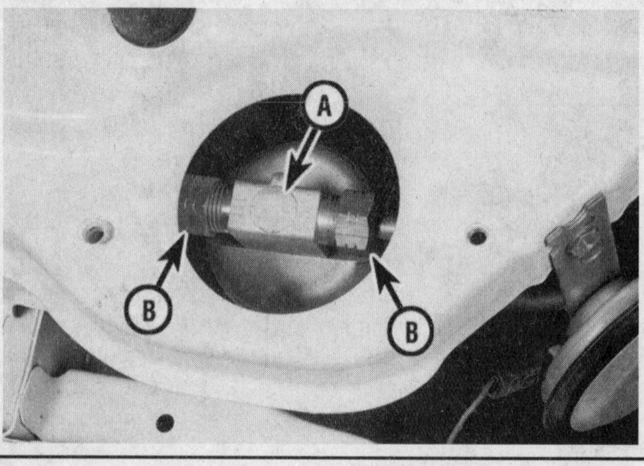

14.11 The sight glass (A) (models so equipped) on top of the receiver/drier can be used to check the refrigerant state of charge - when removing the receiver/drier, disconnect these two connectors (B) (1997 and earlier models shown)

Adding refrigerant

CAUTION:

Refrigerant has changed from the use of R-12 on models through 1994, to the "environmentally friendly" R-134a used in 1995 and later models. The two refrigerants are not compatible, and their oils are also not compatible. Even after purging and evacuating an R-12 system, there is enough residual oil and refrigerant in the hoses and components that simply filling the system with R-134a should not be done by the home mechanic. Special fittings and manifold gauge sets are used on the different refrigerant types so that an accidental hook-up of the two systems cannot be made. When replacing entire components, additional refrigerant oil should be added equal to the amount that is removed with the component being replaced. Refrigerant oils, just like refrigerant R-12 vs. R-134a, are not compatible. Be sure to read the can before adding any oil to the system, to make sure it is compatible with the type of system being repaired.

Note: Because of Federal regulations by the Environmental Protection Agency, R-12 refrigerant is not available for home-mechanic use, however, cans of R-134 refrigerant are commonly available in auto parts stores. Models with R-12 systems will have to be serviced at a dealership or air conditioning shop.

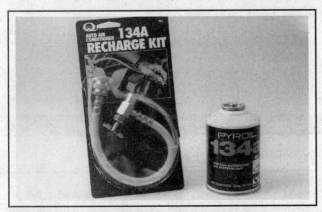

14.13a Refrigerant kit for R-134 recharging

14.13b Connect the kit to the service valve

1994 and earlier models (R-12 systems)

12 Because of Federal regulations implemented by the Environmental Protection Agency, R-12 refrigerant is not available for home-mechanic use. Model years through 1994 use R-12 refrigerant. Have the system discharged, evacuated, charged and leak tested by a qualified shop. Use only refrigerant oil compatible with your system. Refrigerant oils for use with refrigerant R-12 are not compatible with other oils.

1995 and later models (R-134a systems)

▶ **Refer to illustrations 14.13a and 14.13b**

13 Buy an automotive charging kit at an auto parts store (see illustration). A charging kit includes a can of R-134a refrigerant, a tap valve and a short section of hose that can be attached between the tap valve and the system low side service valve. The system low side service valve (charging port) is located on the larger air conditioning tubing line going to the firewall (see illustration).

> ❄❄ **CAUTION:**
>
> **Never add more than one can of refrigerant to the system. If more refrigerant than that is required, the system should be evacuated and leak tested.**

14 Connect the charging kit by following the manufacturer's instructions. Back off the valve handle on the charging kit and screw the kit onto the refrigerant can, making sure first that the O-ring or rubber seal inside the threaded portion of the kit is in place.

> ❄❄ **WARNING:**
>
> **Wear protective eye wear when dealing with pressurized refrigerant cans.**

15 Remove the dust cap from the low-side charging port and attach the quick-connect fitting on the kit hose.

> ❄❄ **WARNING:**
>
> **DO NOT hook the charging kit hose to the system high side! The fittings on the charging kit are designed to fit only on the low side of the system.**

16 Warm the engine to normal operating temperature and turn on the air conditioner. Keep the charging kit hose away from the fan and other moving parts.

17 Turn the valve handle on the kit until the stem pierces the can, then back the handle out to release the refrigerant. You should be able to hear the rush of gas. Add refrigerant to the low side of the system until both the outlet and the evaporator inlet pipe feel about the same temperature. Allow stabilization time between each addition.

18 If you have an accurate thermometer, you can place it in the center air conditioning duct inside the vehicle to monitor the air temperature. A charged system that is working properly, should output air down to approximately 40 degrees F.

19 When the can is empty, turn the valve handle to the closed position and release the connection from the low-side port. Replace the dust cap.

20 Remove the charging kit from the can and store the kit for future use with the piercing valve in the UP position, to prevent inadvertently piercing the can on the next use.

HEATING SYSTEMS

21 If the air coming out of the heater vents isn't hot, the problem could stem from any of the following causes:

   a) *The thermostat is stuck open, preventing the engine coolant from warming up enough to carry heat to the heater core. Replace the thermostat (see Section 3).*
   b) *A heater hose is blocked, preventing the flow of coolant through the heater core. Feel both heater hoses at the firewall. They should be hot. If one of them is cold, there is an obstruction in one of the hoses or in the heater core, or the heater control valve is shut. Detach the hoses and back flush the heater core with a water hose. If the heater core is clear but circulation is impeded, remove the two hoses and flush them out with a water hose.*
   c) *If flushing fails to remove the blockage from the heater core, the core must be replaced. (see Section 12).*

22 If the blower motor speed does not correspond to the setting selected on the blower switch, the problem could be a bad fuse, circuit, switch, blower motor resistor or motor (see Sections 10 and 11).

23 If there isn't any air coming out of the vents:

   a) *Turn the ignition ON and activate the fan control. Place your ear at the heating/air conditioning register (vent) and listen. Most motors are audible. Can you hear the motor running?*
   b) *If you can't (and have already verified that the blower switch and the blower motor resistor are good), the blower motor itself is probably bad (see Section 10).*

24 If the carpet under the heater core is damp, or if antifreeze vapor or steam is coming through the vents, the heater core is leaking. Remove it (see Section 12) and install a new unit (most radiator shops will not repair a leaking heater core).

25 Inspect the drain hose from the evaporator housing located under the vehicle; make sure it is not clogged.

15 Air conditioning receiver/drier - removal and installation

✳✳ WARNING:

The air conditioning system is under high pressure. Do not loosen any hose fittings or remove any components until the system has been discharged. Air conditioning refrigerant should be properly discharged into an EPA-approved recovery/recycling unit by a dealer service department or an automotive air conditioning repair facility. Always wear eye protection when disconnecting air conditioning system fittings.

2000 AND EARLIER MODELS

♦ Refer to illustration 15.4

➡Note: On these models, the receiver/drier is located at the right end of the condenser.

1 Have the refrigerant discharged and recovered by a qualified repair facility.

2 Disconnect the battery negative cable (see Chapter 5).

3 Block the rear wheels so the vehicle can't roll. Jack up the front end at least one foot and place it securely on jackstands. Remove the splash shield and air guide panels from under the front of the vehicle.

4 Disconnect the refrigerant lines from the receiver/drier (see illustration 14.11 and the accompanying illustration). Cap the open fittings immediately to prevent entry of moisture.

5 On 1997 and earlier models, remove the bolt from the receiver/drier clamping band and remove the receiver drier. On 1999 and 2000 models, remove the two nuts that secure the receiver/drier to the mounting bracket on the condenser.

15.4 If the fittings at the receiver/drier are difficult to access, remove the refrigerant line clamp bolt (right arrow) and disconnect the refrigerant line fitting (left arrow) using two wrenches; cap the open fittings immediately (1997 and earlier models shown)

2001 THROUGH 2005 MODELS

➡Note: On these models, the receiver/drier is located at the right end of the condenser. The receiver/drier is an integral component of the condenser. If the receiver/drier must be replaced, you must replace the condenser. However, you might be able to find a separate receiver/drier in the aftermarket that will work.

6 Replace the condenser (see Section 17).

2006 AND LATER MODELS

♦ Refer to illustration 15.10

7 Have the air conditioning system refrigerant discharged and recovered by a qualified repair facility.

8 Raise the front of the vehicle and place it securely on jackstands.

9 Remove the engine compartment under cover.

10 Remove the flange bolt that secures the inlet and outlet air conditioning refrigerant lines to the receiver/drier (see illustration).

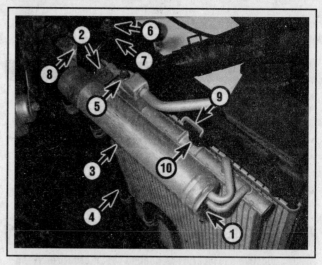

15.10 Receiver/drier and condenser (left side) details (2006 and later models):

1   Refrigerant line flange bolt
2   Receiver/drier mounting bracket bolt
3   Receiver/drier
4   Power steering cooler line
5   Refrigerant line flange bolt
6   Upper left condenser mounting bracket bolt
7   Upper left condenser mounting bracket
8   Upper left condenser mounting bolt
9   Left condenser mounting clip
10   Left condenser mounting clip bracket

11 Remove the receiver/drier mounting bracket bolt and remove the receiver/drier from the condenser.

12 Remove and discard the old refrigerant line O-rings. Always use new O-rings when reattaching the refrigerant line flange to the receiver/drier.

ALL MODELS

13 Installation is the reverse of removal. Replace any O-rings with new ones specifically made for the type of refrigerant in your system and lubricate them with refrigerant oil prior to installation.

✳✳ WARNING:

Do not apply compressor oil to the fitting nuts. Tighten the receiver/drier inlet and outlet fittings securely.

14 Have the system evacuated, charged and leak tested by the shop that discharged it. If the receiver was replaced, have them add about 0.3 ounces of new refrigerant oil to the high pressure side of the compressor. Use only refrigerant oil compatible with your system.

16 Air conditioning compressor - removal and installation

▶ **Refer to illustrations 16.5a and 16.5b**

✳✳ WARNING:

The air conditioning system is under high pressure. Do not loosen any hose fittings or remove any components until the system has been discharged. Air conditioning refrigerant should be properly discharged into an EPA-approved recovery/recycling unit by a dealer service department or an automotive air conditioning repair facility. Always wear eye protection when disconnecting air conditioning system fittings.

1 Have the refrigerant discharged and recovered by a qualified repair facility.

2 Disconnect the negative cable from the battery (see Chapter 5).

3 Remove the drivebelt from the compressor (see Chapter 1).

4 Block the rear wheels so the vehicle can't roll. Jack up the front end at least one foot and place it securely on jackstands. Remove the splash shield and air guide panels from under the front of the vehicle.

5 Disconnect the refrigerant lines and compressor electrical connector (see illustrations). Unbolt the compressor and lower it away from the vehicle.

6 If a new or rebuilt compressor is being installed, follow the directions supplied with the compressor regarding the proper level of refrigerant oil prior to installation.

7 Installation is the reverse of removal. Tighten the compressor mounting bolts securely. Replace any O-rings with new ones specifically for the type of refrigerant in your system and lubricate them with refrigerant oil prior to installation.

✳✳ WARNING:

Do not apply compressor oil to the fitting nuts. Tighten the refrigerant line bolts securely.

8 Have the system evacuated, recharged and leak tested by the shop that discharged it.

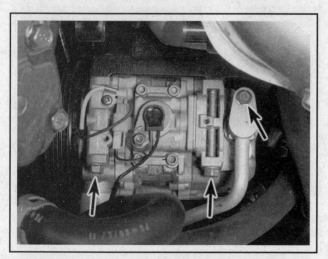

16.5a Disconnect the wiring harness connector at the compressor, then disconnect the upper fitting and upper mounting bolts

16.5b Disconnect the lower fitting and remove the lower mounting bolts

17 Air conditioning condenser - removal and installation

❄❄ **WARNING:**

The air conditioning system is under high pressure. Do not loosen any hose fittings or remove any components until the system has been discharged. Air conditioning refrigerant should be properly discharged into an EPA-approved recovery/recycling unit by a dealer service department or an automotive air conditioning repair facility. Always wear eye protection when disconnecting air conditioning system fittings.

1 Have the refrigerant discharged and recovered by a qualified repair facility.

2 Disconnect the cable from the negative battery terminal (see Chapter 5).

3 Raise the vehicle and place it securely on jackstands. Remove the engine under cover, if equipped.

4 Insert a fin protector such as a sheet of cardboard between the radiator and condenser.

2005 AND EARLIER MODELS

▶ **Refer to illustrations 17.6 and 17.7**

5 Remove the receiver/drier (see Section 15).

6 Disconnect the refrigerant lines (see illustration). Immediately cap the open fittings to keep moisture and contamination out of the system.

7 Remove the mounting nuts and bolts and lift out the condenser (see illustration).

2006 AND LATER MODELS

▶ **Refer to illustration 17.9**

8 Remove the battery cooling duct and the Powertrain Control Module (PCM) cooling duct from the radiator (see illustrations 4.11 and 4.14).

9 Remove the power steering cooler line from the condenser (see illustration 4.11 and accompanying illustration). Do not disconnect the power steering hoses from the cooler line.

10 If you're planning to replace the condenser, remove the receiver/drier (see Section 15). If not, it's not necessary to remove the receiver/drier.

11 Disconnect the refrigerant lines from the receiver/drier (see illustrations 4.11 and 15.10).

12 Remove the upper left mounting bracket bolt and mounting bracket (see illustration 15.10).

13 Remove the upper left and upper right condenser mounting bolts (see illustrations 4.11 and 15.10).

14 Disengage the condenser mounting clips from their corresponding mounting brackets (see illustrations 4.11 and 15.10) and remove the condenser.

ALL MODELS

15 Check the condenser for cracks, damage, refrigerant leakage, bent fins, and distorted or damaged condenser inlet and outlet. Repair or replace the condenser as necessary.

16 Installation is the reverse of removal. Replace any O-rings with new ones specifically for the type of refrigerant in your system and lubricate them with refrigerant oil prior to installation.

❄❄ **WARNING:**

Do not apply compressor oil to the fitting nuts. Tighten the condenser inlet and outlet fittings securely.

17 Have the system evacuated, recharged and leak tested by the shop that discharged it. If the condenser was replaced, have the shop add about 1.0 ounces of new refrigerant oil to the high pressure side of the compressor. Use only refrigerant oil compatible with your system.

17.6 Use a back-up wrench when disconnecting the air conditioning lines (1997 and earlier models shown)

17.7 Remove the condenser mounting bolts and nuts (1997 and earlier models shown)

17.9 Power steering cooler line mounting bracket bolt

Specifications

General

Radiator cap pressure rating	
1997 and earlier	10.7 to 14.9 psi
1999 and later	13.5 to 17.8 psi
Thermostat rating (opening temperature)	
1997 and earlier	188 to 193 degrees F
1999 through 2005	183 to 190 degrees F
2006 and later	176 to 183 degrees F
Refrigerant type	
1994 and earlier	R-12
1995 and later	R-134a
Refrigerant capacity	
1994 and earlier	28.2 ounces
1995 through 2005	21.2 ounces
2006 and later	15.9 ounces

Torque specifications   Ft-lbs (unless otherwise indicated)

➡ **Note: One foot-pound (ft-lb) of torque is equivalent to 12 inch-pounds (in-lbs) of torque. Torque values below approximately 15 foot-pounds are expressed in inch-pounds, because most foot-pound torque wrenches are not accurate at these smaller values.**

Thermostat housing cover bolts	
2005 and earlier	15 to 18
2006 and later	71 to 101 in-lbs
Water pump mounting bolts	
2005 and earlier	14 to 18
2006 and later	
Pulley bolts	13 to 16
Pump bolts	71 to 101 in-lbs
Inlet pipe bolts	14 to 18

Notes

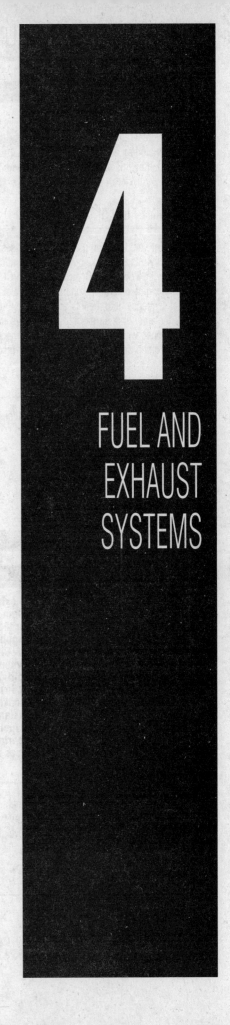

4

FUEL AND EXHAUST SYSTEMS

Section

Reference to other Chapters

1 General information

The fuel system consists of a fuel tank, an electric fuel pump (located in the fuel tank), an EFI/fuel pump relay, fuel injectors, a fuel pressure regulator, an air filter assembly and a throttle body unit. All models covered by this manual are equipped with a Multi Point Fuel Injection (MPFI) system.

MULTI POINT FUEL INJECTION (MPFI) SYSTEM

Multi Point Fuel Injection uses timed impulses to sequentially inject the fuel directly into the intake port of each cylinder. The injectors are controlled by the Powertrain Control Module (PCM). The PCM monitors various engine parameters and delivers the exact amount of fuel, in the correct sequence, into the intake ports. The throttle body serves only to control the amount of air passing into the system. Because each cylinder is equipped with an injector mounted immediately adjacent to the intake valve, much better control of the fuel/air mixture ratio is possible.

FUEL PUMP AND LINES

Fuel is circulated from the fuel tank to the fuel injection system, and back to the fuel tank, through a pair of metal lines running along the underside of the vehicle. An electric fuel pump is attached to the fuel level sending unit inside the fuel tank. All excess fuel is routed back to the fuel tank through a separate return line.

The fuel pump will operate as long as the engine is cranking or running and the PCM is receiving ignition reference pulses from the electronic ignition system (see Chapter 5). If there are no reference pulses, the fuel pump will shut off after 2 or 3 seconds.

EXHAUST SYSTEM

The exhaust system includes an exhaust manifold, a catalytic converter, an exhaust pipe, and a muffler.

The catalytic converter is an emission control device added to the exhaust system to reduce pollutants. A single-bed converter is used in combination with a three-way (reduction) catalyst. Refer to Chapter 6 for more information regarding the catalytic converter.

2 Fuel pressure relief

❊❊ WARNING:

Gasoline is extremely flammable, so take extra precautions when you work on any part of the fuel system. Don't smoke or allow open flames or bare light bulbs near the work area, and don't work in a garage where a gas-type appliance (such as a water heater or a clothes dryer) is present. Since gasoline is carcinogenic, wear fuel-resistant gloves when there's a possibility of being exposed to fuel, and, if you spill any fuel on your skin, rinse it off immediately with soap and water. Mop up any spills immediately and do not store fuel-soaked rags where they could ignite. The fuel system is under constant pressure, so, if any fuel lines are to be disconnected, the fuel pressure in the system must be relieved first. When you perform any kind of work on the fuel system, wear safety glasses and have a Class B type fire extinguisher on hand.

1   Before servicing any fuel system component, you must relieve the fuel pressure to minimize the risk of fire or injury.
2   Remove the fuel filler cap - this will relieve any pressure built up in the tank.

1997 AND EARLIER MODELS

♦ **Refer to illustration 2.7**

3   Remove the cover from beneath the steering column and locate the connector for the circuit opening relay (1993 and earlier models) or fuel pump relay (1994 through 1997 models).

a) *The circuit opening relay connector (1993 and earlier models) has six terminals, one of which is unused. The other five terminals' wire colors are violet, white/red, blue/red, light green and black.*
b) *The fuel pump relay connector (1994 through 1997 models) has six terminals, two of which are unused. The other four terminals' wire colors are white/red, white/red, blue/red and light green.*

4   Start the engine and unplug the circuit opening relay or fuel pump relay connector. Wait for the engine to stall, then turn the ignition key to OFF. Disconnect the cable from the negative terminal of the battery (see Chapter 5).
5   The fuel system is now depressurized.

➡**Note: Place a rag around the fuel line before removing any hose clamp or fitting to prevent any residual fuel from spilling onto the engine.**

6   Connect the circuit opening relay electrical connector and install the under cover.
7   Whenever fuel system pressure has been relieved, the fuel system should be primed before the vehicle is placed back in operation to prevent excessive cranking of the starter, as follows:

a) *Locate the diagnostic connector in the engine compartment.*
b) *Connect the ground and fuel pump terminals together with a short jumper wire (see illustration).*
c) *Turn the key to On for approximately 10 seconds (but don't crank the starter), then turn the key off. Remove the jumper wire from the diagnostic connector.*
d) *Check for any fuel leaks before operating the vehicle.*

2.7 Remove the cap from the diagnostic connector and connect a short jumper wire between the ground terminal (upper arrow) and fuel pump terminal (lower arrow)

2.15 Fuel pump relay location (2006 and later models):

1 *Fuel pump relay*
2 *Fuel pump check connector terminal*

1999 THROUGH 2005 MODELS

8 Remove the knee bolster trim panel (see Chapter 11).

9 Using a flashlight, locate the fuel pump relay, which is located on a small relay box above the accelerator pedal assembly.

10 Remove the relay (it has a six-pin connector) from the relay box.

11 Start the engine and wait for it to stall (it might not even start).

12 After the engine stalls, crank the engine several more times. The fuel system is now depressurized.

13 Turn the ignition switch to OFF, then install the fuel pump relay. Disconnect the cable from the negative terminal of the battery (see Chapter 5).

14 Install the knee bolster trim panel (see Chapter 11).

2006 AND LATER MODELS

▶ **Refer to illustration 2.15**

15 Locate the fuel pump relay in the engine compartment fuse and relay box (see illustration).

16 Remove the relay.

17 Start the engine and wait for it to stall (it might not even start).

18 After the engine stalls, crank the engine several more times. The fuel system is now depressurized.

19 Turn the ignition switch to OFF, then install the fuel pump relay. Disconnect the cable from the negative terminal of the battery (see Chapter 5).

---

3   Fuel pump/fuel pressure - check

✳✳ WARNING:

Gasoline is extremely flammable, so take extra precautions when you work on any part of the fuel system. See the Warning in Section 2.

1997 AND EARLIER MODELS

Fuel pump operation check

▶ **Refer to illustrations 3.7a, 3.7b and 3.7c**

1 Connect the diagnostic connector terminals F/P and GND with a jumper wire (see illustration 2.7).

2 Remove the fuel filler cap.

3 Turn the ignition switch to ON (but don't start the engine).

4 The fuel pump is now activated. Listen at the fuel filler opening for fuel pump noises (the pump is inside the tank, under the package shelf behind the seats).

5 Turn the ignition switch OFF.

6 Remove the jumper wire. Close the cap on the test connector.

7 If the fuel pump did not operate, measure the voltage between the fuel pump connector and ground. To gain access to the connector, remove the trim from the package shelf behind the seats and remove the access panel (see illustrations). Unplug the electrical

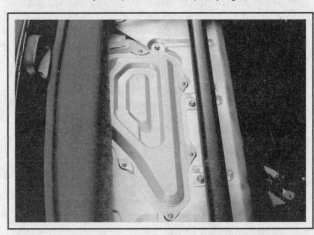

3.7a The fuel pump access panel is located under the package tray (1997 and earlier models shown, 1999 through 2005 models similar)

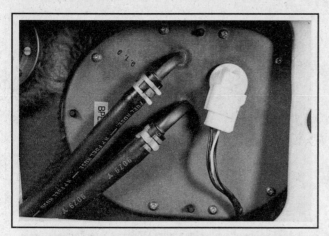

3.7b The electrical connector and fuel feed and return lines are accessible after the panel is removed (1997 and earlier models shown)

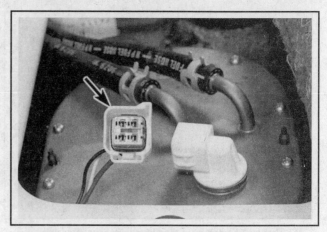

3.7c Unplug the connector to the fuel pump. There should be voltage available at the red/blue wire's terminal in the harness side of the connector; there should be continuity between ground and the black wire's terminal (1997 and earlier models shown, 1999 through 2005 models similar)

3.13 Relieve the fuel pressure, disconnect the fuel feed line from the metal pipe and, using a T-fitting, connect a fuel pressure gauge

connector (see illustration). Connect a voltmeter between the blue/red wire's terminal in the harness side of the connector and a convenient ground (nearby bare metal). With the ignition key in the On position, you should read full battery voltage.

8   If there's no voltage, check the EFI 30-amp fuse and the circuit opening/fuel pump relays (see Section 2, Step 3 for relay location).

9   If there is voltage, check the ground circuit. Connect one probe of an ohmmeter to the black wire's terminal in the harness connector. Connect the other ohmmeter probe to a convenient ground. There should be continuity (little or no resistance).

10 If there is no continuity, check the pump's ground circuit for breaks or poor connections and repair it as necessary.

11 If there is still no continuity, replace the fuel pump (see Section 5).

Fuel pressure check

▶ Refer to illustration 3.13

12 Relieve the fuel system pressure (see Section 2), then disconnect the negative battery cable (see Chapter 5).

13 Disconnect the fuel feed hose from the metal line on the right side of the engine compartment and, using a T-fitting, install a fuel pressure gauge (see illustration).

➡Note: The fuel feed line is the rearmost of the two fuel lines (the forward hose is the return line).

14 Reconnect the negative battery cable, then start the engine. Compare the fuel pressure with the values listed in this Chapter's Specifications.
   a) If the pressure is high, check for a restricted fuel return line. If the line is clear, replace the pressure regulator.
   b) If the pressure is low, pinch the fuel return line. If the pressure goes up, replace the fuel pressure regulator. If the pressure does not increase, replace the fuel filter and re-check the fuel pressure. If the pressure is still low, the fuel pump is probably faulty.

15 Turn the key to Off and remove the jumper wire from the diagnostic connector. Wait five minutes and verify that the fuel pressure remains above the minimum system hold pressure listed in this Chapter's Specifications. If the pressure bleeds down below the minimum, the fuel pressure regulator, the fuel pump or a fuel injector may be leaking.

16 You can check the maximum pressure output of the fuel pump by relieving the fuel pressure, disconnecting the hose that goes to the fuel rail from the T-fitting, and installing a short piece of hose that is capped on the end to the T-fitting (you can install a bolt in the end of the hose and tighten a clamp around it). Turn the key to the On position and activate the fuel pump (see Steps 1, 3 and 4). Compare your findings with the value listed in this Chapter's Specifications.

❊❊ WARNING:

After this check is performed, the fuel pressure cannot be relieved in the normal fashion. It will be necessary to wrap a rag around the hose connected to the T-fitting, then slowly loosen the hose clamp and allow the pressurized fuel to bleed out into the rag.

Fuel pressure regulator check

17 Reconnect the fuel pressure gauge as described in Step 13. Locate the fuel pressure regulator (it's on the rear end of the fuel rail). Disconnect the pressure regulator vacuum hose and plug the hose. Connect a hand-held vacuum pump to the regulator. Start the engine and read the fuel pressure gauge without vacuum applied to the fuel pressure regulator. Apply vacuum to the regulator and check the fuel pressure again. The fuel pressure should decrease as vacuum increases.

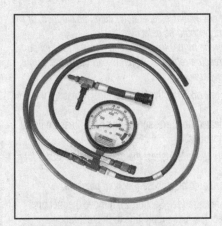

3.34 A typical fuel gauge setup suitable for measuring fuel pressure on 2006 and later models

3.36 To disconnect the fuel line fitting from the fuel rail, rotate the release tab and pull off the fitting (2006 and later models)

3.37 The fuel pressure gauge installed and ready to work:

1   *Inlet side uses existing quick-connect fitting on fuel supply line*
2   *Outlet side uses its own quick-connect fitting to hook up to inlet pipe on fuel rail*

18 Reconnect the vacuum hose to the regulator and check the fuel pressure at idle, comparing your reading with the value listed in this Chapter's Specifications. Disconnect the vacuum hose and watch the gauge - the pressure should increase as soon as the hose is disconnected. If the pressure at idle was too high (with the hose connected), connect a vacuum gauge and check for vacuum in the supply line. If there is no reading on the gauge, check the hose and intake manifold port for a blockage.

19 If the fuel pressure is LOW, pinch the fuel return line shut and watch the gauge. If the pressure doesn't rise, the fuel pump is defective or there is a restriction in the fuel feed line. If the pressure rises sharply, replace the fuel pressure regulator (see Section 14).

20 If the indicated fuel pressure is too high, relieve the fuel pressure (see Section 2), disconnect the fuel return line and blow through it to check for blockage. If there is no blockage, replace the fuel pressure regulator (see Section 14).

21 If the fuel pressure does not fluctuate as described in Step 18, and vacuum is present at the hose, replace the fuel pressure regulator (see Section 14).

22 Depressurize the fuel system (see Section 2). Carefully remove the fuel pressure gauge. Be sure to cover the fitting with a rag before loosening it.

23 Wipe up any spilled gasoline.

24 Start the engine and check for leaks.

1999 THROUGH 2005 MODELS

25 To perform this procedure, you will need a fuel pressure gauge capable of reading 65 or more psi. You'll also need the correct quick-connect fittings to allow you to tee into the fuel system between the No. 1 fuel pulsation damper and the fuel rail.

26 Relieve the fuel pressure (see Section 2), then disconnect the cable from the negative battery terminal (see Chapter 5).

27 Locate the No. 1 fuel pulsation damper, which is located on the right shock tower. Disconnect the fuel line from the outlet side of the No. 1 pulsation damper.

28 Install a fuel pressure gauge between the No. 1 pulsation damper and the fuel line you just disconnected, which goes to the fuel rail.

Verify that the quick-release fittings are fully connected - you should hear a click when you push the fitting onto a fuel pipe.

29 Start the engine and wait for it to settle into its normal idle. Measure the fuel pressure and compare your measurement to the fuel pressure listed in this Chapter's Specifications.

a) *If the pressure is lower than specified, check the fuel lines and hoses for kinks, blockages and leaks. Replace the fuel filter and re-check the fuel pressure. If it's still low, remove the fuel pump (see Section 5) and check the fuel strainer for restrictions. If all these components are okay, the fuel pump could be faulty.*

b) *If the fuel pressure is higher than specified, replace the fuel pressure regulator (see Section 14).*

30 To test the hold pressure, turn off the engine, wait for five minutes and note the indicated fuel pressure, then compare this reading to the hold pressure listed in this Chapter's Specifications.

31 If the hold pressure is low, the problem could be the fuel pump, a leaking injector or a leaking fuel line.

32 Relieve the fuel pressure (see Section 2). Remove the fuel pressure gauge and reconnect the fuel line to the No. 1 fuel pulsation damper.

33 Reconnect the battery, start the engine and make sure that there are no fuel leaks.

2006 AND LATER MODELS

◆ **Refer to illustrations 3.34, 3.36 and 3.37**

34 To perform this procedure, you will need a fuel pressure gauge capable of reading 65 or more psi. You'll also need the correct quick-connect fittings to allow you to tee into the fuel system between the fuel line and the fuel rail (see illustration).

35 Relieve system fuel pressure (see Section 2), then disconnect the cable from the negative battery terminal (see Chapter 5).

36 Disconnect the fuel supply line quick-release connector from the fuel rail (see illustration).

37 Tee the fuel pressure gauge into the fuel system between the fuel supply line and the fuel rail (see illustration). Verify that the fittings are securely connected by pulling on both of them.

38 Locate the fuel pump check connector terminals on the engine compartment fuse and relay box, next to the fuel pump relay (see illustration 2.15). Short the check connector terminals to ground with a jumper wire. Normally, when you turn the ignition key to ON, it activates the pump for two seconds to prime the pump, but Mazda specifies that the pump must run for 10 seconds for the following test, and when you short the fuel pump check connector terminals, the pump will continue to operate as long as the key is turned to ON.

39 Turn the ignition key to ON - NOT to START - and hold it there for 10 seconds, then measure the fuel pressure. To stop the pump, turn the ignition key to OFF.

40 Compare the indicated fuel pressure to the fuel pressure listed in this Chapter's Specifications.

  a) *If the pressure is lower than specified, check the fuel lines and hoses for kinks, blockages and leaks. Remove the fuel pump (see Section 5) and check the fuel strainer for restrictions. If all these components are okay, the fuel filter (which is part of the fuel pump*

assembly and is not available separately) could be clogged, or the fuel pump assembly could be defective.

  b) *If the fuel pressure is higher than specified, replace the fuel pump assembly (the pressure regulator, which is part of the fuel pump, is not available separately).*

41 Turn the ignition key off. Wait five minutes, then measure the hold pressure.

42 Compare the indicated hold pressure to the hold pressure listed in this Chapter's Specifications.

  a) *If the hold pressure is low, inspect the fuel lines and fittings for leaks.*

  b) *A leaking injector could also cause low hold pressure.*

43 Relieve the fuel pressure (see Section 2), remove the fuel pressure gauge and reconnect the fuel supply line to the fuel rail.

44 Reconnect the battery, start the engine and make sure that the quick-connect fitting is not leaking.

4 Fuel lines and fittings - inspection and replacement

❊❊ WARNING:

Gasoline is extremely flammable, so take extra precautions when you work on any part of the fuel system. See the Warning in Section 2.

INSPECTION

1 Once in a while, you will have to raise the vehicle to service or replace some component (an exhaust pipe hanger, for example). Whenever you work under the vehicle, always inspect fuel lines and all fittings and connections for damage or deterioration.

2 Check all hoses and pipes for cracks, kinks, deformation or obstructions.

3 Make sure all hoses and pipe clips attach their associated hoses or pipes securely to the underside of the vehicle.

4 Verify all hose clamps attaching rubber hoses to metal fuel lines or pipes are snug enough to ensure a tight fit between the hoses and pipes.

REPLACEMENT

▶ **Refer to illustration 4.6**

5 If you must replace any damaged sections, use original equipment replacement hoses or pipes constructed from exactly the same material as the section you are replacing. Do not install substitutes

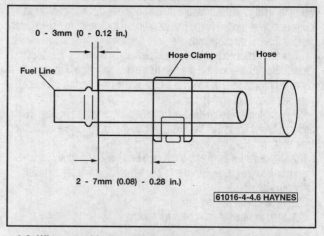

4.6 When attaching a section of rubber hose to a metal fuel line, be sure to overlap the hose as shown, and secure it to the line with a new hose clamp of the proper type

constructed from inferior or inappropriate material or you could cause a fuel leak or a fire.

6 Always, before detaching or disassembling any part of the fuel line system, note the routing of all hoses and pipes and the orientation of all clamps and clips to assure that replacement sections are installed in exactly the same manner. When attaching hoses to metal lines, overlap them as shown (see illustration).

7 Before detaching any part of the fuel system, be sure to relieve the fuel line and tank pressure (see Section 2).

5 Fuel pump/fuel level sending unit - removal and installation

2005 AND EARLIER MODELS

▸ **Refer to illustrations 5.8, 5.9a, 5.9b, 5.10, 5.11, 5.12 and 5.13**

❋❋ WARNING:

Gasoline is extremely flammable, so take extra precautions when you work on any part of the fuel system. See the Warning in Section 2.

1   Remove the fuel tank cap. Depressurize the fuel system (see Section 2).

2   Disconnect the cable from the negative terminal of the battery (see Chapter 5).

3   Remove the package shelf trim behind the seats (see Chapter 11).

4   Remove the fuel pump access cover (see illustration 3.7a).

5   Unplug the electrical connector from the top of the fuel pump (see illustration 3.7b).

6   Disconnect the fuel supply and return hoses from the pump.

7   Remove the fuel pump retaining screws.

8   Carefully lift the fuel pump assembly out of the fuel tank (see illustration).

9   Disconnect the electrical connector and move the hose clamp clear of the pump fitting (see illustrations).

10 Remove the band securing the pump to the bracket (see illustration).

5.8 Lift the fuel pump assembly from the fuel tank at an angle so as not to damage the inlet screen or float arm

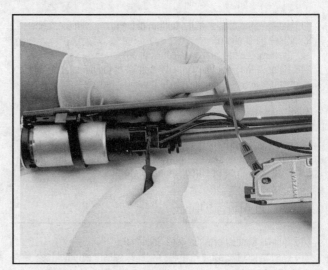

5.9a Disconnect the fuel pump electrical connector . . .

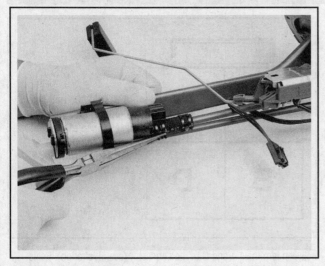

5.9b . . . squeeze the hose clamp and slide it up the hose . . .

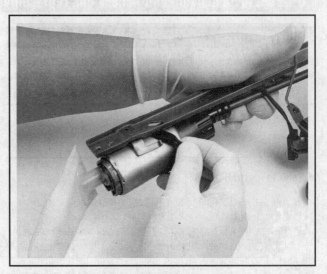

5.10 . . . pull the retaining band off the hook . . .

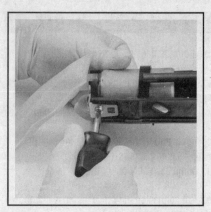

5.11 . . . remove the bracket . . .

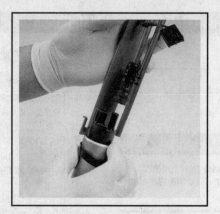

5.12 . . . and remove the fuel pump (1997 and earlier models shown, 1999 through 2005 models similar)

5.13 Remove the inlet filter screen from the pump (1997 and earlier models shown, 1999 through 2005 models similar)

11 Remove the bracket at the bottom of the pump with the rubber mount (see illustration).

12 Remove the fuel pump (see illustration).

13 Remove the sock filter from the bottom of the pump and inspect it for contamination (see illustration). If it is dirty, replace it.

14 Installation is the reverse of removal. Install a new O-ring set (O-ring, cap and spacer) at the hose connection and a new tank seal during installation.

➡**Note: After installing the fuel pump to the bracket, pull the pump down so it is seated tightly against the pad on the bottom of the bracket, then position the hose clamps.**

2006 AND LATER MODELS

15 Relieve the fuel pressure (see Section 2).

16 Disconnect the cable from the negative battery terminal (see Chapter 5).

17 Remove the center console, the quarter-trim, the scuff plate, the tire house trim, the aero board, the front seat back bar garnish and the back trim (see Chapter 11).

18 Remove the fuel pump service hole cover fasteners and remove the cover.

19 Disconnect the electrical connector from the fuel pump.

20 Disconnect the quick-release fitting and disconnect the fuel supply line from the fuel pump.

21 Remove the fuel pump retainer plate screws and remove the retainer plate.

22 Remove the retainer plate gasket.

23 Remove the fuel pump from the fuel tank.

24 With the exception of the fuel level sending unit, the components of the fuel tank are not serviceable separately. If any other fuel pump component is defective, replace the pump as a single assembly.

25 Installation is the reverse of removal.

---

6   Fuel level sending unit - check and replacement

✳✳ WARNING:

Gasoline is extremely flammable, so take extra precautions when you work on any part of the fuel system. See the Warning in Section 2.

CHECK

◆ **Refer to illustration 6.3**

1   The fuel level sending unit is part of the fuel pump assembly mounted in the fuel tank.

2   Remove the fuel pump assembly from the fuel tank (see Section 5).

3   Using an ohmmeter, check the resistance of the sending unit with the float arm completely down (tank empty) and with the arm up (tank full). On 1997 and earlier models, the resistance should change steadily from approximately 110 ohms to approximately 2 to 4 ohms. On 1999 through 2005 models, the resistance should vary from 93-97 ohms to 6.5-7.5 ohms. On 2006 and later models, measure the resistance

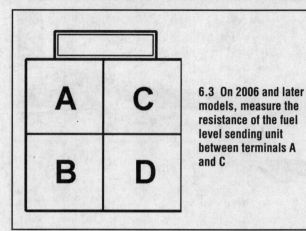

6.3 On 2006 and later models, measure the resistance of the fuel level sending unit between terminals A and C

between terminals A and C of the connector (see illustration). Resistance should vary from 200-205 ohms to 9-11 ohms.

➡**Note: Resistance values are approximate.**

4   If the readings are incorrect, replace the sending unit.

REPLACEMENT

▶ **Refer to illustration 6.6**

5 Remove the fuel pump assembly from the fuel tank (see Section 5).

6 Disconnect the electrical connection to the fuel level sending unit (see illustration).

7 On 2005 and earlier models, remove the nuts securing the sending unit to the bracket and separate the sending unit from the assembly (see illustration 6.6).

8 Installation is the reverse of removal.

6.6 Disconnect the electrical connector and remove the sending unit nuts (arrows)

7 Fuel tank - removal and installation

▶ **Refer to illustrations 7.8, 7.9a, 7.9b, 7.9c, 7.9d and 7.10**

※※ **WARNING:**

Gasoline is extremely flammable, so take extra precautions when you work on any part of the fuel system. See the Warning in Section 2.

1 This procedure is much easier to perform if the fuel tank is empty. Some models may have a drain plug for this purpose. If for some reason the drain plug can't be removed, postpone the job until the tank is empty or siphon the fuel into an approved container using a siphoning kit (available at most auto parts stores).

※※ **WARNING:**

Do not start the siphoning action by mouth!

2 Remove the fuel filler cap to relieve fuel tank pressure. Relieve the fuel system pressure (see Section 2)

3 Detach the cable from the negative terminal of the battery (see Chapter 5).

4 If the tank is full or nearly full, drain the fuel into an approved fuel container.

5 Raise the vehicle and place it securely on jackstands.

6 Familiarize yourself with the layout of the fuel tank assembly before proceeding. Refer to Section 5 and disconnect the fuel pump hoses and electrical connectors.

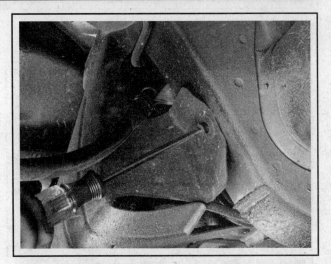

7.8 Remove the tank protector

7 Remove the power plant frame (see Chapter 7A), and the driveshaft and differential (see Chapter 8). At this point, the entire rear suspension/crossmember assembly must be supported with a transmission jack, unbolted from the body and removed from under the vehicle. This will also necessitate disconnecting the brake lines at the crossmember and detaching the parking brake cables from the calipers (see Chapter 9).

8 Remove the tank protector (see illustration). Support the fuel tank with a floor jack. Place a sturdy plank between the jack head and the fuel tank to protect the tank.

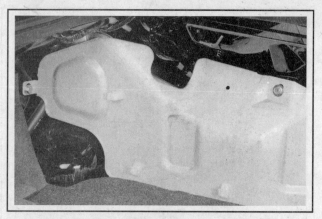

7.9a Remove the access panel inside the trunk

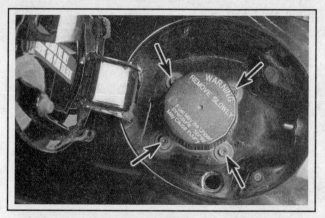

7.9b Remove the filler neck screws (arrows) (also remove the cap)

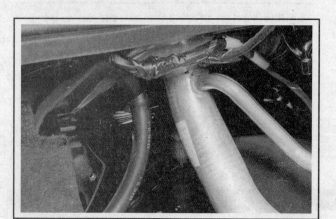

7.9c Detach the overflow hose

7.9d Loosen the clamps that retain the fuel filler hoses to the tank and filler neck

7.10 Remove the fuel tank mounts from the body

9   Inside the trunk, remove the access panel (see illustration). Unbolt the fuel filler neck and detach the hoses at the tank (see illustrations).

➡Note: Be sure to plug the hoses to prevent leakage and contamination of the fuel system.

10 Remove the bolts from the fuel tank retaining brackets (see illustration).

11 Remove the tank from the vehicle.

12 Installation is the reverse of removal. Be sure to bleed the brakes (see Chapter 9).

8 Fuel tank cleaning and repair - general information

1   Any repairs to the fuel tank or filler neck should be carried out by a professional who has experience in this critical and potentially dangerous work. Even after cleaning and flushing of the fuel system, explosive fumes can remain and ignite during repair of the tank.

2   If the fuel tank is removed from the vehicle, it should not be placed in an area where sparks or open flames could ignite the fumes coming out of the tank. Be especially careful inside garages where a gas-type appliance is located, because it could cause an explosion.

9   Air filter housing - removal and installation

2005 AND EARLIER MODELS

▶ **Refer to illustrations 9.1 and 9.3**

1   Unbolt the inlet and outlet ducts and loosen their clamps (see illustration), then disconnect the resonance tubes from the air cleaner housing.

2   Disconnect the mass airflow sensor electrical connector (see illustration 9.1).

3   Remove the attaching bolt(s) (see illustration) and remove the air cleaner assembly from the engine compartment.

4   Installation is the reverse of removal.

2006 AND LATER MODELS

▶ **Refer to illustrations 9.5, 9.6 and 9.7**

5   Loosen the hose clamp and disengage the air intake duct from the air filter housing cover (see illustration).

6   Unclamp the air filter housing cover (see illustration), remove the cover and remove the air filter element.

7   Remove the two filter housing mounting nuts (see illustration), then pull the locator pin out of its insulator grommet and remove the filter housing.

8   Inspect the condition of the insulator grommet. If it's cracked, torn or otherwise deteriorated, replace it.

9   Installation is the reverse of removal.

9.1 Loosen the clamp and unplug the mass airflow sensor connector (1997 and earlier models shown, 1999 through 2005 models similar)

9.3 Remove the air cleaner housing mounting fasteners (1997 and earlier models shown, 1999 through 2005 models similar)

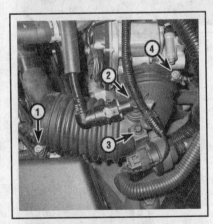

9.5 Air intake duct removal/ installation details

1   Air filter housing-to-air intake duct hose clamp
2   Positive Crankcase Ventilation (PCV) fresh air inlet hose
3   Evaporative Emissions (EVAP) system canister purge solenoid valve bracket
4   Air intake duct-to-throttle body hose clamp

9.6 To remove the air filter housing cover, undo these two spring clamps

9.7 Air filter housing removal/ installation details:

1   Filter housing mounting nuts
2   Filter housing locator pin (underneath this tab); inserted into a rubber insulator grommet located on top of the PCM cover

10 Accelerator cable - removal, installation and adjustment

➡ Note: This Section applies to 2005 and earlier models only.

REMOVAL

▶ Refer to illustrations 10.2, 10.3, 10.4 and 10.5

1   Detach the cable from the negative terminal of the battery (see Chapter 5).
2   Loosen the locknut on the threaded portion of the cable at the plenum (see illustration).
3   Rotate the throttle lever and slip the cable end out of the slot in the lever (see illustration).
4   Detach the cable from the accelerator pedal and release the cable guide attached to the firewall (see illustration).
5   From the engine compartment side of the firewall, pull the cable through the firewall (see illustration).

INSTALLATION AND ADJUSTMENT

▶ Refer to illustration 10.11

6   Installation is the reverse of removal. Make sure the cable casing grommet seats properly in the firewall.
7   To adjust the cable, fully depress the accelerator pedal and check that the throttle is fully opened.
8   Measure the play in the accelerator and compare your measurement to that listed in this Chapter's Specifications.
9   If the throttle is not fully opened and/or if the play is incorrect, loosen the locknuts and adjust the cable accordingly.
10 Tighten the locknuts and recheck the adjustment. Make sure the throttle closes fully when the pedal is released.
11 Press the pedal to the floor and make sure the throttle opens fully. If it doesn't, loosen the pedal adjuster locknut, adjust pedal position with the bolt, then tighten the locknut (see illustration).

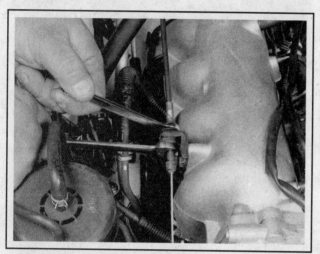

10.2 Loosen the locknuts on the accelerator cable (1997 and earlier models shown, 1999 through 2005 models similar)

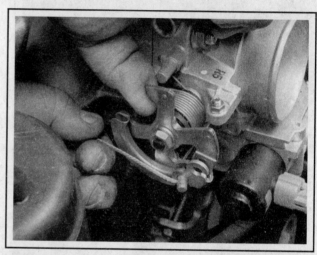

10.3 Rotate the throttle lever and remove the cable end from the slot (1997 and earlier models shown, 1999 through 2005 models similar)

10.4 Slip the cable end out of the top of the accelerator pedal arm (1997 and earlier models shown, 1999 through 2005 models similar)

10.5 Pull the cable through the firewall (1997 and earlier models shown, 1999 through 2005 models similar)

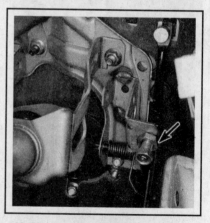

10.11 Loosen the locknut (arrow) and turn the adjusting bolt to adjust the accelerator pedal (1997 and earlier models shown, 1999 through 2005 models similar)

11 Electronic Fuel Injection (EFI) system - general information

1 These models are equipped with an Electronic Fuel Injection (EFI) system. The EFI system is composed of three basic subsystems: fuel system, air induction system and electronic control system.

FUEL SYSTEM

2 An electric fuel pump located inside the fuel tank supplies fuel under constant pressure to the fuel rail, which distributes fuel evenly to all injectors. From the fuel rail, fuel is injected into the intake ports, just above the intake valves, by fuel injectors. The amount of fuel supplied by the injectors is precisely controlled by a Powertrain Control Module (PCM). A pressure regulator controls system pressure in relation to intake manifold vacuum. A fuel filter between the fuel pump and the fuel rail filters fuel to protect the components of the system.

AIR INDUCTION SYSTEM

3 The air induction system consists of an air filter housing, the throttle body and the duct connecting the two. An Intake Air Temperature (IAT) sensor monitors the temperature of the incoming air. This information helps the PCM determine the amount of fuel to be injected by the injectors. The throttle plate inside the throttle body is controlled by the driver. On 2005 and earlier models, the accelerator pedal is connected to the throttle plate by an accelerator cable. On 2006 and later models, there is no accelerator cable; the accelerator pedal is connected to the throttle plate electronically. An Accelerator Pedal Position (APP) sensor at the pedal sends a voltage signal proportional to the pedal angle to the Powertrain Control Module (PCM), which processes this signal in conjunction with other inputs and opens or closes the throttle plate accordingly. As the throttle plate opens, the speed of the incoming air increases, which lowers the temperature of the air. The IAT sends this information to the PCM and the PCM signals the injectors to increase the amount of fuel delivered to the intake ports.

ELECTRONIC CONTROL SYSTEM

4 The Computer Control System controls the EFI and other systems by means of a Powertrain Control Module (PCM), which employs a microcomputer. The PCM receives signals from a number of information sensors which monitor such variables as intake air temperature, throttle angle, coolant temperature, engine rpm, vehicle speed and exhaust oxygen content. These signals help the PCM determine the injection duration necessary for the optimum air/fuel ratio. Some of these sensors and their corresponding PCM-controlled relays are not contained within EFI components, but are located throughout the engine compartment. For further information regarding the PCM and its relationship to the engine electrical and ignition system, see Chapter 6.

12 Electronic Fuel Injection (EFI) system - check

▶ **Refer to illustrations 12.6, 12.7, 12.8 and 12.9**

1 Check the ground wire connections for tightness. Check all wiring and electrical connectors that are related to the system. Loose electrical connectors and poor grounds can cause many problems that resemble more serious malfunctions.

2 Check to see that the battery is fully charged, as the control unit and sensors depend on an accurate supply voltage in order to properly meter the fuel.

3 Check the air filter element - a dirty or partially blocked filter will severely impede performance and economy (see Chapter 1).

4 If a blown fuse is found, replace it and see if it blows again. If it does, search for a grounded wire in the harness related to the system.

5 Check the air intake duct from the air cleaner housing to the intake manifold for leaks, which will result in an excessively lean mixture. Also check the condition of the vacuum hoses connected to the intake manifold.

6 Remove the air intake duct from the throttle body and check for carbon and residue build-up. If it's dirty, clean it with aerosol carburetor cleaner (make sure the can says it's safe for use with oxygen sensors and catalytic converters) and a toothbrush (see illustration).

❋❋ CAUTION:

Be sure not to remove the thin sealing film from the edge of the throttle plate and the area where it seats inside the throttle body.

12.6 With the engine off, use aerosol carburetor cleaner (make sure it is safe for use with catalytic converters and oxygen sensors), a toothbrush and a rag to clean the throttle body - open the throttle plate so you can clean behind it

12.7 Use a stethoscope or a screwdriver to determine if the injectors are working properly - they should make a steady clicking sound that rises and falls with engine speed changes

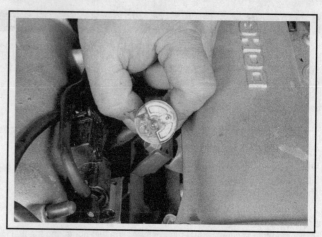

12.8 Install the noid light into the fuel injector electrical connector and check to see that it blinks with the engine running

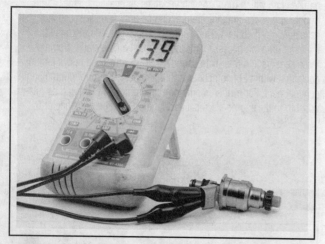

12.9 Using an ohmmeter, measure the resistance across the terminals of the injector (injector removed for clarity)

7   With the engine running, place a stethoscope against each injector, one at a time, and listen for a clicking sound, indicating operation (see illustration). If you don't have an automotive stethoscope you can use a long screwdriver; just place the tip of the screwdriver against the injector body and press your ear against the handle.

8   If there is a problem with an injector, purchase a special injector test light ("noid" light) and install it into the injector electrical connector (see illustration). Start the engine and make sure that each injector connector flashes the noid light. This will test for the proper voltage signal to the injector.

9   With the engine OFF and the fuel injector electrical connectors disconnected, measure the resistance of each injector (see illustration). Compare the measured resistance to the values listed in this Chapter's Specifications. Out of range injectors are probably faulty.

10 The remainder of the system checks should be left to a dealer service department or other qualified repair shop, as there is a chance that the control unit may be damaged if not performed properly.

13 Throttle body - removal and installation

⁂ WARNING:

Gasoline is extremely flammable, so take extra precautions when you work on any part of the fuel system. See the Warning in Section 2.

⁂ WARNING:

The engine must be completely cool before beginning this procedure.

2005 AND EARLIER MODELS

Check

1   Verify that the throttle linkage operates smoothly when the throttle lever is moved from fully closed to fully open.

2   Check the throttle body for wear and deposits.

⁂ CAUTION:

Do not remove the thin seal coating from the throttle valve or bore.

Replacement

▶ **Refer to illustrations 13.9a, 13.9b and 13.10**

3   Detach the cable from the negative terminal of the battery (see Chapter 5).

4   Loosen the hose clamps and remove the air intake duct.

5   Detach the accelerator cable from the throttle lever (see Section 10).

6   If your vehicle is equipped with cruise control, disconnect the

13.9a Depress the tab and disconnect the TPS electrical connector

13.9b Use the same technique to unplug the IAC valve connector

13.10 A typical throttle body is retained by four bolts/nuts

cruise control cable from the throttle linkage. The cruise control cable uses the same end plug as the accelerator cable and is disconnected the same way (see illustration 10.3).

7 Clearly label, then detach, all vacuum hoses from the throttle body.

8 Detach the coolant hoses from the throttle body. Plug the coolant hoses to prevent coolant loss.

9 Disconnect the electrical connectors from the Throttle Position Sensor (TPS) and Idle Air Control (IAC) valve (see illustrations).

10 Remove the four throttle body mounting nuts/bolts (see illustration).

11 Detach the throttle body and gasket from the intake manifold.

12 Using a soft brush and carburetor cleaner, thoroughly clean the throttle body casting, then blow out all passages with compressed air.

❋❋ CAUTION:

Do not clean the throttle position sensor with anything. Just wipe it off carefully with a clean, soft cloth.

13 Installation of the throttle body is the reverse of removal.

14 Be sure to tighten the throttle body mounting nuts/bolts to the torque listed in this Chapter's Specifications.

2006 AND LATER MODELS

▶ **Refer to illustrations 13.17 and 13.18**

15 Drain the coolant (see Chapter 1).

16 Remove the air intake duct (see illustration 9.5).

17 Disconnect the electrical connector from the throttle body (see illustration).

18 Disconnect the coolant hoses from the throttle body (see illustration).

19 Remove the throttle body from the air intake plenum. Remove and discard the old throttle body gasket.

20 Installation is the reverse of removal. Be sure to use a new gasket and tighten the throttle body mounting bolts to the torque listed in this Chapter's Specifications.

13.17 Throttle body electrical connector

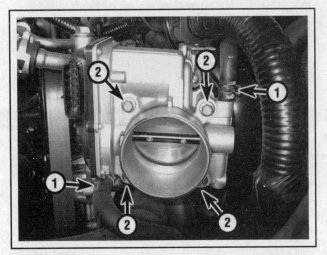

13.18 Throttle body removal/installation details (2006 and later models)

1   *Coolant hoses*

2   *Throttle body mounting bolts*

14 Fuel pressure regulator - removal and installation

1997 AND EARLIER MODELS

♦ Refer to illustrations 14.5 and 14.6

➡Note: On these models, the fuel pressure regulator is mounted on the fuel rail.

1   Relieve the fuel pressure (see Section 2) and detach the cable from the negative terminal of the battery (see Chapter 5).

2   Detach the vacuum hose from the regulator.

3   Place a metal container or shop towel under the fuel return hose.

4   Slide the clamp down the hose and remove the fuel return hose from the regulator.

5   Remove the pressure regulator mounting bolts (see illustration) and detach the pressure regulator from the fuel rail.

6   Use a new O-ring and make sure that the pressure regulator is installed properly on the fuel rail (see illustration).

7   The remainder of installation is the reverse of removal.

1999 THROUGH 2005 MODELS

➡Note: On these models, the fuel pressure regulator is located on the fuel pump/fuel level sending unit.

8   Remove the fuel pump/fuel level sending unit (see Section 5).

9   Disconnect the hose from the pressure regulator, remove the regulator retaining bolt and remove the regulator.

10 Installation is the reverse of removal.

2006 AND LATER MODELS

➡Note: On these models, the fuel pressure regulator is an integral component of the fuel pump/fuel level sending unit. It cannot be replaced separately from the pump. If the regulator is defective, replace the fuel pump assembly.

11 Remove the fuel pump/fuel level sending unit (see Section 5).

12 Swap the fuel level gauge sending unit to the new fuel pump unit.

13 Installation is the reverse of removal.

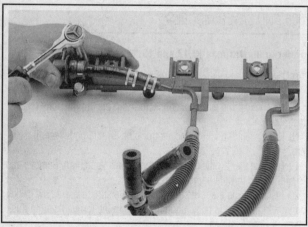

14.5 To remove the fuel pressure regulator from the fuel rail, detach the fuel return hose, remove the two regulator bolts and separate the regulator from the fuel rail (fuel rail removed from engine for clarity)

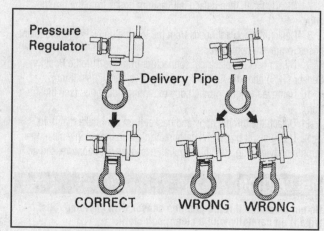

14.6 If the fuel pressure regulator is cocked during installation, it will not seal properly

15 Fuel rail and injectors - removal and installation

2005 AND EARLIER MODELS

♦ Refer to illustrations 15.8a, 15.8b, 15.9a, 15.9b, 15.9c, 15.11a and 15.11b

1   Relieve the fuel pressure (see Section 2).

2   Detach the cable from the negative terminal of the battery (see Chapter 5).

3   Remove the PCV hose from the valve cover and intake manifold.

4   If you're working on a 1993 or earlier model, remove the hose clamps and hoses from the air valve, then unbolt and remove the air valve from the engine side of the air intake plenum.

5   Carefully mark each injector and its electrical connector with a felt pen or paint, then remove the connectors from each injector and set the wire harness aside.

➡Note: Use a small flat blade screwdriver to release each connectors' lock lever while gently pulling the connector.

6   On 1997 and earlier models, detach the vacuum hose from the fuel pressure regulator.

7   Disconnect the fuel lines from the fuel pressure regulator and the fuel rail.

8   Remove the fuel rail mounting bolts and pull the fuel rail off the injectors (see illustrations).

15.8a Remove the bolts that retain the fuel rail to the intake manifold . . .

15.8b . . . and pull the rail off the injectors

15.9a Remove the mounting insulators . . .

15.9b . . . lift the fuel rail and pressure regulator out . . .

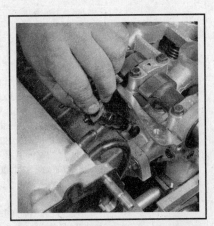

15.9c . . . and remove the injectors from their bores

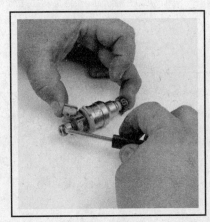

15.11a Pry off the O-ring . . .

9 Remove the mounting insulators, lift out the fuel rail and pressure regulator, then pull the injectors out of their bores (see illustrations).

10 Set the fuel injectors aside in a clearly labeled storage container so they can be returned to the same bores if reused.

11 If you intend to re-use the same injectors, replace the grommets and O-rings (see illustrations).

12 Installation of the fuel injectors is the reverse of removal.

13 Tighten the fuel rail mounting bolts securely.

2006 AND LATER MODELS

▶ **Refer to illustrations 15.18, 15.21 and 15.22**

14 Remove the engine cover.

15 Relieve the system fuel pressure (see Section 2).

16 Disconnect the cable from the negative battery terminal (see Chapter 5).

17 Disconnect the fuel supply line quick-connect fitting from the fuel rail (see illustration 3.36).

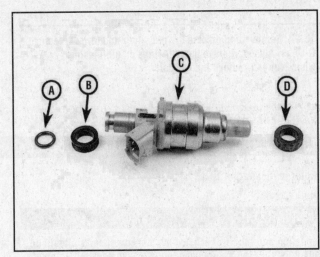

15.11b . . . and remove the grommet and insulator

A   O-ring
B   Grommet
C   Injector
D   Insulator

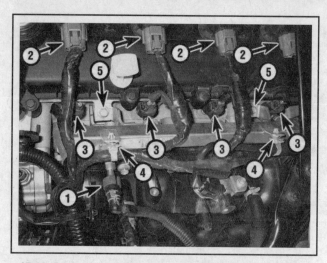

15.18 Fuel rail and injectors removal details:

1 *Fuel supply line quick-connect fitting (see Section 3)*
2 *Ignition coil electrical connectors (see Chapter 5)*
3 *Fuel injector electrical connectors*
4 *Harness clips (detach from brackets with a small screwdriver)*
5 *Fuel rail mounting bolts*

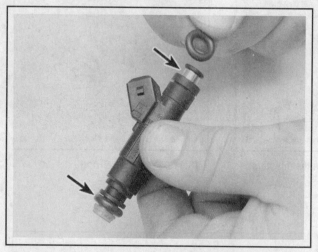

15.22 Remove and discard the old upper and lower injector O-rings. Always replace these O-rings on all injectors whenever you remove the fuel rail

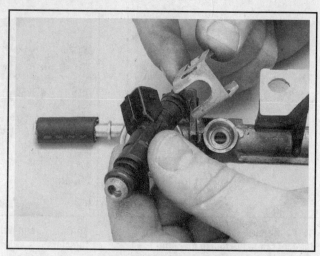

15.21 Remove the retainer clip from each injector, then pull the injector straight out of the fuel rail (if the injector sticks to the injector bore, wiggle and pull at the same time)

18 Disconnect the electrical connectors from the ignition coils and from the fuel injectors, detach the harness clips and set the harness aside (see illustration).

19 Remove the fuel rail mounting bolts.

20 Remove the fuel rail and injectors as a single assembly.

21 Remove the clip that secures each injector to the fuel rail and pull out each injector (see illustration).

22 Remove and discard the old injector O-rings (see illustration). Lightly oil, then install, the new injector O-rings.

23 Lubricate each upper injector O-ring with clean engine oil, then install the injectors into the fuel rail and secure them with the injector clips.

24 Lubricate each lower injector O-ring with clean engine oil, then install the fuel rail and injectors. Be careful not to damage the lower injector O-rings during installation. Tighten the fuel rail bolts securely.

25 Installation is otherwise the reverse of removal. Start the engine and check for leaks.

16 Exhaust system servicing - general information

♦ **Refer to illustration 16.1**

❊❊ WARNING:

Inspection and repair of exhaust system components should be done only after the system components have cooled completely.

1 The exhaust system consists of the exhaust manifold, catalytic converter, the muffler, the tailpipe and all connecting pipes, brackets, hangers and clamps. The exhaust system is attached to the body with mounting brackets and rubber hangers (see illustration). If any of these parts are damaged or deteriorated, excessive noise and vibration will be transmitted to the body.

2 Conducting regular inspections of the exhaust system will keep it safe and quiet. Look for any damaged or bent parts, open seams, holes, loose connections, excessive corrosion or other defects which could allow exhaust fumes to enter the vehicle. Deteriorated exhaust system components should not be repaired - they should be replaced with new parts.

3   If the exhaust system components are extremely corroded or rusted together, they will probably have to be cut from the exhaust system. The convenient way to accomplish this is to have a muffler repair shop remove the corroded sections with a cutting torch. If, however, you want to save money by doing it yourself and you don't have an oxygen/acetylene welding outfit with a cutting torch, simply cut off the old components with a hacksaw. If you have compressed air, special pneumatic cutting chisels can also be used. If you do decide to tackle the job at home, be sure to wear eye protection to guard your eyes from metal chips and work gloves to protect your hands.

4   Here are some simple guidelines to apply when repairing the exhaust system:

    a)   Work from the back to the front when removing exhaust system components.

    b)   Apply penetrating oil to the exhaust system component fasteners to make them easier to remove.

    c)   Use new gaskets, hangers and clamps when installing exhaust system components.

    d)   Apply anti-seize compound to the threads of all exhaust system fasteners during reassembly.

Be sure to allow sufficient clearance between newly installed parts and all points on the underbody to avoid overheating the floor pan and possibly damaging the interior carpet and insulation. Pay particularly close attention to the catalytic converter and its heat shield.

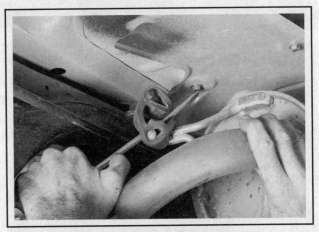

16.1 The rubber hangers can be pried off their posts

> **✳✳ WARNING:**
>
> The catalytic converter operates at very high temperatures and takes a long time to cool. Wait until it's completely cool before attempting to remove the converter. Failure to do so could result in serious burns.

Specifications

Fuel system

Fuel pressure	
1997 and earlier	
Fuel pump pressure (maximum)	
1993 and earlier	64 to 85 psi
1994 through 1997	70 to 95 psi
Fuel pump line pressure (engine idling)	
1996 and earlier	32 to 38 psi
1997	29 to 35 psi
Engine idling (vacuum hose disconnected from pressure regulator)	
1996 and earlier	Not specified (but should be approximately 5 to 10 psi greater than with the hose connected)
1997	41 psi
Fuel system hold pressure (minimum)	
1991 and earlier	50 psi
1992 through 1997	21 psi
1999 through 2005	
Fuel pressure	53 to 61 psi
Fuel hold pressure (after five minutes)	36 psi
2006 and later	
Fuel pressure	50 to 59 psi
Fuel hold pressure (after five minutes)	36 psi

Specifications (continued)

Fuel system (continued)

Fuel injector resistance
- 2000 and earlier ..... 12 to 16 ohms
- 2001 through 2005 ..... 12 to 13 ohms
- 2006 and later ..... 11.4 to 12.6 ohms

Idle Air Control (IAC) valve resistance
- 1993 and earlier ..... 11 to 13 ohms
- 1994 through 1997 ..... 10.7 to 12.3 ohms
- 1999 through 2005 ..... 8.7 to 10.5 ohms
- 2006 and later ..... N/A

Accelerator cable freeplay ..... 3/64 to 1/8 inch

Idle speed

1997 and earlier
- Manual transmission ..... 800 to 900 rpm in neutral
- Automatic transmission ..... 750 to 850 rpm in Park

1999 through 2005 ..... 750 to 850 rpm

2006 and later
- Manual transmission ..... 670 to 770 rpm
- Automatic transmission ..... 700 to 800 rpm

Torque specifications   Ft-lbs (unless otherwise indicated)

➡ **Note: One foot-pound (ft-lb) of torque is equivalent to 12 inch-pounds (in-lbs) of torque. Torque values below approximately 15 ft-lbs are expressed in inch-pounds, since most foot-pound torque wrenches are not accurate at these smaller values.**

Throttle body mounting fasteners
- 2005 and earlier ..... 14 to 19
- 2006 and later ..... 71 to 100 in-lbs

Section

Reference to other Chapters

5

ENGINE ELECTRICAL SYSTEMS

1 General information and precautions

The engine electrical systems include all ignition, charging and starting components. Because of their engine related functions, these components are discussed separately from chassis electrical devices such as the lights, the instruments, etc. (which are included in Chapter 12).

Always observe the following precautions when working on the electrical systems:

a) *Be extremely careful when servicing engine electrical components. They are easily damaged if checked, connected or handled improperly.*

b) *Never leave the ignition switch on for long periods of time (10 minutes maximum) with the engine off.*

c) *Don't disconnect the battery cables while the engine is running.*

d) *Maintain correct polarity when connecting a battery cable from another vehicle during jump starting.*

Always disconnect the negative cable first and hook it up last or the battery may be shorted by the tool being used to loosen the cable clamps.

✳✳ CAUTION:

If the stereo in your vehicle is equipped with an anti-theft system, make sure you have the correct activation code before disconnecting the battery.

It's also a good idea to review the safety-related information regarding the engine electrical systems located in the *Safety First!* section near the front of this manual before beginning any operation included in this Chapter.

2 Battery - emergency jump starting

Refer to the *Booster battery (jump) starting* procedure at the front of this manual.

3 Battery - removal and installation

▶ **Refer to illustrations 3.2a, 3.2b, 3.2c and 3.2d**

➡**Note: The battery is located in the luggage compartment on 2005 and earlier models. On 2006 and later models, it's located in the engine compartment.**

1   Beginning with the negative battery cable, disconnect both cables from the battery terminals.

2   Remove the battery hold-down clamp (see illustrations).

3   Lift out the battery. Be careful, it's heavy.

4   While the battery is out, inspect the carrier (tray) for corrosion.

5   If you are replacing the battery, make sure that you get one that is identical, with the same dimensions, amperage rating, cold cranking amperage rating, etc., as the original.

6   Installation is the reverse of removal.

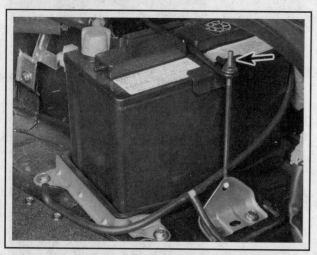

3.2a To remove the battery, detach the negative battery cable first, then the positive cable, remove the hold-down strap nut (arrow) and remove the hold-down strap (2005 and earlier models)

3.2b To remove the battery cover on 2006 and later models, disengage the hose from the two clips on the right end of the cover, then unsnap and remove the cover

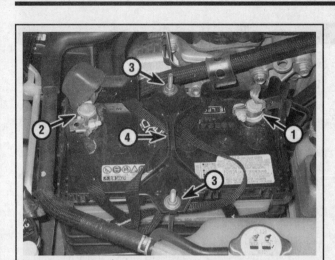

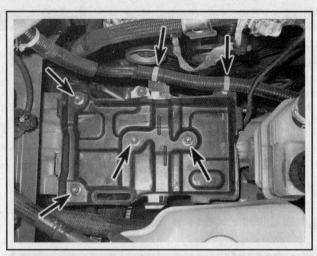

3.2c Battery details (2006 and later models)

1	Negative battery terminal	3	Hold-down clamp nuts
2	Positive battery terminal	4	Hold-down clamp

3.2d To remove the battery tray on 2006 and later models, detach the harness clips from the tray, then remove these four mounting bolts

4   Battery cables - check and replacement

1   Periodically inspect the entire length of each battery cable for damage, cracked or burned insulation and corrosion. Poor battery cable connections can cause starting problems and decreased engine performance.

2   Check the cable-to-terminal connections at the ends of the cables for cracks, loose wire strands and corrosion. The presence of white, fluffy deposits under the insulation at the cable terminal connection is a sign that the cable is corroded and should be replaced. Check the terminals for distortion, missing mounting bolts and corrosion.

3   When removing the cables, always disconnect the negative cable first and hook it up last or the battery may be shorted by the tool used to loosen the cable clamps. Even if only the positive cable is being replaced, be sure to disconnect the negative cable from the battery first (see Chapter 1 for further information regarding battery cable removal).

4   Disconnect the old cables from the battery, then trace each of them to their opposite ends and detach them from the starter solenoid and ground terminals. Note the routing of each cable to ensure correct installation.

5   If you are replacing either or both of the old cables, take them with you when buying new cables. It is vitally important that you replace the cables with identical parts. Cables have characteristics that make them easy to identify: positive cables are usually red, larger in cross-section and have a larger diameter battery post clamp; ground cables are usually black, smaller in cross-section and have a slightly smaller diameter clamp for the negative post.

6   Clean the threads of the solenoid or ground connection with a wire brush to remove rust and corrosion. Apply a light coat of battery terminal corrosion inhibitor, or petroleum jelly, to the threads to prevent future corrosion.

7   Attach the cable to the solenoid or ground connection and tighten the mounting nut/bolt securely.

8   Before connecting a new cable to the battery, make sure that it reaches the battery post without having to be stretched.

9   Connect the positive cable first, followed by the negative cable.

5   Ignition system - general information and precautions

1   The electronic ignition system includes the ignition switch, the battery, the igniter (1993 and earlier models), the ignition coil(s) and the spark plugs. The ignition system is controlled by the Powertrain Control Module (PCM). Using data provided by information sensors which monitor various engine functions (such as rpm, intake air volume, engine temperature, etc.), the PCM ensures a perfectly timed spark under all conditions.

➡ **Note: On 1994 and later models, the igniter function is handled by the PCM.**

2   When diagnosing the electronic ignition system, be sure to make all the necessary ignition system checks before replacing any components, as they are expensive and usually non-returnable.

3   When working on the ignition system, take the following precautions:

a) *Always connect a tachometer in accordance with the manufacturer's instructions. Some tachometers may be incompatible with this ignition system.*

b) *Never allow the ignition coil terminals to touch ground. Grounding the coil could result in damage to the igniter and/or the ignition coil.*

c) *Do not disconnect the battery when the engine is running.*

d) *On 1993 and earlier models, make sure the igniter is properly grounded.*

6   Ignition system - check

❊❊ **WARNING:**

Because of the high voltage generated by the ignition system, extreme care should be taken whenever an operation is performed involving ignition components. This not only includes the igniter, coil and spark plug wires, but related components such as plug connectors, tachometer and other test equipment also.

2000 AND EARLIER MODELS

▶ **Refer to illustration 6.1**

❊❊ **CAUTION:**

The type of spark tester shown in illustration 6.1 is perfectly suitable for pre-OBD II vehicles (manufactured through 1995). But using this old style spark tester on an OBD II-compliant 1996, 1997, 1999 or 2000 vehicle might set a Diagnostic Trouble Code, because each plug wire being tested for spark is disconnected from the plug that it fires, so the plug doesn't fire and the mixture in that cylinder will be excessively rich because it's not being ignited. So if you're checking spark on one of these vehicles, we recommend that you use the newer style of inline spark tester that is installed inline between the spark plug wire and the spark plug (see illustration 6.8), because it allows the plugs to fire while being tested.

1   If the engine turns over but will not start, disconnect the spark plug wire from any spark plug and attach it to a calibrated tester available at most auto parts stores (see illustration). Connect the clip on the tester to a bolt or metal bracket on the engine.

2   Crank the engine and watch the end of the tester or spark plug wire to see if bright blue, well-defined sparks occur.

3   If they do, sufficient voltage is reaching the plug to fire it (repeat the check at the remaining plug wires to verify that they are OK). However, the plugs themselves may be fouled, so remove and check them as described in Chapter 1.

4   If no sparks or intermittent sparks occur, disconnect the plug wires from the coils and check the terminals. Dry out any moisture and clean the terminals (both on the plug wires and inside the coils). Connect an ohmmeter to the ends of each plug wire in turn and measure the resistance. If it exceeds the value listed in this Chapter's Specifications, replace the plug wires as a set.

5   If the plug wires' resistance is within the Specification, reinstall them and repeat the spark test.

6   If there's still inadequate spark, check the primary wire connections at the coils to make sure they're clean and tight.

7   If you're working on a 1993 or earlier model, unplug the ignition coil electrical connector. With the ignition key On, check for battery voltage at the blue wire's terminal in the harness side of the connector. If there is no battery voltage, check the main fuse, ignition switch and wiring harness.

2001 THROUGH 2005 MODELS

▶ **Refer to illustration 6.8**

➡**Note: These models have two ignition coils mounted directly above, and firing the spark plugs for, cylinder numbers 2 and 4. On this type of ignition system, known as a waste-spark system, each coil fires two plugs simultaneously. Each coil also has a short spark plug wire that connects it to the plug for its companion cylinder. The companion cylinder for the coil mounted above cylinder number 2 is cylinder number 3; the companion cylinder for the coil mounted above cylinder 4 is cylinder 1.**

8   If the engine turns over but will not start, detach one of the two coils (see Section 7) from the spark plug that it fires directly and install a newer style inline calibrated ignition tester between the high-tension terminal under the coil and the spark plug (see illustration).

![spark plug wire and tester photograph for 2000 and earlier models]

6.1 To use a calibrated ignition tester (available at most auto parts stores), remove a spark plug wire from one of the spark plugs, connect the wire to the tester and clip the tester to a good ground - if there is enough voltage to fire the plug, sparks will be clearly visible between the electrode tip and the tester body as the engine is cranked

6.8 Spark tester details (1996 and later models)

| 1 | Tester body | 3 | Tester lead |
| 2 | Ignition coil (or spark plug boot) | | |

9   Crank the engine and see if the tester body flashes.

10 If the tester flashes during cranking, sufficient voltage is reaching the plug to fire it. Repeat this test for each of the two coils and for each of their respective companion plugs.

11 If no flashes occur during cranking at either cylinders 2 and 3 or 1 and 4, inspect the primary wire connection at the coil that isn't functioning. Make sure that it's clean and tight.

12 If a coil is functioning but one of the cylinders that it fires still has a misfire condition, the plug might be fouled. Remove and inspect the plug (see Chapter 1) and retest.

13 If no sparks or intermittent sparks occur during cranking at all cylinders, the Powertrain Control Module (PCM) might be defective. Have the PCM checked by a dealer service department. Testing the PCM is beyond the scope of the do-it-yourselfer because it requires expensive special tools. Any further testing of the ignition system should be conducted by a dealer service department or qualified repair shop with the proper tools.

2006 AND LATER MODELS

→Note: These models have four ignition coils, one for each spark plug, mounted directly above each plug. There are no spark plug wires.

14 Remove each ignition coil (see Section 7), then connect an inline tester similar to the one shown in illustration 6.8 between the high-tension terminal under the coil and the spark plug.

15 The test protocol for these models is similar to the one for 2001 through 2005 models (see Steps 8 through 13).

7   Ignition coil - check and replacement

CHECK

1993 and earlier models

▶ Refer to illustrations 7.3 and 7.4

1   Perform the ignition system checks as described in Section 6.

2   Crank the engine and verify that a strong blue spark is visible at the coil wire or spark plug wire.

3   Use an ohmmeter to measure the resistance of the primary coil winding (see illustration). If not within the values listed in this Chapter's Specifications, replace the coil.

4   Use an ohmmeter to measure the resistance of the secondary coil winding (see illustration). If not within the values listed in this Chapter's Specifications, replace the coil.

1994 through 2000 models

5   Perform the ignition system checks as described in Section 6.

6   Use an ohmmeter to measure the resistance of the secondary coil winding (see illustration 7.4). If not within the range listed in this Chapter's Specifications, replace the coil. Primary winding resistance is not tested on these models.

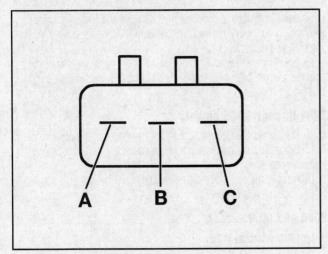

7.3 To check primary resistance on 1993 and earlier models, connect an ohmmeter from terminal A in the coil side of the connector to terminals B and C in turn; if resistance isn't as specified, replace the coil

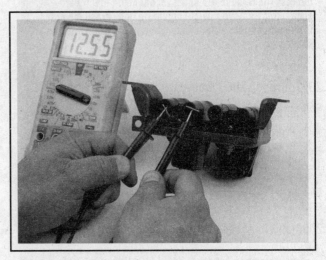

7.4 Connect an ohmmeter between each pair of high-tension towers (1-4 and 2-3) to measure the resistance of the secondary coil windings

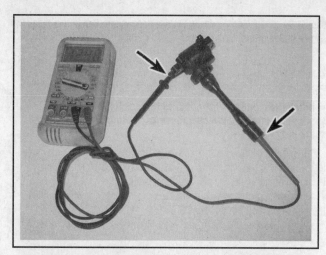

7.8 To measure the secondary resistance of an ignition coil, connect the probes of an ohmmeter to the two high tension terminals (2001 through 2005 models)

7.14 The coil mounting bolts pass through tabs on the bracket - coil cylinder numbers are marked on the bracket; on some models, a coil screw and nut secure a harness retainer (typical 1994 through 2000 models)

a) *Measure the resistance between the left and right terminals and between the center and right terminals. It should be anywhere from high to infinite resistance. If the indicated resistance is zero ohms, replace the coil.*

b) *Measure the resistance between the left and center terminals. It should be several k-ohms. If the indicated resistance is zero ohms or infinite resistance, replace the coil.*

REPLACEMENT

11 Detach the cable from the negative terminal of the battery (see Section 1).

2000 and earlier models

▶ **Refer to illustration 7.14**

12 Unplug the electrical connector(s) from the coil.
13 Label and disconnect the spark plug wires from the coil terminals.
14 Remove the coil assembly mounting bolts and take off the coil assembly. If necessary, remove the screws to separate the coils from the bracket (see illustration).
15 Installation is the reverse of removal. If the coils were separated from the bracket, be sure to install the 1-4 and 2-3 coils in the correct locations.

2001 through 2005 models

16 Disconnect the electrical connector from the ignition coil.
17 Disconnect the spark plug wire boot from the coil's companion cylinder spark plug.
18 Remove the coil mounting bolt and remove the coil.
19 Installation is the reverse of removal.

2006 and later models

Refer to illustration 7.20

20 Disconnect the electrical connector from the ignition coil (see illustration).
21 Remove the coil mounting bolt and remove the coil.
22 Installation is the reverse of removal.

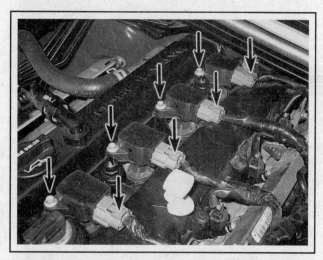

7.20 To remove an ignition coil on a 2006 and later model, depress the release tab and disconnect the electrical connector. Remove the coil mounting bolt, grasp the coil firmly and pull it straight up to disengage it from the spark plug

2001 through 2005 models

Refer to illustration 7.8

7 Perform the ignition checks as described in Section 6.
8 Remove the coil (see Steps 16 through 18). Using an ohmmeter, measure the secondary resistance between the two high tension terminals (see illustration) and compare your measurement to the secondary resistance listed in this Chapter's Specifications. If the indicated resistance is not within specification, replace the coil.

2006 and later models

9 Perform the ignition checks as described in Section 6.
10 Disconnect the electrical connector from the ignition coil (see Step 20). The connector has three terminals: left, center and right. Using an ohmmeter, measure the resistance between the following terminals:

8   Igniter (1993 and earlier models) - replacement

➡Note: A special igniter checker is required to check the function of the igniter. Some automotive parts stores may be able to perform the check for you.

1   Detach the cable from the negative terminal of the battery (see Section 1).

2   Disconnect the electrical connector from the igniter.
3   Remove the screws from the bracket assembly and remove the igniter and bracket assembly from the engine compartment (it's mounted on the right side of the engine compartment).
4   Installation is the reverse of removal.

9   Ignition timing - check and adjustment

◆ Refer to illustration 9.2

➡Note: The following ignition timing procedure applies to 1997 and earlier models. However, if the procedure specified on the VECI label of your vehicle differs from this one, use the procedure found on the VECI label. Ignition timing adjustment on 1999 and later models requires special equipment and should be performed by a dealer service department or other qualified repair shop.

1   Connect a tachometer according to the manufacturer's specifications. External DC power for the tachometer should be obtained by connecting to the single-pin connector on the blue wire near the camshaft position sensor.

2   If you're working on a 1995 or earlier model, locate the diagnostic connector and insert a jumper wire between terminals TEN and GND (see illustration).

3   With the ignition switch off, connect a timing light according to the tool manufacturer's instructions. Most timing lights are powered by the battery. Also, an inductive style pick-up is connected to the number one cylinder spark plug wire.

4   Locate the timing marks on the pointer index and the crankshaft pulley (see illustration 3.6 in Chapter 2, Part A).

5   Start the engine and allow it to warm up to normal operating temperature (upper radiator hose hot). Verify that the engine idle is as listed in this Chapter's Specifications. Aim the timing light at the index pointer. The mark on the crankshaft pulley should line up with the timing indicator. If necessary, loosen the camshaft position sensor hold-down bolt and slowly rotate the camshaft position sensor until the

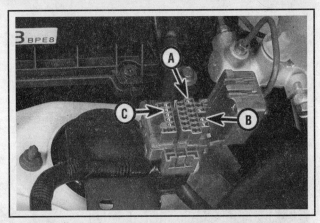

9.2 Attach a jumper wire between terminals TEN and GND of the test connector; connect the tachometer rpm pickup to the IG terminal (1995 and earlier models)

A   GND terminal
B   TEN terminal
C   IG terminal

timing marks align. Tighten the hold-down bolt and recheck the timing.

6   Remove the jumper wire from the diagnostic connector. Operate the throttle to increase engine speed and confirm that the ignition timing advances.

7   Turn the engine off and remove the tachometer and the timing light.

10 Charging system - general information and precautions

The charging system includes the alternator, an internal voltage regulator, a charge indicator, the battery and the wiring between all the components. The charging system supplies electrical power for the ignition system, the lights, the radio, etc. The alternator is driven by a drivebelt at the front of the engine.

The purpose of the voltage regulator is to limit the alternator's voltage to a preset value. This prevents power surges, circuit overloads, etc., during peak voltage output.

The charging system doesn't ordinarily require periodic maintenance. However, the drivebelt, battery and wires and connections should be inspected at the intervals outlined in Chapter 1.

The dashboard warning light should come on when the ignition key is turned to Start, then should go off immediately. If it remains on, there is a malfunction in the charging system. Some vehicles are also equipped with a voltage gauge. If the voltage gauge indicates abnormally high or low voltage, check the charging system (see Section 11).

Be very careful when making electrical circuit connections to a

vehicle equipped with an alternator and note the following:

a) *When reconnecting wires to the alternator from the battery, be sure to note the polarity.*
b) *Before using arc welding equipment to repair any part of the vehicle, disconnect the wires from the alternator and the battery terminals.*
c) *Never start the engine with a battery charger connected.*
d) *Always disconnect both battery leads before using a battery charger.*
e) *The alternator is driven by an engine drivebelt which could cause serious injury if your hands, hair or clothes become entangled in it with the engine running.*
f) *Because the alternator is connected directly to the battery, it could arc or cause a fire if overloaded or shorted out.*
g) *Wrap a plastic bag over the alternator and secure it with rubber bands before steam cleaning the engine.*

11 Charging system - check

1   If a malfunction occurs in the charging circuit, don't automatically assume that the alternator is causing the problem. First check the following items:

a) *Check the drivebelt tension and its condition. Replace it if worn or deteriorated.*

b) *Make sure the alternator mounting and adjustment bolts are tight.*

c) *Inspect the alternator wiring harness and the electrical connectors at the alternator and voltage regulator. They must be in good condition and tight.*

d) *Check the large main fuse in the engine compartment. If it's burned, determine the cause, repair the circuit and replace the fuse (the vehicle won't start and/or the accessories won't work if the fuse blows).*

e) *Check all the fuses that are in series with the charging system circuit. The location of these fuses may vary by year and model but the designations are the same.*

f) *Start the engine and check the alternator for abnormal noises (a growling, shrieking or squealing sound indicates a bad bushing).*

g) *Check the specific gravity of the battery electrolyte. If it's low, charge the battery (doesn't apply to maintenance free batteries).*

h) *Make sure that the battery is fully charged (one bad cell in a battery can cause overcharging by the alternator).*

i) *Disconnect the battery cables (negative first, then positive). Inspect the battery posts and the cable clamps for corrosion. Clean them thoroughly if necessary (see Chapter 1). Reconnect the positive cable, then the negative cable.*

2   Using a voltmeter, check the battery voltage with the engine off. Connect the positive terminal of the voltmeter to the battery positive terminal and the negative terminal of the voltmeter to the battery negative terminal. It should be at least 12.66 volts.

3   Start the engine and check the battery voltage again. It should now be approximately 13.5 to 15.1 volts.

12 Alternator - removal and installation

REMOVAL

2005 and earlier models

▶ **Refer to illustrations 12.2 and 12.3**

1   Detach the cable from the negative terminal of the battery (see Section 1).

2   Detach the electrical connectors from the alternator (see illustration).

3   Loosen the alternator adjustment and pivot bolts (see illustration) and detach the drivebelt.

4   Remove the pivot bolt and the bolt securing the bracket to the engine.

5   Separate the alternator and bracket from the engine.

2006 and later models

▶ **Refer to illustrations 12.9 and 12.12**

6   Remove the battery and the battery tray (see Section 3).

7   Disengage the power steering hose from its support bracket.

8   Remove the serpentine drivebelt (see Chapter 1).

12.2 Disconnect the battery cable (1) and the electrical connector (2) from the alternator (2005 and earlier models)

12.3 Remove the alternator adjusting bolt, bracket bolt (upper arrow) and lower pivot bolt or nut (lower arrow) (1997 and earlier models shown, 1999 through 2005 models similar)

12.9 Alternator assembly details (2006 and later models):

1	Serpentine drivebelt	4	Upper alternator
2	Alternator harness		mounting bolt
	bracket bolt	5	Front air scoop
3	Cable tie		retaining bolt

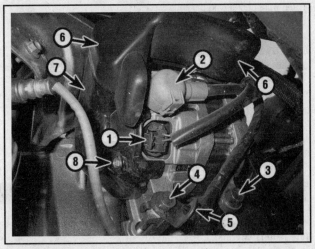

12.12 Alternator assembly details (2006 and later models)

1	Electrical connector	5	Harness bracket
2	Battery cable	6	Front air scoop
3	Lower front mounting bolt	7	Rear air scoop
4	Lower rear mounting bolt	8	Rear air scoop retaining bolt

9   Remove the alternator harness bracket bolt (see illustration).

10 Raise the front of the vehicle and place it securely on jackstands.

11 Remove the engine compartment under-covers.

12 Disconnect the electrical connectors from the alternator (see illustration).

13 Remove the upper alternator mounting bolt (see illustration 12.9).

14 Remove the lower alternator mounting bolts (see illustration 12.12) and remove the alternator.

➡**Note: The lower rear bolt also secures a small bracket for a harness; don't forget to reattach this bracket when you install the lower rear bolt.**

15 Because the backside of the alternator is close to the exhaust manifold, the alternator uses a two-piece plastic scoop to direct cooling air onto its backside (see illustration 12.12). Each part of the scoop is bolted to the alternator. The front part is secured by a single bolt (see illustration 12.9). If you need to, you can remove this bolt and remove the front part of the scoop. The rear part of the scoop (see illustration 12.12) is bolted to the back of the alternator. You can remove this part of the scoop after removing the alternator, then be sure to install it on the new alternator.

INSTALLATION (ALL MODELS)

16 If you are replacing the alternator, take the old alternator with you when purchasing a replacement unit. Make sure that the new/rebuilt unit is identical to the old alternator. Look at the terminals - they should be the same in number, size and locations as the terminals on the old alternator. Finally, look at the identification markings - they will be stamped in the housing or printed on a tag or plaque affixed to the housing. Make sure that these numbers are the same on both alternators.

17 Many new/rebuilt alternators do not have a pulley installed, so you may have to switch the pulley from the old unit to the new/rebuilt one. When buying an alternator, find out the store policy regarding installation of pulleys - some stores will perform this service free of charge.

18 Install in the reverse order of removal.

19 After the alternator is installed on 2005 and earlier models, adjust the drivebelt tension (see Chapter 1).

20 Check the charging voltage to verify proper operation of the alternator (see Section 11).

13 Starting system - general information and precautions

1   The sole function of the starting system is to turn over the engine quickly enough to allow it to start.

2   The starting system consists of the battery, the starter motor, the starter solenoid and the electrical circuit connecting the components. The solenoid is mounted directly on the starter motor.

3   The solenoid/starter motor assembly is installed on the upper part of the engine, next to the transmission bellhousing.

4   When the ignition key is turned to the START position, the starter solenoid is actuated through the starter control circuit. The starter solenoid then connects the battery to the starter motor, which does the

actual work of cranking the engine.

5   The starter motor on a vehicle equipped with a manual transmission can be operated only when the clutch pedal is depressed; the starter on a vehicle equipped with an automatic transmission can be operated only when the transmission selector lever is in Park or Neutral.

6   Always observe the following precautions when working on the starting system:

a) *Excessive cranking of the starter motor can overheat it and cause serious damage. Never operate the starter motor for more than 15 seconds at a time without pausing to allow it to cool for at least two minutes.*

b) *The starter is connected directly to the battery and could arc or cause a fire if mishandled, overloaded or short circuited.*

c) *Always detach the cable from the negative terminal of the battery before working on the starting system.*

14 Starter motor - testing in vehicle

➡**Note: Before diagnosing starter problems, make sure the battery is fully charged.**

1   If the starter motor does not turn at all when the switch is operated, make sure that the shift lever is in Neutral or Park (automatic transmission) or that the clutch pedal is depressed (manual transmission).

2   Make sure that the battery is charged and that all cables, both at the battery and starter solenoid terminals, are clean and secure.

3   If the starter motor spins but the engine is not cranking, the overrunning clutch in the starter motor is slipping and the starter motor must be replaced.

4   If, when the switch is actuated, the starter motor does not operate at all but the solenoid clicks, then the problem lies with either the battery, the main solenoid contacts or the starter motor itself (or the engine is seized).

5   If the solenoid plunger cannot be heard when the switch is actuated, the battery is bad, the circuit is open, or the starter solenoid itself is defective.

6   To check the solenoid, connect a jumper lead between the battery (+) and the ignition switch terminal (the small terminal) on the solenoid. If the starter motor now operates, the solenoid is OK and the problem is

in the ignition switch, Neutral start switch or in the wiring.

7   If the starter motor still does not operate, remove the starter/solenoid assembly for disassembly, testing and repair.

8   If the starter motor cranks the engine at an abnormally slow speed, first make sure that the battery is charged and that all terminal connections are tight. If the engine is partially seized, or has the wrong viscosity oil in it, it will crank slowly.

9   Run the engine until normal operating temperature is reached, then shut it off. Disconnect the primary connectors from the camshaft position sensor (see Chapter 5).

10 Connect a voltmeter positive lead to the battery positive post and connect the negative lead to the negative post.

11 Crank the engine and take the voltmeter readings as soon as a steady figure is indicated. Do not allow the starter motor to turn for more than 15 seconds at a time. A reading of nine volts or more, with the starter motor turning at normal cranking speed, is normal. If the reading is nine volts or more but the cranking speed is slow, the motor is faulty. If the reading is less than nine volts and the cranking speed is slow, the solenoid contacts are probably burned, the starter motor is bad, the battery is discharged or there is a bad connection.

15 Starter motor - removal and installation

➡**Note: The starter/solenoid assembly cannot be repaired using separate components. In the event of failure, exchange the starter/solenoid assembly for a new or rebuilt unit.**

1   Detach the cable from the negative terminal of the battery (see Section 1).

2   Raise the vehicle and support it securely on jackstands.

2005 AND EARLIER MODELS

▶ **Refer to illustrations 15.3a, 15.3b and 15.4**

3   On 1997 and earlier models, remove the starter bracket from the starter. Disconnect the electrical connector from the solenoid. Remove the nut and disconnect the battery cable from the solenoid (see illustrations).

4   Remove the starter mounting bolts and remove the starter (see illustration).

5   Installation is the reverse of removal.

2006 AND LATER MODELS

▶ **Refer to illustration 15.8**

6   Remove the left front wheel.

7   Remove the inner fender liner.

8   Flip open the weatherproof plastic cover (see illustration) and disconnect the battery cable from the B+ stud, and the starter cable from its terminal.

9   Remove the nut from the starter mounting stud (see illustration 15.8) and remove the starter mounting bolt. Note that the starter harness bracket is secured by the starter mounting nut. Be sure to reattach this bracket when installing the starter.

10 Remove the starter through the left wheel well.

11 Installation is the reverse of removal.

15.3a Unbolt the starter bracket (1997 and earlier models; there is no bracket on 1999 through 2005 models)

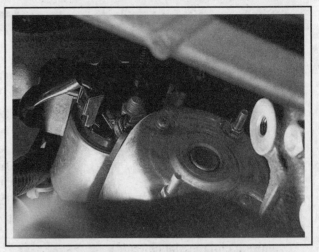

15.3b Disconnect the solenoid electrical connector and detach the battery cable from the top terminal of the solenoid

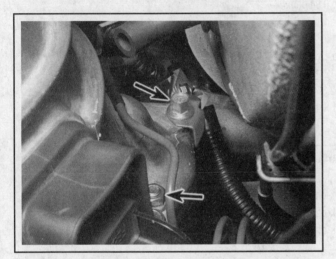

15.4 Remove the upper mounting bolt (note the harness retainer it secures) and the lower mounting bolt and nut

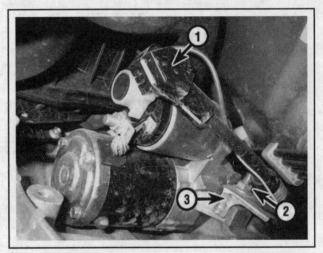

15.8 Starter assembly details

1   Weatherproof cover
2   Starter mounting nut

3   Starter harness
    mounting bracket

Specifications

Ignition timing

➥Note: With test terminals TEN and GND of the Data Link Connector connected with a jumper wire (1995 and earlier models).

1994 and earlier	
Manual transmission	9 to 11 degrees BTDC
Automatic transmission	7 to 9 degrees BTDC
1995 models	1 degree ATDC to 1 degree BTDC
1996 models	10 degrees BTDC
1997 models	9 to 11 degrees BTDC
1999 through 2005	6 to 8 degrees BTDC
2006 and later	Approximately 8 degrees BTDC

Ignition coil resistance (cold)

2005 and earlier	
Primary resistance	
1993 and earlier	0.78 to 0.94 ohms
1994 through 2005	Not available
Secondary resistance	
1993 and earlier	11.2 to 15.2 K-ohms
1994 through 1997	8.7 to 12.9 K-ohms
1999 and 2000	8.24 12.36 K-ohms
2001 through 2005	7 to 11 K-ohms
2006 and later	See text

Spark plug wire resistance (2000 and earlier models)

Cylinder no. 1	4 to 11 k-ohms
Cylinder no. 2	3 to 8 k-ohms
Cylinder no. 3	2 to 6 k-ohms
Cylinder no. 4	1 to 5 k-ohms

Charging system

Charging voltage	
1993 and earlier	14.1 to 14.7 volts
1994 through 1997	14.3 to 14.9 volts
1999 and later	13 to 15 volts

Torque specifications   Ft-lbs (unless otherwise indicated)

➥Note: One foot-pound (ft-lb) of torque is equivalent to 12 inch-pounds (in-lbs) of torque. Torque values below approximately 15 ft-lbs are expressed in inch-pounds, since most foot-pound torque wrenches are not accurate at these smaller values. Alternator mounting bolts

Adjusting bolt	14 to 18
Pivot bolt	28 to 38
Camshaft position sensor mounting bolt	14 to 18
Crankshaft position sensor mounting bolts	70 to 95 inch-lbs
Starter mounting fasteners	
Upper bracket bolt	144 to 192 in-lbs
Lower bracket bolt	28 to 38
Starter-to-engine bolts and nut	28 to 38
Starter cable nut	91 to 104 inch-lbs

6

EMISSIONS
AND ENGINE
CONTROL
SYSTEMS

Section

1   General Information

▶ **Refer to illustrations 1.1 and 1.6**

1   To minimize pollution of the atmosphere from incompletely burned and evaporating gases and to maintain good driveability and fuel economy, a number of emission control systems are used on these vehicles (see illustration). They include the:

Positive Crankcase Ventilation (PCV) system
Evaporative Emission Control (EVAP) system
Deceleration control system (1993 and earlier)
Exhaust Gas Recirculation (EGR) system (1994 and later)
Three-way catalytic converter (TWC) system
Powertrain Control Module (PCM)

2   The Sections in this Chapter include general descriptions, checking procedures within the scope of the home mechanic and component replacement procedures (when possible) for each of the systems listed above.

3   Before assuming an emissions control system is malfunctioning, check the fuel and ignition systems carefully (see Chapters 4 and 5). The diagnosis of some emission control devices requires specialized tools, equipment and training. If checking and servicing become too difficult or if a procedure is beyond the scope of your skills, consult your dealer service department or other repair shop.

4   This doesn't mean, however, that emission control systems are particularly difficult to maintain and repair. You can quickly and easily perform many checks and do most of the regular maintenance at home with common tune-up and hand tools.

➡**Note: The most frequent cause of emissions problems is simply a loose or broken electrical connector or vacuum hose, so always check the vacuum hoses and electrical connectors.**

5   Pay close attention to any special precautions outlined in this

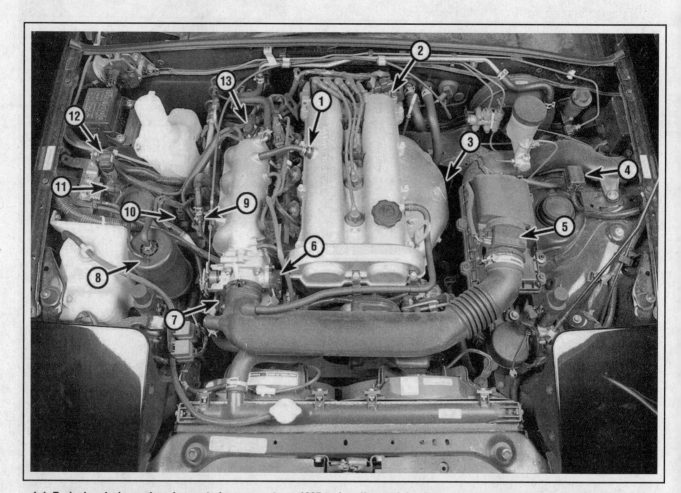

1.1 Typical emission and engine control components on 1997 and earlier models - items may vary with model year of vehicle

1   PCV valve
2   Camshaft Position (CMP) sensor
3   Oxygen sensor (not visible in this photo)
4   Diagnostic connector
5   Mass Airflow (MAF) sensor
6   Throttle Position (TP) sensor
7   Idle Air Control (IAC) valve (underneath throttle body)

8   EVAP canister
9   Exhaust Gas Recirculation (EGR) vent solenoid valve
10 Exhaust Gas Recirculation (EGR) vacuum solenoid valve
11 EVAP canister purge solenoid valve
12 Exhaust Gas Recirculation (EGR) boost sensor
13 Exhaust Gas Recirculation (EGR) valve/valve position sensor

Chapter. It should be noted that the illustrations of the various systems may not exactly match the system installed on your vehicle because of changes made by the manufacturer during production or from year-to-year.

6   The Vehicle Emissions Control Information (VECI) label and a vacuum hose diagram are located on the hood (see illustration). These contain important emissions specifications and setting procedures, and a vacuum hose schematic with emissions components identified. When servicing the engine or emissions systems, the VECI label in your particular vehicle should always be checked for up-to-date information.

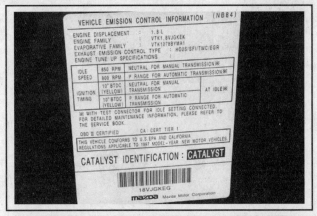

1.6 The Vehicle Emissions Control Information (VECI) label contains such essential information as the types of emission control systems installed on the engine, the idle speed and ignition timing specifications

2   On-Board Diagnostic (OBD) System and trouble codes

1   The PCM (computer) has a built-in self-diagnosis system which detects malfunctions in the system sensors and alerts the driver by illuminating a CHECK ENGINE warning light in the instrument panel. The computer stores the failure code until the diagnostic system is cleared by disconnecting the negative battery cable then depressing the brake pedal for a period of five seconds or longer. The warning light goes out automatically when the malfunction is repaired.

2   The CHECK ENGINE warning light should come on when the ignition switch is placed in the On position; this checks the bulb for proper operation. When the engine is started, the warning light should go out. If the light remains on, the diagnostic system has detected a malfunction or abnormality in the system.

OBTAINING DIAGNOSTIC TROUBLE CODES (DTCS)

1995 and earlier models

3   To determine which sensor or system component is malfunctioning, connect a jumper wire between the TEN and GND terminals at the DIAGNOSTIC test connector (see illustration 9.2 in Chapter 5) in the engine compartment. Make sure the battery voltage is greater than 11 volts, the transmission is in Neutral, the accessories are off, the throttle valve is closed and the engine is at normal operating temperature, then turn the ignition switch to the ON position but do not start the engine.

4   The diagnostic code is the number of flashes indicated on the CHECK ENGINE light. If no codes are stored, the CHECK ENGINE light will come on for a few moments, then go out. If any malfunction has been detected, the light will blink the first digit(s) of the code at a long interval(s) and then blink the second digit of the code at short interval(s). For example, a code 34 (IAC valve) will first blink three long flashes and then pause and blink four quick flashes.

➡Note: If the code is simply a single digit number, the CHECK ENGINE light will flash in the quick mode.

5   The accompanying table indicates the diagnostic code, the system affected, and the corrective action to take.

1996 and later models

▶ Refer to illustrations 2.6a and 2.6b

6   These models are equipped with On-Board Diagnostic II (OBD-II) systems; the Diagnostic Trouble Codes (DTCs) can only be accessed with a scan tool. Professional scan tools are expensive, but relatively inexpensive generic scan tools (see illustrations) are available at most

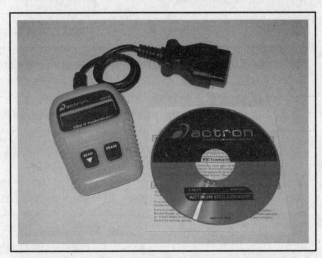

2.6a Simple code readers are an economical way to extract trouble codes when the CHECK ENGINE light comes on

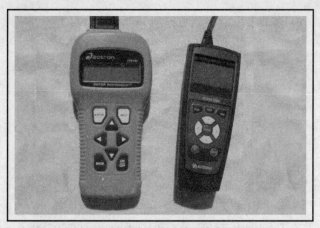

2.6b Scanners like these from Actron and AutoXray are powerful diagnostic aids - they can tell you just about anything that you want to know about your engine management system

auto parts stores. Simply plug the connector of the scan tool into the diagnostic connector, which is located under the driver's side of the dash. Then follow the instructions included with the scan tool to extract the DTCs.

7 Once you have outputted all of the stored DTCs, look them up on the accompanying DTC chart.

8 After troubleshooting the source of each DTC make any necessary repairs or replace the defective component(s).

9 The accompanying tables are a list of the Diagnostic Trouble Codes (DTCs) that can be accessed by a do-it-yourselfer working at home (there are many, many more DTCs available to professional mechanics with proprietary scan tools and software, but those codes cannot be accessed by a generic scan tool). If, after you have checked and repaired the connectors, wire harness and vacuum hoses (if applicable) for an emission-related system, component or circuit, the problem persists, have the vehicle checked by a dealer service department or other qualified repair shop.

CLEARING THE CODES

1995 and earlier models

10 After the self-diagnosis check, remove the jumper wire and close the cover on the DIAGNOSTIC electrical connector. Check the indicated system or component or take the vehicle to a dealer service department to have the malfunction repaired.

11 After repairs have been made, the diagnostic code must be canceled by detaching the cable from the negative terminal of the battery, then depressing the brake pedal for more than five seconds.

12 After cancellation, perform a road test and make sure the warning light does not come on. If the original trouble code is repeated, additional repairs are required.

1996 and later models

13 Clear the DTCs with the scan tool in accordance with the instructions provided by the scan tool's manufacturer.

TROUBLE CODES - 1995 AND EARLIER MODELS

Code	Circuit or system	Corrective action
01	Ignition pulse	Check the ignition coil, igniter and PCM circuitry or components.
02	Ignition Ne-signal	Check the camshaft position sensor and PCM circuitry or components.
03	Ignition G-signal	Check the distributor and PCM circuitry or components.
08	Airflow sensor	Check the airflow sensor circuit from the sensor to the PCM for an open or short circuit or a sensor malfunction.
09	Coolant temperature sensor	Check the coolant temperature sensor circuit for an open or short circuit or a sensor malfunction.
10	Intake air temperature sensor	Check the intake air temperature sensor circuit for an open or short circuit or a sensor malfunction.
12	Throttle position sensor	Check the throttle position sensor circuit for an open or short circuit or a sensor malfunction.
14	Barometric pressure sensor	The barometric pressure sensor is integrated within the PCM. Have the problem diagnosed by a dealer service department or other qualified repair shop.
15	Oxygen sensor	Check the oxygen sensor circuit for an open or short circuit or a sensor malfunction.

TROUBLE CODES - 1995 AND EARLIER MODELS (CONTINUED)

Code	Circuit or system	Corrective action
17	Oxygen sensor has detected a rich or lean condition	Check the fuel and ignition system performance (fuel pressure high or low, leaking fuel injectors, inoperative fuel injector, intake air leaks, ignition misfire, etc.).
26	Solenoid valve (purge control)	Check for an open or short circuit from the solenoid valve to the PCM. Check for an open or short circuit from the solenoid valve to the fuel injection main relay. Check for a defective solenoid valve.
34	IAC valve	Check for an open or short circuit from the IAC valve to the PCM. Check for an open or short circuit from the IAC valve to the fuel injection main relay. Check for a defective IAC valve.

TROUBLE CODES - 1996 AND LATER MODELS

Code	Possible cause
P0010	Intake camshaft position actuator circuit open (bank 1)
P0011	"A" Camshaft position - timing over-advanced
P0012	"A" Camshaft position - timing over-retarded
P0015	"B" Camshaft position - timing over-retarded (bank 1)
P0016	Crankshaft position/camshaft position, sensor A - correlation
P0020	Intake camshaft position actuator circuit open
P0030	HO2S heater control circuit (sensor 1)
P0031	HO2S heater control circuit low (sensor 1)
P0032	HO2S heater control circuit high (sensor 1)
P0037	HO2S heater control circuit low (sensor 2)
P0038	HO2S heater control circuit high (sensor 2)
P0053	HO2S heater resistance (sensor 1)
P0054	HO2S heater resistance (sensor 2)
P0069	Manifold pressure (MAP) sensor - barometric pressure correlation
P0096	Intake air temperature (IAT) sensor 2 - circuit range/performance problem
P0097	Intake air temperature (IAT) sensor 2 - circuit low input
P0098	Intake air temperature (IAT) sensor 2 - circuit high input
P0100	Mass air flow or volume air flow circuit malfunction
P0101	Mass air flow or volume air flow circuit, range or performance problem
P0102	Mass air flow or volume air flow circuit, low input

TROUBLE CODES - 1996 AND LATER MODELS (CONTINUED)

Code	Possible cause
P0103	Mass air flow or volume air flow circuit, high input
P0106	Manifold absolute pressure or barometric pressure circuit, range or performance problem
P0107	Manifold absolute pressure or barometric pressure circuit, low input
P0108	Manifold absolute pressure or barometric pressure circuit, high input
P0110	Intake air temperature circuit malfunction
P0111	Intake air temperature circuit, range or performance problem
P0112	Intake air temperature circuit, low input
P0113	Intake air temperature circuit, high input
P0115	Engine coolant temperature circuit
P0116	Engine coolant temperature circuit range/performance problem
P0117	Engine coolant temperature circuit, low input
P0118	Engine coolant temperature circuit, high input
P0120	Throttle position or pedal position sensor/switch circuit malfunction
P0121	Throttle position or pedal position sensor/switch circuit, range or performance problem
P0122	Throttle position or pedal position sensor/switch circuit, low input
P0123	Throttle position or pedal position sensor/switch circuit, high input
P0125	Insufficient coolant temperature for closed loop fuel control
P0126	Insufficient coolant temperature for stable operation
P0128	Coolant thermostat (coolant temperature below thermostat regulating temperature)
P0130	O2 sensor circuit malfunction (sensor 1)
P0131	O2 sensor circuit, low voltage (sensor 1)
P0132	O2 sensor circuit, high voltage (sensor 1)
P0133	O2 sensor circuit, slow response (sensor 1)
P0134	O2 sensor circuit - no activity detected (sensor 1)
P0135	O2 sensor heater circuit malfunction (sensor 1)
P0137	O2 sensor circuit, low voltage (sensor 2)
P0138	O2 sensor circuit, high voltage (sensor 2)
P0139	O2 sensor circuit, slow response (sensor 2)

Code	Possible cause
P0140	O2 sensor circuit - no activity detected (sensor 2)
P0141	O2 sensor heater circuit malfunction (sensor 2)
P0170	Fuel trim malfunction
P0171	System too lean
P0172	System too rich
P0222	Throttle position or pedal position sensor/switch B circuit, low input
P0223	Throttle position or pedal position sensor/switch B circuit, high
P0245	Turbocharger wastegate solenoid A, low
P0246	Turbocharger wastegate solenoid A, high
P0300	Random/multiple cylinder misfire detected
P0301	Cylinder no. 1 misfire detected
P0302	Cylinder no. 2 misfire detected
P0303	Cylinder no. 3 misfire detected
P0304	Cylinder no. 4 misfire detected
P0325	Knock sensor no. 1 circuit malfunction (bank 1 or single sensor)
P0327	Knock sensor no. 1 circuit, low input (single sensor)
P0328	Knock sensor no. 1 circuit, high input (single sensor)
P0335	Crankshaft position sensor "A" - circuit malfunction
P0339	Crankshaft position sensor "A" - circuit intermittent
P0340	Camshaft position sensor "A" - circuit malfunction
P0400	Exhaust gas recirculation - flow malfunction
P0401	Exhaust gas recirculation - insufficient flow detected
P0402	Exhaust gas recirculation - excessive flow detected
P0403	Exhaust gas recirculation - circuit malfunction
P0404	Exhaust gas recirculation - range or performance problem
P0420	Catalyst system efficiency below threshold
P0421	Warm-up catalyst efficiency below threshold
P0441	Evaporative emission control system, incorrect purge flow

TROUBLE CODES - 1996 AND LATER MODELS (CONTINUED)

Code	Possible cause
P0442	Evaporative emission control system, small leak detected
P0443	Evaporative emission control system, purge control valve circuit malfunction
P0446	Evaporative emission control system, vent control circuit malfunction
P0451	Evaporative emission control system, pressure sensor range or performance problem
P0452	Evaporative emission control system, pressure sensor low input
P0453	Evaporative emission control system, pressure sensor high input
P0455	Evaporative emission (EVAP) control system leak detected (no purge flow or large leak)
P0456	Evaporative emission (EVAP) control system leak detected (very small leak)
P0461	Fuel level sensor circuit, range or performance problem
P0462	Fuel level sensor circuit, low input
P0463	Fuel level sensor circuit, high input
P0464	Fuel level sensor circuit, intermittent
P0470	Exhaust pressure sensor malfunction
P0480	Cooling fan no. 1, control circuit malfunction
P0481	Cooling fan no. 2, control circuit malfunction
P0482	Cooling fan no. 3, control circuit malfunction
P050A	Cold start idle air control system performance (2008 and later)
P050B	Cold start ignition timing performance (2008 and later)
P0500	Vehicle speed sensor malfunction
P0505	Idle control system malfunction
P0506	Idle control system, rpm lower than expected
P0507	Idle control system, rpm higher than expected
P0510	Closed throttle position switch malfunction
P0550	Power steering pressure sensor, circuit malfunction
P0564	Cruise control system, multi-function input signal
P0571	Cruise control/brake switch A, circuit malfunction
P0600	Serial communication link malfunction

Code	Possible cause
P0601	Internal control module, memory check sum error
P0602	Control module, programming error
P0604	Internal control module, random access memory (RAM) error
P0605	Internal control module, read only memory (ROM) error
P0606	PCM processor fault
P0610	Control module - vehicle options error
P0638	Throttle actuator control range/performance problem
P0661	Intake manifold tuning valve control circuit low
P0662	Intake manifold tuning valve control circuit high
P0685	EGM power relay, control - circuit open
P06B8	Internal control module nonvolatile random access memory error
P0703	Torque converter/brake switch B, circuit malfunction
P0704	Clutch switch input circuit malfunction
P0705	Transmission range sensor, circuit malfunction (PRNDL)
P0706	Transmission range sensor circuit, range or performance problem
P0715	Input/turbine speed sensor circuit malfunction
P0720	Output speed sensor malfunction
P0725	Engine speed input circuit malfunction
P0741	Torque converter clutch, circuit performance problem or stuck in Off position
P0742	Torque converter clutch circuit, stuck in On position
P0743	Torque converter clutch circuit, electrical problem
P0751	Shift solenoid A, performance problem or stuck in Off position
P0752	Shift solenoid A, stuck in On position
P0753	Shift solenoid A, electrical problem
P0756	Shift solenoid B, performance problem or stuck in Off position
P0757	Shift solenoid B, stuck in On position
P0758	Shift solenoid B, electrical problem
P0850	Park/Neutral Position (PNP) switch - input circuit malfunction

3 Air Flow Meter/Intake Air Temperature (AFM/IAT) sensor - replacement

➡Note: 1993 and earlier models are equipped with a vane-type airflow sensor with an integral IAT sensor.

1 Disconnect the electrical connector from the sensor.
2 Remove the air intake duct (see Chapter 4).

3 Remove the air filter housing cover (see Chapter 4).
4 Remove the nuts that secure the airflow sensor to the filter housing cover and remove the sensor.
5 Installation is the reverse of removal.

4 Accelerator Pedal Position (APP) sensor - replacement

◆ Refer to illustration 4.2

➡Note: The APP sensor, which is located at the upper end of, and is an integral component of, the accelerator pedal assembly, is used only on 2006 and later models.

1 Remove the knee bolster trim (see Chapter 11).
2 Disconnect the electrical connector from the APP sensor (see illustration).
3 Remove the APP sensor mounting bolts and remove the sensor/pedal assembly.
4 Installation is the reverse of removal.

4.2 Accelerator Pedal Position (APP) sensor details:

1 *Electrical connector*	2 *Mounting bolt*

5 Camshaft Position (CMP) sensor - replacement

1 All models use a sensor to indicate camshaft position. Mazda terminology for this sensor can be confusing. On 1994 and earlier models, Mazda referred to this sensor as the "crankshaft position sensor" or "crank angle sensor" (these models do not have an actual crankshaft position sensor mounted somewhere near the crankshaft). In 1995 (the same year that Mazda added an actual crankshaft position sensor) it began using the standard SAE terminology, Camshaft Position (CMP) sensor. In this book, to avoid confusion, we will refer to all camshaft sensors as Camshaft Position (CMP) sensors and all crankshaft sensors as Crankshaft Position (CKP) sensors.

1997 AND EARLIER MODELS

◆ Refer to illustrations 5.4 and 5.5

➡Note: The CMP sensor on 1994 through 1997 models is located at the left rear corner of the cylinder head, behind the exhaust camshaft. The sensor on 1993 and earlier models is mounted at the right rear corner of the cylinder head, behind the intake camshaft. The procedure for removing and installing either unit is the same.

2 Disconnect the cable from the negative battery terminal (see Chapter 5).

3 Disconnect the electrical connector from the sensor. Mark the relationship of the sensor to the cylinder head.
4 Remove the CMP sensor mounting bolt (see illustration), then pull the sensor straight out to remove it.

5.4 To remove the CMP sensor on 1997 and earlier models, remove the sensor mounting bolt (1994 through 1997 sensor shown, 1993 and earlier sensor similar)

5.5 Replace the old CMP sensor O-ring (1). When installing the CMP sensor, align the drive tang (2) with the slot in the camshaft (1994 through 1997 sensor shown, 1993 and earlier sensor similar)

5.17 CMP sensor removal and installation details (2006 and later model shown, 2001 through 2005 models similar):

1   *Electrical connector*   2   *Mounting bolt*

5   Install a new O-ring onto the sensor housing (see illustration).

6   Align the sensor drive tang with the slot in the camshaft (see illustration 5.5).

7   Insert the sensor into the cylinder head, aligning the marks made in Step 3.

8   If the sensor does not seat completely, recheck the alignment of the drive tang and camshaft slot.

9   Installation is the reverse of removal. Don't tighten the CMP sensor mounting bolt until you've checked ignition timing.

10   Check and, if necessary, adjust the ignition timing (see Chapter 5), then tighten the CMP sensor mounting bolt securely.

1999 AND 2000 MODELS

➡Note: The CMP sensor is located on the upper right front corner of the timing belt cover, near the intake camshaft timing belt sprocket.

11   Disconnect the cable from the negative battery terminal (see Chapter 5).

12   Disconnect the electrical connector from the CMP sensor.

13   Remove the CMP sensor mounting bolt and remove the sensor.

14   Before installing the CMP sensor, inspect it carefully. Make sure that it's free of any metal particles or shavings.

15   Installation is the reverse of removal.

2001 AND LATER MODELS

▶ **Refer to illustration 5.17**

➡Note: On 2001 through 2005 models, the CMP sensor is located on top of and near the right rear corner of the valve cover. On 2006 and later models, the CMP sensor is located on top of and near the left rear corner of the valve cover. The procedure for removing and installing both units is similar.

16   Disconnect the cable from the negative battery terminal (see Chapter 5).

17   Disconnect the electrical connector from the CMP sensor (see illustration).

18   Remove the CMP sensor mounting bolt and remove the sensor.

19   Before installing the CMP sensor, inspect it carefully. Make sure that it's free of any metal particles or shavings.

20   Installation is the reverse of removal.

6   Crankshaft Position (CKP) sensor - replacement

1995 THROUGH 2005 MODELS

▶ **Refer to illustration 6.3**

➡Note: On 1995 through 1997 models, the CKP sensor is located on the lower front part of the engine, to the left of the crankshaft pulley. On 1999 through 2005 models, the CKP sensor is located on the lower front part of the engine, to the right of the crankshaft pulley. The procedure for removing, adjusting and installing both units is similar.

1   Disconnect the cable from the negative battery terminal (see Chapter 5).

2   Trace the wiring harness from the CKP sensor up to its electrical connector and disconnect it. Free the harness from any retainers.

3   Remove the CKP sensor mounting bolt (see illustration) and remove the sensor from its bracket.

4   When installing the CKP sensor, position the sensor so that the gap between the sensor and one of the timing lugs on the timing plate is 0.020 to 0.059 inch, then tighten the sensor mounting bolt securely.

5   Installation is otherwise the reverse of removal.

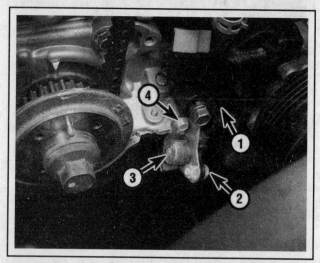

6.3 CKP sensor removal, installation and adjustment details (1995 through 1997 model shown, 1999 through 2005 models similar):

1   Trace the wire from the CKP sensor up to the electrical connector and disconnect it
2   CKP sensor mounting bolt
3   Measure the gap between the CKP sensor and one of the lugs on the timing plate (not shown because crank pulley is removed for clarity)
4   CKP sensor mounting bracket bolt

2006 AND LATER MODELS

Removal

▸ **Refer to illustration 6.10**

➡ **Note: The CKP sensor is located on the lower front part of the engine, to the right of the crankshaft pulley.**

6   Remove the battery and the battery tray (see Chapter 5).
7   Remove the air filter housing (see Chapter 4).
8   Remove the serpentine drivebelt (see Chapter 1).
9   Raise the front of the vehicle and place it securely on jackstands. Remove the engine compartment under-cover.
10   Disconnect the electrical connector from the CKP sensor (see illustration).
11   Remove the CKP sensor mounting bolts and remove the sensor.

Installation

▸ **Refer to illustration 6.13**

12   Bring the No. 1 piston to TDC (see Chapter 2A).
13   Look at the CKP sensor's trigger wheel, or timing plate, that's mounted on the backside of the crankshaft pulley. Note the small teeth that stick out from the circumference of the timing plate. At about ten o'clock there is a blank spot on the edge on the timing plate, where there are no teeth. From this blank area, count five teeth in a counter-clockwise direction, then, using a straightedge, draw a straight line from the center of this fifth tooth through the center of the crankshaft pulley (see illustration).
14   Place the CKP sensor in position, align the center of the sensor with the line that you made in the previous Step, then tighten the sensor bolts securely.
15   The remainder of installation is the reverse of removal.

6.10 CKP sensor removal and installation details (2006 and later models):

1   Sensor electrical connector   3   Crankshaft position sensor
2   Sensor mounting bolts

Empty Space

CKP Sensor

Center Line of CKP Sensor

Paint Mark at 5th Tooth

61016-6-6.13 HAYNES

6.13 CKP sensor alignment details (2006 and later models)

7   Engine Coolant Temperature (ECT) sensor - replacement

♦ Refer to illustrations 7.4a and 7.4b

※ WARNING:

The engine must be completely cool before beginning this procedure.

➡ Note: The ECT sensor is located at the back end of the cylinder head on all models. It is extremely difficult to access. To unscrew it, you will need a long extension, a U-joint and a socket deep enough to fit over the sensor.

1   Disconnect the cable from the negative battery terminal (see Chapter 5).

2   Drain the coolant (see Chapter 1).

3   On 2006 and later models, remove the strut bar (see Chapter 10) and the strut bar reinforcement plate (see Section 4 in Chapter 2A).

4   Disconnect the electrical connector from the ECT sensor (see illustrations).

5   Unscrew and remove the ECT sensor.

6   Wrap the threads of the new ECT sensor with Teflon tape to prevent leaks.

7   Installation is the reverse of removal. Be sure to tighten the ECT sensor securely.

8   Refill the cooling system (see Chapter 1), start the engine and check for leaks.

7.4a On earlier models, don't confuse the coolant temperature gauge sending unit (1) with the ECT sensor (2) (typical 1997 and earlier model)

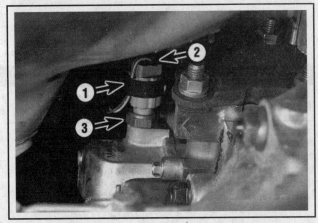

7.4b On 2006 and later models, the ECT sensor is hard to reach. It's easier to see from below (as shown here), but it's easier to access from above

1   *Remove the electrical tape*
2   *Disconnect the electrical connector*
3   *Unscrew the ECT sensor with a deep socket, U-joint and extension*

8   Intake Air Temperature (IAT) sensor - replacement

The IAT sensor is an integral component of the Air Flow Meter (AFM) (1993 and earlier models) or the Mass Air Flow (MAF) sensor (1994 and later models). If the IAT sensor is defective, replace the Air Flow Meter/Intake Air Temperature (AFM/IAT) sensor (see Section 3) or the Mass Air Flow/Intake Air Temperature (MAF/IAT) sensor (see Section 11).

9   Knock sensor - replacement

1999 THROUGH 2005 MODELS

➡ Note: The knock sensor is located on the right side of the engine block, above the oil filter canister.

1   Disconnect the cable from the negative battery terminal (see Chapter 5).

2   Remove the intake manifold support bracket (see Chapter 2A).

3   Disconnect the electrical connector from the knock sensor.

4   Unscrew the knock sensor.

5   Installation is the reverse of removal. Be sure to tighten the knock sensor to the torque listed in this Chapter's Specifications.

2006 AND LATER MODELS

➡**Note: The knock sensor is located on the left side of the engine block, below the intake manifold.**

6 Disconnect the cable from the negative battery terminal (see Chapter 5).

7 Remove the intake manifold (see Chapter 2A).
8 Disconnect the knock sensor electrical connector.
9 Remove the knock sensor mounting bolt and remove the knock sensor.
10 Installation is the reverse of removal. Be sure to tighten the knock sensor mounting bolt to the torque listed in this Chapter's Specifications.

---

10 Manifold Absolute Pressure (MAP) sensor (2006 and later models) - replacement

➡**Note: The MAP sensor is located on the intake manifold plenum, which must be removed to access the MAP sensor.**

1 Disconnect the cable from the negative battery terminal (see Chapter 5).

2 Remove the intake manifold plenum (see Chapter 2A).
3 Remove the MAP sensor from the intake manifold plenum.
4 Installation is the reverse of removal.

---

11 Mass Air Flow/Intake Air Temperature (MAF/IAT) sensor - replacement

1994 THROUGH 2005 MODELS

➡**Note: The MAF/IAT sensor is located on, and is an integral component of, a plastic tube between the air filter housing and the air intake duct. The MAF/IAT sensor is not removable from the tube. If the MAF/IAT sensor is defective, the sensor and the tube are replaced as a single assembly.**

1 Disconnect the cable from the negative battery terminal (see Chapter 5).
2 Remove the air intake duct (see Chapter 4).
3 Remove the MAF/IAT sensor from the air filter housing.
4 Installation is the reverse of removal.

2006 AND LATER MODELS

▶ **Refer to illustration 11.6**

➡**Note: The MAF/IAT sensor is located on the outlet tube part of the air filter housing, next to the air intake duct. The MAF/IAT sensor is removable from the filter housing.**

5 Disconnect the cable from the negative battery terminal (see Chapter 5).
6 Disconnect the electrical connector from the MAF/IAT sensor (see illustration).

11.6 MAF/IAT sensor removal and installation details (2006 and later models):

1 Electrical connector
2 MAF/IAT sensor mounting screws

7 Remove the MAF/IAT sensor mounting screws and remove the MAF/IAT sensor from the air filter housing cover.
8 Installation is the reverse of removal.

---

12 Oxygen sensors - general information and replacement

GENERAL INFORMATION

1 The oxygen sensor monitors the exhaust gases before they have passed through the catalytic converter. Later models equipped with the OBD-II emission control system have an additional oxygen sensor mounted in the exhaust system after the converter (the PCM compares the reading from each sensor to determine the efficiency of the converter). The oxygen content in the exhaust reacts with the oxygen sensor to produce a voltage output which varies from 0.1-volt (high oxygen, lean mixture) to 0.9-volts (low oxygen, rich mixture). The PCM constantly monitors this variable voltage output to determine the ratio of oxygen to fuel in the mixture. The PCM alters the air/fuel mixture ratio by controlling the pulse width (open time) of the fuel injectors. A mixture ratio of 14.7 parts air to 1 part fuel is the ideal mixture ratio

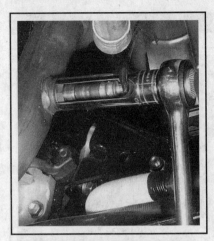

12.10a Use an oxygen sensor socket, if available, to loosen the oxygen sensor (1995 and earlier models shown)

12.10b Typical upstream oxygen sensor location on 1996 and later models (2006 model shown)

12.10c Typical downstream oxygen sensor location on 1996 and later models (2006 model shown)

for minimizing exhaust emissions, thus allowing the catalytic converter to operate at maximum efficiency. It is this ratio of 14.7 to 1 which the PCM and the oxygen sensor attempt to maintain at all times.

2   The oxygen sensor produces no voltage when the oxygen sensor is below its normal operating temperature of about 600-degrees F. During this initial period before warm-up, the PCM operates in open loop mode.

3   If the engine reaches normal operating temperature and/or has been running for two or more minutes, and if the main oxygen sensor is producing a steady signal voltage below 0.70-volts at 1,500 or more rpm, the PCM will set a Code 15.

4   When there is a problem with the oxygen sensor or its circuit, the PCM operates in the open loop mode - that is, it controls fuel delivery in accordance with a programmed default value instead of feedback information from the oxygen sensor.

5   The proper operation of the oxygen sensor depends on four conditions:

   a) *Electrical - The low voltages generated by the sensor depend upon good, clean connections which should be checked whenever a malfunction of the sensor is suspected or indicated.*

   b) *Outside air supply - The sensor is designed to allow air circulation to the internal portion of the sensor. Whenever the sensor is removed and installed or replaced, make sure the air passages are not restricted.*

   c) *Proper operating temperature - The PCM will not react to the sensor signal until the sensor reaches approximately 600-degrees F. This factor must be taken into consideration when evaluating the performance of the sensor.*

   d) *Unleaded fuel - The use of unleaded fuel is essential for proper operation of the sensor. Make sure the fuel you are using is of this type.*

6   In addition to observing the above conditions, special care must be taken whenever the sensor is serviced.

   a) *The oxygen sensor has a permanently attached pigtail and electrical connector which should not be removed from the sensor. Damage to or removal of the pigtail or electrical connector can adversely affect operation of the sensor.*

   b) *Grease, dirt and other contaminants should be kept away from the electrical connector and the louvered end of the sensor.*

   c) *Do not use cleaning solvents of any kind on the oxygen sensor.*

   d) *Do not drop or roughly handle the sensor.*

   e) *The silicone boot must be installed in the correct position to prevent the boot from being melted and to allow the sensor to operate properly.*

REPLACEMENT

▶ Refer to illustrations 12.10a, 12.10b and 12.10c

➡Note: Because it is installed in the exhaust manifold or pipe, which contracts when cool, the oxygen sensor may be very difficult to loosen when the engine is cold. Rather than risk damage to the sensor (assuming you are planning to reuse it in another manifold or pipe), start and run the engine for a minute or two, then shut it off. Be careful not to burn yourself during the following procedure.

7   Disconnect the cable from the negative battery terminal (see Chapter 5).

8   Raise the vehicle and place it securely on jackstands.

9   Carefully disconnect the electrical connector from the sensor pigtail lead.

10 Remove the oxygen sensor from the exhaust system (see illustrations).

11 Anti-seize compound must be used on the threads of the sensor to facilitate future removal. The threads of new sensors will already be coated with this compound, but if an old sensor is removed and reinstalled, recoat the threads.

12 Install the sensor and tighten it securely.

13 Reconnect the electrical connector of the pigtail lead to the main engine wiring harness.

14 Lower the vehicle and reconnect the cable to the negative terminal of the battery.

13 Power Steering Pressure (PSP) switch - replacement

♦ Refer to illustration 13.2

➡Note: The PSP switch is located on the power steering pump on all models.

1 Disconnect the cable from the negative battery terminal (see Chapter 5).

2 Disconnect the electrical connector from the PSP switch (see illustration).

3 Unscrew the switch with a wrench or deep socket. Be prepared to catch some spilled power steering fluid with a shop rag.

4 Installation is the reverse of removal. Be sure to tighten the PSP switch securely.

13.2 Disconnect the electrical connector and unscrew the switch from the power steering pump (2006 model shown)

14 Throttle Position (TP) sensor - replacement

➡Note: The TP sensor, which is located on the throttle body, is used on all models. On 1995 and earlier models, the TP sensor is replaceable separately from the throttle body, but on 1996 through 2005 models there is no way to adjust the TP sensor without special factory tools. We therefore don't recommend removing or replacing the TP sensor on these models at home. On 2006 and later models (which use an electronic throttle body), the TP sensor cannot be replaced separately; on these models, if the TP sensor is defective, replace the throttle body.

CHECK

♦ Refer to illustrations 14.2a, 14.2b, 14.3a, 14.3b and 14.6

1 Disconnect the electrical connector from the TP sensor.

2 Insert a 0.016-inch feeler gauge between the throttle stop screw and the stop lever (see illustrations).

14.2a Inserting a feeler gauge between the stop screw and the stop lever on 1993 and earlier models . . .

14.2b . . . and 1994 and 1995 models

3 With the correct feeler gauge in position, use an ohmmeter to verify that there is no continuity between the specified terminal pairs (see illustrations).

    a) The two lower terminals on 1993 and earlier models, regardless of transmission type.

    b) Terminals C and D on 1994 and 1995 models.

4 On 1993 and earlier models with an automatic transmission, connect the ohmmeter probes to the second terminal from the top and the lowest terminal. Then slowly rotate the throttle lever toward the wide-open position. In the closed throttle position there should be less than 1 k-ohm of resistance and at the wide-open position approximately 5 k-ohms resistance.

5 On 1993 and earlier models with a manual transmission, connect the ohmmeter probes to the top two terminals. Then slowly rotate the throttle lever toward the wideopen position; there should be no continuity until the throttle reaches the wide-open position.

6 If the continuity or resistance is not as specified, adjust the TP sensor.

➡️**Note: Don't adjust the idle speed screw (see illustration); it was pre-set at the factory.**

ADJUSTMENT

🔸 **Refer to illustration 14.9**

7 Disconnect the electrical connector from the TP sensor and verify that the throttle valve is in the closed position.

8 Connect an ohmmeter between the sensor lower terminals (1993 and earlier models) or terminals C and D (1994 and 1995 models) (see illustrations 14.3a and 14.3b).

9 Loosen the two TP sensor attaching screws (see illustration).

1993 and earlier models

10 Insert a feeler gauge of the specified thickness between the throttle stop screw and the stop lever:

    a) With an automatic transmission use a 0.010 inch feeler gauge.

    b) With a manual transmission use a 0.016 inch feeler gauge.

11 Rotate the TP sensor clockwise approximately 30 degrees, then rotate it back (counterclockwise) until there is continuity.

12 Replace the feeler gauge with a gauge of the specified thickness

and verify that there is no continuity:

    a) With an automatic transmission use a 0.016 inch feeler gauge.

    b) With a manual transmission use a 0.027 inch feeler gauge.

13 If there is continuity, repeat Steps 10 through 12.

14 Tighten the two attaching screws.

➡️**Note: Do not move the TP sensor from the set position when tightening the screws.**

15 If you cannot successfully adjust the TP sensor, replace it.

1994 and 1995 models

16 Position the TPS so there is continuity when a 0.012-inch feeler gauge is inserted between the throttle stop screw and stop lever, and no continuity when a 0.016-inch feeler gauge is inserted.

17 Tighten the two attaching screws.

➡️**Note: Do not move the TP sensor from the set position when tightening the screws.**

18 If you cannot successfully adjust the TP sensor, replace it.

REPLACEMENT

19 If adjustment doesn't bring the sensor within specifications, disconnect it, remove the screws and replace it with a new one, then adjust it as described previously.

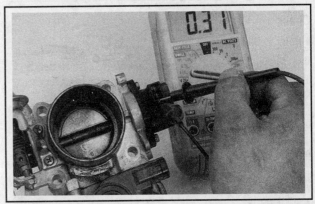

14.3a On 1993 and earlier models, with the feeler gauge in place, there should be no continuity between the two lower TP sensor terminals

14.3b Typical TP sensor terminal configuration on 1994 and 1995 models

14.6 Do NOT adjust the idle speed screw - it's permanently adjusted at the factory

14.9 Loosen the two TP sensor retaining screws (1993 and earlier TP sensor shown, 1994 and 1995 sensor similar)

15 Inhibitor switch/Transmission Range (TR) switch - check, adjustment and replacement

1   On 1994 and earlier vehicles, this switch is referred to as the inhibitor switch or the neutral start switch, because it prevents the engine from starting when the transmission is in gear. On 1995 and later vehicles, the inhibitor switch is replaced by the Transmission Range (TR) switch, which also functions as an inhibitor switch, and tells the Powertrain Control Module (PCM) or the Transmission Control Module (TCM) what gear the transmission is in. Mazda also refers to the inhibitor switch and TR switch as the transmission position switch. In this book we refer to all 1994 and earlier switches as inhibitor switches and to 1995 and later switches as TR switches. All inhibitor switches/TR switches are located on the side of the transmission where the shift linkage from the shift lever inside the vehicle connects to the manual lever on the transmission.

2   To functionally check the inhibitor switch/TR switch, make sure that the engine starts only when the shift lever is in PARK or NEUTRAL. Then, with the ignition key in the ON position, make sure the backup lights come on only when the shift lever is in REVERSE.

3   If the inhibitor switch/TR switch doesn't function as described, raise the vehicle and support it securely on jackstands. Then check, adjust and, if necessary, replace the switch as follows.

1994 AND EARLIER MODELS

Check

♦ **Refer to illustration 15.5**

4   Disconnect the electrical connector from the inhibitor switch, attach the leads of an ohmmeter to the terminals and check for continuity.

5   With the shift lever in PARK or NEUTRAL, there should be continuity between terminals 1 and 2 (see illustration).

6   With the shift lever in REVERSE, there should be continuity between terminals 3 and 4.

7   If the continuity is not as described, try adjusting the inhibitor switch as follows.

Adjustment

8   Put the shift lever in the NEUTRAL position.

9   The neutral start switch is in a black plastic housing located on the side of the transmission, directly under the shift lever of the transmission. The switch is secured by two bolts and has a smaller screw at the bottom of the switch. Loosen the two securing bolts and remove the

screw from the switch body.

10   Rotate the switch and insert a 5/64-inch diameter pin into the alignment hole (where the screw was removed) and through the internal rotor.

11   Tighten the mounting bolts, then remove the pin and install the screw in the hole.

12   Recheck switch operation (see Steps 4 through 6). If the continuity is still not correct, replace the switch.

Replacement

13   Disconnect the cable from the negative battery terminal (see Chapter 5).

14   Remove the retaining nut that secures the shift lever to the manual selector shaft and separate the lever from the shaft.

15   Disconnect the electrical connector, remove the screw and the two retaining bolts and remove the inhibitor switch.

16   Installation is the reverse of removal. Do not tighten the retaining bolts fully until the switch has been adjusted (see Steps 10 and 11).

17   Reconnect the battery (see Chapter 5).

18   To verify that the switch is correctly adjusted, make sure that the engine starts only in PARK or NEUTRAL, then turn the ignition key to ON, put the shift lever in reverse and verify that the backup lights operate. If not, readjust the switch.

1995 THROUGH 1997 MODELS

Check

♦ **Refer to illustration 15.19**

19   With the shift lever in PARK, there should be continuity between terminals B and H, and E and I (see illustration).

20   With the shift lever in REVERSE, there should be continuity between terminals G and I.

21   With the shift lever in NEUTRAL, there should be continuity between terminals B and H.

22   With the shift lever in DRIVE, there should be continuity between terminals C and I

23   With the shift lever in SECOND, there should be continuity between terminals F and I.

24   With the shift lever in LOW, there should be continuity between terminals A and I.

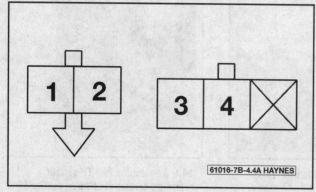

15.5 Inhibitor switch terminal guide (1994 and earlier models)

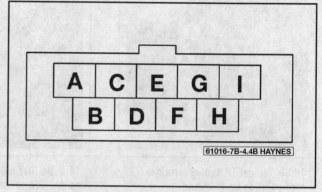

15.19 TR switch terminal guide (1995 through 1997 models)

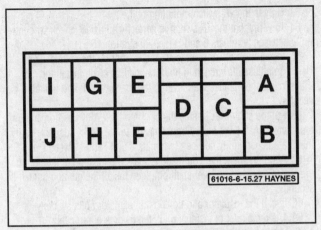

15.27 TR switch terminal guide (1999 through 2005 models)

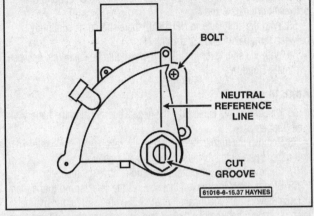

15.37 TR switch adjustment details

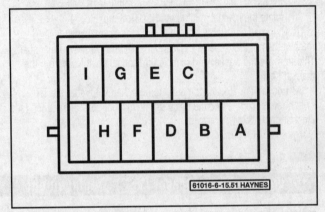

15.51 TR switch terminal guide (2006 and later models)

Adjustment

25 Refer to Steps 8 through 12.

Replacement

26 Refer to Steps 13 through 18.

1999 THROUGH 2005 MODELS

Check

♦ **Refer to illustration 15.27**

27 With the shift lever in PARK, there should be continuity between terminals D and C, and I and B (see illustration).
28 With the shift lever in REVERSE, there should be continuity between terminals I and F.
29 With the shift lever in NEUTRAL, there should be continuity between terminals D and C, and I and J.
30 With the shift lever in DRIVE, there should be continuity between terminals I and H.
31 With the shift lever in SECOND, there should be continuity between terminals I and E.
32 With the shift lever in LOW, there should be continuity between terminals I and G.

Adjustment

♦ **Refer to illustration 15.37**

33 Disconnect the cable from the negative battery terminal (see Chapter 5).
34 Disconnect the selector rod from the manual shaft lever.
35 Rotate the manual shaft to the NEUTRAL position.
36 Loosen the TR switch mounting bolt.
37 Align the groove in the rotating part of the switch with the NEUTRAL reference line on the switch housing (see illustration).
38 Tighten the TR switch mounting bolt.
39 Reconnect the selector rod to the manual shaft lever.
40 Reconnect the battery (see Chapter 5),
41 To verify that the switch is correctly adjusted, make sure that the engine starts only in PARK or NEUTRAL. Then turn the ignition key to ON, put the shift lever in reverse and verify that the backup lights operate. If not, readjust the switch.

Replacement

42 Disconnect the cable from the negative battery terminal (see Chapter 5).
43 Disconnect the electrical connector from the TR switch.
44 Disconnect the selector rod from the manual shaft lever.
45 Remove the manual shaft lever.
46 Unstake the lock washer with a screwdriver, then remove the nut, lock washer and washer.
47 Remove the TR switch.
48 Install and adjust the TR switch (see Steps 34 through 41)
49 When installing the TR switch, be sure to use a new nut, lock washer and washer. Tighten the nut securely and stake the lock washer. Installation is otherwise the reverse of removal.
50 To verify that the switch is correctly adjusted, make sure that the engine starts only in PARK or NEUTRAL, then turn the ignition key to ON, put the shift lever in reverse and verify that the backup lights operate. If not, readjust the switch.

2006 AND LATER MODELS

Check

♦ **Refer to illustration 15.51**

51 With the shift lever in PARK, there should be continuity between terminals A and I, and E and B (see illustration).

52 With the shift lever in REVERSE, there should be continuity between terminals E and C.

53 With the shift lever in NEUTRAL, there should be continuity between terminals A and I and E and H.

54 With the shift lever in DRIVE, there should be continuity between terminals E and D.

Adjustment

55 Disconnect the cable from the negative terminal of the battery (see Chapter 5).

56 Remove the tunnel member (see illustration 5.11 in Chapter 7A) and middle part of the exhaust system (see Chapter 4).

57 Remove the four insulator bolts and remove the insulator.

58 Before removing the nut that secures the selector rod to the manual shaft lever, mark the location of the nut on the slot for the manual lever shaft pin, then remove the nut and separate the manual lever from the selector lever.

59 Disconnect the electrical connector from the TR switch.

60 Rotate the manual shaft to the NEUTRAL position.

61 Using an adjustable wrench to hold the manual shaft lever, remove the nut that secures the manual shaft lever to the manual shaft. Then remove the washer and remove the manual shaft lever from the manual shaft.

62 Loosen the TR switch mounting bolt, then verify that the TR switch reference line and the notch on the manual shaft are aligned (see illustration 15.37).

63 Tighten the TR switch mounting bolt.

64 To verify that the TR switch is correctly adjusted, check for continuity between terminals E and H (see illustration 15.51).

65 Install the manual shaft lever and washer on the manual shaft. Using an adjustable wrench to hold the manual shaft, install the nut that secures the manual shaft lever to the manual shaft and tighten it securely.

66 Put the shift lever (inside the car) into the PARK position and turn the manual shaft lever on the transmission to the PARK position. Verify that there is continuity between terminals A and I and between E and B.

67 Align the mark that you made to mark the location of the nut on the slot for the manual lever shaft pin, then install the nut and tighten it securely.

68 Install the insulator and tighten the insulator bolts securely.

69 The remainder of installation is the reverse of removal.

70 Verify that the TR switch operates correctly (see Steps 51 through 54) before reconnecting the electrical connector to the TR switch.

Replacement

71 Follow Steps 55 through 62.

72 Remove the manual shaft nut, lock washer and washer.

73 Remove the TR switch mounting bolt.

74 Installation is the reverse of removal. Follow Steps 62 through 70.

16 Vehicle Speed Sensor (VSS) - replacement

➡Note: The VSS is located on the transmission.

1 Disconnect the cable from the negative terminal of the battery (see Chapter 5).

2 Raise the vehicle and place it securely on jackstands.

3 Disconnect the electrical connector from the VSS.

4 Remove the VSS mounting bolt and remove the VSS.

5 Installation is the reverse of removal.

17 Powertrain Control Module (PCM) - removal and installation

1993 AND EARLIER MODELS

➡Note: The PCM is located below the right part of the dash, in the right foot well, under the passenger side front floor mat.

1 Disconnect the cable from the negative terminal of the battery (see Chapter 5).

2 Remove the floor mat, then remove the PCM protective cover.

3 Disconnect the electrical connectors from the PCM.

4 Remove the PCM mounting bracket fasteners and remove the PCM.

5 Installation is the reverse of removal.

1994 THROUGH 1997 MODELS

▶ Refer to illustration 17.8

➡Note: The PCM is located behind the passenger seat.

6 Disconnect the cable from the negative terminal of the battery (see Chapter 5).

7 Remove the trim covering the PCM.

8 Remove the PCM mounting bracket nuts (see illustration) and remove the PCM and mounting bracket as a single assembly. Carefully flip the PCM around and disconnect the electrical connectors from the PCM. Each connector has a locking tab which must be disengaged before the connector is unplugged.

9 Separate the PCM from its mounting bracket.

10 Installation is the reverse of removal.

1999 THROUGH 2005 MODELS

➡Note: The PCM is located under the left part of the dash, near the brake pedal bracket.

11 Disconnect the cable from the negative terminal of the battery (see Chapter 5).

12 Remove the knee bolster trim (see Chapter 11).

13 Using a flashlight, locate the PCM, then disconnect the electrical connectors from the PCM and disengage the PCM harness from the harness stud on the pedal bracket.

17.8 To detach the PCM on 1994 through 1997 models, remove these three bracket mounting nuts, then disconnect the electrical connectors at the bottom of the unit

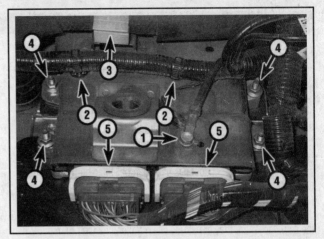

17.18 PCM removal details (2006 and later models):

1	*Ground bolt*	4	*PCM cover nuts*
2	*Harness clips*	5	*PCM electrical connectors*
3	*Radiator hose clip*		

14 Remove the PCM mounting nut and bolt and remove the PCM.

15 Installation is the reverse of removal.

2006 AND LATER MODELS

▶ **Refer to illustration 17.18**

➡**Note: The PCM is located in the engine compartment, under the air filter housing.**

16 Disconnect the cable from the negative terminal of the battery (see Chapter 5).

17 Remove the air filter housing (see Chapter 4).

18 Disconnect the ground wire (see illustration), detach the electrical harness clips and move the harness and coolant hose out of the way. Remove the PCV cover nuts and remove the cover.

19 Flip open the levers that secure the electrical connectors to the PCM and disconnect the connectors.

20 Remove the PCM from the air filter housing insulator.

21 Installation is the reverse of removal.

18 Catalytic converter - description, check and replacement

➡**Note: Because of a federally mandated extended warranty which covers emissions-related components such as the catalytic converter, check with a dealer service department before replacing the converter at your own expense.**

GENERAL DESCRIPTION

1 To reduce hydrocarbon, carbon monoxide and oxides of nitrogen emissions, all vehicles are equipped with a three-way catalyst system which oxidizes and reduces these chemicals, converting them into harmless nitrogen, carbon dioxide and water.

2 On 1997 and earlier models, the catalytic converter is located underneath the vehicle, between the front and rear exhaust pipes.

3 On 1999 and 2000 models, there are two different setups, one for California models and the other for 49-State models:

  a) *California models are equipped with a Warm-Up Three-Way Catalyst (WU-TWC) in addition to the main (Three-Way Catalyst) TWC located underneath the vehicle. The WU-TWC is located between the exhaust manifold flange and the front exhaust pipe flange.*

  b) *49-State models are equipped with a TWC underneath the vehicle, but are not equipped with a WU-TWC.*

4 On 2001 through 2005 models, there is no difference between California and 49-State models: There is one TWC catalyst underneath

the vehicle. It's bolted to the front exhaust pipe at its forward mounting flange, and is an integral component of the rest of the exhaust system.

5 On 2006 and later models, the TWC is an integral component of the exhaust manifold, and is therefore covered in *Exhaust manifold - removal and installation* in Chapter 2A.

CHECK

6 Periodically inspect the catalytic converter-to-exhaust pipe mating flanges and bolts. Make sure that there are no loose bolts and no leaks between the flanges.

7 Look for dents in or damage to the catalytic converter protector. If any part of the protector is damaged or dented enough to touch the converter, repair or replace it.

8 Inspect the heat insulator for damage. Make sure that there is adequate clearance between the heat insulator and the catalytic converter.

REPLACEMENT

9 The catalytic converter is removed as part of exhaust system removal (see Chapter 4).

19 Evaporative Emission Control (EVAP) system - description and component replacement

DESCRIPTION

▶ **Refer to illustrations 19.2a and 19.2b**

1 The Evaporative Emission Control (EVAP) system traps and stores fuel vapors from the fuel tank, throttle body and intake manifold that would normally enter the atmosphere in the form of hydrocarbon (HC) emissions.

2 The EVAP system consists of a charcoal-filled canister, the lines connecting the canister to the fuel tank, a check valve, a rollover valve (some models) and a purge solenoid valve (see illustrations).

3 Fuel vapors are transferred from the fuel tank and throttle body to the canister, where they are stored when the engine isn't running. When the engine is running and the operating conditions are right, a PCM-controlled purge solenoid valve opens the line between the canister and the intake manifold, allowing intake manifold vacuum to pull the vapors from the canister into the manifold, where they're mixed with the incoming air/fuel mixture and consumed in the combustion process.

4 On 1997 and earlier models, the EVAP canister and the canister purge valve are located in the engine compartment.

5 On 1999 and later models, the canister purge valve is also located in the engine compartment, but the EVAP canister is located underneath the vehicle, near the fuel tank.

COMPONENT REPLACEMENT

1997 and earlier models

EVAP canister purge valve

▶ **Refer to illustration 19.6**

6 Disconnect the electrical connector from the canister purge valve (see illustration).

7 Clearly label, then disconnect the vacuum hoses from the purge valve, then remove the purge valve from its mounting bracket.

8 Installation is the reverse of removal.

EVAP canister

9 Clearly label, then disconnect the upper vacuum hoses from the canister. Detach the canister from its mounting bracket, disconnect the lower vacuum hose and remove the canister.

10 Installation is the reverse of removal.

1999 and later models

EVAP canister purge valve

▶ **Refer to illustration 19.11**

11 Disconnect the electrical connector from the canister purge valve (see illustration).

12 Clearly label, then disconnect the vacuum hoses from the purge valve.

13 Remove the purge valve mounting bracket bolt

14 Installation is the reverse of removal

19.2a The EVAP canister is mounted in the engine compartment

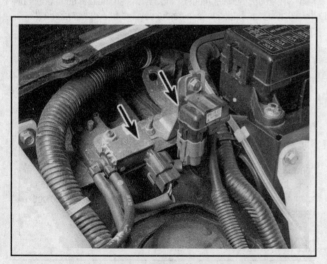

19.2b The purge solenoid valve (left arrow) and EGR boost sensor (right arrow) are mounted on the right inner fender

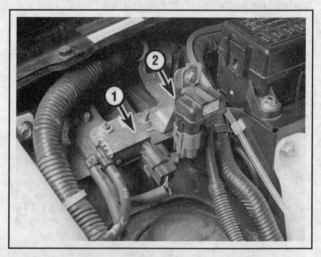

19.6 Typical 1997 and earlier EVAP canister purge valve (1); (2) is the EGR boost sensor

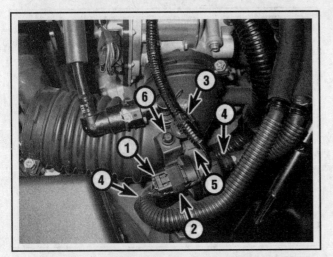

19.11 Typical 1999 and later EVAP canister purge valve details (2006 and later model shown):

1	Electrical connector	4	EVAP lines
2	Tape	5	Purge valve insulator
3	Harness clip	6	Bracket mounting bolt

EVAP canister

▶ Refer to illustration 19.16

15 Raise the vehicle and place it securely on jackstands.

16 Remove the small cross brace below the EVAP canister (see illustration).

17 Clearly label, then disconnect the two EVAP line quick-connect

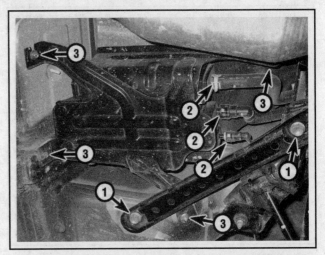

19.16 Typical 1999 and later EVAP canister details (2006 and later model shown):

1	Cross brace bolts	3	EVAP canister mounting bracket fasteners
2	EVAP lines		

fittings, then loosen the hose clamp and disconnect the third EVAP line, from the canister.

18 Remove the EVAP canister mounting bracket fasteners, then remove the canister and mounting bracket as a single assembly.

19 Remove the fasteners that secure the EVAP canister to its mounting bracket and separate the canister from the bracket.

20 Installation is the reverse of removal.

---

20 Exhaust Gas Recirculation (EGR) system - description and component replacement

DESCRIPTION

1 The EGR system reduces oxides of nitrogen (NOx) by recirculating a small amount of exhaust gases from the exhaust manifold back through the intake manifold and the combustion chambers. These spent gases (which don't burn in the combustion process their second time through) lower combustion temperature, which decreases the amount of NOx produced.

COMPONENT REPLACEMENT

2005 and earlier models

▶ Refer to illustration 20.2

➡Note: The EGR valve is located on the right side of the engine, behind the intake manifold.

2 Disconnect the electrical connector from the EGR valve (see illustration).

3 Disconnect the vacuum hose from the EGR valve.

4 Remove the two EGR valve mounting bolts and remove the valve and the old gasket.

5 Installation is the reverse of removal. Be sure to use a new gasket and tighten the bolts securely.

20.2 EGR valve details (2005 and earlier unit shown):

1 Electrical connector
2 Vacuum line
3 Mounting bolts (other bolt not visible)

20.11 EGR valve (2006 and later models) (valve cover removed for clarity):

| 1 | EGR valve | 2 | Electrical connector |

20.12 Unplug the valve position sensor connector (upper arrow), disconnect the vacuum lines and remove the EGR valve mounting bolts (lower arrow; one bolt hidden)

2006 and later models

▶ **Refer to illustrations 20.11 and 20.12**

➡**Note: The EGR valve is located behind the cylinder head. It's extremely difficult to access. The EGR valve mounting bolts are particularly difficult to reach. Unless you have the right combination of tools, these two bolts are extremely difficult to remove and install. Mazda offers a special tool (SST 49 N013 001) for this job. We recommend that you obtain this tool before trying to replace the EGR valve yourself on these models.**

6   Remove the engine cover.

7   Disconnect the cable from the negative battery terminal (see Chapter 5).

8   Drain the engine coolant (see Chapter 1).

9   Remove the strut bar (see Chapter 10), the cowl grille and windshield wiper motor and linkage assembly (see Chapter 12) and the strut reinforcement brace (see illustrations 4.19a and 4.19b in Chapter 2A).

10   Disconnect the heater hose and move the heater pipe out of the way.

11   Disconnect the electrical connector from the EGR valve (see illustration).

12   Using a flashlight and a mirror, locate the EGR mounting bolts, which are located near the lower end of the EGR valve and face toward the firewall. Using the special Mazda tool, or a suitable equivalent tool, remove the EGR valve mounting bolts (see illustration).

13   Tap the EGR valve, if necessary, with a small rubber mallet to knock it loose from the head, then pull the valve up so that you can disconnect the coolant hose from the valve. Remove the EGR valve.

14   Remove and discard the old EGR valve gasket.

15   Make sure that the gasket surfaces of both the head and the EGR valve are clean before installing the new gasket. Tighten the EGR valve bolts securely. Installation is otherwise the reverse of removal.

21 Positive Crankcase Ventilation (PCV) system - description, check and replacement

GENERAL INFORMATION

▶ **Refer to illustration 21.1**

1   The Positive Crankcase Ventilation (PCV) system reduces hydrocarbon emissions by scavenging crankcase vapors. It does this by circulating fresh air from the air cleaner through the crankcase, where it mixes with blow-by gases and is then rerouted through a PCV valve to the intake manifold (see illustration).

2   The main components of the PCV system are the PCV valve, a fresh air intake and the vacuum hoses connecting these components to the engine.

3   To maintain idle quality, the PCV valve restricts the flow when the intake manifold vacuum is high. If abnormal operating conditions (such as piston ring problems) arise, the system is designed to allow excessive amounts of blow-by gases to flow back through the crankcase vent tube into the air cleaner to be consumed by normal combustion.

21.1 The PCV valve is mounted in the valve cover

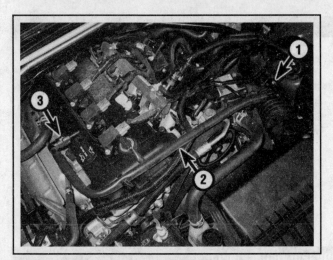

21.12 PCV fresh air inlet hose details (2006 and later models):

1   *Quick-connect fitting at air intake duct*
2   *PCV fresh air inlet hose*
3   *Quick-connect fitting at valve cover*

4   This system directs the blow-by into the throttle body which, over time, can cause an oily residue build up in the area near the throttle plate. Consequently, it is a good idea to periodically clean this residue from the throttle body. Refer to Chapter 4 for this cleaning procedure.

CHECK

➡Note: The following checks apply to PCV valves used on 2005 and earlier models. They do NOT apply to the PCV valve used on 2006 and later models. There is a functional but not an operational check for the PCV valve on 2006 and later models (see Steps 13 through 16).

5   To check the valve, first pull it out of the grommet in the valve cover and shake the valve. It should rattle, indicating that it's not clogged with deposits. If the valve does not rattle, replace it with a new one.

6   Start the engine and allow it to idle, then place your finger over the valve opening. If vacuum is felt, the PCV valve is working properly. If no vacuum is felt, the PCV valve may be bad or the hose may be plugged. Also, check for vacuum leaks at the valve, engine oil filler cap and all the hoses.

REPLACEMENT

2005 and earlier models

7   Pull straight up on the valve to remove it. Check the rubber grommet for cracks and distortion. If it's damaged, replace it.

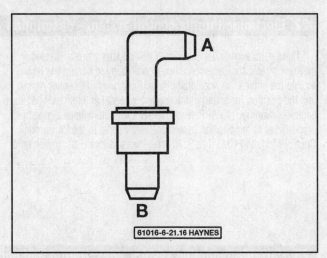

21.16 To test the PCV valve on 2006 and later models:

1   *Apply pressure to port A and verify that there is no airflow through port B*
2   *Apply vacuum to port A and verify that there is airflow through port B*

8   If the valve is clogged, the hose is also probably plugged. Remove the hose and clean it with solvent.

9   After cleaning the hose, inspect it for damage, wear and deterioration. Make sure it fits snugly on the fittings.

10 If necessary, install a new PCV valve.

11 Install the clean PCV hose. Make sure that the PCV valve and hose are secure.

2006 and later models

PCV fresh air inlet hose

▶ **Refer to illustration 21.12**

12 The fresh air inlet hose connects the air intake duct to a pipe on the valve cover (see illustration). Removal of this hose is self evident.

PCV valve and crankcase ventilation hose (PCV hose)

▶ **Refer to illustration 21.16**

13 The crankcase ventilation hose (or PCV hose) connects the PCV valve (which is located on the left side of the block, below the intake manifold) to the intake manifold.

14 Remove the intake manifold (see Chapter 2A).

15 Remove the PCV valve from the crankcase breather plate on the block.

16 To test the PCV valve, apply pressure to port A (see illustration) and verify that there is no airflow out port B. Apply vacuum to port A and verify that there is airflow through port B. If the PCV valve fails either test, replace it.

17 Installation is the reverse of removal.

22 Electronic throttle control system - description

There is no accelerator cable on 2006 and later models. Instead, they use an electronically-controlled throttle body to control the flow of air into the engine. An Accelerator Pedal Position (APP) sensor monitors the position (or angle) of the accelerator pedal at all times when the engine is running. The APP sensor sends a variable voltage signal that's proportional to the position of the accelerator pedal to the Powertrain Control Module (PCM). The PCM processes this input, along with other engine operating conditions, and sends a voltage signal to a solenoid motor inside the throttle body. The solenoid opens and closes the throttle plate in response to this signal. A Throttle Position (TP) sensor inside the throttle body monitors the throttle plate position and sends this information back to the PCM, which uses the TP sensor signal to verify the accuracy of its commands.

23 Variable induction system - description and component replacement

DESCRIPTION

1 2006 and later models use a variable induction system that optimizes power and torque across the range of engine speed operation and improves mileage.

2 Under light load conditions (stop and go driving at lower speeds in town, for example) the intake path is shorter, which improves torque. Under heavier loads (heavy acceleration or high speed driving, for example) the intake path is longer, which improves power.

3 The variable induction system consists of a specially-designed intake manifold, a one-way check valve, vacuum chamber, variable air intake air solenoid valve and shutter valve actuator.

4 The check valve admits intake manifold vacuum into a small vacuum chamber that supplies the vacuum signal to the variable intake air shutter valve actuator. The PCM-controlled variable intake air solenoid valve controls the amount of vacuum metered to the shutter valve actuator. The actuator (a vacuum diaphragm) controls the angle of the variable intake air shutter valve inside the manifold via a link rod that directs incoming air through the shorter or longer intake path in response to a vacuum signal.

COMPONENT REPLACEMENT

Variable intake air solenoid valve

➡Note: The variable intake air solenoid valve is located on top of the intake manifold plenum.

5 Disconnect the cable from the negative terminal of the battery (see Chapter 5).

6 Remove the engine cover.

7 Disconnect the electrical connector from the variable intake air solenoid valve.

8 Disconnect the vacuum line from the variable intake air solenoid valve.

9 Remove the variable intake air solenoid valve mounting bolts and remove the valve.

10 Installation is the reverse of removal.

Shutter valve actuator

➡Note: The intake air shutter valve actuator is located on the backside of the intake manifold plenum. It's impossible to access without removing the intake manifold.

11 Remove the intake manifold (see Chapter 2A).

12 Disconnect the vacuum hose from the shutter valve actuator.

13 Use a screwdriver or a small trim removal tool to disengage the link rod from the shutter valve actuator.

14 Remove the three shutter valve actuator mounting screws and remove the actuator.

15 Installation is the reverse of removal.

24 Variable Valve Timing (VVT) system - description and component replacement

DESCRIPTION

1 2006 and later models use a Variable Valve Timing (VVT) system, which controls intake timing to increase engine torque in the low and mid-speed range and to increase horsepower in the high-speed range.

2 The VVT system consists of the PCM-controlled Oil Control Valve (OCV), which is mounted on top of the cylinder head, and the VVT actuator, which is mounted on the front end of the intake camshaft.

3 The PCM-controlled OCV varies the oil pressure in the VVT actuator, which continually varies the timing of the intake cam in relation to the fixed timing of the exhaust cam.

COMPONENT REPLACEMENT

Oil control valve (OCV)

▶ **Refer to illustration 24.5**

4   Remove the valve cover (see Chapter 2A).

5   Unbolt the OCV (see illustration).

6   Installation is the reverse of removal. Be sure to tighten the OCV mounting bolt securely.

VVT actuator

7   Remove the valve cover (see Chapter 2A).

8   Rotate the crankshaft and note whether there is a hitting noise coming from the VVT actuator each time that the intake camshaft passes through the fully lifted position. If there is, the actuator is not secured to the camshaft. Replace the actuator. Refer to Chapter 2A.

24.5 VVT Oil Control Valve (OCV) (1), OCV mounting bolt (2) and VVT actuator (3)

Torque specifications	Ft-lbs
Knock sensor	
1999 through 2005 models	15 to 25
2006 and later	12 to 17

Notes

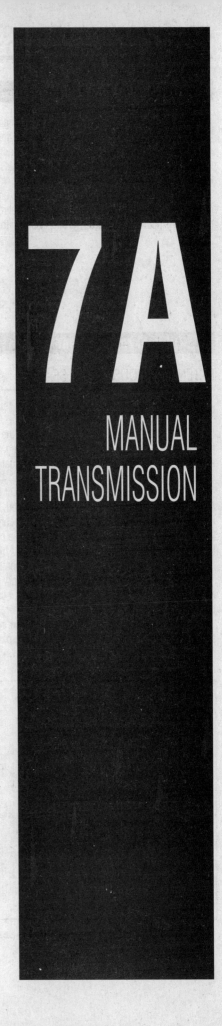

7A

MANUAL TRANSMISSION

Section

1   General information

The vehicles covered in this manual are equipped with either a five- or six-speed manual transmission or an automatic transmission. All information on the manual transmission is included in this Part of Chapter 7. Information on the automatic transmission can be found in Part B of this Chapter.

Because of the complexity of the transmission, unavailability of replacement parts and the special tools necessary, internal repair by the home mechanic is not recommended. The information in this Chapter is limited to general information and removal and installation of the transmission.

Depending on the expense involved in having a faulty transmission overhauled, it may be a good idea to replace the unit with either a new or rebuilt one. Your local dealer or transmission shop should be able to supply you with information concerning cost, availability and exchange policy. Regardless of how you decide to remedy a transmission problem, you can still save a lot of money by removing and installing the unit yourself.

2   Oil seal replacement

EXTENSION HOUSING OIL SEAL

♦ **Refer to illustrations 2.4 and 2.6**

1   Oil leaks frequently occur due to wear of the extension housing oil seal and/or the speedometer drive gear O-ring. Replacement of these seals is relatively easy, since the repairs can usually be performed without removing the transmission from the vehicle.

2   The extension housing oil seal is located at the extreme rear of the transmission, where the driveshaft is attached. If leakage at the seal is suspected, raise the vehicle and support it securely on jackstands. If the seal is leaking, transmission lubricant will be built up on the front of the driveshaft and may be dripping from the rear of the transmission.

3   Refer to Chapter 8 and remove the driveshaft.

4   Using a screwdriver or pry bar, carefully pry the oil seal out of the rear of the transmission (see illustration). Do not damage the splines on the transmission output shaft.

5   If the oil seal cannot be removed with a screwdriver or pry bar, a special oil seal removal tool (available at auto parts stores) will be required.

6   Using a large section of pipe or a very large deep socket as a drift, install the new oil seal (see illustration). Drive it into the bore squarely and make sure it's completely seated.

7   Lubricate the splines of the transmission output shaft and the outside of the driveshaft sleeve yoke with lightweight grease, then install the driveshaft. Be careful not to damage the lip of the new seal.

SPEEDOMETER CABLE DRIVEN GEAR HOUSING O-RING (1997 AND EARLIER MODELS)

♦ **Refer to illustrations 2.9 and 2.11**

8   The speedometer cable driven gear housing is located on the side of the extension housing. Look for transmission oil around the cable housing to determine if the O-ring is leaking.

9   Disconnect the speedometer cable (see illustration).

10 Remove the driven gear housing (see illustration 2.9).

11 Install a new O-ring in the driven gear housing and reinstall the driven gear housing and cable on the extension housing (see illustration).

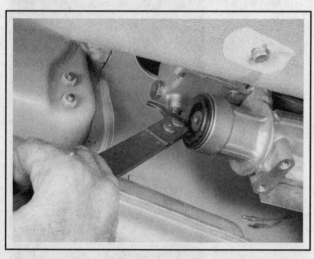

2.4 With the driveshaft removed, pry the seal from the rear end of the transmission

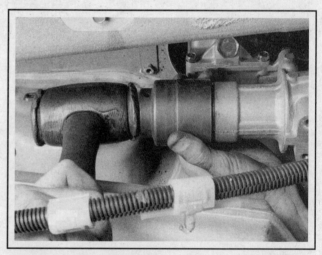

2.6 Tap a new seal in with a socket the same size as the seal

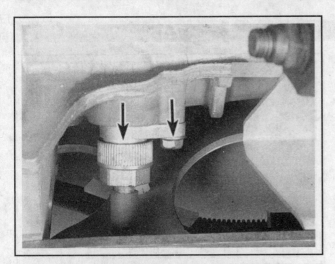

2.9 Unscrew the speedometer cable retaining nut (left arrow); use a wrench on the hex if it's tight. Undo the bolt (right arrow) to remove the driven gear

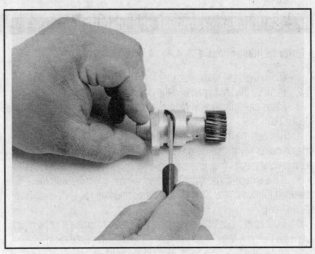

2.11 Pry the old O-ring off the driven gear and install a new one

---

3   Speedometer cable replacement (1997 and earlier models)

▶ **Refer to illustration 3.2**

1   Disconnect the negative cable at the battery (see Chapter 5).

2   Inside the passenger compartment, remove the instrument cluster and pull it back for access (see Chapter 12). Reach behind the cluster, disconnect the speedometer cable by pressing the retaining lever and detaching it from the cluster (see illustration).

3   Push the cable through the firewall into the engine compartment.

4   Raise the vehicle and support it securely on jackstands.

5   Under the vehicle, unscrew the speedometer cable collar and pull the cable from the driven gear housing (see illustration 2.9).

6   Detach the cable from the retaining straps and remove it from the vehicle.

7   To install, push the cable through the firewall into the passenger compartment and seat the firewall grommet securely. Insert the cable into the cluster housing until it clicks in place. Install the cluster.

8   Insert the cable end into the driven gear in the transmission, install the retaining collar and tighten it securely. Secure the cable with the retaining straps.

3.2 Squeeze the retainer tab on the cable (arrow) to free it from the speedometer (instrument cluster removed for clarity)

4 Shift lever - removal and installation

♦ Refer to illustrations 4.3, 4.4a, 4.4b and 4.5

1 Disconnect the negative cable at the battery (see Chapter 5).
2 Remove the shift knob and the console (see Chapter 11).
3 Place the shift lever in Neutral and unbolt the shift lever plate (see illustration).
4 Remove the three retaining bolts and lift the shift lever straight up and out of the transmission (see illustration). Remove the shift lever bushing and gasket (see illustration).
5 If the extension housing has been removed, refill it with the specified lubricant (see Chapter 1) before installing the shift lever (see illustration).
6 Coat both sides of a new gasket with sealant, place it in position, lubricate the shift lever base and lower it into the transmission.
7 Install the retaining bolts. Tighten the bolts securely.
8 Install the shift boot, console and knob.

4.3 Remove four bolts and lift the shift lever boot . . .

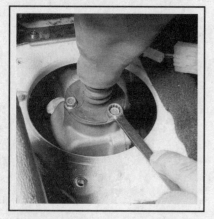

4.4a . . . then remove three bolts to free the lever . . .

4.4b . . . and remove the bushing and gasket (1997 and earlier models shown, later models similar)

4.5 If the extension housing was removed, pour oil into it through the shift lever opening

5 Power plant frame - removal and installation

2005 AND EARLIER MODELS

♦ Refer to illustrations 5.3a, 5.3b, 5.4, 5.5, 5.6a, 5.6b, 5.7 and 5.8

1 The power plant frame is a brace that connects the transmission to the differential.
2 Raise the vehicle and support it securely on jackstands.
3 Detach the wiring harness and ground wire from the power plant frame (see illustrations).
4 Support the transmission with a jack (see illustration).
5 Remove the bracket that connects the power plant frame to the transmission (see illustration).
6 Remove the bolts at the rear end of the power plant frame, then pry out the spacer (see illustrations). Note that the two bolts are different; the reamer bolt goes in the forward hole.

⁂ CAUTION:

Don't remove the spacers from the upper side of the power plant frame. This will degrade the performance of the power plant frame and the entire assembly will have to be replaced.

7 Remove the differential mounting spacer (see illustration). To remove the sleeve that the reamer bolt passes through, thread an M14 x 1.5 bolt into the bottom of the sleeve, then use it as a handle, twisting and pulling to free the sleeve. Once the sleeve is free, you'll need to get the M14 x 1.5 bolt out of the sleeve. To do this, thread an M6 x 1 bolt through the hole in the side of the block and tighten it against the side of the sleeve. Unscrew the M14 x 1.5 bolt, then unscrew the M6 x 1 bolt and remove the sleeve.
8 Unbolt the front end of the power plant frame from the transmission, then remove it from the vehicle (see illustration).

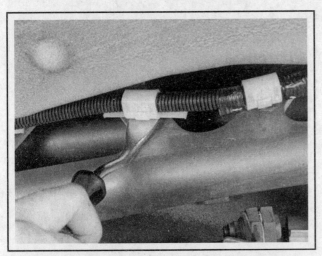

5.3a Free the wiring harness retainers from the power plant frame . . .

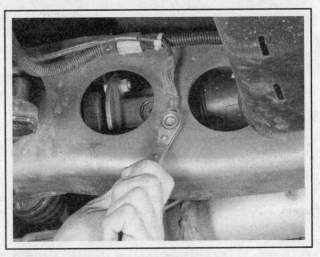

5.3b . . . and unbolt the ground wire

5.4 Support the transmission with a jack; a transmission jack like this one, which can be rented, is adjustable for angle as well as height (1997 and earlier models shown, 1999 through 2005 models similar)

5.5 Unbolt the bracket that connects the transmission to the power plant frame (1997 and earlier models shown, 1999 through 2005 models similar)

5.6a Remove the bolts from the rear of the power plant frame . . .

5.6b . . . and pry out the spacer from the forward lower bolt hole - DO NOT remove the spacers from the upper bolt holes (1997 and earlier models shown, 1999 through 2005 models similar)

5.7 Remove the differential mounting spacer (1997 and earlier models shown, 1999 through 2005 models similar)

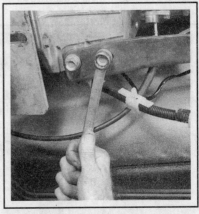

5.8 Unbolt the front end of the power plant frame (1997 and earlier models shown, 1999 through 2005 models similar)

9 Installation is the reverse of the removal procedure, with the following additions:

a) *Install the reamer bolt in the forward hole at the rear of the power plant frame.*

b) *Tighten the bolts at the rear end of the power plant frame, then the bolts at the front end. Be sure to tighten the nuts/bolts securely.*

2006 AND LATER MODELS

▶ **Refer to illustration 5.11**

10 Raise the vehicle and place it securely on jackstands.

11 Remove the four tunnel member mounting bolts (see illustration) and remove the tunnel member.

12 Before removing the power plant frame, support the transmission securely.

13 Remove the eight power plant frame nuts - four at the transmission and four at the differential - and unbolt the power plant frame.

✳✳ CAUTION:

Failure to support the transmission before removing the power plant frame could damage cables and/or electrical wiring connected to the transmission.

5.11 Tunnel member (1) and power plant frame (2) mounting bolts

14 Installation is the reverse of removal. Be sure to tighten all fasteners securely.

6 Manual transmission - removal and installation

REMOVAL

▶ **Refer to illustrations 6.5, 6.6 and 6.10**

1 Disconnect the negative cable from the battery (see Chapter 5).

2 Working inside the vehicle, remove the shift lever (see Section 4).

3 Raise the vehicle and support it securely on jackstands.

4 Remove the splash shield from under the front of the vehicle.

5 Remove the exhaust system components as necessary for clearance (see Chapter 4). On later models, remove the performance rod from under the front of the vehicle (see illustration).

6 Disconnect the speedometer cable and wire harness connectors from the transmission (see illustration). Remove the starter (see Chapter 5) and the clutch release cylinder (see Chapter 8).

7 Remove the driveshaft (see Chapter 8). Use a plastic bag to cover the end of the transmission to prevent fluid loss and contamination.

8 Support the transmission with a jack - preferably a special jack made for this purpose. Safety chains will help steady the transmission on the jack.

9 Remove the power plant frame (see Section 5).

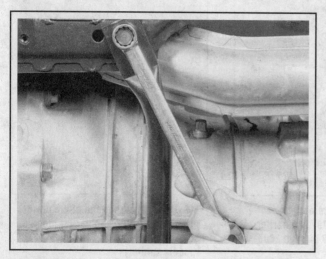

6.5 If the vehicle is equipped with a crossbar or performance rod, removal it

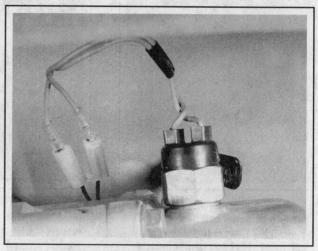

6.6 Follow the wires from the neutral and back-up light switches to the connectors and disconnect them

10 Remove the bolts securing the transmission to the engine (see illustration).

11 Make a final check that all wires and hoses have been disconnected from the transmission, then move the transmission and jack toward the rear of the vehicle until the transmission input shaft is clear of the clutch hub. Keep the transmission level as this is done.

✳✳ CAUTION:

Don't shake the transmission up and down or from side to side in an effort to make it slide out. This may damage the camshaft position sensor on the engine.

12 Once the input shaft is clear, lower the transmission and remove it from under the vehicle.

✳✳ CAUTION:

Don't depress the clutch pedal while the transmission is out of the vehicle.

13 The clutch components can be inspected at this time (see Chapter 8). In most cases, new clutch components should be routinely installed if the transmission is removed.

INSTALLATION

14 If removed, install the clutch components (see Chapter 8).

15 With the transmission secured to the jack as on removal, raise the transmission into position behind the engine and then carefully slide it forward, engaging the input shaft with the clutch plate hub. Do not use excessive force to install the transmission - if the input shaft does not slide into place, readjust the angle of the transmission so it's level and/or turn the input shaft so the splines engage properly with the clutch.

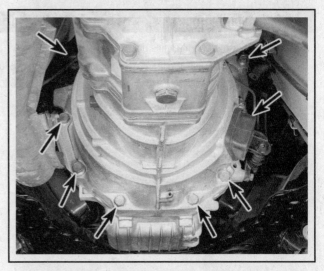

6.10 Remove the transmission-to-engine bolts

16 Install the transmission-to-engine bolts. Tighten the bolts to the torque listed in this Chapter's Specifications.

17 Install the power plant frame. Tighten the bolts securely.

18 Remove the jack supporting the transmission.

19 Install the various items removed previously, referring to Chapter 8 for the installation of the driveshaft and Chapter 4 for information regarding the exhaust system components.

20 Make a final check that all wires, hoses and the speedometer cable have been connected and the transmission has been filled with lubricant to the proper level (see Chapter 1). Lower the vehicle.

21 Working inside the vehicle, install the shift lever (see Section 4).

22 Connect the negative battery cable. Road test the vehicle for proper operation and check for leakage.

7 Manual transmission overhaul - general information

Overhauling a manual transmission is a difficult job for the do-it-yourselfer. It involves the disassembly and reassembly of many small parts. Numerous clearances must be precisely measured and, if necessary, changed with select fit spacers and snap-rings. As a result, if transmission problems arise, it can be removed and installed by a competent do-it-yourselfer, but overhaul should be left to a transmission repair shop. Rebuilt transmissions may be available - check with your dealer parts department and auto parts stores. At any rate, the time and money involved in an overhaul is almost sure to exceed the cost of a rebuilt unit.

Nevertheless, it's not impossible for an inexperienced mechanic to rebuild a transmission if the special tools are available and the job is done in a deliberate step-by-step manner so nothing is overlooked.

The tools necessary for an overhaul include internal and external snap-ring pliers, a bearing puller, a slide hammer, a set of pin punches, a dial indicator and possibly a hydraulic press. In addition, a large, sturdy workbench and a vise or transmission stand will be required.

During disassembly of the transmission, make careful notes of how each piece comes off, where it fits in relation to other pieces and what holds it in place. Be sure to note how the parts are installed as you remove them - this will make it much easier to get the transmission back together.

Before taking the transmission apart for repair, it will help if you have some idea what area of the transmission is malfunctioning. Certain problems can be closely tied to specific areas in the transmission, which can make component examination and replacement easier. Refer to the Troubleshooting Section at the front of this manual for information regarding possible sources of trouble.

Torque specifications	Ft-lbs
Transmission-to-engine bolts	
2005 and earlier	48 to 65
2006 and later	28 to 38

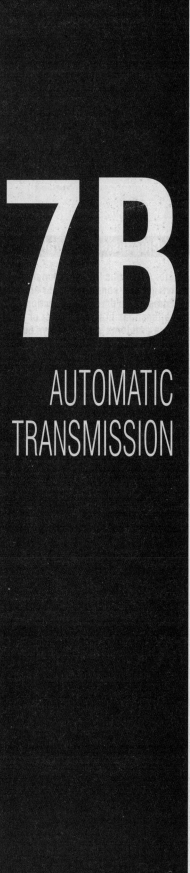

7B

AUTOMATIC TRANSMISSION

Section

Reference to other Chapters

1 General information

All vehicles covered in this manual come equipped with either a five- or six-speed manual transmission or an automatic transmission. All information on the automatic transmission is included in this Part of Chapter 7. Information on the manual transmission can be found in Part A of this Chapter.

Due to the complexity of the automatic transmission and the need for specialized equipment to perform most service operations, this Chapter contains only general diagnosis, routine maintenance, adjustment and removal and installation procedures.

If the transmission requires major repair work, it should be left to a dealer service department or an automotive or transmission repair shop. You can, however, remove and install the transmission yourself and save the expense, even if the repair work is done by a transmission shop.

2 Diagnosis - general

➡ **Note: Automatic transmission malfunctions may be caused by five general conditions: poor engine performance, improper adjustments, hydraulic malfunctions, mechanical malfunctions or malfunctions in the computer or its signal network. Diagnosis of these problems should always begin with a check of the easily repaired items: fluid level and condition (see Chapter 1), shift linkage adjustment and throttle linkage adjustment. Next, perform a road test to determine if the problem has been corrected or if more diagnosis is necessary. If the problem persists after the preliminary tests and corrections are completed, additional diagnosis should be done by a dealer service department or transmission repair shop. Refer to the "Troubleshooting" Section at the front of this manual for information on symptoms of transmission problems.**

PRELIMINARY CHECKS

1 Drive the vehicle to warm the transmission to normal operating temperature.

2 Check the fluid level as described in Chapter 1:

a) If the fluid level is unusually low, add enough fluid to bring the level within the designated area of the dipstick, then check for external leaks (see below).

b) If the fluid level is abnormally high, drain off the excess, then check the drained fluid for contamination by coolant. The presence of engine coolant in the automatic transmission fluid indicates that a failure has occurred in the internal radiator walls that separate the coolant from the transmission fluid (see Chapter 3).

c) If the fluid is foaming, drain it and refill the transmission, then check for coolant in the fluid or a high fluid level.

3 Check the engine idle speed.

➡ **Note: If the engine is malfunctioning, do not proceed with the preliminary checks until it has been repaired and runs normally.**

4 Inspect the shift linkage (see Section 3). Make sure that it's properly adjusted and that the linkage operates smoothly.

FLUID LEAK DIAGNOSIS

5 Most fluid leaks are easy to locate visually. Repair usually consists of replacing a seal or gasket. If a leak is difficult to find, the following procedure may help.

6 Identify the fluid. Make sure it's transmission fluid and not engine oil or brake fluid (automatic transmission fluid is a deep red color).

7 Try to pinpoint the source of the leak. Drive the vehicle several miles, then park it over a large sheet of cardboard. After a minute or two, you should be able to locate the leak by determining the source of the fluid dripping onto the cardboard.

8 Make a careful visual inspection of the suspected component and the area immediately around it. Pay particular attention to gasket mating surfaces. A mirror is often helpful for finding leaks in areas that are hard to see.

9 If the leak still cannot be found, clean the suspected area thoroughly with a degreaser or solvent, then dry it.

10 Drive the vehicle for several miles at normal operating temperature and varying speeds. After driving the vehicle, visually inspect the suspected component again.

11 Once the leak has been located, the cause must be determined before it can be properly repaired. If a gasket is replaced but the sealing flange is bent, the new gasket will not stop the leak. The bent flange must be straightened.

12 Before attempting to repair a leak, check to make sure that the following conditions are corrected or they may cause another leak.

➡ **Note: Some of the following conditions cannot be fixed without highly specialized tools and expertise. Such problems must be referred to a transmission repair shop or a dealer service department.**

Gasket leaks

13 Check the pan periodically. Make sure the bolts are tight, no bolts are missing, the gasket is in good condition and the pan is flat (dents in the pan may indicate damage to the valve body inside).

14 If the pan gasket is leaking, the fluid level or the fluid pressure may be too high, the vent may be plugged, the pan bolts may be too tight, the pan sealing flange may be warped, the sealing surface of the transmission housing may be damaged, the gasket may be damaged or the transmission casting may be cracked or porous. If sealant instead of gasket material has been used to form a seal between the pan and the transmission housing, it may be the wrong sealant.

Seal leaks

15 If a transmission seal is leaking, the fluid level or pressure may be too high, the vent may be plugged, the seal bore may be damaged, the seal itself may be damaged or improperly installed, the surface of the shaft protruding through the seal may be damaged or a loose bearing may be causing excessive shaft movement.

16 Make sure the dipstick tube seal is in good condition and the tube is properly seated. Periodically check the area around the speedometer gear for leakage. If transmission fluid is evident, check the O-ring for damage (see Chapter 7A).

Case leaks

17 If the case itself appears to be leaking, the casting is porous and will have to be repaired or replaced.

18 Make sure the oil cooler hose fittings are tight and in good condition.

Fluid comes out the vent pipe or fill tube

19 If this condition occurs, the transmission is overfilled, there is coolant in the fluid, the case is porous, the dipstick is incorrect, the vent is plugged or the drain back holes are plugged.

---

3   Shift linkage - check and adjustment

CHECK

1   Check the operation of the transmission in each shift lever position (try to start the engine in each gear - the starter should operate in Park and Neutral only). If the engine does not start or starts in any gear other than Park or Neutral, the shift linkage is in need of adjustment or the inhibitor switch/Transmission Range (TR) switch (see Chapter 6) is defective or in need of adjustment.

ADJUSTMENT

⬧ **Refer to illustrations 3.4, 3.6 and 3.11**

2   Disconnect the cable from the negative terminal of the battery (see Chapter 5).

3   On 2005 and earlier models, remove the console upper panel, shift knob, shift lever sleeve and indicator panel.

4   On 2005 and earlier models, loosen the adjustment lever locknut (see illustration).

5   Push the shift lever forward, into Park. Apply the parking brake. Raise the front of the vehicle and support it securely on jackstands. Block the rear wheels.

6   On 2006 and later models, loosen the nut that secures the manual shaft lever to the selector lever (see illustration).

7   Move the shift lever on the transmission all the way to its rear detent (the Park position).

8   With the shift lever inside the vehicle and the shift lever on the transmission in their Park positions, tighten the adjustment locknut securely (see illustration 3.4 or 3.6).

9   Install the indicator panel, shift sleeve and knob.

10 Check the operation of the shift lever to make sure there is a click when shifting from the Park to Low detents, the shifter button returns smoothly and the shift lever lines up with the indicator in each position.

11 If the shift lever is not properly aligned with the indicator on 2005 and earlier models, loosen the four indicator retaining screws and insert a bent piece of heavy gauge wire into the alignment holes (see illustration).

➡**Note: Any further adjustment on 2006 and later models is beyond the scope of the home mechanic.**

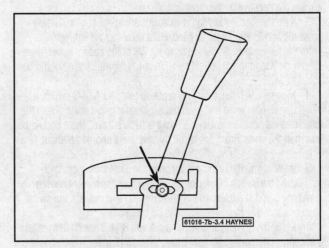

3.4 Loosen the adjustment lever locknut (2005 and earlier models)

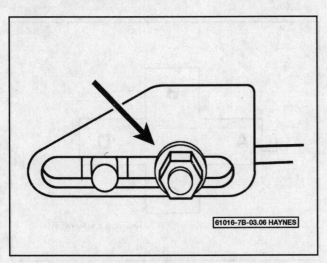

3.6 Manual shaft lever-to-manual selector lever nut (2006 and later models)

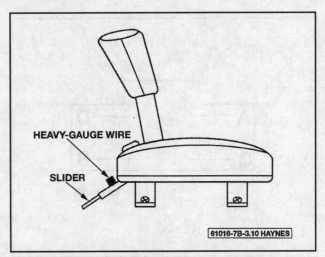

3.11 Range indicator adjustment details (2005 and earlier models)

12 Tighten the indicator mounting screws, starting with the forward left screw and moving in a counterclockwise pattern until all four screws are tight. Install the console upper panel.

13 After adjustment check the operation of the transmission in each shift lever position (try to start the engine in each gear - the starter should operate in Park and Neutral only). Adjust the inhibitor switch/Transmission Range (TR) switch if necessary (see Chapter 6).

4 Kickdown/4-3 switch, solenoid and relay (1993 and earlier) - check and replacement

SWITCH CHECK

▶ **Refer to illustration 4.2**

1　Locate the switch at the top of the accelerator pedal.

2　Without unplugging the connector, insert a voltmeter's positive probe into terminal C (kickdown switch terminal; yellow/green wire) and ground the negative probe (see illustration).

3　Turn the ignition key to On without starting the engine. Slowly press the accelerator pedal by hand while watching the voltmeter. From the fully released position to about 7/8 of the pedal's travel, there should be less than 1.5 volts. From 7/8 to full throttle, there should be about 12 volts.

4　Move the voltmeter positive probe to terminal A (4-3 switch terminal; green-blue wire) and push the accelerator pedal again. From the fully released position to about 5/8 of the pedal's travel, there should be less than 1.5 volts. From 3/4 to full throttle, there should be about 12 volts.

5　If either voltage reading is incorrect, test the switch continuity. Unplug the switch connector and connect an ohmmeter between terminals C and D (kickdown switch terminals) and depress the switch plunger about 1/4 inch. There should be continuity.

6　Move the ohmmeter to terminals A and B (4-3 switch terminals) and depress the switch plunger about 1/8 to 3/16 inch. There should be continuity.

7　If there isn't continuity in Step 5 or 6, replace the switch. If the continuity readings are correct, adjust the switch.

SWITCH ADJUSTMENT

8　Unplug the switch connector (if not already done). Loosen the switch locknuts and unscrew it as far as you can without removing it.

9　Hold the accelerator pedal to the floor. Turn the switch clockwise until you hear it click, indicating the switch is on, then turn it another 1/4-turn clockwise. Release the accelerator pedal.

10 Reconnect the switch electrical connector.

11 Hold the switch so its position won't change and tighten the locknuts.

KICKDOWN RELAY CHECK

▶ **Refer to illustration 4.14**

12 Jack up the vehicle and place it securely on jackstands.

13 Locate the relay; it's the center of the three relays on the left side of the transmission. Unplug the relay.

14 Connect an ohmmeter between relay terminals A and D (see illustration). There should be no continuity.

15 With the ohmmeter still connected, connect a 12-volt battery between terminals B and C. There should now be continuity.

16 If the relay doesn't test correctly, replace it.

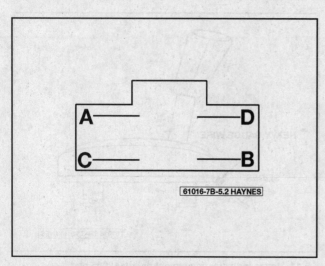

4.2 Kickdown/4-3 switch terminals

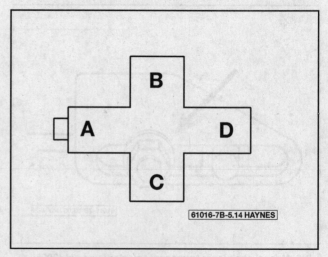

4.14 Kickdown relay terminals

KICKDOWN SOLENOID CHECK

17 Drain about 1-1/8 quarts of fluid from the transmission, then tighten the transmission pan bolts (see Chapter 1).

18 Locate the kickdown solenoid; it's the cylindrical solenoid on the left side of the transmission just forward of the rear extension housing.

Once you've found it, unplug its electrical connector and unscrew it from the transmission.

19 Connect a 12-volt battery between the solenoid terminal and solenoid body. The solenoid plunger should extend each time the battery is connected.

20 If the solenoid doesn't perform correctly, replace it.

21 Refer to Chapter 1 and top up the transmission fluid.

5 Automatic transmission - removal and installation

REMOVAL

1 Disconnect the negative cable from the battery (see Chapter 5).

2 Raise the vehicle and support it securely on jackstands. Remove the splash shield from under the front of the vehicle.

3 Drain the transmission fluid (see Chapter 1), then reinstall the pan.

4 Remove any exhaust components which will interfere with transmission removal (see Chapter 4). On later models, remove the performance rod from under the transmission and the cross rod from under the differential.

5 Remove the torque converter cover.

6 Mark the torque converter and driveplate with white paint so they can be installed in the same position.

7 Remove the torque converter-to-driveplate bolts. Turn the crankshaft for access to each bolt. Turn the crankshaft in a clockwise direction only (as viewed from the front).

8 Remove the starter motor (see Chapter 5).

9 Remove the driveshaft (see Chapter 8).

10 Disconnect the speedometer cable.

11 Detach the wire harness connectors from the transmission.

12 Disconnect the vacuum hoses and oil cooler lines.

13 Disconnect the shift linkage.

14 Support the engine with a jack. Use a block of wood under the oil pan to spread the load.

15 Support the transmission with a jack - preferably a jack made for this purpose. Safety chains will help steady the transmission on the jack.

16 Remove the power plant frame (see Chapter 7A).

17 Remove the bolts securing the transmission to the engine.

18 Lower the transmission slightly and disconnect and plug the transmission fluid cooler lines.

19 Remove the transmission dipstick tube.

20 Move the transmission to the rear to disengage it from the engine block dowel pins and make sure the torque converter is detached from the driveplate. Secure the torque converter to the transmission so it won't fall out during removal. Lower the transmission slowly from the vehicle.

INSTALLATION

21 Prior to installation, make sure the torque converter hub is securely engaged in the pump. The torque converter bolt flange should be at least 7/8-inch in from the transmission-to-engine mating surface on the bellhousing. An accurate measurement can be made by laying a long straightedge across the bellhousing mating surface and measuring with a ruler from the straightedge to a converter mounting bolt hole. If the converter is not in far enough, rotate the converter while pressing in until the converter hub clunks deeper into the pump.

22 With the transmission secured to the jack, raise it into position. Be sure to keep it level so the torque converter does not slide forward. Connect the transmission fluid cooler lines.

23 Turn the torque converter to line up the bolt holes with the holes in the driveplate. The white paint mark on the torque converter and the driveplate made in Step 6 must line up.

24 Move the transmission forward carefully until the dowel pins and the torque converter are engaged.

25 Install the transmission housing-to-engine bolts. Tighten them securely.

26 Install the torque converter-to-driveplate bolts. Tighten the bolts to the torque listed in this Chapter's Specifications.

27 Install the power plant frame. Tighten the bolts and nuts securely.

28 Remove the jacks supporting the transmission and the engine.

29 Install the dipstick tube, using a new O-ring.

30 Install the starter motor (see Chapter 5).

31 Connect the vacuum hose(s).

32 Connect the shift linkage.

33 Plug in the transmission wire harness connectors.

34 Install the torque converter cover.

35 Install the driveshaft.

36 Connect the speedometer cable.

37 Adjust the shift linkage.

38 Install any exhaust system components that were removed or disconnected. On later models, install the performance rod and the cross rod under the differential.

39 Install the splash shield and lower the vehicle.

40 Fill the transmission with the specified fluid (see Chapter 1), run the engine and check for fluid leaks.

Torque specifications	Ft-lbs
Transmission-to-engine bolts	
2005 and earlier	48 to 65
2006 and later	28 to 38
Torque converter-to-driveplate bolts	
1993 and earlier	27 to 39
1994 and later	26 to 36
Fluid pan bolts	See Chapter 1

8

CLUTCH AND DRIVELINE

Section

Reference to other Chapters

1 General information

The information in this Chapter deals with the components from the rear of the engine to the rear wheels, except for the transmission, which is dealt with in Chapters 7A and 7B. For the purposes of this Chapter, these components are grouped into three categories: clutch, driveshaft and driveaxles. Separate Sections within this Chapter offer general descriptions and checking procedures for both groups.

Since nearly all the procedures covered in this Chapter involve working under the vehicle, make sure it's securely supported on sturdy jackstands or a hoist where the vehicle can be easily raised and lowered.

2 Clutch - description and check

1   All vehicles with a manual transmission use a single dry plate, diaphragm spring type clutch. The clutch disc has a splined hub which allows it to slide along the splines of the transmission input shaft. The clutch and pressure plate are held in contact by spring pressure exerted by the diaphragm in the pressure plate.

2   The clutch release system is operated by hydraulic pressure. The hydraulic release system consists of the clutch pedal, a master cylinder, a fluid reservoir, the hydraulic line, a slave cylinder which actuates the clutch release lever and the clutch release (or throw-out) bearing.

3   When pressure is applied to the clutch pedal to release the clutch, hydraulic pressure is exerted against the outer end of the clutch release lever. As the lever pivots, the shaft fingers push against the release bearing. The bearing pushes against the fingers of the diaphragm spring of the pressure plate assembly, which in turn releases the clutch plate.

4   Terminology can be a problem regarding the clutch components because common names have in some cases changed from that used by the manufacturer. For example, the driven plate is also called the clutch plate or disc, the pressure plate assembly is sometimes referred to as the clutch cover, the clutch release bearing is sometimes called a throw-out bearing, and the release cylinder is sometimes called the operating or slave cylinder.

5   Other than replacing components that have obvious damage, some preliminary checks should be performed to diagnose a clutch system failure.

a) *The first check should be of the fluid level in the clutch/brake reservoir (see Chapter 1). If the fluid level is low, add fluid as necessary and inspect the hydraulic clutch system for leaks. If the reservoir has run dry, bleed the system (see Section 8) and retest the clutch operation.*

b) *To check clutch spin down time, run the engine at normal idle speed with the transmission in Neutral (clutch pedal up - engaged). Disengage the clutch (pedal down), wait several seconds and shift the transmission into Reverse. No grinding noise should be heard. A grinding noise would most likely indicate a problem in the pressure plate or the clutch disc.*

c) *To check for complete clutch release, run the engine (with the parking brake applied to prevent movement) and hold the clutch pedal approximately 1/2-inch from the floor. Shift the transmission between 1st gear and Reverse several times. If the shift is not smooth, component failure is indicated. Check the release cylinder pushrod travel. With the clutch pedal depressed completely the release cylinder pushrod should extend substantially. If it doesn't, check the fluid level in the reservoir.*

d) *Visually inspect the clutch pedal bushing at the top of the clutch pedal to make sure there is no sticking or excessive wear.*

e) *Under the vehicle, check that the clutch release lever is solidly mounted on the ball stud.*

3 Clutch components - removal, inspection and installation

✳✳ WARNING:

Dust produced by clutch wear and deposited on clutch components is hazardous to your health. DO NOT blow it out with compressed air and DO NOT inhale it. DO NOT use gasoline or petroleum based solvents to remove the dust. Brake system cleaner should be used to flush the dust into a drain pan. After the clutch components are wiped clean with a rag, dispose of the contaminated rags and cleaner in a labeled, covered container.

REMOVAL

♦ **Refer to illustrations 3.6 and 3.7**

1   Access to the clutch components is normally accomplished by removing the transmission, leaving the engine in the vehicle. If, of course, the engine is being removed for major overhaul, then the opportunity should always be taken to check the clutch for wear and replace worn components as necessary. However, the relatively low cost of the clutch components compared to the time and labor involved in

3.6 Mark the relationship of the pressure plate to the flywheel (in case you're going to reuse the same pressure plate)

3.7 Loosen the pressure plate bolts evenly, a little at a time to prevent warping the pressure plate

gaining access to them warrants their replacement any time the engine or transmission is removed, unless they are new or in near-perfect condition. The following procedures assume that the engine will stay in place.

2   Remove the release cylinder (see Section 7). Hang it out of the way with a piece of wire - it isn't necessary to disconnect the pipe or hose.

3   Remove the transmission from the vehicle (see Chapter 7, Part A). Support the engine while the transmission is out. Preferably, an engine hoist should be used to support it from above. However, if a jack is used underneath the engine, make sure a piece of wood is used between the jack and oil pan to spread the load.

❋❋ CAUTION:

The pick-up for the oil pump is very close to the bottom of the oil pan. If the pan is bent or distorted in any way, engine oil starvation could occur.

4   The release fork and release bearing can remain attached to the transmission for the time being.

5   To support the clutch disc during removal, install a clutch alignment tool through the clutch disc hub.

6   Carefully inspect the flywheel and pressure plate for indexing marks. The marks are usually an X, an O or a white letter. If they cannot be found, scribe marks yourself so the pressure plate and the flywheel will be in the same alignment during installation (see illustration).

7   Slowly loosen the pressure plate-to-flywheel bolts (see illustration). Work in a diagonal pattern and loosen each bolt a little at a time until all spring pressure is relieved. Then hold the pressure plate securely and completely remove the bolts, followed by the pressure plate and clutch disc.

INSPECTION

♦ **Refer to illustrations 3.11 and 3.13**

8   Ordinarily, when a problem occurs in the clutch, it can be attributed to wear of the clutch driven plate assembly (clutch disc). However,

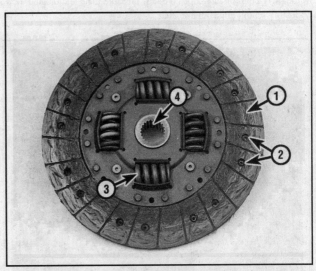

3.11 Examine the clutch disc for evidence of excessive wear, such as smeared friction material, chewed-up rivets, worn hub splines and distorted damper cushions or springs

1   Lining
2   Rivets
3   Damper springs
4   Hub splines

all components should be inspected at this time.

9   Inspect the flywheel for cracks, heat checking, score marks and other damage. If the imperfections are slight, a machine shop can resurface it to make it flat and smooth. Refer to Chapter 2 for the flywheel removal procedure.

10   Inspect the pilot bearing (see Section 5).

11   Inspect the lining on the clutch disc. There should be at least 1/16-inch of lining above the rivet heads. Check for loose rivets, distortion, cracks, broken springs and other obvious damage (see illustration). As mentioned above, ordinarily the clutch disc is replaced as a matter of course, so if in doubt about the condition, replace it with a new one.

12   The release bearing should be replaced along with the clutch disc (see Section 4).

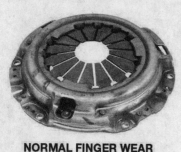

EXCESSIVE WEAR

NORMAL FINGER WEAR   EXCESSIVE FINGER WEAR   BROKEN OR BENT FINGERS

3.13 Replace the pressure plate if any of these conditions are noted

13 Check the machined surface and the diaphragm spring fingers of the pressure plate (see illustration). If the surface is grooved or otherwise damaged, replace the pressure plate assembly. Also check for obvious damage, distortion, cracking, etc. Light glazing can be removed with emery cloth or sandpaper. If a new pressure plate is indicated, new or factory rebuilt units are available.

3.15 Center the clutch disc in the pressure plate with a clutch alignment tool

INSTALLATION

▶ **Refer to illustration 3.15**

14 Before installation, carefully wipe the flywheel and pressure plate machined surfaces clean. It's important that no oil or grease is on these surfaces or the lining of the clutch disc. Handle these parts only with clean hands.

15 Position the clutch disc and pressure plate with the clutch held in place with an alignment tool (see illustration). Make sure it's installed properly (most replacement clutch plates will be marked "flywheel side" or something similar - if not marked, install the clutch disc with the damper springs or cushion toward the transmission).

16 Tighten the pressure plate-to-flywheel bolts only finger tight, working around the pressure plate.

17 Center the clutch disc by ensuring the alignment tool is through the splined hub and into the recess in the crankshaft. Wiggle the tool up, down or side-to-side as needed to bottom the tool. Tighten the pressure plate-to-flywheel bolts a little at a time, working in a criss-cross pattern to prevent distortion of the cover. After all of the bolts are snug, tighten them to the torque listed in this Chapter's Specifications. Remove the alignment tool.

18 Using high-temperature grease, lubricate the inner groove of the release bearing (see Section 4). Also place grease on the release lever contact areas and the transmission input shaft bearing retainer.

19 Install the clutch release bearing (see Section 4).

20 Install the transmission, release cylinder and all components removed previously, tightening all fasteners to the proper torque specifications.

4 Clutch release bearing and lever - removal, inspection and installation

✳✳ WARNING:

Dust produced by clutch wear and deposited on clutch components is hazardous to your health. DO NOT blow it out with compressed air and DO NOT inhale it. DO NOT use gasoline or petroleum-based solvents to remove the dust. Brake system cleaner should be used to flush it into a drain pan. After the clutch components are wiped clean with a rag, dispose of the contaminated rags and cleaner in a labeled, covered container.

REMOVAL

▶ **Refer to illustration 4.3**

1 Disconnect the negative cable from the battery (see Chapter 5).

2 Remove the transmission (see Chapter 7A).

3 Remove the clutch release lever from the ball stud, then remove the bearing from the lever (see illustration).

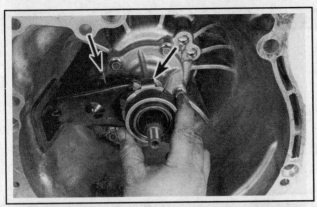

4.3 Reach behind the release lever and disengage the lever from the ball stud by pulling on the retention spring (left arrow), then remove the lever and slide the bearing tangs (right arrow) off the lever

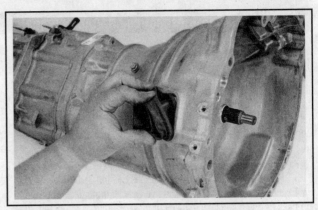

4.5 Replace the release lever boot if it's cracked or deteriorated

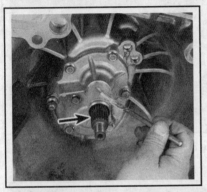

4.6 Apply a light coat of high-temperature grease to the transmission bearing retainer and to the input shaft splines (arrow); also fill the release bearing groove

4.7a Apply high temperature grease to the release lever pivot . . .

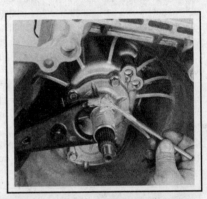

4.7b . . . the fingers that contact the release bearing, and the area that contacts the release cylinder pushrod

INSPECTION

▶ **Refer to illustration 4.5**

4   Hold the bearing by the outer race and rotate the inner race while applying pressure. If the bearing doesn't turn smoothly or if it's noisy, replace the bearing/hub assembly with a new one. Wipe the bearing with a clean rag and inspect it for damage, wear and cracks. Don't immerse the bearing in solvent - it's sealed for life and soaking or dipping in solvent would ruin it. Also check the release lever for cracks and bends.

5   Check the release lever boot for cracks or deterioration (see illustration). If there are problems, pull it out of the hole and install a new one.

INSTALLATION

▶ **Refer to illustrations 4.6, 4.7a, 4.7b and 4.9**

6   Fill the inner groove of the release bearing with high-temperature grease. Also apply a light coat of the same grease to the transmission input shaft splines and the front bearing retainer (see illustration).

7   Lubricate the release lever ball socket and lever ends with high-temperature grease (see illustrations).

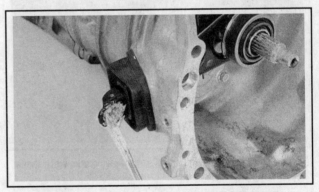

4.9 Apply high temperature grease to the release lever pushrod socket

8   Attach the release bearing to the release lever.

9   Slide the release bearing onto the transmission input shaft front bearing retainer while passing the end of the release lever through the opening in the clutch housing. Push the clutch release lever onto the ball stud until it's firmly seated. Coat the release cylinder pushrod socket in the release lever with high-temperature grease (see illustration).

10 Apply a light coat of high-temperature grease to the face of the release bearing where it contacts the pressure plate diaphragm fingers.

11 The remainder of installation is the reverse of the removal procedure.

5 Pilot bearing - inspection and replacement

▶ **Refer to illustrations 5.1, 5.5 and 5.6**

1   A pilot bearing, pressed into the rear of the crankshaft, supports the front of the transmission input shaft (see illustration). The needle roller bearing is greased at the factory and does not require additional lubrication. The pilot bearing should be inspected whenever the clutch components are removed. Due to its inaccessibility, if you are in doubt as to its condition, replace it with a new one.

2   Remove the transmission (see Chapter 7, Part A).

3   Remove the clutch components (see Section 3).

4   Inspect the bearing for excessive wear, scoring, lack of grease, dryness or obvious damage. If any of these conditions are noted, the bearing should be replaced. A flashlight will be helpful to direct light into the recess.

5   The bearing must be pulled from its hole in the crankshaft, gripping the bearing at the rear. Special tools are available, but you may be able to get by with an alternative tool or fabricated tool. One method that works well is to use a slide-hammer with a small tip that has two adjustable hooks, 180-degrees apart (see illustration). Such tips are commonly available for slide-hammers, and are often included with better-quality slide-hammer kits. A slide-hammer is a tool with many uses, such as pulling dents from body parts and removing seals; you'll use it later for more things than just removing bushings. If a slide-hammer with the correct hooked tip is not available, try to find a hooked tool that will fit into the bearing hole and hook behind the bearing, then clamp a large pair of locking pliers to the tool and strike the pliers, near the jaws, to pull the bearing out.

6   To install the new bearing, lightly lubricate the outside surface with multi-purpose grease, then drive it into the recess with a hammer and a bearing driver or a clutch alignment tool (see illustration). Make sure that the bearing seal faces toward the transmission. Don't allow the pilot bearing to become cocked in the bore. Tap it into place until it's flush with the edge of the bearing bore.

7   Lubricate the pilot bearing with high-temperature grease.

8   Install the clutch components (see Section 3).

9   Install the transmission (see Chapter 7, Part A).

5.1 The pilot bearing is mounted inside the flywheel

5.5 A slide hammer with small puller jaws works well; these can be rented

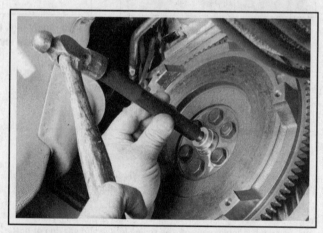

5.6 Drive in the new pilot bearing with a tool the same diameter as the bearing

6 Clutch master cylinder - removal, overhaul and installation

➡ **Note: Before beginning this procedure, contact local parts stores and dealer service departments concerning the purchase of a rebuild kit or a new master cylinder. Availability and cost of the necessary parts may dictate whether the cylinder is rebuilt or replaced with a new one. If you decide to rebuild the cylinder, inspect the bore as described in Step 8 before purchasing parts.**

2005 AND EARLIER MODELS

Removal

▶ **Refer to illustrations 6.2 and 6.3**

1   Open the hood and place rags beneath the clutch master cylinder.

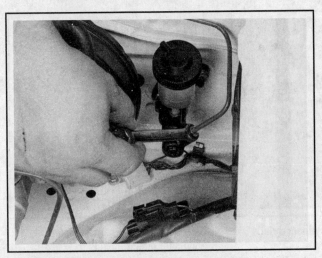

6.2 Loosen the fluid line with a flare nut wrench to prevent
rounding off the nut

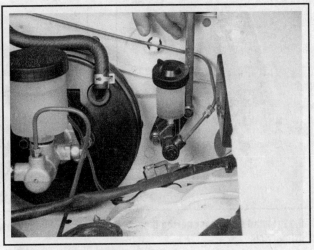

6.3 Remove the mounting nuts and pull the master cylinder
off the firewall

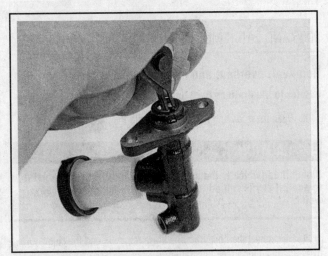

6.5 While holding the piston down, remove the snap-ring
with snap-ring pliers

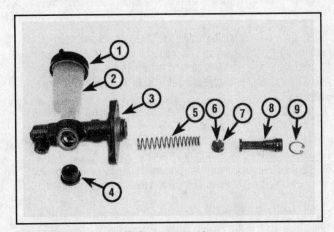

6.6 Clutch master cylinder components

1	Cap	6	Primary cup
2	Reservoir	7	Spacer
3	Master cylinder body	8	Piston and secondary cup
4	Master cylinder grommet		assembly
5	Return spring	9	Snap-ring

❋❋ CAUTION:

**Clutch fluid (which is the same as brake fluid) will cause paint
to peel. If any is spilled, clean it off immediately with soapy
water.**

2   Disconnect the hydraulic line at the clutch master cylinder (see
illustration). If available, use a flare-nut wrench on the fitting, to protect
the fitting from being rounded off.

3   Remove the nuts which attach the master cylinder to the firewall
(see illustration). Pull the master cylinder away from the firewall, again
being careful not to spill fluid from the master cylinder.

Overhaul

◆ **Refer to illustrations 6.5, 6.6 and 6.12**

4   Turn the master cylinder over and allow the trapped fluid to drain
from the fluid line opening into a pan.

5   Place the cylinder in a vise with the piston end up. Push the

piston down with a Phillips screwdriver and remove the snap-ring with
snap-ring pliers (see illustration).

❋❋ CAUTION:

Do not damage the push rod contact surface of the piston.

6   Tap the master cylinder on a block of wood to eject the piston,
spacer, primary cup and spring from inside the bore (see illustration).

➡**Note: If the rebuild kit supplies a complete piston assembly,
ignore the Steps which don't apply.**

7   Carefully remove the seal from the piston.

8   Inspect the bore of the master cylinder for deep scratches, score
marks and ridges. The surface must be smooth to the touch. If the bore
isn't perfectly smooth, the master cylinder must be replaced with a new
or factory rebuilt unit.

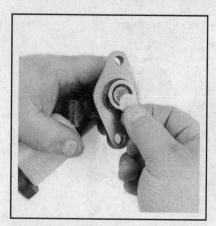

6.12 Install the spacer next to the primary cup

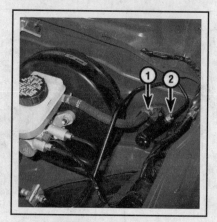

6.20 Clutch master cylinder details

1   Hose clip for brake reservoir fluid supply hose
2   Clutch hydraulic line fitting

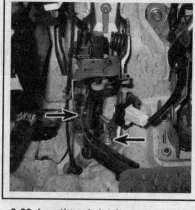

6.22 Location of clutch master cylinder mounting nuts

9   If the cylinder will be rebuilt, use the new parts contained in the rebuild kit and follow any specific instructions which may have accompanied the rebuild kit. Wash all parts to be re-used with brake cleaner, denatured alcohol or clean brake fluid. DO NOT use petroleum-based solvents.

10 Attach a new seal to the piston. The seal lips must face away from the pushrod end of the piston.

11 Lubricate the bore of the cylinder, the spring, primary cup, spacer and piston with plenty of fresh brake fluid.

12 Carefully guide the spring, primary cup, spacer and piston into the cylinder bore (see illustration 6.6 and the accompanying illustration).

13 Again place the cylinder in a vise with the piston end up. Push the piston down with a Phillips screwdriver and install a new snap-ring with snap-ring pliers (see illustration 6.5).

Installation

14 Dab a small amount of grease on the end of the pushrod. Position the master cylinder on the pushrod and against the firewall, installing the mounting nuts finger-tight.

15 Connect the hydraulic line to the master cylinder, moving the cylinder slightly as necessary to thread the fitting properly into the bore. Don't cross-thread the fitting as it's installed.

16 Tighten the mounting nuts and the hydraulic line fitting securely.

17 Fill the clutch/brake fluid reservoir with brake fluid conforming to DOT 3 specifications and bleed the clutch system (see Chapter 1).

18 Check the clutch pedal height and freeplay (see Chapter 1).

2006 AND LATER MODELS

Removal, overhaul and installation

♦ **Refer to illustrations 6.20 and 6.22**

19 Open the hood and place rags beneath the clutch master cylinder.

✸✸ CAUTION:

Clutch fluid (which is the same as brake fluid) will cause paint to peel. If any is spilled, clean it off immediately with soapy water.

20 Disconnect the hose from the brake reservoir and the clutch hydraulic line fitting (see illustration).

21 Inside the vehicle, remove the knee bolster trim panel (the panel below the steering column) and the knee bolster (see Chapter 11).

22 Using a flashlight, locate the two clutch master cylinder mounting nuts (see illustration) and remove them.

23 Remove the clutch master cylinder.

24 If you're rebuilding the master cylinder, refer to Steps 4 through 13.

25 When installing the clutch master cylinder, be sure to tighten the master cylinder mounting nuts to the torque listed in this Chapter's Specifications. Installation is otherwise the reverse of removal (see Steps 14 through 18).

7   Clutch release cylinder - removal, overhaul and installation

➡ **Note: Before beginning this procedure, contact local parts stores and dealer service departments concerning the purchase of a rebuild kit or a new release cylinder. Availability and cost of the necessary parts may dictate whether the cylinder is rebuilt or replaced with a new one. If it's decided to rebuild the cylinder, inspect the bore as described in Step 7 before purchasing parts.**

2005 AND EARLIER MODELS

Removal

♦ **Refer to illustrations 7.2 and 7.3**

1   Raise the vehicle and support it securely on jackstands.

7.2 The release cylinder's fluid line fitting (left arrow) and bleed valve (right arrow) are accessible from under the left side of the vehicle

7.3 After disconnecting the fluid line, unbolt the release cylinder from the transmission

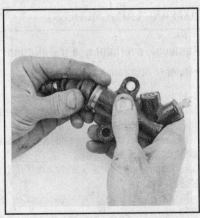

7.4 Remove the pushrod and boot

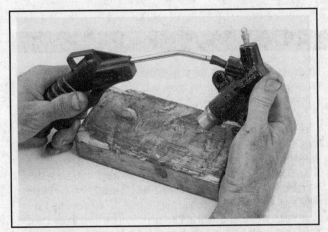

7.5 Blow low-pressure air into the fluid line fitting to remove the piston - DO NOT get your fingers in the way!

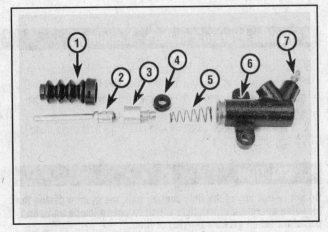

7.6 Clutch release cylinder components

1 Boot	5 Spring
2 Pushrod	6 Cylinder body
3 Piston	7 Bleed valve
4 Cup (wide side faces into cylinder)	

2   Disconnect the hydraulic line at the release cylinder (see illustration). If available, use a flare-nut wrench on the fitting, which will prevent the fitting from being rounded off. Have a small can and rags handy, as some fluid will be spilled as the line is removed. Cap the fluid line.

3   Remove the release cylinder mounting bolts (see illustration). Remove the release cylinder.

Overhaul

▶ **Refer to illustrations 7.4, 7.5 and 7.6**

4   Remove the pushrod and the boot (see illustration).

5   Tap the cylinder on a block of wood to eject the piston and seal. If the piston won't come out easily, blow low-pressure air into the fluid line fitting (see illustration).

❋❋ WARNING:

The piston can shoot out forcefully enough to cause injury. Don't use any more air pressure than necessary. Be sure to point the open end of the cylinder at a block of wood. Keep your fingers out of the way.

6   Remove the spring from inside the cylinder (see illustration).

7   Carefully inspect the bore of the cylinder. Check for deep scratches, score marks and ridges. The bore must be smooth to the touch. If any imperfections are found, the release cylinder must be replaced with a new one.

8   Using the new parts in the rebuild kit, assemble the components using plenty of fresh brake fluid for lubrication. Note the installed direction of the spring and the seal.

Installation

9   Install the release cylinder on the clutch housing. Make sure the pushrod is seated in the release fork pocket.

10   Connect the hydraulic line to the release cylinder. Tighten the connection.

11   Fill the clutch master cylinder with brake fluid (conforming to DOT 3 specifications).

12   Bleed the system (see Section 8).

13   Lower the vehicle.

2006 AND LATER MODELS

Removal, overhaul and installation

♦ **Refer to illustration 7.15**

14 Raise the vehicle and place it securely on jackstands.

15 Locate the clutch release cylinder on the left side of the transmission bellhousing (see illustration).

16 Disconnect the hydraulic line from the transmission bellhousing and from the release cylinder.

17 Remove the release cylinder mounting bolts and remove the release cylinder.

18 If you're rebuilding the release cylinder, refer to Steps 4 through 8.

19 When installing the clutch release cylinder, be sure to tighten the release cylinder mounting bolts to the torque listed in this Chapter's Specifications. Installation is otherwise the reverse of removal (see Steps 9 through 13).

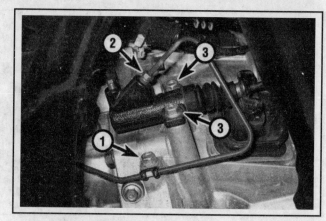

7.15 Clutch release cylinder details

1   Clutch hydraulic line clip
2   Clutch hydraulic line fitting
3   Clutch release cylinder mounting bolts

8   Clutch hydraulic system - bleeding

1 The hydraulic system should be bled of all air whenever any part of the system has been removed or if the fluid level has been allowed to fall so low that air has been drawn into the master cylinder. The procedure is similar to bleeding a brake system.

2 Fill the clutch/brake reservoir with new brake fluid conforming to DOT 3 specifications.

✳✳ CAUTION:

Do not re-use any of the fluid coming from the system during the bleeding operation or use fluid which has been inside an open container for an extended period of time.

3 Locate the bleeder valve on the clutch release cylinder (next to the fitting for the hydraulic fluid line) (see illustration 7.2). Remove the dust cap which fits over the bleeder valve and push a length of plastic

hose over the valve. Place the other end of the hose into a clear container with about two inches of brake fluid in it. The hose end must be submerged in the fluid.

4 Have an assistant depress the clutch pedal and hold it. Open the bleeder valve on the release cylinder, allowing fluid to flow through the hose. Close the bleeder valve when fluid stops flowing from the hose. Once closed, have your assistant release the pedal.

5 Continue this process until all air is evacuated from the system, indicated by a full, solid stream of fluid being ejected from the bleeder valve each time and no air bubbles in the hose or container. Keep a close watch on the fluid level in the reservoir; if the level drops too low, air will be sucked back into the system and the process will have to be started all over again.

6 Install the dust cap and lower the vehicle. Check carefully for proper operation before placing the vehicle in normal service.

9   Clutch switch - check and replacement

CHECK

♦ **Refer to illustrations 9.4a and 9.4b**

1 Check the clutch pedal adjustment (see Chapter 1).

2 Verify that the engine will not start when the clutch pedal is released. Verify that the engine will start when the clutch pedal is depressed all the way.

3 If the clutch switch doesn't perform as described, adjust and if necessary, replace it.

4 Locate the switch on the clutch pedal assembly and unplug the electrical connector (see illustrations).

5 Connect an ohmmeter between the terminals of the switch. Verify that there is continuity between the switch terminals when the switch is On (pedal depressed).

6 Verify that no continuity exists between the switch terminals when the switch is Off (pedal released).

7 If the switch fails either of the tests, replace it.

REPLACEMENT

2005 and earlier models

8 Unplug the electrical connector (see illustration 9.4a). Loosen the locknuts and remove the switch.

9 Installation is the reverse of removal.

10 Adjust the pedal height (see Chapter 1)

11 Verify again that the engine doesn't start when the clutch pedal is released, and does start when the pedal is depressed.

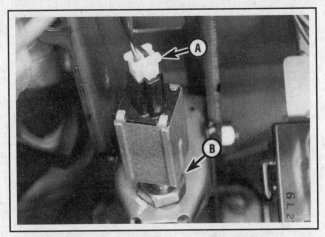

9.4a Clutch switch details (2005 and earlier models)

A   *Connector*
B   *Upper locknut (lower locknut hidden)*

2006 and later models

12 Disconnect the electrical connector from the switch (see illustration 9.4b).

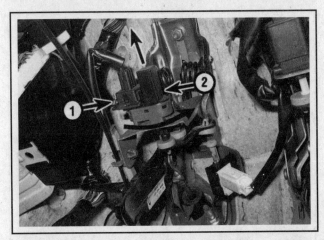

9.4b Clutch switch assembly details (2006 and later models)

1   *Electrical connector*
2   *Switch*

13 To unlock the switch from its mounting bracket, rotate it counter-clockwise, then pull it out.
14 Installation is the reverse of removal.

10 Driveshaft - inspection

1   Raise the rear of the vehicle and support it securely on jackstands.
2   Crawl under the vehicle and visually inspect the driveshaft. Look for any dents or cracks in the tubing. If any are found, the driveshaft must be replaced.
3   Check for any oil leakage at the front and rear of the driveshaft. Leakage where the driveshaft enters the transmission indicates a defective transmission rear seal. Leakage where the driveshaft enters the differential indicates a defective pinion seal.
4   While under the vehicle, have an assistant turn the rear wheel so the driveshaft will rotate. As it does, make sure the universal joints are operating properly without binding, noise or looseness.
5   The universal joints can also be checked with the driveshaft motionless, by gripping your hands on either side of the joint and attempting to twist the joint. Any movement at all in the joint is a sign of considerable wear. Lifting up on the driveshaft will also indicate movement in the universal joints.
6   Finally, check the driveshaft mounting bolts at the ends to make sure they are tight.

11 Driveshaft - removal and installation

▶ **Refer to illustrations 11.4 and 11.5**

1   Raise the rear of the vehicle and support it securely on jackstands.
2   On 2006 and later models, remove the tunnel member (see illustration 5.11 in Chapter 7A).
3   If necessary, remove the middle part of the exhaust system (see Chapter 4).
4   Mark the relationship of the driveshaft to the differential companion flange (see illustration).

11.4 Mark the relationship of the differential and driveshaft to ensure correct installation

11.5 Hold the driveshaft from turning with a rod while you undo the nuts

5 Remove the bolts and separate the driveshaft from the differential companion flange (see illustration). Pull the driveshaft toward the rear to remove it.

6 Wrap a plastic bag tightly around the extension housing of the transmission to prevent fluid loss.

7 Installation is the reverse of removal. Be sure to align the reference marks made during removal.

12 Driveaxles - general information and inspection

1 Power is transmitted from the differential to the wheels through a pair of driveaxles. The inner end of each driveaxle is splined into the differential side gears. The outer ends of the driveaxles are splined to the axle hubs and locked in place by a large locknut.

2 The inner ends of the driveaxles are equipped with sliding constant velocity joints, which are capable of both angular and axial motion. Each inner joint assembly consists of a tripod bearing and a joint housing (outer race) in which the joint is free to slide in and out as the driveaxle moves up and down with the wheel. The joints can be disassembled and cleaned in the event of a boot failure (see Section 14), but if any parts are damaged, the joints must be replaced as a unit.

3 The outer CV joints are the "ball joint" type which have ball bearings running between an inner race and an outer cage, allowing angular but not axial movement. The outer joints should be cleaned, inspected and repacked, but they cannot be disassembled. If an outer joint is damaged, it must be replaced along with the axleshaft (the outer joint and axleshaft are sold as a single component).

4 The boots should be inspected periodically for damage and leaking lubricant. Torn CV joint boots must be replaced immediately or the joints can be damaged. Boot replacement involves removal of the driveaxle (see Section 13).

➡**Note: Some auto parts stores carry "split" type replacement boots, which can be installed without removing the driveaxle from the vehicle. This is a convenient alternative; however, the driveaxle should be removed and the CV joint disassembled and cleaned to ensure the joint is free from contaminants such as moisture and dirt which will accelerate CV joint wear.**

The most common symptom of worn or damaged CV joints, besides lubricant leaks, is a clicking noise in turns, a clunk when accelerating after coasting and vibration at highway speeds. To check for wear in the CV joints and driveaxle shafts, grasp each axle (one at a time) and rotate it in both directions while holding the CV joint housings, feeling for play indicating worn splines or sloppy CV joints. Also check the driveaxle shafts for cracks, dents and distortion.

13 Driveaxles - removal and installation

REMOVAL

▶ **Refer to illustrations 13.2, 13.4, 13.7, 13.10, 13.11a and 13.11b**

1 Set the parking brake.

2 If the design of the vehicle's wheels allows access to the driveaxle hub locknuts without removing the wheels, loosen the rear wheel lug nuts 1/4 turn. Using a hammer and punch, unstake the driveaxle hub locknut and loosen it 1/4 turn (see illustration). Raise the vehicle and support it securely on jackstands. Remove the wheels.

3 If the wheels must be removed for access to the locknut, loosen the rear wheel lug nuts 1/4 turn. Raise the vehicle and support it securely on jackstands. Remove the wheels, then unstake the locknut (see illustration 13.2).

4 Remove the driveaxle hub locknut. To prevent the hub from turning, wedge a prybar between two of the wheel studs and allow the prybar to rest against the ground (see illustration).

5 On 2005 and earlier models, remove the pivot bolt that secures the upper end of the rear knuckle (see Chapter 10). This will allow the

13.2 Bend back the staked portion of the locknut (shown here being staked) and unscrew it

13.4 Either hold the brakes on or use a large prybar to immobilize the hub while loosening the driveaxle hub nut

13.7 Hold the hub with a rod so it won't turn and push the driveaxle free with a puller

13.10 On early models, mark the relationship of the driveaxle inner CV joint to the differential output shaft, then remove the nuts and washers - to prevent the driveaxle from turning, insert a screwdriver between the nut and the CV joint housing

13.11a On later models, mark the relationship of the inner CV joint and the differential housing . . .

13.11b . . . then pry the CV joint out, taking care not to gouge the differential

knuckle to swing out far enough to provide removal clearance for the driveaxle.

6   On 2006 and later models, remove the ABS sensor and the rear brake caliper (see Chapter 9) and secure them out of the way. Disconnect the stabilizer bar link from the rear trailing link and disconnect all four links from the rear knuckle (see Chapter 10).

7   Loosen the driveaxle from the hub splines with a puller that will attach to the wheel studs (see illustration). These can be rented.

✷✷ CAUTION:

Applying force to the end of the driveaxle, beyond just breaking it loose from the hub, can damage the driveaxle or differential.

8   On 2005 and earlier models, pull the top end of the knuckle outward and detach the driveaxle from the hub. After withdrawing the outer end of the driveaxle from the rear knuckle on 2006 and later models, support the knuckle by reattaching it to the rear upper lateral link (see Chapter 10). Don't let the driveaxle hang by the inner CV joint after the outer end has been detached from the steering knuckle, as the inner joint could become damaged. Support the outer end of the driveaxle with a piece of wire, if necessary.

9   Place a drain pan underneath the differential to catch any lubricant that may spill out when the driveaxles are removed.

10   On 1996 and earlier models, where the driveaxle is attached with nuts to the differential output shaft flange, mark the relationship of the inner CV joint and output shaft, then remove the nuts and washers (see illustration).

11   On 1997 and later models, where the driveaxle fits directly into the differential, mark the relationship of the inner CV joint and differential (see illustration). Gently pry the inner CV joint out of the differential, being careful not to damage the dust cover or oil seal (see illustration).

INSTALLATION

▶ **Refer to illustration 13.12**

12 Installation is the reverse of the removal procedure, but with the following additional points:

    a) *On 1996 and earlier models, fit the inner driveaxle end over the studs on the differential output shaft, then install the washers and nuts and tighten them to the torque listed in this Chapter's Specifications.*

    b) *On 1997 and later models, install a new clip on the end of the driveaxle inner CV joint (see illustration), apply molybdenum based grease to the splines and wipe the differential oil seal with differential oil. With the end gap of the clip facing up, push the driveaxle sharply in to seat the clip on the inner CV joint in the groove of the differential side gear.*

13.12 Replace the driveaxle retaining clip before installing the shaft

    c) *Install a new driveaxle hub locknut, tighten it to the torque listed in this Chapter's Specifications and stake the locknut with a punch (see illustration 13.2).*

    d) *Install the wheel and lug nuts, lower the vehicle and tighten the lug nuts to the torque listed in the Chapter 1 Specifications.*

    e) *Check the differential lubricant and add, if necessary, to bring it to the proper level (see Chapter 1).*

✳✳ CAUTION:

The sharp edges of the driveaxle snap-ring can slice or puncture the oil seal.

14 Driveaxle boot replacement and CV joint inspection

➡**Note: If the CV joints must be overhauled (usually due to torn boots), explore all options before beginning the job. Complete rebuilt driveaxles are available on an exchange basis, which eliminates much time and work. Whichever route you choose to take, check on the cost and availability of parts before disassembling the vehicle.**

1 Remove the driveaxle (see Section 13).

INNER CV JOINT AND BOOT

Disassembly

▶ **Refer to illustrations 14.3, 14.4, 14.5, 14.6, 14.7 and 14.9**

2 Mount the driveaxle in a vise with wood-lined jaws (to prevent damage to the axleshaft). Check the CV joint for excessive play in the radial direction, which indicates worn parts. Check for smooth operation throughout the full range of motion for each CV joint. If a boot is torn, disassemble the joint, clean the components and inspect for damage due to loss of lubrication and possible contamination by foreign matter.

3 Pry the boot clamp retaining tabs up with a small screwdriver and slide the clamps off the boot (see illustration).

4 Slide the boot back on the axleshaft and pry the wire ring ball retainer from the outer race (see illustration).

5 Mark the relationship of the outer race to the axleshaft and pull the outer race off the inner bearing assembly (see illustration).

6 Mark the inner race, cage and axleshaft end to ensure that they are reassembled in the same relative positions (see illustration).

7 Remove the snap-ring from the groove in the axleshaft with a pair of snap-ring pliers (see illustration).

8 Slide the inner bearing assembly off the axleshaft.

9 Using a small screwdriver or piece of wood, pry the balls from

14.3 Pry the clamp retaining tabs up with a small screwdriver and slide the clamps off the boot

14.4 Pry the wire ring ball retainer out of the outer race, then slide the outer race (housing) off the bearing assembly

14.5 Use paint or a felt-tip marker to mark the outer race and axleshaft - DO NOT use a punch or scribe

14.6 Apply marks to the inner race, cage and axleshaft

14.7 Remove the outer snap-ring

14.9 Pry the balls out of the cage, but be careful not to nick or scratch them

14.10a Align the lands of the inner race with the window of the cage . . .

14.10b . . . then remove the inner race from the cage

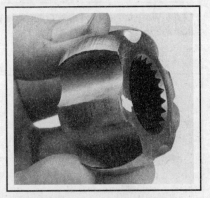

14.11a Check the inner race lands and grooves for pitting and score marks

the cage (see illustration). Be careful not to scratch the inner race, the balls or the cage.

Inspection

▶ **Refer to illustrations 14.10a, 14.10b, 14.11a and 14.11b**

10 Align the inner race lands with the windows and pull the race out of the cage (see illustrations).

11 Clean the components with solvent to remove all traces of grease. Inspect the cage and races for pitting, score marks, cracks and other

signs of wear and damage. Shiny, polished spots are normal and will not adversely affect CV joint performance (see illustrations).

Reassembly

▶ **Refer to illustrations 14.13, 14.14, 14.17, 14.19, 14.20, 14.21a and 14.21b**

12 Insert the inner race into the cage and align the matchmarks.

13 Press the balls into the cage windows with your thumbs (see illustration).

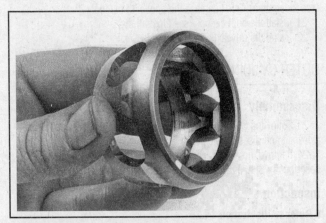

14.11b Check the cage for cracks, pitting and score marks (shiny spots are normal and don't affect operation)

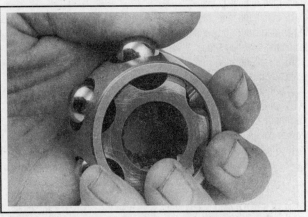

14.13 Press the balls into the cage through the windows using thumb pressure only

14.14 Wrap the splined area of the axle with tape to prevent damage to the boot when installing it

14.17 Pack the inner race and cage assembly full of CV joint grease (also note that the larger diameter side, or bulge, is facing the axleshaft end)

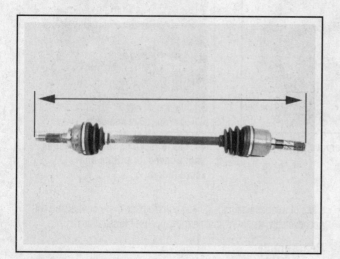

14.19 Adjust the driveaxle to the specified length (on early models, measure from the outer end to the inner flange)

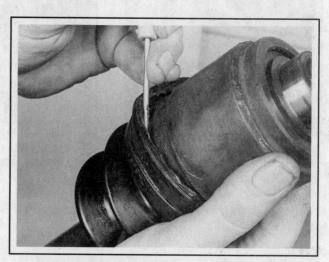

14.20 Equalize the pressure inside the boot by inserting a small, dull screwdriver between the boot and the outer race

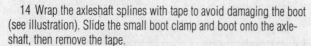

14 Wrap the axleshaft splines with tape to avoid damaging the boot (see illustration). Slide the small boot clamp and boot onto the axleshaft, then remove the tape.

15 Install the inner race and cage assembly on the axleshaft with the larger diameter or bulge of the cage (and the previously applied marks) facing the axleshaft end.

16 Install the snap-ring in the groove. Make sure it's completely seated by pushing on the inner race and cage assembly.

17 Fill the outer race and boot with the specified type and quantity of CV joint grease (normally included with the new joint boot kit). Pack the inner race and cage assembly with grease, by hand, until grease is worked completely into the assembly (see illustration).

18 Slide the outer race down onto the inner race, aligning the matchmarks, and install the wire ring retainer.

19 Wipe any excess grease from the axle boot groove on the outer race. Seat the small diameter of the boot in the recessed area on the axleshaft. Push the other end of the boot onto the outer race and move the race in or out to adjust the driveaxle to the length listed in this Chapter's Specifications (see illustration).

20 With the axle set to the proper length, equalize the pressure in the boot by inserting a dull screwdriver between the boot and outer race (see illustration). Don't damage the boot with the tool.

21 Install the boot clamps (see illustrations).

22 Install the driveaxle as described in Section 13.

OUTER CV JOINT AND BOOT

Disassembly

23 Following Steps 1 through 9, remove the inner CV joint from the axleshaft and disassemble it.

24 Remove the outer CV joint boot clamps, using the technique described in Step 3. Slide the boot off the axleshaft.

Inspection

▶ **Refer to illustration 14.26**

25 Thoroughly wash the inner and outer CV joints in clean solvent

14.21a To tighten a new clamp, bend the tang down . . .

14.21b . . . and fold the tabs over to hold it in place

14.26 After the old grease has been rinsed away and the solvent blown out with compressed air, rotate the outer joint housing through its full range of motion and inspect the bearing surfaces for wear and damage; if any of the balls, the race or the cage look damaged, replace the driveaxle and outer joint assembly

and blow them dry with compressed air, if available.

➡Note: Because the outer CV joint cannot be disassembled, it's difficult to wash away all the old grease and rid the bearing of solvent once it's clean. But it's imperative the job be done thoroughly, so take your time and do it right.

26 Bend the outer CV joint housing at an angle to the driveaxle to expose the bearings, inner race and cage (see illustration). Inspect the bearing surfaces for signs of wear. If the bearings are damaged or worn, replace the driveaxle.

Reassembly

27 Slide the new outer boot onto the driveaxle. It's a good idea to wrap vinyl tape around the splines of the shaft to prevent damage to the boot (see illustration 14.14). When the boot is in position, add the specified amount of grease (included in the boot replacement kit) to the outer joint and the boot (pack the joint with as much grease as it will hold and pout the rest into the boot). Slide the boot on the rest of the way and install the new clamps (see illustrations 14.21a and 14.21b).

28 Clean and reassemble the inner CV joint by following Steps 11 through 21, then install the driveaxle as described in Section 13.

15 Differential pinion oil seal - replacement

▶ Refer to illustrations 15.5, 15.6a, 15.6b, 15.6c, 15.7 and 15.8

1 Raise the rear of the vehicle and place it securely on jackstands. Remove the rear wheels and brake calipers (see Chapter 9).

2 Remove the rear half of the exhaust system (see Chapter 4).

3 Mark the driveshaft and companion flange for ease of realignment during assembly, then remove the driveshaft (see Section 11).

4 Remove the drain plug from the differential housing and allow the differential lubricant to drain into a container (see Chapter 1). When the draining is complete, install the drain plug.

5 Using an inch-pound torque wrench, slowly turn the pinion shaft nut and measure the amount of torque necessary to start the pinion shaft turning (see illustration). Write down this figure.

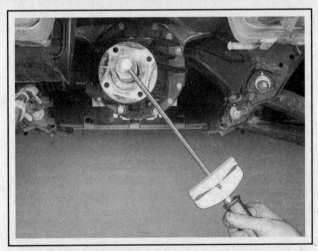

15.5 Turn the pinion shaft with an inch-pound torque wrench to measure the torque at which it starts to turn - a beam-type torque wrench works best for this

15.6a Mark the relationship of the nut and pinion shaft

15.6b Hold the shaft from turning with a rod and two of the bolts while you undo the nut

15.6c If the differential wasn't drained, position a pan to catch the oil; the flange may pull off by hand but if not, use a puller

15.7 Pry the pinion seal out with a seal remover or screwdriver, taking care not to gouge the seal bore

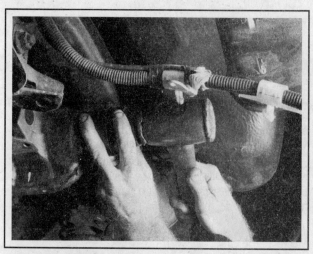

15.8 Tap a new seal squarely into the bore, using a tool the same diameter as the seal

6   Mark the relationship of the pinion nut and companion flange (see illustration). Using a suitable tool, hold the companion flange and remove the pinion nut (see illustration). Remove the companion flange, using a puller if necessary (see illustration).

7   After noting what the visible side of the oil seal looks like, carefully pry it out of the differential with a screwdriver or pry bar (see illustration). Be careful not to damage the splines on the pinion shaft or disturb the position of the shaft.

8   Clean the oil seal mounting surface, then tap the new seal into place, taking care to insert it squarely as shown (see illustration).

9   Inspect the splines on the pinion shaft for burrs and nicks. Remove any rough areas with a crocus cloth. Wipe the splines clean.

10   Install the companion flange, aligning it with the marks made during removal. Gently tap the flange on with a soft-faced hammer until you can start the pinion nut on the pinion shaft.

11   Using a suitable tool, hold the companion flange while tightening the pinion nut to the minimum torque listed in this Chapter's Specifications. Continue tightening, taking frequent rotational torque measurements, using the inch-pound torque wrench, until the measurement recorded in Step 5 is reached. Increase the nut torque in small increments and check the preload after each increase.

✳✳ CAUTION:

Under no circumstances should the pinion nut be backed off to reduce pinion bearing preload.

12   Install the driveshaft, brake calipers and wheels.
13   Fill the differential with oil (see Chapter 1).
14   Lower the vehicle and test drive it to check for leaks.

16 Differential output shaft (driveaxle) oil seal - replacement

◆ **Refer to illustrations 16.4, 16.5 and 16.6**

1 Raise the rear of the vehicle and support it on jackstands.
2 Drain the differential lubricant (see Chapter 1).
3 Remove the driveaxle (see Section 13).
4 On early models, gently pry out the differential output shaft with two prybars (see illustration).

➡ **Note: Be ready to catch the output shaft as it comes out.**

5 Pry out the seal with a seal removal tool or screwdriver (see illustration).
6 Use a hammer and a seal driver, large socket or section of pipe to install the new seal (see illustration).
7 Install a new circlip on the splined end of the output shaft or driveaxle (see Section 13).
8 Apply a film of differential oil to the lips of the seal, then install the output shaft (early models) and the driveaxle (see Section 13).
9 Fill the differential with oil (see Chapter 1).

16.4 On early models, two large pry bars can be used to remove the output shafts from the differential, but be careful where you pry and how hard - you might break the aluminum differential housing

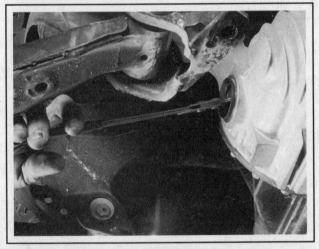

16.5 Pry the seal out with a seal remover or screwdriver, taking care not to gouge the seal bore

16.6 Tap a new seal squarely into the bore, using a tool the same diameter as the seal

17 Differential assembly - removal and installation

1 Loosen the rear wheel lug nuts. Raise the vehicle and place it securely on jackstands. Remove the rear wheels.
2 Remove the exhaust system (see Chapter 4).
3 Support the transmission securely, then remove the power plant frame (see Chapter 7A).

✳✳ **CAUTION:**

Failure to support the transmission before removing the power plant frame could damage cables and/or electrical wiring connected to the transmission.

4 Remove the driveshaft (see Section 11).
5 On vehicles with ABS, detach both rear wheel ABS sensors and their harnesses from the rear knuckles and secure them safely out of the way, so that they won't be damaged during this procedure.

2005 AND EARLIER MODELS

◆ **Refer to illustration 17.9**

6 On 1997 and earlier models, disconnect the speedometer cable.
7 On 1996 and earlier models, remove the nuts that secure the

17.9 With the differential supported by a jack, remove the differential mounting tubes (later models) and upper mounts (all models)

A   Differential mounting tube bolts
B   Upper differential mounts

inner CV joints to the differential output shaft flanges (see illustration 13.10). To give yourself sufficient clearance to separate the inner CV joints from the output shaft flanges, remove the upper control arm-to-rear knuckle pivot bolt (see illustration 13.13 in Chapter 10), then pull the knuckle out (away from the vehicle). After disengaging the inner

ends of the driveaxles from the differential output shaft flanges, support the driveaxles with wire so that they're not hanging by the outer CV joints.

8   If you're working on a 1997 through 2005 model, with inner CV joints that are splined directly into the differential, you must completely remove the driveaxles (see Section 13).

9   Remove the differential mounting tubes, if equipped (see illustration).

10 Support the differential securely, then remove the mounting nuts from the upper mount on each side of the differential (see illustration 17.9).

11 Move the differential forward, then lower and remove it.

2006 AND LATER MODELS

12 Remove the driveaxles (see Section 13).

13 Using a flashlight, locate the two bolts that secure the differential mount (which is located on top of the differential) to brackets on the rear suspension crossmember. Lower and remove the differential and the differential mount as a single assembly.

14 Remove the four nuts that secure the differential mount to the differential and remove the differential mount.

ALL MODELS

15 Installation is the reverse of removal. Be sure to tighten all fasteners securely. Refer to Chapter 7A to install the power plant frame.

16 Check the differential oil level (see Chapter 1) and top it up if necessary.

Specifications

Clutch

Fluid type	See Chapter 1
Pedal freeplay	See Chapter 1
Driveaxle standard length	
1993 and earlier	25.299 to 26.681 inches
1994 and 1995	25.228 to 25.622 inches
1996 and 1997	30.209 to 30.602 inches
1999 through 2005	30.42 to 30.81 inches
2006 and later	
Left driveaxle	30.65 to 31.04 inches
Right driveaxle	32.22 to 32.62 inches

Torque specifications

	Ft-lbs
Clutch master cylinder mounting nuts	14 to 18
Clutch release cylinder bolts	
2005 and earlier	12 to 16
2006 and later	14 to 19
Clutch pressure plate-to-flywheel bolts	
2005 and earlier	14 to 19
2006 and later	19 to 24
Driveshaft-to-differential flange nuts	
1997 and earlier	21 to 22
1999 and later	37 to 43
Driveaxle/hub locknut	
1997 and earlier	160 to 216
1999 through 2005	174 to 235
2006 and later	173 to 203
Differential pinion nut	
1997 and earlier	87 to 130
1999 through 2005	95 to 208
2006 and later	111 to 280
Wheel lug nuts	See Chapter 1

Notes

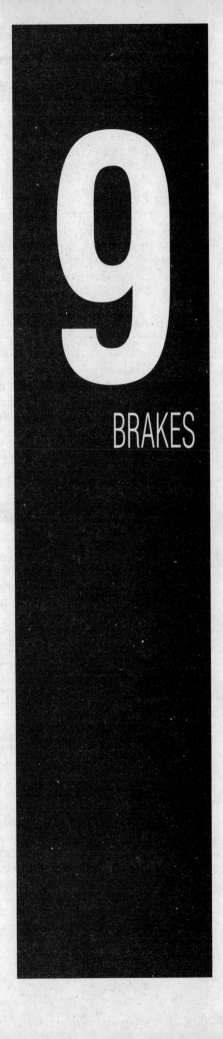

9

BRAKES

Section

Reference to other Chapters

1 General information

The vehicles covered by this manual are equipped with hydraulically operated front and rear brake systems. The front and rear brakes are disc type. Both the front and rear brakes are self-adjusting; the disc brakes automatically compensate for pad wear.

HYDRAULIC SYSTEM

The hydraulic system consists of two separate circuits. The master cylinder has separate reservoirs for the two circuits, and, in the event of a leak or failure in one hydraulic circuit, the other circuit will remain operative. A dual proportioning valve on the firewall provides brake balance between the front and rear brakes.

POWER BRAKE BOOSTER

The power brake booster, utilizing engine manifold vacuum and atmospheric pressure to provide assistance to the hydraulically operated brakes, is mounted on the firewall in the engine compartment.

PARKING BRAKE

The parking brake operates the rear brakes only, through cable actuation. It's activated by a lever mounted in the center console.

SERVICE

After completing any operation involving disassembly of any part of the brake system, always test drive the vehicle to check for proper braking performance before resuming normal driving. When testing the brakes, perform the tests on a clean, dry, flat surface. Conditions other than these can lead to inaccurate test results.

Test the brakes at various speeds with both light and heavy pedal pressure. The vehicle should stop evenly without pulling to one side or the other. Avoid locking the brakes, because this slides the tires and diminishes braking efficiency and control of the vehicle.

Tires, vehicle load and wheel alignment are factors which also affect braking performance.

2 Anti-lock Brake System (ABS) - general information

The Anti-lock Brake System (ABS) is designed to maintain vehicle steerability, directional stability and optimum deceleration under severe braking conditions and on most road surfaces. It does this by monitoring the rotational speed of each wheel and controlling the brake line pressure to each wheel during braking. This prevents the wheel from locking up.

COMPONENTS

Hydraulic unit

The ABS hydraulic unit consists of a hydraulic pump and a solenoid valve body.

a) *The electric pump provides hydraulic pressure for the system.*
b) *The solenoid valve body modulates brake line pressure during ABS operation. The valve body contains three valves - one for each front wheel and one for both of the rear wheels.*

Wheel speed sensors

These sensors are located at each wheel, generate small electrical pulsations when the toothed rotors are turning, sending a signal to the electronic controller indicating wheel rotational speed.

The front speed sensors are mounted at the front wheel hubs in close relationship to the toothed rotors, which are mounted on the inside of the wheel hubs.

The rear wheel sensors are bolted to the toe control hubs. These rotors are also mounted to the inside of the wheel hubs.

ABS control unit

The electronic controller is mounted under the right side of the dash and is the brain of the ABS system. The function of the control module - consisting of microprocessors and the related circuits needed for their operation - is to accept and process information received from the wheel speed sensors to control the hydraulic line pressure, avoiding wheel lock-up. The controller also constantly monitors the system, even under normal driving conditions, to find faults within the system.

If a problem develops within the system, an ABS indicator light will glow on the dashboard. A diagnostic code will also be stored in the controller, which, when retrieved by a service technician, will indicate the problem area or component.

DIAGNOSIS AND REPAIR

If a dashboard warning light comes on and stays on while the vehicle is in operation, the ABS system requires attention. Although a special electronic ABS diagnostic tester is necessary to properly diagnose the system, the home mechanic can perform a few preliminary checks before taking the vehicle to a dealer service department or other repair shop which is equipped with a tester.

a) *Check the brake fluid level in the reservoir.*
b) *Check that all electrical connectors are securely connected.*
c) *Check the fuses.*
d) *Follow the wiring harness to each wheel and check that all connections are secure and that the wiring is not damaged.*

If the above preliminary checks do not rectify the problem, the vehicle should be diagnosed and repaired by a dealer service department or other qualified repair shop.

3   Disc brake pads (front) - replacement

♦ Refer to illustrations 3.1, 3.4, 3.5a, 3.5b, 3.6a, 3.6b, 3.7, 3.8, 3.9, 3.10a, 3.10b, 3.10c, 3.10d, 3.11 and 3.12

❊❊ WARNING:

Dust created by the brake system is harmful to your health. Never blow it out with compressed air and don't inhale any of it. Clean the brake assembly with brake cleaner before any brake work is performed. An approved filtering mask should be worn when working on the brakes. Do not, under any circumstances, use petroleum-based solvents to clean brake parts. Use brake system cleaner.

1   Loosen the front wheel lug nuts, raise the front of the vehicle and place it securely on jackstands. Remove the wheel.

➡ **Note:** *Work on one brake assembly at a time, using the opposite side brake assembly for reference if necessary. Wash the* brake assembly with brake system cleaner before beginning work (see illustration).

2   If you are checking the brake pads for wear, see Chapter 1. Inspect the brake disc carefully as described in Section 5. If machining is necessary, follow the brake disc removal procedure in Section 5.

3   Open the hood and remove the cap from the brake fluid reservoir.

4   Use a C-clamp to push the caliper piston back into its bore to make room for the new pads (see illustration). As the piston is pressed inward, watch the fluid level in the brake fluid reservoir rise, being careful to remove any excess so that fluid will not spill over.

5   Remove the lower caliper bolt and pivot the caliper up off the pads (see illustration). Slide the caliper upper bolt out of the bracket and tie the caliper up so it doesn't hang by the brake hose (see illustration).

6   Remove the anti-rattle springs from the pads (see illustrations).

3.1 Always wash the brakes with brake cleaner before caliper removal

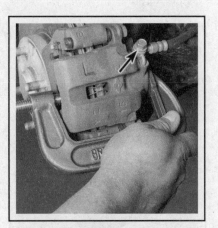

3.4 Depress the piston inward fully to make room for the new pads - don't unscrew the banjo fitting bolt unless the caliper is being overhauled

3.5a Remove the lower lockbolt and pivot the caliper upward . . .

3.5b . . . then slip the upper bolt out of the bracket and tie the caliper up so it doesn't hang by the brake hose

3.6a Remove the upper spring from the pads; note how the ends fit into holes in the pad backing plates (not used on 2006 and later models)

3.6b Remove the lower spring (not used on 2006 and later models)

3.7 Check the boots and replace them if they're cracked or deteriorated

3.8 Remove the pads and shims, then remove the clips from the bracket

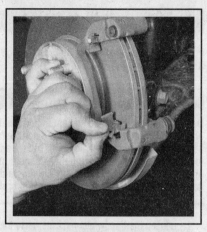

3.9 Place the upper and lower clips in the bracket

3.10a Clip the shims onto the backs of the pads

3.10b Apply anti-squeal compound to the brake pad backing plates where the piston and caliper fingers contact them

3.10c Make sure the clips are in place . . .

7   Check the rubber boots for cracks or deterioration and install new ones if any problems are found (see illustration).

8   Remove the pads, shims (there's one on each pad) and the clips (see illustration).

9   Install new clips in the caliper bracket notches (see illustration).

10 Install new shims on the backs of the pads (see illustration). Apply a coating of anti-squeal compound to the caliper contact areas on the shims (see illustration). Be careful not to get any on or near the brake pad friction surfaces. Install the pads between the clips (see illustrations).

11 Coat the upper mounting (lock) bolt with high-temperature brake grease (see illustration). With the caliper piston pressed all the way into the bore, slip the upper bolt into its bushing (make sure the boot is installed), then pivot the caliper down over the pads.

12 Apply high-temperature brake grease to the lower bolt (see illustration). Push the bolt through the caliper and boot into the bushing, then thread the bolt into the caliper and tighten it to the torque listed in this Chapter's Specifications.

13 Repeat Steps 4 through 12 for the opposite wheel brake pad replacement.

14 Check the brake fluid level and remove or add brake fluid as necessary. Reinstall the reservoir cap.

❊❊ WARNING:

Press the brake pedal several times and recheck the brake fluid level in the reservoir before driving the vehicle.

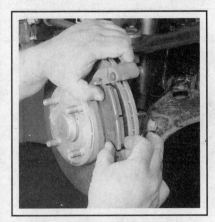

3.10d . . . then position the pads between the clips and press them against the disc. On 2005 and earlier models, install the anti-rattle springs

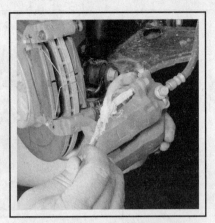

3.11 Coat the pin end of the upper bolt with high-temperature grease

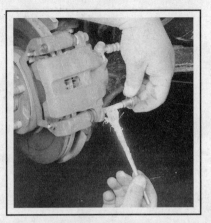

3.12 Coat the pin end of the lower lockbolt with high-temperature grease, then tighten it to the specified torque

4 Disc brake caliper (front) - removal, overhaul and installation

✳✳ WARNING:

Dust created by the brake system is harmful to your health. Never blow it out with compressed air and don't inhale any of it. An approved filtering mask should be worn when working on the brakes. Do not, under any circumstances, use petroleum-based solvents to clean brake parts. Use brake system cleaner.

➡Note: If an overhaul is indicated (usually because of fluid leakage), explore all options before beginning the job. New and factory rebuilt calipers are available on an exchange basis, which makes this job quite easy. If you decide to rebuild the calipers, make sure a rebuild kit is available before proceeding. Always rebuild the calipers in pairs - never rebuild just one of them.

4.6 Using a wood block as a cushion, use compressed air to ease the piston out of its bore - make sure your hands or fingers are not between the piston and caliper

REMOVAL

1 Loosen the front wheel lug nuts, raise the front of the vehicle and place it securely on jackstands. Remove the wheel and prepare for disassembly.

2 Remove the brake hose banjo bolt and disconnect the brake hose from the caliper (see illustration 3.4). Plug the brake hose to keep contaminants out of the brake system and to prevent losing any more brake fluid than is necessary.

➡Note: Don't disconnect the hose if you are only removing the caliper for access to other components.

3 Remove the caliper mounting bolts (lock bolts) and remove the caliper.

OVERHAUL

⬦ Refer to illustrations 4.6, 4.7 and 4.8

4 Clean the exterior of the caliper with brake system cleaner (never use gasoline, kerosene or any petroleum-based solvents), then place the caliper on a clean workbench.

5 Before you remove the piston, place a wood block or some rags between the piston and caliper to prevent damage as it is removed.

6 To remove the piston from the caliper, apply compressed air to the brake fluid hose connection on the caliper body (see illustration). Use only enough pressure to ease the piston out of its bore.

✳✳ WARNING:

Be careful not to place your fingers between the piston and the caliper, as the piston may come out with some force.

4.7 Pry the dust boot out of the caliper bore with a screwdriver - make sure you don't nick or gouge anything

4.8 Remove the seal from the piston using a plastic or wooden tool, such as a pencil

7 Carefully pry the dust boot out of the caliper body (see illustration).

8 Using a wooden or plastic tool, remove the piston seal from the groove in the caliper bore (see illustration). Metal tools may cause bore damage.

9 Remove the caliper bleeder valve. Discard all rubber parts.

10 Inspect the mating surfaces of the piston and caliper bore wall. If there is any scoring, rust, pitting or bright areas, replace the complete caliper unit with a new one. Crocus cloth can be used to remove light corrosion and stains.

11 If these components are in good condition, wash them with brake system cleaner and allow them to dry.

12 To reassemble the caliper, you should already have the correct rebuild kit for your vehicle.

13 Submerge the new piston seal and the piston in brake fluid and install the piston seal in its groove in the caliper bore.

14 Install the piston into the caliper bore. Do not force the piston into the bore, but make sure it is squarely in place, then apply firm (but not excessive) force by hand to install it.

15 Install the new piston dust boot and work it into the caliper groove.

16 Reinstall the bleeder screw and rubber cap.

17 Clean the bolt sleeves and lightly coat them with high-temperature grease. Reinstall the sleeves.

18 At this time, inspect the brake disc to be sure that it is reusable (see Section 5).

INSTALLATION

19 Install the caliper by reversing the removal procedure. Remember to replace the copper sealing washers (gaskets) at the brake hose-to-caliper connection (new washers normally come with the rebuild kit). Tighten the mounting bolts (lock bolts) to the torque listed in this Chapter's Specifications.

20 Bleed the brake circuit according to the procedure in Section 10. Make sure there are no leaks from the hose connections. Test the brakes carefully before returning the vehicle to normal service.

5 Brake disc - inspection, removal and installation

INSPECTION

▶ Refer to illustrations 5.3, 5.4a, 5.4b, 5.5a and 5.5b

1 Loosen the wheel lug nuts, raise the vehicle and support it securely on jackstands. Remove the wheel and install the lug nuts to hold the disc in place. It may be necessary to place washers under the nuts so the disc is held tightly to the hub.

2 Remove the brake caliper as outlined (front brakes see Section 4, rear brakes see Section 7) but it is not necessary to disconnect the brake hose. After removing the caliper bolts, suspend the caliper out of the way with a piece of wire (see illustration 3.5b).

3 Visually inspect the disc surface for score marks and other damage. Light scratches and shallow grooves are normal after use and may not always be detrimental to brake operation, but deep scoring - over 0.039-inch (1.0 mm) - requires refinishing by an automotive machine shop. Be sure to check both sides of the disc (see illustration). If pulsating has been noticed during application of the brakes, suspect disc runout.

5.3 The brake pads on this vehicle were obviously neglected, as they wore down to the rivets and cut deep grooves into the disc - wear this severe means the disc must be replaced

5.4a To check disc runout, mount a dial indicator as shown and rotate the disc

5.4b Using a swirling motion, remove the glaze from the disc surface with sandpaper or emery cloth

5.5a The minimum wear dimension is cast into the back side of the disc

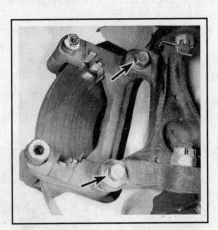

5.5b Use a micrometer to measure disc thickness

5.6a Remove the bolts and lift off the caliper bracket . . .

5.6b . . . the disc can then be slipped off the wheel studs

4   To check disc runout, place a dial indicator at a point about 1/2-inch from the outer edge of the disc (see illustration). Set the indicator to zero and rotate the disc slowly by hand. The indicator reading should not exceed the specified allowable runout limit. If it does, the disc must be refinished by an automotive machine shop.

➡**Note: The discs should be resurfaced regardless of the dial indicator reading, as this will impart a smooth finish and ensure a perfectly flat surface, eliminating any brake pedal pulsation or other undesirable symptoms related to questionable discs. At the very least, if you elect not to have the discs resurfaced, remove the glaze from the surface with emery cloth or sandpaper, using a swirling motion (see illustration).**

5   It is critical that the disc is not machined to a thickness less than the specified minimum thickness. The minimum wear (or discard) thickness is cast into the inside of the disc (see illustration). The disc thickness can be checked with a micrometer (see illustration).

REMOVAL

▶ **Refer to illustrations 5.6a and 5.6b**

6   Unbolt the brake caliper bracket, then remove the disc from the hub (see illustrations).

INSTALLATION

7   Place the disc in position over the wheel studs.

8   Install the caliper bracket. Tighten the bracket bolts to the torque listed in this Chapter's Specifications.

9   Install the caliper and brake pads (see Sections 4 and 3).

10 Install the wheel, then lower the vehicle to the ground. Tighten the lug nuts to the torque listed in the Chapter 1 Specifications.

11 Check the fluid level in the brake reservoir. Remove or add fluid as needed. Depress the brake pedal a few times to bring the brake pads into contact with the disc. Bleeding won't be necessary unless the brake hose was disconnected from the caliper. Check the operation of the brakes carefully before driving the vehicle.

6 Disc brake pads (rear) - replacement

▶ Refer to illustrations 6.7a, 6.7b, 6.8, 6.9a, 6.9b, 6.10, 6.12 and 6.13

✳✳ WARNING:

Disc brake pads must be replaced on both rear wheels at the same time - never replace the pads on only one wheel. The dust created by the brake system is harmful to your health. Never blow brake dust out with compressed air and don't inhale any of it. An approved filtering mask should be worn when working on the brakes. Do not, under any circumstances, use petroleum-based solvents to clean brake parts. Use brake system cleaner only!

1 Remove the cap from the brake fluid reservoir.

2 Loosen the wheel lug nuts, raise the rear of the vehicle and support it securely on jackstands. Block the wheels at the opposite end.

3 Remove the wheels. Work on one brake assembly at a time, using the assembled brake for reference if necessary.

4 If checking brake pads for wear, see Chapter 1. Inspect the brake disc carefully, as outlined in Section 5.

5 If machining is necessary, follow the information in Section 5 to remove the disc, at which time the pads can be removed as well.

6 Open the hood, and carefully remove the cap from the brake fluid reservoir.

7 On 2005 and earlier models, remove the plug from the manual adjustment gear screw (see illustrations).

8 On 2005 and earlier models, pull the brake caliper piston into the caliper by rotating the manual adjustment gear counterclockwise with an Allen wrench (see illustration). As the piston is pulled inward, watch the fluid level in the brake fluid reservoir rise, being careful to remove any excess so the fluid will not spill over.

9 On 2005 and earlier models, remove the caliper lower mounting bolt (lock bolt) (see illustration) and swing the caliper up for access to the brake pads (see illustration).

10 On 2006 and later models, remove the upper and lower caliper mounting bolts (see illustration). Remove the caliper and suspend it from the shock absorber coil spring with a piece of wire to protect the brake hydraulic hose and the parking brake cable.

11 Remove the M-shaped spring from the caliper.

6.7a Rear brake caliper details (2005 and earlier models)

A	Manual adjustment plug	G Brake hose banjo bolt
B	Caliper lower mounting (lock) bolt	H Bleeder valve cap
C	Lower pad spring	I Caliper bracket lower mounting bolt (upper bolt not visible)
D	Upper pad spring	
E	Brake pads	J Parking brake cable bracket bolt
F	Pin boots	

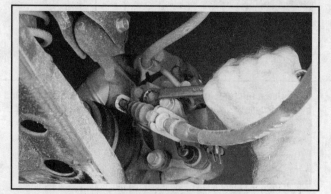

6.7b Remove the manual adjustment plug

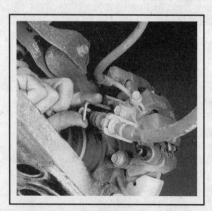

6.8 Using an Allen wrench, rotate the manual adjustment gear counterclockwise to retract the brake pads (2005 and earlier models only)

6.9a Unscrew the caliper lower mounting bolt . . .

6.9b . . . and pivot the caliper upward to expose the pads

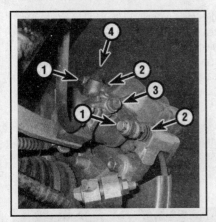

6.10 Rear brake caliper details
(2006 and later models)

1   Caliper mounting bolts
2   Pin boots
3   Brake hose banjo bolt
4   Brake bleeder valve cap

6.12 Swing the caliper up and
remove the pads

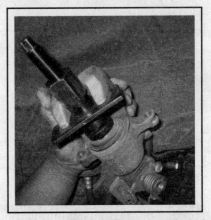

6.13 On 2006 and later models, use
a brake piston retraction tool (shown)
or a pair of needle-nose pliers to
retract the piston into the caliper

12 Remove the brake pads, shim plates and the caliper guide plates (see illustration).

13 On 2006 and later models, retract the piston into the caliper with a special tool (see illustration) or with a pair of large needle-nose pliers. Rotate the piston clockwise into the caliper bore until the piston is fully retracted. As the piston is pulled into the caliper, watch the fluid level in the brake fluid reservoir; if the fluid level rises too high, remove the excess fluid to prevent a spill.

14 With the new replacement brake pads ready, apply a light coating of anti-squeal compound to the brake pad backing plates (see illustration 3.10b). Be careful to not get any on or near the brake pad friction surfaces.

15 With the caliper piston pushed inward fully, install the new pads with the outer shim and the inner shim.

16 Reinstall the caliper guides and, on 2005 and earlier models, the M-shaped spring. Rotate the caliper down over the pads.

17 Reinstall the caliper lower mounting bolt (lock bolt) tightening it to the torque listed in this Chapter's Specifications.

18 If you're working on a 2005 or earlier model, turn the manual adjustment gear clockwise (see illustration 6.8) until the brake pads contact the brake disc. Then turn the manual adjustment gear 1/3 turn counterclockwise.

19 Reinstall the manual adjustment gear plug and tighten it securely.

20 Check the brake fluid reservoir level and remove or add brake fluid as necessary. Reinstall the brake fluid reservoir cap.

21 Repeat Steps 6 through 20 for the opposite wheel brake pad replacement.

22 After the job has been completed, firmly depress the brake pedal a few times to bring the pads into contact with the disc. Check the level of the brake fluid, adding some if necessary. Check the operation of the brakes carefully before placing the vehicle into normal service.

7   Disc brake caliper (rear) - removal and installation

✳✳ WARNING:

Dust created by the brake system is harmful to your health. Never blow it out with compressed air and do not inhale any of it. An approved filtering mask should be worn when working on the brakes. Do not, under any circumstances, use petroleum-based solvents to clean brake parts. Use brake system cleaner.

➡**Note: Due to the complexity of the rear calipers on these models, we do not recommend overhauling them. Replacing them as a pair with rebuilt units will provide better service for less cost.**

REMOVAL

1   Loosen the rear wheel lug nuts, raise the rear of the vehicle and place it securely on jackstands. Remove the wheel.

2   Remove the parking brake cable from the caliper.

3   Remove the brake hose banjo bolt and disconnect the brake hose from the caliper (see illustration 6.7a). Plug the brake hose to keep contaminants out of the brake system and to prevent losing any more brake fluid than is necessary.

4   Remove the rear disc manual adjustment gear plug (see illustration 6.7b).

5   Move the brake caliper piston inward by rotating the manual adjustment gear counterclockwise (see illustration 6.8).

6   Remove the lower caliper mounting bolt (lock bolt) (see illustration 6.7a).

7   On 1994 and later models, remove the caliper upper mounting bolt.

8   Remove the caliper from the bracket.

INSTALLATION

9   Install the caliper by reversing the removal procedure. Remember to replace the copper sealing washers (gaskets) at the brake hose-to-caliper connection.

10 Turn the manual adjustment gear clockwise until the brake pads contact the brake disc, then turn the adjustment gear 1/3 turn counter-clockwise. Reinstall the plug and tighten it securely.

11 Bleed the brake circuit according to the procedure in Section 10. Make sure there are no leaks from the hose connections. Test the brakes carefully before returning the vehicle to normal service.

8   Master cylinder - removal, overhaul and installation

➡Note: Before deciding to overhaul the master cylinder, check on the availability and cost of a new or factory rebuilt unit and also the availability of a rebuild kit. If you decide to rebuild the cylinder, inspect the bore as described in Step 12 before purchasing parts.

REMOVAL

▶ Refer to illustrations 8.1a and 8.1b

1   Follow the wiring harness from the master cylinder to the electrical connector for the fluid level warning switch (see illustrations). Unplug the connector.

2   Carefully remove the brake fluid reservoir cap and remove as much fluid as possible from the reservoir with a syringe. Check continuity of the level sensor; continuity should be measured when fluid level is below the MIN level.

3   Place rags under the fittings and prepare caps or plastic bags to cover the ends of the lines once they are disconnected.

❋❋ CAUTION:

Brake fluid will damage paint. Cover all body parts and be careful not to spill fluid during this procedure. Loosen the fittings at the ends of the brake lines where they enter the master cylinder (see illustration 8.1a or 8.1b). To prevent rounding off the flats, use a flare-nut wrench, which wraps around the fitting hex. On 2006 and later models, loosen the hose clamp (see illustration 8.1b) and disconnect the hose that connects the brake master cylinder reservoir to the clutch master cylinder. Be prepared to catch any spilled brake fluid with a shop rag.

4   Remove the nuts and washers attaching the master cylinder to the power brake booster (see illustration 8.1a or 8.1b).

5   Pull the brake lines away from the master cylinder and plug the ends to prevent contamination. Slide the proportioning valve mounting bracket off the studs.

6   Pull the master cylinder off the studs to remove it. Again, be careful not to spill the fluid as this is done.

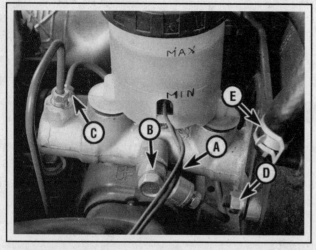

8.1a Brake master cylinder mounting details (2005 and earlier models)

A   Warning light switch harness
B   Brake line union bolt
C   Flare nuts
D   Left mounting nut (right mounting nut hidden)
E   Power brake booster vacuum hose

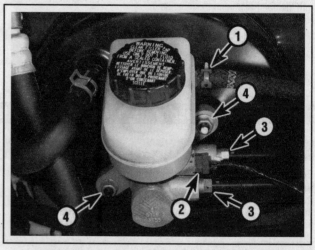

8.1b Brake master cylinder mounting details (2006 and later models)

1   Hose clamp for brake fluid hose to clutch master cylinder
2   Brake fluid level sensor electrical connector
3   Brake hydraulic line fittings
4   Master cylinder mounting nuts

8.8a The brake fluid reservoir on 2005 and earlier models is retained by a screw

8.8b After the reservoir has been removed, pull the grommets from the master cylinder body; if they're hard, cracked or damaged, or have been leaking, replace them (2005 and earlier models)

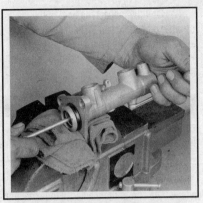

8.9 Using a Phillips screwdriver, depress the pistons, then remove the stopper bolt or screw; be sure to replace the sealing washer for the stopper bolt

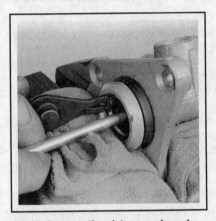

8.10 Depress the pistons again and remove the snap-ring with a pair of snap-ring pliers

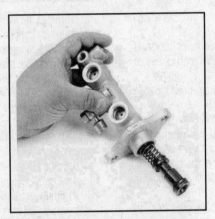

8.11a After the snap-ring has been removed, the primary (No. 1) piston assembly can be removed

8.11b If necessary, tap the master cylinder against a block of wood to eject the secondary piston

OVERHAUL

2005 and earlier models

▶ Refer to illustrations 8.8a, 8.8b, 8.9, 8.10, 8.11a, 8.11b and 8.11c

7   Before attempting the overhaul of the master cylinder, obtain the proper rebuild kit, which will contain the necessary replacement parts and also any instructions which are specific to your model.

8   Remove the reservoir retaining screw, pull off the reservoir and remove the grommets (see illustrations).

9   Place the cylinder in a vise and use a punch or Phillips screwdriver to depress the pistons until they bottom against the other end of the master cylinder. Hold the pistons in this position and remove the stopper bolt or screw from the master cylinder (see illustration).

10   Carefully remove the snap-ring at the end of the master cylinder (see illustration).

11   The internal components can now be removed from the bore (see illustrations). Make a note of the proper order of the components so they can be returned to their original locations.

➡Note: The two springs are different, so pay particular attention to their installed order.

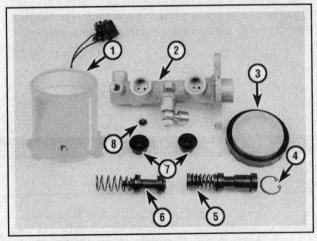

8.11c 2005 and earlier brake master cylinder details

1	Reservoir	5	Primary piston
2	Master cylinder body	6	Secondary piston
3	Reservoir cap	7	Reservoir grommets
4	Snap-ring	8	Stopper bolt or screw

12 Carefully inspect the bore of the master cylinder. Any score marks or other damage mean that a new master cylinder is required. DO NOT attempt to hone the bore.

13 Replace all parts included in the rebuild kit, following any instructions in the kit. Clean all re-used parts with brake system cleaner.

✳✳ WARNING:

Do not use any petroleum-based solvents. During reassembly, lubricate all parts liberally with clean, fresh brake fluid.

14 Push the assembled components into the bore, bottoming them against the end of the master cylinder, then install the stopper bolt.

15 Push in on the primary piston again and install the new snap-ring, making sure it's seated properly in the groove.

16 Install the reservoir grommets, reservoir and reservoir mounting screw.

17 Before installing the master cylinder, it should be bench bled. Since you'll have to apply pressure to the master cylinder piston and, at the same time, control flow from the brake line outlets, the master cylinder should be mounted in a vise, with the jaws of the vise clamping on the mounting flange.

18 Insert threaded plugs into the brake line outlet holes and snug them down so no air will leak past them, but not so tight that they cannot be easily loosened.

19 Fill the reservoir with brake fluid of the recommended type (see Chapter 1).

20 Remove one plug and push the piston assembly into the bore to expel the air from the master cylinder. A large Phillips screwdriver can be used to push on the piston assembly.

21 To prevent air from being drawn back into the master cylinder, the plug must be replaced and tightened before releasing the pressure on the piston.

22 Repeat the procedure until only brake fluid is expelled from the brake line outlet hole. When only brake fluid is expelled, repeat the procedure at the other outlet hole and plug. Be sure to keep the master cylinder reservoir filled with brake fluid to prevent the introduction of any additional air into the master cylinder system while bleeding it.

23 Since high pressure is not involved in the bench bleeding procedure, an alternative to the removal and replacement of the plugs with each stroke of the piston assembly is available. Before pushing in on the piston assembly, remove the plug as described in Step 20. Before releasing the piston, however, instead of replacing the plug, simply put your finger tightly over the hole to keep air from being drawn back into the master cylinder. Wait several seconds for brake fluid to be drawn from the reservoir into the bore, then depress the piston again, removing your finger as brake fluid is expelled. Be sure to put your finger back over the hole each time before releasing the piston, and when the bleeding procedure is complete for that outlet, replace the plug and tighten it before going on to the other port.

2006 and later models

24 On these models, the master cylinder is not rebuildable. You must install a rebuilt or new master cylinder unit. The reservoir is also available separately, so you can replace just the reservoir, if necessary. At the dealer, the reservoir comes with new grommets as well.

25 If the old grommets between the reservoir and the master cylinder (see illustration 8.8b) are leaking, replace them.

INSTALLATION

26 Install the master cylinder and proportioning valve bracket over the studs on the power brake booster, install the washers, and tighten the nuts only finger-tight at this time.

27 Thread the brake line flare nuts into the master cylinder. Since the master cylinder is still loose, it can be moved slightly so the flare nuts thread in easily by hand. Be careful not to strip the threads as the fittings are tightened.

28 Connect the remaining brake line to the master cylinder with the union bolt, using a new sealing washer on each side of the fitting.

29 Tighten the master cylinder mounting nuts and union bolt to the torque listed in this Chapter's Specifications. Tighten the brake line flare nuts securely using a flare-nut wrench.

30 Fill the master cylinder reservoir with fluid, then bleed the master cylinder and the brake system (see Section 10). To bleed the master cylinder on the vehicle, have an assistant depress the brake pedal and hold it down while you loosen the fitting to allow air and fluid to escape. Tighten the fitting, then allow your assistant to return the pedal to its rest position. Repeat this procedure on all fittings until the fluid is free of air bubbles. Check the operation of the brake system carefully before driving the vehicle.

9   Brake hoses and lines - inspection and replacement

INSPECTION

1 About every six months, with the vehicle raised and supported securely on jackstands, the rubber hoses which connect the steel brake lines with the front and rear brake assemblies should be inspected for cracks, chafing of the outer cover, leaks, blisters and other damage. These are important and vulnerable parts of the brake system and inspection should be complete. A light and mirror will be helpful for a thorough check. If a hose exhibits any of the above conditions, replace it with a new one.

REPLACEMENT

Front brake hose
▶ Refer to illustrations 9.3 and 9.4

2 Loosen the wheel lug nuts, raise the vehicle and support it securely on jackstands. Remove the wheel.

3 At the frame bracket, unscrew the brake line fitting from the hose (see illustration). Use a flare-nut wrench to prevent rounding off the corners and hold the hose fitting with an open-end wrench.

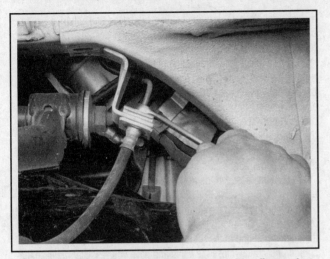

9.3 Unscrew the brake line threaded fitting with a flare-nut wrench to protect the fitting corners from being rounded off

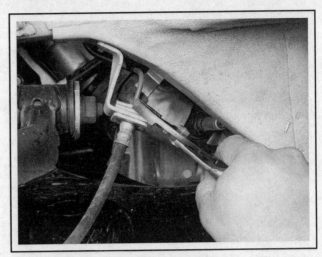

9.4 Pull off the U-clip with a pair of pliers

4 Remove the U-clip from the female fitting at the bracket with a pair of pliers (see illustration), then pass the hose through the bracket.

5 At the caliper end of the hose, remove the banjo fitting bolt, then separate the hose from the caliper. Note that there are two copper sealing washers on either side of the fitting - these sealing washers should be replaced with new ones during installation.

6 To install the hose, pass the caliper fitting end through any bracket, as necessary, then connect the fitting to the caliper with the banjo bolt and new copper sealing washers. Make sure the locating lug on the fitting is engaged with the hole in the caliper, then tighten the bolt to the torque listed in this Chapter's Specifications.

7 Push the hose support into the strut bracket and install the U-clip, as necessary. Make sure the hose is not twisted between the caliper and any brackets.

8 Route the hose into the frame bracket, again making sure it is not twisted, then connect the brake line fitting, starting the threads by hand. Install the U-clip, then tighten the fitting securely.

9 Bleed the caliper (see Section 10).

10 Install the wheel and lug nuts, lower the vehicle and tighten the lug nuts to the torque listed in the Chapter 1 Specifications.

Rear brake hose

11 The rear brake hose serves as the flexible connection between two rigid metal lines, one on the body and the other on the suspension. Both ends of the hose are attached to these metal lines with threaded fittings and U-clips. Refer to Steps 2, 3 and 4. Bleed the wheel cylinder (see Section 10).

Metal brake lines

12 When replacing brake lines, be sure to use the correct parts. Don't use copper tubing for any brake system components. Purchase steel brake lines from a dealer or auto parts store.

13 Prefabricated brake line, with the tube ends already flared and fittings installed, is available at auto parts stores and dealer parts departments. If pre-bent lines are not available, remove the defective line and purchase a straight section of brake line (with the fittings attached and the ends flared) that measures as close as possible to the length of the original line (including the bends). Using the proper tubing bending tools, bend the new line to resemble the original.

14 When installing the new line, make sure it is securely supported in the bracket(s) and has plenty of clearance between moving or hot components.

15 After installation, check the master cylinder fluid level and add fluid as necessary. Bleed the brake system (see Section 10) and test the brakes carefully before driving the vehicle in traffic.

10 Brake hydraulic system - bleeding

▶ Refer to illustration 10.8

❉❉ WARNING:

Wear eye protection when bleeding the brake system. If the fluid comes in contact with your eyes, immediately rinse them with water and seek medical attention. Do not get any brake fluid on the brake pads.

➡Note: Bleeding the hydraulic system is necessary to remove any air that manages to find its way into the system when it has been opened during removal and installation of a hose, line, caliper or master cylinder.

1 If a brake line is disconnected at the brake master cylinder, or if air has entered it due to low fluid level in the brake master cylinder reservoir, start bleeding the brakes at the wheel cylinder or caliper farthest from the brake master cylinder, and move to the next closest wheel cylinder or caliper until all four wheels are bled.

10.8 When bleeding the brakes, a hose is connected to the bleed screw at the caliper or wheel cylinder and then submerged in brake fluid - air will be seen as bubbles in the tube and container (all air must be expelled before moving to the next wheel)

2 If a brake line was disconnected only at a wheel, then only that caliper or wheel cylinder must be bled.

3 If a brake line is disconnected at a fitting located between the master cylinder and any of the brakes, that part of the system served by the disconnected brake line must be bled.

4 Remove any residual vacuum from the brake power booster by applying the brake several times with the engine off.

5 Remove the master cylinder reservoir cover and fill the reservoir with brake fluid. Reinstall the cover.

➡Note: Check the fluid level often during the bleeding operation and add fluid as necessary to prevent the fluid level from falling low enough to allow air bubbles into the master cylinder.

6 Have an assistant on hand, as well as a supply of new brake fluid, a clear plastic container partially filled with clean brake fluid, a length of plastic, rubber or vinyl tubing to fit over the bleeder valve and a wrench to open and close the bleeder valve.

7 For a brake system bleeding of all four wheels, begin at the right rear wheel; remove the bleeder cap and attach the vinyl hose to the bleeder valve. Loosen the bleeder valve slightly, then tighten it to a point where it is snug but can still be loosened quickly and easily. If bleeding only specific wheels or portions of the brake system, follow the appropriate Steps below.

8 Place one end of the tubing over the bleeder valve and submerge the other end in brake fluid in the container (see illustration).

9 Have the assistant depress the brake pedal and hold it down firmly.

10 While the pedal is held down, open the bleeder valve just enough to allow a flow of fluid to leave the valve. Watch for air bubbles to exit the submerged end of the tubing. When the fluid flow slows after a couple of seconds, close the valve and have your assistant release the pedal.

11 Repeat Steps 9 and 10 until no more air is seen leaving the tubing, then tighten the bleeder valve securely and proceed to the left rear wheel, the right front wheel and the left front wheel, in that order, and perform the same procedure. Be sure to check the fluid in the master cylinder reservoir frequently, keeping it about 3/4 full during bleeding.

➡Note: Always use new, fresh brake fluid. Old fluid or fluid from an opened container contains moisture which can boil, rendering the brakes useless.

12 At the end of the operation, refill the master cylinder with fluid to the MAX mark on the reservoir.

13 Check the operation of the brakes. The pedal should feel solid when depressed, with no sponginess. If necessary, repeat the entire brake system bleeding.

✳✳ WARNING:

Do not operate the vehicle if you are in doubt about the effectiveness of the brake system.

11 Power brake booster - check, removal and installation

OPERATING CHECK

1 Depress the brake pedal several times with the engine off and make sure there's no change in the pedal reserve distance (distance from the pedal to the floor).

2 Depress the pedal and start the engine. If the pedal goes down slightly, operation is normal.

AIRTIGHTNESS CHECK

3 Start the engine and turn it off after one or two minutes. Depress the brake pedal slowly several times. If the pedal depresses less each time, the booster is airtight.

4 Depress the brake pedal while the engine is running, then stop the engine with the pedal held depressed. If there is no change in the pedal reserve travel after holding the pedal for 30 seconds, the booster is airtight.

➡Note: If the airtightness check fails in either Step above, first try checking and/or replacing the power brake booster vacuum hose/check valve and repeat the airtightness check.

REMOVAL

▶ Refer to illustration 11.10

5 Power brake booster units shouldn't be disassembled. They require special tools not normally found in most automotive repair stations or shops. Because of its critical relationship to brake performance, the booster should be replaced with a new or rebuilt one.

6 Disconnect the vacuum hose/check valve leading from the engine to the booster (see illustration 8.1). Be careful not to damage the hose when removing it from the booster fitting.

7 Remove the brake master cylinder (see Section 8).

8 Remove the steering column lower finish panel (see Chapter 11).

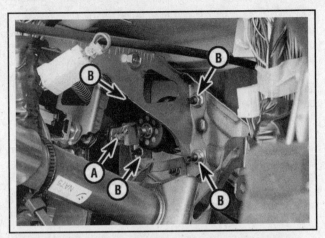

11.10 To disconnect the power brake booster pushrod from the brake pedal, remove the retaining clip and clevis pin (A); to detach the booster from the firewall, remove the four mounting nuts (B, one nut hidden)

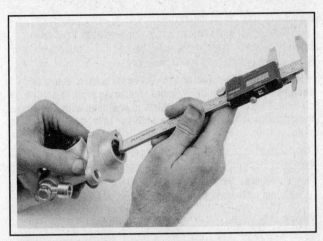

11.15a Measure the distance from the master cylinder pocket to the end of the cylinder body . . .

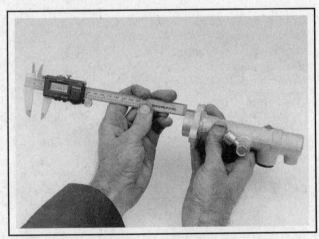

11.15b . . . then measure the distance from the mounting surface to the end of the cylinder body. Subtract this measurement from the first one; that will tell you the depth of the pocket from the mounting surface . . .

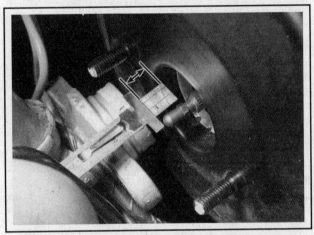

11.15c . . . now measure the protrusion of the cylinder pushrod past the mounting surface; it should be slightly less than the depth of the pocket

9 Remove the pedal return spring.

10 Locate the pushrod clevis connecting the booster to the brake pedal (see illustration). Remove the cotter pin from the clevis pin with pliers and pull out the clevis pin.

11 Remove the four nuts holding the brake booster to the firewall (see illustration 11.10). You may need a light to see the mounting nuts.

12 Slide the booster straight out from the firewall until the studs clear the holes. Be careful not to tear or damage the brake booster gasket between the firewall and the booster.

INSTALLATION

▶ **Refer to illustrations 11.15a, 11.15b, 11.15c and 11.15d**

13 Installation is basically the reverse of removal. Tighten the booster mounting nuts to the torque listed in this Chapter's Specifications. Be sure to use a new clevis retaining clip if the old clip is loose.

14 When installing the power brake booster vacuum hose/check valve, be sure to install the vacuum hose/check valve with the arrows on

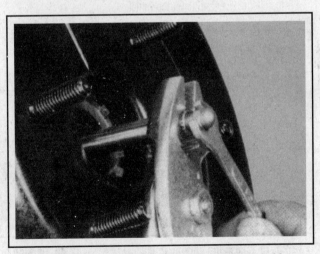

11.15d To adjust the length of the booster pushrod, hold the serrated portion of the rod with a pair of pliers and turn the adjusting screw in or out, as necessary, to achieve the desired setting

the vacuum hose toward the engine.

15 If the power brake booster unit is being replaced, the clearance between the master cylinder piston and the pushrod in the power brake booster must be measured and, if necessary, adjusted.

→**Note: This step applies to non-ABS models only. Vehicles equipped with ABS require special measuring tools to set the clearance accurately. If your vehicle is equipped with ABS, have the adjustment done by a Mazda dealer or other qualified repair shop.**

Using a depth micrometer or vernier caliper, calculate the distance from the pocket of the primary piston to the master cylinder mounting flange (see illustrations). Next, with the engine running for vacuum applied to the power brake booster (or vacuum applied by a vacuum pump,

if desired), measure the distance from the end of the vacuum booster pushrod to the mounting face of the booster where the master cylinder mounting flange seats (see illustration). Subtract the depth of the piston pocket from the protrusion of the pushrod to calculate the clearance and compare your findings with the values listed in this Chapter's Specifications. If not, turn the adjusting screw on the end of the power booster pushrod until the clearance is within the specified limit (see illustration).

16 After the final installation of the master cylinder and brake hoses and lines, the brake pedal height and freeplay must be adjusted and the brake system must be bled. See the appropriate Sections of this Chapter for the procedures.

12 Parking brake - adjustment

♦ **Refer to illustrations 12.2a, 12.2b, 12.4a and 12.4b**

1 The parking brake lever, when properly adjusted, should travel the number of clicks listed in the Chapter 1 Specifications, when a moderate pulling force is applied. If it travels less than the specified minimum number of clicks, the parking brake may not be releasing completely and could cause the rear brakes to drag. If the lever can be pulled up more than the specified maximum number of clicks, the parking brake may not hold adequately on an incline, allowing the car to roll.

2 To gain access to the parking brake cable adjuster, remove the lever cover (see illustrations).

3 Securely block the front wheels so the vehicle won't roll. Jack up the rear end just until the tires are off the ground, then place it securely on jackstands. Place the transmission in Neutral and release the parking brake completely.

4 Turn the adjusting nut until the desired travel is attained (see illustrations).

5 Pull the parking brake lever one click. The parking brake warning light should come on. Release the lever and make sure the rear wheels turn freely.

6 Install the cover and lower the vehicle.

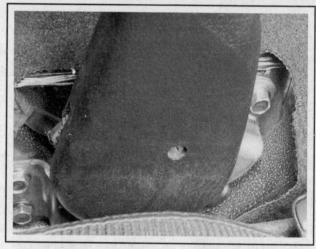

12.2a On 2005 and earlier models, remove the screw and detach the parking brake cover

12.2b To access the parking brake cable adjusting nut on 2006 and later models, carefully pry loose the parking brake lever boot

12.4a Parking brake adjusting nut (2005 and earlier models)

12.4b Parking brake adjusting nut (2006 and later models)

13 Parking brake cables - replacement

1   Make sure the parking brake lever is fully released. Loosen the rear wheel lug nuts. Raise the vehicle and place it securely on jackstands. Remove the rear wheels.

2   Remove the center console (see Chapter 11).

3   Remove the exhaust pipe (see Chapter 4) and, if necessary, the driveshaft (see Chapter 8).

2005 AND EARLIER MODELS

Equalizer-to-brake lever cable

▶ Refer to iliustrations 13.4a and 13.4b

4   Remove the cable adjusting nut (see illustration 12.4a). Remove the return spring and front parking brake cable (see illustrations).

5   Pry out the rubber grommet from the floorpan and pull the front parking cable out.

6   Installation is the reverse of removal. Apply a light coat of grease to the portion of the cable end that engages with the equalizer. Also coat the sealing edge of the rubber grommet with silicone to ensure that it remains watertight.

Equalizer-to-rear caliper cables

▶ Refer to illustrations 13.8 and 13.9

7   Remove the parking cable mounting bolts located along the vehicle chassis.

8   Remove the parking cable retaining clips at the equalizer (see illustration).

9   Detach the parking brake cable from the caliper (see illustration). Free the cable ends from the equalizer and pull the cable out from under the vehicle.

10 Installation is the reverse of removal. Apply a light coat of grease to the portion of the cable end that engages with the equalizer.

11 Adjust the parking brake when the parking brake cable is reinstalled (see Section 12).

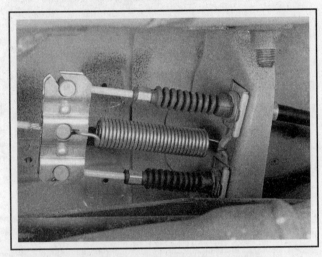

13.4a Under the vehicle, remove the return spring . . .

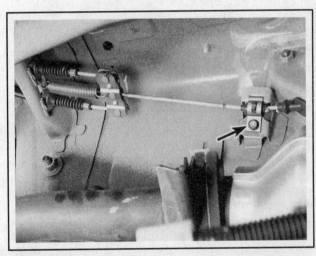

13.4b . . . then unbolt the grommet and remove the front parking cable

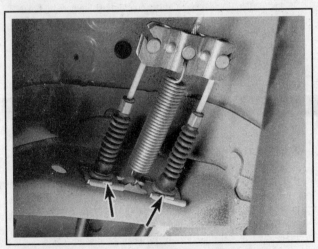

13.8 Remove the retaining clips at the equalizer (arrows) and detach the forward end of the parking brake cable

13.9 Loosen the cable nut and detach the end of the cable from the lever

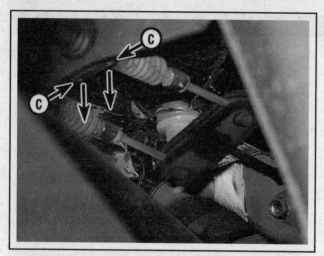

13.16 On 2006 and later models, use needle nose pliers to pull down and remove the retainer clip (C) that secures each of the rear parking brake cables to this crossmember, which is located immediately behind the equalizer

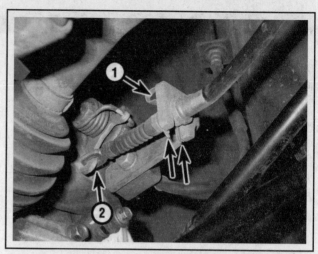

13.21 Parking brake cable connection at the rear brake caliper (2006 and later models):

1   *Cable retainer clip (pull up to remove)*
2   *Disengage the cable end from the parking brake lever on the caliper*

2006 AND LATER MODELS

Front parking brake (parking brake lever-to-equalizer) cable

▸ **Refer to illustration 13.16**

12 Disconnect the electrical connector from the parking brake switch.

13 Remove the cable adjusting nut (see illustration 12.4b).

14 Peel back the carpeting to access the bolt that secures the parking brake lever on the right side of the lever.

15 Remove the other two parking brake lever bolts, lift up the parking brake lever assembly and disengage the front parking brake cable from the lever.

16 Working underneath the vehicle, locate the equalizer (see illustration). Use needle nose pliers to pull down and remove the two clips that secure the two rear parking brake (equalizer-to-rear caliper) cables to the crossmember behind the equalizer.

17 Disconnect the two rear parking brake cables from the equalizer.

18 Remove the screws that secure the insulator where the front cable goes through the pan.

19 Remove the front parking brake cable by pulling it out through the hole in the pan from underneath the vehicle.

20 Installation is the reverse of removal. Adjust the parking brake cable (see Section 12).

Rear parking brake (equalizer-to-rear caliper) cables

▸ **Refer to illustration 13.21**

21 Disconnect the rear cables from the rear brake calipers (see illustration).

22 Trace the forward routing of each rear cable to its bolted clips, remove the bolts and detach the clips (there's one bolted clip for the left cable and two for the right cable).

23 Continue tracing the cables forward to the two clips that secure both cables together. To disengage the cables from these clips, pry open each clip with a screwdriver and pull out the cable.

24 Disconnect the rear cables from the equalizer. You might have to disconnect the front cable (see Steps 12 through 18) to give yourself enough slack to work the plug ends of the rear cables out of the equalizer. Remove the rear parking brake cables.

25 Installation is the reverse of removal. Adjust the parking brake system (see Section 12).

14 Brake pedal - check and adjustment

PEDAL HEIGHT

▸ **Refer to illustration 14.1**

1   Measure the pedal height (see illustration) and compare your measurement to the pedal height listed in this Chapter's Specifications.

2   If the pedal height is incorrect, adjust it as follows:

3   Unplug the electrical connector from the brake light switch.

4   Loosen the brake light switch locknut and turn the brake switch until it does not contact the pedal.

5   Loosen the pushrod locknut.

6   Adjust the pedal height by turning the pedal pushrod.

7   Tighten the pushrod locknut.

8   Turn the brake light switch until it lightly contacts the pedal stopper, then turn the brake light switch an additional 1/2 turn.

9   Tighten the brake light switch locknut.

10 Plug in the brake light switch electrical connector.

11 Check that brake lights come on when the brake pedal is depressed, and go off when the brake pedal is released.

12 Check the pedal freeplay (see below).

PEDAL FREEPLAY

13 Stop the engine if it's running, and depress the brake pedal several times until there's no more vacuum left in the booster.

14 Gently press the pedal by hand until you feel some resistance, then measure the distance between the fully released pedal and the point at which you feel resistance (see illustration 14.1). Compare your measurement with the pedal freeplay listed in this Chapter's Specifications. If the pedal freeplay is incorrect, adjust it as follows:

15 Adjust the brake pedal pushrod to obtain the specified pedal freeplay, then adjust the brake light switch as described. If the pedal freeplay cannot be adjusted properly, troubleshoot the brake system.

PEDAL RESERVE

16 Start the engine, depress the brake pedal a few times, then press down hard and hold it.

17 Pedal reserve travel is measured from the floor to the top of the pedal while it is held depressed (see illustration 14.1). Compare your measurement to the pedal reserve listed in this Chapter's Specifications.

18 If the pedal reserve is less than specified, check the adjustment of

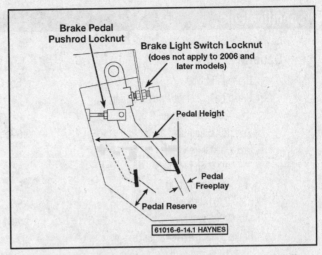

14.1 Brake pedal height, freeplay and reserve travel details

the power brake booster pushrod-to-master cylinder piston clearance. If the brake pedal feels spongy, bleed the brake system (see Section 10).

15 Brake light switch - check and replacement

CHECK

1 The brake light switch is located on a bracket at the top of the brake pedal. The switch activates the brake lights at the rear of the vehicle when the pedal is depressed.

2 To check the brake light switch, simply note whether the brake lights come on when the pedal is depressed and go off when the pedal is released. If they do not function correctly, adjust the switch as described in Section 14 (adjusting the switch is part of brake pedal adjustment).

3 If the lights still do not come on, either the switch is not getting voltage, the switch itself is defective, or the circuit between the switch and the lights is defective. There is always the remote possibility that all of the brake light bulbs are burned out, but this is not very likely.

4 Use a voltmeter or test light to verify that there's voltage present at one side of the switch connector. If no voltage is present, troubleshoot the circuit from the switch to the fuse box. If there is voltage present, check for voltage on the other terminal when the brake pedal is depressed. If no voltage is present, replace the switch. If there is voltage present, troubleshoot the circuit from the switch to the brake lights (see the wiring diagrams at the end of Chapter 12).

REPLACEMENT

▶ **Refer to illustration 15.6**

5 Remove the knee bolster trim panel (see Chapter 11). If you need still more room, remove the knee bolster.

6 Disconnect the electrical connector from the brake light switch (see illustration).

7 On 2005 and earlier models, loosen the brake light switch locknut

(see illustration 14.1) and unscrew the switch from the brake pedal bracket.

8 On 2006 and later models (see illustration 15.6), rotate the switch counterclockwise and pull it out of the brake pedal bracket.

9 Installation is the reverse of removal.

10 Adjust the brake pedal (see Section 14) and, on 2005 and earlier models, the brake light switch (see Section 14). No switch adjustment is necessary on 2006 and later models; when the electrical connector is reconnected to the switch, the clearance between the brake pedal and the switch is automatically adjusted, but only the first time. If you remove the switch, then install it again, the automatic mechanism will not function.

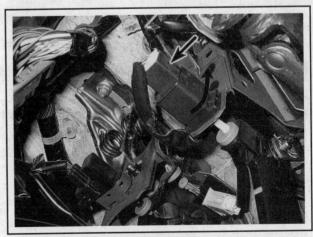

15.6 To disengage the brake light switch from brake pedal bracket on 2006 and later models, turn the switch counterclockwise and pull it out of its mounting hole in the bracket

Specifications

General

Brake fluid type	See Chapter 1
Brake pedal height - pedal-to-carpet	
2005 and earlier	6-3/4 to 7-1/8 inches
2006 and later	6-9/16 inches
Brake pedal freeplay	
1997 and earlier	5/32 to 1/4 inch
1999 and 2000	5/32 to 21/64 inch
2001 through 2005	5/32 to 15/32 inch
2006 and later	5/64 to 3/16 inch
Brake pedal reserve distance	
1999 and earlier	3-3/4 inches
2000 through 2005	3-11/16 inches
2006 and later	4-13/64 inches (minimum)
Brake light switch-to-pedal clearance	See text
Power brake booster pushrod-to-master cylinder piston clearance	
2000 and earlier	
Non-ABS models	0.004 to 0.016 inch
ABS models	Not available
2001 and later (all ABS models)	0.004 to 0.016 inch
ABS sensor-to-toothed wheel clearance	
1995 through 2005 (front and rear)	0.012 to 0.043 inch
2006 and later	
Front	0.012 to 0.057 inch
Rear	0.032 to 0.062 inch

Disc brakes

Minimum brake pad thickness	See Chapter 1
Disc thickness	Refer to the dimension cast into the disc
Disc runout limit (front or rear)	
1993 and earlier	0.004 inch
1994 and later	0.002 inch

Parking brake

Parking brake lever travel	See Chapter 1

Torque specifications   Ft-lbs (unless otherwise indicated)

➡ **Note: One foot-pound (ft-lb) of torque is equivalent to 12 inch-pounds (in-lbs) of torque. Torque values below approximately 15 foot-pounds are expressed in inch-pounds, because most foot-pound torque wrenches are not accurate at these smaller values.**

Brake hose-to-caliper banjo bolts	16 to 22
Front caliper lockbolts (2005 and earlier)	58 to 65
Front caliper bolts (2006 and later)	16 to 23
Front caliper bracket bolts	
2005 and earlier	36 to 51
2006 and later	58 to 75

Torque specifications (continued)   Ft-lbs (unless otherwise indicated)

➡Note: One foot-pound (ft-lb) of torque is equivalent to 12 inch-pounds (in-lbs) of torque. Torque values below approximately 15 foot-pounds are expressed in inch-pounds, because most foot-pound torque wrenches are not accurate at these smaller values.

Rear caliper lockbolt(s)	
1997 and earlier	
Lower	25 to 29
Upper (1994 through 1997 models)	33 to 36
1999 through 2005	25 to 29
2006 and later	15 to 18
Rear caliper bracket bolts	36 to 49
Master cylinder-to-brake booster nuts	
2005 and earlier	87 to 144 in-lbs
2006 and later	120 to 192 in-lbs
Power brake booster mounting nuts	14 to 19
Wheel lug nuts	See Chapter 1

Notes

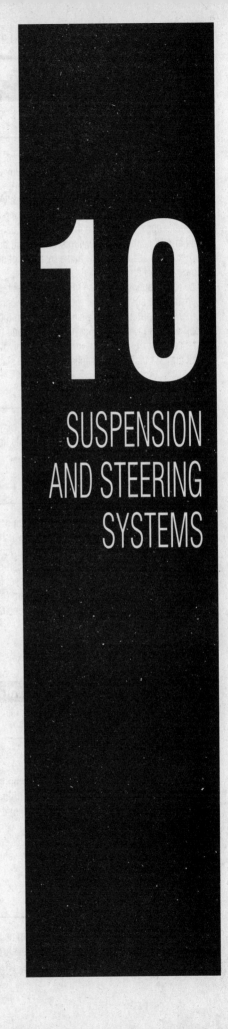

10

SUSPENSION
AND STEERING
SYSTEMS

Section

Reference to other Chapters

1 General information

SUSPENSION

The fully-independent front suspension allows each wheel to compensate for road surface irregularities without any appreciable effect on the other wheel. The suspension at each front wheel consists of a shock absorber/coil spring assembly situated between the upper control arm support and the lower control arm. A steering knuckle is located between the upper and lower arms by a pair of balljoints, one in each control arm. A stabilizer bar controls vehicle roll during cornering. The stabilizer bar is attached to the frame by a pair of steel clamps and to the lower control arms by links.

The rear suspension is also fully independent. Like the front suspension, the suspension at each rear wheel consists of a shock absorber/coil spring assembly situated between the upper control arm support and the lower control arm. A knuckle and hub assembly is located between the upper and lower arms by pivot bolts, one in each control arm. A stabilizer bar similar to the front stabilizer bar is utilized.

STEERING

The steering system consists of a rack-and-pinion type steering gear connected to the steering knuckles by adjustable tie-rods. Power steering is optional.

PRECAUTIONS

Frequently, when working on the suspension or steering system components, you may come across fasteners which seem impossible to loosen. These fasteners on the underside of the vehicle are continually subjected to water, road grime, mud, etc., and can become rusted or frozen, making them extremely difficult to remove. In order to unscrew these stubborn fasteners without damaging them (or other components), be sure to use a generous amount of penetrating oil and allow it to soak in for a while. Using a wire brush to clean exposed threads will also ease removal of the nut or bolt and prevent damage to the threads. Sometimes a sharp blow with a hammer and flat-faced punch (do not use a sharp-pointed or sharp-edged punch) will break the bond between nut and bolt threads, but care must be taken to prevent the punch from slipping off the fastener and ruining the threads. Heating the stuck fastener and surrounding area with a torch sometimes helps too, but this is not recommended because of the obvious dangers associated with heat and flame sources. Long breaker bars and extensions will increase leverage, but never use an extension on a ratchet - the ratcheting mechanism could be damaged. Sometimes tightening the nut or bolt first will help to break it loose. Fasteners that require drastic measures to remove should always be replaced with new ones.

Since most of the procedures dealt with in this Chapter involve jacking up the vehicle and working underneath it, a good pair of jackstands will be needed. A hydraulic floor jack is the preferred type of jack to lift the vehicle, and it can also be used to support certain components during various operations.

✳✳ WARNING:

Never, under any circumstances, rely on a jack to support the vehicle while working on it.

✳✳ WARNING:

Whenever any of the suspension or steering fasteners are loosened or removed they must be inspected and, if necessary, replaced with new ones of the same part number or of original equipment grade, material strength, size, quality and design. Torque specifications must be followed for proper reassembly and component retention. Never attempt to heat or straighten any suspension or steering components. Instead, replace any bent or otherwise damaged part with a new one.

2 Stabilizer bar (front) - removal, inspection and installation

REMOVAL

▶ **Refer to illustrations 2.3a, 2.3b and 2.4**

1 Raise the vehicle and support it securely on jackstands.

2 Remove the under cover from under the front (see Chapter 11).

3 Remove the bracket bolts (see illustrations). Lower the brackets away from the frame.

4 Unbolt the link at each end of the stabilizer bar (see illustration).

5 Take the stabilizer bar out from under the vehicle and remove the rubber bushings.

INSPECTION

6 Check the rubber bushings and link grommets for cracks and tears. Replace all damaged bushings; replace the links if the grommets are damaged.

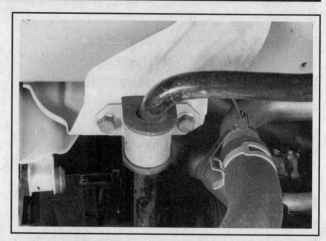

2.3a To detach the front stabilizer bar from the body, unbolt the brackets (2005 and earlier models)

2.3b Front stabilizer bar details; left side shown, right side identical (2006 and later models)

1	Bracket bolts	4	Lower link ballstud nut
2	Bracket	5	Link
3	Upper link ballstud nut	6	Bushing

2.4 Stabilizer bar link fasteners (2005 and earlier models)

INSTALLATION

7   Align the rubber bushings with the marks on the stabilizer, then install the brackets and bolt them to the frame.

8   Install the links.
9   Tighten the bracket bolts and link bolts to the torque listed in this Chapter's Specifications.
10 Install the undercover, then lower the vehicle.

3   Strut bar - removal and installation

1999 THROUGH 2005 MODELS

Removal

1   Remove the nut and through-bolt from each end of the strut bar and remove the strut bar.
2   If the strut bar mounting bolts are difficult to pull out of the bracket, it's because there is too much tension on the strut bar. Loosen the two turnbuckle locknuts, then back off (counterclockwise when viewed from the left side of the engine compartment) the turnbuckle adjustment nut in the center of the strut bar.

❋❋ CAUTION:

Do NOT adjust this turnbuckle unless absolutely necessary. It's already pre-set; if it is loosened, readjustment will be required when the strut bar is installed.

3   If you're replacing the front shock absorbers, remove the nuts that secure the two strut mounting brackets to the top of the shock towers and remove the brackets.

Installation

4   If you removed the strut bar brackets to service the shock absorbers, install the brackets and secure them with the bracket mounting nuts, but don't tighten them yet. Install the strut bar and tighten the strut bar through-bolts/nuts to the torque listed in this Chapter's Specifications, then tighten the strut bar bracket nuts to the torque listed in this Chapter's Specifications.
5   If you loosened the turnbuckle, install the strut bar and secure it to the brackets with the two through-bolts and nuts, but don't fully tighten them yet. Tighten the turnbuckle nut (clockwise when viewed from the side of the engine compartment) until it's snug, tighten the turnbuckle locknuts securely, then tighten the two through-bolts to the torque listed in this Chapter's Specifications.

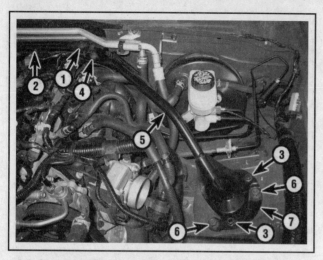

3.6 Strut bar assembly details (left side shown, right side identical)

1	Strut bar center joint mounting nut	5	Left strut bar
2	Strut bar center joint	6	Left strut bar mounting plate nuts
3	Left strut bar mounting nuts	7	Left strut bar mounting plate
4	Left strut bar mounting nut		

2006 AND LATER MODELS

▶ **Refer to illustration 3.6**

6   Remove the nut from each end of the strut bar center joint (see illustration) and remove the center joint.

7   Remove the three left strut bar mounting nuts and remove the left strut bar.

8   Remove the three right strut bar mounting nuts and remove the right strut bar.

9   If you're replacing the front shock absorbers, remove the strut bar mounting plate nuts and remove the strut bar mounting plates.

10   Installation is the reverse of removal. Be sure to tighten all fasteners to the torque listed in this Chapter's Specifications.

4   Shock absorber/coil spring assembly (front) - removal, inspection and installation

2005 AND EARLIER MODELS

Removal

▶ **Refer to illustrations 4.2, 4.4, 4.5a and 4.5b**

1   Loosen the front wheel lug nuts, raise the vehicle, place it securely on safety stands and remove the front wheel.

2   Mark the spring with paint so the assembly can be reinstalled with the correct orientation (see illustration).

3   Loosen the lower control arm pivot bolts so the control arm can drop lower than its normal installed position. Support the control arm so it doesn't strain the brake hose.

4   Remove the shock absorber's lower bolt and nut (see illustration).

5   Working in the engine compartment, remove the shock absorber's upper mounting nuts (see illustration). Pry down on the lower control arm, lower the shock absorber/coil spring assembly free of the fender and take it off the vehicle (see illustration).

Inspection

6   Check the shock absorber body for leaking fluid, dents, cracks and other obvious damage which would warrant replacement.

7   Check the coil spring for chips or cracks in the spring coating (this will cause premature spring failure due to corrosion). Inspect the spring seat for cuts and general deterioration.

4.2 Mark the outside of the spring with paint so the shock/coil spring assembly can be installed in the correct location

4.4 Remove the bolt and nut from the lower end of the shock/coil spring assembly . . .

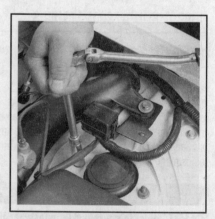

4.5a . . . and the two nuts from the upper end - DO NOT REMOVE THE CENTER NUT UNDER THE CAP!

4.5b Pry the lower control arm downward and remove the shock/coil spring assembly

4.12 To remove the strut mounting plate, remove these three nuts

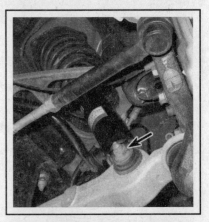

4.13 To disconnect the lower end of the shock absorber from the lower control arm, remove this nut and bolt

8   If any undesirable conditions exist, proceed to the shock absorber disassembly procedure (see Section 5).

➡Note: When disposing of a used damper, return it to your automotive parts store or dealer - they are gas charged and require special disposal procedures.

Installation

9   Installation is the reverse of removal. Be sure to tighten all fasteners to the torque listed in this Chapter's Specifications.

➡Note: Before tightening the fasteners, raise the outer end of the lower control arm to simulate normal ride height.

2006 AND LATER MODELS

Removal

▶ Refer to illustrations 4.12 and 4.13

10   Loosen the front wheel lug nuts, raise the vehicle and place it securely on jackstands. Remove the front wheels.

11   Remove the strut bar (see Section 3).

12   Remove the strut mounting plate nuts and the strut mounting plate (see illustration).

➡Note: The nuts that secure the mounting plate also secure the upper end of the shock absorber to the shock tower.

13   Remove the nut and bolt that secure the lower end of the shock absorber to the lower control arm (see illustration).

14   Disconnect the upper control arm (see Section 6), then remove the upper control arm and shock absorber.

➡Note: The shock absorber cannot be removed unless you remove the upper control arm with it.

Inspection

15   Inspect the shock absorber/coil spring assembly as described in Steps 6 through 8.

Installation

16   Installation is the reverse of removal.

➡Note: Before tightening the fasteners, raise the outer end of the lower control arm to simulate normal ride height.

5   Shock absorber/coil spring - replacement

1   If the shock absorbers or coil springs exhibit the telltale signs of wear (leaking fluid, loss of damping capability, chipped, sagging or cracked coil springs) explore all options before beginning any work. The shock absorbers are not serviceable and must be replaced if a problem develops. However, assemblies complete with springs may be available on an exchange basis, which eliminates much time and work. Whichever repair/replacement method you choose, check on the cost and availability of parts before disassembling your vehicle.

✳✳ WARNING:

Disassembling the shock absorber/coil spring is potentially dangerous and utmost attention must be directed to the job, or serious injury may result. Use only a high-quality spring compressor

and carefully follow the manufacturer's instructions furnished with the tool. After removing the coil spring from the assembly, set it aside in a safe, isolated area.

DISASSEMBLY

▶ Refer to illustration 5.4

2   Remove the shock absorber/coil spring assembly following the procedure described in the previous Section. Mount the assembly in a vise. Line the vise jaws with wood or rags to prevent damage to the unit and do not tighten the vise excessively.

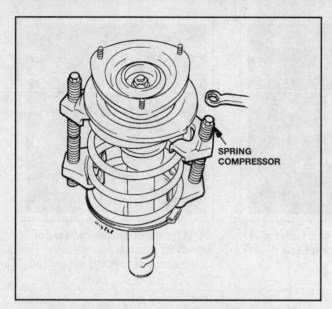

5.4 Install the spring compressor according to the tool manufacturer's instructions and compress the spring until all pressure is relieved from the upper spring seat

3   Pry the cap from the top center of the shock/coil spring assembly. Loosen the damper shaft nut that's beneath the cap, but DO NOT remove it yet!

4   Following the tool manufacturer's instructions, install the spring compressor (which can be obtained at most auto parts stores or equipment yards on a daily rental basis) on the spring and compress it sufficiently to relieve all pressure from the upper spring seat (see illustration). This can be verified by wiggling the spring.

5   Remove the damper shaft nut. It may be necessary to hold the shaft from turning while loosening the nut.

6   Remove the nut and washer. Mark the outer side of the spacer plate and mounting plate so they can be reinstalled in the same orientation to the spring. Remove the spacer plate and mounting plate. Check the mounting plate for cracking and general deterioration. If there is any doubt about its condition, replace it.

7   Lift the rebound stopper (the accordion-like rubber piece) from the damper shaft. Check the rubber for cracking and hardness, replacing it if necessary.

8   Carefully lift the compressed spring from the assembly and set it in a safe place.

✳✳ WARNING:

Keep the ends of the spring pointed away from your body.

REASSEMBLY

9   Place the coil spring onto the lower insulator, with the end of the spring resting in the step (lowest part of the insulator) (see illustration 4.2).

10 Extend the damper rod to its full length and install the rebound stopper.

11 Install the mounting plate and spacer plate so their paint marks will face outward when the shock/coil spring assembly is installed (see illustration 4.2).

12 Install the damper shaft nut and partially tighten it.

13 Remove the spring compressor tool.

14 Tighten the damper shaft nut to the torque listed in this Chapter's Specifications.

15 Install the shock/coil spring assembly following the procedure outlined previously (see Section 4).

6   Upper and lower control arms (front) - removal and installation

2005 AND EARLIER MODELS

Upper control arm

Removal

▶ **Refer to illustrations 6.4a, 6.4b and 6.5**

1   Loosen the front wheel lug nuts, raise the vehicle, place it securely on jackstands and remove the front wheel. If you're working on a model equipped with ABS, detach the retaining band that secures the wheel speed sensor harness.

2   Remove the under cover from the front of the vehicle (see Chapter 11).

3   Remove the shock absorber lower mounting bolt (see Section 4). Support the lower control arm from below.

4   Remove the cotter pin and nut from the upper balljoint, then separate the balljoint from the upper control arm with small puller (see illustrations).

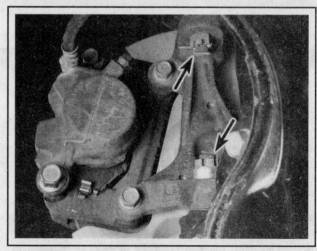

6.4a The upper and lower balljoint stud nuts are secured by cotter pins (arrows)

6.4b Remove the cotter pin and partially loosen the nut, then use a small puller to separate the balljoint stud from the knuckle

6.5 Hold the bolt head (right arrow) with a wrench and remove the nut (left arrow)

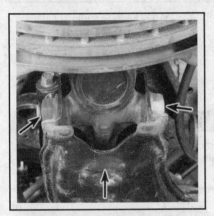

6.14 Remove the pivot bolt and nut (upper arrows) from the outer end of the control arm - also remove the balljoint bolt (lower arrow); it's accessible from the top of the control arm

6.15a Mark the position of the adjusting cams (arrows) . . .

6.15b . . . then remove the pivot bolts and nuts from the inner end of the control arm

5   Hold the pivot bolt with a wrench and loosen the nut (one long bolt passes through the front and rear pivot points of the upper control arm) (see illustration). Remove the nut and take the upper control arm off the vehicle.

Inspection

6   Inspect the front and rear bushings in the lower control arm. If either bushing is torn or cracked, take the control arm to an automotive machine shop and have the old bushings pressed out and new ones pressed in.

7   Check the balljoint dust boot for cracks or deterioration. If there are any problems, carefully tap the dust boot off of the control arm with a hammer and chisel. Be sure not to hit the balljoint stud with the chisel.

8   Pack the inside of a new dust boot with grease, then press the dust boot onto the balljoint stud with a 1-1/8 inch socket. Leave a small gap (no more than 3/64 inch) between the dust boot and the control arm. Don't push the dust boot on too far or the retaining ring will be damaged.

Installation

9   Installation is the reverse of the removal procedure. Tighten the balljoint nut to the torque listed in this Chapter's Specifications, then install a new cotter pin. Before tightening the remaining fasteners to the torque values listed in this Chapter's Specifications, raise the outer end of the lower control arm with a floor jack to simulate normal ride height.

10 Have the wheel alignment checked and, if necessary, adjusted.

Lower control arm

▶ Refer to illustrations 6.14, 6.15a and 6.15b

11 Loosen the front wheel lug nuts, raise the vehicle, place it securely on jackstands and remove the front wheel.

12 Disconnect the stabilizer bar link bolt from the lower control arm (see illustration 2.4).

13 Remove the shock absorber lower bolt (see Section 5).

14 Remove the balljoint through-bolt and the upper bolt that secure it to the lower control arm (see illustration).

15 Remove the inner pivot bolts that secure the lower control arm to the frame (see illustrations). Lower the inner end of the arm away from the frame, pull it away from the balljoint and remove it from under the vehicle.

16 Inspect the front and rear bushings in the lower control arm. If either bushing is torn or cracked, take the control arm to an automotive

6.21 Upper control arm details

1   Brake hose bracket bolt
2   Upper control arm pivot bolts/nuts

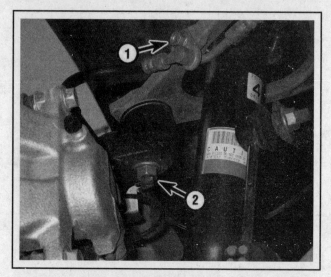

6.22 Upper control arm-to-steering knuckle balljoint details

1   Brake hose brake bolt
2   Upper control arm balljoint stud nut

machine shop and have the old bushings pressed out and new ones pressed in.

17 Installation is the reverse of the removal procedure. Tighten the balljoint bolts to the torque listed in this Chapter's Specifications while the vehicle is still raised. Before tightening the remaining fasteners to the torque values listed in this Chapter's Specifications, raise the outer end of the lower control arm with a floor jack to simulate normal ride height.

18 Have the wheel alignment checked and, if necessary, adjusted.

2006 AND LATER MODELS

19 Loosen the wheel lug nuts, raise the vehicle and place it securely on jackstands. Remove the front wheels.

20 Detach the ABS wheel speed sensor from the steering knuckle, set it aside and suspend it safely out of the way.

✳✳ CAUTION:

Failure to detach the ABS wheel speed sensor could result in damage to the ABS sensor harness during either of the following procedures, which could cause the ABS system to malfunction.

Upper control arm

▶ Refer to illustrations 6.21 and 6.22

21 Unbolt the brake hose bracket from the upper control arm (see illustration).

22 Disconnect the upper control arm balljoint from the steering knuckle (see illustration).

✳✳ CAUTION:

Make sure that you detach the brake hose from the upper control arm before you separate the upper arm balljoint from the steering knuckle.

23 Remove the upper control arm pivot bolts/nuts (see illustration 6.21).

24 Disconnect the shock absorber (see Section 4), then remove the upper control arm and shock absorber.

➡**Note: The upper control arm cannot be removed unless you remove the shock absorber with it.**

25 Installation is the reverse of removal. Be sure to tighten all fasteners to the torque listed in this Chapter's Specifications.

Lower control arm

▶ Refer to illustrations 6.28a and 6.28b

26 Unbolt the front brake caliper mounting bracket (see Chapter 9). Remove the caliper and bracket as a single assembly from the steering knuckle and suspend the caliper safely out of the way.

27 Remove the steering knuckle (see Section 9).

28 Mark the position of the caster adjusting cam (see illustration), then loosen the lower control arm rear pivot bolt/nut (see illustration).

29 Mark the position of the camber adjusting cam, then remove the lower control arm front pivot bolt/nut and remove the lower control arm.

30 Installation is the reverse of removal. Be sure to tighten all fasteners to the torque listed in this Chapter's Specifications.

➡**Note: Before tightening any fastener that runs through a rubber bushing, raise the outer end of the lower control arm with a floor jack to simulate normal ride height.**

Have the wheel alignment checked and, if necessary, adjusted.

6.28a Before loosening the lower control arm mounting fasteners, mark the positions of the caster and camber adjusting cams

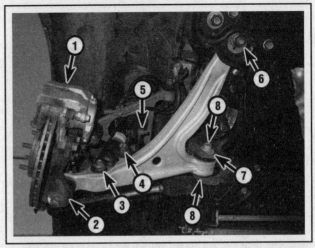

6.28b Lower control arm removal and installation details (rear view)

1 Front brake caliper
2 Steering knuckle
3 Shock absorber-to-lower arm bolt/nut
4 Stabilizer bar link lower bolt/nut
5 Stabilizer bar link upper bolt/nut
6 Lower control arm rear mounting bolt/nut and caster adjusting cam
7 Camber adjusting cam
8 Lower control arm front pivot bolt/nut

7 Balljoints - replacement

2005 AND EARLIER MODELS

Upper balljoints

1 The upper balljoint boot can be replaced separately, but the balljoint itself is replaced as a single unit with the upper control arm. Refer to Section 6 for upper control arm procedures.

Lower balljoints

▶ Refer to illustrations 7.3a, 7.3b, 7.4 and 7.5

2 Loosen the wheel lug nuts, raise the vehicle and support it securely on jackstands. Remove the wheel.

3 Support the lower control arm with a jack. Remove the cotter pin from the balljoint stud nut (see illustration). Loosen the nut, but don't remove it from the stud (see illustration).

7.3a Pull the cotter pin out of the stud nut . . .

7.3b . . . partially loosen the nut . . .

7.4 . . . and use a small puller to separate the stud from the knuckle, then remove the nut and lift the knuckle up and off the balljoint stud

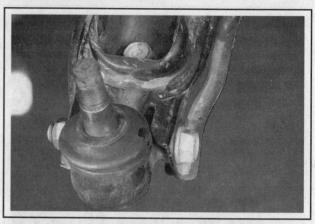

7.5 Remove the balljoint through-bolt and upper bolt to detach the balljoint from the lower control arm

4   Separate the balljoint from the steering knuckle with a small puller and lift the steering knuckle off the balljoint stud (see illustration 6.4b and the accompanying illustration).

5   Remove the balljoint mounting bolts and nut (see illustration).

6   To install the balljoint, insert the balljoint threaded stud through the hole in the lower control arm and install the nut, but don't tighten the nut yet.

7   Install the balljoint mounting bolts and nut. Tighten the balljoint bolts and nut to the torque listed in this Chapter's Specifications.

8   Place the steering knuckle onto the balljoint stud and tighten the balljoint stud nut to the torque listed in this Chapter's Specifications, then secure it with a new cotter pin.

9   Install the wheel and lug nuts. Lower the vehicle and tighten the lug nuts to the torque listed in the Chapter 1 Specifications.

2006 AND LATER MODELS

10 The balljoints on the upper and lower control arms cannot be serviced separately from the control arms. You can purchase new dust boots, but if a balljoint must be replaced, you must replace the control arm.

11 The balljoints can be detached from the steering knuckle using the same methods described earlier in this Section.

8   Hub and bearing assembly (front) - removal and installation

✳✳ WARNING:

Dust created by the brake system is harmful to your health. Never blow it out with compressed air and do not inhale any of it. Do not, under any circumstances, use petroleum-based solvents to clean brake parts. Use brake system cleaner only.

➡Note: The front wheel bearings are part of the hub and bearing assembly and are not serviced separately.

REMOVAL

♦ Refer to illustrations 8.3, 8.4, 8.5, 8.6 and 8.7

1   Loosen the wheel lug nuts, raise the vehicle and support it securely on jackstands. Remove the wheel.

2   Remove the brake caliper, caliper bracket and brake disc (see Chapter 9).

3   Place a dial indicator against the hub (see illustration). Push the hub all the way in and set the indicator to zero. Pull the hub out as far as it will go and note the reading (hub endplay). If it exceeds 0.002 inch, undo the locknut as described in Steps 4 and 5 and try retightening it to the torque listed in this Chapter's Specifications. If this doesn't bring endplay within the specified range, you'll need to replace the entire hub.

✳✳ WARNING:

If retightening the locknut does correct excessive end- play, don't reuse the locknut - remove it and install a new one.

4   Remove the grease cap from the hub (see illustration).

5   Bend back the staked portion of the locknut with a hammer and punch, then undo the locknut (see illustration).

➡Note: If you're planning to try retightening the locknut to correct excessive endplay, grind away all of the staked portion after the nut is removed. Otherwise you won't be able to torque it accurately.

6   Pull the hub and bearing assembly off the spindle (see illustration). If it doesn't come off easily, use a puller.

7   If necessary, unbolt the brake disc shield and take it off the knuckle (see illustration).

INSPECTION

♦ Refer to illustrations 8.8a and 8.8b

8   Check the bearings inside the hub (see illustrations). Spin them with your fingers and check for roughness, looseness or noise. If these problems are found, or if grease has been leaking from the bearings, replace the hub and bearing assembly.

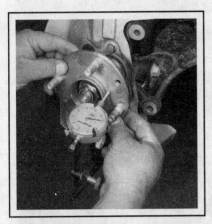

8.3 Check endplay of the hub and bearing assembly with a dial indicator

8.4 Tap the bearing cap free with a hammer and chisel

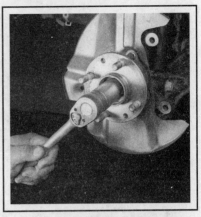

8.5 To remove the hub and bearing assembly, remove the center hub locknut

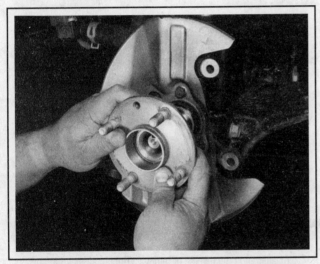

8.6 Remove the hub and bearing assembly from the spindle

8.7 The brake disc shield is secured by bolts

8.8a Check the spindle outer bearing . . .

8.8b . . . and inner bearing for roughness, looseness, noise and leaking grease

8.10a Tighten a new locknut to the specified torque . . .

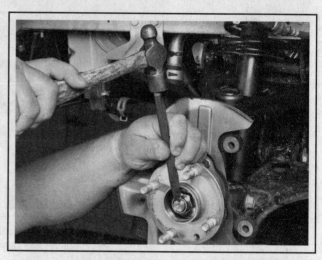

8.10b . . . then stake (punch) the locknut lip down into the spindle groove, to prevent the locknut from loosening

9   Check the wheel studs and the ABS sensor ring (if equipped) for damage. These can be pressed off and new ones pressed on by an automotive machine shop.

INSTALLATION

▶ **Refer to illustrations 8.10a and 8.10b**

10 Installation is the reverse of removal. Be sure to clean off the

spindle and lubricate it with wheel bearing grease. Install a new locknut, tighten it to the torque listed in this Chapter's Specifications, then stake the locknut with a hammer and punch (see illustrations).

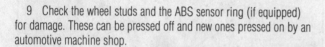

9   Steering knuckle - removal and installation

1   Loosen the wheel lug nuts, raise the vehicle and support it securely on jackstands. Remove the wheel.
2   Remove the brake caliper, bracket and disc (see Chapter 9).
3   Remove the hub and bearing assembly (see Section 8).
4   If the vehicle is equipped with ABS, remove the bolt and detach the ABS wheel speed sensor from the knuckle.
5   Detach the tie-rod from the knuckle (see Section 17).
6   Detach the balljoints from the knuckle, then remove the steering knuckle from the vehicle.

7   Installation is the reverse of removal. Tighten all steering and suspension fasteners to the torque listed in this Chapter's Specifications.

➡**Note: Before tightening any fastener that runs through a rubber bushing, raise the outer end of the lower control arm with a floor jack to simulate normal ride height.**

Use new cotter pins on the balljoint nuts. Tighten the wheel lug nuts to the torque listed in the Chapter 1 Specifications.

10 Shock absorber/coil spring assembly (rear) - removal, inspection and installation

2005 AND EARLIER MODELS

Removal

▶ **Refer to illustrations 10.4 and 10.5**

1   Loosen the rear wheel lug nuts. Raise the rear of the vehicle and place it securely on jackstands. Remove the rear wheels.
2   If you're working on the left side of the vehicle, remove the pro-

tector shield for the fuel tank filler pipe.
3   Support the lower control arm from below. Remove the lower link from the stabilizer link so the lower control arm can drop below its normal position (see Section 11).

✳✳ **CAUTION:**

Don't let the lower arm pull on the brake hose when it drops.

10.4 Hold the shock/coil spring assembly's lower bolt (arrow) with a socket, undo the nut and pull out the bolt

10.5 Remove the two nuts at the top - DO NOT REMOVE THE CENTER NUT!

10.13 Rear shock absorber details

1   Lower shock absorber bolt
2   Upper shock absorber bolt

4   Remove the shock absorber's lower bolt and nut (see illustration).

5   Working in the trunk, remove the upper mounting nuts (see illustration). Lower the shock absorber/coil spring assembly free of the fender and remove it from under the vehicle.

Inspection

6   Inspection and replacement of the damper unit or coil spring are the same as for front shock absorber/coil spring assemblies (see Section 5).

Installation

7   Installation is the reverse of removal. Tighten the fasteners to the torque listed in this Chapter's Specifications.

➥Note: Before tightening any fastener that runs through a rubber bushing, raise the rear knuckle with a floor jack to simulate normal ride height.

2006 AND LATER MODELS

Removal

▶ Refer to illustrations 10.13, 10.15 and 10.16

8   Loosen the rear wheel lug nuts. Raise the vehicle and place it securely on jackstands. Remove the rear wheels.

9   Remove the clip that secures the parking brake cable to the bracket at the rear brake caliper, disconnect the cable from the rear caliper and set the cable aside (see Chapter 9).

10   Remove the rear brake caliper assembly and suspend it safely out of the way with wire (see Chapter 9).

11   Disconnect the inner end of the rear upper lateral link (see Section 13).

12   Remove the nut from the upper end of the rear stabilizer link (see Section 11).

13   Remove the shock absorber lower bolt (see illustration).

14   Inside the trunk, remove the carpeting (see Chapter 11).

15   To remove the left shock absorber, remove the metal shield in the trunk that protects the fuel filler neck (see illustration).

16   Remove the upper shock absorber mounting nuts (see illustration).

10.15 To remove the fuel filler neck shield, remove these bolts

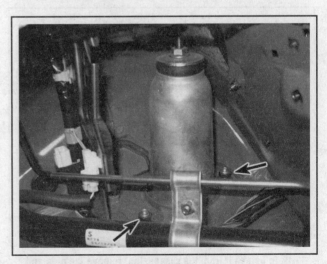

10.16 Upper shock absorber mounting nuts

17 Remove the shock absorber retaining bolt from the underside of the wheel well (see illustration 10.13) and remove the shock absorber.

Inspection

18 Inspection and replacement of the damper unit or coil spring are the same as for front shock absorber/coil spring assemblies (see Section 5).

Installation

19 Installation is the reverse of removal. Tighten the fasteners to the torque listed in this Chapter's Specifications.

→Note: **Before tightening any fastener that runs through a rubber bushing, raise the rear knuckle with a floor jack to simulate normal ride height.**

11 Stabilizer bar (rear) - removal and installation

2005 AND EARLIER MODELS

♦ **Refer to illustrations 11.2 and 11.3**

1 Loosen the rear wheel lug nuts. Raise the rear of the vehicle and place it securely on jackstands. Remove the rear wheels.

2 Unbolt the stabilizer bar from the upper ends of the links (see illustration).

3 Unbolt the stabilizer bar bushing clamps from the body (see illustration). The stabilizer bar can now be removed from the vehicle. Pull the bushings off the stabilizer bar using a rocking motion.

4 Unbolt the lower ends of the stabilizer link on each side of the vehicle and remove the links.

5 Check the bushings for wear, hardness, distortion, cracking and other signs of deterioration, replacing them if necessary. Also check the stabilizer bar link bushings for the same conditions, and replace if necessary.

6 Using a wire brush, clean the areas of the bar where the bushings ride. Installation is the reverse of the removal procedure. Apply rubber lubricant to the bushings prior to installation.

✳✳ CAUTION:

Do not use petroleum-based products or brake fluid, as these will damage the rubber.

7 Install the bushings at the stabilizer bar brackets with the bushing flat bottom/split facing the crossmember, and with the bushing located on the stabilizer bar at the installation position line painted on the stabilizer bar. On the left side of the vehicle, center the inner edge of the bushing in the light-colored paint mark between the two dark paint marks. On the right side, position the inner end of the bushing just inside the dark paint mark.

8 Install and tighten the stabilizer bar bracket bolts and link bolts to the torque listed in this Chapter's Specifications.

9 Install the wheel and lug nuts, then lower the vehicle. Tighten the wheel lug nuts to the torque listed in the Chapter 1 Specifications.

2006 AND LATER MODELS

♦ **Refer to illustration 11.12**

10 Loosen the rear wheel lugs nuts. Raise the vehicle and place it securely on jackstands. Remove the rear wheels.

11 Detach the ABS wheel speed sensor from the rear knuckle, set it aside and suspend it safely out of the way.

✳✳ CAUTION:

Failure to detach the ABS wheel speed sensor could result in damage to the ABS sensor harness during the following procedure, which could cause the ABS system to malfunction.

11.2 To detach it from the suspension, remove the nuts and bolts from the links (arrows)

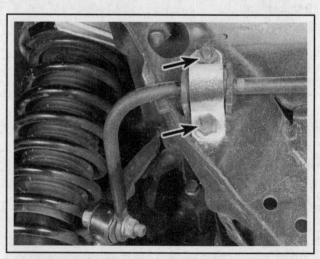

11.3 To detach the rear stabilizer bar from the body, unbolt the brackets

12 Remove the stabilizer bar bracket bolts (see illustration) and remove the brackets.

13 Remove the link rod nuts and remove the stabilizer bar.

14 Inspect the condition of the stabilizer bar bracket bushings. If they're cracked, torn or deteriorated, replace them.

15 Installation is the reverse of removal. Tighten the fasteners to the torque listed in this Chapter's Specifications.

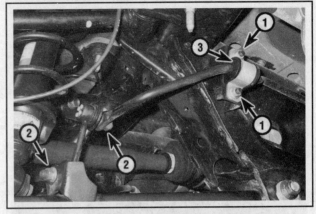

11.12 Rear stabilizer bar details; left end shown, right end identical

1 *Stabilizer bar bracket bolts*
2 *Stabilizer bar link nuts*
3 *Stabilizer bar bracket bushing*

12 Upper and lower control arms (rear) - removal, inspection and installation

➥Note: This Section applies to 2005 and earlier models only.

LOWER CONTROL ARM

Removal

▶ Refer to illustrations 12.4, 12.5a and 12.5b

1 Loosen the rear wheel lug nuts, raise the rear of the vehicle and support it securely on jackstands. Remove the wheel.

2 Support the lower arm with a floor jack.

3 Unbolt the lower end of the shock absorber/coil spring assembly and the stabilizer bar link from the control arm (see Sections 10 and 11).

4 Clean the area around the wheel alignment adjusting cam bolts, located at the inner pivot points of the control arm (see illustration). Mark the positions of the adjusting cams so you can return rear wheel alignment to near its correct setting on installation.

5 Remove the outer pivot bolt from the control arm (see illustration). Remove the inner pivot bolts (see illustration), then take the control arm off the vehicle.

12.4 Mark the position of the cam plate on each lower control arm pivot bolt

12.5a Remove the outer bolt . . .

12.5b . . . and the inner bolts; the bolt heads face each other on installation

12.13 Remove one outer bolt and nut and two inner bolts and nuts to free the rear upper control arm

Inspection

6   Follow the inspection procedures described in Section 6. The bushings at inner and outer ends of the control arms can be pressed out and new ones pressed in.

Installation

7   Install the control arm inner pivot bolts. Line up the cam plates in the positions marked on removal.

8   Install the control arm inner and outer pivot bolts, but don't tighten them completely yet. Install the stabilizer bar link bolt and shock absorber lower bolt, but don't tighten them completely yet.

9   Raise the rear knuckle with a floor jack to simulate normal ride height, then tighten the suspension fasteners to the torques listed in this Chapter's Specifications. Install the wheel and lug nuts, then lower the vehicle. Tighten the wheel lug nuts to the torque listed in the Chapter 1 Specifications.

10   Have rear wheel alignment checked and, if necessary, adjusted.

UPPER CONTROL ARM

▶ **Refer to illustration 12.13**

11   Loosen the wheel lug nuts, raise the vehicle and support it securely on jackstands. Remove the wheel.

12   Support the lower control arm with a floor jack.

13   Remove the pivot bolt at the outer end of the upper control arm and the two pivot bolts at the inner end (see illustration). Take the control arm off the vehicle.

14   Install the control arm inner and outer pivot bolts. Raise the lower control arm with a floor jack to simulate normal ride height, then tighten the fasteners to the torque values listed in this Chapter's Specifications.

15   Install the wheel and lug nuts, then lower the vehicle. Tighten the wheel lug nuts to the torque listed in the Chapter 1 Specifications.

16   Have the rear wheel alignment checked and, if necessary, adjusted.

13 Rear multi-link suspension components - removal and installation

➡ **Note: This Section applies to 2006 and later models only.**

1   Loosen the rear wheel lug nuts. Raise the vehicle and place it securely on jackstands. Remove the rear wheel.

2   Detach the ABS wheel speed sensor and harness clip from the rear knuckle, then set the ABS sensor and harness aside and suspend it safely out of the way.

✳✳ CAUTION:

Failure to detach and set aside the ABS wheel speed sensor could result in damage to the ABS sensor harness during any of the following procedures; damage to the harness could cause the ABS system to malfunction.

TOE CONTROL LINK

▶ **Refer to illustration 13.3**

3   Loosen, but don't remove, the nut from the toe control link balljoint stud (see illustration), install a balljoint tool, and push the balljoint stud out of the rear knuckle. Remove the nut and separate the balljoint stud from the knuckle.

4   Mark the position of the toe control link cam (see illustration 13.3).

Remove the toe control link pivot bolt and remove the link.

5   If the balljoint or the bushing on the toe control link is damaged, replace the toe control link. Neither the balljoint nor the bushing is available separately. The only part available separately is a new balljoint dust boot.

6   Installation is the reverse of removal. Be sure to tighten all fasteners to the torque listed in this Chapter's Specifications.

➡ **Note: Before tightening any fastener that runs through a rubber bushing, raise the rear knuckle with a floor jack to simulate normal ride height.**

7   Have the rear wheel alignment checked and, if necessary, adjusted.

LOWER TRAILING LINK

8   Remove the lower trailing link-to-rear knuckle bolt (see illustration 13.3).

9   Remove the lower trailing link pivot bolt (see illustration 13.3) and remove the lower trailing link.

10   Installation is the reverse of removal. Tighten the fasteners to the torque listed in this Chapter's Specifications.

➡ **Note: Before tightening any fastener that runs through a rubber bushing, raise the rear knuckle with a floor jack to simulate normal ride height.**

13.3 Rear multi-link suspension details (front view)

1. *Toe control link balljoint stud pinch bolt/nut*
2. *Toe control link balljoint*
3. *Mark the position of the toe control link pivot bolt cam*
4. *Toe control link pivot bolt*
5. *Lower trailing link-to-rear knuckle bolt*
6. *Lower trailing link pivot bolt*
7. *Lower lateral link balljoint*
8. *Mark the position of the lower lateral pivot bolt cam*
9. *Lower lateral link pivot bolt*

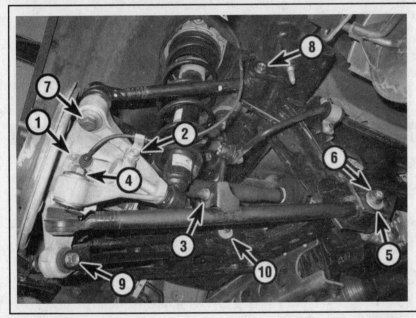

13.11 Rear multi-link suspension details (rear view)

1. *Rear-wheel ABS speed sensor retaining bolt*
2. *ABS harness clip bolt*
3. *Rear stabilizer bar link nut*
4. *Lower lateral link balljoint stud nut*
5. *Mark the position of the lower lateral link pivot bolt cam*
6. *Lower lateral link pivot bolt/nut*
7. *Upper lateral link balljoint stud nut*
8. *Upper lateral link pivot bolt*
9. *Lower trailing link-to-rear knuckle bolt*
10. *Mark the position of the toe control link pivot bolt cam*

LOWER LATERAL LINK

▸ **Refer to illustration 13.11**

11 Disconnect the stabilizer bar link rod from the lower lateral link (see illustration).

12 Loosen, but don't remove, the nut (see illustration 13.11) from the lower lateral link balljoint stud, install a balljoint tool, and push the balljoint stud out of the rear knuckle. Remove the nut and separate the balljoint stud from the knuckle.

13 Mark the position of the lower lateral link cam. Remove the lower lateral link pivot bolt and remove the lower lateral link.

14 If the balljoint or the bushing on the lower lateral link is damaged, replace the lower lateral link. Neither the balljoint nor the bushing is available separately. The only part available separately is a new balljoint dust boot.

15 Installation is the reverse of removal. Be sure to tighten all fasteners to the torque listed in this Chapter's Specifications.

➥**Note: Before tightening any fastener that runs through a rubber bushing, raise the rear knuckle with a floor jack to simulate normal ride height.**

16 Have the rear wheel alignment checked and, if necessary, adjusted.

UPPER LATERAL LINK

17 Loosen, but don't remove, the nut (see illustration 13.11) from the upper lateral link balljoint stud, install a balljoint tool, and push the balljoint stud out of the rear knuckle. Remove the nut and separate the balljoint stud from the knuckle.

18 Remove the upper lateral link pivot bolt and nut (see illustration 13.11) and remove the upper lateral link.

19 If the balljoint or the bushing on the upper lateral link is damaged, replace the lower lateral link. Neither the balljoint nor the bushing is available separately. The only part available separately is a new balljoint dust boot.

20 Installation is the reverse of removal. Be sure to tighten all fasteners to the torque listed in this Chapter's Specifications.

➡**Note: Before tightening any fastener that runs through a rubber bushing, raise the rear knuckle with a floor jack to simulate normal ride height.**

UPPER TRAILING LINK

♦ **Refer to illustration 13.21**

21 Loosen, but don't remove, the nut from the upper trailing link balljoint stud (see illustration), install a balljoint tool, and push the balljoint stud out of the rear knuckle. Remove the nut and separate the balljoint stud from the knuckle.

22 Remove the upper trailing link pivot bolt (see illustration 13.21) and remove the upper trailing link.

23 If the balljoint or the bushing on the upper trailing link is damaged, replace the upper trailing link. Neither the balljoint nor the bushing is available separately. The only part available separately is a new balljoint dust boot.

24 Installation is the reverse of removal. Be sure to tighten all fasten-

13.21 Upper trailing link details

1   Upper trailing link balljoint stud nut
2   Upper trailing link pivot bolt

ers to the torque listed in this Chapter's Specifications.

➡**Note: Before tightening any fastener that runs through a rubber bushing, raise the rear knuckle with a floor jack to simulate normal ride height.**

14 Rear knuckle and hub assembly - removal and installation

1   Loosen the wheel lug nuts, raise the vehicle and support it securely on jackstands. Remove the wheel.

2   Remove the brake caliper, bracket and disc (see Chapter 9). Remove and set aside the ABS sensor, if equipped.

3   Remove the driveaxle/hub nut and break the driveaxle free from the hub splines (see Chapter 8).

2005 AND EARLIER MODELS

4   Support the lower control arm with a floor jack. Remove the outer pivot bolts from the upper and lower control arms to separate the knuckle from the vehicle (see Sections 12 and 13). Support the driveaxle so as not to damage the driveaxle boot.

5   Installation is the reverse of removal. Tighten the fasteners to the torque listed in this Chapter's Specifications.

➡**Note: Before tightening any fastener that runs through a rubber bushing, raise the rear knuckle with a floor jack to simulate normal ride height.**

Tighten the driveaxle hub nut to the torque listed in Chapter 8 Specifi-

cations. Install the wheel and lug nuts. Lower the vehicle and tighten the lug nuts to the torque listed in the Chapter 1 Specifications.

2006 AND LATER MODELS

6   Disconnect the ABS speed sensor and harness (see illustration 13.11) and set them safely aside.

7   Unbolt the lower end of the shock absorber from the knuckle.

8   Disconnect the toe-control link, the upper and lower trailing links and the upper and lower lateral links from the rear knuckle (see Section 13).

9   Pull the rear knuckle and hub assembly off the driveaxle. Support the driveaxle assembly to protect the outer CV joint boot while the knuckle is disconnected and removed from the multi-link suspension.

10 Installation is the reverse of removal. Be sure to tighten all fasteners to the torque listed in this Chapter's Specifications.

➡**Note: Before tightening any fastener that runs through a rubber bushing, raise the rear knuckle with a floor jack to simulate normal ride height.**

15 Rear hub and bearing assembly - removal and installation

Due to the special tools and expertise required to press the hub and bearing from the rear knuckle, this job should be left to a professional mechanic. However, the knuckle and hub can be removed and the

assembly taken to a dealer service department or other repair shop. See Section 14 for the rear knuckle and hub removal procedure.

16 Steering wheel - removal and installation

✳✳ WARNING:

All models are equipped with airbags. The airbag is armed and can deploy (inflate) whenever the battery is connected. To prevent accidental deployment (and possible injury), turn the ignition key to LOCK and disconnect the negative battery cable whenever working near airbag components. After the battery is disconnected, wait at least two minutes before beginning work (the system has a back-up capacitor that must fully discharge). For more information see Chapter 12.

REMOVAL

▶ **Refer to illustrations 16.4a, 16.4b and 16.5**

1   Turn the ignition key OFF, then disconnect the cable from the negative terminal of the battery (see Chapter 5). Wait at least two minutes before proceeding. Disconnect the electrical connector for the airbag wiring harness below the dash (see Chapter 12).

2   Turn the steering wheel so the wheels are pointing straight ahead, turn the ignition key to the Lock position and remove the key.

✳✳ WARNING:

Follow the airbag servicing instructions prior to proceeding with any steps that may involve the airbag system:

DO NOT disassemble any airbag component.
DO NOT attempt repair of the airbag system wiring harness.
DO NOT inspect or check the airbag system using an ohmmeter, because this can cause inadvertent deployment of the airbag.
DO NOT disconnect the airbag module with the ignition switch ON - this could cause inadvertent airbag deployment.
DO NOT handle or carry the airbag with the trim cover facing you.

When handling the airbag, DO NOT set the airbag module down with the trim cover facing down.
Contact a dealer for proper disposal of a used airbag.

3   Remove the airbag attaching screws and detach the airbag module from the steering wheel. Disconnect the module electrical connectors (see Chapter 12).

✳✳ WARNING:

Set the airbag module down with the trim side facing up.

4   Remove the steering wheel locknut (see illustration), then mark the relationship of the steering shaft to the hub (if marks do not already exist or do not line up) to simplify reinstallation and ensure steering wheel alignment (see illustration).

5   Pull the steering wheel off the shaft. Rock the steering wheel from side to side as you pull (see illustration). If the steering wheel is stuck, use a steering wheel puller to disconnect the steering wheel from the shaft.

INSTALLATION

6   Make sure that the front wheels are facing straight ahead.

7   To install the wheel, align the mark on the steering wheel hub with the mark on the shaft and slip the wheel onto the shaft. Install the nut and tighten it to the torque listed in this Chapter's Specifications.

8   Plug in the electrical connector for the airbag module and flip down the locking tab.

9   Make sure the airbag module electrical connector is positioned correctly and that the wires do not interfere with anything, then install the airbag module and tighten the retaining screws to the torque listed in this Chapter's Specifications.

10 Connect the negative battery cable. Reconnect the electrical connector for the airbag wiring harness under the dash.

16.4a Remove the steering wheel nut

16.4b Make alignment marks on the steering wheel and column

16.5 Rock the wheel back and forth to free it - use a steering wheel puller if it's stuck

17 Tie-rod ends - removal and installation

REMOVAL

▶ **Refer to illustrations 17.2 and 17.4**

1   Loosen the wheel lug nuts. Raise the front of the vehicle, support it securely on jackstands, block the rear wheels and set the parking brake. Remove the front wheel.

2   Remove the cotter pin (see illustration) and loosen the nut on the tie-rod end stud.

3   Hold the tie rod with a pair of locking pliers or wrench and loosen the jam nut enough to mark the position of the tie-rod end in relation to the threads (see illustration 17.2).

4   Disconnect the tie rod from the steering knuckle arm with a puller (see illustration).

5   Unscrew the tie-rod end from the tie-rod.

INSTALLATION

6   Thread the tie-rod end to the marked position on the tie-rod and insert the tie-rod stud into the steering knuckle arm. Tighten the jam nut securely.

7   Install the castle nut on the stud and tighten it to the torque listed in this Chapter's Specifications. Install a new cotter pin. If the hole for the cotter pin does not line up with one of the slots in the nut, tighten the nut an additional amount until it slides through easily; DO NOT loosen the nut.

8   Install the wheel and lug nuts. Lower the vehicle and tighten the lug nuts to the torque listed in the Chapter 1 Specifications.

9   Have the alignment checked by a dealer service department or an alignment shop.

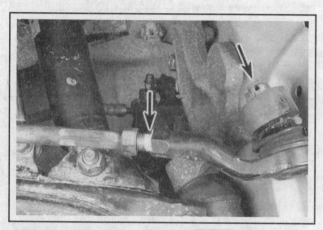

17.2 Remove the cotter pin from the castle nut (right arrow) and loosen - but don't remove - the nut; loosen the jam nut, then mark the position of the tie-rod end in relation to the threads (left arrow)

17.4 Disconnect the tie-rod end from the steering knuckle arm with a puller

18 Steering gear boots - replacement

▶ **Refer to illustration 18.3**

1   Loosen the lug nuts, raise the vehicle and support it securely on jackstands. Remove the wheel.

2   Remove the tie-rod end and jam nut (see Section 16).

3   Remove the steering gear boot clamps (see illustration). Slide the boot off.

4   Before installing the new boot, wrap the threads and serrations on the end of the steering rod with a layer of tape so the small end of the new boot is not damaged during installation.

5   Place a new inner clamp over the steering gear.

6   Slide the new boot into position on the steering gear until it seats in the groove in the steering rod and install clamps. Tighten the clamps securely.

7   Remove the tape and install the tie-rod end jam nut and tie-rod end (see Section 16).

8   Install the wheel and lug nuts. Lower the vehicle and tighten the lug nuts to the torque listed in the Chapter 1 Specifications.

9   Have the alignment checked by a dealer service department or an alignment shop.

18.3 Slide the small clamp off the end of the boot, then untwist the large clamp

19 Steering gear - removal and installation

✳✳ WARNING:

All models are equipped with airbags. Make sure the steering shaft is not turned while the steering gear is removed or you could damage the airbag system. To prevent the shaft from turning, turn the ignition key to the lock position before beginning work or run the seat belt through the steering wheel and clip the seat belt into place. Make sure the ignition switch is OFF.

REMOVAL

♦ Refer to illustrations 19.2, 19.3a, 19.3b, 19.5a, 19.5b, 19.5c, 19.5d and 19.5e

1 Disconnect the cable from the negative terminal of the battery (see Chapter 5). Wait at least two minutes before proceeding. Loosen the front wheel lug nuts, raise the front of the vehicle and support it securely on jackstands. Apply the parking brake and remove the wheels.

Remove the engine undercover splash shield.

2 If equipped with power steering, place a drain pan under the steering gear. Detach the power steering pressure and return lines (see illustration) and cap or cover the ends to prevent excessive fluid loss and contamination.

3 Mark the relationship of the steering column universal joint at the steering gear input shaft. Remove the steering column universal joint pinch bolt (see illustrations).

4 Separate the tie-rod ends from the steering knuckle arms (see Section 17).

5 Support the steering gear and remove the steering gear bracket mounting bolts (see illustrations). Separate the steering column shaft from the steering gear input shaft and remove the steering gear assembly.

✳✳ WARNING:

Do NOT turn the steering wheel while the steering gear is removed. If the steering wheel is inadvertently turned, check the clockspring for damage and adjust the clockspring connector, if necessary (see Chapter 12).

19.2 Squeeze the return line clamp (left arrow) and slide it off the hose; undo the pressure line fitting (right arrow) with a flare nut wrench

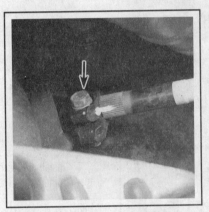

19.3a Mark the relationship of the universal joint to the steering gear input shaft and remove, don't just loosen, the U-joint pinch bolt (2005 and earlier models)

19.3b Mark the relationship of the intermediate shaft U-joint to the steering gear, remove the bolt that secures the U-joint to the steering gear input shaft and separate the intermediate shaft U-joint from the input shaft (2006 and later models)

19.5a Remove the steering gear bracket bolts (two on the rear not visible) (2005 and earlier models)

19.5b The rear bolts can be reached with a flex-head ratchet and socket (2005 and earlier models)

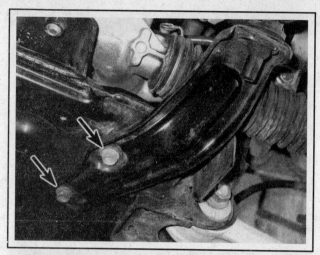

19.5c On 2006 and later models, remove these two radiator support brackets (left bracket shown)

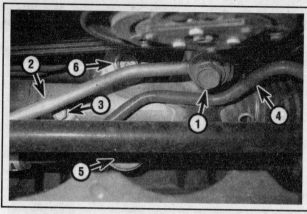

19.5d Steering gear details - left end (2006 and later models)

1   Pressure line banjo bolt
2   Pressure line
3   Return line clip bolt
4   Return line (fitting, not visible, connects to steering gear at left side of input shaft boss)
5   Left front mounting bolt
6   Left rear mounting bolt

6   Check the steering gear mounting grommets for excessive wear or deterioration, replacing them if necessary.

INSTALLATION

7   Raise the steering gear into position and connect the steering gear input shaft and the steering shaft universal joint, aligning the marks.

8   Install the steering gear mounting brackets and bolts and tighten them to the torque listed in this Chapter's Specifications.

9   Connect the tie-rod ends to the steering knuckle arms (see Section 17).

10 Install the universal joint pinch bolt and tighten it to the torque listed in this Chapter's Specifications.

11 If equipped with power steering, connect the power steering pressure and return hoses to the steering gear and fill the power steering pump reservoir with the recommended fluid (see Chapter 1).

12 Lower the vehicle and bleed the steering system (see Section 21).

13 Have the alignment checked by a dealer service department or alignment shop.

19.5e Steering gear details - right end (2006 and later models)

1   Return hose clamp   *4   Right front mounting bolt*
2   Return line   *5   Right rear mounting bolt*
3   Return line clip bolt

20   Power steering pump - removal and installation

REMOVAL

1   Disconnect the cable from the negative battery terminal (see Chapter 5).

2   Using a large syringe or suction gun, suck as much fluid out of the power steering fluid reservoir as possible. Place a drain pan under the vehicle to catch any fluid that spills out when the hoses are disconnected. Cap or cover the hoses to prevent entry of dirt or other contaminants.

2005 and earlier models

♦ **Refer to illustrations 20.4 and 20.8**

3   Remove the drivebelt (see Chapter 1).

4   Loosen the clamp and disconnect the fluid return hose from the pump (see illustration). Detach the electrical connector from the pressure sensor on the pump, if applicable.

5   Remove the pressure line-to-pump fitting (see illustration 20.4), then detach the line from the pump.

20.4 Power steering pump mounting details (2005 and earlier models)

A   *Sensor connector*
B   *Pressure line fitting*
C   *Return line clamp*
D   *Pivot bolt*

20.8 Hold the adjusting bolt (arrow) with a wrench, undo the nut and remove the bolt

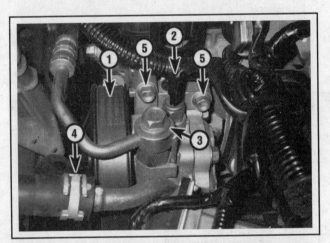

20.12 Power steering pump details (2006 and later models)

1   *Drivebelt*
2   *PSP switch electrical connector*
3   *Pressure line banjo bolt*
4   *Return line hose clamp*
5   *Upper pump mounting bolts*

20.15 Power steering pump lower mounting bolt location

6   Check the pressure line O-rings and replace if necessary.

7   Raise the front of the vehicle and place it securely on jackstands.

8   Loosen the pivot bolt/nut and adjuster bolt (see illustration 20.4 and the accompanying illustration), and remove the drivebelt (see Chapter 1).

9   Remove the pivot, adjuster and mounting bolts/nuts, then remove the pump from the vehicle.

10 If access to engine components is required, remove the pump mounting bracket mounting bolts and remove the mounting bracket.

2006 and later models

▶ **Refer to illustrations 20.12 and 20.15**

11 Remove the drivebelt (see Chapter 1).

12 Disconnect the electrical connector from the Power Steering Pressure (PSP) switch (see illustration).

13 Remove the pressure line banjo bolt and disconnect the pressure line.

14 Loosen the return hose clamp and disconnect the return hose from the return line.

15 Remove the two upper pump mounting bolts and the lower mounting bolt (see illustration).

16 Installation is the reverse of removal.

INSTALLATION

17 Installation is the reverse of removal. Be sure to tighten the pressure line fitting to the torque listed in this Chapter's Specifications. Adjust the drivebelt tension following the procedure described in Chapter 1.

18 Top off the fluid level in the reservoir (see Chapter 1) and bleed the system (see Section 21).

21 Power steering system - bleeding

1 Following any operation in which the power steering fluid lines have been disconnected, the power steering system must be bled to remove all air and obtain proper steering performance.

2 Before starting the engine and with the front wheels in the straight ahead position, check the power steering fluid level and, if low, add fluid until it reaches the L (Low) mark on the dipstick.

3 Start the engine and allow it to run at fast idle. Recheck the fluid level and add more new, fresh power steering fluid if necessary to reach the L mark on the dipstick.

4 Bleed the system by turning the wheels from side to side, without hitting the stops. This will work the air out of the system. Continuously check the reservoir and keep the reservoir full of fluid as this is done.

5 When the air is worked out of the system, return the wheels to the straight ahead position and keep the vehicle running for several more minutes before shutting it off, or road test as follows before shutting the engine off.

6 Road test the vehicle to be sure the steering system is functioning normally and is noise-free.

7 Recheck and top off the power steering fluid level to the F (Full) mark on the dipstick while the engine is at normal operating temperature. Add fluid if necessary (see Chapter 1).

22 Wheels and tires - general information

♦ **Refer to illustration 22.1**

All vehicles covered by this manual are equipped with metric-sized fiberglass or steel belted radial tires (see illustration). Use of other sizes or types of tires may affect the ride and handling of the vehicle. Don't mix different types of tires, such as radials and bias belted, on the same vehicle as handling may be seriously affected. It is recommended that tires be replaced in pairs on the same axle, but if only one tire is being replaced, be sure it's the same size, type, structure and tread design as the other, with the same or better tread wear rating, traction rating, and temperature rating.

Because tire pressure has a substantial effect on handling and wear, the pressure on all tires should be checked at least once a month or before any extended trips (see Chapter 1). Make sure that tires are not worn below the tread depth wear indicators molded into the tread or depth measured is at least the recommended depth in your owner's manual or as recommended by the tire manufacturer.

These models are factory-equipped with either steel or aluminum wheels. If alkaline compounds (road salt or saltwater) get on aluminum wheels, flush both the outside and inside the wheels with water soon. Wheels must be replaced if they are bent, dented, leak air, have elongated bolt holes, are heavily rusted or corroded, have wobble that is noticeable visually (the radial runout is excessive) or if the lug nuts will not stay tight. Wheel repairs that use welding or peening are not recommended. Never use a temporary spare for more than the prescribed driving distance and speed, and do not use the temporary spare wheel with a standard tire.

When installing/demounting tires, make sure the tire shop uses a "non-contact" tire mounting machine if you have aluminum wheels. Tire and wheel balance is important in the overall handling, braking, and performance of the vehicle. Unbalanced wheels can adversely affect

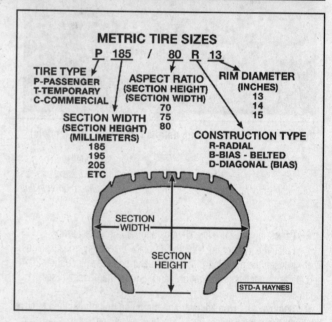

22.1 Metric tire size code

handling and ride characteristics as well as tire life. Whenever a tire is installed on a wheel, the tire and wheel should be balanced by a shop with the proper equipment. Make sure the tire shop uses an off-vehicle tire balancer whenever balancing the wheels/tires, or damage to the front transaxle could result.

Rotate tires front to back, and back to front. Do not include "Temporary Use Only" spare tire in the tire rotation.

23 Wheel alignment - general information

▶ **Refer to illustration 23.1**

A wheel alignment refers to the adjustments made to the wheels so they are in proper angular relationship to the suspension and the ground. Wheels that are out of proper alignment not only affect vehicle control, but also increase tire wear. The front end angles normally measured are camber, caster and toe-in (see illustration). On the front end, camber, caster, toe-in and maximum steering angle are adjustable. The only adjustments possible on the rear are camber and toe-in. The other angles should be measured to check for bent or worn suspension parts.

Getting the proper wheel alignment is a very exacting process, requiring complicated alignment machines to perform the job properly. Because of this, you should have a shop with a four-wheel alignment machine and technician with the proper training to properly perform these tasks. However, we give the following information describing the basic idea of what is involved with wheel alignment so you can better understand the process and deal intelligently with the shop that does the work.

Toe-in is the turning in of the wheels. The purpose of a toe specification is to ensure stability with controlled parallel rolling of the wheels. In a vehicle with zero toe-in, the distance between the front edges of the wheels will be the same as the distance between the rear edges of the wheels. The actual amount of toe-in is normally only a fraction of an inch. On the front end, toe-in is adjusted by the tie-rod end position on the tie-rod. On the rear end, it is adjusted by an adjuster on the rear suspension lower control arm. Incorrect toe-in will cause the tires to wear , by making them scrub excessively on the road surface, and will cause the vehicle to be less stable, especially during straight line driving.

Camber is the tilt of the wheels from vertical when viewed from the end of the vehicle. When the wheels tilt out at the top, camber is positive (+). When the wheels tilt in at the top, camber is negative (-). The amount of tilt is measured in degrees from vertical; this measurement is the camber angle. This angle affects the amount of tire tread which contacts the road and compensates for changes in the suspension geometry when the vehicle is cornering or traveling over varying surfaces. It is adjusted on the front and rear ends by turning the adjusting cam bolts at the inner end of the lower control arm.

Caster is the tilting of the front steering axis from the vertical. A tilt toward the rear is positive caster and a tilt toward the front is negative caster. Caster is for directional stability by causing the steering to tend to return to center.

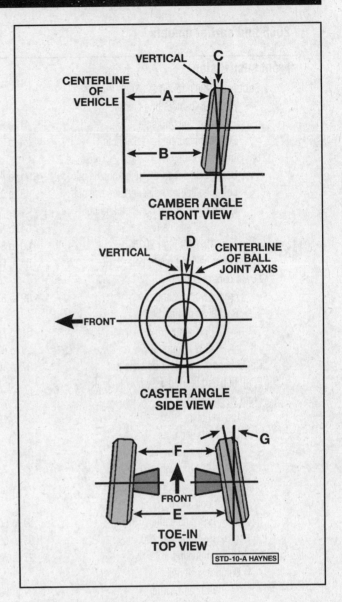

23.1 Camber, caster and toe-in angles

A minus B = C (degrees camber)
D = degrees caster
E minus F = toe-in (measured in inches)
G = toe-in (expressed in degrees)

Torque specifications	Ft-lbs

2005 and earlier models

Front suspension

Strut bar (1999 through 2005)	
Strut bar-to-mounting bracket	
through-bolts/nuts	41 to 59
Strut bar mounting bracket nuts	24 to 29
Balljoints	
Upper balljoint-to-steering knuckle nut	31 to 44
Lower balljoint-to-steering knuckle nut	43 to 57
Lower balljoint through-bolt and nut	
1997 and earlier	54 to 68
1999 through 2005	69 to 88
Lower balljoint upper bolt	54 to 68
Lower control arm	
Front pivot bolt and nut	69 to 83
Rear pivot bolt and nut	
1997 and earlier	61 to 76
1999 through 2005	69 to 83
Upper control arm pivot bolt and nut	87 to 101
Front hub and bearing assembly locknut	123 to 160
Front stabilizer bar	
Bracket bolts	14 to 19
Link bolts and nuts	
1997 and earlier	27 to 39
1999 through 2005	32 to 44
Shock absorber/coil spring assembly	
Lower bolt and nut	
1997 and earlier	54 to 68
1999 through 2005	69 to 86
Upper mounting nuts	22 to 26
Damper shaft nut	
1997 and earlier	24 to 33
1999 through 2005	12 to 17

Rear suspension

Upper control arm pivot bolts and nuts	
1997 and earlier	34 to 49
1999 through 2005	40 to 56
Lower control arm	
Outer pivot bolt and nut	
1997 and earlier	47 to 54
1999 through 2005	63 to 73
Inner pivot bolts and nuts	54 to 70
Rear stabilizer bar	
Bracket bolts	15 to 20
Link bolts and nuts	
1997 and earlier	27 to 39
1999 through 2005	32 to 44

Rear suspension

Rear shock absorber/coil spring assemblies

Lower bolt and nut	54 to 68
Upper mounting nuts	22 to 26
Damper shaft nut	
1997 and earlier	24 to 33
1999 through 2005	12 to 17

Steering

Steering gear bracket bolts	
1997 and earlier	34 to 43
1999 through 2005	55 to 77
Steering column-to-gear pinch bolt	14 to 19
Power steering pressure hose fitting	
1997 and earlier	24 to 34
1999 through 2005	12 to 17
Steering wheel nut	29 to 36
Tie-rod end-to-steering knuckle nut	
1997 and earlier	22 to 32
1999 through 2005	32 to 41
Wheel lug nuts	See Chapter 1

2006 and later models

Front suspension

Strut bar	
All fasteners (except strut bar mounting plate nuts)	12 to 20
Strut bar mounting plate nuts	34 to 46
Upper balljoint nut	41 to 53
Lower balljoint nut	80 to 104
Upper control arm pivot bolts	62 to 72
Front shock absorber/coil spring assembly	
Lower bolt and nut	58 to 76
Damper shaft nut	28 to 34
Upper mounting nuts (front suspension brace plate nuts)	34 to 46
Lower control arm pivot bolts/nuts (front and rear)	87 to 101
Stabilizer bar	
Stabilizer link rod-to-lower control arm nut	32 to 45
Link rod-to-stabilizer bar nut	32 to 45
Stabilizer bar bracket bolts	26 to 37

Rear suspension

Shock absorber/coil spring assembly

Upper mounting nuts	34 to 46
Upper mounting bolt	17 to 23
Lower mounting bolt/nut	65 to 88
Damper shaft nut	29 to 34

Torque specifications	Ft-lbs
Rear suspension (continued)	
Stabilizer bar	
Link rod-to-stabilizer and link rod-to-rear	
lower lateral link	32 to 45
Stabilizer bar bracket nuts	13 to 20
Suspension links	
Rear lateral links	
Rear lower lateral link	
Rear lower lateral link-to-	
crossmember bracket pivot bolt/nut	87 to 101
Rear lower lateral balljoint stud-to-	
knuckle nut	80 to 100
Rear upper lateral link	
Rear upper lateral link-to-	
crossmember bracket pivot bolt/nut	56 to 75
Rear upper lateral link balljoint	
stud-to-knuckle nut	80 to 100
Rear trailing links	
Rear lower trailing link	
Rear lower trailing link-to-	
crossmember bracket pivot bolt	56 to 75
Rear lower trailing link-to-	
knuckle bolt	56 to 75
Rear upper trailing link	
Rear upper trailing link-to-crossmember	
bracket pivot bolt/nut	56 to 75
Rear upper trailing link balljoint	
stud-to-knuckle nut	54 to 69
Toe control link	
Toe control link-to-crossmember	
bracket pivot bolt/nut	52 to 70
Toe control link balljoint stud-to-	
knuckle pinch bolt/nut	23 to 31
Steering	
Steering gear bracket bolts	55 to 77
Steering column-to-pinion gear pinch bolt	13 to 20
Steering wheel nut	29 to 36
Tie-rod end-to-steering knuckle nut	35 to 44
Power steering pressure hose fitting	22 to 32
Wheel lug nuts	See Chapter 1

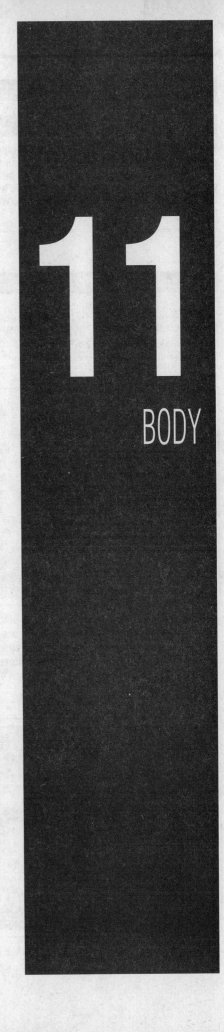

11

BODY

Section

1   General information

✳✳ WARNING:

The models covered by this manual are equipped with Supplemental Restraint Systems (SRS), more commonly known as airbags. Always disable the airbag system before working in the vicinity of any airbag system components to avoid the possibility of accidental deployment of the airbags, which could cause personal injury (see Chapter 12).

Certain body components are particularly vulnerable to accident damage and can be unbolted and repaired or replaced. Among these parts are the hood, doors, tailgate, liftgate, bumpers and front fenders.

Only general body maintenance practices and body panel repair procedures within the scope of the do-it-yourselfer are included in this Chapter.

2   Repair minor paint scratches

No matter how hard you try to keep your vehicle looking like new, it will inevitably be scratched, chipped or dented at some point. If the metal is actually dented, seek the advice of a professional. But you can fix minor scratches and chips yourself. Buy a touch-up paint kit from a dealer service department or an auto parts store. To ensure that you get the right color, you'll need to have the specific make, model and year of your vehicle and, ideally, the paint code, which is located on a special metal plate under the hood or in the door jamb.

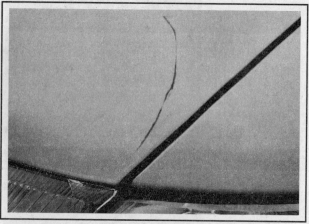

Make sure the damaged area is perfectly clean and rust free. If the touch-up kit has a wire brush, use it to clean the scratch or chip. Or use fine steel wool wrapped around the end of a pencil. Clean the scratched or chipped surface only, not the good paint surrounding it. Rinse the area with water and allow it to dry thoroughly

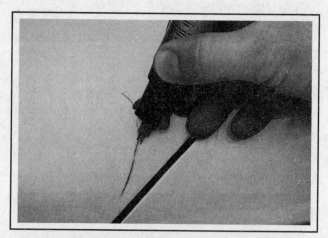

Thoroughly mix the paint, then apply a small amount with the touch-up kit brush or a very fine artist's brush. Brush in one direction as you fill the scratch area. Do not build up the paint higher than the surrounding paint

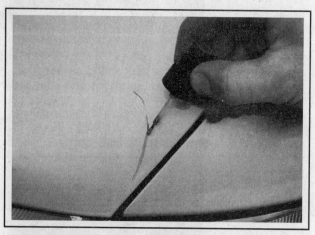

If the vehicle has a two-coat finish, apply the clear coat after the color coat has dried

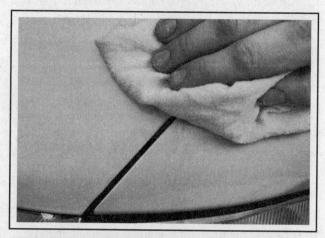

Wait a few days for the paint to dry thoroughly, then rub out the repainted area with a polishing compound to blend the new paint with the surrounding area. When you're happy with your work, wash and polish the area

3   Body repair - minor damage

PLASTIC BODY PANELS

The following repair procedures are for minor scratches and gouges. Repair of more serious damage should be left to a dealer service department or qualified auto body shop. Below is a list of the equipment and materials necessary to perform the following repair procedures on plastic body panels.

> *Wax, grease and silicone removing solvent*
> *Cloth-backed body tape*
> *Sanding discs*
> *Drill motor with three-inch disc holder*
> *Hand sanding block*
> *Rubber squeegees*
> *Sandpaper*
> *Non-porous mixing palette*
> *Wood paddle or putty knife*
> *Curved-tooth body file*
> *Flexible parts repair material*

Flexible panels (bumper trim)

1   Remove the damaged panel, if necessary or desirable. In most cases, repairs can be carried out with the panel installed.

2   Clean the area(s) to be repaired with a wax, grease and silicone removing solvent applied with a water-dampened cloth.

3   If the damage is structural, that is, if it extends through the panel, clean the backside of the panel area to be repaired as well. Wipe dry.

4   Sand the rear surface about 1-1/2 inches beyond the break.

5   Cut two pieces of fiberglass cloth large enough to overlap the break by about 1-1/2 inches. Cut only to the required length.

6   Mix the adhesive from the repair kit according to the instructions included with the kit, and apply a layer of the mixture approximately 1/8-inch thick on the backside of the panel. Overlap the break by at least 1-1/2 inches.

7   Apply one piece of fiberglass cloth to the adhesive and cover the cloth with additional adhesive. Apply a second piece of fiberglass cloth to the adhesive and immediately cover the cloth with additional adhesive in sufficient quantity to fill the weave.

8   Allow the repair to cure for 20 to 30 minutes at 60-degrees to 80-degrees F.

9   If necessary, trim the excess repair material at the edge.

10   Remove all of the paint film over and around the area(s) to be repaired. The repair material should not overlap the painted surface.

11   With a drill motor and a sanding disc (or a rotary file), cut a "V" along the break line approximately 1/2-inch wide. Remove all dust and loose particles from the repair area.

12   Mix and apply the repair material. Apply a light coat first over the damaged area; then continue applying material until it reaches a level slightly higher than the surrounding finish.

13   Cure the mixture for 20 to 30 minutes at 60-degrees to 80-degrees F.

14   Roughly establish the contour of the area being repaired with a body file. If low areas or pits remain, mix and apply additional adhesive.

15   Block sand the damaged area with sandpaper to establish the actual contour of the surrounding surface.

16   If desired, the repaired area can be temporarily protected with several light coats of primer. Because of the special paints and techniques required for flexible body panels, it is recommended that the vehicle be taken to a paint shop for completion of the body repair.

STEEL BODY PANELS

▶ **See photo sequence**

Repair of dents

17   When repairing dents, the first job is to pull the dent out until the affected area is as close as possible to its original shape. There is no point in trying to restore the original shape completely as the metal in the damaged area will have stretched on impact and cannot be restored to its original contours. It is better to bring the level of the dent up to a point that is about 1/8-inch below the level of the surrounding metal. In cases where the dent is very shallow, it is not worth trying to pull it out at all.

18   If the backside of the dent is accessible, it can be hammered out gently from behind using a soft-face hammer. While doing this, hold a block of wood firmly against the opposite side of the metal to absorb the hammer blows and prevent the metal from being stretched.

19   If the dent is in a section of the body which has double layers, or some other factor makes it inaccessible from behind, a different technique is required. Drill several small holes through the metal inside the damaged area, particularly in the deeper sections. Screw long, self-tapping screws into the holes just enough for them to get a good grip in the metal. Now pulling on the protruding heads of the screws with locking pliers can pull out the dent.

20   The next stage of repair is the removal of paint from the damaged area and from an inch or so of the surrounding metal. This is easily done with a wire brush or sanding disk in a drill motor, although it can be done just as effectively by hand with sandpaper. To complete the preparation for filling, score the surface of the bare metal with a screwdriver or the tang of a file or drill small holes in the affected area. This will provide a good grip for the filler material. To complete the repair, see the Section on filling and painting.

Repair of rust holes or gashes

21   Remove all paint from the affected area and from an inch or so of the surrounding metal using a sanding disk or wire brush mounted in a drill motor. If these are not available, a few sheets of sandpaper will do the job just as effectively.

22   With the paint removed, you will be able to determine the severity of the corrosion and decide whether to replace the whole panel, if possible, or repair the affected area. New body panels are not as expensive as most people think and it is often quicker to install a new panel than to repair large areas of rust.

23   Remove all trim pieces from the affected area except those which will act as a guide to the original shape of the damaged body, such as headlight shells, etc. Using metal snips or a hacksaw blade, remove all loose metal and any other metal that is badly affected by rust. Hammer the edges of the hole in to create a slight depression for the filler material.

24   Wire-brush the affected area to remove the powdery rust from the surface of the metal. If the back of the rusted area is accessible, treat it with rust inhibiting paint.

25   Before filling is done, block the hole in some way. This can be done with sheet metal riveted or screwed into place, or by stuffing the hole with wire mesh.

26   Once the hole is blocked off, the affected area can be filled and painted. See the following subsection on filling and painting.

These photos illustrate a method of repairing simple dents. They are intended to supplement Body repair - minor damage in this Chapter and should not be used as the sole instructions for body repair on these vehicles.

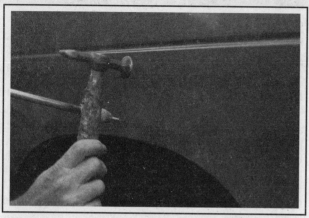

1 If you can't access the backside of the body panel to hammer out the dent, pull it out with a slide-hammer-type dent puller. Tap with a hammer near the edge of the dent to help 'pop' the metal back to its original shape, about 1/8-inch below the surface of the surrounding metal

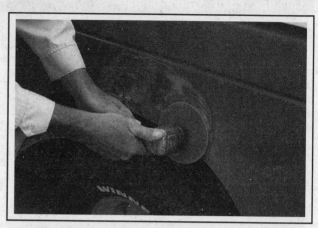

2 Using coarse-grit sandpaper, remove the paint down to the bare metal. Clean the repair area with wax/silicone remover.

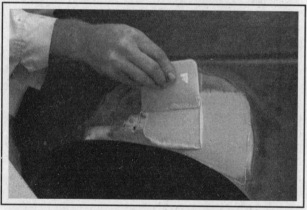

3 Following label instructions, mix up a batch of plastic filler and hardener, then quickly press it into the metal with a plastic applicator. Work the filler until it matches the original contour and is slightly above the surrounding metal

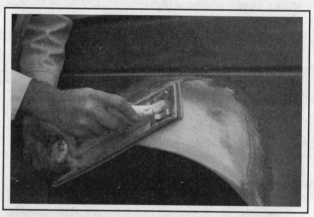

4 Let the filler harden until you can just dent it with your fingernail. File, then sand the filler down until it's smooth and even. Work down to finer grits of sandpaper - always using a board or block - ending up with 360 or 400 grit

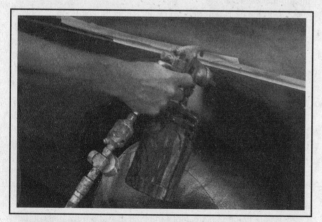

5 When the area is smooth to the touch, clean the area and mask around it. Apply several layers of primer to the area. A professional-type spray gun is being used here, but aerosol spray primer works fine

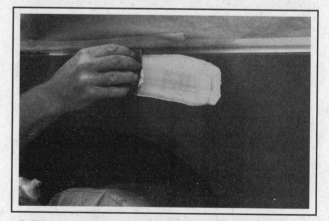

6 Fill imperfections or scratches with glazing compound. Sand with 360 or 400-grit and re-spray. Finish sand the primer with 600 grit, clean thoroughly, then apply the finish coat. Don't attempt to rub out or wax the repair area until the paint has dried completely (at least two weeks)

Filling and painting

27 Many types of body fillers are available, but generally speaking, body repair kits which contain filler paste and a tube of resin hardener are best for this type of repair work. A wide, flexible plastic or nylon applicator will be necessary for imparting a smooth and contoured finish to the surface of the filler material. Mix up a small amount of filler on a clean piece of wood or cardboard (use the hardener sparingly). Follow the manufacturer's instructions on the package, otherwise the filler will set incorrectly.

28 Using the applicator, apply the filler paste to the prepared area. Draw the applicator across the surface of the filler to achieve the desired contour and to level the filler surface. As soon as a contour that approximates the original one is achieved, stop working the paste. If you continue, the paste will begin to stick to the applicator. Continue to add thin layers of paste at 20-minute intervals until the level of the filler is just above the surrounding metal.

29 Once the filler has hardened, the excess can be removed with a body file. From then on, progressively finer grades of sandpaper should be used, starting with a 180-grit paper and finishing with 600-grit wet-or-dry paper. Always wrap the sandpaper around a flat rubber or wooden block, otherwise the surface of the filler will not be completely flat. During the sanding of the filler surface, the wet-or-dry paper should be periodically rinsed in water. This will ensure that a very smooth finish is produced in the final stage.

30 At this point, the repair area should be surrounded by a ring of bare metal, which in turn should be encircled by the finely feathered edge of good paint. Rinse the repair area with clean water until all of the dust produced by the sanding operation is gone.

31 Spray the entire area with a light coat of primer. This will reveal any imperfections in the surface of the filler. Repair the imperfections with fresh filler paste or glaze filler and once more smooth the surface with sandpaper. Repeat this spray-and-repair procedure until you are satisfied that the surface of the filler and the feathered edge of the paint are perfect. Rinse the area with clean water and allow it to dry completely.

32 The repair area is now ready for painting. Spray painting must be carried out in a warm, dry, windless and dust free atmosphere. These conditions can be created if you have access to a large indoor work area, but if you are forced to work in the open, you will have to pick the day very carefully. If you are working indoors, dousing the floor in the work area with water will help settle the dust that would otherwise be in the air. If the repair area is confined to one body panel, mask off the surrounding panels. This will help minimize the effects of a slight mismatch in paint color. Trim pieces such as chrome strips, door handles, etc., will also need to be masked off or removed. Use masking tape and several thickness of newspaper for the masking operations.

33 Before spraying, shake the paint can thoroughly, then spray a test area until the spray painting technique is mastered. Cover the repair area with a thick coat of primer. The thickness should be built up using several thin layers of primer rather than one thick one. Using 600-grit wet-or-dry sandpaper, rub down the surface of the primer until it is very smooth. While doing this, the work area should be thoroughly rinsed with water and the wet-or-dry sandpaper periodically rinsed as well. Allow the primer to dry before spraying additional coats.

34 Spray on the top coat, again building up the thickness by using several thin layers of paint. Begin spraying in the center of the repair area and then, using a circular motion, work out until the whole repair area and about two inches of the surrounding original paint is covered. Remove all masking material 10 to 15 minutes after spraying on the final coat of paint. Allow the new paint at least two weeks to harden, then use a very fine rubbing compound to blend the edges of the new paint into the existing paint. Finally, apply a coat of wax

4 Body repair - major damage

1 Major damage must be repaired by an auto body shop specifically equipped to perform body and frame repairs. These shops have the specialized equipment required to do the job properly.

2 If the damage is extensive, the frame must be checked for proper alignment or the vehicle's handling characteristics may be adversely affected and other components may wear at an accelerated rate.

3 Due to the fact that all of the major body components (hood, fenders, etc.) are separate and replaceable units, any seriously damaged components should be replaced rather than repaired. Sometimes the components can be found in a wrecking yard that specializes in used vehicle components, often at considerable savings over the cost of new parts.

5 Upholstery, carpets and vinyl trim - maintenance

UPHOLSTERY AND CARPETS

1 Every three months remove the floormats and clean the interior of the vehicle (more frequently if necessary). Use a stiff whiskbroom to brush the carpeting and loosen dirt and dust, then vacuum the upholstery and carpets thoroughly, especially along seams and crevices.

2 Dirt and stains can be removed from carpeting with basic household or automotive carpet shampoos available in spray cans. Follow the directions and vacuum again, then use a stiff brush to bring back the "nap" of the carpet.

3 Most interiors have cloth or vinyl upholstery, either of which can be cleaned and maintained with a number of material-specific cleaners or shampoos available in auto supply stores. Follow the directions on the product for usage, and always spot-test any upholstery cleaner on an inconspicuous area (bottom edge of a backseat cushion) to ensure that it doesn't cause a color shift in the material.

4 After cleaning, vinyl upholstery should be treated with a protectant.

➡ **Note: Make sure the protectant container indicates the product can be used on seats - some products may make a seat too slippery.**

❊❊ **CAUTION:**

Do not use protectant on vinyl-covered steering wheels.

5 Leather upholstery requires special care. It should be cleaned regularly with saddlesoap or leather cleaner. Never use alcohol, gasoline, nail polish remover or thinner to clean leather upholstery.

6 After cleaning, regularly treat leather upholstery with a leather conditioner, rubbed in with a soft cotton cloth. Never use car wax on leather upholstery.

7 In areas where the interior of the vehicle is subject to bright sunlight, cover leather seating areas of the seats with a sheet if the vehicle is to be left out for any length of time.

VINYL TRIM

8 Don't clean vinyl trim with detergents, caustic soap or petroleum-based cleaners. Plain soap and water works just fine, with a soft brush to clean dirt that may be ingrained. Wash the vinyl as frequently as the rest of the vehicle.

9 After cleaning, application of a high-quality rubber and vinyl protectant will help prevent oxidation and cracks. The protectant can also be applied to weather-stripping, vacuum lines and rubber hoses, which often fail as a result of chemical degradation, and to the tires.

6 Fastener and trim removal

▶ Refer to illustration 6.4

1 There is a variety of plastic fasteners used to hold trim panels, splash shields and other parts in place in addition to typical screws, nuts and bolts. Once you are familiar with them, they can usually be removed without too much difficulty.

2 The proper tools and approach can prevent added time and expense to a project by minimizing the number of broken fasteners and/or parts.

3 The following illustration shows various types of fasteners that are typically used on most vehicles and how to remove and install them (see illustration). Replacement fasteners are commonly found at most auto parts stores, if necessary.

4 Trim panels are typically made of plastic and their flexibility can help during removal. The key to their removal is to use a tool to pry the panel near its retainers to release it without damaging surrounding areas or breaking-off any retainers. The retainers will usually snap out of their designated slot or hole after force is applied to them. Stiff plastic tools designed for prying on trim panels are available at most auto parts stores (see illustration). Tools that are tapered and wrapped in protective tape, such as a screwdriver or small pry tool, are also very effective when used with care.

Fasteners

This tool is designed to remove special fasteners. A small pry tool used for removing nails will also work well in place of this tool

A Phillips head screwdriver can be used to release the center portion, but light pressure must be used because the plastic is easily damaged. Once the center is up, the fastener can easily be pried from its hole

Here is a view with the center portion fully released. Install the fastener as shown, then press the center in to set it

This fastener is used for exterior panels and shields. The center portion must be pried up to release the fastener. Install the fastener with the center up, then press the center in to set it

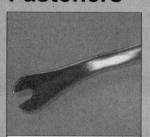

This type of fastener is used commonly for interior panels. Use a small blunt tool to press the small pin at the center in to release it . . .

. . . the pin will stay with the fastener in the released position

Reset the fastener for installation by moving the pin out. Install the fastener, then press the pin flush with the fastener to set it

This fastener is used for exterior and interior panels. It has no moving parts. Simply pry the fastener from its hole like the claw of a hammer removes a nail. Without a tool that can get under the top of the fastener, it can be very difficult to remove

7 Hinges and locks - maintenance

Once every 5000 miles, or every four months, the hinges and latch assemblies on the doors, hood and trunk should be given a few drops of light oil or lock lubricant. The door latch strikers should also be lubricated with a thin coat of grease to reduce wear and ensure free movement. Lubricate the door and trunk locks with spray-on graphite lubricant.

8 Windshield and fixed glass - replacement

Replacement of the windshield and fixed glass requires the use of special fast-setting adhesive/caulk materials and some specialized tools. It is recommended that these operations be left to a dealer or a shop specializing in glass work.

9 Hood - removal, installation and adjustment

➡Note: The hood is heavy and somewhat awkward to remove and install - at least two people should perform this procedure.

REMOVAL AND INSTALLATION

▶ **Refer to illustration 9.1**

1 Use a scribe or felt tip marker to make marks around the hinges to ensure proper alignment during reinstallation (see illustration).
2 Use blankets or pads to cover the cowl area of the body and fenders. This will protect the body and paint as the hood is removed.
3 Disconnect the windshield washer tube at the hood.
4 Have an assistant support the hood. Remove the hinge-to-hood bolts.
5 Lift off the hood.
6 Installation is the reverse of removal.

ADJUSTMENT

▶ **Refer to illustration 9.10**

7 Fore-and-aft and side-to-side adjustment of the hood is done by moving the hinge plate slot after loosening the bolts.
8 Use a scribe or felt tip marker to make a line around the entire hinge plate so you can judge the amount of movement (see illustration 9.1).
9 Loosen the bolts or nuts and move the hood into correct alignment. Move it only a little at a time. Tighten the hinge bolts and carefully lower the hood to check the position.
10 If necessary after installation, the entire hood latch assembly can be adjusted up-and-down as well as from side-to-side on the radiator support so the hood closes securely, and is flush with the fenders. To make the adjustment, use a scribe or felt tip marker to make a line around the hood latch mounting bolts to aid alignment when reinstalling (see illustration), then loosen the bolts and reposition the latch assembly to align with the striker on the hood, as necessary. Following adjustment, retighten the mounting bolts.
11 The hood latch assembly, as well as the hinges, should be periodically lubricated with white lithium-base grease to prevent binding and wear.

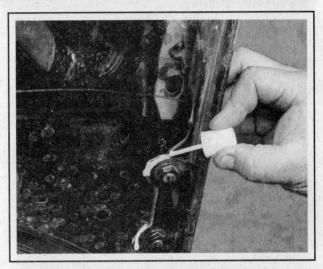

9.1 Before removing the hood, mark around the hinges

9.10 Mark the position of the hood latch before loosening the bolts

10 Hood release latch and cable - removal and installation

LATCH

2005 and earlier models

♦ Refer to illustration 10.2

1   Use a scribe or felt tip marker to make a line around the latch to aid alignment when reinstalling, then remove the hood latch mounting bolts (see illustration 9.10). Remove the latch.

2   Disconnect the hood release cable by removing the cable retaining clip near the hood latch and disengaging the cable from the latch assembly (see illustration).

3   Installation is the reverse of removal.

➡Note: Adjust the latch so the hood engages securely when closed and the hood bumpers are slightly compressed (see Section 9).

2006 and later models

♦ Refer to illustration 10.5

4   Trace the electrical lead from the latch to the electrical connector and disconnect it.

5   Pull the hood release cable out of its retaining bracket (see illustration), then disengage the cable end from the slot in the latch mechanism.

6   Remove the latch assembly mounting bolts and remove the latch.

7   Installation is the reverse of removal.

CABLE

♦ Refer to illustration 10.12

8   Disconnect the hood release cable from the latch.

9   Attach a piece of thin wire or string to the end of the cable and unfasten all remaining cable retaining clips.

10 On 1997 and earlier models, remove the driver's side kick panel. Then remove the release lever mounting bolts and detach the hood release lever.

11 On 1999 through 2005 models, detach the hood release lever

from the knee bolster trim panel below the steering column. The hood release lever is secured by a press fit into a slot in the trim panel. To disengage it from the trim panel, pull it straight down.

12 On 2006 and later models, the hood release lever is secured to the trim panel at the lower left corner of the instrument panel by three small mounting tabs and a single larger mounting tab. To remove it, pull the release lever as if you were releasing the hood release latch and insert a tape-wrapped screwdriver into the slot (see illustration). Pry each tab loose by pulling the screwdriver handle toward you so that the screwdriver tip forces each tab down and disengages it from the trim panel. Pull the release lever assembly down and toward you to disengage the large mounting tab at the front end of the release lever assembly.

13 Pull the cable and grommet rearward into the passenger compartment until you can see the wire or string. Ensure that the new cable has a grommet attached, then remove the old cable from the wire or string and replace it with the new cable.

14 Working in the engine compartment, pull the wire or string back through the firewall.

15 Installation is the reverse of removal.

➡Note: Push on the cable grommet with your fingers from inside the passenger compartment to seat the grommet into the firewall correctly.

10.2 Pry off the retaining clip

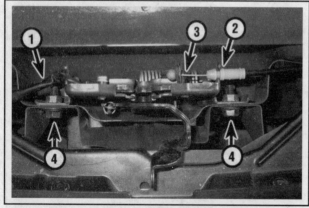

10.5 Hood release latch assembly details

1	Electrical lead	4 Hood release latch
2	Cable bracket	mounting bolts
3	Cable slot	

10.12 To disengage the hood release lever from the dash on 2006 and later models, lift up the lever, then insert a small tapped screwdriver into this slot and pry the middle mounting tab loose

11 Bumpers - removal and installation

→Note: The bumper assembly is heavy and somewhat awkward to remove and install - support the bumper when the bolts are removed - have an assistant help you when performing this procedure.

1   On 1997 and earlier models, raise the headlights. Apply the parking brake, raise the vehicle and support it securely on jackstands.

2   Disconnect the cable from the negative battery terminal (see Chapter 5) and disconnect any wiring that would interfere with bumper removal.

1997 AND EARLIER MODELS

Front bumper

▶ Refer to illustrations 11.4, 11.5a, 11.5b, 11.6, 11.7, 11.8a, 11.8b, 11.8c, 11.9, 11.10a and 11.10b

3   Remove the under cover splash shield. Open the hood. Remove the screws from both side marker lights and remove the lights.

4   Remove the upper radiator shroud (see illustration).

5   Remove the set plate and upper retainer (see illustrations).

6   Remove the lower bolts that secure the front fascia to the bumper reinforcement (see illustration).

7   Inside the air intake opening, remove the fascia screws and the license plate bracket (see illustration).

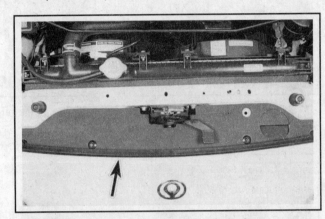

11.4 Remove the upper radiator shroud (arrow) . . .

11.5a . . . the retainer . . .

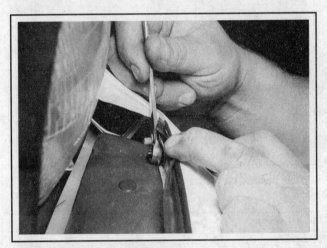

11.5b . . . and the set plate

11.6 Unbolt the underside of the fascia (arrows)

11.7 Inside the grille opening, remove the license plate bracket (inner arrows) and detach the fascia (outer arrows)

11.8a On each side, remove the support strap (arrows) . . .

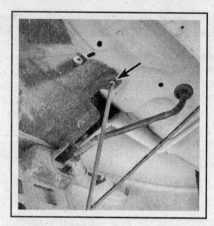

11.8b . . . the set plate . . .

11.8c . . . and the retaining nuts (arrows)

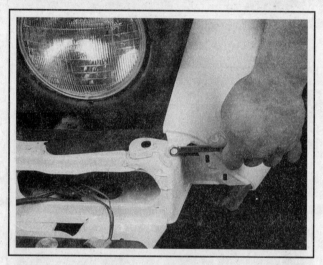

11.9 Remove the fender-to-fascia bolt

11.10a Remove the bolts from the underside of the reinforcement . . .

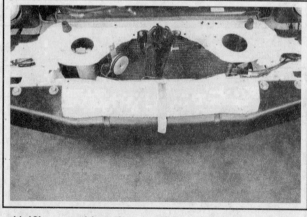

11.10b . . . and from the upper side

8   Under each side of the vehicle, remove the support strap, set plate and two mounting nuts (see illustrations).

9   Remove the fascia-to-fender bolt on each side and take the front fascia off the vehicle (see illustration).

10   Remove the bumper reinforcement bolts and lower the bumper away from the vehicle (see illustrations).

11   Installation is the reverse of the removal procedure.

Rear bumper

12   Remove the rear side marker lights (see Chapter 12).

13   Under the vehicle, remove the splash shield from the rear of each wheel well.

14   Remove the bumper mounting nuts and take the bumper off the vehicle.

15   Installation is the reverse of the removal procedure.

1999 THROUGH 2005 MODELS

Front bumper

16   Open the hood and remove the two bolts along the upper trailing edge of the bumper.

17   In each wheel well, remove the two bolts located at the upper rear corner of the bumper. One bolt faces straight down and the other bolt faces forward.

18   Underneath the bumper, remove the six bolts located along the lower trailing edge of the bumper, three at each end.

19   Remove the bumper assembly.

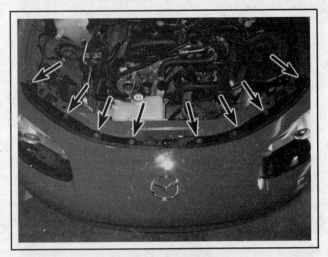

11.31 Front bumper cover upper fasteners

11.32 Front bumper-to-engine under cover fasteners

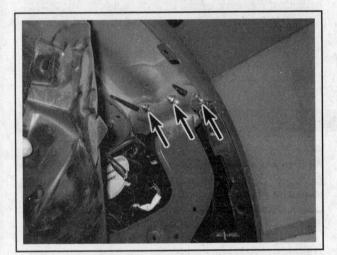

11.33 The front bumper fasteners are accessed through the wheel wells (right side shown)

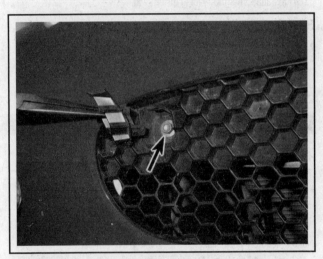

11.35 To access the two front bumper bolts located in the grille, remove the trim cover, then remove the bolt (right side shown)

20 If you're disassembling the bumper for repairs or replacement, detach the license plate holder, then remove the five bolts that secure the air dam skirt to the bumper and remove the skirt.

21 Installation is the reverse of removal.

Rear bumper

22 Remove the license plate light (see Chapter 12).

23 Remove the rear taillight assemblies (see Chapter 12).

24 Remove the two bolts, one on each side of the license plate area, from the rear part of the bumper.

25 In each wheel well, remove the bolt located at the upper forward corner of the bumper. This bolt faces straight up.

26 Remove the five bolts located along the rear outer edge of the wheel well.

27 Underneath the vehicle, remove the two bolts, one on each side, that are located just behind the wheel well. These bolts face straight down.

28 Remove the two clips, one on each inner side of the bumper, just behind the wheel wells.

29 Remove the bumper.

30 Installation is the reverse of removal.

2006 AND LATER MODELS

Front bumper

▶ **Refer to illustrations 11.31, 11.32, 11.33 and 11.35**

31 Open the hood and remove the eight fasteners that secure the upper trailing edge of the bumper (see illustration).

32 Detach the front bumper from the engine under covers (see illustration).

33 Remove the front wheels, then detach the front wheel well splash shields as necessary (see Section 12) to allow access to the rest of the bumper fasteners accessed through the wheel wells (see illustration).

34 Disconnect the electrical connectors from the sidemarker lights. If the vehicle is equipped with fog lights, disconnect the electrical connectors from the fog lights.

35 Remove the trim covers from the grille, then remove the two bumper fasteners located in the grille area (see illustration).

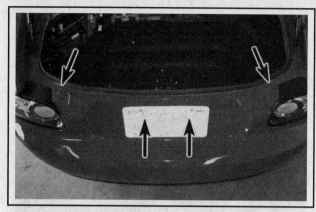

11.38 To detach the upper part of the rear bumper, remove these fasteners

36 Remove the front bumper assembly.
37 Installation is the reverse of removal.

Rear bumper

▶ **Refer to illustration 11.38**

38 Remove the fasteners that secure the upper part of the rear bum-

per (see illustration). Remove the license plate and remove the other two screws that secure the upper part of the bumper.
39 Remove the rear taillights (see Chapter 12).
40 Remove the rear wheels, then detach the back part of each rear wheel well splash shield as necessary to access the lower bumper fasteners.
41 Remove the lower bumper fasteners from the upper end of each corner of the bumper, where it attaches to the underside of the sheet-metal along the trailing edge of wheel well.
42 Besides the fasteners, the rear bumper is also secured to the vehicle body by three bumper sliders. There's one bumper slider below the license plate area and the other two sliders are located at each upper corner of the bumper, between the taillight receptacles and the wheel wells, at the seams between the bumper and the body. With an assistant at one side of the vehicle, pull out the two ends of the bumper cover out to disengage them from the bumper sliders. When the ends are both disengaged, pull off the center part of the bumper from the back of the vehicle. Be careful! Without an assistant helping you support the bumper during this final step, the bumper might pop off, fall to the floor and be damaged when you disengage it from the sliders.
43 When installing the rear bumper, spread the ends of the bumper apart, then lift the bumper into position. Press the bumper against the three bumper sliders to engage it with the sliders.
44 Installation is otherwise the reverse of removal.

12 Fender (front) - removal and installation

2005 AND EARLIER MODELS

▶ **Refer to illustration 12.4**

1 Refer to Section 11 and remove the front bumper.
2 Loosen the front wheel lug nuts, raise the front of the vehicle and place it securely on jackstands. Remove the front wheel.
3 Remove the splash shield fasteners and remove the splash shield.
4 Remove the bolts along the top of the fender (see illustration).
5 Remove the nut at the rear of the fender and work the fender loose from the vehicle.

✳✳ CAUTION:

Don't force the fender off. If it won't come easily, check again to make sure all fasteners have been removed.

2006 AND LATER MODELS

▶ **Refer to illustrations 12.6a, 12.6b, 12.8 and 12.9**

6 Remove the front wheel and remove the splash shields (see illustrations).

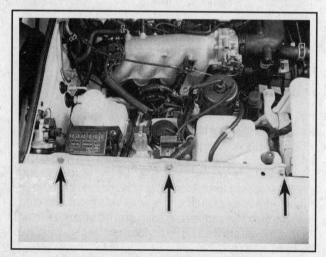

12.4 Remove the bolts along the top of the fender

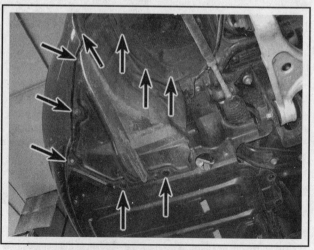

12.6a Front fender splash shield fasteners; left side shown (not all fasteners visible)

12.6b Main fender splash shield fasteners; right side shown (not all fasteners visible)

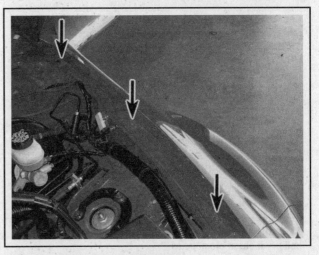

12.8 Upper fender mounting bolts

7   Remove the front bumper (see Section 11).
8   Remove the bolts along the upper edge of the fender (see illustration).
9   Remove the bolt at the upper rear corner of the fender (see illustration). Remove the fender.
10 Installation is the reverse of removal.

12.9 Rear fender mounting bolt

13 Trunk lid - removal, installation and adjustment

→Note: The trunk lid is heavy and somewhat awkward to remove and install - at least two people should perform this procedure.

2005 AND EARLIER MODELS

✳✳ WARNING:

The trunk lid is heavy enough to cause injury if the balance spring isn't in position. If you need to remove the balance spring, remove the trunk lid first.

Removal and installation

♦ Refer to illustrations 13.3 and 13.5

1   Open the trunk lid and cover the edges of the trunk compartment with pads or cloths to protect the painted surfaces when the lid is removed.
2   Disconnect any cables or wire harness connectors attached to the

trunk lid that would interfere with removal.
3   Make alignment marks around the hinge mounting nuts with a marking pen (see illustration).

13.3 Mark the position of the hinges on the trunk lid

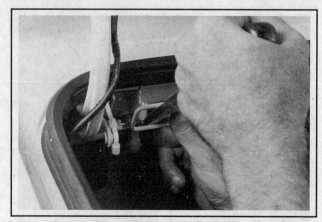

13.5 Slip a taped screwdriver through the balance spring and pry it out of the notches

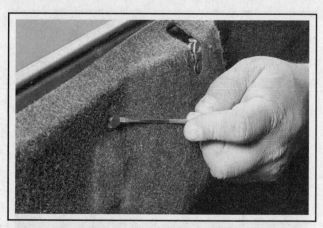

13.10a Pry the button up and pull the plastic rivets out of the trim panel

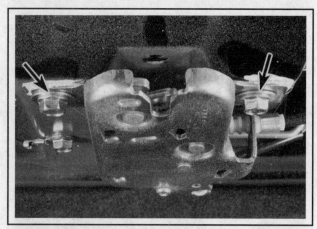

13.10b Remove the latch bolts

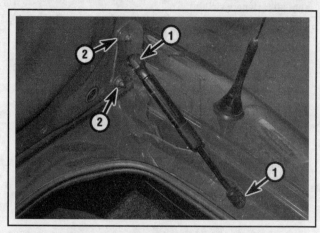

13.14 Trunk lid removal details (right side shown)

1   Strut rod spherical bearing protective clips
2   Trunk lid hinge nuts

4   While an assistant supports the trunk lid, remove the lid-to-hinge nuts on both sides of the trunk and lift it off.

5   If you need to remove the balance spring, wrap a screwdriver with tape to protect the paint, then insert it through the end of the balance spring and pry it out of the notch (see illustration).

6   Installation is the reverse of removal.

➡**Note: When reinstalling the trunk lid, align the hinges with the marks made during removal.**

Trunk lid adjustment

▶ **Refer to illustrations 13.10a and 13.10b**

7   Fore-and-aft and side-to-side adjustment of the trunk lid is accomplished by moving the lid in relation to the hinge after loosening the bolts or nuts.

8   Scribe a line around the entire hinge plate as described earlier in this Section so you can determine the amount of movement.

9   Loosen the nuts and move the trunk lid into correct alignment. Move it only a little at a time. Tighten the hinge nuts and carefully lower the trunk lid to check the alignment.

10   If necessary after installation, the entire trunk lid striker assembly can be adjusted up and down as well as from side to side on the trunk lid so the lid closes securely and is flush with the rear quarter panels. To do this, remove the trunk trim panel for access, then scribe a line around the trunk striker assembly to provide a reference point. Then loosen the bolts and reposition the striker as necessary (see illustrations). Following adjustment, retighten the mounting bolts.

Balance spring adjustment

11   The balance spring should raise the trunk lid 2-3/4 to 12 inches when the lock is unlocked. If the trunk lid rises more or less than this, reposition the balance spring in its notches to increase or reduce spring tension.

2006 AND LATER MODELS

▶ **Refer to illustration 13.14**

12   Disconnect the trunk lid wiring harness connector, remove the clips that secure the trunk lid harness and set the harness safely aside where it won't be damaged during trunk lid removal.

13   Mark the position of both hinges on the trunk lid (see illustration 13.3).

14   Pry off the protective clips from each end of the two trunk lid struts (see illustration). With an assistant holding up the trunk lid, pry loose the spherical bearings at each end of the two trunk lid struts and remove both struts.

15 With the assistant holding the trunk lid, remove the trunk lid hinge bolts and remove the trunk lid.

16 When installing the trunk lid, make sure that the hinges are aligned with the marks that you made prior to disassembly, then tighten the hinge bolts securely. Again, having an assistant there to help is a good idea.

17 Installation is otherwise the reverse of removal. Be sure to install the clamping bands over the spherical bearings at each end of the struts.

18 Check the alignment of the trunk lid striker in relation to the latch (see Section 14).

14 Trunk lid latch, striker and lock cylinder - removal and installation

2005 AND EARLIER MODELS

Trunk lid latch

▶ Refer to illustrations 14.3 and 14.4

1 Open the trunk, remove the trunk trim panel for access, then scribe a line around the trunk striker assembly to provide a reference point to aid the installation procedure.

2 Detach the retaining bolts and remove the latch (see illustration 13.10b).

3 Disconnect the trunk release cable from the latch (see illustration).

4 If you need to remove the striker, unbolt it from the trunk lid (see illustration).

5 Installation is the reverse of removal. See Section 13 for adjustment procedures.

Trunk lock cylinder

▶ Refer to illustrations 14.7 and 14.8

6 Open the trunk and remove the trim panel (see illustration 13.10a).

7 Pry the retaining clip loose from the actuator rod and separate the actuator rod from the lock cylinder (see illustration).

8 Remove the retaining bolts and take the lock cylinder out of the rear body panel (see illustration).

9 Installation is the reverse of removal.

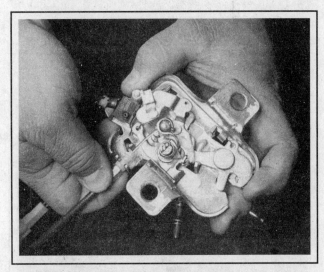
14.3 Turn the latch over and detach the opener cable

14.4 Remove the striker bolts

14.7 Pry the retaining clip off the rod and pull the rod free of the lock cylinder

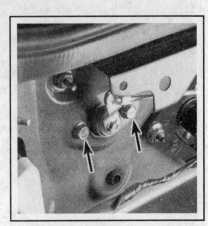
14.8 Remove the bolts to detach the lock cylinder from the trunk

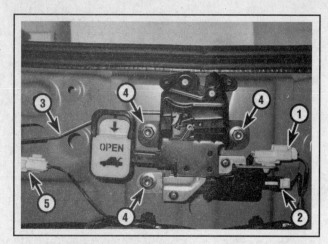

14.12 Trunk lid latch details

1 Trunk compartment light electrical connector
2 Trunk lid opener electrical connector
3 Actuator rod
4 Trunk lid latch mounting bolts
5 Key lock cylinder electrical connector

2006 AND LATER MODELS

Latch

♦ **Refer to illustration 14.12**

10 Remove the trunk trim from the rear area of the trunk around the trunk lid latch.

11 Disengage the trunk lid latch actuator rod from the key lock cylinder (see illustration 14.22).
12 Disconnect the electrical connectors from the trunk lid latch (see illustration).
13 Remove the latch mounting bolts and remove the latch.
14 Installation is the reverse of removal. Close the trunk lid and verify that the striker engages the latch correctly.
15 If necessary, adjust the position of the striker in relation to the latch (see Steps 16 through 20).

Striker adjustment

Refer to illustration 14.17

16 Remove the trim from the trunk in the area around the striker.
17 Loosen the striker bolts (see illustration).
18 Move the striker up, down, left or right as necessary, then retighten the bolts and verify that the striker engages the latch properly.
19 Repeat the previous Step until the striker is correctly aligned with the latch. Tighten the latch bolts securely.
20 Install the trunk trim.

Key lock cylinder

♦ **Refer to illustration 14.22**

21 Remove the trunk trim from the area around the key lock cylinder.
22 Disengage the trunk lid latch actuator rod from the key lock cylinder (see illustration).
23 Trace the electrical lead to its connector (see illustration 14.12) and disconnect it.
24 Remove the key lock cylinder mounting nuts and remove the key lock cylinder.
25 Installation is the reverse of removal.

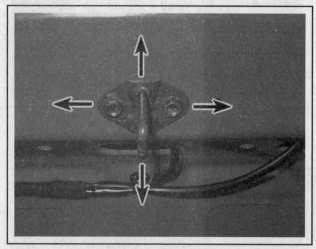

14.17 To adjust the striker, loosen the bolts and move the striker as necessary until it's correctly aligned with the latch

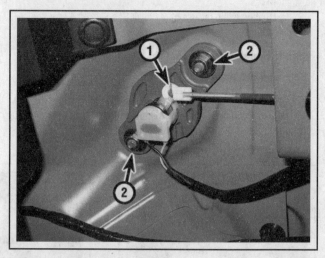

14.22 Key lock cylinder details

1 Trunk lid latch actuator rod
2 Key lock cylinder mounting nuts

15 Door trim panel - removal and installation

2005 AND EARLIER MODELS

▶ **Refer to illustrations 15.1, 15.2a, 15.2b, 15.3, 15.5, 15.7a and 15.7b**

1   On manual window models, remove the window crank by working a cloth back-and-forth behind the handle to dislodge the retainer (see illustration). A special tool is available for this purpose, but it is not essential. With the retainer removed, pull off the handle. On power window models, disconnect the battery, pry out the switch assembly, unplug the electrical connector and remove the switch assembly.

2   Pry the trim cap from the upper arm rest screw, then remove the screws and arm rest (see illustrations).

3   Remove the screw from the inside door handle cover (see illustration).

4   Lift up the inside door handle and remove the trim cover.

5   Insert a special trim panel removal tool, a wide putty knife, or a thin screwdriver between the door trim panel and door to disengage the door trim retaining clips. Work around the outer edge until the panel is loose (see illustration).

6   Make sure all of the door trim retaining clips are disengaged. Remove the door trim panel from the vehicle by gently pulling it upwards and out, while disconnecting any electrical connectors.

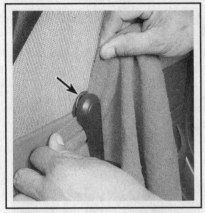

15.1 Work a cloth up behind the manual window regulator handle and move it back-and-forth until the retainer is pushed up so you can remove it

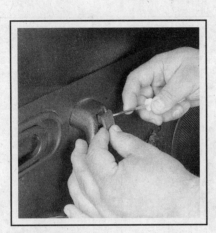

15.2a Pry out the trim cap . . .

15.2b . . . and remove the three arm rest screws (1997 and earlier shown)

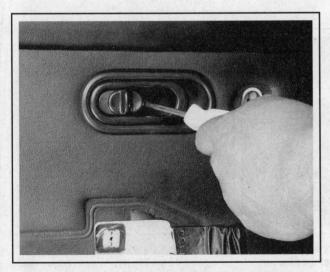

15.3 Remove the screw from the handle cover and lift out the cover (1997 and earlier shown)

15.5 Use a trim panel removal tool to detach the trim panel retaining clips, then pull the door trim up and out to remove it

7 For access to inside the door, remove the plastic watershield. Peel back the plastic cover, taking care not to tear it (see illustration). To remove the watershield completely, you'll need to remove the inside handle and peel back the separate handle watershield (see illustration).

8 To install the door trim panel, first press the watershield back into place. If necessary, add more sealant to hold it in place. Install the inside handle if it was removed.

9 Prior to installation of the door trim panel, be sure to reinstall any clips which may have come out of the door trim panel during removal.

10 Place the door trim panel in position, making sure that any door panel electrical connectors are connected or routed through the panel as necessary. Press the door trim panel into place until the clips are seated.

11 The remainder of installation is the reverse of the removal steps.

If the vehicle has manual windows, place the clip on the window crank, then push the crank onto the shaft until the clip engages.

2006 AND LATER MODELS

♦ **Refer to illustrations 15.12a, 15.12b, 15.14, 15.15 and 15.16**

12 Remove the trim cover from the inside door handle and remove the trim panel retaining screw (see illustration), then remove the trim cap from the upper end of the door pull (see illustration).

13 Remove the retaining screws from the inside door handle and from the upper end of the door pull.

14 Remove the trim cap from inside the cup holder and remove the retaining screw (see illustration).

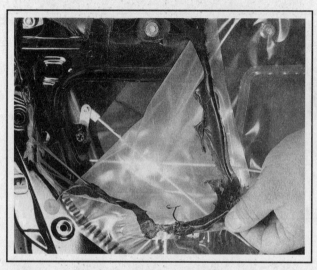

15.7a If the plastic watershield is peeled off carefully, it can be reused

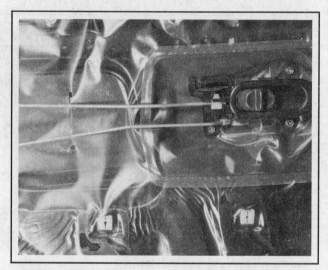

15.7b Remove the inside handle screws and peel off the handle watershield (1997 and earlier shown)

15.12a Carefully pry out the trim cover from the inside door handle recess. When installing this cover, make sure that the tab (1) seats fully into the slot (2)

15.12b Carefully pry of the trim cap from the upper end of the door pull, then remove the retaining screws from the inside door handle and the upper end of the door pull

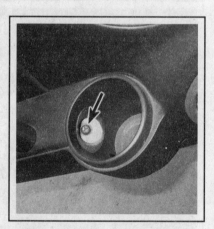

15.14 Remove the trim cap from inside the cup holder and remove this retaining screw

15 Remove the door trim panel (see illustration). Use a trim panel removal tool to pry loose the clips. Start from the bottom of the trim panel and work around the perimeter until all the fasteners have been released from the door.

16 Pull the trim panel away from the door slightly and disengage the cable ends from the inside door handle. To disengage each cable end, align the foot on the lower end of the connecting pin with the elongated hole in the handle lever, then lift the pin straight up (see illustration).

17 Disconnect all electrical connectors from the backside of the trim panel and remove the trim panel.

18 When installing the door trim panel, start with the upper edge. Align the three clips along the upper edge and pull down on the trim panel to engage the clips, then pop all the other clips into place.

19 Installation is otherwise the reverse of removal.

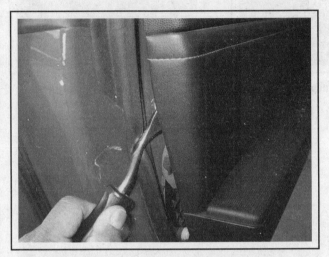

15.15 Use a trim panel removal tool to pry off the door trim panel

15.16 To disengage the cables from the inside door handle, align the foot on the lower end of each cable end pin with the elongated hole in the handle lever, then pull the pin straight up

16 Door - removal, installation and adjustment

➡**Note: The door is heavy and somewhat awkward to remove and install - at least two people should perform this procedure.**

REMOVAL AND INSTALLATION

▶ **Refer to illustrations 16.7, 16.8a and 16.8b**

1 Lower the window completely in the door and then disconnect the negative cable from the battery (see Chapter 5).

2 Open the door all the way and support it on jacks or blocks covered with rags to prevent damaging the paint.

3 Remove the door trim panel and watershield (see Section 15).

4 Remove the door speaker (see Chapter 12).

5 Unplug all electrical connectors, ground wires and harness retaining clips from the door.

➡**Note: It's a good idea to label all connections to aid the reassembly process.**

6 Working through the door speaker hole and the door opening, detach the rubber conduit between the body and the door. Then pull the wiring harness through the conduit and remove it from the door.

7 Pull out the pin out of the door stop strut (see illustration). Remove the nuts and detach the door stop strut from the door.

16.7 Remove the stop strut pin; you'll need to remove the trim panel and watershield to detach the stop strut from the door

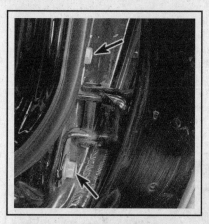

16.8a Remove the lower hinge bolts . . .

16.8b . . . and the upper hinge bolts

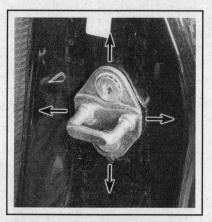

16.11 Adjust the door lock striker by loosening the mounting screws and gently tapping the striker in the desired direction

8   Mark around the door hinges and hinge bolts to aid alignment when reinstalling (see illustrations).

9   Remove the hinge-to-door bolts and carefully detach the door.

10 Installation is the reverse of removal. Adjust and securely tighten the door hinge bolts and striker bolts, if removed, as described below.

ADJUSTMENT

▶ Refer to illustration 16.11

11 Following installation, locate the alignment marks made during door removal. Make sure the door is aligned properly and adjust it if necessary as follows:

a) Up-and-down and forward-and-backward adjustments are made by loosening the hinge-to-body bolts and moving the door, as necessary. A special offset tool may be required to reach some of the bolts.

b) In-and-out and up-and-down adjustments are made by loosening the door side hinge bolts and moving the door, as necessary. A special offset tool may be required to reach some of the bolts.

c) The door lock striker can also be adjusted both up-and-down and sideways to provide a positive engagement with the locking mechanism. This is done by loosening the screws and moving the striker by hand or by lightly tapping with a soft-faced hammer, as necessary (see illustration).

d) Check the alignment of the wedge attached to the lower part of the doorjamb with the dovetail in the door. Adjust if necessary by loosening the wedge screws and moving the wedge up or down.

17 Door latch, lock cylinder and handles - removal and installation

2005 AND EARLIER MODELS

1   Remove the door trim panel and the plastic watershield (see Section 15).

Door latch

2   Reach inside the door and disconnect the control links from the latch.

3   Mark the location of the door latch prior to removal. Remove the latch retaining screws from the end of the door.

4   Detach the door latch.

5   Installation is the reverse of removal. Align the door latch and tighten the door latch screws securely.

Outside handle

▶ Refer to illustration 17.6

6   Through the door inside access hole, remove the outside handle retention nuts (see illustration).

17.6 Pry up the retaining clip (left arrow) and remove the control rod from the lock cylinder; remove the nuts (right arrow; one nut hidden) to detach the outside handle from the door

7 Remove the control rod from the lock cylinder (see illustration 17.6).

8 Use a pliers or screwdriver to pry the retaining clip upwards and off of the lock cylinder.

9 Pull the outside handle and lock cylinder from the door.

10 Installation is the reverse of removal.

Inside handle

11 Refer to Section 15 for removal and installation.

2006 AND LATER MODELS

Door unit

▶ **Refer to illustration 17.14**

➡**Note: The door unit is the metal inner door panel that protects the trim panel from moisture, just like the plastic watershield used on earlier models. The door unit must be removed to remove the door latch and actuator, the outside door handle, the window glass, the window glass regulator and the outside power mirror.**

12 Remove the door trim panel (see Section 15).

13 Remove the door speaker (see Chapter 12).

14 Disconnect the electrical connectors for the power mirror, the door lock actuator and the power window motor, remove all door unit fasteners and remove the door unit (see illustration).

15 Installation is the reverse of removal.

Door latch and lock actuator

▶ **Refer to illustrations 17.18 and 17.19**

16 Remove the door trim panel (see Section 15) and the door unit (see Steps 12 through 14).

17 Disconnect the cables from the inside door handle and the door lock knob.

18 Disengage the rods from the key lock cylinder and the outside door handle (see illustration).

19 Remove the door latch retaining screws (see illustration) and remove the latch and lock actuator.

20 Installation is the reverse of removal.

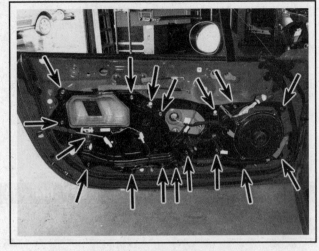

17.14 Door unit mounting fastener locations

Outside door handle

▶ **Refer to illustration 17.23**

21 Remove the door trim panel (see Section 15) and the door unit (see Steps 12 through 14).

22 Disengage the rod from the outside door handle (see illustration 17.18).

23 From inside the door, remove the cover from the door handle retaining bolt, then remove the retaining bolt (see illustration).

24 Firmly grasp the rear part of the outside door handle with one hand and with the other hand pull the door handle lever out (as if you were opening the door) and remove the rear part of the outside handle. Pull the rear part of the outside door handle out, away from the door, to disengage the locking tab (see illustration 17.23) from the mounting hole. Be careful not to scratch the paint.

25 To install the outside door handle, insert the locking tab through the mounting hole in the door (see illustration 17.23), push the rear part of the handle assembly toward the door, align the mounting bolt hole in the handle with the mounting bolt hole in the door, install the door

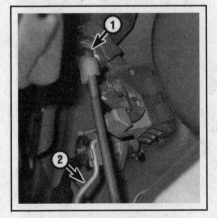

17.18 Outside door handle actuator rod (1) and key lock cylinder actuator rod (2)

17.19 Door latch mounting screws

17.23 Outside door handle cover and bolt (1). To remove the outside door handle, pull the mounting tab out, then back (2)

handle retaining bolt and tighten it securely. Install the bolt cover.

26 The remainder of installation is the reverse of removal.

Key lock cylinder

27 Remove the door trim panel (see Section 15), the door window glass (see Section 18), the door unit (see Steps 12 through 14) and the outside door handle (see Steps 22 through 24).

28 Disengage the rod from the key lock cylinder (see illustration 17.18).

29 Rotate the key lock cylinder so that the tab on the lock cylinder is aligned with the notch in the door.

30 Remove the key lock cylinder by pulling it out of the door from the outside.

31 To install the key lock cylinder, align the tab on the cylinder with the notch in the door, insert the cylinder into the door, then rotate the cylinder clockwise. Installation is otherwise the reverse of removal.

---

18 Door window glass - removal, installation and adjustment

2005 AND EARLIER MODELS

Removal and installation

1 Remove the door trim panel, the inside handle and the plastic watershields (see Section 15).

2 Open the window to approximately 7-1/2 inches from the fully open position.

3 Remove the outside trim along the top edge of the door. It's secured by a screw at the front and rear ends and clips along its length.

4 Disconnect the negative battery cable (see Chapter 5).

5 Place a rag inside the door panel to help prevent scratching the glass. Remove the nuts from the bottom of the glass.

6 Remove the glass by pulling it away from the regulator and up and out of the door.

7 Installation is the reverse of removal.

Adjustment

▶ **Refer to illustration 18.9**

8 Window glass vertical adjustment is by means of the upper stoppers mounted in the lower edge of the glass. Loosen the stopper screws, position and hold the glass fully closed in the door frame, and lightly tighten the adjustment screws. Wind the window slowly, checking for smooth travel. Adjust vertically and horizontally to obtain full closure with smooth travel as the window is wound up and down.

9 Window glass in-and-out adjustment is done by moving the lower ends of the rear channel and regulator in or out. To do this, loosen the channel and regulator nuts in the bottom of the door (see illustration). Move the channel and regulator in or out as necessary to obtain correct alignment of the glass when the window is closed, then tighten the nuts.

2006 AND LATER MODELS

Door window glass

▶ **Refer to illustrations 18.12 and 18.13**

10 Lower the door window glass so that the top of the glass is 4.33 inches above the beltline molding.

11 Remove the door trim panel (see Section 15) and the door unit (see Section 17).

12 Remove the glass stopper retaining bolts (see illustration) and remove the glass stoppers.

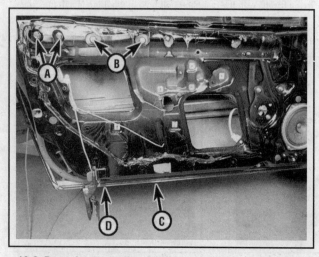

18.9 Door glass mounting details

A   Rear channel upper nut and bolt
B   Regulator upper bolts
C   Regulator lower nut (in bottom of door)
D   Rear channel lower nut (in bottom of door)

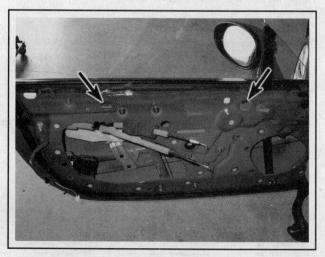

18.12 Door window glass stopper bolts

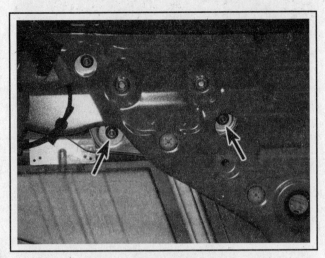

18.13 Door window glass-to-regulator nuts

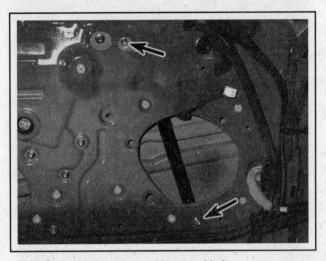

18.17 Door window glass guide nut and bolt

13 Remove the nuts that secure the door window glass to the regulator (see illustration).

14 To remove the door window glass, pull it up and out of the door, tilting the upper edge of the glass inward (toward the vehicle).

15 Installation is the reverse of removal.

Quarter glass

▶ **Refer to illustration 18.17**

16 Remove the door trim panel (see Section 15), the door unit (see Section 17) and the door window glass (see Steps 10 through 14).

17 Remove the nut and bolt (see illustration), then remove the door glass guide.

18 Remove the nuts, then remove the door quarter glass from the door glass guide.

19 Installation is the reverse of removal.

---

19 Window regulator - removal and installation

2005 AND EARLIER MODELS

▶ **Refer to illustration 19.5**

1 Remove the door trim panel, inside handle and watershields (see Section 15).

2 Remove the door glass (see Section 18).

3 Mark or measure the location of the manual or power window regulator assembly for reinstallation alignment.

4 For power windows, disconnect the power window electrical connector.

5 Unbolt the window regulator assembly and remove the regulator through the door frame access hole (see illustration 18.9 and the accompanying illustration).

6 Remove the door glass run channel as necessary (see illustration 18.9).

7 Installation is the reverse of removal. During installation, apply multi-purpose grease to the regulator rollers.

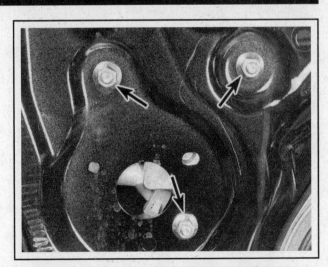

19.5 The cranking portion of the regulator is secured by three bolts

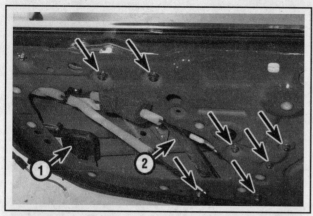

19.9 Regulator retaining nuts, power window motor (1) and regulator (2)

2006 AND LATER MODELS

▶ **Refer to illustration 19.9**

8   Remove the door trim panel (see Section 15), the door unit (see Section 17) and the door window glass (see Section 18).

9   Remove the window regulator retaining nuts (see illustration), then remove the regulator. Start with the motor, then angle the regulator mechanism properly so that you can work it through the access hole.

10   Installation is the reverse of removal.

20 Outside mirrors - removal and installation

▶ **Refer to illustration 20.2**

1   If you're working on a vehicle with power mirrors, disconnect the negative cable from the battery. Remove the inner door panel, inside handle and both watershields (see Section 15). Reach into the door and unplug the mirror wiring connector.

2   Rotate the mirror to expose the mounting screws (see illustration). Undo the screws and take the mirror off.

3   Installation is the reverse of removal.

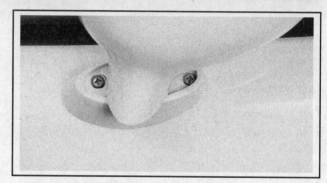

20.2 Rotate the mirror to expose the screws

21 Steering column covers - removal and installation

▶ **Refer to illustrations 21.2a and 21.2b**

1   Remove the steering column lower cover screws.

2   Separate the upper and lower covers and take them off (see illustrations).

3   Installation is the reverse of the removal procedure.

21.2a Lower steering column cover screw locations (1997 and earlier models shown, other models similar)

21.2b With the screws removed, separate the upper and lower cover halves

22 Center console - removal and installation

1 Disconnect the negative battery cable (see Chapter 5).

2005 AND EARLIER MODELS

▶ **Refer to illustrations 22.2, 22.3a, 22.3b, 22.4, 22.5 and 22.6**

2 Unscrew the shift knob (see illustration).
3 Lift out the ashtray and remove the screw beneath it (see illustrations).
4 Open the storage compartment and remove the screw(s) at the bottom (see illustration).

5 Remove the screw at the lower front of the console on each side (see illustration).
6 Lift the console up and unplug the electrical connectors (see illustration). Lift the console off the shift lever.
7 Installation is the reverse of the removal procedure.

2006 AND LATER MODELS

▶ **Refer to illustrations 22.9a, 22.9b, 22.10, 22.11a and 22.11b**

8 Unscrew and remove the shift lever knob.

22.2 Unscrew the shift knob

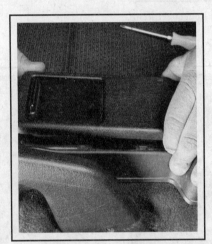

22.3a Lift out the ashtray . . .

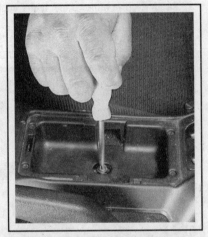

22.3b . . . and remove the screw beneath it

22.4 Remove the screw(s) from the bottom of the storage compartment

22.5 Remove one screw from the lower front on each side

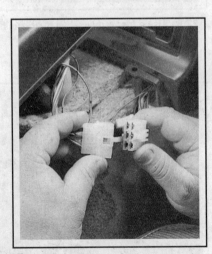

22.6 Lift the console partway out and unplug its electrical connectors

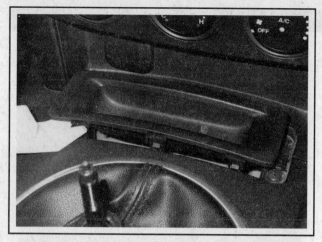

22.9a Use a trim removal tool to pry out the front cover from the center console

9   Remove the front and rear trim covers (see illustrations).
10 Remove the parking brake lever boot (see illustration).
11 Remove the console retaining screws (two at the front, one in the bottom of the cup holder receptacle and two at the rear) (see illustrations).
12 Lift up the console and disconnect the electrical connectors from the power window main switch and the gear position indicator.
13 Installation is the reverse of removal.

22.9b Use a trim removal tool to pry out the rear cover from the center console

22.10 Use a trim removal tool to pry loose the parking brake lever boot

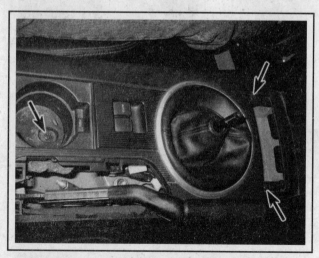

22.11a Center console front screw locations

22.11b Center console rear screw locations

23 Dashboard trim panels - removal and installation

2005 AND EARLIER MODELS

1   Dashboard trim panels include the center trim panel and instrument cluster bezel.

Center trim panel

▶ **Refer to illustrations 23.2a, 23.2b, 23.2c and 23.2d**

2   Pry out the left air duct louver (see illustration). Remove the center panel screw inside the left louver and the two screws at the bottom (see illustrations). Pull the center panel outward, disengaging the clip on each side. Unplug the panel's electrical connector and take the panel off (see illustration). Installation is the reverse of removal.

Instrument cluster bezel

▶ **Refer to illustrations 23.4a, 23.4b and 23.4c**

3   Remove the driver's side airbag module, steering wheel and column (see Chapter 10). Remove the steering column lower and upper covers (see Section 21).

4   Remove the screws from the underside of the instrument cluster bezel (see illustration). Pull the bezel out to detach its clips (see illustrations).

5   Installation is the reverse of removal.

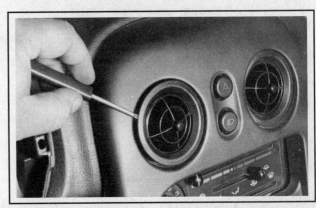

23.2a Pry the louvers out of their holes (they're secured by clips)

23.2b Remove the screw inside the left louver hole

23.2c Remove the horizontal screw and the vertical screw (arrow) at the bottom of the panel

23.2d Pull the panel out and unplug its electrical connector

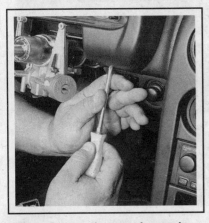

23.4a Remove the screw from under each side of the instrument cluster bezel

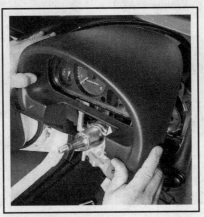

23.4b Pull the bezel out . . .

23.4c . . . disengaging its clips

2006 AND LATER MODELS

Side panels

▶ Refer to illustration 23.6

➡Note: This procedure applies to either side panel.

6   Using a trim removal tool, carefully pry the side panel out from the end of the dash to disengage the mounting clips (see illustration). Pull the panel rearward to disengage the mounting tab at the lower end of the panel and remove the panel.

7   When installing the side panel, make sure that it snaps back into place.

Left vent trim panel

▶ Refer to illustration 23.8

8   Using a trim removal tool, carefully pry loose the left vent trim panel (see illustration).

9   When installing the left vent trim panel, make sure that it snaps back into place.

Instrument cluster trim panel

▶ Refer to illustration 23.10

10   Using a trim removal tool, carefully pry loose the four instrument cluster trim panel retaining clips from the instrument panel (see illustration) and remove it.

11   Installation is the reverse of removal.

Side walls

▶ Refer to illustration 23.12

12   Using a trim removal tool or a taped screwdriver, carefully pry the side wall away from the center panel unit while simultaneously pulling the side wall toward the rear of the vehicle (see illustration).

✳✳ CAUTION:

Trying to simply pry off the side wall might damage the mounting clips, pins and tab.

23.6 Pry off the side panel with a trim removal tool

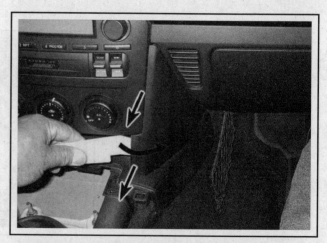

23.8 Pry off the left vent trim panel with a trim removal tool

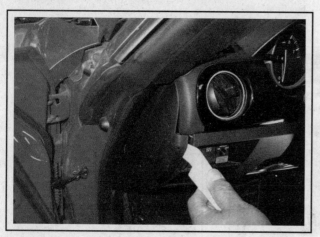

23.10 Pry loose the instrument cluster trim panel

23.12 Pry the trailing edge of the side wall out, away from the center panel unit, and simultaneously pull the side wall to the rear to disengage the retaining clip and pin

13 When installing the side wall, first push it forward to engage the clips and pins that face forward with their respective mounting holes. Push it inward, toward the center panel to snap the remaining clips, pins and tab into place.

Knee bolster trim panel

▶ **Refer to illustration 23.14**

14 Pull the knee bolster trim panel rearward to disengage the clips at the upper corners. Pull the lower edge of the panel down to disengage the clips at the lower corners (see illustration).

15 Installation is the reverse of removal.

Knee bolster

▶ **Refer to illustration 23.17**

16 Remove the knee bolster trim panel.

17 Remove the knee bolster mounting screws (see illustration) and remove the knee bolster.

18 Installation is the reverse of removal.

Console panel

▶ **Refer to illustrations 23.21 and 23.22**

19 Remove the center console (see Section 22).

20 Remove the side walls (see Step 12).

21 Remove the console panel retaining screws (see illustration).

22 Pull the console panel to the rear to disengage the locator pin and mounting tab from each side (see illustration).

23 Disconnect the electrical connectors from the console panel and remove the panel.

24 When installing the console panel, make sure that the tab and pin on each side are correctly aligned with their corresponding installation holes, then push the panel forward until the tabs and pins snap into place.

25 Installation is otherwise the reverse of removal.

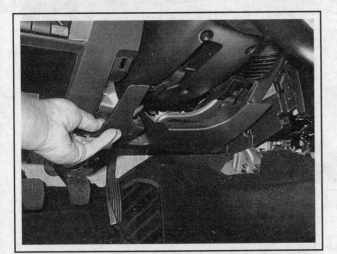

23.14 Pull the knee bolster trim panel rearward to disengage the clips at the upper corners, then pull down the lower edge of the panel to disengage the clips at the lower corners

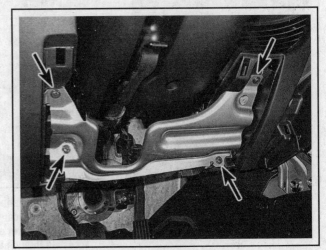

23.17 Knee bolster mounting screws

23.21 Console panel retaining screws

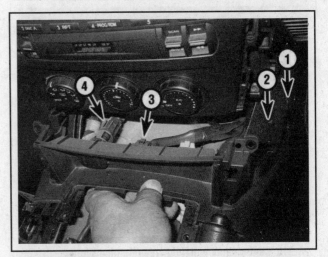

23.22 Console panel details

1	Locator pin	4 Accessory socket
2	Mounting tab	electrical connector
3	Electrical connector	

Glove box

▶ Refer to illustration 23.26

26 To disconnect the glove box stoppers from the sides of the box, twist each stopper in a counterclockwise direction and work it out of its mounting hole in the box (see illustration).

27 Open the glove box as far as it will go, then disengage the hinge pins from their receptacles and remove the glove box.

28 Installation is the reverse of removal.

Center panel unit

▶ Refer to illustrations 23.30, 23.31a, 23.31b and 23.32

29 Remove the knee bolster trim panel, the knee bolster, the side walls and the glove box.

30 If equipped, remove the center panel installation bolt (see illustration).

31 Remove the center panel retaining screws (see illustrations).

32 Pull out the center panel unit and disconnect the antenna lead from the radio. Disconnect the electrical connectors from the radio and the heater and air conditioning control assembly. Disconnecting the antenna lead and the electrical connector from the radio is extremely difficult on these models because the space behind the radio and the heater and air conditioning control assembly is extremely tight. Before disconnecting them, disengage the harness clip (see illustration) to put enough slack in the harness to disconnect the connectors. Access the harness clip and connectors from the left side of the glove box receptacle.

33 If you are replacing the heater and air conditioning control assembly, refer to Chapter 3. If you are replacing the radio, refer to Chapter 12.

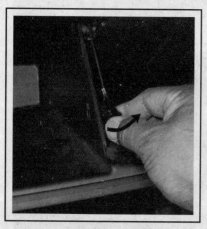

23.26 To disengage the stoppers from the glove box, twist them and pull them out

23.30 The installation bolt, if equipped, is located on the left side of the center panel unit and is accessed through the cavity for the knee bolster

23.31a Center panel unit left side retaining screw

23.31b Center panel unit right side retaining screw

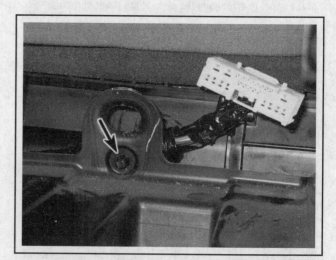

23.32 Before you even try to disconnect this large multi-pin connector from the radio, disengage this harness clip by squeezing it with a pair of needle nose pliers and pushing it through its bracket

34 Installation is the reverse of removal.

⁂ CAUTION:

When installing the center panel unit, make sure that the wiring harness and antenna lead are not snagged between the unit, the dashboard and/or the firewall. If the wiring harness or the antenna lead is pinched or kinked, it might cause the radio and/or the heater and air conditioning control assembly to malfunction.

Right vent trim panel

▶ **Refer to illustrations 23.36a and 23.36b**

35 Remove the side walls (see Step 12), the glove box and the center panel unit (see Steps 26 through 32).

36 Remove the three vent trim panel retaining screws (see illustrations). Two of the screws are located in the upper part of the cavity for the center panel unit; the third screw is located in the roof of the cavity for the glove box, above the glovebox latch.

37 Grasp the vent trim panel firmly and carefully pull it straight back to disengage the mounting clips.

38 Installation is the reverse of removal.

23.36b Third vent trim panel screw, located in the upper part of the glove box cavity, above the glove box striker

Switch panel

▶ **Refer to illustration 23.41**

39 Remove the left side panel, the left vent trim panel, the knee bolster trim panel and the knee bolster.

40 Disengage the hood release lever from the switch panel (see Section 10).

41 Remove the switch panel retaining screws (see illustration), pull off the switch panel and disconnect the electrical connectors.

42 Installation is the reverse of removal.

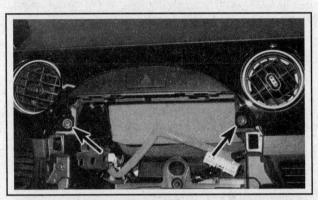

23.36a Right vent trim panel screws

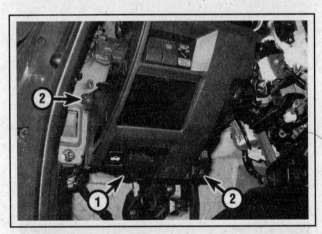

23.41 Switch panel details

1 *Hood release lever*
2 *Lower mounting screws (upper screws, not shown, are behind left vent trim panel)*

24 Instrument panel - removal and installation

⁂ WARNING:

All models are equipped with airbags. The airbag is armed and can deploy (inflate) whenever the battery is connected. To prevent accidental deployment (and possible injury), turn the ignition key to LOCK and disconnect the negative battery cable whenever working near airbag components. After the battery is disconnected, wait at least two minutes before beginning work (the system has a back-up capacitor that must fully discharge). See Chapter 12 for more information.

1 Turn the ignition key OFF, then disconnect the cable from the negative terminal of the battery. Wait at least two minutes before proceeding.

⁂ WARNING:

Follow the airbag servicing instructions prior to proceeding with any steps that may involve working around the airbags.

DO NOT disassemble any airbag component.

DO NOT attempt repair of airbag system wiring harness.

DO NOT inspect or check the airbag system using an ohmmeter, because this can cause inadvertent deployment of the airbag.

DO NOT disconnect the airbag module (SAS) with the ignition switch ON - this could cause inadvertent airbag deployment.

DO NOT handle or carry the airbag with the trim cover facing you when it has been removed and is live (has not been deployed).

When handling the airbag, DO NOT set the airbag module down with the trim cover facing down.

DO NOT touch a deployed airbag for at least 15 minutes - it can be extremely hot.

Contact a dealer for proper disposal of a used airbag.

2005 AND EARLIER MODELS

♦ **Refer to illustrations 24.3, 24.9a, 24.9b, 24.10, 24.13, 24.14a, 24.14b and 24.14c**

2   Remove the center console (see Section 22).

3   Remove the top strikers, sun visors and adapters (see illustration). Pull the header trim away from the body to detach its six clips. Disengage the pin on the header trim and take the trim off.

4   Pull the A-pillar trim on each side away from the body to detach the three clips. Disengage the trim pin from the body and take the A-pillar trim off.

5   Remove the radio (see Chapter 12).

6   Remove the instrument cluster (see Chapter 12).

7   Open the glove compartment, undo its hinge screws and take the glove compartment out.

8   On 1994 and later models:

   a) Remove the passenger side airbag module as follows:

   b) Disconnect the airbag electrical connector.

   c) Remove the airbag retaining screws from inside the glove compartment area (glove compartment removed).

   d) Lift out the passenger side airbag assembly.

   e) Remove the driver's side airbag module and the steering wheel (see Chapter 10).

9   Remove the lower cover from under the steering wheel (see illustration). Unplug the instrument panel electrical connectors below the column (see illustration).

10   Remove the steering column mounting bolts and lower the steering column away from the dashboard (see illustration).

11   Detach the hood release knob or lever from the instrument panel.

12   Disconnect the heater control assembly wires and cables from the heater/blower unit (see Chapter 3).

13   Pry out the center hole cover on the top of the dashboard at the windshield vent panel (see illustration). Remove the screw at the center of the windshield vent panel.

14   Pry out the bolt covers in the right and left side panels at the ends of the dashboard as well as at the bottom of the center panel (see illustrations). Remove the instrument panel mounting bolts located beneath the covers.

15   Carefully remove the instrument panel while disconnecting any remaining electrical connectors.

16   Installation is the reverse of removal. When reinstalling the instrument panel and reconnecting the heater controls, see Chapter 3 for control adjustment.

2006 AND LATER MODELS

♦ **Refer to illustrations 24.31, 24.35a, 24.35b and 24.35c**

17   Remove the driver's airbag and the steering wheel (see Chapter 10).

18   Remove the steering column covers (see Section 21).

19   Remove the steering column switches (see Chapter 12).

20   Remove the instrument cluster trim panel (see Section 23).

21   Remove the instrument cluster (see Chapter 12).

22   Remove the knee bolster trim panel and the knee bolster (see Section 23).

23   Unbolt and lower the steering column.

24   Remove the center console (see Section 22).

25   Remove the glove box (see Section 23).

26   Remove the side walls (see Section 23).

27   Remove the center panel unit (see Section 23).

28   Remove the side panels (see Section 23).

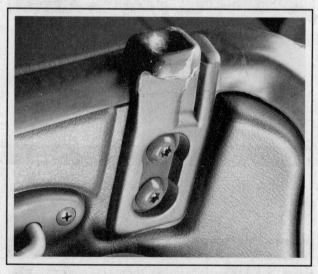

24.3 Remove the top latch strikers and sun visors so the header panel can be removed

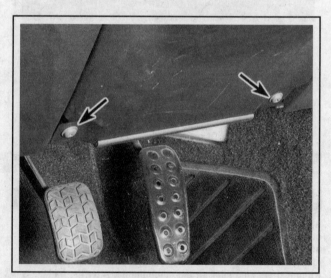

24.9a Remove the screws and remove the panel from beneath the steering column

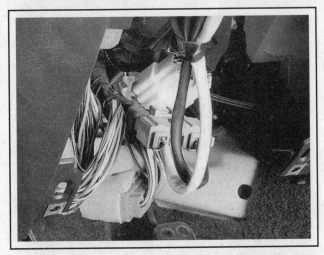

24.9b Unplug the electrical connectors

24.10 Unbolt the steering column and lower it away from the dashboard

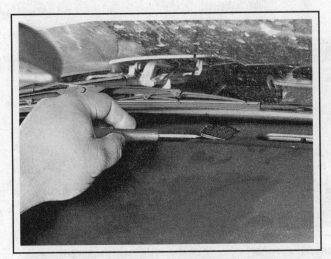

24.13 Pry the cover from the screw at the top center of the instrument panel and remove the screw

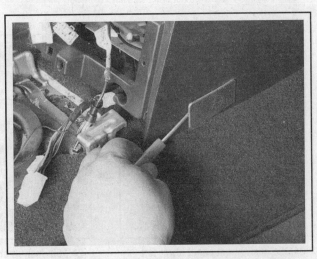

24.14a Uncover and remove the screw at each side of the lower center panel

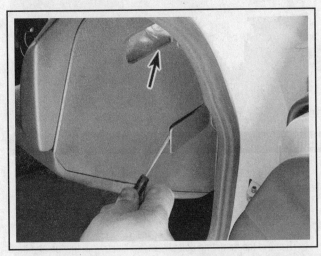

24.14b Pry the upper cover (arrow) and lower cover from the screws on each side of the instrument panel

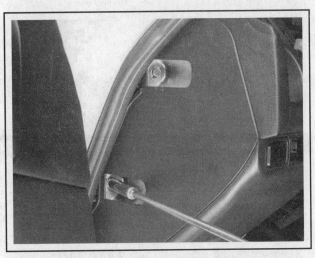

24.14c Remove the screws and lift the panel out

29 Remove the hood release lever (see Section 10).

30 Using a trim removal tool, carefully pry off the A-pillar trim panels.

31 Using a trim removal tool, carefully pry off the left and right door opening scuff plates (see illustration).

32 Remove the left and right kick panels.

33 Remove the interior fuse and relay box.

34 Disconnect all electrical harness connectors.

35 Remove the instrument panel mounting nuts and bolts:

a) Left and right end bolts (two at each end of the instrument panel, in the same vicinity as the side panels)

b) Left and right lower corner bolts (two at each end) (see illustrations)

c) Center vertical support bolts, at the lower end of the vertical support to the left of the center panel unit (see illustration)

d) Center bolt, above and to the left of the center vertical support bolts, accessed through the instrument cluster cavity; bolt faces down

36 Remove the instrument panel.

37 Installation is the reverse of removal.

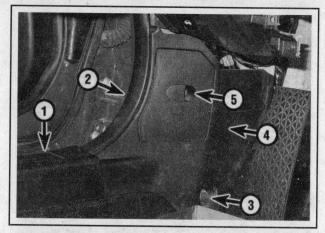

24.31 Scuff plate and kick panel details (left side shown, right side similar)

1 Scuff plate
2 Seaming wedge
3 Kick panel fastener
4 Kick panel
5 Fuse box

24.35a Instrument panel lower left mounting bolts

24.35b Instrument panel lower right mounting bolts

24.35c Instrument panel vertical support bolts

25 Convertible top - removal, installation and adjustment

REMOVAL AND INSTALLATION

1 Zip the rear window open. Pad the rear window on both sides with towels to protect it from scratches, then lower the top.

2 Remove the scuff plate from each doorsill.

3 Remove the cover and protector from each end of the beltline molding, then pull up the seaming welt that covers the edge of the door opening.

4 Pull out one of the quarter trim panels to detach its clips. Disengage the two pins and pull the panel out. Do the same with the other quarter trim panel.

5 Remove the screws and plastic rivets and detach the package tray trim panel.

6 Remove the mounting bolt at each front corner of the top and the nuts around the beltline. Lift the top off the vehicle, being careful not to scratch the window.

7 Installation is the reverse of the removal steps.

ADJUSTMENT

▶ **Refer to illustration 25.8**

8   Lift the cover to expose the top latch adjusting nut (see illustration). Turn the nut clockwise to decrease the clearance between the top and the windshield header, or counterclockwise to increase it.

25.8 Pull back the cover and turn the nut to adjust the top latches

---

26 Detachable hard top - removal, installation and adjustment

REMOVAL AND INSTALLATION

➡**Note: The hard top is heavy and somewhat awkward to remove and install - at least two people should perform this procedure.**

1   Open the windows all the way. If the vehicle has a rear window defogger, locate its electrical connector at the left lower corner of the top and unplug it.
3   Lower the sun visors and open the latches at the top of the windshield.
3   Open the latch on each side of the top at the lower corner.
4   Hold the forward part of the top with one hand and have an assistant do the same on the other side. Press down on the rear deck latches to free the top from the mounting studs on the rear deck. Move the top back just enough to clear the studs and lift it straight up and off the vehicle.
5   Installation is the reverse of removal. Make sure the convertible top is lower all the way before you install the hard top.

ADJUSTMENT

6   The side and top latches are adjusted in the same way as the convertible top latches (see illustration 25.8).
7   To adjust the mounting studs on the rear deck, loosen their bolts. Move the plates forward, backward or sideways as needed and tighten the bolts.

---

27 Seats - removal and installation

▶ **Refer to illustrations 27.3a and 27.3b**

1   Disconnect the seat belt buckle electrical connector near the floor.
2   Remove the seat forward/back travel release handle cover at the side of the seat.
3   Remove the seat rail retaining bolts at the floor, disconnect the electrical connector, and lift the seats from the vehicle (see illustrations).
4   Installation is the reverse of removal.

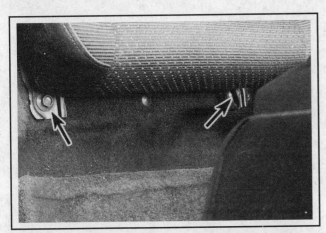

27.3a Detach the seat rail bolt covers (if equipped), and remove the front seat rail bolts from the floor

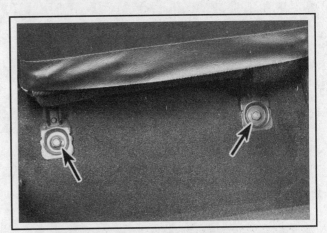

27.3b Remove the rear seat rail bolts, detach the electrical connector and remove the seat from the vehicle

28 Seat belts - check

1   Check the seat belts, buckles, latch plates and guide loops for any obvious damage or signs of wear.

2   Make sure the seat belt reminder light comes on when the key is turned on.

3   The seat belts are designed to lock up during a sudden stop or impact, yet allow free movement during normal driving. The retractors should hold the belt against your chest while driving and rewind the belt when the buckle is unlatched. Check the retractor on each seat belt locks when the belt is quickly pulled.

➡**Note: Do not remove the belt retractor covers or disassemble the retractors, as the ELR (Emergency Locking Retractor) has a spring that will unwind and cannot be rewound.**

4   If any of the above checks reveal problems with the seat belt system, disconnect the negative battery cable (see Chapter 5), and replace the seat belt components and retractor assemblies as necessary.

12

CHASSIS ELECTRICAL SYSTEM

Section

1 General information

The electrical system is a 12-volt, negative ground type. Power for the lights and all electrical accessories is supplied by a lead/acid-type battery which is charged by the alternator.

This Chapter covers repair and service procedures for the various electrical components not associated with the engine. Information on the battery, alternator, ignition system and starter motor can be found in Chapter 5.

It should be noted that when portions of the electrical system are serviced, the cable should be disconnected from the negative battery terminal to prevent electrical shorts and/or fires.

2 Electrical troubleshooting - general information

A typical electrical circuit consists of an electrical component, any switches, relays, motors, fuses, fusible links or circuit breakers related to that component and the wiring and electrical connectors that link the component to both the battery and the chassis. To help you pinpoint an electrical circuit problem, wiring diagrams are included at the end of this book.

Before tackling any troublesome electrical circuit, first study the appropriate wiring diagrams to get a complete understanding of what makes up that individual circuit. Trouble spots, for instance, can often be narrowed down by noting if other components related to the circuit are operating properly. If several components or circuits fail at one time, chances are the problem is in a fuse or ground connection, because several circuits are often routed through the same fuse and ground connections.

Electrical problems usually stem from simple causes, such as loose or corroded connections, a blown fuse, a melted fusible link or a bad relay. Visually inspect the condition of all fuses, wires and connections in a problem circuit before troubleshooting it.

If testing instruments are going to be utilized, use the diagrams to plan ahead of time where you will make the necessary connections in order to accurately pinpoint the trouble spot.

The basic tools needed for electrical troubleshooting include a circuit tester or voltmeter (a 12-volt bulb with a set of test leads can also be used), a continuity tester, which includes a bulb, battery and set of test leads, and a jumper wire, preferably with a circuit breaker incorporated, which can be used to bypass electrical components. Before attempting to locate a problem with test instruments, use the wiring diagram(s) to decide where to make the connections.

VOLTAGE CHECKS

Voltage checks should be performed if a circuit is not functioning properly. Connect one lead of a circuit tester to either the negative battery terminal or a known good ground. Connect the other lead to a electrical connector in the circuit being tested, preferably nearest to the battery or fuse. If the bulb of the tester lights, voltage is present, which means that the part of the circuit between the electrical connector and the battery is problem free. Continue checking the rest of the circuit in the same fashion. When you reach a point at which no voltage is present, the problem lies between that point and the last test point with voltage. Most of the time the problem can be traced to a loose connection.

➡Note: Keep in mind that some circuits receive voltage only when the ignition key is in the Accessory or On position.

FINDING A SHORT

One method of finding shorts in a circuit is to remove the fuse and connect a test light or voltmeter in its place to the fuse terminals. There should be no voltage present in the circuit. Move the wiring harness from side to side while watching the test light. If the bulb goes on, there is a short to ground somewhere in that area, probably where the insulation has rubbed through. The same test can be performed on each component in the circuit, even a switch.

GROUND CHECK

Perform a ground test to check whether a component is properly grounded. Disconnect the battery and connect one lead of a self-powered test light, known as a continuity tester, to a known good ground. Connect the other lead to the wire or ground connection being tested. If the bulb goes on, the ground is good. If the bulb does not go on, the ground is not good.

CONTINUITY CHECK

A continuity check is done to determine if there are any breaks in a circuit - if it is passing electricity properly. With the circuit off (no power in the circuit), a self-powered continuity tester can be used to check the circuit. Connect the test leads to both ends of the circuit (or to the "power" end and a good ground), and if the test light comes on the circuit is passing current properly. If the light doesn't come on, there is a break somewhere in the circuit. The same procedure can be used to test a switch, by connecting the continuity tester to the power-in and power-out sides of the switch. With the switch turned On, the test light should come on.

FINDING AN OPEN CIRCUIT

When diagnosing for possible open circuits, it is often difficult to locate them by sight because oxidation or terminal misalignment are hidden by the electrical connectors. Merely wiggling an electrical connector on a sensor or in the wiring harness may correct the open circuit condition. Remember this when an open circuit is indicated when troubleshooting a circuit. Intermittent problems may also be caused by oxidized or loose connections.

Electrical troubleshooting is simple if you keep in mind that all electrical circuits are basically electrical current running from the battery, through the wires, switches, relays, fuses and fusible links to each electrical component (light bulb, motor, etc.) and to ground, from which it is passed back to the battery. Any electrical problem is an interruption in the flow of electricity to the electrical component and back to the battery.

3 Fuses - general information

▶ **Refer to illustrations 3.1a, 3.1b, 3.1c, 3.1d, 3.1e, 3.3 and 3.4**

1   The electrical circuits of the vehicle are protected by a combination of fuses, circuit breakers and fusible links. The main fuse and relay block is located in the engine compartment on the passenger side and the interior fuse box is located under the instrument panel on the driver's side of the dashboard (see illustrations).

2   Each of the fuses is designed to protect a specific circuit, and the various circuits are identified on the fuse panel itself. The main fuse block in the engine compartment supplies circuits with high current draws, such as the fuel injection, headlights, cooling fan, etc. The interior fuse box, under the driver's side instrument panel, supplies current to the remainder of the circuits; interior lights, radio, door locks, power windows, instrument panel, wipers, exterior lights, etc.

3.1a On 2005 and earlier models, the engine compartment fuse and relay box is located in the right rear corner of the engine compartment

3.1b On 1997 and earlier models, the interior fuse box is located near the driver's side kick panel

3.1c The fuses and a fuse puller are beneath the cover (on 1999 through 2005 models, the interior fuse box can be accessed through a small cover in the lower left corner of the instrument panel)

3.1d On 2006 and later models, the engine compartment fuse and relay box is located in the right rear corner of the engine compartment

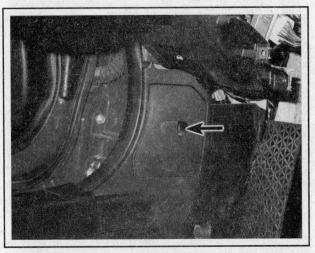

3.1e On 2006 and later models, the interior fuse and relay box is located in the left kick panel. To access it, open this door

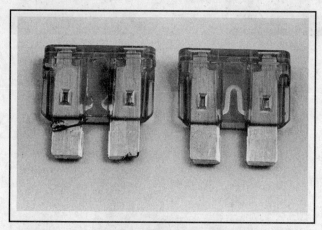

3.3 When a fuse blows, the element between the terminals melts - the fuse on the left is blown, the fuse on the right is good

3.4 The main fuse is secured by a bolt on each side (one bolt not visible); each bolt also secures a wire terminal (typical 1997 and earlier model shown; 1999 through 2005 models similar)

3   With the exception of the 80-amp main fuse, miniaturized fuses are employed in the main fuse block and the fuse box. These are compact fuses, with blade terminal design.

➡**Note: When replacing a fuse, do not attempt to use pliers - always use the fuse puller tool supplied in the fuse box cover for safe removal and replacement, without damaging the fuse itself or neighboring fuses.**

If an electrical component fails, always check the fuse first. The best way to check the fuses is with a test light. Check for power at the exposed terminal tips of each fuse. If power is present at one side of the fuse but not the other, the fuse is blown. A blown fuse can be identified by visually inspecting it (see illustration).

4   To replace the 80-amp main fuse, disconnect the negative cable from the battery (see Chapter 5). Open the fuse box cover. Undo the fuse box mounting nuts and remove the fuse box from the engine compartment sidewall. Undo the screw on each side of the fuse (see illustra-

tion). Remove the fuse and install a new one. Don't forget to reinstall the two fuse wires (one is secured by each of the fuse screws).

5   Be sure to replace blown fuses with the correct type. Fuses of different ratings are physically interchangeable, but only fuses of the proper rating should be used. Replacing a fuse with one of a higher or lower value than specified is not recommended. Each electrical circuit needs a specific amount of protection. The amperage value of each fuse is molded into the fuse body.

6   If the replacement fuse immediately fails, this indicates a more serious problem than just a failed or defective fuse. Don't replace it again until the cause of the problem is isolated and corrected. In most cases, this will be a short circuit in the wiring caused by a broken or deteriorated wire, or a failed electrical component.

➡**Note: If the fuse box Room fuse is burned out, the dashboard malfunction light will be On; to replace, turn the ignition switch to Lock and install the new fuse.**

4   Relays - general information

▶ **Refer to illustrations 4.2, 4.4 and 4.6**

1   Many electrical accessories in the vehicle use relays to transmit the electrical signal to the component. If the relay is defective, that component will not operate properly. Relay locations vary by model year.

2   The circuit opening relay or fuel pump relay, turn signal/flasher relay and timer/buzzer unit are located under the dashboard on the driver's side (see illustration). On early models the horn relay is in this location; on later models the headlight retractor relay is here.

3   The fuel injection main relay and cooling fan relay are located in the engine compartment fuse/relay block.

4   The side marker/tail/license/tail illumination (TNS) relay and headlight relay are located on the left side of the engine compartment (see illustration). On early models the headlight retractor relay is in this location; on later models the horn relay is here.

5   The rear defogger relay (on models so equipped) is in the trunk.

6   On later models, the air conditioning and condenser fan relays are located in the engine compartment (see illustration).

7   If a faulty relay is suspected, it can be removed and tested by a dealer or other qualified shop. Defective relays must be replaced as a unit.

4.2 Relays are located under the driver's side of the instrument panel . . .

4.4 . . . on the left side of the engine compartment . . .

4.6 . . . and, on some models, on the right side of the engine compartment

5   Turn signal/hazard flashers - check and replacement

✳✳ WARNING:

All models are equipped with airbags. The airbag is armed and can deploy (inflate) anytime the battery is connected. To prevent accidental deployment (and possible injury), turn the ignition key to LOCK and disconnect the negative battery cable whenever working near airbag components. After the battery is disconnected, wait at least two minutes before beginning work (the system has a back-up capacitor that must fully discharge). For more information see Section 24.

1   On 2005 and earlier models, the turn signal/hazard flasher unit is located under the left end of the instrument panel. Remove the knee bolster trim panel (see Chapter 11) to access it. On 2006 and later models, the turn signal/hazard flasher unit is located on the backside of the switch panel at the lower left corner of the instrument panel. You might be able to reach the flasher by simply removing the knee bolster trim panel and the knee bolster, then reaching through the opening to get at the backside of the switch panel. If not, you'll have to remove the switch panel, which involves removing other trim panels as well (see Chapter 11, Section 23).

2   When the flasher unit is functioning properly, an audible click can be heard during its operation. If the turn signals fail on one side or the other and the flasher unit does not make its characteristic clicking sound, a faulty turn signal bulb is indicated.

3   Flasher relay check: With the ignition switch on, operate the turn signal switch right and left, checking that the front and rear turn signals are flashing; actuate the Hazard warning switch and check that both front and rear signals flash.

4   If only one side fails to flash properly, check for burnt out bulbs.

5   If both turn signals fail to flash, the problem may be a blown fuse, a faulty flasher unit, a failed bulb, a broken switch or a loose or open electrical connection. If a quick check of the fuse box indicates that the turn signal fuse has blown, check the wiring for a short before installing a new fuse.

6   To replace the flasher, remove the flasher from its mounting bracket and disconnect the electrical connector.

7   Make sure that the replacement unit is identical to the original. Compare the old one to the new one before installing it.

8   Installation is the reverse of removal.

6   Steering column switches - removal and installation

✳✳ WARNING:

All models are equipped with airbags. The airbag is armed and can deploy (inflate) anytime the battery is connected. To prevent accidental deployment (and possible injury), turn the ignition key to LOCK and disconnect the negative battery cable whenever working near airbag components. After the battery is disconnected, wait at least two minutes before beginning work (the system has a back-up capacitor that must fully discharge). For more information see Section 24.

2005 AND EARLIER MODELS

▶ **Refer to illustration 6.5**

1   Disconnect the negative battery cable (see Chapter 5).

2   Disable the driver's airbag and remove the airbag assembly (see Chapter 10).

3   Remove the steering wheel (see Chapter 10).

4   Remove the steering column upper and lower covers (see Chapter 11).

6.5 Combination switch assembly details

1 Mounting screws
2 Clockspring alignment marks

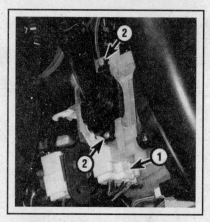

6.9a Turn signal switch details

1 Electrical connector
2 Switch mounting screws

6.9b Windshield wiper/ washer switch

1 Electrical connector
2 Switch mounting screws

5 Remove the combination switch retaining screws (see illustration).

6 Disconnect the electrical connectors and slide the combination switch off the column.

> **✳✳ WARNING:**
>
> **Handle the combination switch/clockspring assembly very carefully. Damage to the clockspring could cause an airbag system failure, resulting in serious personal injury.**

7 Installation is the reverse of removal. Ensure the clockspring is centered properly before installing the combination switch/clockspring assembly onto the steering shaft as follows:

 a) *Position the front wheels pointing straight ahead.*

 b) *Gently rotate the clockspring inner hub clockwise to the end of its stop. Do not force it against the stop.*

 c) *Rotate the clockspring 2-3/4 turns counterclockwise.*

 d) *Align the mark on the inner hub with the mark on the housing (see illustration 6.5).*

2006 AND LATER MODELS

Refer to illustrations 6.9a and 6.9b

8 Remove the steering column covers (see Chapter 11).

9 Disconnect the electrical connector from the switch (see illustrations).

10 Remove the switch retaining screws and remove the switch.

11 Installation is the reverse of removal.

7 Interior switches - replacement

2005 AND EARLIER MODELS

Hazard flasher switch

▶ **Refer to illustration 7.2**

1 Remove the center trim panel (see *Dashboard trim panels - removal and installation* in Chapter 11).

2 Remove the hazard flasher switch mounting screws (see illustration) and remove the hazard flasher switch.

3 Installation is the reverse of removal.

Dimmer switch or power mirror switch

4 Remove the knee bolster trim panel (see Chapter 11).

5 These switches are secured to the knee bolster trim panel by tabs on the sides of the units. Depress the tabs and push the switch out of the trim panel.

6 Installation is the reverse of removal. Make sure that the switch snaps into place.

7.2 Hazard flasher switch retaining screw (1997 and earlier unit shown; 1999 through 2005 unit similar)

Power window switch

7 Carefully pry the power window switch out of the center console with a small taped screwdriver.

8 Disconnect the electrical connector from the power window switch.

9 Installation is the reverse of removal. Make sure that the switch snaps into place.

2006 AND LATER MODELS

Hazard flasher switch

10 Remove the left and right side covers, the glove box, the center panel unit and the right (passenger's side) vent trim panel (see Chapter 11).

11 Remove the hazard flasher retaining screws and pull the hazard flasher off the dash. Disconnect the electrical connector and remove the hazard flasher unit.

12 Installation is the reverse of removal.

Power mirror switch

13 Remove the door trim panel (see Chapter 11).

14 Depress the retaining tab and remove the power mirror switch panel from the door trim panel.

15 Remove the power mirror switch mounting screws and remove the switch.

16 Installation is the reverse of removal.

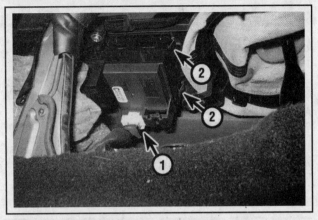

7.18 Power window switch details

1   *Electrical connector*   2   *Release tabs*

Power window switch

▶ **Refer to illustration 7.18**

17 Detach and raise up one side of the center console (see Chapter 11).

18 Disconnect the electrical connector, then depress the power window switch tabs (see illustration) and push the switch up and out of the console.

19 Installation is the reverse of removal.

8 Ignition switch - replacement

▶ **Refer to illustration 8.5**

✳✳ WARNING:

All models are equipped with airbags. The airbag is armed and can deploy (inflate) anytime the battery is connected. To prevent accidental deployment (and possible injury), turn the ignition key to LOCK and disconnect the negative battery cable whenever working near airbag components. After the battery is disconnected, wait at least two minutes before beginning work (the system has a back-up capacitor that must fully discharge). For more information see Section 24.

1 Disconnect the negative battery cable (see Chapter 5).

2 Disable the driver's airbag.

3 Remove the steering column upper and lower covers and under cover (see Chapter 11).

4 Disconnect the electrical connector from the switch.

5 Remove the screw and separate the switch from the steering lock assembly (see illustration).

6 Installation is the reverse of removal.

8.5 Ignition switch removal details

1   *Electrical connector*
2   *Ignition switch mounting screw*

9   Ignition key lock cylinder - removal and installation

♦ **Refer to illustration 9.4**

9.4 The steering lock assembly is secured by two break-off bolts

❋❋ WARNING:

All models are equipped with airbags. The airbag is armed and can deploy (inflate) anytime the battery is connected. To prevent accidental deployment (and possible injury), turn the ignition key to LOCK and disconnect the negative battery cable whenever working near airbag components. After the battery is disconnected, wait at least two minutes before beginning work (the system has a back-up capacitor that must fully discharge). For more information see Section 24.

1   Disconnect the negative battery cable (see Chapter 5).
2   Disable the driver's airbag.
3   Remove the steering column upper and lower covers and under cover (see Chapter 11). If necessary, unbolt the steering column and lower it for access to the lock cylinder bolts.
4   The steering lock assembly is secured by break-off bolts (see illustration). To remove them, cut a screwdriver slot in the top of each bolt with a hammer and chisel, then unscrew the bolts. Another method is to drive the bolts in a counterclockwise direction with the hammer and chisel.

5   Once the bolts are removed, lower the steering lock assembly away from the steering column.
6   Install the new steering lock assembly and secure it with two new break-off bolts, tightening them until their heads snap off.
7   The remainder of installation is the reverse of the removal steps.

10 Headlight - bulb replacement and aim adjustment

BULB REPLACEMENT

1997 and earlier models

♦ **Refer to illustrations 10.2, 10.3 and 10.4**

1   Turn the headlight switch to raise the headlights, then disconnect the negative battery cable (see Chapter 5).
2   Remove the screws at the side of the headlight bezel, then remove the bezel (see illustration).
3   Remove the headlight retaining ring (see illustration).
4   Pull the bulb out of the housing and unplug its wiring connector (see illustration). Remove the bulb.
5   Reverse the removal steps to install the new bulb.
6   Switch on the headlights and check for proper operation.

➡**Note: The headlight bulb replacement procedure steps in this Section do not affect headlight aim. However, be sure to check the headlight aim is correct and adjust if necessary.**

10.2 Remove the screws and the headlight bezel

10.3 Remove the bulb retaining ring screws, rotate the retaining ring counterclockwise about one-eighth of a turn and remove the retaining ring

10.4 Pull the headlight bulb assembly straight out of the housing and unplug the connector

10.9 Headlight electrical connector (2006 and later model shown, 1999 through 2005 models similar)

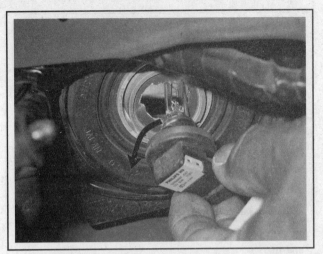

10.10 To remove the bulb from the headlight housing, turn it counterclockwise and pull it out (2006 and later model shown; 1999 through 2005 models similar)

1999 and later models

→Note: 1999 and later models use removable halogen headlight bulbs instead of a sealed beam housing. On 1999 through 2005 models, a single halogen bulb is used for both high- and low-beam. On 2006 and later models there are two bulbs: a halogen type high-beam similar to the bulb used on 1999 through 2005 models, and a High Intensity Discharge (HID) bulb for low-beam.

Halogen headlight bulbs

▶ Refer to illustrations 10.9 and 10.10

✳✳ WARNING:

Halogen gas-filled bulbs are under pressure and can shatter if the surface is scratched or the bulb is dropped. Wear eye protection and handle the bulb carefully, grasping only the base of the bulb. Do not touch the surface of the bulb with your fingers,

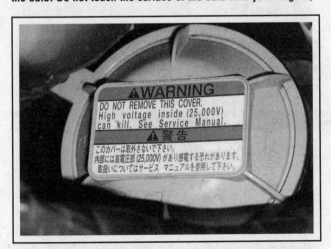

10.12 If you see this type of cover over a headlight bulb with this warning, do NOT remove it

because the oil from your skin could cause the bulb to overheat and prematurely fail. If you do accidentally touch the bulb surface, clean it with rubbing alcohol.

7   Disconnect the cable from the negative battery terminal (see Chapter 5).

8   If you're replacing a right side bulb, remove the windshield washer fluid reservoir (see illustration 5.1b in Chapter 3) and set it aside. Don't disconnect the fluid reservoir hoses.

9   Disconnect the electrical connector from the bulb (see illustration).

10 Rotate the bulb counterclockwise and pull it out of the headlight housing (see illustration).

11 To install a new bulb, align the lugs on the bulb base with the cutouts in the headlight housing, insert the bulb into the housing and turn it clockwise until it locks into place. The remainder of installation is the reverse of removal.

High Intensity Discharge (HID) headlight bulbs

▶ Refer to illustration 10.12

✳✳ WARNING:

2006 and later models use High Intensity Discharge (HID) low-beam bulbs instead of halogen bulbs. According to the manufacturer, the high voltages produced by this system can be fatal in the event of a shock. Also, the voltage can remain in the circuit even after the headlight switch has been turned to OFF and the ignition key has been removed. Therefore, for your safety, we don't recommend that you try to replace one of these bulbs yourself. Instead, have this service performed by a dealer service department or other qualified repair shop.

12 If you see this cover with this warning (see illustration) over a headlight bulb, do NOT remove the cover and do not try to replace the bulb yourself.

10.13 The aiming screws are below the headlight and to one side

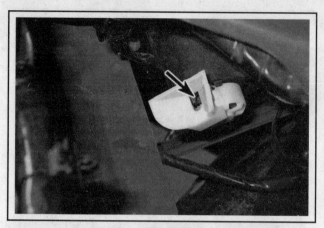

10.16 Vertical headlight adjuster screw

HEADLIGHT AIM ADJUSTMENT

▶ **Refer to illustrations 10.13 and 10.16**

➡**Note: It is important that the headlights are aimed correctly. If adjusted incorrectly they could blind the driver of an oncoming vehicle and cause a serious accident or seriously reduce your ability to see the road. The headlights should be checked for proper aim every 12 months and any time a new headlight is installed or front end body work is performed. It should be emphasized that the following procedure is only an interim step which will provide temporary adjustment until the headlights can be adjusted by a properly equipped shop.**

13 On 1997 and earlier models, there are two adjustment screws (one to the side controlling left-and-right movement and one below the light for up-and-down movement) that are accessible from the front of the headlight housing (see illustration), with the headlights raised.

14 1999 and 2000 models have a vertical adjustment screw on the backside of each headlight housing. There is no horizontal adjustment screw on these models. Using a Phillips screwdriver, rotate the adjuster screw clockwise to move the beam up, or counterclockwise to move the beam down.

15 2001 through 2005 models have both a horizontal and a vertical adjustment screw on the backside of each headlight housing. The upper screw is the vertical adjuster; the lower screw is the horizontal adjuster. Using a Phillips screwdriver, rotate the vertical adjuster screw clockwise to move the beam up, or counterclockwise to move the beam down. Rotate the horizontal adjuster screw clockwise to move the beam to the

right, or counterclockwise to move the beam to the left.

16 2006 and later models have a vertical adjustment screw (see illustration) on the backside of each headlight housing. There is no horizontal adjustment screw on these models. Using a Phillips screwdriver, rotate the adjuster screw clockwise to move the beam up, or counterclockwise to move the beam down.

17 There are several methods of adjusting the headlights. The simplest method requires a blank wall, masking tape and a level floor.

   a) Position masking tape vertically on the wall in reference to the vehicle centerline and the centerlines of both headlights.
   b) Position a horizontal tape line in reference to the centerline of all the headlights.

➡**Note: It may be easier to position the tape on the wall with the vehicle parked only a few inches away.**

   c) Adjustment should be made with the vehicle parked 25 feet from the wall, tire air pressure adjusted with the tires cold, sitting level, the gas tank half-full and no unusually heavy load in the vehicle.
   d) Starting with the low beam adjustment, position the high intensity zone so it is two inches below the horizontal line and two inches to the side of the headlight vertical line, away from oncoming traffic. Turn the headlight adjustment screws (see illustration 10.13) until the desired level has been achieved.
   e) With the high beams on, the high intensity zone should be vertically centered with the exact center just below the horizontal line.

➡**Note: It may not be possible to position the headlight aim exactly for both high and low beams. If a compromise must be made, keep in mind that the low beams are the most used and have the greatest effect on driver safety.**

11 Headlight housing - removal and installation

1997 AND EARLIER MODELS

1 Turn the headlight switch On to raise the headlights, then disconnect the negative battery cable (see Chapter 5).

2 Remove the headlight bulb (see Section 10).

3 Remove the headlight assembly side mounting nut from each side of the assembly, then lift the assembly off.

4 Installation is the reverse of removal. Refer to Section 10 for headlight bulb installation and adjustment.

1999 AND LATER MODELS

5 Disconnect the cable from the negative battery terminal (see Chapter 5).

6 Remove the front bumper (see Chapter 11).

7 Disconnect the electrical connectors from the headlight housing.

8 On 1999 through 2005 models, remove the two upper headlight housing bolts and remove the headlight housing.

9 On 2006 and later models, remove the upper bolt and clip, the inner bolt and the two lower bolts and remove the headlight housing.

10 Installation is the reverse of removal.

12 Headlight retractor motor and circuit - adjustment, check and component replacement

ADJUSTMENT

▶ **Refer to illustrations 12.3a and 12.3b**

1 Raise the headlights and disconnect the negative cable from the battery (see Chapter 5).

2 Pry the link on the retractor motor free from the arm on the headlight lid.

3 Lower the headlight lid by hand until it rests against the stopper (see illustrations). The lid should be flush with the body. If it isn't, raise the lid and adjust the stopper as necessary.

4 Reconnect the actuator link to the arm and reconnect the negative cable to the battery. Operate the headlights with the switch and check the adjustment again.

CHECK

Retractor motor

▶ **Refer to illustration 12.5**

5 Unplug the retractor motor electrical connector and identify its

terminals (see illustration). Make sure the retractor linkage is in good condition and properly connected.

6 Using jumper wires, connect the positive terminal of a 12-volt battery to motor terminal 1 and the battery's negative terminal to motor terminal 2.

7 Using another wire, connect the battery positive terminal to terminals 3 and 4 in turn. The headlight lid should raise when voltage is connected to terminal 3, and lower when voltage is connected to terminal 4. If the motor doesn't perform as described, replace it.

Retractor/hazard flasher switch

▶ **Refer to illustration 12.9**

8 Remove the console center panel (see Chapter 11).

9 To test the retractor portion of the switch, connect an ohmmeter between terminals 1 and 3 (see illustration). With the retractor switch in the Off position, there should be continuity. With the switch in the On position, there should be continuity between terminals 2 and 3.

10 To test the hazard flasher portion of the switch, connect the ohmmeter between terminals 4 and 5. There should be continuity with the hazard switch in the On position.

11 If the switch doesn't perform as described, replace it.

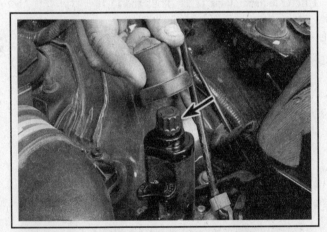

12.3a Pull off the cover and turn the knob to raise or lower the headlights manually

12.3b Adjust headlight lid position with the stopper (arrow)

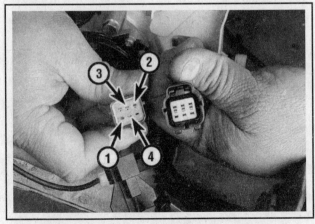

12.5 Retractor motor terminal identification

12.9 Retractor switch terminal identification

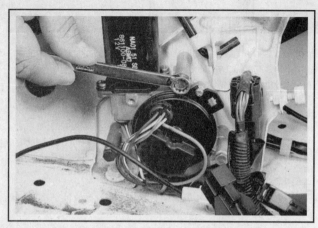

12.12 Unbolt the retractor motor

REPLACEMENT

♦ **Refer to illustration 12.12**

12 To remove the retractor motor, unplug its wiring connector and pry the link off the arm. Unbolt the motor and take it out (see illustration).

13 To remove the switch, undo its mounting screws and take it out of the center panel.

14 Installation is the reverse of the removal steps.

13 Bulb replacement

2005 AND EARLIER MODELS

Front turn signal and parking light

♦ **Refer to illustration 13.2**

1 Open the hood.

2 Reach behind the light assembly. Twist the light bulb holder (socket) counterclockwise and pull it out of the light assembly (see illustration).

3 While holding the socket, push the bulb into the socket and turn it counterclockwise to remove it. Replace the bulb.

4 Installation is the reverse of removal.

Side marker lights (front and rear)

♦ **Refer to illustrations 13.5 and 13.6**

5 Remove the lamp assembly screws (see illustration).

6 Pull the lamp assembly out of the body panel (see illustration). Twist the bulb socket counterclockwise and remove it from the lamp assembly. Pull out the bulb and push a new one in.

7 Installation is the reverse of removal.

Rear brake, turn signal, tail and back-up lights

♦ **Refer to illustrations 13.9a, 13.9b and 13.10**

8 Open the trunk lid.

9 To replace a turn signal bulb, twist the socket counterclockwise and pull it out of the panel (see illustration). While holding the socket, push the bulb into the socket and turn it counterclockwise to remove it (see illustration). Replace the bulb.

10 To replace a brake or backup light bulb, remove the light housing/bulb socket holder (see illustration). While holding the housing, push the bulb into the socket and turn it counterclockwise to remove it. Replace the bulb.

11 Installation is the reverse of removal.

License plate light

♦ **Refer to illustration 13.13**

12 Open the trunk lid.

13.2 Rotate the bulb holder to remove the combination light (turn signal) bulb from the housing

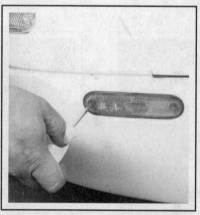

13.5 Remove the housing securing screws and pull out the housing . . .

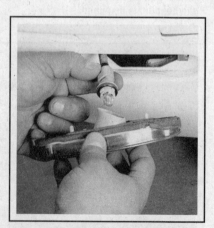

13.6 . . . twist the bulb socket, free it from the housing and pull out the bulb

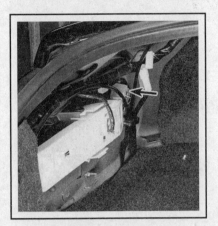

13.9a Twist the turn signal bulb socket and pull it out . . .

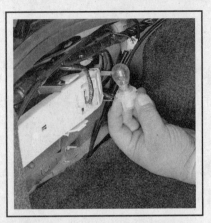

13.9b . . . then press the bulb into the socket and turn counterclockwise to remove

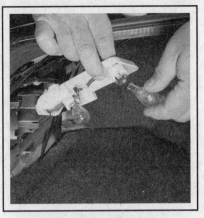

13.10 Remove the taillight bulb holder (socket) to replace the tail and brake light bulbs

13.13 From inside the trunk, twist the license plate bulb socket and pull it out, then press the bulb into its socket and turn it counterclockwise to remove it

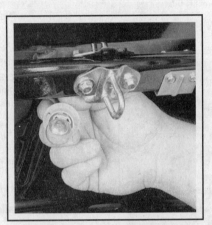

13.16 Twist the high-mounted brake light socket and pull it free; press the bulb into its socket and turn it counterclockwise to remove it

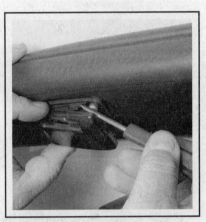

13.18a Pry out the overhead light lens . . .

13 Twist the socket counterclockwise and pull it out of the panel (see illustration). While holding the socket, push the bulb into the socket and turn it counterclockwise to remove it. Replace the bulb.

14 Installation is the reverse of removal

High-mounted brake light

▶ Refer to illustration 13.16

15 Open the trunk lid.

16 Twist the socket counterclockwise and pull it out of the panel (see illustration). While holding the socket, push the bulb into the socket and turn it counterclockwise to remove it. Replace the bulb.

17 Installation is the reverse of removal

Interior and trunk lights

▶ Refer to illustrations 13.18a, 13.18b and 13.19

18 For the interior light, pry the light lens off, and pry the bulb from its holder (socket) (see illustrations). Replace the bulb and press the light lens in place.

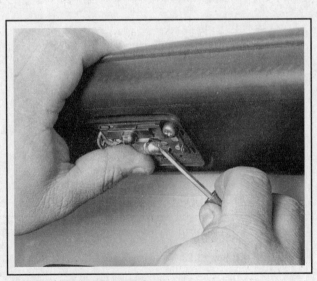

13.18b . . . then pry out the bulb

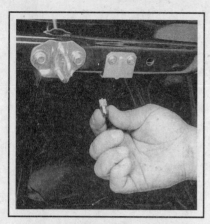

13.19 Pull the trunk light bulb out of the socket

13.20 The instrument cluster light bulbs are removed from the backside of the cluster - rotate the socket 90-degrees counterclockwise and pull it out

13.23 Front turn signal bulb electrical connector

13.28 Front parking light bulb electrical connector

19 For the trunk light, open the trunk and pull out the bulb (see illustration). Press in the new bulb.

Instrument cluster illumination

▶ Refer to illustration 13.20

20 To gain access to the instrument cluster illumination light(s), the instrument cluster will have to be removed (see Section 17). The bulb(s) can then be removed and replaced from the rear of the cluster (see illustration).

2006 AND LATER MODELS

Front turn signal bulb

▶ Refer to illustration 13.23

21 Loosen the front wheel lug nuts, raise the vehicle and place it securely on jackstands. Remove the front wheel.

22 Remove the fasteners from the front wheel well splash shield (see *Fender - removal and installation* in Chapter 11) and peel back the splash shield to gain access to the headlight housing.

23 Disconnect the electrical connector from the front turn signal bulb (see illustration).

24 Remove the bulb socket from the headlight housing, then remove the bulb from the socket.

25 Installation is the reverse of removal.

Front parking light bulb

▶ Refer to illustration 13.28

26 Loosen the front wheel lug nuts, raise the vehicle and place it securely on jackstands. Remove the front wheel.

27 Remove the fasteners from the front wheel well splash shield (see *Fender - removal and installation* in Chapter 11) and peel back the splash shield to gain access to the headlight housing.

28 Disconnect the electrical connector from the front parking light bulb (see illustration).

29 Remove the bulb socket from the headlight housing, then remove the bulb from the socket.

30 Installation is the reverse of removal.

Front sidemarker bulb

▶ Refer to illustration 13.33

31 Loosen the front wheel lug nuts, raise the vehicle and place it securely on jackstands. Remove the front wheel.

32 Remove the fasteners from the front wheel well splash shield (see *Fender - removal and installation* in Chapter 11) and peel back the splash shield to gain access to the front sidemarker light.

33 Disconnect the electrical connector from the front sidemarker light bulb (see illustration).

34 Remove the bulb socket from the front sidemarker light housing, then remove the bulb from the socket.

35 If you need to replace the front sidemarker assembly, slide the housing up to disengage the lower release tab, then push out the upper tab and remove the housing.

36 Installation is the reverse of removal.

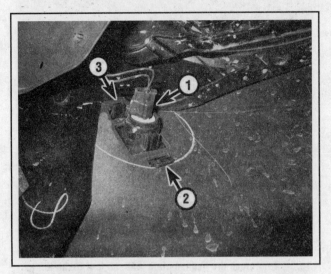

13.33 Front sidemarker light details

1   *Electrical connector*
2   *Lower mounting tab*
3   *Upper mounting tab*

13.39 Fog/driving light bulb electrical connector

13.43 Center high-mount brake light details

1   *Electrical connector*
2   *Mounting clip access holes*

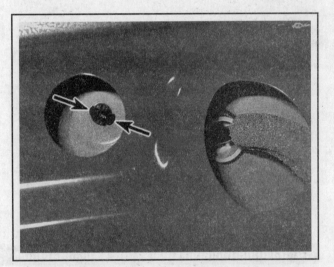

13.44 To disengage each center high-mount brake light mounting clip, squeeze the two tabs together and push out the clip

Fog/driving light bulb

▶ **Refer to illustration 13.39**

37 Loosen the front wheel lug nuts, raise the vehicle and place it securely on jackstands. Remove the front wheel.

38 Remove the fasteners from the front wheel well splash shield (see *Fender - removal and installation* in Chapter 11) and peel back the splash shield to gain access to the fog/driving light.

39 Disconnect the electrical connector from the fog/driving light bulb (see illustration).

40 Turn the fog/driving light bulb socket counterclockwise to remove it from the fog/driving light housing. The fog light bulb, the bulb socket and the mounting flange are a one-piece assembly.

41 Installation is the reverse of removal.

Center high-mount brake light assembly

▶ **Refer to illustrations 13.43 and 13.44**

42 Open the trunk lid and remove the trim panel from the forward part of the trunk.

43 Trace the center high-mount brake light electrical lead to the electrical connector and disconnect it (see illustration).

44 Working through the access holes in the underside of the trunk lid, use a pair of needle nose pliers to squeeze the tabs together on each of the four center high-mount brake light mounting clips and release all four clips (see illustration). Pull off the center high-mount brake light assembly.

45 Installation is the reverse of removal.

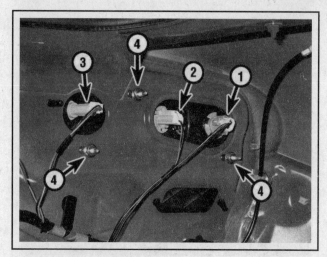

13.47 Taillight assembly details

1   Brake light/taillight bulb electrical connector
2   Rear turn signal bulb electrical connector
3   Back-up light bulb electrical connector
4   Taillight housing retaining nuts

Brake light/taillight, rear turn signal and back-up light bulbs

▶ Refer to illustration 13.47

46 Open the trunk lid and remove the trunk end and side trim.

47 Rotate the socket counterclockwise for the bulb that you're replacing (see illustration) and pull it out of the taillight housing.

48 To remove the bulb from the socket, pull it straight out of the socket.

49 If you need to replace the taillight assembly, disconnect the electrical connectors, remove the three housing mounting nuts and pull off the housing.

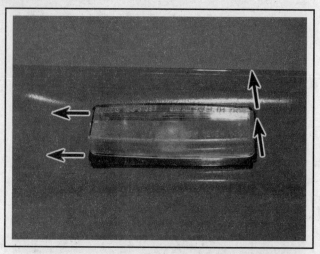

13.50 To remove the license plate lens, slide it to the left to disengage the mounting tab and disengage the right end

License plate light bulb

▶ Refer to illustration 13.50

50 Open the trunk lid. To free the license plate light housing from the trunk lid, slide the housing to the left to disengage the mounting tab, then pull the right end out of the trunk lid (see illustration). Remove the bulb from the socket.

51 Installation is the reverse of removal.

Map light bulb or trunk light bulb

52 Carefully pry off the lens with a small screwdriver.
53 Remove the old bulb and install a new bulb.
54 Make sure that the lens snaps into place.

14   Daytime Running Lights (DRL) - general information

1   The Daytime Running Lights (DRL) system, used on some models, turns the headlights on whenever the engine is started. The only exception is when the engine is on when the parking brake is engaged. Once the parking brake is released, the lights will remain on as long as the ignition switch is on, even if the parking brake is later applied.

2   The DRL system supplies reduced voltage to the headlights so they won't be too bright for daytime use, while prolonging headlight life.

15   Radio and speakers - removal and installation

☀☀ WARNING:

Later models are equipped with airbags. The airbag is armed and can deploy (inflate) anytime the battery is connected. To prevent accidental deployment (and possible injury), turn the ignition key to LOCK and disconnect the negative battery cable whenever working near airbag components. After the battery is disconnected, wait at least two minutes before beginning work (the system has a back-up capacitor that must fully discharge). For more information see Section 24.

2005 AND EARLIER MODELS

Radio

▶ Refer to illustrations 15.3a, 15.3b and 15.4

1   Disconnect the negative cable at the battery (see Chapter 5).

2   If you're working on a 1995 or earlier model, remove the console center panel (see Chapter 11). Remove the four screws that secure the radio.

15.3a Carefully pry the service hole cover from each side of the radio . . .

15.3b . . . then insert the special tools to disengage the fasteners (1997 and earlier models shown, 1999 through 2005 models similar)

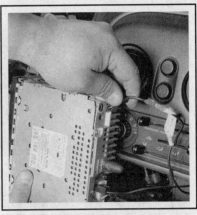

15.4 Pull the radio out of the instrument panel and disconnect the electrical connectors and antenna lead

15.8a Remove the speaker attaching screws . . .

15.8b . . . then unplug the electrical connector

15.14 Radio mounting screws (right side shown, left side identical)

3 If you're working on a 1996 or later model, pry out the service cover at each end of the radio (see illustration). Insert the special removal tools into the mounting holes to disengage the radio (see illustration).

4 Pull the radio out far enough to unplug the electrical connector and the antenna lead and remove the radio (see illustration).

5 Installation is the reverse of removal.

Speakers

6 Disconnect the negative cable at the battery (see Chapter 5).

Door speakers

▶ **Refer to illustrations 15.8a and 15.8b**

7 Remove the front door trim panel (see Chapter 11).

8 Remove the speaker retaining screws/nuts. Unplug the electrical connector and remove the speaker (see illustrations).

9 Installation is the reverse of removal.

Headrest speakers (some models)

10 Remove the seat (see Chapter 11). Remove the seatback portion of the seat cover.

11 Remove the speaker grille, then remove the speaker retaining screws/nuts. Unplug the electrical connector and remove the speaker.

12 Installation is the reverse of removal.

2006 AND LATER MODELS

Radio

▶ **Refer to illustration 15.14**

13 Remove the center panel unit (see Dashboard trim panels - removal and installation in Chapter 11).

14 Remove the four radio mounting screws (see illustration) and remove the radio from its mounting bracket.

15 Installation is the reverse of removal.

15.17 Door tweeter details

1	*Electrical connector*	*2*	*Tweeter mounting screws*

15.21 Door speaker details

1	*Electrical connector*	*2*	*Speaker mounting screws*

Speakers

Door tweeter

♦ **Refer to illustration 15.17**

➡**Note: The door tweeter is mounted on the backside of the door trim panel.**

16 Remove the door trim panel (see Chapter 11).
17 Disconnect the electrical connector from the tweeter (see illustration).

18 Remove the tweeter mounting screws and remove the tweeter.
19 Installation is the reverse of removal.

Door speaker

♦ **Refer to illustration 15.21**

20 Remove the door trim panel (see Chapter 11).
21 Disconnect the electrical connector from the speaker (see illustration).
22 Remove the speaker mounting screws and remove the speaker.
23 Installation is the reverse of removal.

16 Antenna - removal and installation

♦ **Refer to illustrations 16.1, 16.3 and 16.4**

1 Open the trunk and unplug the antenna cable (see illustration).

➡**Note: The antenna may be tested if desired, by checking continuity at the antenna cable plug end. The antenna should have full continuity (no resistance).**

2 Place masking tape around the antenna base to protect the paint.
3 On models with manual antennas, unscrew and remove the mast (see illustration).

4 On all models, unscrew and remove the antenna base (see illustration).
5 On models with power antennas, turn the ignition key to On, turn the radio switch to On, then, after the antenna fully extends, gently pull on the mast - the mast and nylon rack gear will pull out of the antenna assembly.
6 To remove the antenna assembly, raise the trunk and remove the trunk side trim on the side with the antenna. Disconnect the antenna

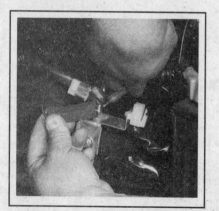

16.1 Unplug the antenna cable

16.3 On manual antenna models, unscrew the mast

16.4 Unscrew the antenna base with a wide-bladed screwdriver, a coin or snap-ring pliers

connector, electrical connectors (on power antenna models) and bolt or nut, then lift out the antenna assembly.

7   Installation is the reverse of removal. To install the antenna mast on power antenna models:

a) Turn the ignition switch and radio to ON.
b) Wait until the power antenna stops operating (you hear no more noise from it).

c) Insert the antenna mast into the power antenna assembly.
d) Make sure the antenna mast rack gear fits into the pinion gear within the power antenna assembly.
e) Turn the ignition switch to LOCK. The power antenna will operate, retracting the antenna mast.
f) After the antenna mast is retracted, install and tighten the mounting nut securely.

17 Instrument cluster - removal and installation

2005 AND EARLIER MODELS

▶ **Refer to illustration 17.3**

✷✷ WARNING:

All models are equipped with airbags. The airbag is armed and can deploy (inflate) anytime the battery is connected. To prevent accidental deployment (and possible injury), turn the ignition key to LOCK and disconnect the negative battery cable whenever working near airbag components. After the battery is disconnected, wait at least two minutes before beginning work (the system has a back-up capacitor that must fully discharge). For more information see Section 24.

1   Disconnect the cable from the negative battery terminal (see Chapter 5).
2   Remove the steering wheel (see Chapter 10). Remove the steering column upper and lower covers and the instrument cluster bezel (see Chapter 11).
3   Remove the instrument cluster retaining screws and pull the cluster away from the dashboard (see illustration).
4   Disconnect the speedometer cable from the instrument cluster.

➡Note: Lubrication of a noisy speedometer cable may be done by injecting lithium grease or other suitable lubricant into the speedometer cable housing when disconnected from the instrument cluster.

5   Unplug the electrical connectors and remove the cluster.
6   Installation is the reverse of removal.

2006 AND LATER MODELS

▶ **Refer to illustrations 17.8a and 17.8b**

7   Remove the steering column covers, the cluster trim panel and the knee bolster trim panel (see Chapter 11).
8   Remove the three instrument cluster mounting screws (see illustrations). The two lower screws are located at the lower left (shown) and lower right corners of the cluster.
9   Pull out the cluster and disconnect the electrical connectors from the backside of the cluster.
10   Installation is the reverse of removal.

17.3 Remove the cluster mounting screws and pull the cluster out so the speedometer cable can be disconnected

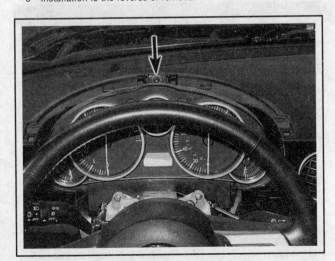

17.8a Upper instrument cluster mounting screw

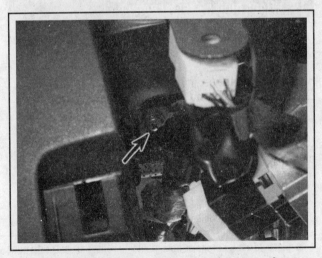

17.8b Lower left instrument cluster mounting screw - lower right screw not shown

18 Horn - check and replacement

CHECK

1   Disconnect the electrical connector from the horn (it's near the hood latch).
2   Test the horn by carefully connecting battery voltage to the two horn terminals with jumper wires from the battery.
3   If the horn doesn't sound, replace it. If it does sound, the problem lies in the steering wheel horn switch, horn relay (see Section 5) or the wiring between components.

REPLACEMENT

2005 and earlier models

▶ Refer to illustration 18.4

4   Disconnect the electrical connector and remove the bracket bolt (see illustration).
5   Installation is the reverse of removal.

2006 and later models

▶ Refer to illustration 18.8

6   Raise the front of the vehicle and place it securely on jackstands.
7   Remove the front engine compartment under cover.
8   Disconnect the electrical connector from the horn (see illustration).
9   Remove the horn mounting nut and remove the horn.
10 Installation is the reverse of removal.

18.4 Disconnect the horn electrical connector and remove the horn mounting bolt

18.8 Horn mounting details

1   Electrical connector   2   Mounting nut

19 Wiper motor - replacement

1   Disconnect the cable from the negative battery terminal (see Chapter 5).

2005 AND EARLIER MODELS

▶ Refer to illustrations 19.4 and 19.6

2   Remove the cowl grille (it's located forward of the lower edge of the windshield). Remove the baffle cover (it's above and behind the wiper motor).
3   Unplug the electrical connector from the wiper motor.
4   Remove the wiper linkage retaining nut and the rear mounting bolt (see illustration). Pull the linkage arm off the shaft.
5   Unbolt the engine compartment fuse block and move it aside.
6   Remove the wiper motor front mounting bolts, then rotate the

motor counterclockwise and remove it from the vehicle (see illustration).
7   Installation is the reverse of removal.

2006 AND LATER MODELS

▶ Refer to illustrations 19.8, 19.9a, 19.9b and 19.10

8   Remove the protective trim caps (see illustration), remove the windshield wiper arm nuts and remove the windshield wiper arms.
9   Using a trim removal tool, carefully pry off the cowl trim panel (see illustrations).
10 Disconnect the electrical connector(s) from the wiper motor (see illustration).
11 Remove the wiper motor/linkage assembly mounting bolts and

19.4 Remove the wiper motor-to-linkage nut (left arrow), detach the linkage arm and remove the rear mounting bolt (right arrow)

19.6 Remove the two front wiper motor mounting bolts (arrows); the lower bolt also secures a ground wire

19.8 Remove the protective trim cap and nut from each wiper arm

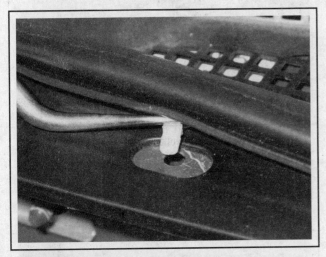

19.9a Using a trim removal tool, pry up the locator pins on the underside of the cowl trim panel . . .

19.9b . . . and remove the cowl trim panel

remove the wiper motor and linkage as a single assembly. Place the wiper motor/linkage assembly on a clean work surface.

12 Using a trim removal tool, carefully pry off the link arm balljoints from the motor crank arm.

13 Remove the motor crank arm mounting nut, note the orientation of the arm in relation to the motor, then remove the crank arm from the shaft.

14 Remove the motor mounting bolts and detach the motor from its mounting bar.

15 When reassembling the motor and linkage, make sure that you install the crank arm at the same angle in relation to the motor that it was in before you removed it. Installation is otherwise the reverse of removal.

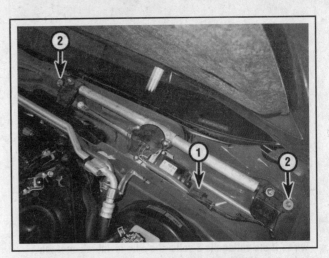

19.10 Windshield wiper motor/linkage assembly removal details

1 Electrical connector(s)   *2 Mounting bolts*

20 Rear window defogger - check and repair

1   The rear window defogger consists of a grid of horizontal heater filament elements baked onto the glass surface.

2   Small breaks in the element can be repaired without removing the rear window.

CHECK

▶ **Refer to illustrations 20.6, 20.7 and 20.9**

3   Turn the ignition switch and defogger system switch to ON. If the defogger doesn't work at all, check both the DEFOG fuse in the passenger compartment fuse block and the WIPER fuse in the engine compartment fuse block.

4   Determine which side of the window defogger heat grid is negative (connected to ground), and which side is positive (connected to 12 volts).

5   When measuring voltage during the next two tests, wrap a piece of aluminum foil around the tip of each voltmeter probe.

6   Press the foil-covered positive voltmeter probe against the positive side of the defogger grid with your finger (see illustration).

7   Using the voltmeter negative probe, check the voltage at the center of each heater filament element (see illustration). If the voltage is 5 volts, the wire is okay (there is no break). If the voltage is high (10 to 12 volts), the wire is broken between the center of the element and the positive end. If the voltage is 0-volts the wire is broken between the center of the element and ground.

8   Connect the negative lead to a good body ground. The reading should stay the same.

9   To find the break, place the voltmeter positive lead against the defogger positive terminal. Place the voltmeter negative lead with the foil strip against the heat wire at the positive terminal end and slide

it toward the negative terminal end. The point at which the voltmeter deflects from zero to several volts is the point at which the heater filament element is broken (see illustration). Make note of the location of the area of the heater filament break.

➡ **Note: If the heat element is not broken, the voltmeter will indicate no voltage at the positive end of the heat element but gradually increase to about 12-volts.**

20.6 When measuring the voltage at the rear window defogger grid, wrap a piece of aluminum foil around the negative probe of the voltmeter and press the foil against the wire with your finger

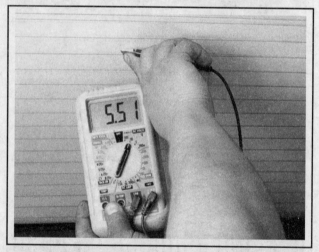

20.7 To determine if a wire has broken, place the voltmeter positive lead against the defogger positive terminal and check the voltage with the negative lead at the center of each wire - if the voltage is 5-volts, the wire is unbroken; if the voltage is 10-volts, the wire is broken between the center of the wire and the positive end; if the voltage is 0-volts, the wire is broken between the center of the wire and ground

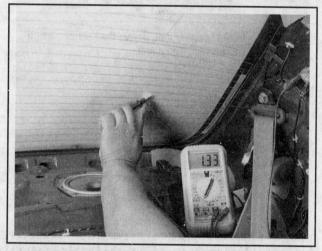

20.9 To find the break, place the voltmeter positive lead against the defogger positive terminal, place the voltmeter negative lead with the foil strip against the heat wire at the positive terminal end and slide it toward the negative terminal end - the point at which the voltmeter deflects from zero to several volts is the point at which the wire is broken

REPAIR

▶ **Refer to illustration 20.15**

10 Repair the break in the element using a repair kit specifically recommended for this purpose, such as DuPont paste No. 4817 (or equivalent). Included in this kit is plastic conductive epoxy.

11 Prior to repairing a break, turn off the system and allow it to cool off for a few minutes.

12 Lightly buff the element area with fine steel wool, then clean it thoroughly with rubbing alcohol.

13 Use masking tape to mask off the area being repaired.

14 Thoroughly mix the epoxy, following the instructions provided with the repair kit.

15 Apply the epoxy material to the slit in the masking tape, overlapping the undamaged area about 3/4-inch on either end (see illustration).

16 Allow the repair to cure for 24 hours before removing the tape and using the system.

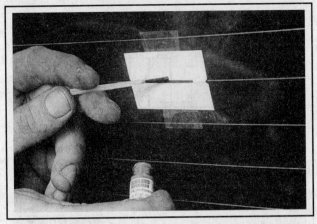

20.15 To use a defogger repair kit, apply masking tape to the inside of the window at the damaged area, then brush on the special conductive coating

21 Electric side-view mirrors - general information

1 The electric side-view mirrors can be adjusted up-and-down and left-to-right by a driver's side switch located on the left door trim panel. On models with factory-installed dual power mirrors, each mirror is also equipped with a heater grid behind the mirror glass to clear the mirror surface of fog, ice or snow. On these models, the mirror heater grid is an integral component of each mirror. If a heater grid fails, replace the mirror (see Chapter 11). The heater grid switches and the heated mirror system indicator light are integral components of the heater/air conditioning control panel on the dash. If one of these components fails, replace the heater/air conditioning control assembly (see Chapter 3). The heated mirror relay is located in one of the fuse and relay boxes.

2 The power mirror control switch has a LEFT-RIGHT selector switch that allows you to send voltage to the side-view mirror that you want to adjust. With the ignition switch in the ACC position, roll down the windows and operate the mirror control switch through all functions (left-right and up-down) for both the left and right side-view mirrors.

3 Listen carefully for the sound of the electric motors running in the mirrors.

4 If you can hear the motors but the mirror glass doesn't move, the problem is probably a defective drive mechanism inside the mirror, which will necessitate replacement of the mirror.

5 If the mirrors don't operate and no sound comes from the mirrors, check the fuse in one of the fuse and relay boxes (see Section 3).

6 If the fuse is OK, refer to Chapter 11 and remove the door panel for access to the back of the mirror control switch, without disconnecting the wires attached to it. Turn the ignition ON and check for voltage at the switch. There should be voltage at one terminal. If there's no voltage at the switch, check for an open in the wiring between the fuse panel and the switch.

7 If there's voltage at the switch, disconnect it. Check the switch for continuity in all its operating positions. If the switch does not have continuity, replace it.

8 Reconnect the switch. Locate the wire going from the switch to ground. Leaving the switch connected, connect a jumper wire between this wire and ground. If the mirror works normally with this wire in place, repair the faulty ground connection.

9 If the mirror still doesn't work, remove the mirror and check the wires at the mirror for voltage. Check with the ignition key turned to ON and the mirror selector switch on the appropriate side. Operate the mirror switch in all its positions. There should be voltage at one of the switch-to-mirror wires in each switch position, except the neutral (off) position.

10 If voltage is not present in each switch position, check the wiring between the mirror and control switch for opens and shorts.

11 If there's voltage, remove the mirror and test it off the vehicle with jumper wires. Replace the mirror if it fails this test.

22 Cruise control system - description and check

2005 AND EARLIER MODELS

▶ **Refer to illustration 22.7**

1 The cruise control system maintains vehicle speed with a cruise control unit (computer), located in the passenger compartment under the dashboard behind the heater blower unit, a speed sensor to signal the cruise control unit, and an actuator located in the engine compartment. The actuator is connected to the throttle linkage by a cable. The cruise control system also consists of the steering wheel cruise control switches, speed sensor in the instrument cluster, brake light switch, clutch switch for vehicles with manual transmissions, and associated wiring. Some features of the system requires special testers and diagnostic procedures which are beyond the scope of the home mechanic.

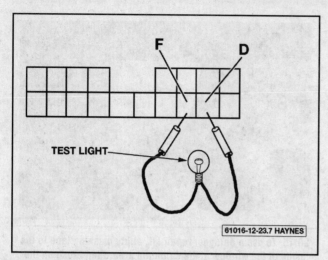

22.7 Cruise control unit (under dash) electrical connector and test light hookup - 1996 and earlier shown

Listed below are some general procedures that may be used to locate common problems.

2   Check the METER and STOP fuses at the fuse box (see Section 3).

3   Have an assistant operate the brake pedal while you check the operation of the brake lights (voltage from the brake switch - and clutch switch on vehicles with manual transmission - deactivates the cruise control).

4   If the brake lights don't come on or don't shut off, correct the problem and retest the cruise control. Check the clutch switch (see Chapter 8).

5   Visually inspect the vacuum hose connected to the actuator, check the control cable between the cruise control actuator and the throttle linkage, and replace as necessary.

6   Check the control cable freeplay as follows: Remove the cable clip and adjust the nut so that the actuator control cable freeplay is approximately 1/32 inch to 3/16 inch when the cable is pressed lightly by your finger.

7   A quick test of the remainder of the 1996 and earlier cruise control system is performed as follows, using a 1.4 watt test light with probes connected between terminals D and F of the cruise control connector (see illustration), located under the dash on the cruise control unit behind the heater blower unit (see Chapter 3 for access). Connect the test light with the cruise control connector still connected to the cruise control unit, and with the Terminal D probe pushed through open Terminal D hole to the electrical connector pin on the control unit.

8   Turn the ignition switch ON, and shift the gear selector lever to D on automatic transmission vehicles, or to any gear except Neutral on manual transmission vehicles. Check the cruise control Main switch is OFF (Main indicator light is OFF).

9   Press the Resume/Accel switch and the main switch simultaneously to activate the system test. The Main indicator light will come on. Then operate each switch described below and obtain the two-digit problem code numbers (light flashes; first set of flashes is the first digit of the problem code and then the second set of flashes is the second digit of the problem code). Example: Three flashes, a slight delay, then five flashes, indicates problem Code 35.

10   Pressing Set/Coast switch, problem Code 21 indicates trouble with the cruise control switch.

11   Pressing Resume/Accel switch, problem Code 22 indicates trouble with the cruise control switch.

12   Depressing brake pedal, problem Code 31 indicates trouble with the brake light switch.

13   Turning Ignition switch ON, shift the gear selector lever to P or N on automatic transmission vehicles, or depressing the clutch on manual transmission vehicles, problem Code 35 indicates trouble with the neutral safety switch (see Chapter 6) or clutch switch (see Chapter 8).

14   Test drive the vehicle above 25 MPH, problem Code 37 indicates trouble with the speed sensor or trouble (electrical short or open) in the cruise control system wiring harness.

15   Finally, test drive the vehicle to determine if the cruise control is now operating properly. If the problem is not found with the above procedures, immediately take the vehicle to a dealer service department or an automotive electrical specialist for further diagnosis and repair.

2006 AND LATER MODELS

16   The Powertrain Control Module (PCM) controls the cruise control system electronically via the electronic throttle control system. If you have problems with the cruise control system, check for the presence of trouble codes stored in the PCM (see Chapter 6). If that doesn't turn up any problems, have it checked by a dealer service department or other qualified repair shop.

23   Power window system - general information

1   The power window system controls the electric motors, mounted inside the doors, that lower and raise the windows. The power window system consists of the control switches, the fuse, the circuit breaker, the motors, the window regulators (the scissor-like mechanisms that raise and lower the window glass) and the wiring connecting the switches to the motors. When the ignition switch is turned to ON, current flows through the power window fuse in the engine compartment fuse and relay box to a circuit breaker located in the instrument panel wiring harness (located near the parking brake pedal). From there, current flows to the power window switches.

2   The power windows are wired so that they can be lowered and raised from the master control switch by the driver or by passengers using remote switches located at each passenger window. Each window has a separate motor that is reversible. The position of the control switch determines the polarity and therefore the direction of operation.

3   The power window system will only operate when the ignition switch is turned to ON. In addition, a window lockout switch at the master control switch can, when activated, disable the power window switches on the other doors. Always check these items before troubleshooting a window problem.

4   These procedures are general in nature, so if you can't find the problem using them, take the vehicle to a dealer service department.

5   If the power windows don't work at all, check the fuse or circuit breaker.

6   If only the rear windows are inoperative, or if the windows only operate from the master control switch, check the window lockout switch for continuity in the unlocked position. If it doesn't have continuity, replace it.

7   Check the wiring between the switches and the fuse for continuity. Repair the wiring, if necessary.

8   If only one window is inoperative from the master control switch, try the control switch at the window that doesn't work.

➡**Note: This doesn't apply to the driver's door window.**

9   If the same window works from one switch, but not the other, check the switch for continuity.

10   If the switch tests OK, check for a short or open in the wiring between the affected switch and the window motor.

11   If one window is inoperative from both switches, remove the trim panel from the affected door (see Chapter 11), then check for voltage at the switch and at the motor while operating the switch. First check for voltage at the electrical connectors for the circuit. With the ignition key turned to ON and the connectors all connected, backprobe at the designated wire (see the wiring diagrams at the end of this Chapter) with a grounded test light. Pushing the driver's window switch to the DOWN position, there should be voltage at one terminal. Pushing the same switch to the UP position, there should be voltage at another terminal. If these voltage checks are OK, disconnect the electrical connector at the driver's motor, and check it for voltage when the switch is operated.

12   If voltage is reaching the motor and the switch is OK, disconnect the door glass from its regulator (see Chapter 11). Move the window up and down by hand while checking for binding and damage. Also check for binding and damage to the regulator. If the regulator is not damaged and the window moves up and down smoothly, replace the motor. If there's binding or damage, lubricate, repair or replace parts, as necessary.

13   If voltage isn't reaching the motor, check the wiring in the circuit for continuity between the switches and motors (see the wiring diagram at the end of this Chapter).

14   If you have to replace the main power window switch, pry it out of the door trim panel, then disconnect the electrical connector(s) from the switch.

15   When you're done, test the windows to confirm that the window system is functioning correctly.

24 Airbag system - general information

These models are equipped with a Supplemental Restraint System (SRS), more commonly known as "airbags." This system is designed to protect the driver and front seat passenger from serious injury in the event of a head-on or frontal collision. It consists of airbag modules in the center of the steering wheel and the passenger side of the instrument panel, and a sensing/diagnostic unit located inside the passenger compartment.

AIRBAG MODULES

The airbag modules contain a housing incorporating the cushion (airbag) and inflator unit. The inflator assembly is mounted on the back of the housing over a hole through which gas is expelled, inflating the bag almost instantaneously when an electrical signal is sent from the system. The specially wound wire that carries this signal to the driver's module is called a clockspring. The clockspring is a flat, ribbon-like electrically conductive tape which is wound many times so that it can transmit an electrical signal regardless of steering wheel position.

CENTRAL AIRBAG SENSING/DIAGNOSTIC UNIT

The airbag sensing/diagnostic unit contains the safing sensor and an on-board microprocessor which monitors the operation of the system. It checks this system every time the vehicle is started, causing the "AIRBAG" warning light to go on, then off, if the system is operating properly. If there is a fault in the system, the light will go on and stay on and the airbag sensing/diagnostic unit will store fault codes indicating the nature of the fault. If the AIRBAG light goes on and stays on, the vehicle should be taken to your dealer immediately for service.

SERVICING COMPONENTS NEAR THE AIRBAG SYSTEM

Nevertheless, there are times when you need to remove the steering wheel, radio or service other components on or near the instrument panel. At these times, you'll be working around components and wiring harnesses for the airbag system. Airbag system wiring is easy to identify; they're all covered by a bright yellow conduit. Do not unplug the connectors for the airbag system wiring, except to disable the system. And do not use electrical test equipment on the airbag system wiring. ALWAYS DISABLE THE AIRBAG SYSTEM BEFORE WORKING NEAR THE AIRBAG SYSTEM COMPONENTS OR RELATED WIRING.

Disabling the airbag system

1   Turn the steering wheel to the straight ahead position, place the ignition switch in Lock and remove the key.

2   Disconnect the cable from the negative battery terminal (see Chapter 5).

3   Wait two minutes for the back-up capacitor to discharge.

Enabling the airbag system

4   Connect the cable to the negative battery terminal.

5   Turn the ignition key to On and verify that the "AIRBAG" warning light comes on for approximately six seconds, then goes off.

25 Wiring diagrams

Since it is not possible to include all wiring diagrams for every year covered by this manual, the following diagrams are those that are typical and most commonly needed.

Prior to troubleshooting any circuits, check the fuse and circuit breakers to make sure they are in good condition. Make sure the battery is properly charged and has clean, tight cable connections (see Chapter 1).

When checking the wiring system, make sure that all electrical connectors are clean, with no broken or loose pins. When unplugging an electrical connector, do not pull on the wires, only on the connector housings themselves.

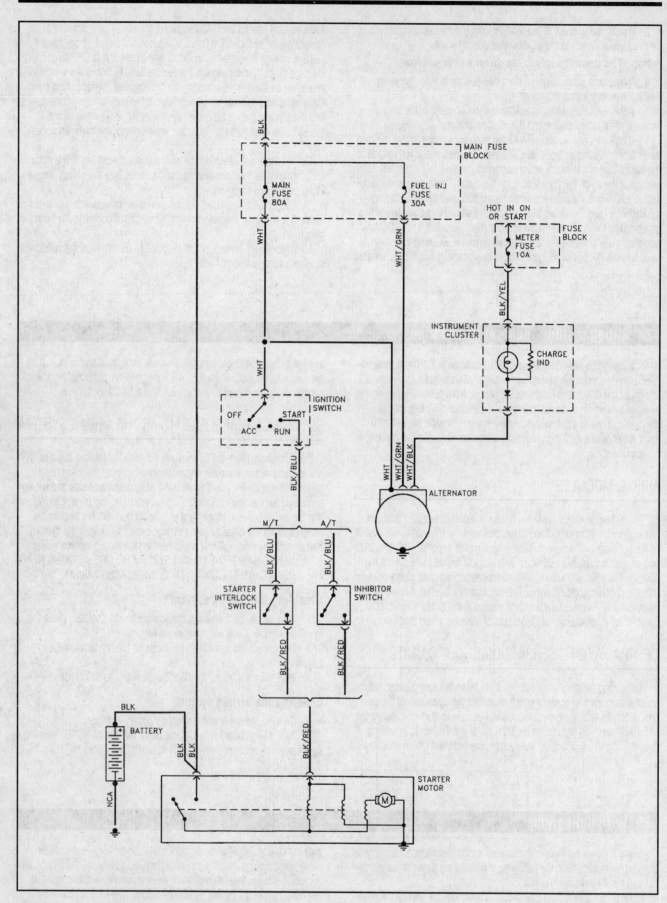

Starting and charging system - 1993 and earlier models

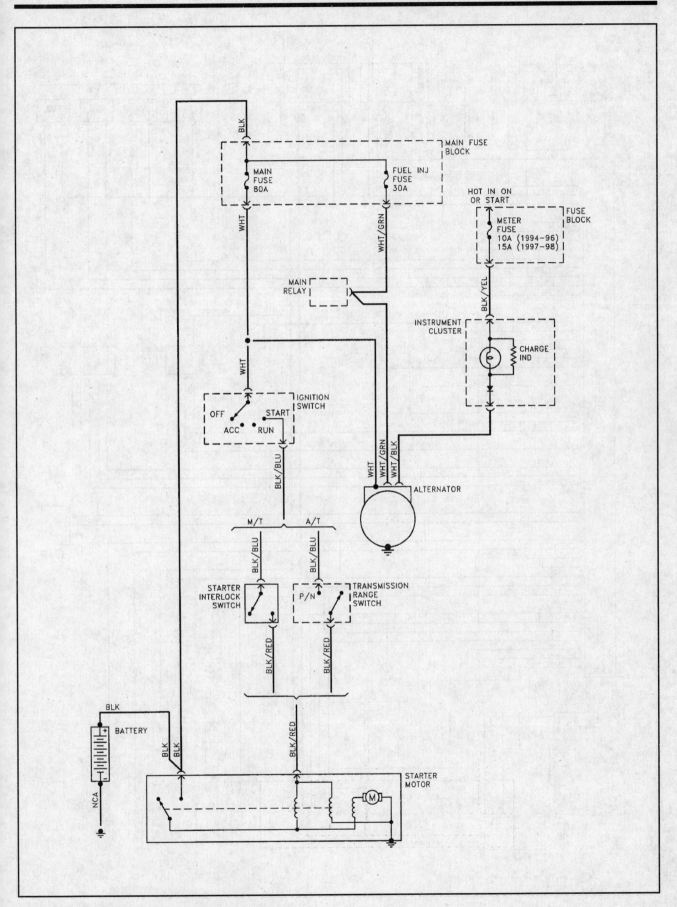

Starting and charging system - 1994 and later models

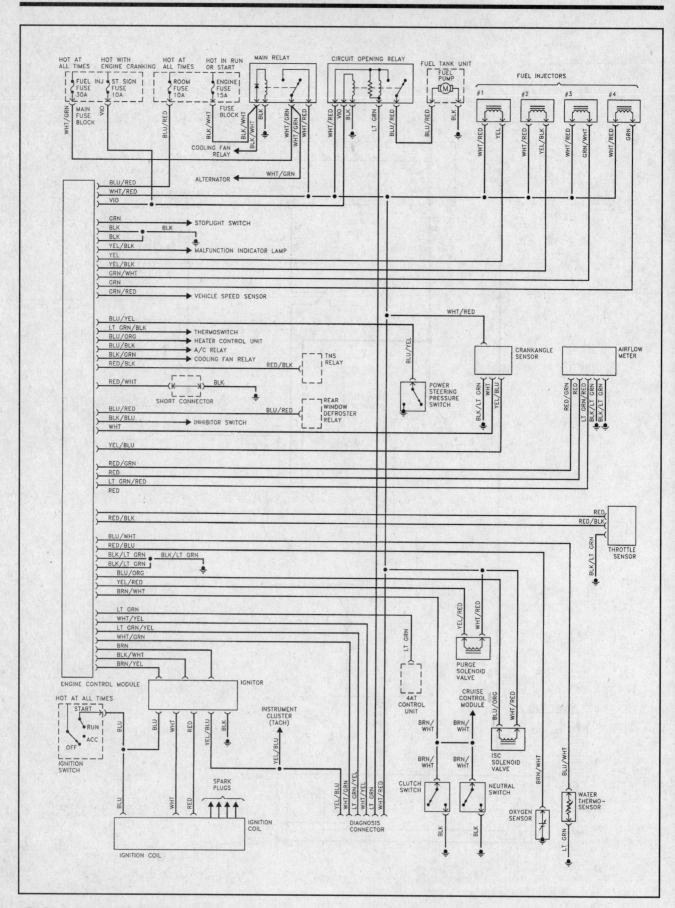

Engine control system - 1993 and earlier models

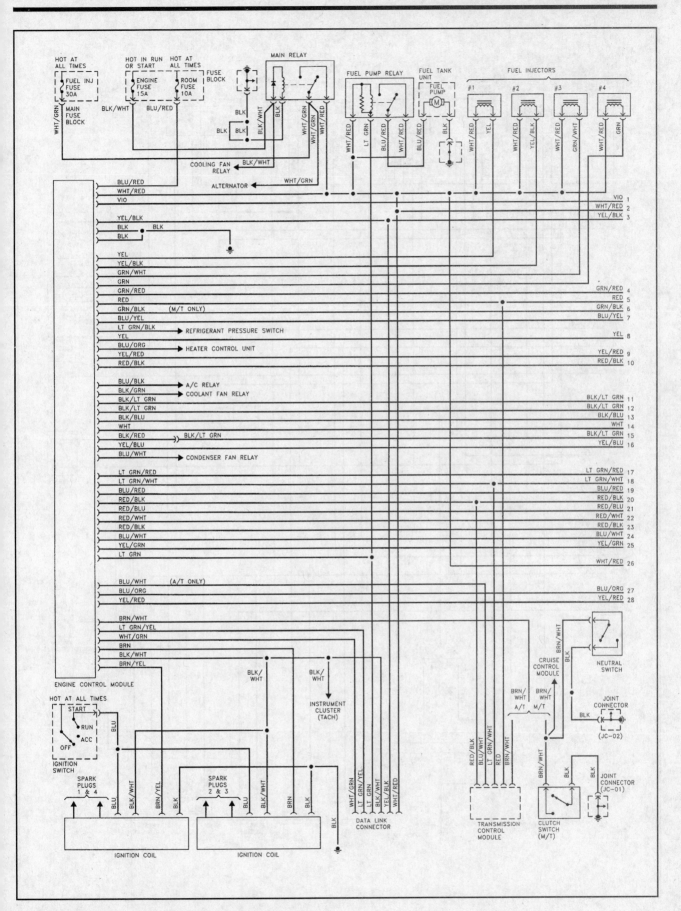

Engine control system - 1994 and 1995 models (page 1 of 2)

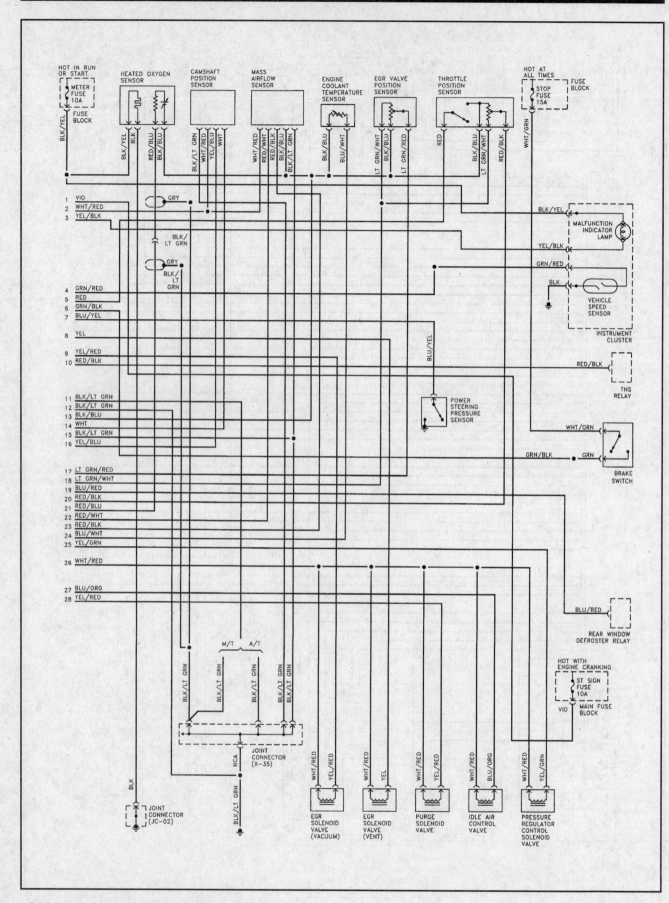

Engine control system - 1994 and 1995 models (page 2 of 2)

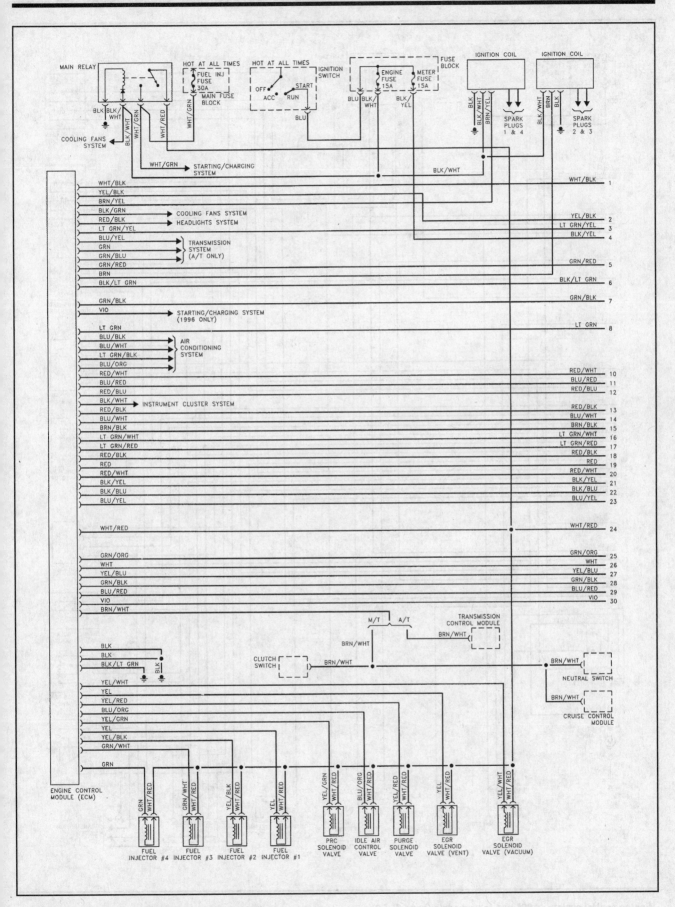

Engine control system - 1996 and later models (page 1 of 2)

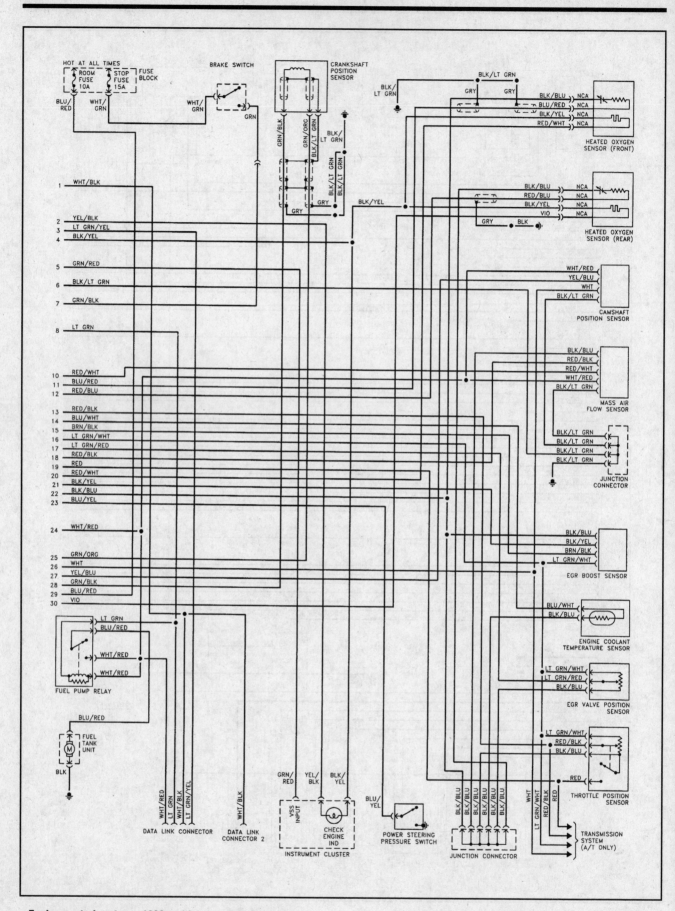

Engine control system - 1996 and later models (page 2 of 2)

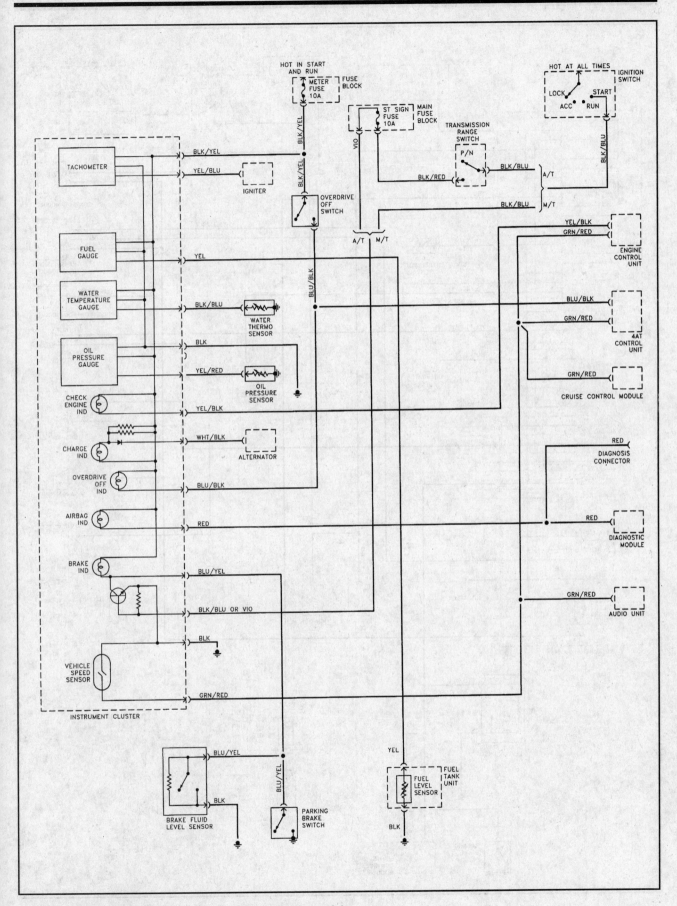

Engine gauges and warning light systems - 1993 and earlier models

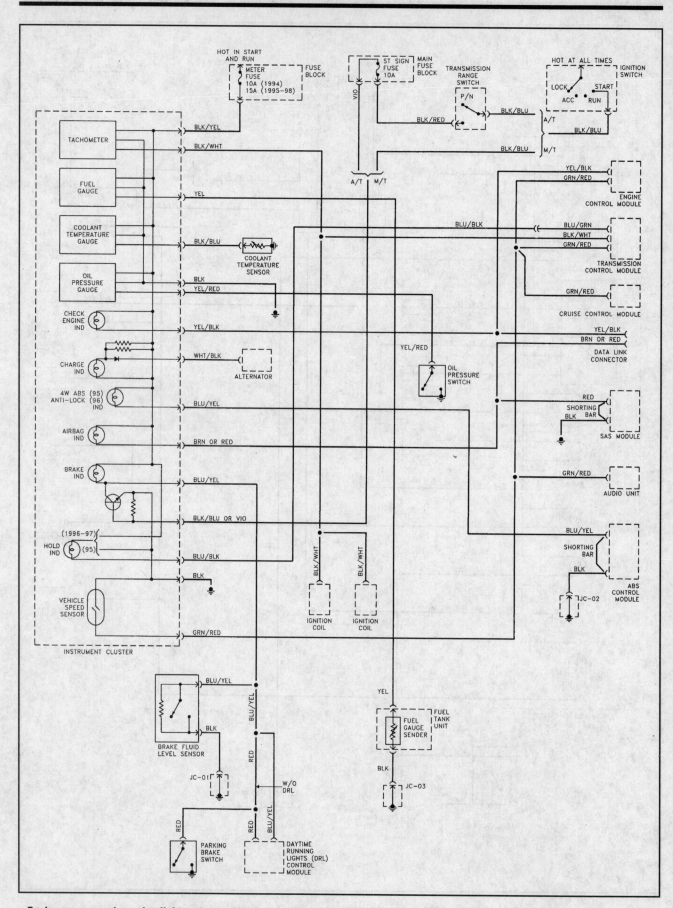

Engine gauges and warning light systems - 1994 and later models

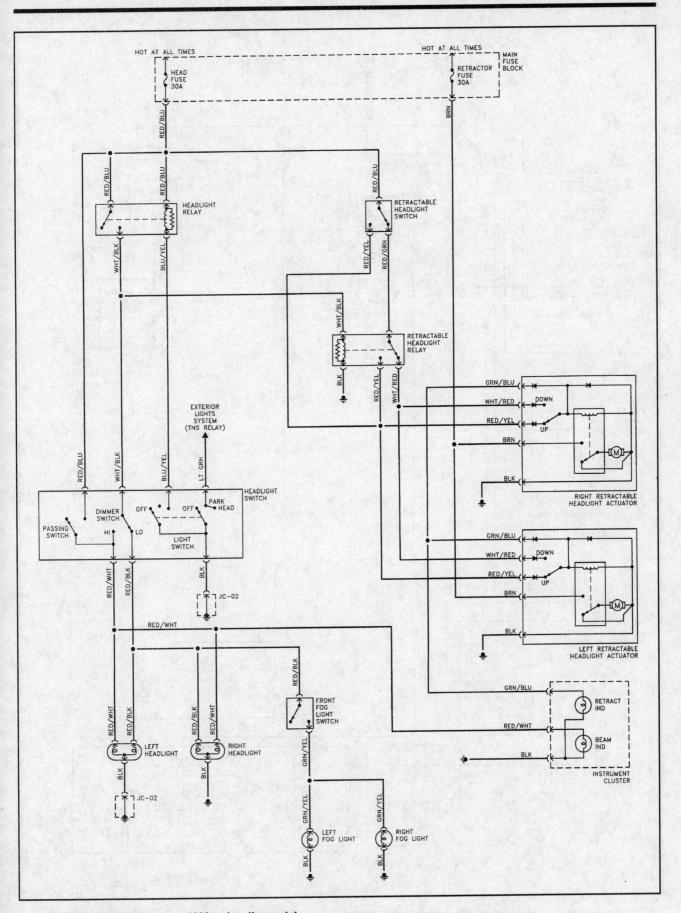

Headlight and fog light systems - 1993 and earlier models

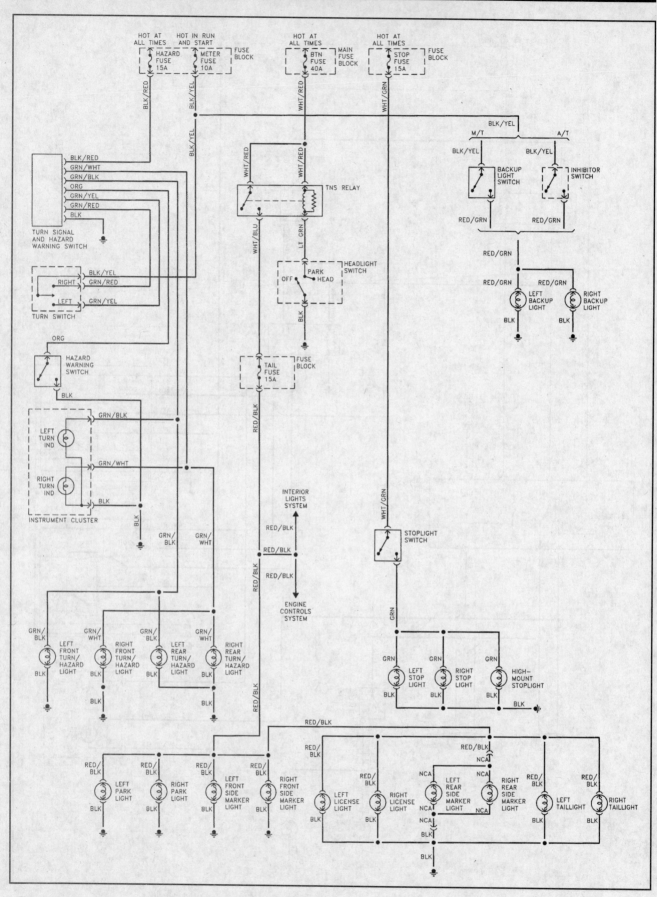

Exterior lighting system (except headlights and fog lights) - 1993 and earlier models

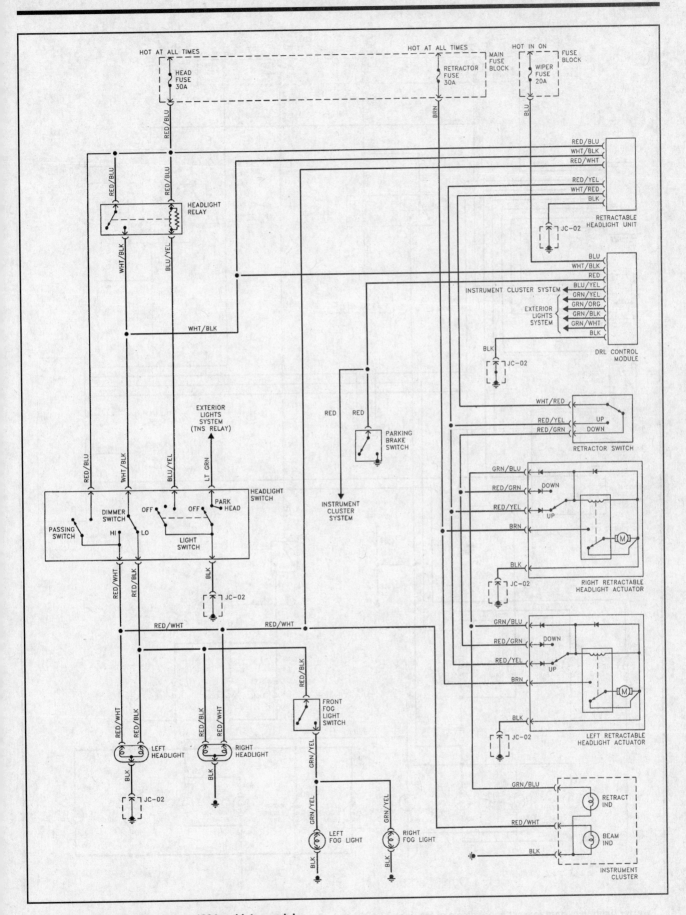

Headlight and fog light systems - 1994 and later models

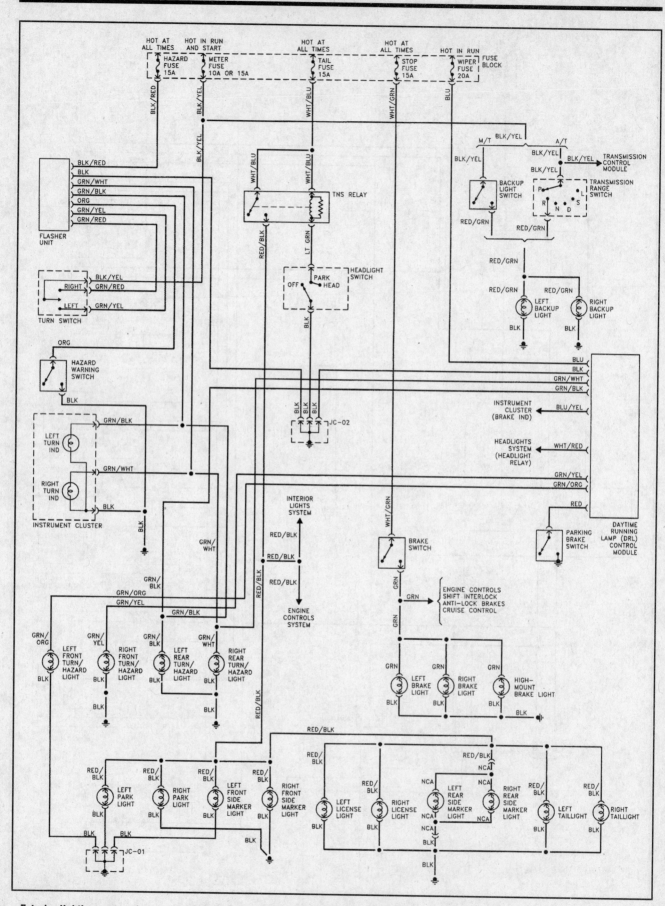

Exterior lighting system (except headlights and fog lights) - 1994 and later models

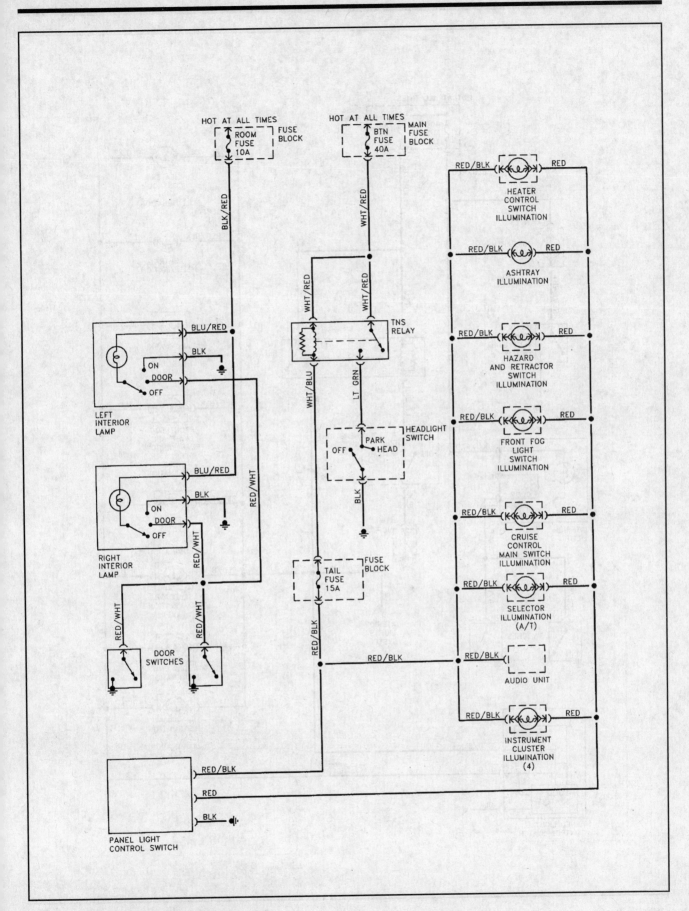

Interior lighting system - 1993 and earlier models

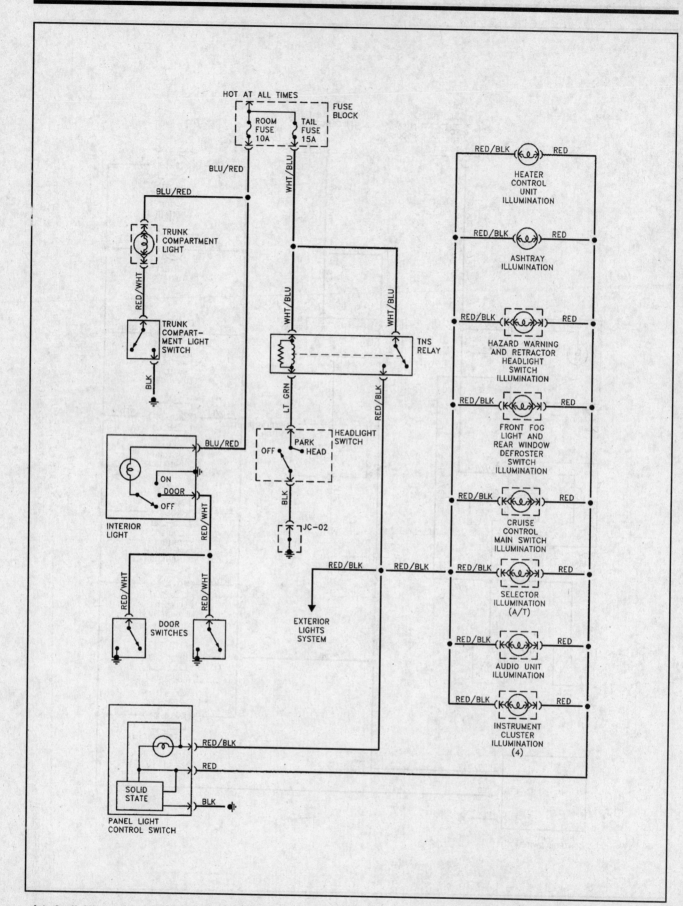

Interior lighting system - 1994 and later models

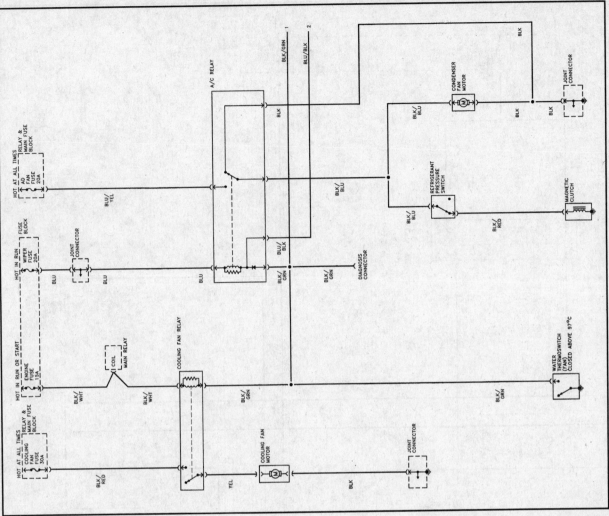

Heating and air conditioning system (includes engine cooling fan system) – 1993 and earlier models (1 of 2)

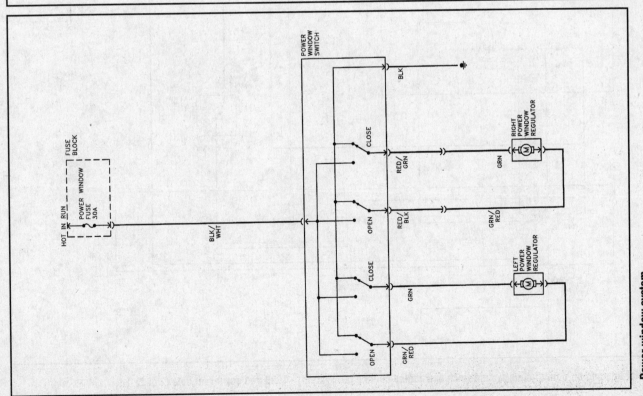

Power window system

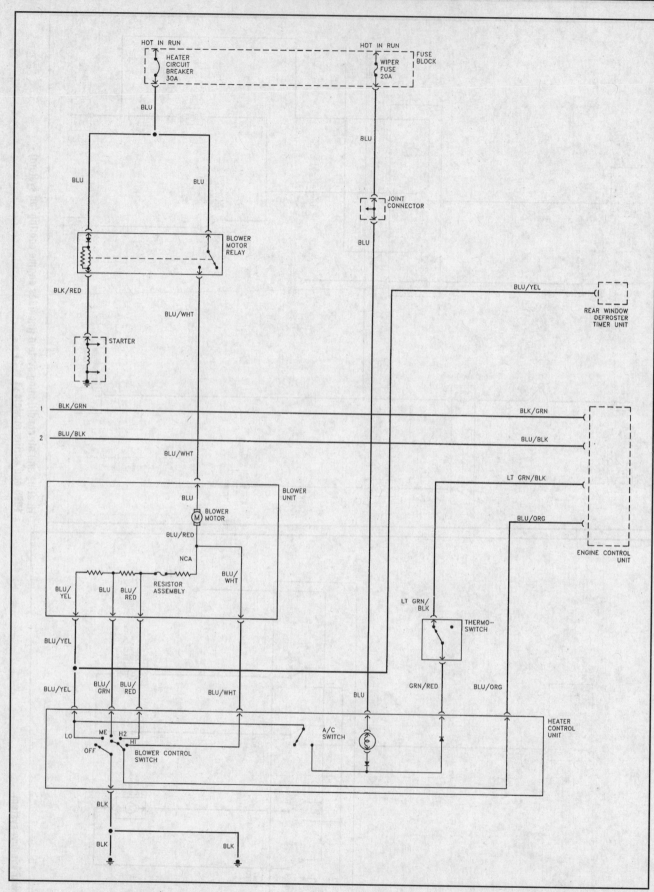

Heating and air conditioning system (includes engine cooling fan system) - 1993 and earlier models (2 of 2)

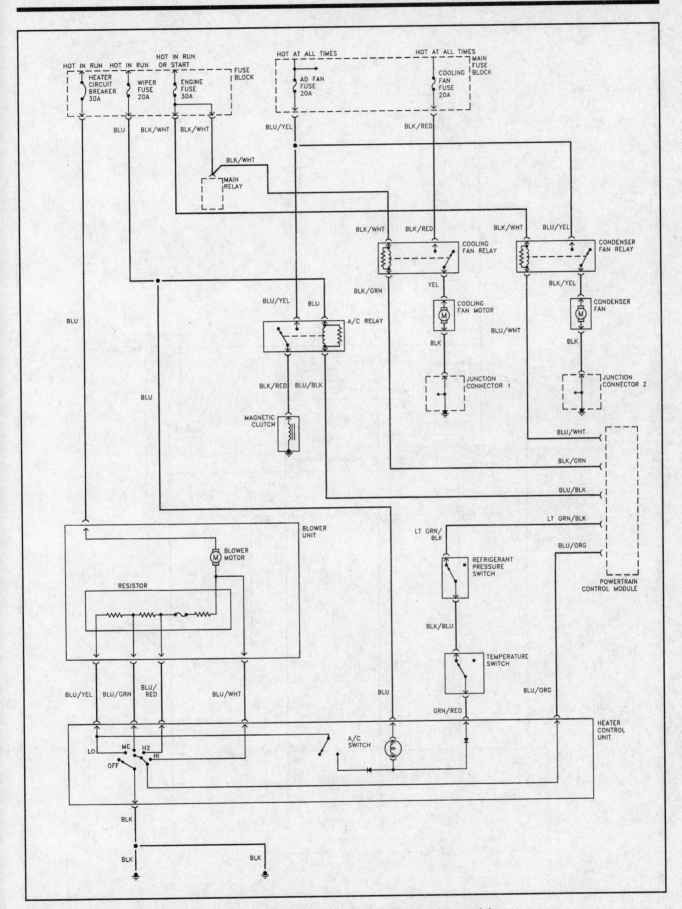

Heating and air conditioning system (includes engine cooling fan system) - 1994 and later models

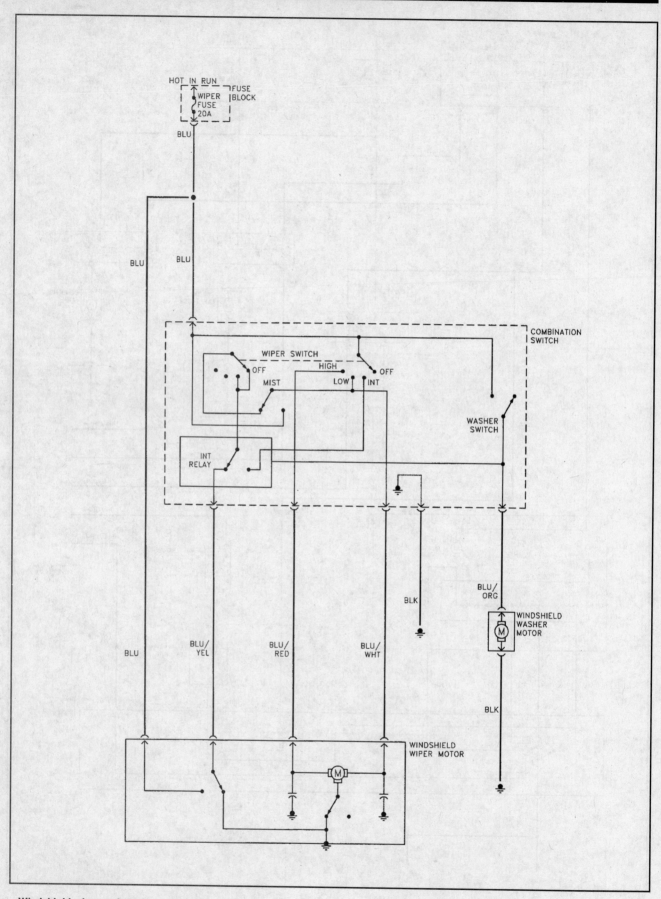

Windshield wiper and washer system

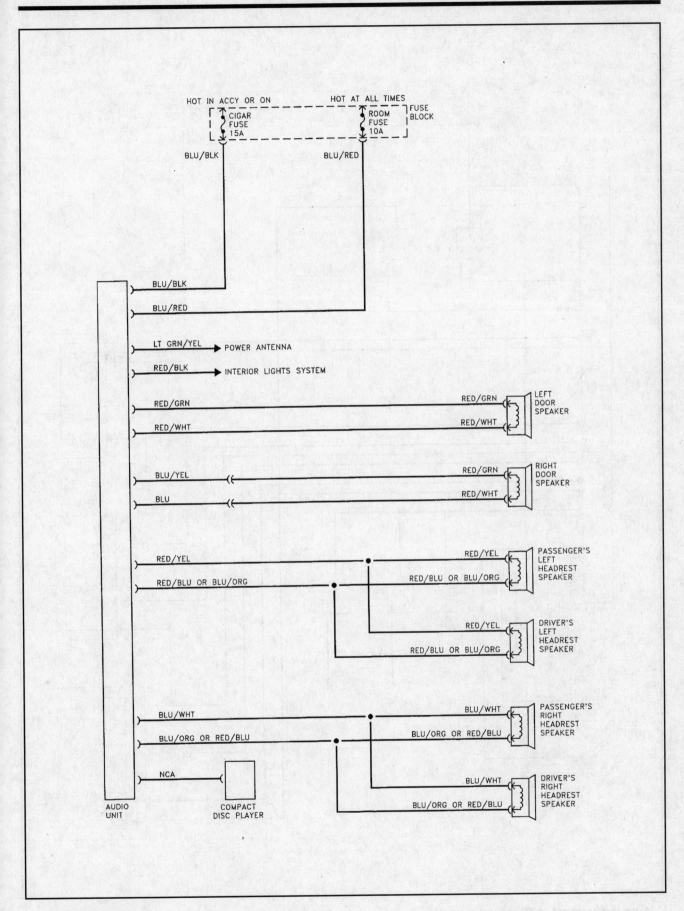

Typical stereo system

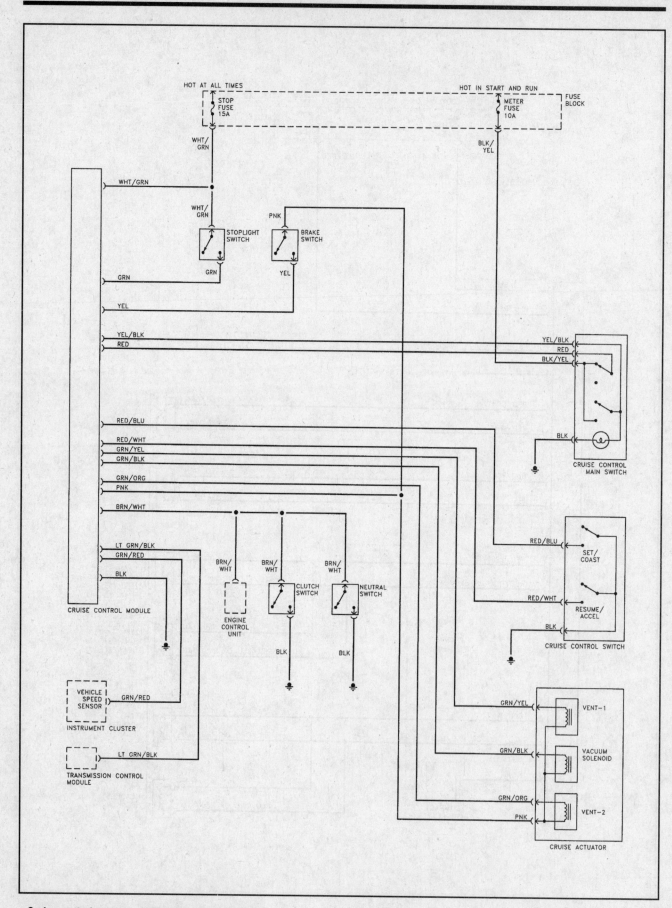

Cruise control system - 1993 and earlier models

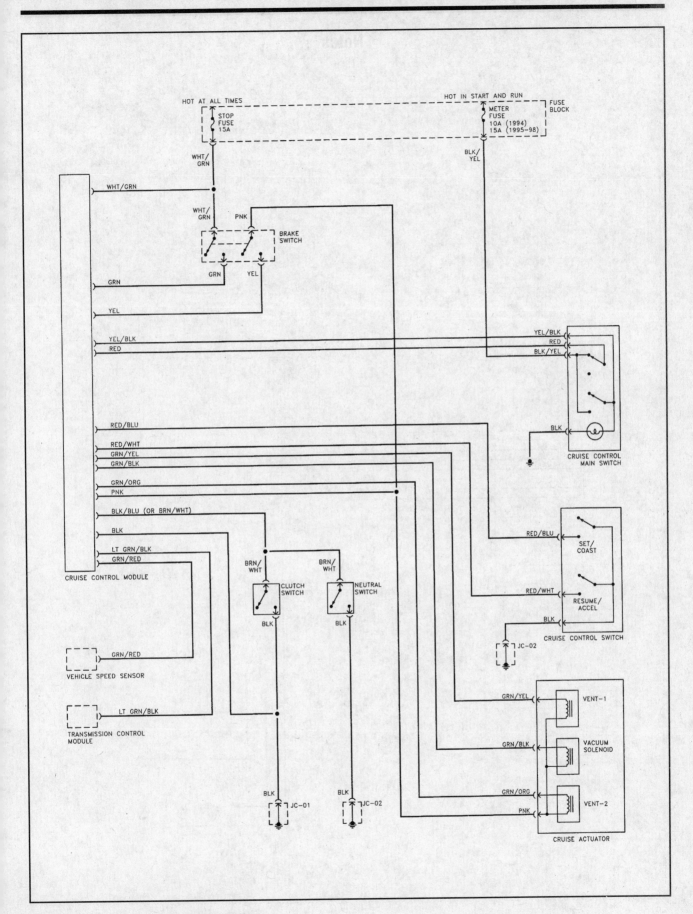

Cruise control system - 1994 and later models

Notes

GLOSSARY

AIR/FUEL RATIO: The ratio of air-to-gasoline by weight in the fuel mixture drawn into the engine.

AIR INJECTION: One method of reducing harmful exhaust emissions by injecting air into each of the exhaust ports of an engine. The fresh air entering the hot exhaust manifold causes any remaining fuel to be burned before it can exit the tailpipe.

ALTERNATOR: A device used for converting mechanical energy into electrical energy.

AMMETER: An instrument, calibrated in amperes, used to measure the flow of an electrical current in a circuit. Ammeters are always connected in series with the circuit being tested.

AMPERE: The rate of flow of electrical current present when one volt of electrical pressure is applied against one ohm of electrical resistance.

ANALOG COMPUTER: Any microprocessor that uses similar (analogous) electrical signals to make its calculations.

ARMATURE: A laminated, soft iron core wrapped by a wire that converts electrical energy to mechanical energy as in a motor or relay. When rotated in a magnetic field, it changes mechanical energy into electrical energy as in a generator.

ATMOSPHERIC PRESSURE: The pressure on the Earth's surface caused by the weight of the air in the atmosphere. At sea level, this pressure is 14.7 psi at 32°F (101 kPa at 0°C).

ATOMIZATION: The breaking down of a liquid into a fine mist that can be suspended in air.

AXIAL PLAY: Movement parallel to a shaft or bearing bore.

BACKFIRE: The sudden combustion of gases in the intake or exhaust system that results in a loud explosion.

BACKLASH: The clearance or play between two parts, such as meshed gears.

BACKPRESSURE: Restrictions in the exhaust system that slow the exit of exhaust gases from the combustion chamber.

BAKELITE: A heat resistant, plastic insulator material commonly used in printed circuit boards and transistorized components.

BALL BEARING: A bearing made up of hardened inner and outer races between which hardened steel balls roll.

BALLAST RESISTOR: A resistor in the primary ignition circuit that lowers voltage after the engine is started to reduce wear on ignition components.

BEARING: A friction reducing, supportive device usually located between a stationary part and a moving part.

BIMETAL TEMPERATURE SENSOR: Any sensor or switch made of two dissimilar types of metal that bend when heated or cooled due to the different expansion rates of the alloys. These types of sensors usually function as an on/off switch.

BLOWBY: Combustion gases, composed of water vapor and unburned fuel, that leak past the piston rings into the crankcase during normal engine operation. These gases are removed by the PCV system to prevent the buildup of harmful acids in the crankcase.

BRAKE PAD: A brake shoe and lining assembly used with disc brakes.

BRAKE SHOE: The backing for the brake lining. The term is, however, usually applied to the assembly of the brake backing and lining.

BUSHING: A liner, usually removable, for a bearing; an anti-friction liner used in place of a bearing.

CALIPER: A hydraulically activated device in a disc brake system, which is mounted straddling the brake rotor (disc). The caliper contains at least one piston and two brake pads. Hydraulic pressure on the piston(s) forces the pads against the rotor.

CAMSHAFT: A shaft in the engine on which are the lobes (cams) which operate the valves. The camshaft is driven by the crankshaft, via a belt, chain or gears, at one half the crankshaft speed.

CAPACITOR: A device which stores an electrical charge.

CARBON MONOXIDE (CO): A colorless, odorless gas given off as a normal byproduct of combustion. It is poisonous and extremely dangerous in confined areas, building up slowly to toxic levels without warning if adequate ventilation is not available.

CARBURETOR: A device, usually mounted on the intake manifold of an engine, which mixes the air and fuel in the proper proportion to allow even combustion.

CATALYTIC CONVERTER: A device installed in the exhaust system, like a muffler, that converts harmful byproducts of combustion into carbon dioxide and water vapor by means of a heat-producing chemical reaction.

CENTRIFUGAL ADVANCE: A mechanical method of advancing the spark timing by using flyweights in the distributor that react to centrifugal force generated by the distributor shaft rotation.

CHECK VALVE: Any one-way valve installed to permit the flow of air, fuel or vacuum in one direction only.

CHOKE: A device, usually a moveable valve, placed in the intake path of a carburetor to restrict the flow of air.

CIRCUIT: Any unbroken path through which an electrical current can flow. Also used to describe fuel flow in some instances.

CIRCUIT BREAKER: A switch which protects an electrical circuit from overload by opening the circuit when the current flow exceeds a predetermined level. Some circuit breakers must be reset manually, while most reset automatically.

COIL (IGNITION): A transformer in the ignition circuit which steps up the voltage provided to the spark plugs.

COMBINATION MANIFOLD: An assembly which includes both the intake and exhaust manifolds in one casting.

COMBINATION VALVE: A device used in some fuel systems that routes fuel vapors to a charcoal storage canister instead of venting them into the atmosphere. The valve relieves fuel tank pressure and allows fresh air into the tank as the fuel level drops to prevent a vapor lock situation.

COMPRESSION RATIO: The comparison of the total volume of the cylinder and combustion chamber with the piston at BDC and the piston at TDC.

CONDENSER: 1. An electrical device which acts to store an electrical charge, preventing voltage surges. 2. A radiator-like device in the air conditioning system in which refrigerant gas condenses into a liquid, giving off heat.

CONDUCTOR: Any material through which an electrical current can be transmitted easily.

CONTINUITY: Continuous or complete circuit. Can be checked with an ohmmeter.

COUNTERSHAFT: An intermediate shaft which is rotated by a mainshaft and transmits, in turn, that rotation to a working part.

CRANKCASE: The lower part of an engine in which the crankshaft and related parts operate.

CRANKSHAFT: The main driving shaft of an engine which receives reciprocating motion from the pistons and converts it to rotary motion.

CYLINDER: In an engine, the round hole in the engine block in which the piston(s) ride.

CYLINDER BLOCK: The main structural member of an engine in which is found the cylinders, crankshaft and other principal parts.

CYLINDER HEAD: The detachable portion of the engine, usually fastened to the top of the cylinder block and containing all or most of the combustion chambers. On overhead valve engines, it contains the valves and their operating parts. On overhead cam engines, it contains the camshaft as well.

DEAD CENTER: The extreme top or bottom of the piston stroke.

DETONATION: An unwanted explosion of the air/fuel mixture in the combustion chamber caused by excess heat and compression, advanced timing, or an overly lean mixture. Also referred to as "ping".

DIAPHRAGM: A thin, flexible wall separating two cavities, such as in a vacuum advance unit.

DIESELING: A condition in which hot spots in the combustion chamber cause the engine to run on after the key is turned off.

DIFFERENTIAL: A geared assembly which allows the transmission of motion between drive axles, giving one axle the ability to turn faster than the other.

DIODE: An electrical device that will allow current to flow in one direction only.

DISC BRAKE: A hydraulic braking assembly consisting of a brake disc, or rotor, mounted on an axle, and a caliper assembly containing, usually two brake pads which are activated by hydraulic pressure. The pads are forced against the sides of the disc, creating friction which slows the vehicle.

DISTRIBUTOR: A mechanically driven device on an engine which is responsible for electrically firing the spark plug at a predetermined point of the piston stroke.

DOWEL PIN: A pin, inserted in mating holes in two different parts allowing those parts to maintain a fixed relationship.

DRUM BRAKE: A braking system which consists of two brake shoes and one or two wheel cylinders, mounted on a fixed backing plate, and a brake drum, mounted on an axle, which revolves around the assembly.

DWELL: The rate, measured in degrees of shaft rotation, at which an electrical circuit cycles on and off.

ELECTRONIC CONTROL UNIT (ECU): Ignition module, module, amplifier or igniter. See Module for definition.

ELECTRONIC IGNITION: A system in which the timing and firing of the spark plugs is controlled by an electronic control unit, usually called a module. These systems have no points or condenser.

END-PLAY: The measured amount of axial movement in a shaft.

ENGINE: A device that converts heat into mechanical energy.

EXHAUST MANIFOLD: A set of cast passages or pipes which conduct exhaust gases from the engine.

FEELER GAUGE: A blade, usually metal, or precisely predetermined thickness, used to measure the clearance between two parts.

FIRING ORDER: The order in which combustion occurs in the cylinders of an engine. Also the order in which spark is distributed to the plugs by the distributor.

FLOODING: The presence of too much fuel in the intake manifold and combustion chamber which prevents the air/fuel mixture from firing, thereby causing a no-start situation.

FLYWHEEL: A disc shaped part bolted to the rear end of the crankshaft. Around the outer perimeter is affixed the ring gear. The starter drive engages the ring gear, turning the flywheel, which rotates the crankshaft, imparting the initial starting motion to the engine.

FOOT POUND (ft. lbs. or sometimes, ft.lb.): The amount of energy or work needed to raise an item weighing one pound, a distance of one foot.

FUSE: A protective device in a circuit which prevents circuit overload by breaking the circuit when a specific amperage is present. The device is constructed around a strip or wire of a lower amperage rating than the circuit it is designed to protect. When an amperage higher than that stamped on the fuse is present in the circuit, the strip or wire melts, opening the circuit.

GEAR RATIO: The ratio between the number of teeth on meshing gears.

GENERATOR: A device which converts mechanical energy into electrical energy.

HEAT RANGE: The measure of a spark plug's ability to dissipate heat from its firing end. The higher the heat range, the hotter the plug fires.

HUB: The center part of a wheel or gear.

HYDROCARBON (HC): Any chemical compound made up of hydrogen and carbon. A major pollutant formed by the engine as a byproduct of combustion.

HYDROMETER: An instrument used to measure the specific gravity of a solution.

INCH POUND (inch lbs.; sometimes in.lb. or in. lbs.): One twelfth of a foot pound.

INDUCTION: A means of transferring electrical energy in the form of a magnetic field. Principle used in the ignition coil to increase voltage.

INJECTOR: A device which receives metered fuel under relatively low pressure and is activated to inject the fuel into the engine under relatively high pressure at a predetermined time.

INPUT SHAFT: The shaft to which torque is applied, usually carrying the driving gear or gears.

INTAKE MANIFOLD: A casting of passages or pipes used to conduct air or a fuel/air mixture to the cylinders.

JOURNAL: The bearing surface within which a shaft operates.

KEY: A small block usually fitted in a notch between a shaft and a hub to prevent slippage of the two parts.

MANIFOLD: A casting of passages or set of pipes which connect the cylinders to an inlet or outlet source.

MANIFOLD VACUUM: Low pressure in an engine intake manifold formed just below the throttle plates. Manifold vacuum is highest at idle and drops under acceleration.

MASTER CYLINDER: The primary fluid pressurizing device in a hydraulic system. In automotive use, it is found in brake and hydraulic clutch systems and is pedal activated, either directly or, in a power brake system, through the power booster.

MODULE: Electronic control unit, amplifier or igniter of solid state or integrated design which controls the current flow in the ignition primary circuit based on input from the pick-up coil. When the module opens the primary circuit, high secondary voltage is induced in the coil.

NEEDLE BEARING: A bearing which consists of a number (usually a large number) of long, thin rollers.

OHM: (Ω) The unit used to measure the resistance of conductor-to-electrical flow. One ohm is the amount of resistance that limits current flow to one ampere in a circuit with one volt of pressure.

OHMMETER: An instrument used for measuring the resistance, in ohms, in an electrical circuit.

OUTPUT SHAFT: The shaft which transmits torque from a device, such as a transmission.

OVERDRIVE: A gear assembly which produces more shaft revolutions than that transmitted to it.

OVERHEAD CAMSHAFT (OHC): An engine configuration in which the camshaft is mounted on top of the cylinder head and operates the valve either directly or by means of rocker arms.

OVERHEAD VALVE (OHV): An engine configuration in which all of the valves are located in the cylinder head and the camshaft is located in the cylinder block. The camshaft operates the valves via lifters and pushrods.

OXIDES OF NITROGEN (NOx): Chemical compounds of nitrogen produced as a byproduct of combustion. They combine with hydrocarbons to produce smog.

OXYGEN SENSOR: Use with the feedback system to sense the presence of oxygen in the exhaust gas and signal the computer which can reference the voltage signal to an air/fuel ratio.

PINION: The smaller of two meshing gears.

PISTON RING: An open-ended ring with fits into a groove on the outer diameter of the piston. Its chief function is to form a seal between the piston and cylinder wall. Most automotive pistons have three rings: two for compression sealing; one for oil sealing.

PRELOAD: A predetermined load placed on a bearing during assembly or by adjustment.

PRIMARY CIRCUIT: the low voltage side of the ignition system which consists of the ignition switch, ballast resistor or resistance wire, bypass, coil, electronic control unit and pick-up coil as well as the connecting wires and harnesses.

PRESS FIT: The mating of two parts under pressure, due to the inner diameter of one being smaller than the outer diameter of the other, or vice versa; an interference fit.

RACE: The surface on the inner or outer ring of a bearing on which the balls, needles or rollers move.

REGULATOR: A device which maintains the amperage and/or voltage levels of a circuit at predetermined values.

RELAY: A switch which automatically opens and/or closes a circuit.

RESISTANCE: The opposition to the flow of current through a circuit or electrical device, and is measured in ohms. Resistance is equal to the voltage divided by the amperage.

RESISTOR: A device, usually made of wire, which offers a preset amount of resistance in an electrical circuit.

RING GEAR: The name given to a ring-shaped gear attached to a differential case, or affixed to a flywheel or as part of a planetary gear set.

ROLLER BEARING: A bearing made up of hardened inner and outer races between which hardened steel rollers move.

ROTOR: 1. The disc-shaped part of a disc brake assembly, upon which the brake pads bear; also called, brake disc. 2. The device mounted atop the distributor shaft, which passes current to the distributor cap tower contacts.

SECONDARY CIRCUIT: The high voltage side of the ignition system, usually above 20,000 volts. The secondary includes the ignition coil, coil wire, distributor cap and rotor, spark plug wires and spark plugs.

SENDING UNIT: A mechanical, electrical, hydraulic or electro-magnetic device which transmits information to a gauge.

SENSOR: Any device designed to measure engine operating conditions or ambient pressures and temperatures. Usually electronic in nature and designed to send a voltage signal to an on-board computer, some sensors may operate as a simple on/off switch or they may provide a variable voltage signal (like a potentiometer) as conditions or measured parameters change.

SHIM: Spacers of precise, predetermined thickness used between parts to establish a proper working relationship.

SLAVE CYLINDER: In automotive use, a device in the hydraulic clutch system which is activated by hydraulic force, disengaging the clutch.

SOLENOID: A coil used to produce a magnetic field, the effect of which is to produce work.

SPARK PLUG: A device screwed into the combustion chamber of a spark ignition engine. The basic construction is a conductive core inside of a ceramic insulator, mounted in an outer conductive base. An electrical charge from the spark plug wire travels along the conductive core and jumps a preset air gap to a grounding point or points at the end of the conductive base. The resultant spark ignites the fuel/air mixture in the combustion chamber.

SPLINES: Ridges machined or cast onto the outer diameter of a shaft or inner diameter of a bore to enable parts to mate without rotation.

TACHOMETER: A device used to measure the rotary speed of an engine, shaft, gear, etc., usually in rotations per minute.

THERMOSTAT: A valve, located in the cooling system of an engine, which is closed when cold and opens gradually in response to engine heating, controlling the temperature of the coolant and rate of coolant flow.

TOP DEAD CENTER (TDC): The point at which the piston reaches the top of its travel on the compression stroke.

TORQUE: The twisting force applied to an object.

TORQUE CONVERTER: A turbine used to transmit power from a driving member to a driven member via hydraulic action, providing changes in drive ratio and torque. In automotive use, it links the driveplate at the rear of the engine to the automatic transmission.

TRANSDUCER: A device used to change a force into an electrical signal.

TRANSISTOR: A semi-conductor component which can be actuated by a small voltage to perform an electrical switching function.

TUNE-UP: A regular maintenance function, usually associated with the replacement and adjustment of parts and components in the electrical and fuel systems of a vehicle for the purpose of attaining optimum performance.

TURBOCHARGER: An exhaust driven pump which compresses intake air and forces it into the combustion chambers at higher than atmospheric pressures. The increased air pressure allows more fuel to be burned and results in increased horsepower being produced.

VACUUM ADVANCE: A device which advances the ignition timing in response to increased engine vacuum.

VACUUM GAUGE: An instrument used to measure the presence of vacuum in a chamber.

VALVE: A device which control the pressure, direction of flow or rate of flow of a liquid or gas.

VALVE CLEARANCE: The measured gap between the end of the valve stem and the rocker arm, cam lobe or follower that activates the valve.

VISCOSITY: The rating of a liquid's internal resistance to flow.

VOLTMETER: An instrument used for measuring electrical force in units called volts. Voltmeters are always connected parallel with the circuit being tested.

WHEEL CYLINDER: Found in the automotive drum brake assembly, it is a device, actuated by hydraulic pressure, which, through internal pistons, pushes the brake shoes outward against the drums.

MASTER INDEX

A

NOTES